11/48c

GROSSMAN'S GUIDE

to Wines, Spirits, and Beers

FIFTH REVISED EDITION

GROSSMAN'S
GUIDE *to Wines,*
Spirits, and Beers

FIFTH REVISED EDITION

HAROLD J. GROSSMAN

New York • CHARLES SCRIBNER'S SONS

1 3 5 7 9 11 13 15 17 19   C/MD   20 18 16 14 12 10 8 6 4 2

Printed in the United States of America
Library of Congress Catalog Card Number 73-5187
ISBN 0-684-13528-0

Acknowledgements

FRANCE: Jean-Pierre Gachelin
Richard L. Blum, Jr.
Michel L. Dreyfus
Charles Meuhler

GERMANY: Peter Sichel

ITALY: Donald Sozzi

CALIFORNIA: Frank Bartholomew
Terrence McInnes

AMERICA: Charles Fournier
Donald F. Marsh

SPAIN: Rafael Aguilar
Luther Conant

PORTUGAL: Elleseva Sayers

YUGOSLAVIA & BALKANS: John Nanovic

ARGENTINA & RUSSIA: Frank Feinberg

RUMS: H. B. Estrada

VODKA: Thomas G. Cockerill

BOURBON: Alfred Durante

BEER: Dr. J. B. Bockelmann
Thomas P. Hawkes

TRADE ABBREVIATIONS: Paul Schack

GENERAL CONSULTANTS: Henry Ogden Barbour
Harriet Lembeck

Contents

vii

Publisher's Foreword to the Fifth Edition

In The thirty years that have passed since Scribners published the first edition of *Grossman's Guide to Wines, Spirits, and Beers,* Harold J. Grossman's book has established itself as a standard reference work for everyone interested in this field, professional and amateur alike.

It has been revised periodically as was necessary over this period and this is now the fifth such revised edition. Books, unlike some wines, do not always improve through aging—particularly reference books—and the late Harold Grossman recognized the author's responsibility to keep his work as useful as possible by making the necessary changes and additions dictated by trends in the marketplace. At the time of his death he was at work on revising the fourth edition.

Following Mr. Grossman's death in 1967 the responsibility of revising the book fell upon his widow and former co-worker Florence L. Grossman, but upon her death in 1971 the responsibility has devolved upon his publishers. In this we have been generously helped by such experts in the field as Gordon Bass and Julius Wile, who were not only colleagues of Mr. Grossman but long-time friends as well. The challenging task of coordinating all the necessary textual changes and at the same time preserving the tone and character of Mr. Grossman's own work was assumed by Mr. Robert Scharff and the reader can see for himself how admirably he has performed that assignment.

CHARLES SCRIBNER'S SONS

GROSSMAN'S GUIDE

to Wines, Spirits, and Beers

FIFTH REVISED EDITION

1. Introduction

THE beginnings of the liquor industry are lost in the mazes of the past, almost as old as man himself, and our knowledge of it is made up of widely scattered information from the dawn of time in every language written or spoken. The entire subject lacks finality. It is continually developing and consequently is always intriguing. Like living things, it is subject to growth and fluctuations, and in that fact lies, perhaps, its chief fascination.

The development and improvement of the quality of alcoholic beverages have been a natural result of the advance of science and civilization. The role of science has been limited to assuring uniformity of quality and sound products year in and year out, for mysterious Mother Nature still insists she will have something to say in the matter, even when it comes to distilled spirits.

The vine, the brewing kettle, and the still have accompanied the spread of Christianity, establishing certain honorable traditions which the trade proudly upholds today. It is also interesting to note the esteem in which the wine trade is held abroad. It was the first "trade" considered sufficiently honorable and dignified for a member of the aristocracy to engage in, and many of the leading European firms are directed by men of noble families.

In England a wine merchant is consulted in matters pertaining to wines, spirits, or beers just as a lawyer is in legal matters. The confidence thus placed in him gives the merchant a keen consciousness of his responsibility. Also, as he knows that the business he builds will be continued by his sons and grandsons, family pride leads him to pass on an impeccable reputation. It is not unusual to find firms that have been doing business under the same name in the same place for hundreds of years—in some cases more than 400 years. This is the European custom and we are happy to note that it is beginning to take hold in the United States.

One of the leading Champagne shippers illustrated this point when he told me: "When I ship my wine, my name appears on the label. It is I who guarantee the quality. My reputation is more important to me than any pecuniary profit I may derive from the sale. It took my forebears 200 years to establish this reputation for shipping wines of quality, and rest assured that I am going to pass on as good a name to my successors as I received." It is men of this type who have placed the wine and spirit trade on the high plane which has become traditional.

Based on these traditions, certain firms have established their brands so well that the public asks for their product by the name of the shipper. This has been particularly true in the case of Cognac and whiskies, but since Prohibition made our public "age conscious," many people have been buying "numbers" rather than brands in whose name we have confidence. This has happened in the case of wines, as well. It is true that certain wines do improve with age—up to a point—but there are other wines which are more pleasant if drunk when young, as is the case with light white wines, whose charm lies in their freshness.

The industry as a whole is today a most important part of our business life, employing, directly or through allied enterprises, millions of men. It is one of the three most important sources of tax revenue for the Federal treasury and the several State treasuries.

Just as Prohibition is bad, so is excess, and in no case is this more true than in the use of alcoholic beverages. There is no better word of advice on this point than that which Lord Chesterfield gave to his son, in the letter dated London, March 27, 1747:

"Were I to begin the world again with the experience I now have of it, I would lead a life of real, not imaginary pleasures. I would enjoy the pleasures of the table, and of wine; but stop short of the pains inseparably annexed to an excess of either."

The leaders of the industry are unanimous in preferring that more people drink and enjoy beverages, rather than that the individual drink more.

It is gratifying to note the moderation exercised by the public in the use of alcoholic beverages since Repeal. A per capita consumption of less than two gallons of spirits per year indicates an average of three-fifths of an ounce per day. Wine consumption is a little over one-half of an ounce, while the beer average is about 7 ounces. A people whose alcoholic beverage consumption is so low may, without fear of contradiction, be called temperate.

The Guide has been divided into five main sections: wines; spirits; beers and ales; uses, merchandising, control, and so forth; and finally, the Appendices which contain useful, quick reference data. All of the material has been carefully cross-indexed so as to simplify the book's use for reference purposes.

Condensed information on the entire industry is given, including the description of a product, its method of production, selling, care, and uses in public and private places. Naturally the practices described are those generally used in the United States, unless otherwise specified.

It is our hope that libraries will find the Guide a comprehensive source of information on all phases of the subject; that producers, vintners, distillers and brewers will find it valuable as a general reference and in equipping their sales representatives with information about the other phases of the industry, which will enable them to win the confidence of their customers; that the wholesale distributor will find it invaluable as a training manual for his staff, and as a reference book. The various Appendices also have been compiled with a view to practical use.

Particular care has been taken in providing information on every phase of the industry for the use of retail establishments, whether off-premise (stores), or on-premise (hotels, restaurants, or clubs).

After reading the book through, it may be useful to review certain chapters at the time when one is featuring the promotion of particular products. For example, during the Christmas season, there is an opportunity to sell liqueurs in their fancy bottles. It is good business to be posted on these, and to refer to the Guide if one is asked for a liqueur whose style or character may have been forgotten.

It is also advisable for the hotel, restaurant, or club manager to keep his service personnel well-informed. After all, they are his sales staff and they cannot be expected to increase the sale of beverages if they are not familiar with them. This applies equally to the wholesaler or distributor. The sales staff which is trained and can give information will become salesmen instead of order takers.

While the Guide has been designed primarily to be of use to the trade, it is our earnest hope that it will be read by the most important person to the entire industry—the consumer. It is to please and serve him that the industry constantly strives. A greater familiarity with the beverages which are discussed in detail in this book would, we believe, not only aid him in purchasing with assurance, but would, perhaps, point out to him many intriguing qualities which he may have overlooked, and therefore increase his enjoyment.

To provide the reader with practical information, to increase his knowledge and enjoyment, and above all, to impart something of the fascination of the subject is the purpose of this Guide.

2. Definitions

It is important to explain what we mean by the various terms we use, so that there may be no misconceptions. The definitions and axioms which follow are important because they are the basic elements on which the book is built. Unless we understand the same things by the same words, there may be some confusion in reading the book. These, then, are the tools with which we are to work:

what is alcohol?

Alcohol is a volatile, colorless liquid with an ethereal odor, obtained through the fermentation of a sugar-containing liquid. There are many members of the alcohol family, but ethyl is the best-known alcohol and the one which concerns us most, as it is the principal alcohol to be found in all alcoholic beverages. Chemically, alcohols are hydroxides of organic radicals. There is nothing in alcohol which, in itself, is poisonous or injurious to man's health.

what is an alcoholic beverage?

Literally, any potable liquid containing from $\frac{1}{2}$ of 1 per cent up to $75\frac{1}{2}$ per cent of ethyl alcohol by volume is an alcoholic beverage. However, social and economic factors enter the picture, and we find that, for the purposes of taxation, the Federal and several State Governments have set certain definite standards as to what constitutes an alcoholic beverage. Whereas beers containing as little as 2 per cent of alcohol by volume are taxable, certain bitters and medicinal compounds, which often contain upwards of 40 per cent, are not taxed because they are not considered alcoholic beverages in the tax sense. In 1919 the Congress of the United States established by law that an alcoholic beverage containing more than $\frac{1}{2}$ of 1 per cent of alcohol by volume was intoxicating, yet in later years, liqueurs containing 12 per cent of alcohol by volume were permitted to be sold as "non-alcoholic" cordials. One might draw the conclusion that, by 1930, 12 per cent of alcohol in a liqueur was not as intoxicating as 1 per cent was in beer.

4

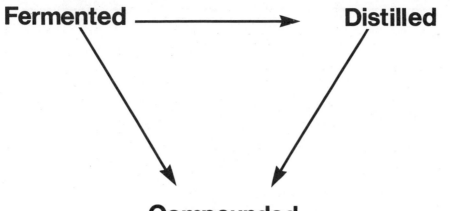

Fermented ——————————▶ **Distilled**

Compounded

For purposes of classification all alcoholic beverages fall into one of three basic categories: 1) fermented beverages which are made from grains and fruits with alcoholic strengths ranging from 7 to 14 percent; 2) distilled or spirit beverages which result from a pure distillation of fermented beverages; and 3) compounded beverages which are made by combining either a fermented beverage or spirit with flavoring substances.

Wine is the naturally fermented juice of freshly gathered ripe grapes, which have been pressed at or near the place where gathered. The Federal Alcohol Administration's regulations, however, give a broader use to the term and say that it may be applied to the fermented juice of other fruits, or even herbs, such as blackberry, elderberry, peach, and dandelion wines. Wine is more than just water and alcohol. The Bible calls it the blood of the grape. Wine is a living thing in a constant state of change. — *what is wine?*

A spirit is a potable alcoholic beverage obtained from the distillation of an alcohol-containing liquid. It makes very little difference whether the original liquid contained a small or a large amount of alcohol. Once the principles of distillation are applied, nearly all of the alcohol may be separated from the liquid. In this process, however, it is inevitable that certain other matters will also be separated and it is these congeners, which we may call impurities, that give the several spirits their distinct character after the spirit has been matured in wood and the congeners, or impurities, have fully developed. — *what is a spirit?*

Beer is a liquor fermented from cereals and malt, flavored with hops. — *what is beer?*

There are only two colors in wine—red and white.
Any wine containing the slightest tinge of red is a red wine. — *axioms*

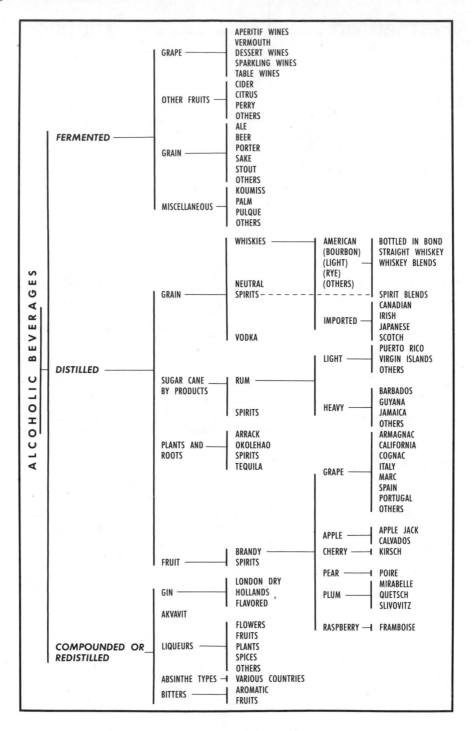

White wines range from the very palest straw-color to deep, dark brown. There is no wine that is absolutely colorless.

Red wines are generally dry. (Exceptions are Porto and Port-type wines, some Italian and one or two Hungarian table wines, and, of course, kosher wines.)

White wines vary in sweetness, from the extreme dryness of a Manzanilla to the rich sweet lusciousness of a Tokay Eszencia.

The word "dry" is used in the wine trade to describe the opposite of sweet. Literally, it means lacking in sugar.

FOUR MAIN CLASSIFICATIONS OF WINES

LIGHT BEVERAGE (Natural still wines).   Red and white Bordeaux, Burgundy, Italian, Rhine, Moselle, Alsatian, Spanish, Portuguese, Tokay, Hungarian table wines, American, California, etc. Alcoholic content 14 per cent or less.

SPARKLING.   Champagne, sparkling Burgundy, Asti Spumante, sparkling Moselle, etc. Alcoholic content 14 per cent or less.

FORTIFIED.   Sherry, Port (Porto), Madeira, Marsala, Malaga, etc. Alcoholic content over 14 but not over 24 per cent.

Bottle Sketches

Typical or standard shapes of bottles generally used in wine trade for packaging their products.

FROM LEFT TO RIGHT. *Champagne and sparkling wines; Bordeaux wines; Burgundy still wines; Alsatian, Rhine, Moselle, and Hungarian white table wines; Chianti; Tokay.*

FROM LEFT TO RIGHT. *Portuguese crackling Rosé; Bocksbeutel for Steinwein; Sherry; Port, Madeira, and Marsala; Italian sweet Vermouth; French dry Vermouth.*

AROMATIZED. Vermouth, both Italian and French, quinined wines, etc. Alcoholic content 15½ to 20 per cent.

Wines with less than 14 per cent alcohol will improve after bottling. Fortified and aromatized wines will improve very little or not at all, with the exception of Vintage Ports (Portos).

CLASSIFICATION OF SPIRITS

BRANDIES. Cognac, Armagnac, Spanish, Greek, Israeli, Italian, American, Kirsch (cherry brandy), Calvados (Apple Jack), Slivovitz, etc.

WHISKIES. Scotch, Irish, Canadian, American Rye, Bourbon, Light, etc.

RUMS. Jamaica, Demerara, Cuban, Puerto Rican, Martinique, Haitian, Batavia Arak, etc.

GINS. English London dry and Old Tom, American gins similar to these two, Hollands, etc.

VODKAS. Russian, Polish, American, Zubrowka, Starka, Okhotnichya, Pertsovaka, etc.

OTHER SPIRITS. Akvavit, Okolehao, Tequila, Bitters, etc.

LIQUEURS. Generic types such as Menthe, Cacao, Anise, Blackberry Curaçao, etc., are produced in many countries. In addition there are a large number of proprietary specialties which have earned international popularity, such as: Benedictine, Drambuie, Galliano, Chartreuse, Southern Comfort, Kahlua, etc.

Spirits mature—improve—as long as they are stored in porous containers, usually wood, though sometimes, notably in Holland, in earthenware crocks, where the action of the air mellows the spirit through oxidation.

Spirits do not improve in glass. Once bottled they remain unchanged.

CLASSIFICATION OF MALT BEVERAGES

BEERS are the light-colored brews commonly called lager. Alcoholic strength about 4 per cent by volume.

ALES are darker, and more bitter brews. Alcoholic strength about 4.5 per cent by volume.

PORTER and STOUT are very full-bodied, rich malt brews. Alcoholic strength about 4.5 per cent by volume.

SAKÉ is a specially treated and refermented brew made in Japan. Alcoholic strength of 14 to 16 per cent by volume.

Beer is a product more delicate than milk. It is extremely sensitive to light and heat, and should be kept in a dark, cold storeroom.

3. Fermentation

THE way to tell a story, someone wisely said, is to begin at the beginning, go straight on to the end, and then stop. The story of alcoholic beverages must begin with an understanding of the process whereby alcohol is obtained. Alcohol can be produced only from sugar or a product which can be changed into a sugar. "First catch your rabbit," advised the old cookbook. First have your sugar, and it is an easy matter to transform it into alcohol by the natural process of fermentation.

Fermentation is the result of chemical changes by which the molecule of sugar is split into two molecules of ethyl alcohol and two molecules of carbon dioxide gas. The gas escapes into the air and the alcohol remains. The metamorphosis that takes place is like that which changes milk into cheese or the lowly caterpillar into the lovely butterfly. Nature provides its own chemical agents to see that the job is accomplished efficiently in each case. The agent in fermentation is a yeast. Yeast, being a living plant organism, capable of self-reproduction, has as many individual strains as there are people on earth, a number of which have been identified and given long scientific names. But the yeast in grape juice, whose job it is to change the juice into wine, is called saccharomycetes (also spelled saccharomyces).

It might be said that the transforming of grape juice into wine by the process of fermentation could be left entirely to nature without any interference from man, except in the case of sparkling, fortified, or other such wines. And this is true—up to a point. Grass grows quite naturally in the fields in a wild state, but it takes constant care to make an attractive lawn. Wine left too long to ferment upon its husks will draw color from the skins, if they are those of black grapes, and it will also draw from the pips, stalks, or the small pedoncules, more acidity and tannin, and more of the unsuitable acids, which would prove objectionable later. It is man's job, therefore, to control the process of fermentation, leaving most of the work to the yeasts or saccharomycetes.

The yeasts or saccharomycetes appear when the grapes begin to ripen. They settle on the outside of the skins to await the time when the grapes are gathered and the juice expressed. The yeasts then can perform their mission in life of causing the grape juice to ferment and become wine. The grapes themselves are not affected by their presence, since their action does not commence until the juice is expressed and there is oxygen present. In other words, eliminate the air, and the grape juice will not ferment, even though it is chuck full of saccharomycetes. However, under favorable temperature conditions (15° to 20° C, not over 85° F.) they perform their function. They cause a terrific commotion and change to take place, yet remain unaffected themselves. They work violently at first, when there is an abundance of grape sugar to work upon, and more quietly as it is changed into alcohol and carbon dioxide, until all the sugar has been used up or the wine attains an alcoholic strength of around 14 per cent, when their action will be inhibited and the fermentation process is completed.

The saccharomycetes, or catalytic agent, in other words, produced a new product, ethyl alcohol, and what was originally must (unfermented grape juice)

Grape must fermenting.

has now become wine. But the importance of this agent does not end with its chemical action. It has a definite influence on the character of the wine itself. It is a living plant organism and is influenced by climate, soil, and geographical conditions existing in each wine-producing region, much as human beings are influenced by their environment.

A good case in point is to be found in the white wines of Burgundy and Champagne. In both instances, the Pinot grape is used, yet two more distinct and different white wines are hard to find. Admittedly, the soil difference is a contributing factor, but the character of the yeasts or saccharomycetes has much to do with explaining this phenomenon.

Still another example appears in the Sherry district at Jerez, Spain, where the yeast develops as a film upon the surface of the wine, known as the "flower," is found to be entirely different from that in the Manzanilla warehouses of San Lucar de Barrameda on the seacoast.

To sum up, the process known as fermentation is one which consists mainly in the splitting up of each molecule of grape sugar present in grape juice into two molecules of alcohol and two molecules of carbon dioxide. But it must be remembered (1) that there are other fermentable substances in grape juice besides grape sugar; (2) that there are other catalysts which render possible subsidiary fermentations which take place at the same time or later, and are responsible for the presence, in wine, of compounds which did not exist in the grape juice.

Grape juice, indeed, is a very complex aqueous solution. It contains, besides water and grape sugar, acids and other substances, most of them in very small quantities, either of a vegetable or of a mineral origin.

1. Substances, other than water, which are the same in must and wine: grape sugar, saccharomycetes, acids, cellulose, essential oils, mucilage, etc.

2. Substances other than ethyl alcohol, present in wine, but not in must: glycerine, various acids, alcohols other than ethyl, esters, aldehydes, etc.

We have been discussing fermentation in wine, in which sugar is naturally present in the form of grape sugar in the grape juice. It is also present in other fruits, most particularly in sugar cane, whose juice, properly treated, gives us the sugar we use in our coffee and, as a by-product, molasses which, when fermented, produces the alcohol which we distill off and eventually call rum.

However, alcoholic beverages are often obtained from basic ingredients which contain no natural sugar but which are rich in starch, such as grains, cereals, potatoes, etc. This is possible because, under the proper conditions, the starches can be converted into sugar (maltose and dextrin) by the action of the diastase which is the principal enzyme contained in malt (usually barley malt). Once the sugar is there, yeast will gladly finish the job of fermentation.

4. Wine in General

THE vintner's life, like the policeman's, is not a happy one, even when Mother Nature is most co-operative. Making wine is not merely a matter of gathering grapes, pressing them, and leaving them to ferment. It is not the simplest and most profitable of agricultural pursuits, when one considers that every vine must be carefully watched, pruned down so that all its strength will not go into the stalk but into producing grapes of rich quality, sprayed against the many diseases always waiting to attack at a moment's notice. The vintner must take care that birds, who love the grapes, do not eat up the entire crop; he must gather the grapes when they are just ripe, press them, and see that conditions favorable to a perfect fermentation are present. He must watch carefully over the casks of new wine to make sure that the *mycodermae aceti* (vinegar yeasts) which are in the air do not get in and steal the show; and after the wine gets in the bottle, he hopes that eventually it will reach an appreciative buyer. Add to this his eternal worry over too much rain or too little sunshine, and it is a wonder that men have the courage to carry on such an arduous task, particularly when you consider that one out of every three vintages are apt to be below normal.

Man has made wine almost as long as he has husbanded the earth. Paleontologists have found evidence of masses of grape pips, skins, and stems, which apparently had been crushed by prehistoric man. No one knows when wine was first made. It is possible that a cliff dweller who had gathered wild grapes to use their sweet juice as a thirst-quencher returned from a hunting trip, picked up the vessel which he had left, and discovered, to his amazement and delight, that the grape juice had become a different drink, one that made him happy—the grape juice had fermented and become wine.

The Egyptians credit Osiris, and the Greeks Dionysus, with the gift of wine, while the Hebrews say Noah first introduced it. At all events, the numerous references in the Bible indicate that not only wine but stronger beverages were made, as indicated by the following words:

13

Yayin—the Hebrew word most often used to describe wine.
Homer—fresh, young, unmixed wine.
Tiros—strong wine.
Sekhor—strong drink.
Meseg—mixed wines.

Phoenician traders introduced the vine into Europe at the Mediterranean coastal trading posts they established, and later the Roman legions carried it into Gaul, Germany, and across the Channel into England. Although England is one of wine's best markets, it has never been able to produce wine successfully in commercial quantities.

The greatest single influence upon wine has been the Church. Indeed, the development of the vine has accompanied the spread of Christianity. Wine was needed for sacramental functions, and the good fathers recognized its food value. Since they made the wine for their own use and not for commercial purposes, they were more interested in quality than in quantity and their every effort was directed toward improving the vines and perfecting the quality of the wines they made. As a result, the vintners outside the Church began to follow their example and the general standard of wine-making was raised to a higher level.

Evidences of their work still exist in France today. The vineyards of Châteauneuf-du-Pape near Avignon were started by Pope Clement V in the early fourteenth century, and they still produce wines which we enjoy at the present time. Dom Pérignon, the Bénédictine monk of the Abbey of Hautvillers, probably did more for Champagne than any other man, and as we lift the sparkling wine we still hear echoed in our ears his rapturous cry as he first sipped Champagne, "Oh, come quickly! I'm drinking stars!"

It was men of the Church, too, who first made elixirs from wine and brandy, combined with herbs and plants, which were originally used for medicinal purposes. The two most notable examples, with their secret formulas still in use today after hundreds of years, are the famed Bénédictine and Chartreuse liqueurs.

Even in the United States, the vinicultural history of California begins with the efforts of Fray Junipero, a Dominican missionary, who planted around the missions vines he had brought from Spain.

But while the development of viniculture was greatly stimulated by the Church, the making of wine antedates it by thousands of years. Archaeologists have translated the Laws of Hammurabi, the lawgiver king of Babylonia, handed down some 4100 years ago. Among them are regulations governing innkeepers and the manner in which their hostelries could be conducted. The penalties called for the loss of a limb for permitting riotous drinking on the premises, and in extreme cases—death. They seem to have been rather trying for the unfortunate violators but they indicate, as did our more recent "noble experiment," that man will not be made temperate by force or by stringent prohibitory laws. It is apparent that the majority of people, from the beginning, have enjoyed alcoholic beverages temperately, and that there has always been a small minority who abuse the privilege to their own and their fellows' detriment. Attempts to protect this minority have led to periodic restrictions over the rest for more than four thousand years.

The vine has played an important part in our own land, as well as throughout the world. In the year 1000, a small band of intrepid Vikings discovered America which they dubbed "Vineland the Good" because of the wild profusion of grape vines they found growing on our shores, and for 600 years thereafter the country was referred to, in Icelandic literature, as Vineland. One of the first concerns of the early European settlers on our Eastern seaboard was the cultivation of the vine, both native and imported. These efforts, unfortunately, were doomed to failure for reasons which are discussed in the chapter on American wines. However, it is interesting to note that some twenty, or more than half of the known grape species of the world, are indigenous to North America.

The American influence, oddly enough, has been felt in every viticultural region in Europe, not because of our taste for wine or our lack of it, but because of a certain grape pest (*phylloxera vastatrix*) which reached Europe with a shipment of American vine plants imported for experimental purposes. In every part of viticultural Europe havoc was caused by the insatiable appetite of the phylloxera before an effective remedy was found. Chemicals, sprays, turning over the land, were of no avail. After twenty-odd years of suffering and experimentation, it was found that the phylloxera did not attack the American plants, which have much hardier roots. Thereupon, the European varieties (*Vitis Vinifera*) were grafted on American roots (*Vitis Aestivalis*, *Vitis Riparia*, or *Vitis Labrusca*). For this reason, there are people who say that our wines must be just as good as the European, because "their grapes grow from American vines." It is important to understand that the grape continues to have the identical character which it had prior to the grafting on the American roots.

Although man had been making wine and beer since time immemorial, it was not until the early 1860's that anyone actually knew how the miracle was performed. It was the great scientist, Louis Pasteur, who, by his revolutionary researches in the field of vinous and malt fermentation, proved conclusively that fermentation was caused by the presence of minute organisms called "ferments." He further demonstrated that if grape juice or brewers' wort is exposed to air from which these minute organisms have been removed, no change takes place, but if ordinary air is present, the miracle of fermentation takes place. Based on Pasteur's studies, the business of wine making and brewing began a new era. Exact scientific knowledge replaced guesswork. Certain things no longer "just happened"; the vinters understood at last how they happened and why; and they knew at last what to do about it.

Wine, like a human being, is born, passes through adolescence, matures, grows old, and, if not drunk in time, becomes senile and finally dies. Its life span, like that of man, is unpredictable at the time of birth. It suffers from maladies to which some succumb while others recover. Some wines are aristocrats, some plebeians, but the mass of wines are just sturdy, honest, good fellows. Yet all are interesting, more so as one gets to know them better, because no two vintages of the same wine, or any two wines, are ever identical. Each has its own individuality. There will be family resemblances and characteristics which can be recognized quite readily, but the more one studies the subject and notes these intriguing differences, the greater will be the enjoyment from wines.

tasting—what to look for

Three factors govern the appreciation of wine—color, aroma, and taste. Wine offers a three-fold sensory appeal. That is why those who love wine first hold the glass to the light, then smell it, and finally taste it. The pleasure of anticipation is half the fun, and in drinking wine, each step in the process adds to the enjoyment.

A wine must be clear and brilliant, have a clean, pleasant bouquet, and should have a clean, sound, pleasant taste on the palate. There is beauty in its brilliant color, whether it be the amber of a white wine, reminding us of golden sunshine, or the warm ruby depth of a red wine. The color also gives the first indication of the wine's body; the deeper the color, the fuller it will be. Naturally, this applies to wines of the same type. Two totally dissimilar wines cannot be compared.

After the appeal to the eye, the sense of smell is pleased by the subtle, pleasant perfume which a wine gives off in the form of esters. As a matter of fact, more than three-fourths of our sense of taste is actually our ability to smell. The bouquet, aroma, perfume—call it what you will—of a wine tells much of what the taste will be. In subsequent chapters, in describing the taste of wines, we shall be forced to use what may seem to be strange comparisons. We shall refer to some wines as having a strawberry, violet, or flowery bouquet. In other words, we shall try to give a taste picture in terms of familiar experiences.

Finally, after the aroma of the wine has promised a certain taste, the palate should confirm it, and add the after-taste which is experienced after the wine has been swallowed.

If wine is being "tasted" critically, with a view to purchasing or salability, it should be compared with a similar wine of the same price to establish the fact of its quality. Is the taste more pleasing? Is the quality better than the wine with which it is being compared? Tasting is a business and should be carried out very carefully and seriously. But in drinking wine for pleasure, enjoyment should not be encumbered by any critical analysis of its delicate nuances. The important thing, in this instance, is the pleasure which the wine gives. Do not be hypercritical.

CULINARY USES OF WINE

IT is not necessary to be a professional chef in order to use wine in cooking. A knowing dash of wine in the pot seasons, tenderizes, imparts rare flavor and bouquet. Alcohol? By some mysterious alchemy, alcohol quickly evaporates when heat is applied, leaving the blessing of wine's flavorful bouquet.

Wine in cooking goes back to the first viniculturists—and that is a long, long time ago. They looked upon wine as food and used it as naturally in cooking as they would any other ingredient.

Why do you use herbs? For flavoring of course. Jars of dried herbs of every description are found in racks in every kitchen. If you use them with a heavy hand, all you taste is the herb and every dish will seem to taste alike.

If you look upon wine as the most delicate of all flavorings you will realize its potentiality in cooking. Knowing how to use it is easier than you think.

The French are recognized as the world's best cooks. They make the most of the ingredients they use to create superb dishes from soups to desserts. Their use of wine in cooking gives the simplest dish an elusive, subtle flavor. They know from long experience that wine will produce the best results if handled delicately. Too much will spoil the effect. It is not the wine you taste in the finished dish but rather the goodness of the food itself which the wine enhances.

Carême, who was chef to George IV of England, and later to the Rothschilds, wrote in his memoirs that his thoughts were first turned to the art of the cuisine by the delightful aromas which tantalized him as he stood one day, all but starving, outside a Paris restaurant. That aroma was produced by the wine in which the dishes were being cooked. From that moment on his course was set. Carême became the greatest of all chefs. He was able to produce a thousand different tastes with his seasonings, just as a painter with a few colors can create an infinite variety of nuances and tones. Wine was one of the principal ingredients he used.

In America, which is the melting pot of peoples from every country in the world, one can find every type of food. Many dishes have been adapted and simplified. But we have our own heritage. In Colonial days Sherry, Port, and Madeira were the favorite wines of hospitality, and soups, shellfish, and desserts were prepared with these wines. (*The Williamsburg Art of Cookery* compiles a collection of recipes culled from *The Compleat Housewife* printed in 1742.) See page 516 for a list of recommended modern cookbooks which feature cooking with wine.

THE THERAPEUTIC VALUE OF WINE

"WINE," said Pasteur, "is the most healthful and hygienic of beverages." From the earliest days it has been looked upon as a natural remedy for man's ills. In ancient times it must have been invaluable to physicians whose medical knowledge was limited, and European doctors today use it extensively in their practice. In Europe, indeed, where oenotherapy has long been practiced with success, doctors regularly prescribe various wines in cases of anemia, arteriosclerosis, constipation, diarrhea, malaria, pneumonia, illness of the liver, kidneys, gall bladder, and so forth.

However, it is as an aid to recovery during the convalescent period that wine can give its best service. Many of the tonics prescribed by physicians, to say nothing of the many patent medicines, could not be made without such wines as Sherry, Madeira, Porto, or Tokay. All of these wines, rich in minerals, easily assimilated by the system, are used daily to help those who are run down, anemic, or fatigued. Champagne is the first food permitted after an abdominal operation. It is almost the only nourishment the stomach will receive and hold after the operative shock. The medicinal value of Champagne and other sparkling wines in cases of sea sickness is well known. Sherry, rich in iron, is mentioned in the pharmacopoeia.

It is a significant fact that in the Médoc district (Bordeaux wine region) of France, there are nearly twice as many octogenarians per 100,000 population as there are in the whole of France outside that district. Claret forms part of the daily diet of these old people. Incidentally, they also boast more golden wedding anniversary celebrations than any other section of France. Wine, in France, is called "the milk of the aged."

More important, however, than its medicinal properties is the fact that throughout the ages man has looked upon wine as a food. The Bible refers to it in this sense time and again, for example, in Isaiah: "Until I come and take you away to a land like your own land, a land of corn and wine, a land of bread and vineyards." And later, "Thus saith the Lord, As the new wine is found in the cluster, and one saith Destroy it not; for a blessing is in it."

There is a blessing in it. Wine is a food and an aid to health. A quart of wine containing 10 per cent of alcohol furnishes 850 calories, or the alimentary equivalent of a pound of meat, or 20 ounces of milk, or a pound of bread.

In "Tables of Food Values—Revised and Enlarged" by Alice V. Bradley, published by Chas. A. Bennett Co., Inc., Peoria, Illinois, copyright 1956, caloric values of several wines are given as follows:

TYPE OF WINE	CALORIES PER OUNCE	AVERAGE PORTION	CONTENT
California Red Table Wine	18	4 oz.	72
California White Table Wine	22.5	4 oz.	90

TYPE OF WINE	CALORIES PER OUNCE	AVERAGE PORTION	CONTENT
California Chablis, Rhine	17.5–20	4 oz.	70/80
Catawba (sweet)	30.25	4 oz.	121
Champagne (dry)	21.25	4 oz.	85
Champagne (sweet)	29.25	4 oz.	117
Red Bordeaux	16.75	4 oz.	67
Moselle Wine	16.75	4 oz.	67
Madeira	32.5	2 oz.	65
Malaga	43.5	2 oz.	87
Port (California)	43.25	2 oz.	86.5
Port (Imported)	38.75	2 oz.	77.5
Sherry (California)	36	2 oz.	72
Sherry (Imported, dry)	32	2 oz.	64
Vermouth (dry, French)	27.25	2 oz.	54.5
Vermouth (sweet, Italian)	43.5	2 oz.	87

All light wines contain vitamins, particularly B and C, which are important to the digestive tract as they help activate the secretions of the ductless glands whose proper functioning is so necessary to our general well-being. As can be seen from the chemical composition of wine it contains valuable alcohols, acids, and minerals in minute quantities.

Intemperance is almost unknown in wine-drinking nations such as France, Italy, and Spain. There are two reasons for this: first, the wine is used as food and consumed at meal times: second, while everyone drinks, drunkenness is looked upon by these practical people as a wasteful use of a good thing and consequently it is frowned upon.

In the United States as recently as 1963 only 35 per cent of the wine consumed was table wine, while wines containing more than 14 per cent alcohol constituted almost 65 per cent. In recent years wine has become more and more a part of our regular diet so that by 1972 wines under 14 per cent constituted over 70 per cent of our consumption, while wines of higher alcoholic content have fallen to approximately 25 per cent. Our per capita consumption of table wines is just about one and a half gallons, but it is a healthy improvement over the nine-tenths of a gallon in 1963.

THE WINE LABEL IN GENERAL

EVERY label which appears on the bottle of an alcoholic beverage sold in the United States must be approved by the DATF (Department of Alcohol, Tobacco, and Firearms) of the U.S. Treasury Department. It is mandatory that the public be furnished with clear, correct information as to the product, the contents, the country of origin, and the U.S. importer. Additional information is permitted. You can be sure that the label will bear as much information as it is legally entitled to, to describe the origin and character of the wine the bottle contains. Among these items which may be mentioned or included on a label according to United States regulations are the following:

A. Vintage. This is the year in which all the grapes used to make the wine were gathered, pressed, and the juices fermented into wine.

B. Village, parish, district, or state in which the grapes were grown.

C. Vineyard in which all the grapes grew.

D. Type or variety of wine.

E. Registered, trade-marked brand.

F. Official governmental guarantee to the wine's authenticity of proper labeling.

G. Shipper's name and address.

H. Vineyard owner's name and address.

I. Wine bottled by the vineyard owner.

J. Special reserve quality.

K. Wine made from extra-fine grapes.

L. Bottled at the vineyard owner's cellars.

M. Country of origin.

Specific labeling laws or labeling information of the various wine-producing countries of the world are given in the upcoming chapters.

OPPOSITE PAGE. *There are six basic types of wine labels:*
TOP-LEFT. Estate or Chateau Bottled *wines are those where the grapes are grown, processed and bottled on the same property.*
TOP-RIGHT. Domaine Bottling *refers to wines from which the grapes are grown, processed and bottled by the owner but not necessarily on one property.*
MIDDLE-LEFT. Regional Bottling *refers to wines made from grapes grown in one Parish or region. If wine or grapes from out of the area are used, local custom or law controls the percentage.*
BOTTOM LEFT. Generic Bottling *refers to wines which use a name originating elsewhere to identify in general the type of wine but has no real meaning in use or law. Terms such as Burgundy, Sauternes or Claret indicate the general type of wine and is always preceded by the name of the actual locality of origin.*
MIDDLE RIGHT. Varietal Bottling *indicates the wine by the grape from which it is made. The proportion of wine from that grape may vary from 51 to 100 percent, depending on local law.*
BOTTOM RIGHT. Monopole or Brand Labeling *is used where the actual name of the wine has no real significance but gains consumer identification and acceptance through the use of advertising or other consumer marketing techniques.*

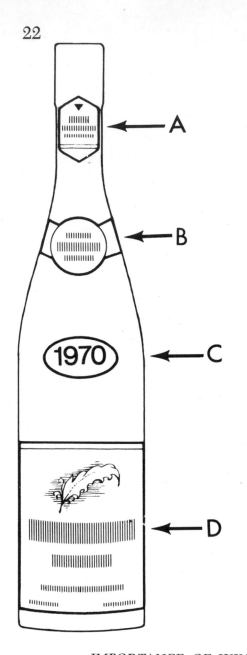

This is a composite bottle showing the placement of some of the other labels often used by the wine trade.

A — *A. Identification seal or label sometimes used by geographical groups or associations (of shippers) as a supplementary guarantee of origin and authenticity.*

B — *B. Shipper's or importer's label.*

C — *C. Vintage label, if applicable, and the information does not appear on the main label.*

D — *D. Main label, which bears the name and type of the wine.*

IMPORTANCE OF WINE IN THE ECONOMY OF THE NATION

THE world's greatest wine-producing and consuming nation is France. The per capita consumption is almost 29 gallons. To satisfy this demand, 7 per cent of the arable land, or some four million acres, is planted in vineyards.

These vineyards are owned by 1,500,000 individuals who give employment to many more. Figures of the other important wine-producing and consuming nations of Europe—Italy, Spain, and Germany—are comparable.

In contrast, the American consumption figures are absurd. People with a far lower standard of living, recognizing the food value of wine, use twenty times as much as our less than one and two-thirds gallons per capita. However, more important is the fact that 25 per cent of our consumption is fortified wine containing over 14 per cent of alcohol, while in the wine-consuming countries of Europe and South America practically all the wine the people drink is light table wine of less than 14 per cent alcohol.

If we could increase our consumption of light wines in this country to one-quarter of the French rate, or a little less than eight gallons per capita, i.e., about four glasses of wine per week, we would require, on the basis of the French figures, some three and a half million acres of land, involving some two million farmers, and the employment of perhaps two or three times as many persons. And this would be only the beginning. Distribution and sale, the allied industries such as bottle makers, label printers, and so on, would add to the employables, because of this increase in wine consumption. This appears even more desirable when you consider that the opportunities offered to the small farmers would help to create more independent, self-reliant men, such as the country wants as the backbone of the nation.

As a means of encouraging this, the several State Governments and the Federal administration should recognize that for actual revenue-through-taxation, wine is a woefully poor contributor. The present tax rates average:

	FEDERAL	STATE
Light wines under 14 per cent	$ .17 per gal.	$.10 per gal.
Fortified wines up to 21 per cent	.67 per gal.	.10 per gal.
Natural sparkling wines, 14 per cent	3.40 per gal.	.53$\frac{1}{3}$ per gal.

The State tax rates shown are those levied in New York. Each State levies its own taxes, and there is some variation, while in most of the so-called Controlled or Monopoly States there is no specific tax as such, since the State sells to its citizens at a profit.

In 1939, when the Federal excise taxes were $.05 and $.10 per gallon respectively, the Federal Government and the several States collected through wine excise and fortifying taxes some $15,000,000. In 1952, when total volume had almost doubled and the Federal taxes had been increased by more than 200 per cent over 1939, tax collections increased to a little over $100,000,000. In the 1972 calendar year, Federal wine tax collections amounted to over $186,000,000 compared to $180,000,000 in calendar year 1971. In fact the annual rate of collections has risen approximately 27 per cent in just three years. The prospect now is that, at *current* rates, government and state revenues from wine sales will double in less than a decade.

The only Federal tax increase in wine since 1952 was a jump from $2.72 to $3.40 for natural sparkling wines. This is a most illogical excise tax rate since it is exactly twenty times the 17 cent rate for light wines. But all in all, the tax from wine is rarely as much as 4 per cent of the total tax revenue from alcoholic beverages. Generally speaking, these taxes are low and quite reasonable when compared to those levied on beers and spirits. However, it is the high license fees, both for production and sale, which are the greatest hindrances to a more rapid expansion of wine-making, and which tend to increase the cost of the wine to the consuming public.

So long as wine is looked upon as an alcoholic beverage and not as a food its wide use will be curtailed. When the day arrives on which wine can be made and sold freely with a minimum of special tax and license burden, when it can be distributed through outlets that sell other foods, much as coffee and tea are sold today, then and then only is our country likely to become a wine-drinking nation. Then the Federal and State treasuries will derive an increased revenue from wine through the larger income tax payments of the farmers, who will turn to wine-making when they find it profitable.

The picture is not too discouraging. Wine consumption has reached over 350,000,000 gallons—over four times as much as in 1939—according to Wine Institute figures. This means many more acres planted to vineyards, greater employment in the vineyards and at the wineries and in every phase of the industry. It is to be hoped that it will continue to prosper.

5. The Wines of France

IN any discussion of wines, it is natural that France should be uppermost in our minds. "The French," said the old history book, "are a gay people, fond of dancing and light wines." The former statement is open to question, but there is no doubt about the wines. In fact, although the largest wine-producing nation in the world, France still imports slightly more wine than she exports.

There are some who would have us believe that much wine is shipped from the United States to France which returns here later as French wine with high-sounding names. To the best of our knowledge, *there is no foundation of fact in this statement.* In the first place, our wines are too expensive for French needs, and in the second place, France has a glut of fine wines but a shortage of cheap, ordinary wine of high alcohol strength.

It is her fine wine which France exports, and let it be observed here that it is this policy of exporting only such goods as will enhance her reputation, whether wine or chefs or clothes, which has made the French the most astute merchandisers in the world, and given her a position from which she sets the fashion in the art of good living. Poor wine, badly made dresses, and downright bad cooking there are in France, but they stay there.

It is not, however, because of the quantity of wine she produces or drinks, but because of the quality and variety of wines that she offers to the world, that France comes at the head of our list. In every Department but two, the vine is cultivated.

France is politically subdivided into ninety-five Departments, which are further subdivided into Communes or Parishes (counties). The three most important Departments, as far as controlled appellation of wines are concerned, are the Gironde (Bordeaux—Clarets and white wines), Côte d'Or, (Burgundy—red and white, Saône-et-Loire, and Rhône, and Marne (Champagne). After these leaders come the Departments of Yonne (Chablis), Bas-Rhin and Haut-Rhin (Alsace), Maine et Loire (Anjou), Indre et Loire (Vouvray), and the various Departments along the Rhône River, which produce the famous Côtes-du-Rhône wines.

The wines from each section are so markedly different and have such individual characteristics, that they have been accepted as basic types. Their names are often misused and the wines imitated in almost all wine-producing countries, so that, in order to study the wines of the country properly, we must take each geographical division separately. Each will be considered in the order of its importance to the wine trade in general.

APPELLATION CONTRÔLÉE

ALTHOUGH the vine has been cultivated commercially in Gaul since the Roman occupation, and with greater care and intelligence than in other countries, it is only within recent years that regulatory laws have been passed, guaranteeing the authenticity of origin and place names commonly found on wine labels.

The first delimitary laws were passed after the 1911 "Champagne wars." This came about when the vignerons who were making their wine exclusively from grapes grown within the province of La Champagne rose up in arms against certain merchants who imported grapes at low prices from outside the traditional Champagne region and sold their Champagne at cut prices. The riots resulted in laws that fixed the boundaries within which the grapes must be grown to produce wine legally entitled to the name Champagne.

Since then, further laws have fixed the geographic limits of all the major wine, the Cognac and the Armagnac districts. More recently these laws have been amplified to fix the physical limits of the world-famous vineyards as well as setting the maximum quantity of quality wine each may produce of a given vintage. By setting the legal maximum of quantity an assurance of maintenance of quality is attained. Under this law, called *Appellation d'Origine*, the production of each vineyard is controlled. The vineyard owner is obliged to report to his local board, who in turn reports to the central or national board of *Appellation Contrôlée* wines located in Paris. Wines produced under this system of control of origin and quality will bear the phrase *Appellation Contrôlée* on the label, which becomes a French Government guarantee of origin and to a certain degree quality as well.

The basic conditions for a wine to be entitled to an *appellation contrôlée* are set up by the Institut National des Appellations d'Origine des Vins et Eaux-de-Vie, an official body whose members belong either to the French civil service or to the wine industry.

Some of these conditions are: District boundaries according to the nature of the soil; grape varieties; methods of pruning; maximum quantity of wine per acre allowed to be produced, and sugar and alcohol content of the wine. Growers and shippers must follow these regulations if they wish to label their wines with the name of the vineyard, the commune, or the district. There are exceptions: Very old bottles of wine do not carry the *appellation contrôlée* statement because most of the laws date from 1935 and the following years, though some of them are older.

Controls are exercised by technicians to make sure that these regulations are enforced. The quality regulations, of course, increase in stringency in relation to the fame of the place of origin of the wine. For example, a wine entitled to be labeled "Pommard" *Appellation Contrôlée,* if it comes from any vineyard of the Pommard zone, has a minimum of $10\frac{1}{2}$ per cent of alcohol and was fermented from a must that had 189 grams of sugar per liter. But, for the wine to have the legal right to be labeled "Pommard Epenots" *Appellation Contrôlée* it must be made entirely from grapes grown in the *Les Epenots* vineyard of the Pommard zone. It must also have a minimum alcoholic content of 11 percent and been fermented from a must that contained a minimum of 198 grams of sugar per liter. In both cases the maximum quantity of wine which may legally be produced is 14 hectoliters (369.85 gallons) per acre.

Some wines, not so well known, bear on their labels the letters V.D.Q.S. (*Vins Délimités de Qualité Supérieure*) which indicate that they are high-quality wines of specified origin. They are subject to regulations similar to those of *appellation contrôlée* wines. That is, these wines have been harvested from strictly defined vineyards and vines, by traditional methods. The label shows that the wine has been officially analyzed, tasted and pronounced good, conforming to standards set jointly by the I.N.A.O. and the Ministry of Agriculture. V.D.Q.S. wines, about sixty of them, are grouped into seven general areas, including reds, whites, and rosés (see Appendix F.). Someday the VDQS wines may be combined into the Appellation Controlée.

There are also wines under the category of *Appellation Simple* which must come entirely from the district named and finally non-appellation wines which may be blends from various districts and even various countries.

1. BORDEAUX

history FIFTY years before the birth of Christ, Burdigalia (Bordeaux) was the chief town and commercial center of Biturigis Vivisi. Later, in the fourth century, it was made the capital of Aquitania Secunda. Its fame, then as now, was irrevocably linked with the excellence of its wines, which were praised by Columella, renowned Roman writer of the first century.

Through his marriage with Eleanor of Aquitaine in 1152, Henry of Anjou acquired the Sénéchaussée of Bordeaux (Gascony) and the vast Duchy of Guienne. Two years later he became King Henry II of England, and for 300 years Gascony belonged to the English crown. Its wines enjoyed wide popularity in the islands, a taste which exists to this day.

The history of the famous wines of Bordeaux began more than 2,000 years ago. We do not know who first produced a wine of the Claret type, but the poet Ausonius sang of its charms and virtues during the Roman occupation. The famous Château Ausone is supposed to be his vineyard.

What is Claret? The term is applied to the red wines produced in the Department of the Gironde. Bordeaux is the main city and seaport of the district. Therefore, while Claret is a type of wine, it also has a very definite geographical origin in Bordeaux. All Bordeaux red wines are Clarets, and *only* Bordeaux red wines are Clarets. Only wines produced from grapes grown within the borders of the Department of the Gironde are entitled to be called

Bordeaux and even then part of the area is excluded because of the nature of the soil.

If France is first as a wine-producing country, the Bordeaux district (Gironde) may be regarded as the heart of the French wine trade. The district produces three distinct varieties of wine, equally distinguished: magisterial Clarets of great breeding; clean, dry, white Graves; and luscious, golden Sauternes. *types of wines*

The Bordelais viticultural region is divided into five main and three lesser districts, namely: *geography*

Médoc	Côtes
Graves	Entre-Deux-Mers
Sauternes	Palus
St. Emilion	
Pomerol	

There is a further subdivision, the "Commune" or "Parish." The Parish is a geographical, political, and formerly religious subdivision, as a Parish priest and church were required to administer the spiritual needs of a community. The Church worked out such a perfect geographical subdivision that the State saw no reason to change it, and took it over in toto.

One would think that rich soil would be required to produce fine wine. *soil* Nothing could be further from the truth. In fact, the soil of the Bordeaux wine region is mainly gravel, limestone, sand with a clay subsoil. More unfriendly soil for agriculture would be difficult to find, and yet the vine flourishes best in just this type of soil. Where no other crop can be grown successfully, the vine gives the best quality of wine grape. This is equally true in the other famous viticultural regions of Europe.

The principal or informing vine used in the production of the great Clarets *the grape* is the Cabernet Sauvignon. Growing in small, close-set bunches, its violet-scented grapes are small and sweet. Few, if any vineyards, however, are planted with only one variety of vine, and Cabernet-Franc (also called Bouchet), Merlot, Malbec, Carmenère, and Petit Verdot are also planted. The best white wines are made from the Semillon, the Sauvignon Blanc, and the Muscadelle.

The vine in Bordeaux is not allowed to grow wild; in fact, it is cut down close to the ground after the vintage, so that the winter appearance of a vineyard is that of a bare field, dotted with an orderly series of stumps. The vines are not allowed to grow more than two and a half to three and a half feet high, so that what strength they derive from the soil will go into producing grapes of quality rather than trailing vine.

districts   MÉDOC. The most important subdivision is the Médoc, which forms a triangular peninsula, stretching north some fifty miles from Bordeaux to Soulac, varying in width from six to ten miles. It lies between the Garonne and Gironde Rivers on the east, and the sea on the west. Only Clarets° are produced in the fifty-three Parishes which make up the Médoc, of which the four most important, so far as we are concerned, are Pauillac, St. Julien, Margaux, and St. Estèphe.

GRAVES. The second district in importance is Graves which takes its name from the gravelly or pebbly quality of the soil. The Graves stretches for some twenty-five miles to the southwest of Bordeaux, for the most part level plain, which becomes more hilly to the south. Here are produced both red and white wines. The most important Parishes of the Graves are Pessac, Léognan, and Martillac.

ST. EMILION AND POMEROL. Third in importance are the St. Emilion and Pomerol districts. There are five Parishes in the former; the Parish of Pomerol is important enough to be considered a separate district. They are all situated on somewhat hilly ground north of the Dordogne River, in the immediate vicinity of the town of Libourne. The wines from these vineyards, because of their depth of color and fullness of body, are considered the Burgundy wines of the Bordeaux district.

SAUTERNES. Where the Graves terminates, we come to a district smaller than the Island of Manhattan, but viticulturally favored as are few regions in the world. Entirely distinct from all the other wines of Bordeaux, and having an excellence all their own, are the rich, luscious, highly perfumed wines of the Sauternes. The *Sauternais* or *Pays du Sauternes* (Sauternes Country) lies to the southeast of Graves and on the left bank of the Garonne River. Five Parishes comprise the Sauternes country: Sauternes, Bommes, Fargues, Preignac, and Barsac. The wines from any of these Parishes are known by the regional name of Sauternes. Barsac, for example, is a Sauternes.

PALUS, CÔTES, AND ENTRE-DEUX-MERS. In these districts are produced the smaller but useful wines, both red and white, which are generally shipped simply as Bordeaux Blanc or Bordeaux Rouge, or under the shipper's brand name.

the making   The vintage in Bordeaux usually begins sometime during the last two weeks
of the wine   of September. The *vendangeurs* (vintagers)—men, women, and children—are organized in groups under a foreman, who supervises the work to see that only ripe, sound grapes are picked, and that the work is thoroughly and conscientiously done. The bunches of grapes are cut off the vine with special pruning shears and are placed in small baskets which, when full, are emptied

---

° Exceptions are: the good, dry white wines Pavillon Blanc du Château Margaux and Château La Dame Blanche, and the Rosé de Lascombes, which is produced at Château Lascombes.

into large wooden, hodlike receptacles known as *hottes*. The *porte-hotte* (hod-carrier) takes his full *hotte* to a two-wheeled wagon or a truck which has two tubs called *douils*, into which he dumps the grapes. The vintager in charge of the cart pushes the grapes down firmly until the *douil* is filled.

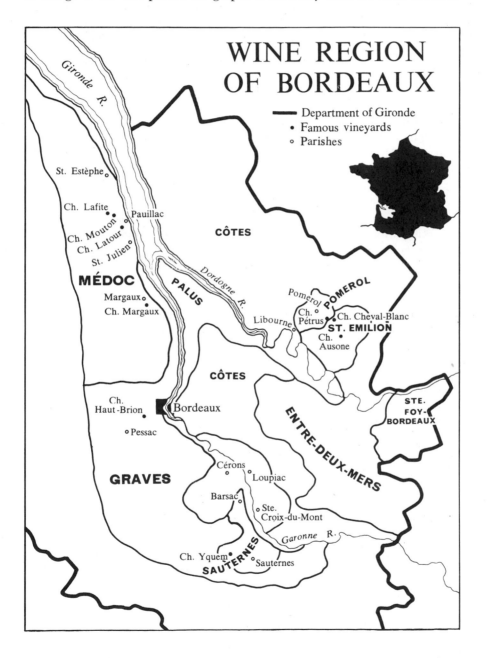

WINE REGION OF BORDEAUX

— Department of Gironde
• Famous vineyards
○ Parishes

A solidly packed *douil* will produce a *barrique* (cask) of 225 liters of wine. When both *douils* are filled, the cart, drawn either by horses or oxen, proceeds to the *pressoir* or *cuvier* (pressing house) where, amidst a great deal of bustle and activity, pressing operations are going on.

Here the grapes are passed through a mechanical "crushing" device above a large fermenting vat. The purpose of "crushing" is simply to break the skins so that the juice will run out freely. The grapes, without further pressing, together with the free flowing juice, drop down into the vat.

The juice is now known as *must*. The grape skins and pips remain in the must during fermentation, to give the wine color and body.

The juice of the usual wine grapes is quite colorless. The color in red wine is obtained from the inside of the grape skin. Grape juice will not dissolve the pigment, but alcohol will, and it is the alcohol formed during fermentation that extracts or dissolves the color in the skins. It is for this reason that a white wine may be made from black-skinned grapes by the simple process of separating the juice from the skins before fermentation begins. The most notable example of this is Champagne.

However, in the making of the white wines of Bordeaux and of most of the other wine regions, white grapes are used almost exclusively and after the *égrappage*° or destemming, the grapes are pressed by means of mechanical presses and the expressed juice is run off into casks.

The saccharomycetes or yeasts which are present on the skins of the grapes begin to multiply with amazing rapidity in the favorable element of grape juice and plenty of air, and fermentation begins almost at once. At first it is violent and quite boisterous. In fact, the verb "to ferment" comes from the Latin *fervere*, "to boil," and if one looks into a vat of fermenting must, it looks like boiling liquid. The escaping gas causes the surface to boil, bubble, and hiss angrily. However, it gradually simmers down as less and less sugar remains, until there is hardly any left. During the period of violent fermentation, the skins, pips, and all the other residue in the must float to the top, forming a cap three or four feet thick. If the cap forms too quickly, it will be broken up with wooden appliances to ensure plenty of air for the saccharomycetes. The grape juice, or must, which is slowly becoming wine, remains at the bottom.

This first, or violent fermentation may take from a week to a month, depending on temperature and climatic conditions. The average time is two weeks.

As soon as the first fermentation is completed, the new wine is "racked" (drawn off) into clean, sulphured barriques of 225 liters, which are placed in the *chai* (warehouse) or cellar, if the vineyard boasts such a luxury. Fer-

---

° The stems are removed in a special apparatus called the *égrappoir*. The destemming operation is known as the *égrappage*.

mentation continues slowly until the little sugar remaining has been used up. This continued period of fermentation causes a certain amount of boiling over, so the cask is not closed tightly. A water seal is used in the bung, which permits the gas to escape but does not allow any air to enter.

During the first few months, because of boiling over and evaporation, there will be a certain loss of wine, which will leave an air space into which the bad ferments are prone to penetrate, ready to undo all the good work of the yeasts making the wine sick or even turning it to vinegar. The preventative is to keep the cask filled up to the bung with sound wine. The casks are refilled twice a week during the first two months and every two weeks thereafter until the wine falls bright (clear) five or six months later.

During this period of continued activity, the wine throws off certain impurities and superfluous solid matter which are deposited at the bottom of the cask and are known as the lees, consisting principally of cream of tartar, tartrate of lime, yeast cells, coloring, and albuminous material.

It is not good for the new wine to remain too long in contact with the lees, so the new wine is racked into fresh casks three times during the first year: in the early spring, March or April; in June, when the vine flowers; and in October. The operation of racking must be performed on a clear dry day to ensure a bright, clear wine. Wine racked or bottled on a muggy or stormy day will be dull in appearance.

With the third racking, the bung is driven home and the cask stored so that the bung is on the side, entirely covered with wine. This assures complete closure and prevents the entrance of any air. Of course, while the wine is in the wood, it will be in contact with the air it breathes through the porous wood, and its development continues.

Since World War II improvements in methods of vinification have made it possible to bottle Clarets earlier than has been customary. Today the lighter-bodied wines are ready for bottling after two years in wood and the fuller-bodied Clarets in big years may require two and a half years development in cask, but the traditional three years or more is no longer practiced.

Before bottling, the wine is subjected to one last operation, which is fining, i.e., clarifying. The heavier solids have precipitated of their own weight to form the lees, but a few lighter particles may remain in suspension, floating in the wine. In order to ensure only perfectly clear, bright wine being bottled, it must be fined. This, too, is done on clear, dry days somewhat as follows: A small amount of albuminous material, which may be either isinglass, gelatine, ox-blood, or white of egg, is mixed with a little wine and poured into the cask. This protein matter combines with part of the tannin in the wine, forming an insoluble tannate film, which slowly precipitates, acting as a filter, carrying with it all such extraneous matter as is the cause of wine's turbidity, leaving the wine in a brilliant condition for bottling. The fining process takes one or two weeks.

A clear, dry day must be selected for bottling, and once a cask is broached, the entire contents must be bottled and the bottles corked. Much as a human being accustomed to an active outdoor occupation dislikes the confinement of an office job, so the wine resents the change from the cask to the confinement of the bottle. It usually takes several months for it to accustom itself to the change. During this period the wine is not drinkable because it is suffering from a disease known in the wine trade as bottle-sickness. After the bottle-sickness period, it takes up its development in the bottle, which will continue until it reaches its prime. If it is not drunk, it will become senile and die. Red wines which have suffered man's ingratitude in this manner can easily be recognized. They have lost color, have no bouquet, flavor, or body. They are dead and lifeless. It has been my misfortune to examine during years past several famous pre-war cellars amply stocked with very old vintages of great repute. The sixty- or seventy-year-old Clarets and Burgundies were all in this condition.

It is difficult to say how long a Claret will live. No two vintages are alike, just as no two people are alike. While the less successful vintages reach their peak in ten to fifteen years, better vintages will continue to improve for thirty, forty, or even fifty years. Naturally, the older the wine becomes, the greater the amount of deposit there will be in the bottle, and the more delicate it will be. Consequently it is difficult to ship it around. This is a natural phenomenon and is to be expected of all wines, particularly red wines. In the course of time, the wine throws off some of its bitartrates, and in the case of red wines, a certain amount of tannin, also, which make up the deposit that settles on the side or bottom of the bottle, depending upon how it is stored. The sediment, however, in no way affects the quality of the wine; it is simply one proof of age.

An extremely old Claret, fit to drink, is almost an impossibility in America today, as it could not withstand the rigors of an ocean voyage. However, there is no reason why a young wine laid down in this country should not mature just as well as in Bordeaux, and be just as enjoyable.

Bordeaux wine trade   There are more than 4,000 vineyards in the Bordeaux wine region, each of which is called *château*, meaning castle. In many cases the property boasts a medieval castle, but when the term is used as generally as it is in Bordeaux, the majority of these "castles" are simply farmhouses used only for pressing grapes and storing wine.

Obviously, if each of the 4,000 odd vineyard owners were to attempt to sell his wines direct to the buyers from all over the world, there would be no end of confusion. Because of this, there evolved many generations ago clearing houses in the form of the Bordeaux Wine Merchants, brokers who buy the wine from the different vineyard owners, sometimes bottled, but more often, and in larger quantities, in the wood. The broker ships the wine as he receives it, or blends it with wine from other vineyards and bottles it, not under the château or vineyard name, but under his own proprietary brand. With few exceptions, the vineyard owner never markets his own wines, but depends on the wine merchant to do it for him.

The Bordeaux wine trade has developed four types of labels to help promote *labeling* the sale of its wines. These are:

(A) Château bottled
(B) Château wine bottled by a cooperative or by a wine merchant
(C) Monopole or trade-mark brand
(D) District or Parish label
(E) Varietal label

There are two distinct types of labels used on château wines. The first, "château bottled," indicates that the wine has been produced, cared for, and bottled at the vineyard property where the grapes were grown. It has on the label or capsule the phrase, *Mise en bouteilles au château*, which means "placed in the bottle at the château." The vineyard owner delivers this wine to the wine merchant or shipper, bottled, labeled, and cased. The cork will always be branded with the château name and vintage year. Examples: Château Lafite-Rothschild, Château Latour, Château Olivier, Château Yquem.

The second type of label, "Château wine, bottled by the wine merchant," indicates that the wine has been produced at the château named on the label, but has been purchased in the cask and bottled by the shipper in his Bordeaux cellars. In this case, the phrase, *Mise (mis) en bouteilles au château*, will not appear, but the shipper's name will appear on the label. Examples: Château Lafite-Rothschild, Château Latour, Château Yquem. This will differ from the "château bottled" in that each shipper designs his own label.

There are some châteaux that do not practice château bottling at all; they have found it more profitable to sell their wines in wood to the different wine merchants who bottle them. So you will often find Château Pontet-Canet, Château Léoville-Barton and Château Langoa-Barton being sold under different labels.

Whereas château bottling guarantees authenticity of origin and should guarantee quality, this does not necessarily hold, as many châteaux bottle their wines only during good years, while others bottle their wine every year. Consequently, because of changing vintage conditions, château bottlings vary greatly in quality from year to year. This has a direct influence on the price governing each vintage and explains why a younger vintage will sometimes fetch a much higher price than an older one of the same wine. A good example is the 1969 Château Latour which costs better than two and a half times as much as the less desirable 1965.

In order to take care of his customer's needs in every part of the world,

36

TOP LEFT. *Chateau bottled. Note the phrase ``Mis en bouteille au chateau.''*
TOP RIGHT. *Château wine bottled by a wine merchant.*
BOTTOM LEFT. *An example of new French varietal label.*
BOTTOM-RIGHT. *Monopole or trade-mark brand. Note the word "depose" in lower right hand corner, meaning registered brand.*

the Bordeaux shipper must always have a wide assortment of château wines. Although there is no "Wine Stock Market" in Bordeaux, château bottlings are traded in somewhat the same manner as stocks and bonds on our exchange. Through the centuries the trade has evolved a system that is eminently fair and satisfactory, both to the vineyard owner and to the shipper.

Suppose, for instance, that the 1959 vintage of Château Latour totaled 100,000 bottles, all château bottled. Eight wine merchants agree to buy up the entire vintage and split it among them. Each of them would then have the same wine to offer to the trade, identical in every respect as to labeling, capsules, cases, etc., and their price would be more or less the same. Along comes a ninth merchant who needs this wine for one of his customers. As the eight merchants have cornered the market on this wine, he must buy from one of the original purchasers and pay him a profit, making a profit for himself on the sale. Therefore, when buying château bottled Bordeaux wines, shop for the lowest price, as it is all the same wine.

The third type of label is the *Monopole* or private brand. Each shipper has his own private brand label on which he stakes his reputation for honesty, and his knowledge and ability as a wine merchant. This is almost invariably a blend of various wines from different parts of the Bordeaux region, which the shipper maintains year in and year out at the same standard of quality; e.g.: Prince Blanc, Le Cardinal, Mouton Cadet, Ruban Rouge, Lion d'Or.

The fourth is the Parish or District label. A bottle so labeled contains wine produced in the Parish or District named, i.e., Médoc (wine in this bottle was produced in the Médoc District). This wine does not necessarily come from one vineyard but may be from several in the Parish or District named. It will be a blended wine, bottled by the shipper at his Bordeaux cellars. For this reason, it is possible to obtain wines bearing identical names and vintages from different shippers of widely varying quality and price. The explanation is that one shipper may have used better quality wine in his blend, while another feels that price is more important than quality. After all, the Bordeaux shipper, like any other businessman, tries to satisfy his customers' needs. Beware of bargains. Compare prices. You get what you pay for in wine or shoelaces.

The Varietal label is the fifth type. This term has been used in the United States to indicate that the grape variety named on the label predominates in the wine itself. At least 51 per cent of the wine must be made from the grape named. The purpose was to break away from generic names which were not definitive and to identify more precisely the nature of the wine. This practice was used in Europe only in Alsace, Switzerland, Italy and a few other regions. In recent years the shippers of Bordeaux, Burgundy and the Loire have sought to promote their wines by using Varietal labels. The French authorities require the use of 100 per cent of the grapes named, and it has been difficult for many shippers to develop acceptable wines. A high proportion of the wines of France have traditionally been made of two or more grape varieties.

the vintage　　There seems to be some confusion as to the exact meaning of the word "vintage" in reference to wines, whether they are imported or produced in the United States. The word has several meanings which it would be well to explain.

1. Vintage means the gathering of the grapes and pressing them and making wine therefrom. There is a vintage every year.

2. The date on a bottle of wine signifies the year in which the wine was produced, the vintage year.

3. Some vineyards bottle and date every year's production; others date only the better years.

4. Certain regions, notably Champagne and Porto, date only the wines of exceptional years. Since this is not done every year, the dated wines are known as "vintage" wines.

A vintage chart, judiciously used, can be helpful, but it is important to remember table wines are living things which are constantly changing. No two wines, even of the same district, are going to develop at a constant rate. Furthermore, not all the wines made in a great year are great, and not all the wines made in a relatively poor year are poor. Sweeping generalities of this kind cannot be applied, when one considers the thousands of vineyards involved. However, the chances are better for good wines resulting when conditions are generally favorable, and with these reservations in mind, a vintage chart can be useful to you. (See complete vintage chart, Appendix B, page 461.)

CLASSIFIED GROWTHS

IN 1855 a number of Bordeaux wines were to be exhibited at the Exposition in Paris. There was some question about the order in which the wines should be shown as, inevitably, there was rivalry among the 4,000-odd vineyard owners as to who produced the finest wine. In order to settle the matter once and for all, a jury was selected to taste and classify the outstanding Clarets and Sauternes in order of merit. Although this was done nearly a century ago, these classifications still hold, for the most part, and are accepted the world over. Sixty-one Clarets were chosen and classified in five classes or groups, while twenty-one Sauternes were grouped in two main classes and one special class. (See Appendix F) Below the fifth growth in the Médoc and the second growth in the Sauternes are further classifications in descending order as follows:

Grands crus exceptionnels
Crus bourgeois supérieurs
Crus bourgeois
Crus premiers artisans
Crus artisans
Crus paysans

In 1953 the leading wines of Graves were officially classified. In 1959, they were again classified and this time thirteen red and eight white were selected. Then, in 1955 and again in 1969 an official classification was made of the top Clarets of Saint-Emilion. Twelve were chosen as "First Classified Great Growths" and 72 as "Great Classified Growths." Both of these classifications have been effected by the *Institut National des Appellations d'Origine des Vins et Eaux-de-Vie.*

Because of the world demand and the high prices of the great classified growths more and more of the so-called "petits châteaux" from all the regions of Bordeaux are being sold and are replacing the district or parish labels in the market.

notes on the classified Claret growths

To differentiate between a classified Claret and crû bourgeois is easy. To tell the difference between a second and a third growth is more difficult. Most of these sixty-one vineyards produce excellent wines whose main differences lie in nuances of nose (bouquet), body, and delicacy, easily apparent to the connoisseur, but not to the layman. However, certain basic, distinguishing marks are apparent in wines from different Parishes or sections. For example, the wines of the Pauillac (Lafite, Latour, Mouton, etc.) have more body than those of Margaux (Château Margaux), which have finesse and delicacy; while the Clarets of the Graves (Haut-Brion, La Mission-Haut-Brion, Haut-Bailly, etc.) are fuller than the Médoc wines mentioned. Even fuller and sturdier are the Pomerol (Pétrus, Certan) and St. Emilion (Ausone, Cheval Blanc, Belair, etc.).

CHÂTEAU LAFITE-ROTHSCHILD. Lafite is spelled with one "f" and one "t" and should not be confused with similar names: Laffite, Laffitte, etc.

Through the centuries many legends, wearing the aura of antiquity, have come to us. According to a document dated 1355, Château Lafite belonged to a certain Jean de Lafite. In 1868 Baron James de Rothschild acquired it at private auction for the reputed sum of one hundred sixty-five thousand pounds, and it is still held by his heirs. In a good year Château Lafite-Rothschild has a magnificent deep color, softness and delicacy of flavor, and a violet bouquet.

CHÂTEAU LATOUR, also a first growth, takes its name from an ancient tower. This, according to legend, is the only remaining vestige of the original castle of St. Lambert, supposedly destroyed by Du Guesclin when the English were driven out of Gascony. The retiring English, say the ancient tales, left a vast fortune buried in or near the tower. But the fortune, as we well know, was buried not below but above the ground, for the great wines of Château Latour have more body and a more pronounced flavor than either Lafite or Margaux.

CHÂTEAU MARGAUX, in true medieval splendor, once boasted a stout fortress surrounded by moats a hundred feet wide, which were connected to the Gironde by canals so that boats could sail up to its very gates. In 1447, it was the property of Baron François de Montferrand. After him, it passed through many hands until, in 1879, it came to Count Pillet-Will who held it until after the war. Today it is owned by a corporation. The wines of Château Margaux are generous without being too full-bodied, refreshing, and with a delightfully fragrant bouquet. In one of the best parts of its vineyard a limited quantity of fine white wine is produced from the Semillon and Sauvignon Blanc grape varieties. It is labeled Pavillon Blanc du Château Margaux.

CHÂTEAU HAUT-BRION, in the Parish of Pessac in the Graves, is the fourth and last of the first growths, and the only wine of the sixty to be chosen from outside the Médoc. It is, in fact, almost in the suburbs of Bordeaux. Haut-Brion, pronounced O-Bree-ON, is, according to some chroniclers, the French spelling of O'Brien, and this is possible, as there must have been some Irishmen in Gascony during the English period. As far back as the fourteenth century, at the Court of Pope Clement V, these wines were highly regarded. From 1801 to 1804 the lord and master of the Château was Napoleon's nemesis, my lord Talleyrand. Though they lack the softness and lightness of their fellow first growths, these wines are renowned for their full, generous body and beautiful color. This superb vineyard has been the property of Clarence Dillon, the American financier, for a number of years.

Almost from the publication of the classification of 1855 there have been violent disagreements as to its validity. Outspoken among the dissidents were the owners of Château Mouton-Rothschild who did not accept tamely having their wine rated below the first four and as a result adopted the challenging motto:

Premier ne puis	First I cannot be
Second ne daigne	Second I do not deign to be
Mouton suis.	Mouton I am.

In 1973, after much work by the Baron Phillipe de Rothschild, the vineyard was classified in Bordeaux as a first growth. (The 1855 classification remains unchanged.) The Baron then wrote a new motto:

First, I am
Second, I was
But Mouton does not change.

Aerial view of the beautiful Château La Mission-Haut-Brion at Pessac, Graves. (Courtesy Mr. Henri Woltner, Bordeaux)

Judging by the prices Mouton usually fetches, this move was more than justified. Over the years Mouton has consistently brought more money than the average of the four first growths. Of course, the Minister of Agriculture may well have opened up Pandora's Box. Although the 1855 classification is still amazingly accurate many inequities have developed. On the basis of market prices alone Château Pétrus of Pomerol and Château Cheval Blanc of Saint Emilion deserve top classification among the clarets of Bordeaux.

Getting back to the 1855 classifications, well-known second growths in the American market are the wines of Châteaux Léoville-Las Cases, Léoville-Barton, Lascombes, Gruaud-Larose, Brane-Cantenac, which is one of my favorites, with its traditional raspberry flower aroma, Rausan-Ségla, Cos d'Estournel, and Montrose.

Among the third growths, Châteaux Kirwan, Palmer, and Calon-Ségur are fairly well-known in America, while among the fourth growths, the wines of Châteaux Branaire-Duluc, Talbot, and Beychevelle are often seen here.

Finally, there are the fifth growths of which the better known in the United States are Châteaux Pontet-Canet, Grand-Puy-Lacoste, Pédesclaux, Cantemerle, Lynch-Bages, and Mouton-Baron Philippe, which was formerly known as Mouton d'Armailhacq. There are too many people who turn up their noses at fifth growths, considering them poor or even inferior. What they forget or overlook is that fifth growths are still part of that special group of sixty wines that were selected from among all the hundreds and thousands of better red wines of Bordeaux. The fact is that they are still great wines even though they do not pretend to be the peers of the first growths.

When we asked M. Jean Cruse why they had never château-bottled their wine, he explained that by doing so they would be in competition with all the other classed growth château bottled wine, with the burden of being a fifth growth, whereas each shipper who sold Pontet-Canet (and all of them did) felt he was selling his own name and his own label, and consequently had a more personal interest in selling it. This merchandising policy was extraordinarily successful. However, since World War II the entire production of Pontet-Canet, which averages some 270,000 bottles annually, has been bottled and distributed by only two houses, Cruse et Fils Frères and Barton & Guestier.

GRAVES CLARETS.   The fine Clarets of the Graves region were not classified officially in 1855. They had to wait a century, until 1953, when an official quality classification was at last made and published. (For the complete list of the Graves classified growths see Appendix F, page 486.) From the Graves come such outstanding wines as Châteaux La Mission-Haut-Brion, Pape Clément, Haut-Bailly, and Smith-Haut-Lafitte. They are fuller bodied and not quite as delicate as the wines of the Médoc, but Graves Clarets make up in richness what they lack in finesse.

ST. EMILION AND POMEROL.   Politics or jealousy must have had something to do with the 1855 classification, that the wines of Châteaux Ausone and Cheval Blanc in St. Emilion, and Pétrus, L'Evangile, and Vieux-Château-Certan in Pomerol were not included. These wines, because of their deep color, rich bouquet, and fullness of body, are called the "Burgundies" of Bordeaux. Ausone, whose average yield is quite small, Cheval Blanc, and Pétrus all produce magnificent wines which almost invariably command prices equal to the great Médoc Clarets. St. Emilion Clarets were finally classified in 1955 and again in 1969 (see Appendix F, page 486.)

Still other wines of great repute are Châteaux Belair, Pavie, Canon, Magdelaine, and Clos Fourtet in St. Emilion, and Fleur-Pétrus, La Conseillante, Petit-Village, Nenin, and Trotanoy in Pomerol. In spite of their excellence, these wines are not known well enough in America, but they will be with time.

WHITE WINES OF BORDEAUX

MORE white wine than red is made in the Graves (pronounced *grahv*). The white wines are clean, dry, fresh and have a pleasant, fruity bouquet of their own.

Most of the Graves wines are shipped by the Bordeaux houses under private brand labels as standard blends; each house having several brands varying in quality and dryness, in order to please the tastes of their several world markets. The paler the color, the drier the wine will be. There are several outstanding château bottled white Graves: Châteaux Olivier, Carbonnieux, and Haut-Brion Blanc. Of these the best known in this country is Château Olivier, an estate whose castle and vineyards were renowned in the twelfth century. Here the Prince of Wales, known as Edward the Black Prince, had a hunting lodge during the time when Aquitaine was an English domain and he was "Governor General of Gascony."

The ancient legends of these old châteaux have the perfume and enchantment of the wines themselves. It is related of Château Carbonnieux that, in order to convince a certain Sultan of Turkey of the merits of French wine (wine being prohibited to the Faithful by the Koran), Château Carbonnieux was shipped to him labeled "Mineral Water of Carbonnieux." So impressed was the Commander of the Faithful upon drinking the wine, that he exclaimed: "When they have water that is so pure and so agreeable, how can the French drink wine?"

These wines are extremely dry, with a clean, invigorating quality that has made them favorites of connoisseurs in all English-speaking lands.

The grape varieties in the Graves are the Semillon, the Sauvignon Blanc, and the Muscadelle, principal among them being the Semillon which gives the wines their luscious, golden finesse, velvetiness, and aroma. Although the same grape varieties are used in the Graves as in the Sauternes, a dry wine is produced because the grapes are gathered when they are ripe, and not left to hang on the vine until over-ripe, as is done in the Sauternais.

The Sauvignon Blanc produces a wine that is full in body, rich in bouquet; the Muscadelle produces a highly perfumed wine, but its principal use is to act as the preacher to marry the others. In other words, it is used to knit the wines made from the Semillon and Sauvignon into a uniform blend, and also to give a slight Muscat undertone to the wine—very delicate in these wines, but much stronger in the Sauternes. It is used less and less today.

There are five Parishes in the Sauternais: Sauternes, which gives the regional name to the entire section, Bommes, Fargues, Preignac, and Barsac. Wine produced from grapes grown in any of these five Parishes is legally permitted to be called Sauternes.

There is a pronounced difference in the way Sauternes are made as compared to the Graves. In fact, originally the wine resembled the Graves. But many years ago, it seems, the owner of a château, reputedly at Yquem, in this district was away on a hunting trip. He was delayed and therefore did not return in time to order the gathering of the grapes when they were ripe. As his men had no authority to start this work, they waited for the master to appear, some four weeks later. The grapes were over-ripe, shrivelled and had a mold covering them, but the owner decided to gather them, none the less, and see what could be done. To his own surprise as well as that of everyone else, the wine which developed from these over-ripe grapes was unlike anything they had seen before, but it was delicious—very rich, luscious, and highly perfumed.

Today we understand what happened. When the grapes reach a certain stage of maturity beyond the full stage of ripeness, a new mold settles upon them, known technically as the *Botrytis Cinerea*.

When gathering grapes in the Sauternais they do not begin until the sun is high, about half-past eight in the morning, and they stop before the sun goes down, because the dew would wash off some of the Botrytis Cinerea. The French call this condition of over-ripeness *pourriture noble*, meaning noble rottenness. They are not, of course, rotten, as rotten grapes are removed lest they spoil the wine; they are merely over-ripe. Only bunches which are in a perfect condition of over-ripeness are picked, and therefore a vineyard may be gone over as many as eight times before all the grapes are gathered, a procedure which naturally adds to the cost of production.

Leaving the grapes on the vine until they attain *la pourriture noble* has the following results: the water in the grapes is evaporated by the sun and the sugar concentrated. This gives a smaller yield of juice or must per acre, but it insures an abundance of richness. Sauternes, consequently, are always rich, sweet wines, when compared to Graves or white Burgundies. In this sense there is no such thing as a "dry" Sauternes.

The wines of the five Sauternes Parishes are all very similar in character. The important point to remember is that they are all sweet. Sweetness and dryness, or course, are relative qualities. Some Sauternes are sweeter and richer than others, but compared with white wines from the Graves or any other section of the Bordeaux wine region, they are so much softer, sweeter, and fuller bodied, that there is no need to quibble over the statement that Sauternes is sweet.

This does not mean that a rather dry-tasting wine cannot be produced. The Appellation of Origin law and its *Appellation Contrôlée* regulations do not prevent production of such a wine in the Sauternais, but they forbid its being labeled Sauternes or Barsac. It can only be labeled Bordeaux Blanc.

In the disastrously poor year of 1968 some rather dry-tasting wine was produced even at the famous Château d'Yquem, and it, too, could only be bottled as Bordeaux Blanc.

Of the five Parishes entitled to the use of the regional term Sauternes, Barsac is the most enterprising. While the vintners in the Parishes of Bommes, Fargues, and Preignac are content to market their wines simply as Sauternes, those of Barsac insist that their wines be known by the name of their Parish. To say that the wines of Barsac are identical to those of the Parish of Sauternes is as wrong as to say that Barsac wines are dry—as many people believe. The wine of Barsac lacks the softness and finesse of the Sauternes, but taste it and you know that you have a wine you can figuratively put your teeth into. So far as sweetness is concerned, there is little difference; that is, when château bottled wines are compared.

the question of Barsac

However, comparing Sauternes and Barsac shipped under the label of a Bordeaux wine merchant is another story. These are blended wines, and when the shipper blends, he can do anything he pleases. He can blend for sweetness, relative dryness, perfume, or body. He knows perfectly well that if his Sauternes and Barsac are identical, there is no purpose in buying both wines. So he blends one wine more for sweetness than the other, thereby establishing two different wines. There is no consistency among shippers as to which of the two wines will be the sweeter.

Château Olivier, with its moat, at Léognan, Graves. (Courtesy Louis Eschenauer, Bordeaux)

Haut
Sauternes
and Haut
Barsac

Haut in French means high, but it has no "official" bearing on the Sauternes and Barsac of the region. It is usually so labeled for the American market and generally denotes a better grade of wine. As a rule, these wines cost more than the simple Sauternes or Barsac of the same vintage and the same shipper and are generally sweeter. "Haut" has no geographical significance, as there is no portion of Barsac or the Sauternes region known or designated as Haut Barsac or Haut Sauternes.

sulphur

Because these wines are rich in sugar, it is difficult to keep them from refermenting during unseasonably warm weather. The only preventive is to sulphur the casks well before they are filled. The sulphur fumes sterilize the cask, destroying any bacteria which might be present, and, when the wine is poured in, act as a deterrent on the yeasts remaining in the wine, as they are always ready to continue their fermentation job under the least provocation.

In the classification of 1855, as explained on page 38, the wines of the great Sauternes vineyards were classed in order of merit in the same manner as the Clarets. This embraced twenty growths, which, due to the split-up of several vineyards, is today twenty-three. (See Appendix F.)

Famed Château Yquem, whose crenelated walls and towers enclose the residence, offices, winery and cellars, in the heart of Sauternes. (Courtesy Marquis Bertrand de Lur Saluces)

CHÂTEAU YQUEM. In the fourteenth century when Edward II was King of England, his wine merchant and buyer in Bordeaux was Pierre Ayquem (also spelled Eyquem). It was he or one of his descendants who gave the family patronym to the vineyard whose storied wines have evoked more and greater hyperbole than almost any other wine since the celebrated Falernians of Roman times. A few of these are:

"The extravagance of perfection"
"A ray of sunshine concentrated in a glass"
"A ray more brilliant than the sun's"

In fact, in 1859 the Grand Duke Constantine of Russia paid the fabulous sum of 20,000 gold francs for a tun (1,200 bottles) of the 1847 vintage. This was about $3.50 per bottle, an unheard-of price in those days.

There is no question about Yquem's wines being in a class by themselves, meriting the apparent exaggerations of poets intoxicated by such perfection. The finer vintages of Château Yquem combine a richness of perfume, a depth of vinosity and fullness of body all in perfect balance. There are differences between vintages and some are sweeter than others. Yquems will vary from a sweet to a deep luscious richness.

CHÂTEAU LA TOUR BLANCHE. According to ancient documents, this fine vineyard was at one time the property of Messire Jean Saint-Marc de La Tour Blanche, Treasurer General of the King. Sometime after the French Revolution, its ownership passed to M. Osiris, who bequeathed the entire property to the State for a viticultural school.

Château La Tour Blanche is generally ranked as the first Sauternes after Yquem. Its wines are always elegant, full, and rich.

Please note the spelling of "La Tour" as two words. Many people confuse Château La Tour Blanche, the Sauternes, with Château Latour, the Claret.

CHÂTEAU DE RAYNE-VIGNEAU. Property for generations of the Vicomtes de Pontac, Vigneau has had a glorious history. Its most notable exploit consisted of defeating the best German wine in a blind tasting at the World's Fair of 1867 and being selected as the finest white wine of that age. The two wines in question were a Château Vigneau 1861 and a Rhine wine of the same vintage.

CHÂTEAU SUDUIRAUT. Bordering Château Yquem, it was formerly controlled by the crown and today its label bears the legend "ancien cru du Roy" (former property of the King). It is vigorous with a rich aroma.

CHÂTEAU GUIRAUD (formerly Bayle). A beautiful property which includes a fine vineyard—about 150 acres in extent—a part of 350 acres and a lovely old château. The wine of Château Guiraud is famed for its delicacy, perfume, and body.

CHÂTEAUX COUTET AND CLIMENS.   These two first growths, situated in the Parish of Barsac, possess the typical firmness and elegant bouquet of Barsac Sauternes. They are Sauternes and just as rich as the other growths of Bommes, Fargues, Preignac, or Sauternes.

CHÂTEAUX LAFAURIE-PEYRAGUEY, CLOS HAUT-PEYRAGUEY, RIEUSSEC, RABAUD-PROMIS, and SIGALAS-RABAUD, the other first growths, are all excellent wines which are available on this market.

Among the second growths, the best known in our market are *Château Filhot* in the Parish of Sauternes, which is the property of the Marquis Bertrand de Lur Saluces (Yquem) and *Château Myrat*, in the Parish of Barsac. Although classed as second growths, they are none the less very excellent wines possessing a fine rich bouquet and body.

In addition to the major districts discussed in detail above there are others which produce distinguished, useful and usually less expensive wines. For example, Entre-Deux-Mers, "between two seas", a large section lying between the Garonne and Dordogne rivers before they meet, produces a vast quantity of white wine, some dry and some sweet, and Bourg and Blaye across the Gironde from the Médoc produce rather mediocre white wines and robust fruity red wines, some of exceptional quality.

2. BURGUNDY

"NONE other will I have," (*Aultre n'Aray*) said Duke Philip the Good, of Burgundy, when he set his heart on marrying the beautiful Princess Isabelle. This thoroughly typical phrase was adopted as the ducal motto of the House of Burgundy. It represents the attitude of Burgundians then and now, proud of their race, their lineage, and their wines. It was their wont to style themselves "Dukes of Burgundy and Lords of the finest wines in Christendom." Positive, virile, forthright are words which may be applied alike to men and wine of Burgundy.

history   The history of wine in Burgundy dates back to Caesar's conquest of Gaul and is almost as turbulent as the political story of the region. The Roman legions planted vines from Italy, and when the wine began competing with that of the mother country, the Emperor Domitian ordered the vines uprooted and the fields planted in corn. This was in 96 A.D. Fortunately, the edict was enforced only half-heartedly, and was finally rescinded entirely by the Emperor Probus in 278 A.D.

Long before the wine of the region was known by the regional term Burgundy, the Church—which here, as elsewhere, had a strong influence in the development of quality wines—had made famous among medieval gourmets the names of such vineyards as Clos de Bèze, Corton-Charlemagne, Romanée, Clos de Vougeot, Meursault, and Montrachet.

First known as wine of Auxerre, since the wine went to Paris and the outside world by boat down the river Yonne from the "port" of Auxerre; and later as wine of Beaune; it was not until the sixteenth century that it acquired the name Burgundy. When Petrarch advised Pope Urban V to remove from Avignon to Rome, according to legend, his Holiness demurred because his entourage complained: "There is no Beaune wine in Italy, and without Beaune wine how unhappy we would be." This difficulty seemingly was overcome during the Pontificate of Gregory XII.

geography

From time immemorial, wine has been Burgundy's chief source of fame, but, unlike other wine regions, Burgundy wines do not all come from one concentrated geographical locale. Due to the acquisitiveness of her Dukes, who reached out on all sides for more and more land, wine produced in every part of the Duchy became known simply as Burgundy. This wine-producing region includes four separate districts.

First in importance is the "True Burgundy," known today as the *Côte d'Or,* or Golden Slope, which is divided into the Côte de Nuits and Côte de Beaune. This is a string of low-lying hills, extending some 38 miles from Dijon on the north to Santenay in the south, the width of the vineyards being from 550 to 600 yards. Second, further south lies the Mâconnais and Beaujolais. Third, about halfway between Dijon and Paris, in the Department of the Yonne, there are a few thousand acres of vineyards around the town of Chablis, which produce the famous white wine of the same name. And finally, between the Côte d'Or and the Mâconnais lies the Côte Chalonnaise.

The soil of the Côte d'Or, rich in iron, is chalky, argillaceous, and rocky. The slopes take their name from the burnished gold appearance they present in the late fall when the leaves have fallen off the vine and the ground is exposed.

grape varieties

The fine red wines come from the Pinot Noir, while the white wines of repute are produced from the Chardonnay. The Pinot is a noble plant which produces quality but not quantity, and here, as nowhere else, is the *vigneron* tempted to increase his output at the sacrifice of quality.

The other red grape variety in Burgundy which predominates in the south is the Gamay, a more productive variety which gives a poor wine in the Côte d'Or, but in the clay and granite soil of Macon and Beaujolais, produces an extremely enjoyable red wine. The other white grape of Burgundy is the Aligoté which is a highly productive white wine grape yielding copious quantities of agreeable but undistinguished and short-lived white wine. It must always bear the name of the grape on the label.

vineyards   The most famous vineyards are found on the slopes with a southern exposure. They neither extend to the summit of the hills nor reach the lower plains. The fine vineyards form something like a wide continuous ribbon laid along the gentle slopes, rarely dropping below the 800 foot elevation or rising above the 1,000 foot level. The plain is some 700 feet above sea level, and the higher hills are 1,500 feet.

It is on these slopes that the Pinot seems to do best and the Gamay is rarely to be found. On the plains and summits, however, the Gamay is most in evidence. Wines resulting from an admixture of the two varieties are known as *Passe-tous-grains*.

In Burgundy, as in other viticultural regions, the phylloxera did its devastating work, and today most of the vineyards have been replanted with American phylloxera-resisting roots on which the native Pinot and Gamay have been grafted. The last native stocks were removed in the early 1950s.

The laws controlling the origin and labeling of wines limit the production of the vineyards which are capable of producing fine wines in order to ensure the highest quality possible, thus forcing the *vigneron* to prune his vines properly. As the quantity is strictly limited, he does everything in his power to aid the vine in giving quality.

The system of vineyard ownership in Burgundy is different from that of any other viticultural region of France, and duplicated to any extent only in Germany. To begin with, the vineyards are all very small. The largest, Clos de Vougeot, is only some 126 acres, and La Romanée is just about 2 acres, the average being under 25 acres. Not only are the vineyards extremely small, but, with rare exceptions, they are held by anywhere from three to as many as sixty-odd owners, each proprietor having title to a small parcel of the vineyard. This is in some way a contrast to the Bordeaux system, where some of the well-known vineyards are owned by one person or corporation, and the entire product is controlled by one management.

At Clos de Vougeot, for example, there are sixty-six owners who cultivate their individual parcels of the vineyard, gather the grapes from their own vines, press them, and vinify the resultant must. As the human element enters into production, it is understandable that, although the same Pinot variety is planted in the entire vineyard, and all the operations of making the wine take place at the same time, there may be sixty-six different wines produced, all legally entitled to the appellation of Clos de Vougeot.

It is apparent that under this system there can be no château bottling, as is practiced in Bordeaux. However, "estate bottling" has received great impetus since Repeal in the United States. American connoisseurs began to demand château bottled Burgundies, and "estate bottling," usually followed by the name of the owner, was the answer.

While this has been good merchandising on their part and benefits the consumer, since in theory the Burgundians would strive to offer only the very

WINE REGIONS OF BURGUNDY

°Dijon

Fixin °

Gevrey-Chambertin

Chambertin-Clos de Bèze

Morey-St. Denis °

Clos de Tart

Bonnes Mares •

Les Musigny

Chambolle-Musigny °

Clos Vougeot •

Vougeot

Les Grands Echézeaux •

Flagey-Echézeaux

Richebourg •

Vosne-Romanée

Romanée-Conti

La Tâche •

La Grand Rue

Nuits-St. Georges

Les Cailles

Les St. Georges •

Premeaux

Comblanchien

Pernand-Vergelesses °

Corton-Charlemagne

Le Corton •

Les Pougets

Clos du Roi •

Aloxe-Corton

Les Grèves •

Les Fèves

Beaune

Les Epenots

Les Rugiens •

Pommard

Volnay

Les Santenots

Auxey-Duresses °

Meursault

Les Genevrières

Les Charmes

Puligny-Montrachet

Bâtard-Montrachet

Le Montrachet

Chassagne-Montrachet

Chevalier-Montrachet

Santenay °

°Chagny

CÔTE DE NUITS

LA CÔTE D'OR

CÔTE DE BEAUNE

• Famous vineyards

° Parishes

best quality, "estate bottling" only guarantees the authenticity of vineyard origin and the fact that the wine comes from the grapes of a single producer, and has not been blended with wines from any other producer or from any other vineyard. As a matter of fact, the practice of "estate bottling" has proliferated so since World War II, it is not uncommon today to see "estate bottlings" of wines labeled *Gevrey-Chambertin, Chambolle-Musigny, Vosne-Romanée,* etc., which in our opinion contradicts the entire meaning and objective of the system. For example, a wine labeled *Gevrey-Chambertin* is a blend of wines produced in any part of the Gevrey-Chambertin Parish. When the label also states it is "estate bottled" the blend is made entirely of wines from the producer's vineyard holdings in Gevrey-Chambertin. These can be, though not necessarily, parcels in the great *Le Chambertin* and also from the most poorly rated vineyards in the parish. We believe that "estate bottling" should be reserved and practiced only for the unblended wine of the great vineyards which are bottled by the actual producer who is a proprietor, no matter how small his holding.

Not all of the growers ship their own wines, and if the shippers were to keep each grower's wines separate their lists would not only be interminable but also very confusing. For this reason, it has been only natural for shippers to buy, say, Clos de Vougeot from several growers, blend these wines together, and offer them as their own (the shippers') quality of Clos de Vougeot. This also tends to equalize the price.

labeling   A Burgundy wine will bear the best-known or most famous name to which it is legally entitled. If the name of the vineyard whence it originates is world-famous, rest assured that is the name under which the wine will travel. If the Parish, however, is more renowned than the vineyard, then the wine will travel under the Parish name. If neither is well-known, it will go forth as Côte de Nuits, or Côte de Beaune, or simply as red or white Burgundy.

For example, wine from the Chambertin vineyard will invariably be shipped as Chambertin, while wine from the Les Epenots vineyard in the Parish of Pommard will reach our table labeled Pommard, because it is a better-known name than Les Epenots, even though Les Epenots is considered one of the finer growths or vineyards of the Parish.

Wine from any vineyard in the Parishes of Comblanchien, or Corgoloin, will be labeled Côte de Nuits or simply Bourgogne rouge, because neither the vineyards nor the Parishes are well known outside the district. Most of the red wines of the Parishes of Meursault, Puligny-Montrachet, and Chassagne-Montrachet suffer the same fate and get out to the world as Côte de Beaune, because these Parishes, while world-famous for their white wines, are not too well known for their reds.

The famous vineyards of the Côte d'Or have not been officially classified, as were those of Bordeaux, but the studied judgment of wine lovers, who have drunk these wines and matched one against another for over a millennium, have established a hierarchy of Burgundy wines which is generally accepted. At least the prices these great wines fetch indicate the present-day Burgundy devotees are in agreement with the order of classification. (See table of great Burgundy vineyards, Appendix F.)

The most costly red wine of Burgundy is that of Romanée-Conti, a rather small vineyard in the Parish of Vosne-Romanée. Like all things, its price is governed by supply and demand. The area planted in vines is only a little more than four and a half acres. Its two big rivals, Chambertin and Clos de Vougeot, both much larger vineyards, produce great wines, honorably challenging Romanée-Conti's place in the Burgundy sun. Unquestionably the first vineyard among the white wines is Le Montrachet (pronounced Moan-rah-SHAY).

notes on the wines of the Côte d'Or

The wines of the Côte de Nuits are generous, full-bodied, having a deep fruity, vinous bouquet. They develop less rapidly than those of the Côte de Beaune and should be kept longer, so that their early roughness will develop that full roundness characteristic of the great Burgundies.

The wines of the Côte de Beaune, on the other hand, having less body, develop more rapidly and are ready for drinking sooner. They show a pleasant, fruity bouquet, a softness and finesse, and are tenderly supple, which makes them most agreeable wines at all times.

ROMANÉE-CONTI. The accepted king of Burgundy, whose wines always have all the qualities of a great wine: body, vinosity, bouquet, and character; they are rich and long lived.

CHAMBERTIN. Napoleon, so the story goes, would drink no other wine, and planned all his great military and civil victories when warmed by the generous fire of Chambertin. But, the sad tale continues, when he was before Moscow, his supply became exhausted, with the resulting disastrous retreat from Russia. Knowing his penchant for Chambertin, the allies generously permitted that he be supplied with it at St. Helena.

No one knows the origin of the vineyard of Chambertin. It is lost in obscurity. But like all ancient vineyards, it is rich in legends. The story connected with it throws some light on the entire Burgundy viticultural development. In the year 630, according to the records, the Duc de Amalgaire gave a parcel of vineyard, with an area of some 35 acres, to the Abbey of Bèze. Henceforth the vineyard was known as Clos de Bèze, and in time its wines acquired much renown. Sometime later, and before 1219, when we have our next parchment record, a peasant named Bertin owned the field bordering Clos de Bèze. In his simple way he reasoned that if he planted the same grape varieties as grew in the famous Clos de Bèze vineyards, his wines should be good, too. The French word for field is *champ*, and the vineyard then must have been known as Champ de Bertin. This was finally contracted to the

Ancient Château de Clos Vougeot, set in the very center of the vineyard, property of the Confrérie des Chevaliers du Tastevin, at Vougeot, Côte d'Or. (Photo courtesy of the Confrérie)

present Chambertin, and since 1219 the wines from the two vineyards have been confused and looked upon as one and the same. Today, the total area of Chambertin and Chambertin-Clos de Bèze is 67½ acres, and the wines go out to the world either under the name of Chambertin or Chambertin-Clos de Bèze. Both wines are big, heady wines which acquire a firm roundness with age. They have the qualities which make great wines—color, bouquet, body, and finesse.

CLOS DE VOUGEOT.   These are fruity wines, having flavor, color, body, bouquet, and an infinite grace and character. The elegance of its wines has merited Clos de Vougeot an honor which is today traditional. During the Napoleonic wars, one Colonel Bisson, marching past the gates of the Clos de Vougeot at the head of his column, ordered that a roll be beat and that his men present arms before a vineyard whose wines were so magnificent.

The Little Corporal, it is said, conqueror on the fields of Austerlitz and Marengo, and now become all-powerful Emperor, heard of the excellent wines made at Vougeot. He sent word to one Dom Gobelet, the last clerical cellarmaster prior to the French Revolution, saying that it would please him to taste these superlative wines. "If he is that curious," replied the venerable Cistercian haughtily, "let him come to my house."

The beautiful imposing Château du Clos de Vougeot is situated on the upper slopes in the very center of the vineyard. For many centuries it belonged to the Cistercian Abbey of Cîteaux. The earliest available records of the Abbey vineyard ownership date back to 1110. The present Château was begun in the thirteenth century and completed sometime in the sixteenth. Its primary function was to serve as the pressing house and cellars for the wine production activities of the Cistercian Order, who owned it until the French Revolution when it was secularized. Today, the Château is the property of the Confrérie des Chevaliers du Tastevin, the society of Burgundy wine lovers. All of the great ceremonies, functions, and dinners of the Confrérie are held there.

LES MUSIGNY AND LES BONNES MARES. These two great rival vineyards lie in the Parish of Chambolle-Musigny. Both these wines are known for their finesse, suppleness, and elegance, but, although they are similar in character, Les Musigny is the bigger of the two. In 1882, the leaders of the Parish decided that the sale of all its wines would be increased if the Parish were to adopt the name of its most famous vineyard, and therefore Chambolle became Chambolle-Musigny. This system has been adopted by the Parishes of Gevrey-*Chambertin*, Flagey-*Echézeaux*, Vosne-*Romanée*, Nuits-*Saint-Georges*, Aloxe-*Corton*, Puligny-*Montrachet*, and Chassagne-*Montrachet*.

ROMANÉE, ROMANÉE-ST.-VIVANT, RICHEBOURG, LA TÂCHE, LA GRANDE RUE. The Parish richest in great vineyards is Vosne-Romanée. These vineyards vary in size from the bare 2 acres of La Romanée, 15 acres for La Tâche, 20 acres of Les Richebourg, to the almost 24 acres of Romanée-Saint-Vivant. The wines of these great growths differ, but it would take one long accustomed to drinking them to identify these differences. Suffice it to say that they all have beautiful color, a deep bouquet and flavor, and that they have body, elegance, and, above all, breed.

LES GRANDS ECHÉZEAUX. These 23 acres of vineyard lie across the road from Clos de Vougeot, and there is a close resemblance between the wines. There was a time, long past, when the vineyard belonged to the Abbey of Saint-Vivant and was considered a part of Vosne, and to this day it is thought of in the same breath with the wines of Vosne-Romanée. Its wines are big and colorful, having much character and breed.

CLOS DE TART, CLOS DES LAMBRAYS, LES SAINT-GEORGES. The first two vineyards, with an acreage of 17½ and 22½ respectively, lie in the Parish of Morey-St. Denis. The 20 acres of the Saint-Georges are in the Parish of Nuits-Saint-Georges. These three great vineyards of the Côte de Nuits have rich wines, with color, body, and character, though not to the same extent as Chambertin, for example, or Clos de Vougeot.

The last commune of Côte de Nuits before you reach Dijon has the odd name of Fixin. Here the wines are similar to those of Gevrey-Chambertin and sometimes their equal. Perrières (not to be confused with Clos des Perrières of Meursault) and Clos du Chapitre produce good strong Burgundy wines. The Appellation of Côte de Nuits-Villages is restricted to the wines of the five communes of Fixin, Brochon, Prissey, Camblanchien and Corgoloin.

CÔTE DE BEAUNE

THE ancient medieval city of Beaune is the headquarters or capital of the Burgundy wine trade. Most of the great shipping houses have their cellars in the city itself and it is in Beaune that we find the world-famous Hospices de Beaune.

HOSPICES DE BEAUNE. There are many well preserved examples of Beaune's long history—churches, parts of the old city wall, and battlements—all still in use in one way or another, but her proudest monument is *Les Hospices*

Central courtyard of 15th Century Hospices de Beaune, where the annual Hospices' wine auctions are held on the third Sunday of November. (Courtesy Julius Wile)

de Beaune. This is a charitable hospital that was built in 1443. It has rendered continuous, uninterrupted, and devoted service to the poor of the region for over 500 years, wars or revolution notwithstanding.

The *Hôtel-Dieu* or hospital is an exquisite example of Flemish architectural style. It is a four-story-high block-square building, surmounted by a slanting roof whose slates are arranged in a classic pattern of green, yellow, and black. The cobble-stoned open central courtyard—the Court of Honor—had been the locale for the annual Hospices wine auctions.

Over the centuries modern improvements have been adopted in the care of the sick, but some of the original wards, kitchens, chapels, and the museum have been preserved in their original state of the fifteenth century. The museum contains many works of art including paintings of Nicholas Rolin and his wife, Guigone de Salins, and the magnificent altarpiece of the Last Judgment, all on wood, which she commissioned the Flemish painter Roger Van der Weyden (1440–1464) to paint expressly for the Hospices de Beaune.

In 1441 Pope Eugene IV authorized the creation of the Hospices de Beaune as a hospital to care for the poor and indigent people of Beaune. Nicolas Rolin, tax collector during the reign of Louis XI, and his wife donated the property and erected the building. They also gave the Hospices several parcels of vineyards so that the Hospices might be supported by the sale of the wines therefrom. The legend of the period has it that Nicolas Rolin could well afford to provide such a charity for the poor as he had created so many of them. However true or false that may be, the Hospices de Beaune has proved to be a remarkable institution.

Its principal support has always come from the sale of wines produced from vineyards that have been willed to the Hospices by devout Burgundians. Today these comprise some thirty-two parcels which are known by the names of the donors. (See Appendix F, page 489, for the list.)

For over four centuries the Hospices wines were sold privately but since the year 1859 they have been sold at public auction on the third Sunday of November in Les Halles de Beaune. All of the Hospices de Beaune vineyards are located in the Côte de Beaune, from Aloxe-Corton to Meursault, but because they represent the first real opportunity for buyers to taste the wines of each vintage, the prices fetched at the auction determine to a great extent the rating of the vintage for all Burgundy wines. For example, in 1972, they produced °F 7,609,604, nearly a 17 per cent increase when compared to 1971. Often these figures are more than the individual wines are really worth, but the factors of charity and publicity unquestionably influence the bidding.

LE CORTON, CLOS DU ROI, LES BRESSANDES. In the Parish of Aloxe-Corton lie the famous vineyards of Le Corton, with an area of 28¼ acres, Clos du

°F—francs

58

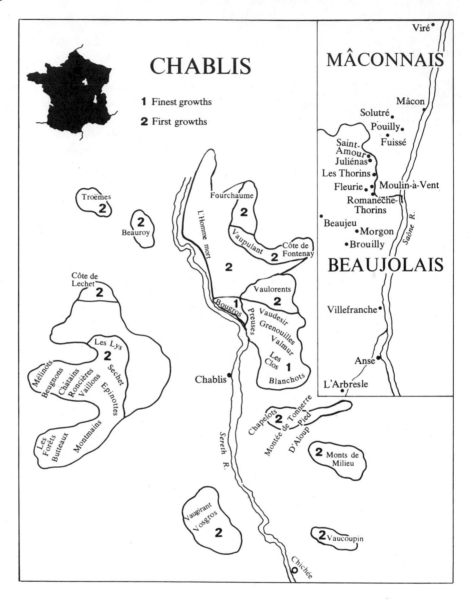

CHABLIS

1 Finest growths
2 First growths

MÂCONNAIS

Viré
Mâcon
Solutré
Pouilly
Fuissé
Saint-Amour
Juliénas
Les Thorins
Fleurie
Moulin-à-Vent
Romanéche-Thorins
Beaujeu
Morgon
Brouilly

BEAUJOLAIS

Villefranche

Anse
L'Arbresle

Troèmes
Beauroy
Fourchaume
Vaupulant
Côte de Fontenay
Côte de Lechet
Vaulorents
Bougros
Preuses
Vaudesir
Grenouilles
Valmur
Les Clos
Blanchots
Les Lys
Mélinots
Beugnons
Châtains
Roncières
Vaillons
Sechet
Epinottes
Les Forêts
Butteaux
Montmains
Chablis
Chapelots
Montée de Tonnerre
Pied D'Aloup
Monts de Milieu
Serein R.
Vaugirant
Vosgros
Vaucoupin
Chichée

Roi with 26¼ acres, and Les Bressandes with some 42½ acres. Corton is considered by many to be the best red wine of the Côte de Beaune. It is usually a solid and robust wine. With bottle ripeness it expands and possesses a wealth of bouquet, roundness, body, and breed, which can be compared with the great Côte de Nuits wines. Clos du Roi and Les Bressandes are also big wines but they are more like Beaune wines in character. They have a lovely color, aroma, and finesse. The wines from Les Pougets vineyard are always very fine, with excellent color, flavor, and body.

VERGELESSES. Ile des Vergelesses and Les Basses-Vergelesses, with an area of 23⅓ and 44⅔ acres respectively, in the Parish of Pernand, are renowned for their finesse and distinction.

LES FÈVES, LES GRÈVES. These are the two outstanding examples from Beaune itself. Les Fèves, with 10⅔ acres, and Les Grèves, with 79½ acres, produce wines noted for their fine, rich softness and elegance.

LES RUGIENS-BAS, LES EPENOTS. The Parish name, Pommard, is probably the most famous Burgundy wine name. It is certainly far better known than that of its finest vineyard, Rugiens. For that reason most of its wine comes to our table labeled simply Pommard and because of the insistent demand, its price is usually somewhat high. Should you come upon authentic and properly matured examples of Pommard-Rugiens, Pommard-Epenots, La Platière, or Les Garollières, you will find them generally delicate, fruity, well-rounded wines of character.

VOLNAY, MONTHÉLIE, AUXEY-DURESSES, CHASSAGNE-MONTRACHET. The red wines of Volnay and Monthélie are lighter in color, elegant, and delightful; those of Auxey-Duresses are somewhat like those of Pommard and Volnay, and the red wines of Chassagne-Montrachet have a richness and fullness that remind one of those of the Côte de Nuits.

The Appellation of Côte de Beaune-Villages is restricted to 16 communes in the Côte de Beaune.

The Chalonaise lies just south of the Côte de Beaune. The soil, the grapes and the wines are quite similar although they do not often attain the same quality. The four communes having Appellations are Rully, Mercurey, Givry and Montagny. A considerable amount of sparkling wine is produced in the Chalonaise.

MÂCONNAIS AND BEAUJOLAIS

ON the rolling low hills immediately south of the Chalonaise lie the districts of Mâcon and Beaujolais. It is hard to tell where one begins and the other leaves off, but as the wines they produce are so similar in character, we can consider them as one region.

In the Côte d'Or, the Gamay grape variety is used for quantity rather than quality, but in the Beaujolais it produces the fine wines and is used extensively. Most of the wines go to market under the regional name of Macon or Beaujolais, Macon Supérieur or Beaujolais Supérieur. The better growths or "Crus" of Beaujolaise are limited to nine—Brouilly, Chénas, Chiroubles, Côte de Brouilly, Fleurie, Juliénas, Morgon, Moulin-a-Vent and Saint Amour. The Appellation Beaujolais-Villages is permitted to the wines of some 39 communes.

The wines of the region have a clear brilliant color and a fairly light body, when compared with those of the Côte d'Or. Their primary characteristic is fresh fruitiness. They are most pleasant while in the fresh vigor of youth, and for this reason should not be kept for many years. In France, most of these wines are drunk before they are two or three years old.

WHITE WINES OF BURGUNDY

ALL of the main subdivisions of the Burgundy wine region produce white wines, each of which is of an individual character and has its following. The Mâconnais gives us Pouilly-Fuissé; the Department of the Yonne, or Lower Burgundy, Chablis; and the Côte d'Or, or rather the Côte de Beaune, produces, in the Parishes of Meursault, Puligny-Montrachet, and Chassagne-Montrachet, the great white wines. In addition, several vineyards in other Parishes produce white wines of repute. In Aloxe-Corton we have the renowned Corton-Charlemagne, so named in honor of the great Emperor. Right in the center of the Clos de Vougeot vineyard there are some 5 acres planted with white Chardonnay grapes from which Clos Blanc de Vougeot is made, and at the famous Musigny vineyard in Chambolle-Musigny a limited amount of Musigny Blanc is produced by Comte Georges de Vogüé. They are all distinguished wines, possessing full flavor and body.

For the making of white wines the *plant noble* is the Chardonnay (Chardonet). Other varieties of grape are used, but to a very minor degree, excepting the Aligoté which is found in many vineyards.

The wine which the world knows as Chablis is unique and possesses a character all its own. The distinguishing characteristic, which is not to be found in every vintage, is an austere flinty quality, much prized by those who have had the good fortune to encounter it. Chablis is, perhaps, the driest and palest of table wines. Its color should be a pale straw-gold. We have seen Chablis which was brownish in color, but it tasted as it looked and not as Chablis should—dry and crisp.

The much prized "flinty" quality is known as *pierre-à-fusil* (gun flint). This flinty taste is like the sharp, metallic tang most of us have experienced when, as children, we were dared to taste metal on a frosty morning. Chablis has the same effect. Added to this is its delicate, fruity bouquet and herein lies its cooling, refreshing quality. Although in good years, Chablis is a long lived wine, we prefer it young and fresh. There is no wine that can match Chablis with oysters. They were made for each other, and you will agree with me if you try this combination.

There are a few outstanding vineyards in the Chablis region, which are listed below, but "estate bottling" is rare, and most of the wine reaches us labeled simply Chablis or Chablis Premier vin. These are blended wines, the blend being made of wines from several vineyards. "Premier vin" indicates that the wines are of superior quality and some from special vineyards (twenty-nine of them). The reputation of the shipper is your best guarantee of quality.

The Chablis Grand Cru vineyards: Les Clos, Vaudésir, Valmur, Grenouilles, Blanchots, Preuses, Bougros and La Moutonne. The first seven Grand Crus have been accepted for many years but La Moutonne has never received official recognition from the Minister of Agriculture, although the quality of the wine and the price brought in the open market substantiate its position. Actually, there is apt to be some argument over the question of the greatest white wine. There can be no hesitation, however, in regard to Le Montrachet. It is one of the world's great white wines, full-bodied and robust, yet possessing an elegance, perfume, and dignity hard to match. Coming from a rather small vineyard, only $18\frac{3}{4}$ acres in extent—half of which lies in the Parish of Puligny and half in that of Chassagne—the wines are in such demand that they usually fetch prices equal to those of the great red growths of the Côte de Nuits.

Besides Le Montrachet, which H. Warner Allen has called the Château Yquem of Burgundy, there are two other vineyards of great repute to be found in the two Parishes. Le Bâtard-Montrachet lies in both Parishes, while the Chevalier-Montrachet growth is in the Parish of Puligny-Montrachet. The wines of these two growths are very much like those of Le Montrachet, and while very fine do not quite reach its heights of quality. All of these wines are quite pale in color, have a wealth of bouquet and finesse, and are never cheap.

The Parish of Meursault boasts four vineyards of repute, which, in the order of their importance are: Les Perrières, Les Genevrières, Les Charmes-Dessus and La Goutte-d'Or. The wines of these vineyards are not as big as those of Montrachet but they are full-bodied, dry, have finesse and elegance.

Meursault-La Goutte-d'Or obtains its name from its golden color. It does not possess the finesse of the others. By the way, Montrachet means "bald hill," while Meursault denotes "mouse jump."

In the Parish of Aloxe-Corton, some white wine is made at the famous Le Corton vineyard, and much more in the Charlemagne vineyard, which, at one time, is said to have belonged to the great Emperor. Some very fine white wine is also produced at Clos de Vougeot. These wines are excellent and must be included in any list of white Burgundies, but these Parishes are still more famed for their great red wines.

Until recently, the great wine districts of Bordeaux and Burgundy produced no vin rosé for export. What little was made was usually drunk right in the neighborhood. In Bordeaux the growers and shippers have noted the rising popularity of pink wines and Bordeaux rosés are now available in many American wine shops. A few Burgundy district rosés are also beginning to make an appearance.

The process of making "vin rosé" is similar to that of making red wine. In fact, rosés are wines that started out to be red wines. As we know, red wines get their color pigment on the inside of the red or black grapes' skin. This is dissolved by the alcohol produced during fermentation. If the grapes are removed before all of the coloring pigment has been dissolved, the resulting wine will be a light red or pink color. This is the method used for the quality rosés. The best grape varieties are Gamay, Grenache, Pinot Noir, and Cabernet Franc.

Rosés are at their peak when they are young and fresh. Like white wines, they should always be lightly chilled. They are not wines that call for pomp or ceremony, no need to sniff them solemnly or swirl them in our mouth.

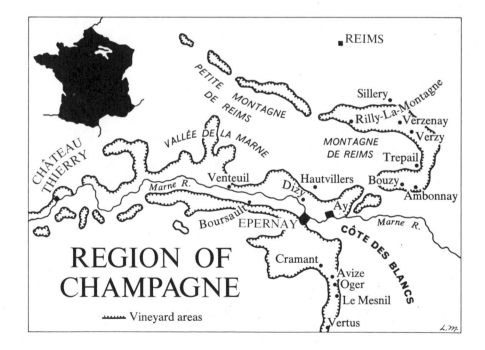

REGION OF CHAMPAGNE

⎍⎍⎍⎍ Vineyard areas

They are noted for a tart fruitiness. On the whole most Burgundy and Bordeaux rosés are quite dry.

For details on the various Burgundy vintages, see page 488.

SPARKLING BURGUNDY

THE discovery of sparkling wine in Champagne set off the spark which became a conflagration in all the wine-producing regions of Europe, and even to this day sparkling wine continues to be made with more or less success wherever wine grapes grow. Burgundy's sparkling wine has enjoyed the greatest amount of public acceptance after Champagne, throughout the world. This has been primarily because of fashion and because its wines were best for the making of this type of wine, the most pleasant, and the prettiest to look at.

Sparkling wines are made in Burgundy from white, rosé or pink, and red wines. They are made in the approved sparkling Champagne method, which is explained in the section on Champagne. In most instances, good sound wines are used, but never the great wines. Obviously, the great wines will fetch much higher prices as still wines.

Pink sparkling Burgundy is usually labeled *Oeil de Perdrix* (partridge eye).

As a general rule, sparkling Burgundies are sweeter than Champagne. This is due to the fact that at the time the sediment is removed, the loss of wine is replaced with a substantial dosage of syrup made from wine and the finest rock-sugar candy.

Sparkling Burgundy, and for that matter all red sparkling wines wherever they may be produced, will be much fuller bodied than Champagne because the red wines from which they are produced are fuller bodied by nature. Sparkling Burgundy, i.e., all sparkling red wines, show the sediment, which deposits naturally, within a relatively short time—eighteen months to two years. Avoid purchases in excess of the normal requirements of six months' consumption.

There was a recent controversy on the subject of whether or not sparkling Burgundy is sold in France. Sparkling wine of Burgundy is sold in substantial volume in France under the name of *Bourgogne Mousseux*, which means "sparkling Burgundy," and it is drunk mostly by the Burgundians themselves.

3. CHAMPAGNE

THE word Champagne is synonymous with happiness, gaiety, laughter, for it is the joyous wine of festive occasions. "Champagne," said André L. Simon, "has always been, still is, and will ever be an extravagant wine, and the most charming and fascinating of wines."

There is a difference between La Champagne and Le Champagne. The former is the name of the ancient French Province, part of which is today the Department of La Marne; the latter is the wine produced in this long-famous wine region.

Wine has been made in Champagne since the early Roman times, since Caesar came and saw and conquered Gaul. That early wine, however, was a still wine, and even today a still Champagne is made. However, Champagne has become known throughout the world as a sparkling white wine, whose sparkle is due to a secondary fermentation that takes place within the tightly corked bottle.

history · The history of the province and of its wine is intertwined, part of the same fabric. The most important city, Reims, was named for Saint Remi, one of its first archbishops, who, in the year 496 A.D. converted the first Frankish King, Clovis, to Christianity, and at the baptism presented Clovis with a cask of Champagne from his own vineyard.

Henri IV of France prided himself on the fact that he was a vineyard owner and vintner. His vineyard properties were near Ay, and he had a pressing house and cellars in the town. They still stand and may be seen today by anyone visiting this charming little town, which is the center of the region producing the finest "black" grapes of La Champagne. Henri was fond of styling himself *Roi de France et de Navarre et Sire d'Ay* (King of France and Navarre and Lord of Ay).

It was not until the seventeenth century that the sparkling wine we associate with the name of Champagne came into use. Some say that Dom Pérignon, a pious Bénédictine monk who was treasurer and head cellarer of the Abbey of Hautvillers near Epernay, is the man who put the bubbles in Champagne. Like the Parson Weems' story of George Washington and the cherry tree, this legend cannot stand too close examination. However, Dom Pérignon did more for Champagne than any man who preceded him. For nearly half a century (1668–1715) he was in charge of wine-making, and, more important, he received the wines which came to the Abbey in the form of tithes from the peasant vineyard owners of the Parish. Being an excellent taster, he soon observed that the wines of one vineyard were consistently dry, those of another richer and fuller bodied, while those of a third possessed more finesse. He decided to try blending these wines to produce a more balanced and uniform wine, and the result was that he made better wines than any which had been produced before, and to this day the system is followed.

It was Dom Pérignon, too, who was first to use the bark of the cork tree as a stopper for Champagne bottles. Although cork bark had been used in other wine regions, Dom Pérignon introduced it in the Champagne region to replace the bits of tow soaked in oil as a stopper, making it possible to retain the sparkle in the wine for a much longer period of time. The vineyard farmers revere his name, have erected statues to his memory, and, in 1939, celebrated the tercentenary of his birth.

The region which produces Champagne is the most northerly wine-producing section of France. It lies chiefly in the Department of the Marne, with parts of the Departments of the Haute Marne and the Aube included. As you will note from the map, to the east is Alsace, and to the south, Burgundy. The Marne River forms an important line of division. North of the Marne are grown only black grapes, around the towns of Ay and Hautvillers, and in the Montagne (mountain) de Reims section at Mailly, Verzy, Verzenay, Bouzy, and Ambonnay. South of the river lies the Côte des Blancs, where white grapes are grown—around the towns of Cramant, Avize, Oger, Le Mesnil, and at Vertus. The soil of the country is quite chalky, a quality which does much to give grapes, grown from the same vines as that used in Burgundy to the south, such a different character. *geography*

The informing grape varieties are Pinot Noir and Chardonnay, the same varieties grown in the Burgundy region, and Pinot Meunier, a black grape. *grape varieties*

THE CHAMPAGNE VINTAGE

SINCE the wine is a blend of wines made from grapes grown in a number of different vineyard, no vineyard name appears on the label, and consequently the name of the "blender" or shipper, which is always there, takes on importance. Each important shipper owns vineyards in the various districts named above, but as a rule his own vineyards do not produce enough grapes for his needs, so he has to buy additional quantities from the smaller vineyard owners, who are not shippers.

The actual vintaging operations begin at the end of September or the early part of October, depending on weather conditions. Their success requires the discipline and organization of an army. The pickers, ranging in age from seven to seventy, are split into groups under the direction of a sergeant; a group of more experienced workers acts as sorters, and the work of the entire vineyard is under the direction of a head vintager, whose responsibility it is that the work is done rapidly and efficiently. In charge of all the vineyards is the chief of the vintage, who goes from vineyard to vineyard supervising the gathering and seeing to it that the grapes keep moving to the press. The chief cellarer is in charge at the pressing house, and in command of the entire operation is the *régisseur,* or general production manager of the house.

The ripe grapes are gathered in baskets, called *paniers.* When the *panier* is full it is taken to the side of the road where experienced sorters cull out any green, over-ripe, or defective grapes to assure that only perfect, sound

The épluchage. *Highly skilled workers select only perfect bunches (culling out any imperfect grapes) before the caques are trucked to the wine press.* (Courtesy C.I.V.C., Epernay)

fruit goes to the press. This selection process is called *épluchage* and is practiced by some of the leading producers. After the *épluchage*, the grapes are placed in *caques* or *clayettes* (large baskets) and set to one side until trucks can cart them to the pressing house.

Although most of the very large firms have several pressing houses, it is usual for the grapes to be pressed at the cellars in the town where the firm is located. Large hydraulic presses are used which will hold exactly 8,800 pounds. Each basket is weighed and marked to ensure the exact quantity being placed in the press. The amount of grapes which make one loading of a press is called a *marc*. From each *marc*, four pressings or qualities of juice are obtained. They are known as *cuvée, première taille, deuxième taille, rebèche*.

Pressure is applied twice for the cuvée, and after each pressure the grapes are worked toward the center of the press with wooden shovels. For the première and deuxième tailles, pressure is applied only once. For the rebèche, the marc is removed to a smaller press. The houses which pride themselves on the quality of their wines use only the cuvée and première taille pressings, selling the wine resulting from the deuxième taille in cask to those who will buy it. Rebèche wine cannot be used for champagne; it is sold as ordinary wine.

As the juice is expressed from the grapes, it gushes out from the bottom of the press through a channel and is gathered in a cistern below the presses, whence it is transferred at once into casks where the must ferments into wine.

Each cask is carefully marked with the name of the vineyard where the grapes were grown.

The casks are not completely filled, and the bung is left open so that the carbonic acid gases created and the overflow of impurities may escape. When the first violent fermentation subsides and the wine becomes quiet, the bung is driven home and the wine rests through the winter months.

Some of the natural sugar will remain unfermented, because the cold weather arrests the action of the saccharomycetes or yeasts, which are hibernating creatures. In the spring, when the sap begins to rise in the vines, the wine will begin to work again, and the interrupted work of fermentation will commence anew where it left off. Before this happens, however, the *régisseur* and the *maître de chai* (head cellarer) carefully taste the wines and decide what proportions of wines of different vineyards are to go into the cuvée (the blend). The decision having been made, the new wines are pumped, in the agreed proportions, into large blending vats, where they are thoroughly married. At this point a small amount of the finest cane rock sugar candy,

LEFT. *Typical Champagne hydraulic press, showing cistern into which the freshly expressed* must *is flowing.*

RIGHT. *Highly skilled workman deftly performing the* remuage *operation of shaking the sediment down onto the inner surface of the cork.* (Courtesy of C.I.V.C., Epernay)

dissolved in old wine, is added to the blend, to assure uniform secondary fermentation. This process is called the *dosage de tirage* (bottling dosage). The quantity of sugar varies from year to year, depending on the natural sugar the new wine contains. The wine is then immediately bottled and corked. The corks are held in place by metal clips known as *agrafes*.

The bottles are stacked on their sides in the cellars which are hewn out of the solid chalk subsoil of the region.

The yeasts discover the additional sugar, realize that they have not finished their job, and go back to work with vim, creating additional alcohol and carbonic acid gas. As the gas cannot escape it finally becomes a component part of the wine.

During the first couple of years, the stacks of bottles are examined for breakage. This is an inevitable expense as there are bound to be a few imperfect bottles which cannot stand the strain of the 70 to 80 pounds pressure developed by the newly created gas. In the early days the percentage of breakage was terrific (sometimes as much as every other bottle), but today, with improved bottle manufacture and the scientific use of the saccharometer to measure the exact sugar content of the wine, breakage has been reduced to less than one per cent.

Then the bottles are restacked, this time head down. They remain in this position until they are to be prepared for shipment. The time varies, some wine being shipped when it has been in the bottle three to four years, but the usual time is six or more years after the vintage, when it is a vintage wine.

remuage   The action of fermentation is like a fire. Where there is fire, there are ashes. As a result of the secondary fermentation which has taken place in the bottle, "ashes" have been left in the form of a sediment which must be removed, as one of the shipper's aims is to offer a clear and brilliant wine. Removal of the sediment is not an easy job as it may adhere to the bottle or may float in the wine. This long, hard, tedious job is accomplished as follows: the bottles are placed in specially built racks, called *pupitres*. At first the bottles are at an angle of some 45 degrees, the angle being gradually increased until the bottles are standing perpendicularly, head down. Every day or so an expert workman will grasp each bottle, give it a shake (*remuage*), and let it fall back into its slot on the rack with a small jolt. The object of this daily remuage is to shake the sediment down on to the cork. This operation takes from three to four months. When the wine is perfectly clear, the bottles are stood head down in baskets, in which they are transferred to an upper chamber of the cellars to have the sediment removed.

Only those bottles that are going to be shipped at once have the sediment removed at this time. The bottles that are to be held for later shipment are returned to the cellars where they are stored, head down, so that the sediment will always remain on the cork.

Sometimes the sediment has hardened as a crust on the inner surface of the cork, but to make sure that it won't slip back into the wine when the bottle is turned, the neck of the bottle is dipped in a brine solution which freezes a little wine on the cork with the sediment.

A skilled workman, wearing a leather apron and often a wire-covered mask to protect his face from a bursting bottle, grasps the bottle. Standing opposite a barrel surmounted with a shield, he releases the *agrafes* (clips holding the cork) with a pair of pliers. The cork flies out, taking the frozen bit of sediment with it. He gives the neck of the bottle two sharp raps to loosen any bit of sediment which may have adhered to the neck of the bottle. A small amount of the wine will foam out. He examines this foam to be sure that the wine has a perfectly clean bouquet, and then hands the bottle to another workman sitting nearby who will add the *liqueur d'expédition* (shipping dosage).

dégorgement

The wine which has been lost during the disgorging of the sediment must be replaced. This is done by adding wine from previously disgorged bottles. Some markets, however, like sweeter wines than others and for these markets a small amount of a sweetening liqueur is added. This *liqueur d'expédition* is made up of the finest cane rock sugar candy, dissolved in old wine.

liqueur d'expédition

The shipping cork is now driven in by machine and tightly wired down. The labels and the metal or leadfoil capsule dressing are put on. When this is accomplished, it is ready to start its journey to our table, to help us celebrate our most joyous and triumphant moments.

corking and labeling

Because tastes vary, and some people prefer a dry and others a sweet Champagne, the shippers have adopted a simple system of marking their labels, so that you will know just how sweet the wine in the bottle is. The following list should serve as a general guide to denote the varying qualities of sweetness. All shippers use these descriptive terms. There is, however, a certain degree of variation. Thus, while a *Brut* is always drier than an *Extra Sec*, one shipper's *Brut* may be slightly drier than another's.

labeling

Brut or *Nature*	very, very dry	.5 to 1.5 per cent sweetening
Extra Sec or *Extra Dry*	somewhat sweeter but fairly dry	1.5 to 3 per cent sweetening
Sec or *Dry*	medium sweet	3 to 5 per cent sweetening
Demi Sec	quite sweet	5 to 7 per cent sweetening
Doux	very sweet	7 per cent or more sweetening

As in other wine-producing regions, the quality of the grapes and the resultant wine vary greatly according to the summer weather conditions. Three qualities of vintage are possible: 1. Disastrously bad, when the wine is thin and has little character. No reputable house will bottle it. 2. Fairly good wines, lacking some quality which can be made up by blending with wines of a previous vintage. 3. Fine, well-balanced wines which need no assistance and can stand on their own feet. This last will happen two, three, or possibly four times in a decade. Bottles of wine in the third category will be dated with the year in which the grapes which produced them were grown. These are known as vintage wines. Wines of the second category, blends of several vintages, are not dated and are known in the trade as non-vintage wines.

The minimum standards specified under the existing *Appellation Contrôlée* regulations establish that non-vintage Champagne must be matured in bottle one year and vintage wines three years. However, the leading producers usually age their wines, non-vintage and vintage, at least four years and often longer before they ship them to market.

vintage wines   Knowledge of Champagne vintages is important. For use in America, we recommend younger wines, because fine old vintage Champagne is one of the most delicate of all wines. A fine vintage will develop and mature nobly with the years if it is properly stored and undisturbed, but it does not travel properly when old and has a tendency to become heavy. On the other hand, young wines have a light fruity freshness which is their most charming characteristic. Late disgorged Champagnes are the only exception to these general comments. Many of the fine French Champagne producers store small quantities of various vintages undisgorged in their cellars for their personal use on great occasions. The House of Bollinger is the first and only champagne producer to market a late disgorged Champagne with its "R.D." *Recemment Dégorgé* (recently disgorged). The distinctive "R.D." label in gold and black shows both the vintage date and the date of disgorgement. Limited quantities of the best vintages are put aside and left undisturbed for ten years, then disgorged and shipped. Late disgorged Champagnes not only retain all their qualities but also benefit considerably from longer maturity.

Champagne vintages   There is no useful purpose to be gained in discussing storied vintages which, even if obtainable, would no doubt be tired and disappointing. The great vintages of the forties and fifties were: 1943, 1945, 1947, 1949, 1953, 1955, and 1959. Details on the more recent Champagne vintages may be found on page 471.

non-vintage   Wine is produced every year, regardless of quality. In the years when the quality is not up to "vintage" standards, it is helped by blending with wines kept in reserve from successful previous crops and shipped as a wine without a vintage date on the label. These are the Champagne houses' standard wines. Non-vintage Champagne is always less expensive than vintage, but this does not mean that the quality is necessarily less. Many non-vintage wines of the great houses are very fine.

The first Champagne salesman was the Marquis de Sillery, of the seventeenth century. He was one of the richest vineyard owners of the region, and in great favor at court. He introduced sparkling Champagne at court and was the first to ship it to England. *English market*

What the Marquis de Sillery did for sparkling Champagne in France, St. Evremond did in London. Soldier, writer, philosopher, and courtier, he was last but not least a gourmet and a connoisseur. Having incurred the displeasure of his king, he left France and settled in London where he became one of the brightest lights of London society. He made it the fashion to drink Champagne, and the English ever since have been recognized as the most discriminating connoisseurs of fine Champagne and are the region's best customers outside of France.

Wines of every degree of sweetness are shipped to London, although the driest, or *Brut* wines predominate. The fine wines are sent to London. Indeed, because of this, some Americans prefer to buy their Champagne through English wine merchants, paying the added English profit, in order to be sure they are getting the best wine—the wine selected for the English market. The leading French brands, however, are shipped to America in the identical quality that they are to England.

Traditionally, in the production of Champagne both "white" and "black" grapes are used. However, some houses produce some wines that are obtained entirely from the white Chardonnay which grows south of Épernay in the region known as the Côte de Blancs. Such wines are usually lighter in color and body. They are also dry and elegant wines and generally more costly. They are labeled "Blanc de Blancs" and are usually shipped as Brut wines. *Blanc de Blancs*

Once a bottle of Champagne is broached, it must be consumed in its entirety because the gas escapes and it is impractical to recork it. For this reason the shippers bottle the wine in various sized containers to meet as many situations as possible. Each bottle has a name: *bottle sizes*

Split	6½ oz.
Half bottle	13 oz.
Imperial bottle	26 oz.
Magnum (2 bottles)	52 oz.

Rarely Ever Shipped

Jeroboam (4 bottles)	104 oz.
Rehoboam (6 bottles)	156 oz.
Methuselah (8 bottles)	208 oz. (1.65 gals.)
Salmanazar (12 bottles)	312 oz. (2.44 gals.)
Balthazar (16 bottles)	416 oz. (3.3 gals.)
Nebuchadnezzar (20 bottles)	520 oz. (4.07 gals.)

Champagne as is the case with most wines develops better in a large container than in a small one, but it is a good point to know that the shippers do not mature their champagnes in any other sizes than the half bottles, imperial bottles, magnums, and infrequently in jeroboams. All other sizes are filled by decanting from bottles. Therefore, the best size to use is the magnum if there are enough people in the party, and the next best is the bottle.

uses of Champagne

Champagne is one of the most delicate and delightful of all wines, but because it takes so long and is so costly to produce, it can never be a cheap wine. This puts it in a class by itself as the "glamor" wine. It is indispensable at weddings, receptions, and formal banquets, but its uses do not stop there. Champagne is just as much at home with oysters as it is with ham or dessert. For instance, many people do not enjoy an extremely dry Brut with strawberry mousse, but a Sec is very pleasant to them.

A cold glass of Champagne makes a delightful apéritif or, if it is preferred, it can be made into the ever popular Champagne cocktail by adding a cube of sugar on which a dash of bitters has been allowed to soak, and a twist of lemon peel. Champagne also finds its use in the kitchen.

Champagne Rosé—Pink Champagne

In response to the demands of fashion some shippers offer Champagne Rosé. In nearly all cases it is produced by adding the desired proportion of red table wine of the Champagne—generally from Bouzy or Ambonnay—at the time of *dégorgement*. It is usually a vintage wine, always Brut quality, ergo, extremely dry and very elegant in character.

Vin mousseux relates to all sparkling wines but the name Champagne may only be used for sparkling wine made in the delimited district of Champagne. Almost every wine region of France produces a vin mousseux, and the designation may be used for all French sparkling wines regardless of the method used for production. There are only about fifteen French Mousseux which carry an Appellation Contrôlée. All other labels are monopoles.

Vin mousseux-mèthode champenoise is used for Champagne as well as throughout the rest of France. *Vin Mousseux-Produit en cuve close* uses the Charmat or bulk process. This designation would probably apply to the recently developed exchange method which uses bottle fermentation but is chilled, dumped, filtered and rebottled all in a matter of minutes. Finally we have the production of sparkling wine by artificial carbonation. The label must carry the designation *Vin Mousseux Gazéifié.*

In the United States it is very difficult to market a sparkling wine which does not bear the word Champagne. For some reason New York or California Champagne is more acceptable than a fine French Mousseux made with the mèthode champenoise. For the past several years France has exported as much or more mousseux as they have Champagne itself but very little of it comes to the United States.

4. ALSACE—FRENCH RHINE WINES

ALSACE is the bone over which the Frank and Teuton dogs of war have been scrapping for hundreds of years, the buffer province on the left bank of the Rhine which extends from Strasbourg south to Switzerland, and lies between the Rhine and the Vosges Mountains.

history   Alsace has been an important wine-producing region since the Roman conquerors occupied the Valley of the Rhine. Undoubtedly they planted the vine in Alsace before they did in Germany. The vines they brought from Italy were not the same as those which flourish there today, but the records do not show when the change occurred.

During the half-century of German suzerainty, the Alsatian identity of these fine wines was submerged, and while much wine was made, it was all consumed in Germany or used for blending purposes. Quantity rather than quality was the order.

The Alsatian vintner's life has never been an easy one. There is a record that in 1473 the vintage was so abundant that 35 gallons of wine were exchanged for a basket of turnips.

"... a fertile country," wrote Julius Wile recently, "fields and valleys waving with grain, hillsides covered with symmetric rows of vines marching up and up until they merge with the orchards, bearers of the fruits from which are distilled the famous eaux-de-vie d'Alsace, *Quetsch, Mirabelle* (plum brandies), and *Kirsch* (cherry brandy); and the orchards finally give way to the mighty forests which top the hills and cover the Vosges Mountains—forests filled with game—deer, wild boar, fox, hare, and all varieties of birds. . . .

"There is an atmosphere in Alsace—one of close alliance between man and soil, an aura of maturity combined with a freshness of spirit, of physical youngness that one finds even in the aged, of a people that has known the past, lives in the present, and does not fear the future; of a life that includes the good things of old and yet leaves space for the changes of today.

"It is something of all this that one finds in their wines. Wines that are firm and winy, and at the same time fresh, flowery and delicate—white wines of distinctive characteristics, not the finest wines of France, but worthy of their own separate place in the sun."

geography   Beginning in the north and continuing southward, the towns whose surrounding vineyards are famous are:

BARR.   Whose wine from the famous "Clos Gaensbroennel" hill vineyard was popular on the French Line luxury liners of yesteryear.

RIBEAUVILLÉ AND RIQUEWIHR.   In the center of the region. They have long

Typical vintage scene in Alsace, the vineyards being at the edge of the village, with its traditional bell tower. Note the hotte *carried on the vintager's back.*

enjoyed the reputation of producing the best Alsatian wines.

AMMERSCHWIHR.   The well-known vineyards are Kaefferkopf and Beblenheim with the renowned growth: Sonnenglanz.

COLMAR.   The center of the Alsatian wine trade.

GUEBWILLER AND THANN.   Almost in the shadows of Switzerland, the southernmost towns of the region. There is a hill at Guebwiller called "Kitterle" or "leg-cutter." These leg-cutter wines are said to have been one of Napoleon's favorites.

grapes and
labeling

In Alsace the name of the wine is generally determined by the grape variety from which it is made, instead of from the name of the place or the vineyard. There are exceptions, and often the name of the nearest town or village is used in conjunction with the grape name, as in Traminer of Ribeauvill. The label on a true bottle of Alsatian wine will include the following elements:

1. The words, "Vin D'Alsace," or perhaps, some slight variant such as, "Vin Fin D'Alsace," or, "Grand Vin D'Alsace."

2. The grape variety name.

3. Shipper-grower's address, which must be an actual postal address.

If a wine qualifies as above, and in addition has 11 per cent or more alcohol, it is called by any of several designations, such as: "Grand Cru, Grand Vin, Reserve Exceptionnelle." These wines usually not only meet the standards mentioned but are the vintner's best.

What is of utmost importance is the name of the shipper-producer, which may or may not be coupled with the grape name or otherwise displayed, but which in any case will appear as the address. The sensible way of knowing which wine to buy, apart from preference of grape variety, is in Alsatian wine as every wine the proved reputation and standards of the man who makes it and stakes his sales upon it.

WHEN TO DRINK ALSATIAN WINES

As they are delicate, light, flowery wines, they may be served with almost all foods and they are particularly attractive as luncheon wines. They are all white wines and should be served well chilled. They are, of course, ideal summer wines and are quite delightful in cups, punches, or for spritzers.

The growing of the vine and the vintage do not differ radically from other white wine regions in France except that, because of its more northerly location and cooler climate, the vines are trained high and allowed to reach for the sun. The grape varieties do not ripen at the same time and since many vineyards are planted with three, four or more varieties they must be picked over several times during the vintage. In the case of the Gewürz-traminer, only very ripe (preferably *pourriture noble*) grapes are picked to ensure richness of body and perfume.

Alsatian wines are generally bottled when very young, in the spring or summer, following the vintage. They are at their best when relatively young since freshness is one of their most pleasant characteristics. Occasionally, however, some of the better wines are capable of attaining great age (10–20 years) retaining their fruit and vigor.

Since 1971, only wines produced from a small number of grapes are entitled to the Appellation Contrôlée Vin d'Alsace. Allowed for the production are:

WHITE WINE: Gewürztraminer, Riesling, Pinot Gris (Tokay d'Alsace), Muscat, Pinot Blanc (Klevner), Sylvaner, Chasselas (Gutedel).
RED WINE: Pinot Noir.
ROSÉ WINE: Clairet-Schillerwein, Pinot Noir.

Up to January 1, 1980 the Appellation Contrôlée may be used on white wines produced from the following grapes: Knipperle, Goldriesling, Meunier, Chardonnay, Muller-Thurgau. The denomination "Edelzwicker" may be used if it contains one or more of the permitted grapes. Since January 1, 1973, Traminer is no longer recognized and the denomination "Zwicker," which formerly meant a blend of ordinary wines, also disappears.

Grand Cru indicates an Appellation Controlée wine of superior quality produced under special conditions and with an official examination. All Alsatian wines must be bottled in the green Alsace Flute, a tall slim bottle. The most important and popular wine of Alsace is the Riesling. It has a greenish yellow color, fine fruity bouquet and flavor and is quite dry.

The Gewürztraminer is a higher quality and truly extraordinary wine. Gewürz means spicy, and the wines develop a highly aromatic flowery bouquet and rich flavor not as dry as the Rieslings.

5. RHÔNE WINES

TRAVELING southward, the turbulent Rhône River cuts its swath to the Mediterranean. Along its route there are three widely separated sections which produce red, pink, and white wines of repute.

The principal grape varieties of the Côtes du Rhône are the Syrrah (sometimes called Sirrac, Sirah, Petite Sirah or Serrine, which is also used extensively in California), Grenache, and Vionnier—a white grape. *grape varieties*

At Châteauneuf-du-Pape, the wine is the result of judicious blending of as many as ten grape varieties. Baron P. Le Roy Boiseaumariée, President of the Syndicate of Vineyard Owners of Châteauneuf-du-Pape, stated in 1932 that the choice of grapes to produce a perfect Châteauneuf-du-Pape, are:

1st group	For warmth, richness, and roundness	Grenache and Cinsault	20 per cent
2nd group	For solidity, keeping power, color, and the right flavor	Mourvèdre and Syrrah	40 per cent
3rd group	For vinosity, agreeableness, freshness, and bouquet	Counoise and Picpoul	30 per cent
4th group	For finesse, fire, and brilliance	Clairette and Bourbouenc	10 per cent

The red wines of Châteauneuf-du-Pape traditionally have been big, slow-to-develop wines, but today with more modern methods of vinification they are ready for drinking somewhat sooner. Another post-World War II development is the production of small quantities of white wine at Châteauneuf-du-Pape. It is a pleasant wine of body, flavor, and character, although not as fine as the red.

On the west bank of the Rhone, across and downstream from the ancient Roman city of Vienne, lie the vineyards which produce Côte Rôtie (Roasted Slope).

The wines of Côte Rôtie are very deep in color, have a rich headiness, and roughness which it takes them some years to throw off. As they grow older, they lose some of their color, throw a rather heavy deposit, and rid themselves of their youthful harshness. Twelve to fifteen years is the youngest at which Côte Rôtie should be drunk.

Some white wine is produced at Condrieu and at Château Grillet. Production from both is very small and it is rare to find these wines in commerce. If you are fortunate enough to come across any Château Grillet, you will find it to be pale in color, medium-bodied but with a wealth of character and a magnificent bouquet. It will be expensive.

history   Some thirty miles south, on the left bank of the Rhône near Tain, the renowned hill of Hermitage rises up majestically. A crusader, returning from the Holy Land, decided to settle on these heights and live the contemplative life of a hermit. From the East he had brought with him a vine-cutting which he planted. According to legend, it was the first Syrrah° brought to the Rhône. He tended his vine patiently and eventually it bore fruit from which he made a fine wine which soon had people beating a track to his retreat.

The vineyards of Hermitage are less than 400 acres in extent and produce both red and white wines. The red wines, which Prof. Saintsbury called the "manliest of wines," are big, full-bodied, strong, deep-colored, and have marvelous keeping qualities. The white wines are full, medium dry, and have a deep bouquet. When old they have an amber gold color and lovely mellowness.

For seventy years, 1305–1377, the Papacy was occupied by Frenchmen, who, fearful of the perils of Rome, maintained the Holy See at Avignon. This period is sometimes called the "Babylonian Captivity" of the Popes. The first of the Avignon Popes was Clement V, who, as a native of Bordeaux and Archbishop of Bordeaux, was familiar with viticulture, and left us the legacy of that grand Graves Claret—Château Pape Clément, which he is said to have owned.

When Clément V decided to settle the Holy See at Avignon, he built a fortress-palace just outside the town. This edifice with its lands was dubbed the new château of the Pope, Châteauneuf-du-Pape. As wine is important to a man from Bordeaux, Clément had vines planted, which still produce today the wine that is known as Châteauneuf-du-Pape.

These are the best-known wines of the Côtes du Rhône, although they are not quite equal in quality to Côte Rôtie or Hermitage. They do not have as much color or body, but they do have finesse and they are pleasant.

Tavel Rosé

Across the river from Avignon is the town of Tavel, which gives its name to one of the most delightful of all the pink (Vin Rosé) wines. Tavel combines the dryness of a red wine with the fresh lightness of a white. It has a delightful rosé color, clean, fresh, dry, and usually has a lovely, fruity bouquet and flavor. Tavel is best when young, about five years old. It should be served chilled, like a white wine.

Côtes du Rhône wines are bottled in the same type of bottle used in Burgundy. They are more like Burgundy in character than any other wines. For these reasons many people have been confused, and on many a wine card Châteauneuf-du-Pape is erroneously listed as a Burgundy.

° This vine is thought to have come from Shiraz, Persia. It was brought by the knight Sir Gaspard de Sterimberg on his return from the Albigensian Crusade in 1124, when he became a hermit at the Chapel of St. Christophe at Hermitage.

PLACE ON THE MENU OF BORDEAUX, BURGUNDY, AND RHÔNE WINES

THE place on the menu of any wine is a matter of personal taste and opinion. Fortunately, most wines lend themselves to many foods, and personal preference is the final deciding factor.

Bordeaux   Speaking of Clarets in general, we would say that they go well with almost all foods except those we get from the sea. Experience has shown that a perfectly dry wine, one completely lacking in sugar, will taste better with foods that are not sweet. Of course, you can drink a Claret with fish and it will do you no physical harm, but you will enjoy the wine much more if it accompanies a meat dish. This is especially true if the Claret is a fine old château bottling.

The white, crisp, dry Graves, on the other hand, is more catholic in its tastes and may be served with all foods. It shines its brightest in the company of fish, and does nobly with fowl and white meats.

Sauternes, the perennial favorite of our American table, is a wine that a vast number of people enjoy with all manner of food, so here again personal taste is the deciding factor. As the wine is sweet and has a rich perfume it does not seem to us appealing with dry-tasting foods, though we find it agreeable with a dessert, particularly honeydew melon.

Burgundy   Red Burgundies, being perfectly dry, are like Clarets in being somewhat unsatisfactory with fish. As they have much more body, however, they are pleasant with fuller-bodied and richer (though not sweet) foods. Game or ripe cheese shows them off to the best advantage. Having greater fullness of body, they are headier wines to drink than Clarets, and therefore are more appealing in the winter than in the summer.

White wines are at home with all foods, but a good crisp Chablis or a fresh Pouilly-Fuissé with freshly opened oysters is food for the gods. In ordering wine, it is a good rule to match the dish that will show it off best, and it is my experience that fish accentuates the qualities of white Burgundies.

Rhône wines   The red wines of the Côtes du Rhônes, being full bodied and quite similar to Burgundy in character, may be served with the same type of food: roasts, game, or cheese.

The white wines are at home with most foods, but are best with fish, white meats, or fowl.

A cold bottle of Tavel is a delightful luncheon wine with most dishes and it will be found to be a happy choice on a summer evening when the weather indicates a wine that is refreshing.

OTHER WINES OF FRANCE

THE LOIRE VALLEY

THE château country of the tourist folder—issued by the *Commissariat National du Tourisme*—is not, as you might suppose, the Bordeaux wine region, but that part of France of which Dumas wrote in his enchanting and exciting novels. Because of its proximity to Paris, the people of fashion in the time of the several Louis had to have a château in the Loire valley. The wines of the region were pleasant and the courtiers at the royal court vied with each other showing off the wines from their Loire properties, thus making them quite popular in fashionable court circles.

It is a fact that almost the entire length of the valley of the Loire is a series of wine-producing vineyard areas from which come a variety of pleasant wines, none of which is bone dry. On the contrary, one of their most charming characteristics is the touch of sweetness. They are mostly white table wines, but their medium sweet rosé wines are abundant too. Some red table wines are produced, especially from Touraine: Chinon and Bourgueil. A great deal of sparkling wine is also made at Vouvray near Tours in Touraine, Saumur, and Anjou, of which Angers is the principal city.

POUILLY FUMÉ. South of Paris, the town of Pouilly sur Loire lies on the right bank of the Loire. The vineyards about Pouilly are planted with a grape variety that is the *Sauvignon* but which is known locally as the *Blanc Fumé*. The wine is called *Pouilly Fumé* and should not be confused with the Pouilly-Fuissé of Burgundy, because they are certainly dissimilar. The Burgundian Pouilly-Fuissé is a very crisp, austere dry wine, while the Pouilly Fumé of the Loire is a delicate, soft, charmingly pleasant dry wine.

POUILLY-SUR-LOIRE, named for the district, is another white wine, but is made from the Chasselas grape variety. It is less delicate, but makes a very satisfying drink.

SANCERRE, QUINCY, REUILLY. On the left bank of the river opposite Pouilly we find Sancerre, while a little further east on the Cher River is the town of Quincy. The vineyards of these regions produce white wines that are similar in character to Pouilly Fumé, but somewhat lighter and not quite as elegant.

VOUVRAY, ANJOU, SAUMUR. These are wine districts that produce most of the pleasantly medium-dry sparkling wine of the Loire. The leading producers make their wines by the *méthode champenoise,* but they do not claim their sparkling wines are Champagne. They are lovely. Anjou also produces large quantities of rosé wine. Some of the most popular rosé wines in the United States are the Anjou rosés. This popularity is due unquestionably to their touch of sweetness.

CHINON. This district produced Rabelais, lover of the good life, and a red wine made from Cabernet Franc grapes. Rabelais consumed Chinon in vast amounts and praised it lavishly. It may be that his judgment was befuddled by local patriotism, still it is pleasing and satisfying. It should be drunk young and do not be afraid to chill it. From nearby Bourgueil comes a similar red wine.

CÔTEAUX DU LAYON. The vineyards along the banks of Layon River, a tributary to the Loire, produce delightful, medium-sweet or very sweet white wines from the Chenin blanc grape. These wines are not too well known outside of France, but eventually they will be.

MUSCADET. On both banks of the Loire (but mostly on the left bank), as it flows into the Atlantic near Nantes, the vineyards are planted with a white grape called Muscadet. The light, fairly dry wine produced from them is also called Muscadet (Moose-kah-DAY). It is pleasant, inexpensive, and becoming increasingly popular in America.

CÔTES DE PROVENCE

ALL along the Mediterranean coast, from Narbonne to the Italian border, are vineyards that produce rosé wine. But probably the strongest, heartiest vin rosé comes from Côtes de Provence, which runs from the Italian border along the Mediterranean coast west to the Rhône River, and from the island of Corsica. Corsican rosé is much in demand along the French coast opposite the island because its almost rough quality makes it a good complement to the highly seasoned fish dishes so popular in the area.

Côtes de Provence rosés are grown between Aix-en-Provence and St. Raphaël, and are fine and fruity. Tasted young, they have a delightful bouquet. Older, these wines lose some bouquet but gain in smoothness and fullness of body. Other wines of the Côtes de Provence include Cassis, Bandol, Palette, and, near Nice, Bellet.

LANGUEDOC

WEST of the Côtes de Provence, along the plain from Nîmes to Narbonne, and extending down to Perpignan, huge quantities of ordinary table wine (*vins de consommation courante*) are grown. This area is known as the "Midi." This is actually the old Languedoc Province, and the great wines here are made from Costières du Gard, Clairette du Languedoc, Minervois, and Corbières.

ROUSSILLON

IN the Department of Pyrénées-Orientales are grown many of the same grape varieties which we have grown successfully in California. They include the Grenache, Mataro, Carignan, Macabeu, and Muscatel.

Near the Mediterranean, but stretching even farther south to the sunny frontiers of Spain, come the sweet dessert wines of Rivesaltes, Maury, and Banyuls. Near Montpellier, to the north, are two more Muscatel wines— Frontignan and Lunel.

BÉARN

ALSO in the Pyrénées and a former part of the Royaume de Navarre are the famous vineyards of Jurançon which produce a rich, mellow wine of breed and character from the Manseng grape. Around Pau, Rosé de Béarn, a fine pink wine, is produced.

JURA

THIS region near Switzerland was famous in the past for its wines, but today only the Rosé d'Arbois and the wines of Château d'Arlay and Châlon retain some of this fame. The former, according to French wine experts, rivals Tavel rosés. The latter are legendary and are interesting in a special way. The Savagnin grapes are vintaged as late as possible, sometimes in December, and fermentation takes place in vats which have been cut out of the rock. Because of the late vintage, fermentation is rather slow. Some wines are then racked into very old casks which have held many previous vintages, and they remain in wood seven to eight years—the normal length of time for white wine being one to two and a half years—before they are ready for bottling.

During this period a film forms on the surface of the wine in the cask and performs its miraculous work. To the best of my knowledge, this is the only wine, except for Sherry, in which this flowering phenomenon occurs. As a result of this, Château-Châlon develops an alcoholic content, usually about 15 per cent, which gives extraordinary keeping qualities. It is said to live seventy years and more, and to have an austere dryness coupled with an intense vinosity, such as one encounters in a very old, dry Sherry.

Nearby, a few miles due west of Château-Châlon, not far away from Arbais, lies one of the oldest vineyards we know about, Château d'Arlay, which produces wine similar to Château-Châlon, as well as red and white table wines. But it is the white or rather straw-colored *vin de paille*° that is most distinguished. Only wines of better than average quality vintages are bottled. The twenty acres that comprise the vineyard can produce upwards of 30,000 bottles, but the quantity is usually less.

For many generations the straw or yellow wines of Château d'Arlay were reserved for the use of the family, but in recent years Count de Vogüé has

---

° The term comes from the fact that the grapes are spread upon straw (*paille*) to dry for a period of time, before pressing.

permitted the export sale of a certain number of bottles per year. A few cases are shipped to the United States, where it can be obtained in a few fine restaurants and retail stores.

COUNTRY WINES OF FRANCE

WHILE France has always been synonymous with great wines, only recently have Americans in large numbers begun to discover that France produces reasonably priced reds, whites and rosés as well. In most countries the moderately priced French wines sell in much higher ratio to expensive wines. Here in the United States it is an "inverted pyramid" with the expensive French wines selling proportionately better than the lesser priced wines. It was to create a better equilibrium, and thus not to have to rely so much on "high-priced" wines, that the French wine industry decided in 1972 to put together a promotional program called the "Country Wines of France."

There are over 450 Appellation Contrôlée and V.D.Q.S. wine growing areas in France and the wines selected for the program came from nine of the largest producing areas. Later, as the campaign proved most successful, three other regions' wines were added. Thus there now are five reds (Bordeaux Red, Côtes du Rhone, Corbières, Roussillon, Languedoc), five whites (Alsace, Entre-Deux-Mers, Cadillac, Muscadet, Macon Blanc) and two rosés (Anjou Rosé, Côtes de Provence Rosé).

The Country Wines of France were selected according to several criteria. First, they are reasonably priced quality wines. Second, they are produced in substantial quantity, which assures a certain price stability and adequate continuing supply. In fact, these regions produce annually a total of more than 50,000,000 cases of wine—the largest of them producing seven million cases and the smallest over a million and a half cases. The third criterion is their quality, indicated on the labels by the words Appellation Contrôlée or V.D.Q.S.

The wines come from the same regions or close to the regions where wines are produced which are quite familiar to Americans. For instance, the Macon Blanc from near the Chablis region, the Côtes du Rhone near the Châteauneuf-du-Pape, and the Bordeaux and Bordeaux Supérieur from vineyards near such famous names as Margaux, St. Julien and St. Emilion. All these wines have the same strict control of grape variety, production per acre, vinification methods and the final tasting to give approval of the wines.

6. The Wines of Italy

THE length of the Via Latina was once dotted with statues of Bacchus which *history*
were destroyed as pagan idols with the march of Christianity. The cult of
Dionysus, during the Golden Age of Greece, taught man the contemplation
of his own divinity, and wine was an important part of the cult's ritual. All
Hellas honored the vine and spread the cult to Rome and Asia Minor. Plato
records that Socrates drank unbelievable quantities of wine but he was never
drunk.

It is unquestionable that we owe to the Romans the spread of the vinification
of the grape; however, we are inclined to wonder at Martial who speaks of
"immortale Falernum" with a reverence that bears on idolatry, when we
consider that this wine was generally diluted. It is also difficult to believe
the ancient historians when they speak of the merits of 150 to 200 year old
wine or to understand how wine could have been preserved so long and still
be good.

The Romans were good agriculturists and good vintners but they must have
been limited to naturally fermented wines. These, however, were of great
strength, concentrated to the consistency of jelly, and served only after dilution
with water; spiced and flavored with such substances as aloes, myrrh, resin,
pitch, sea water, marble dust, perfumes, spices, and herbs.

The Romans had capable wine makers, familiar with the use of cork and
glass. From the Greeks they took the method of lining their *amphorae* and
dolias with pitch or resin, for these earthenware containers were porous.
Apparently they also used oak barrels, but these were never in such general
use as the earthenware vessels.

After the fall of the Roman Empire, the Church took up the work of
cultivating the vine, and the barons, under the sway of the Church, cooperated,
for "mighty was the thirst of the Templar."

In the fourteenth and fifteenth centuries, which brought the Renaissance
not only of the arts but of the spirit, it became fashionable to live well, even
if one had to live dangerously. The literature of the Renaissance is full of

85

Castello della Sala in the heart of the Orvieto wine region. (Courtesy Julius Wile, New York.)

references to wines and vines. The banquets of the Medicis and the Barberinis were supreme exhibitions of aesthetic magnificence, with wines served in golden goblets and toasts sung in immortal rhymes.

Of Italy's beauty, poetry, sky, and climate the world's literature is full. The vine grows everywhere, profusely, almost wantonly, as though flaunting the bounty of nature through the fertility of her soil. In fact, Italy is one vast vineyard, from her snow-covered Alpine borders in the north to the volcanic southern tip of the boot.

From birth the Italian absorbs with no conscious effort the love of the vine. Wine is the common drink, inexpensive, natural, and sound. Because no germs harmful to man can live in wine, it is a safer drink than water which is often polluted with typhoid, and as a result the per capita consumption is high, 29.3 gallons, as compared with about one and one-half gallons in the United States. The quantity seems prodigious, and yet drunkenness is practically unknown and is considered shameful when it occurs. According to D'Annunzio, wine should be permitted to intelligent men and prohibited to the stupid.

Because the vine grows so luxuriantly and bears so abundantly throughout Italy, it is often said that the Italian vintner is more concerned with quantity than with quality. This is not altogether true. Of course, most of the wine made year after year by the vintners of the world is just plain, wholesome wine. If it is the product of the fermentation of sound, ripe grapes, it will be an honest wine, a drink within the reach of the masses.

The chief assurance of the quality of the wine is the reputation of the vintner, of course, but the product should be judged by its intrinsic value as well. If the wine is brilliant, of clean bouquet, free from extraneous odors of mold or artificial flavoring, if it is pleasant to the taste and there is no taint of sourness, then you have a good wine.

Italy has often been called "The Vineyard of the World." Where nature is so bountiful, man is prone to leave things in the lap of the gods. Vines were permitted to luxuriate over fertile plains, to climb at will over fence and tree, and grow in festoons. Pruning was carelessly done, and many varieties were grown without selection as to suitability, in all parts of the country. All this is in strong contrast with the conditions in other countries, where nature has been less lavish, and man has had to substitute infinite patience and hard labor for ideal soil conditions.

The Wine Law of 1963

MUCH of the push behind the upswing of the Italian wine industry in the past several years has come from a new government and industry policy of tighter control of all aspects of wine production. The Italian Wine Law of 1963—a Presidential Decree—passed on July 12, 1963 consolidated and defined all legal aspects with which the wine industry must comply. Its basic aim is to protect the name of origin and the sources of musts and wines, and to provide measures for the prevention of fraud and unfair competition.

The law delimits zones of production so that the same type of natural environment is provided for the production of grapes for a specific type of wine. There are three different denominations, graded as follows:

1. *Denominazione Semplice* (Simple Denomination) is just a simple statement of the region of production; e.g., *Rosso Toscano,* a red wine from anywhere inside the region of Tuscany. Such wines do not carry any official guarantee of quality; there are no set standards.

2. *Denominazione di Origine Controllata* (Controlled Denomination) is an appellation reserved for wines which have met stipulated standards of quality. The label must state the zone of origin and it must be produced from grapes traditionally cultivated in an area—the zones are determined by decree of the Ministry of Agriculture and Forestry. DOC wines are subject to testing and may wear a DOC label in addition to their own. All vineyards producing such wines are listed in an official register.

3. *Denominazione di Origine Controllata e Garantita* (Controlled and Guaranteed) is awarded only to fine wines attaining certain qualities of excellence required by the government. To be controlled and guaranteed, a wine must be bottled and sealed with a govenment seal by the producer or someone who takes full responsibility for it. A government inspector can test and analyze the wine at any time. The bottle label of such wine must state that the origin of the wine is controlled and guaranteed, the net content of the bottle, the name of the grower and bottler, the place of bottling, and also the alcoholic strength. It must be remembered that this top category of Italian wines will be awarded only to certain wines from certain producers, rather than whole regions.

Over the years the Wine Law of 1963 should result in more reliable Italian wine for everyone. It is hoped that eventually all the best wines of Italy will be "controllata e garantita," but the overall plan is very much in the embryo stage. That is because the Law is so comprehensive—covering every phase of grape cultivation and wine production, with strict controls all along the line—putting the entire plan into effect will be a long-term operation. Varieties of grapes permitted to be grown in specific zones are determined by the natural conditions of the locality, such as type of soil, position of the vineyard, and geographic location within a defined area. Within the broad area designated as suitable for the production of Chianti, for example, only a small part in the center of the area may be used for wine to be named "Chianti Classico."

The Law also requires that wine or must has to be made from traditional, high-quality grape varieties, rather than from hybrid vines. Production practices must also conform with approved practices for planting, cultivation, fertilization, and maximum allowed yields. To bear the area name, the wine must be bottled in the area.

Great strides have already been made in this program. But due to the fact

TOP. *Modern scientifically planted vineyard.*
BOTTOM. *Vineyards planted in the more traditional style of Italy. The wines are trellised or bowered between fruit or olive trees.* (Courtesy Fratelli Folonari, Brescia.)

that the Law has not taken full effect at present, we have made no reference to DOC zones or controlled and guaranteed wines in our descriptions of Italian wines in this chapter.

labeling   Although compliance with the Law and its terms are at the moment a voluntary situation, most of the better producers appear anxious to obtain the certification of guarantee for export. But since it is a voluntary thing, it is still up to the customer to read the label before purchasing a bottle of Italian wine. On the other hand, the *Instituto Commercio Estero* (Institute of Foreign Commerce) has adapted a seal which is applied on every bottle exported to the United States and Canada, which indicates that the wine contained therein has met the standards of the Italian regulations for these countries.

geography   The map of Italy shows the most casual reader that it lies in the same latitude as Canada and New England. Naples, generally thought of as a semitropical city, is in the same latitude as New York.

The entire Italian peninsula is covered with mountains. In the west and north lie the majestic, snow-capped Alps, toward the east the Venetian Alps —the picturesque needles of the Dolomites. Winters are long and bitter, but the valleys are fertile and the natives frugal and hard-working; so in spite of the handicaps of weather, snow, ice, erosion, and avalanche, the vine thrives, and some of the finest vines are grown on forbidding ledges, carefully terraced and tended.

The peninsula is split by the Apennine chain from the Po to the very tip of Calabria. While the Apennines are not as forbidding as the Alps, they are rocky and bleak, and submit only to the constant struggle of industrious peasants whose forebears have fought the elements for 2,000 years.

The northern part of Italy is cold; the eternal snows and glaciers cool the sirocco from the south. The south is semi-tropical with a climate much like that of Florida. Sicily is the island of eternal sunshine. The vine grows profusely in all of Italy, yet so varied are the climatic conditions, the soil, the methods of cultivation, and the varieties of vines used, that Italy probably could satisfy the nicest requirement of any connoisseur.

grape varieties   From the River Po down to the Vesuvius territory, with its hot, sandy, volcanic soil, Italy runs the entire gamut of varieties of grapes. There are so many types of vines that it is next to impossible to make a complete estimate.

To add to the general confusion, the same grape variety is often grown in several districts, and in each case gives its name to the wine. In other cases, the wine takes its name from the town or village around which the grapes were grown. It is possible, for instance, to get two Vernaccias, one from Verona in the northern part of Venetia, the other grown in Sardinia. Now it stands

WINE REGIONS OF ITALY

A-1 Chianti Classico   A-4 Rufina
A-2 Montalbano   A-5 Colli Senesi
A-3 Colli Fiorentini   A-6 Colli Aretini
A-7 Colline Pisane
B Moscatello-Brunello di Montalcino
C Vin Nobile di Montepulciano
D Vini Tipici dell'Elba

to reason that grapes grown in the mountainous region of the north where the soil is watered by glacier-fed rivers lacking in mineral salts will have a flat taste compared to wine produced from the same grape but grown in volcanic soil containing a great many minerals. And yet they both have the same name.

The principal vines and the regions in which they are cultivated are:

PRINCIPAL GRAPE VARIETIES OF ITALY

VINE	WHERE GROWN	CHARACTERISTICS
Aleatico-Nero	Tuscany, Piedmont, Emilia, Marche, Latium, and Apulia (red wines)	Produces a sweet and aromatic wine. Seldom fermented alone; usually with Trebbiano and Sangiovese, while in Piedmont it is mixed with Bracchetto.
Barbera	Piedmont (red wines)	The most common vine in Piedmont. Prefers clay soils, good drainage, and well-exposed hillsides.
Bracchetto	Piedmont, near Acqui and Alessandria (red wines)	Produces a pleasant light wine of delicate flavor and brilliant red color.
Cortese	Piedmont and Liguria (white wines)	Gives fine, light, dry wine with a delicate aroma. Grows best in porous clay.
Grignolino	Piedmont (red wines)	Said to be identical with Kadarka of Hungary.
Malvasia	Piedmont, Tuscany, Marche, Abruzzi, and Sicily (white dessert wines)	Used for rich liquorous wine and table grapes. A small amount used in Tuscany for Chianti.
Moscato	(Subdivided into three varieties)	
1. Moscato-Semplice di Canelli	Piedmont (white dessert wines)	Grows in poor soils, sandy, high altitudes, sunny slopes. Used for sparkling wines because it has property of secondary fermentation.
2. Moscato-Zibibbo	Sicily (really on the Island of Pantelleria) (white dessert wines)	Originally brought to Sicily in the Middle Ages by Arabs from the town of Zibib, Arabia. This vine is

VINE	WHERE GROWN	CHARACTERISTICS
		also found in the Malaga district of Spain. Produces an individual rich wine, also fine raisins.
3. Moscato-Fior d'Arancio	Sicily and Calabria (white dessert wines)	Wines with an aroma of orange blossoms. *Fior d'Arancio* means flower of orange.
Nebbiolo	Piedmont, Lombardy (red wines, both still and sparkling)	The most aristocratic vine of the north. Difficult of cultivation, it is slow-growing, ripens late, suffers from damp seasons and grows best on high elevations, on slopes well exposed to the south.
Passeretta	Piedmont, Apulia, and Sicily (white dessert wines)	Came originally from Smyrna. Used to add flavor to Moscato. *Passeretta* means shrivelled or withered.
Pinot	Piedmont, Lombardy (red wines)	The Burgundian *Pinot Noir*, it needs dry poor soils and high elevations to produce its best.
Pinot	Piedmont, Lombardy, and Sicily (white wines)	The Burgundian Chardonnay, grown by specialists in the Pinerolo, Piedmontese and at Casteldaccia, Sicily.
Riesling-Italiano	Austrian Venetia, Tristino, also on hillsides surrounding Lake Como (white wines)	Grows best in dry fertile soils, giving a light, dry white wine with the typical Riesling character.
Sangiovese	Tuscany, Romagna, and Abruzzi (red wines)	The genius or base of Chianti of which it forms 70 per cent, the other 30 per cent being made up of Trebbiano, Canaiolo Nero, and Malvasia.
Trebbiano	Piedmont, Romagna and Tuscany (white wines)	One of the easiest grapes to grow, as it prospers in almost any exposure in clay soils.
Vernaccia	Lombardy, Tuscany, Venetia, Sicily, and	Formerly grown in all parts of Italy, today principally in Sardinia and

VINE	WHERE GROWN	CHARACTERISTICS
	Sardinia	Sicily where it produces a highly
	(white wines)	alcoholic white wine.

PIEDMONT

PIEDMONT, the section of Italy which produces the best-known wines, is the most austere region in the country. The wines are hardy, masculine, travel well, and improve with age. From the glaciers of the Alpine banks the land descends in a series of charming valleys and fertile plains to the River Po, from which it again rises gradually to the hills of Monferrato where the vine is cultivated with religious fervor. Piedmont is entirely surrounded by hills, forming a cup at the bottom of which it gets very hot. This is where the famous wines, Barolo and Asti Spumante, are grown.

The region is ruled by Torino, the home of Vermouth, and the center of industry. It is the richest market for wines in the region. The Piedmontese are tenacious, industrious, and faithful to their land. Their vineyards are neat and symmetrical.

Barolo is a little village, crowning a hill of *tufa* which undoubtedly is an extinct volcano. On this hill the Nebbiolo grapes grow best, and they give the finest and most justly celebrated red wine Italy has. In good years, Barolo can be classed as one of the kings of wine.

Opera Pia Barolo stands for the "good works of Barolo." A family named Falletti, the Marchesi of Barolo, were vineyard owners who did much to popularize the wines of Barolo. The last Marchesa, a charitable woman, devoted both time and money to the poor, and her activities were known as OPB (Opera Pia Barolo) when they were passed on to the hands of a committee at the time of her death in 1864. The company which owns and operates the vineyards in Barolo today is a direct successor to this committee.

Barolo in a good year is a big, full-bodied wine, with a ruby-red color which takes on a brownish shade as it ages. It is generous yet austere, rich in alcohol but always a soft, velvety wine with an unmistakable violet bouquet. It should be on all well-balanced wine lists.

The hills surrounding the town of Barolo are dotted with picturesque villages. The Nebbiolo grape is also grown here but because of differences of soil, the flavor is not as fine as that of the Barolo, and the wine produced is called Barbaresco. The Barbaresco district lies just northeast of Alba, with the hillside vineyards surrounding the old red-towered remnant of Barbaresco Castle on the crest of the hill, and the tiny hamlet of perhaps a dozen stone houses. Barbaresco wines are quicker in maturing than Barolos.

It is interesting to note that in Julius Caesar's *Commentaries* there is a reference to these wines which he greatly appreciated and wanted to introduce to Rome. The particular wine he referred to came from the little village of

Morra (Murra). "From Murra," he wrote, "we brought the best wine to our city of Rome."

Other red wines of the Piedmont region are Gattinara, made from the Nebbiolo grape grown near Vercelli, a wine with a dry, pleasant flavor and a slightly bitter undertone; and Grignolino, made from the grape of the same name. This is a light, rather rough wine. Dolcetto is light, faintly bitter, and is the carafe wine of the region. It does not have the character of the Grignolino.

Barbera is the half-brother of Barolo; dry, rough, and coarse, a wine that will pucker your lips, but if you are a native, you will like it. Barbera, Nebbiolo, and Freisa are red wines which can be dry as well as sweet—when sweet they are generally creaming or "crackling" (slightly sparkling). The Freisa is so named for its raspberry bouquet. These wines are often made sparkling, and are sold as sparkling red wine.

From the Cortese Bianco is produced Cortese, a light-bodied, straw-colored wine with a greenish cast. It has a delicate, pleasant, and fresh aroma.

Asti, the sparkling wine center of Italy and the home of the famous white Asti Spumante, is an active little town with a great historical background. It was here that Barbarossa was defeated. The hills of Asti are now honeycombed with cellars excavated for the purpose of storing the fermented juice of the moscato, which is sold throughout the world as Asti Spumante. Bismarck showed such predilection for it that he exclaimed: "I want one good bottle for each of my officers. It will serve to keep their heavy heads awake."

The actual production zone of Asti muscat wine lies south of the town. The vineyards along the rugged banks of the Belbo around Canelli produce the most highly prized moscatos of all. The first producer of Asti Spumante, and today the largest in Italy, is located at Canelli.

Asti Spumante is the most popular Italian sparkling wine. It is a delicious wine with a pleasant, decidedly sweet, muscat flavor which gives it a lovely fresh fruitiness. Most of the shippers have changed over from bottle fermentation to bulk (Charmat) fermentation. Aside from the time and expense saving they claim that the fragrance of the muscat grape is preserved much better under this method.

Many of the Italian sparkling wine producers do maintain the mèthode champenoise for the production of drier wines made from transplanted French grapes including the white Pinot. Also used are local grapes and Lacrima Christi which, technically, is made from the dry wines of that name shipped up from vineyards on the slopes of Mt. Vesuvius (see page 105). In recent years this point has been more carefully enforced.

LOMBARDY

THE Swiss Alps frame with breathtaking beauty the lake region of Lombardy, and the surrounding hills have a corrugated appearance as row upon row of carefully tended vineyards extend as far as the eye can see. The River Adda splits the valley of Valtellina, and Milano lies to the south, wearing the filigree crown of the Duomo (Milan's famous Cathedral).

The best wines of Lombardy come from the Sondrio region, formerly Swiss. They were known as Veltlines wines and today are called Valtellina. Both red and white wines are made. Sassella, the finest Valtellina wine, has a bright ruby color, a delicate fruity bouquet, and fine body.

Inferno is a lighter-bodied red wine, which has a nutty flavor. When labeled simply Valtellina, it is a light-bodied, straw-colored, fresh-tasting wine with a fine aroma.

Frecciarossa is the name of a hillside in the beautiful rolling hills around Casteggio, a town near Pavia. Here Dr. Giorgio Odero has his lovely villa surrounded by one of the most carefully tended vineyards in Italy. During the last century his father not only planted fine French vines but more importantly adopted French methods of planting, cultivation, and vinification. Dr. Odero bottles only the wine of his own production and is one of the very few in Italy who can boast château bottling. Frecciarossa produces red, rosé, white, and ambrato wine. They are fine, full-flavored, full-bodied, of excellent character.

Near charming Lake Garda is produced a pleasant light white wine called Lugana. It is most enjoyable when young, and especially so with a freshly caught broiled trout . . . yes, fresh from Lake Garda, the region from which we receive the lovely Rosé Chiaretto del Garda. This is a very dark rosé, with a gentle flavor, soft-texture, and a hint of bitterness, like almonds, which is common to the best red wines of this region of Italy. Franciacorta, Cellatica, and Red Botticino are light, flavorful reds, but they are not as popular or well known as the Chiaretto.

VENETIA (VERONA)

THE morning sun rising above the Adriatic gilds the *guglie* of the Dolomites in the north, long before it touches the golden cupolas of San Marco. The land drops precipitously from rugged mountain to dismal swamp. In the intervening space rushes the River Adige. Here, at storied, romantic Verona where you can visit the houses of the Montagues and Capulets . . . where you can stand in the courtyard and gaze up at Giulietta's balcony and visualize the poetic trysts of the fated lovers, there also stands majestically the Palazzo Scaglieri, where Cangrande toasted his guests with Vernaccia and where Dante Alighieri found refuge and his protection.

Here, too, is Lake Garda along whose shores are produced bright red Bardolino and dry white Lugana . . . and in the long, narrow Valpolicella valley, running north from Verona, the Corvina, Molinara, Negrara, and other grape varieties join to produce one of Italy's loveliest red table wines.

It is called Valpolicella, the wine into which Hildebrand (Saint and Pope Gregory VII—1020–1085) hoped his nose would forever be dipped. Valpolicella is more than a good wine, it is a fine wine, ruby in color, of delicate bouquet, softness, and a slight bitter tang.

An even finer Valpolicella produced in limited quantities is called Recioto Amarone della Valpolicella. It is made entirely with grapes taken from the upper part of the bunch, i.e., the grapes which have benefited most from the sun, and will be the best, the ripest. To the imaginative person these grapes represent the "ears" of the bunch, ergo *Recioto*, which means ears. An Amarone Valpolicella is usually a soft, well-balanced wine of great character.

Some Recioto Nobile is made also from Recioto grapes which have developed *pourriture noble*. It is a pleasant, sparkling red wine, on the sweet side.

From the vineyards about the ancient walled city of Soave the Garganega and ubiquitous Trebbiano grapes produce the very appropriately named Soave. It is really suave white wine, light, fairly dry, with a pleasant, subtle bouquet, soft velvety texture, and a bit of piquant bitter undertone.

A wine similar to the Soave, the Garganega di Gambelare, is produced in the bordering province of Vicenza. Other excellent white wines, such as the Pinot (white) or the Vespaiola, are found in the same area. Recently, especially in the Breganza region, the production of good red wines has become much better; they are being obtained from imported vines such as Merlot, Pinot Noir, and Cabernet.

In the Adige valley, red wines are in the majority. They range from ordinary to very good. The Merlot, for example, is a good wine here, while some fine white wine is obtained from the Riesling (Italian version, not the Rhine Riesling) and Traminer. An enjoyable, dry sparkling wine is made in Trento, but little reaches our shores.

The province of Bolzano (Upper Adige) produces a wide variety of quality wines, but the best known are Santa Maddelena and Caldaro—dry, red wines—and Lagrein—a dry, fresh rosé with a harmonious flavor.

The white wines produced in the province of Treviso are of excellent quality. The best known are the Colli di Congeliano and the Valdobbiadene which come mainly from the Prosecco grape. The Collio Gariziano and Verdiso are the standard light dry white wines of the region. Raboso is the local red.

EMILIA

WE now come down to the richest and most fertile region of the Po Valley. On the hills around Bologna, home of the sausage, the subsoil is chalky like that of the Champagne region of France. Along the valley of the Trebbia is grown the fine Trebbiano grape, which is greatly in demand for making sparkling wine. However, it is curious to note that the unfermented must

Vineyards growing right up to the remains of the medieval fortress and battlements which protected the ancient city of Soave, near Verona. (Courtesy Fratelli Folonari, Brescia)

obtained from these grapes is nearly all exported to northern countries for the making of sparkling wines. The reason for this is that the perennial floods of the Po make it difficult to preserve dry cellars and the wines cannot be stored. However, a delightful sparkling red wine, Lambrusco, enjoys a merited reputation. It is a lively, grapey wine which goes well with rich Bolognese food. Another popular restaurant wine of Bologna is Albana, a good medium-dry white wine.

Here, too, is the tiny Republic of San Marino, famous for its Sangiovese wine. This is a dry, robust, well-rounded ruby red wine, somewhat harsh and peppery.

TUSCANY

To the poets, this region is Arcady—the home of Dante, Boccaccio, the Borgias, St. Francis of Assisi, St. Catherine of Siena. It bears the marks of the orgies and extravaganzas of its sinners and the pious virtues of its saints.

To most people it is the home of Italian wines, for the mention of Chianti immediately brings forth the picture of the typical straw-covered flask with the red, white, and green stripes. Of all containers for wine, it is the most picturesque and the most unsatisfactory: delicate, difficult to pack, to fill, and to cork.

After many years of acrimonious squabbling, it appears that agreement has finally been attained in defining the geographical boundaries of the region legally entitled to call its wine true Chianti. This area is subdivided into seven districts, all of which lie on the beautiful rolling hillsides about and between Firenze (Florence) and Siena. (See map.)

Here the vine grows profusely and produces enormous quantities of fruit. As you go farther south, the appearance of the vineyards is very different from the orderly, well-tended ones of the north. Where nature is lavish, the vines are left more and more to their own devices. They are allowed to grow wild, their only support being from weeping willows and poplars which are set up as props, the vines being festooned from one tree to another.

There are exceptions to this manner of doing things, of course, the principal one being the vast vineyard of the Barone Ricasoli, the largest grower in Tuscany, whose Brolio Chianti has world distribution. To the present Baron's grandfather must go the credit for having brought Piedmontese viticultural methods into Tuscany. The Brolio vineyards are today an example of scientific cultivation, the cellars are perfection, and the work of improvement in vinification has set an example which other vineyard owners have followed.

Chianti is made from several different grape varieties. The informing grape is the Sangiovese, which makes up about 70 per cent of the marc, the other 30 per cent being Trebbiano, Canaiolo Nero, and Malvasia. In the finer vineyards, some Cabernet and Malbec grapes will be included.

Vinification is much the same as in other red wine, and the wine ferments out at between $10\frac{1}{2}$ and 13 per cent of alcohol, depending on vintage conditions.

Three qualities of Chianti are generally produced; the wine for early home consumption, a better quality for bottling in the traditional *fiaschi*, and the best quality for long aging. Great improvements have been made in the vinification and subsequent care of the wine during the present century. However, it is not uncommon for Chianti to be kept in vats up to six years before bottling. Chianti contains a substantial amount of bitartrates, which makes for a rough, harsh, but full-bodied wine.

A process called *governo* is unique in Tuscany. It consists of setting aside a small per cent of the harvest on trays to become raisins. These are then pressed late in the year and the fermenting juice added to the new Chianti. This provokes a slow secondary fermentation which imparts the typical tangy Chianti taste. On the other hand, some large producers have adopted advanced methods of treatment through refrigeration and judicious filtration, thus producing much softer and more rounded wine, without loss of its native character.

All red wines must acquire bottle ripeness, during which time they throw off their youthful roughness. Chianti is not given this opportunity when the raffia-covered *fiasco* is used, because the shipper must pack and ship promptly. If he does not, he runs the risk of the raffia deteriorating, with consequent

View from Brolio Castle of the vineyard, winery, and offices in the heart of the Tuscan Chianti hills. (Courtesy of Barone Bettino Ricasoli, Florence)

loss through bottle breakage. Thus the best-quality Chianti is always found in the regular Claret style bottle, since the wine will have to rest and develop in the bottle for years. Such Chianti will be splendid, soft, rounded, mellow wine of great character.

Originally the Chianti flask was made for home consumption, not for export. It was not corked, and the wine was protected against the air by a film of olive oil.

For all its roughness, young Chianti is an ideal wine to drink with rich, well-seasoned, oily foods, because its tartness is just the thing to help digest this rich food. Older Chiantis with bottle age have more ubiquitous uses.

From Montepulciano, near Siena, comes another wine on the style of Chianti, called Vin Nobile, as well as the Vernaccia di San Gimignano, a light, dry, pleasant white wine, with a slightly bitter after-taste.

White wine has always been made in Tuscany since white grapes such as the Trebbiano and Malvasia are grown in abundance. A few years ago White Chianti was shipped to our market, but this was short lived. It was prohibited to name any white wine "Chianti," even though it be produced in the Chianti district. It may be labeled "White Tuscan Wine," but only red Chianti can be shipped.

The historical Island of Elba provides us with a clean, very pleasant light, dry white wine labeled simply Vino dell'Elba. This wine is shipped in an intriguing bottle molded into the shape of a fish, thus subtly implying that it is an ideal fish wine, which it is.

The traditional white wine for which Tuscany justifiably does claim some fame is her Vin Santo, a rich, generous, sweet dessert wine, with a delicate muscat flavor. Practically all vintners in the region produce some. The white Trebbiano and Malvasia grapes are gathered when fully ripened and the bunches are strung on poles which are suspended under the attic-roof of the house. There they remain to dry out until late December when they will be pressed and the rich juice ferments very slowly during the cold winter months.

MARCHE AND UMBRIA

THE region of Marche on the Adriatic side of the peninsula is very hilly and exposed to the north wind. Not many great wines are grown in this region, but one in particular demands attention: the very fine, light white wine, Verdicchio dei Castelli di Jesi.

It was at Ravenna, Marche's principal city, that Martial complained of the

102

The old traditional method of transporting wine in the Chianti region of Tuscany.
(Courtesy Julius Wile, New York)

dishonesty of a wine seller who indeed "hath given me pure wine." In those days it was customary to improve the natural flavor of wine with resin and other extraneous flavorings.

Verdicchio di Castelli Jesi is one of Italy's distinguished white wines and the most crisply dry. It has a pale greenish cast, a delicate bouquet and flavor. It is customarily shipped in a graceful green, amphora-like bottle.

Another very similar wine, while not as well known, is the Verdicchio di Matelica. The same grapes are used as for the first Verdicchio, but in different blending proportions. In general, the reds of Marche are looked on as good ordinary wines, but some are of a quality which enables them to almost challenge the most famous Tuscan wines. The best known are Rosso Piceno, Sangiovese di Romagna, Rosso Conero, and Montepulciano di Abruzzi.

Across the peninsula to the Mediterranean side we come to Umbria, where the beautiful cities of Assisi, Perugia, and Orvieto are located. It is a land of pastoral beauty, temperate climate, rolling hills through which flows the

Tevere (Tiber). The well-drained soil is especially suitable to the growing of fine white wines.

After Chianti, Orvieto is the most widely known wine of Italy. Traditionally, Orvieto wines have been bottled in a long-necked *fiasco* similar to the Chianti flask, without question the most impractical bottle for them. As a white wine it must be chilled. If this is done in a wine cooler filled with ice, it is impossible to dry it off satisfactorily and it will drip water over everyone and everything. Fortunately, at least one shipper is now bottling his Orvieto in a distinctive, dumpy glass bottle which makes for neater, "drier" serving.

The white wines of Orvieto are both dry (*secco*) and semi-dry (*abboccato*). Both are light straw-colored and have a fruity freshness, with a bitter undertone. An excellent Orvieto rosé is also produced. It is a dry wine with character.

Trebbiano grapes hanging from the attic rafters to dry out before being pressed for the making of Vin Santo. (Courtesy of Barone Bettino Ricasoli, Florence)

LATIUM

LATIUM was the home of Horace, and his poetry tells of Tusculum, now called Frascati; of the wines that he grew and the trees that he loved so well.

The proud Romans left the shores of the Tiber for the pleasures of the countryside, and on the hills adjacent to Rome they built their villas. Hence the wines produced on the estates of these nobles are called "Vini dei Castelli Romani."

Chiefly white wines are made, as the conditions of soil and climate are not particularly favorable for red wines.

In Rome, every restaurant offers Frascati and they are never quite the same in any two, running the entire gamut from delightful to just ordinary wine. Frascati is most enjoyable when young, when it can be a lovely fresh fruity wine, with a touch of sweetness.

A little further north around the ancient town of Montefiascone on Lake Bolsena is produced the dry and semi-dry, golden-hued Moscatelo, with its fruity and elegant bouquet, which is poetically named Est! Est!! Est!!! While the wine is very good per se, the manner in which it got its name is most interesting.

As the story goes, a long time ago—perhaps four or five centuries—a German bishop named Fuger was on his way to the Vatican to pay his respects to the Holy Father. Being a man of taste and discrimination, he sent his secretary-valet ahead to find suitable accommodations. Where the food, and especially the wine, was good, the valet was to write with chalk the word *Est* on the wall of the inn. When this good man tasted the wines at Montefiascone he could not describe them truthfully with just one "It is," so he chalked on the wall of the Albergo Est! Est!! Est!!! (It is! It is!! It is!!!) When the bishop arrived he agreed with his valet's judgment. In fact, he tarried so long and drank so freely that he finally died at Montefiascone, without ever reaching Rome.

On his tomb, in Montefiascone, one may read today the inscription that his faithful valet had carved upon the stone: "Est, Est, Est, et propter nimium est, Johannes De Fuger, dominus meus, mortuus est," which means: It is, it is, it is, and though too much it is, my master Johannes De Fuger, dead is."

The sequel to the story is that the grateful vintners of Montefiascone who produce Est! Est!! Est!!! commemorate the anniversary of Bishop De Fuger's demise by spilling a barrel of Est! Est!! Est!!! wine over his tomb. So we may presume that his bones have continued throughout the centuries to enjoy uninterruptedly the wine he loved so well.

CAMPANIA

THIS region, dominated by Vesuvius, is one of the most beautiful spots on

The bottle label of Est! Est!! Est!!! shows the Bishop De-Fuger's arrival at the Monte-fiascone Inn.

earth. "See Naples and die," people say of it. The dust of the volcano spreads imperceptibly over the land and fertilizes it. Hot springs and fissures evidence the volcanic nature of the soil. The climate is ideal, and vegetation is luxuriant—three crops a year are rotated on farms. The vine is intensely cultivated, for the area is limited and the demand world-wide. Falernum, prized by the Romans, has fallen from popularity, and in its stead rules Lacrima Christi, which is brought up by northern vintners who subject it to a secondary fermentation in the bottles. This sparkling wine is always rather sweet.

The still Lacrima Christi, made in the shadow of Vesuvius, is a golden wine, not too dry, with a softness, delicacy, and somewhat aromatic bouquet which it gets from the hot volcanic soil. Some red Lacrima Christi is also made.

Today you can get both red and white Falerno, but this modern wine does not evoke the poetic rhapsodies of its ancient namesake, Falernum, of which Juvenal IX tells that Sufeja was able to drink some 35 gallons at a sitting without getting drunk, simply by tickling his throat with a peacock's feather. Gragnano, a dark red, rich, fruity wine, comes closer to the storied ancient. Red Vesuvio, made from the Aglianico grape, and red and white Ravello are also popular wines in the region.

In this magical setting, surrounded by blue waters, lies Capri. Little original Capri wine is available, and most of it is used by the islanders themselves.

It is a light, fresh, delightful wine, usually white, but occasionally red. Prince Patrizi exports small quantities, and those who can purchase real Capri are lucky indeed. More often than not, what we get is wine from the neighboring island of Ischia.

On the island there are innumerable dispensaries where the product is consumed on the premises. The most famous dispenser is a Swede named Moll, patronized by the late Count Zeppelin. Because he sells his wine on credit, he has been for many years a favorite of impecunious college boys, who sing:

"O Moll, O Moll, O Moll,	"O Moll, O Moll, O Moll,
Beve quanto si vuol	Drink as much as you can
Pagare quando si puol!"	Pay whenever you can!"

Just around the corner, so to speak, on the southern slope of the Sorrento peninsula and just above Amalfi lies the pleasant town of Ravello, where legend has it Richard Wagner had the dream that inspired his great opera "Parsifal." For many centuries its red and white wines have been highly regarded, but more recently, since the turn of the century, Ravello has become even better-known for the delightfully crisp, dry rosé it now produces.

APULIA

ONE of the most interesting wine-growing regions of Italy is Apulia, which produces full wines, abundant in esters, high in alcoholic content, and in great demand for blending. The liquorous, warm, nectar-like Moscato di Salento is typical of the region. Of the red wines, Santo Steffano and Castel del Monte, when properly aged, are excellent, while a rosé type of the latter has a dry, delicate, velvety taste.

In the neighborhood of Foggia, the fine white wines of San Severo and Torre Giulia are grown. This wine is as attractive as it is generous; full flavored yet dry, with a delightful aroma.

In the sweet wine group, the Apulia region produces several fine aromatic varieties, including Moscati di Trani (made from the Muscat Blanc), Moscato di Salento (also called Salento Bianco Liquoroso), and Aleatico di Puglia (made from the Aleatico).

CALABRIA

HERE, in a wild country of bare high mountains and fertile valleys, a country of contrasts, of chilly winds and tropical shores, the vine is cultivated extensively. It produces only good local wines of rather light alcoholic content. Much *vin ordinaire* comes from this section.

Savuto du Rogliano, Pollino, and Ciró di Calabria are red table wines, while Greco di Gerace is a dessert wine, made from the Moscato-Fior d'Arancio, which gives the wine a bouquet reminiscent of orange blossoms.

SICILY

HOMER speaks of Sicily as the land where "spontaneous wine from weighty clusters flow." The Sicilians," said Plato, "build as if they were always to live, and sup as if they never were to sup again."

The soil of Sicily is incomparable for growing the grape, and so varied that every variety of vine finds suitable space.

The first to appreciate the enchanting beauty of the island were the English, who practically monopolized the output of Marsala, Lord Nelson's favorite wine.

The volcanic regions of the occasionally active Etna produce a wine of great strength and aggressive bouquet which is much in demand for blending with weaker wines in northern countries.

The western part of the island is planted with the French Pinot and the Arabian Zibibbo vine, the latter producing wines that are liquorous and aromatic. The Pinot is an importation of Duke Salaparuta, whose desire to improve viticulture in Sicily and to raise the standard of living of the natives has been crowned with success at Casteldaccia. The wine of Salapurata is called Corvo.

Corvo is a fine, dry, rather austere wine of much character, with the hot fieriness of Sicily racing through it. Although both red and white are produced, the red has a greater appeal to us. These are the only light wines of note shipped from Sicily, which is better known for her sweet dessert wines.

Four of these wines which are shipped to America, and can be obtained from most Italian wine importers are: Moscato di Noto, from Syracuse; Moscato Zucco, from near Palermo; Moscato di Pantelleria, a small island between Sicily and Tunis, where the Zibibbo Muscat grape produces an excellent, dark-hued, full, rich, and mellow wine; and the Malvasia di Lipari which has a typical Malmsey richness and flavor.

Sicily to most of us means Marsala, an excellent wine some Italians will tell you is Italy's "cream Sherry," a mistake to make as it labels the wine as an imitation, which it is not.

Marsala is a fortified wine obtained from the Insolia and Calaretto grapes. It is sweet, dark walnut brown in color, and has a rather acid undertone, due to the volcanic nature of the soil in which the grapes grow. In this respect, it comes closer to Madeira than it does to Sherry, but it does not resemble either. No, Marsala is an individual wine with its own character. It is a blended wine, and each maintains a Solera system on the order of the Jerez houses.

Marsala also finds many uses in the kitchen, where it is indispensable for the making of zabaglione, scaloppine alla Marsala, and numerous sauces and desserts. In Italy there is a prepared egg and Marsala drink which is imported extensively into the United States under the trade name of *Marvo*.

SARDINIA

THE cork, the olive, and the vine grow well in the island of Sardinia. The wines are mostly heady, liquorous, and strong. "Drink this wine," said an unknown poet, "thou needest no garlands." Like nearby Sicily, Sardinia is better known for dessert wines than for table wines, but her well-known Vernaccia del Campidano is an exception. It is an amber-colored wine, dry and tonic, with a delicate almond-blossom bouquet and a pleasingly bitter tang. Nuragus is another good dry white wine, but Sardinia's two best-known red wines—Cannonau and Oliena—are too sweet and heavy for most visitors to the island.

Moscato del Tempio and Malvasia of Sardinia are two white dessert wines with the characteristic flavor of the grape varieties from which they are made, while the Giro di Sardegna is a red dessert wine on the order of Port.

OF ITALIAN WINES IN GENERAL

THE wines of Italy run the gamut of the wines of the world. The method of naming most wines after the grape makes the selecting of wines by type somewhat difficult. As a general rule, a northern wine will be better than a southern wine.

Many fine Italian wines do not travel well and never reach our shores, so we have discussed those wines which are obtainable in this country.

Italian wines have a rough, downright earthiness. They are strong, masculine wines, with a positiveness that is disarming.

The lighter beverage wines may be used in the same manner as any light white or red wine, though the rougher, sturdier wines will be found to give greatest enjoyment when served with rich, well-seasoned foods. The dessert wines may be enjoyed after dinner, or in the afternoon or evening.

7. The Wines of Germany

SAILING down the Rhine, between its vine-clad hills of Nibelung legend, the orderly beauty makes a profound impression. But it is rare for one to recall that this is due to centuries of unremitting toil. Considering the perfect weather conditions that are required to produce a good wine even in such temperate regions as Bordeaux or Burgundy, one must marvel at the courage and tenacity of the vineyard owners of the Rhine and Moselle valleys, the most northerly wine region in Europe.

No vintner has ever had a more discouraging or difficult task than these Rhenish farmers, but they have triumphed magnificently over the tremendous odds nature has stacked against them. Poor soil, lack of sunshine, a short summer, precipitous hillsides to be terraced, to which the vines cling precariously, and natural diseases of the vine—these handicaps merely spur these undaunted men on to greater efforts. Their courage deserves our admiration, and their success our gratitude, for their patience and their toil have given us some of the world's great wines.

In Germany, as in France, the traditions of wine are entwined with the *history* very roots of its history. As far back as the time of Charlemagne (800 A.D.) the vineyards of the Rhine, probably planted by the Romans of Caesar's time, enjoyed great fame.

During the eighteenth century, most of the Rhine wine shipped to England was labeled "Hochheimer." The English, ever atrocious linguists, found difficulty in pronouncing this word and promptly shortened it to "Hock." Today, in all English-speaking countries, the term Hock, or Hocks, means Rhine wine. This, however, does not include the wines of the Moselle or from Franconia.

Here, too, the monastic orders of the church did much to develop viticulture. Johannisberg (Hill of St. John) takes its name from the Chapel of St. John, erected in 853 A.D. by the Benedictine monks of St. Alban's at Mainz. On this storied hill is the castle (schloss) whose vineyard produces what are recognized to be some of the finest Rhine wines.

109

geography   German viticulture is found in three main geographical districts: the Rhine valley, and its tributaries, the Nahe and the Main; the Moselle valley and its tributaries, the Saar and the Ruwer; Lower Franconia, a small district on the Main around Würzburg, and its famous Steinwein; and more recently, since World War II, the Baden-Württemberg region is regaining attention as an important quality wine producer. (The Baden-Bodensee area is along the Rhine from Lake Constance to above Baden-Baden opposite Alsace, while the Württemberg area includes vineyards on both sides of the Neckar River.)

The Rhine valley, like all Gaul, is divided into three parts: the Rheingau, which embraces the right bank of the river, from above Lorch to and including Hochheim on the Main; the Rheinhesse, which includes the land on the left bank of the river from Worms to Bingen, and that lying between the Nahe and the Rhine; and finally, the Rheinpfalz, or Palatinate, which forms a triangle between the Rhine, the Haardt Mountains, and the French border.

Rising in the Vosges Mountains, the Moselle River wanders through Lorraine, becomes part of the Franco-German border, continues northward to form the border between Luxemburg and Germany, enters Germany proper where it is joined by the Saar, and a little further along by the Ruwer, from which point it winds and twists through its sinuous and picturesque course until it reaches the Rhine at Coblenz.

Viticulturally, the valley is divided into three parts: the Upper Moselle, from Wasserbillig (in Luxemburg) to Trier with its famous Cathedral of Trèves; the Middle Moselle, from Trèves to Traben-Trarbach, twin cities on opposite sides of the river; and the Lower Moselle, from there to Coblenz.

The Middle Moselle section is the most important from the standpoint of the number of famous vineyards; the Saar has a few excellent wines; while the Lower Moselle produces none of importance.

Although the wines produced along the Main, between Homburg and Schweinfurt, are bottled in the standard *bocksbeutel* and sold as Steinwein, true Steinwein comes only from the Steinmantel which forms the south and southwest slopes of the hills around Würzburg (of Würzburger beer fame) in Unterfranken (Lower Franconia).

Up to the turn of the century the regions of Baden Bodensee, Württemberg, with some 100,000 acres of vines made Bavaria the largest wine-producing area of Germany. The destructions of pests, disease, and wars reduced the vineyards by over 60 per cent. It is only since World War II that serious efforts have been made to reestablish production of better quality wines.

soil   As in other fine wine regions, the soil is most forbidding, being suited to no other crop. It is extremely rocky. The vineyards are planted along the steep, terraced slopes of the hills. The terraces are very narrow and must be constantly maintained, a task which must be carried on by hand. The slopes

WINE REGIONS OF GERMANY

Lilli Mautner

are so steep that carts cannot be used. In the Moselle valley there is a predominance of slate to which is attributed the "slatey" dryness of the wines.

grape varieties

The informing grape, the plant noble of the Rhine and Moselle vineyards, is the Riesling. It is a small grape which does not produce abundantly and ripens very late but one which, when nature smiles, gives a glorious wine, full of character, perfume, and body.

The Ostreicher or Sylvaner is grown in the Rheinhesse, the Rheinpfalz, and lower Franconia.

The Traminer is mainly grown in Baden and the Palatinate and in recent years has been planted to some extent in both Rheinhessen and the Rheingau. In these latter regions it is used for blending with Riesling. The Traminer grape is soft and spicy, with low acidity, and the Riesling grape gives it balance and longer life.

The Burgunder is the Pinot Noir of Burgundy and Champagne fame, which is used to produce the few red Hocks of the Rheingau, Ahr valley, and Rheinhesse. It is not her red wines, however, which on the whole are rather thin and commonplace, on which Germany's vinicultural fame rests, but the magnificence of her white wines.

The Müller-Thurgau is another grape variety to gain favor. It is the result of crossing the Riesling with the Sylvaner. Today some 17 per cent of all German vineyards contain Müller-Thurgau grapes. It is found in nearly all districts, although the top Rheingau and Moselle vineyards are still planted 111 entirely to Riesling. The main attraction of the Muller-Thurgau is that it bears a generous crop and ripens earlier than the other varieties. This variety produces very pleasant, mostly light-bodied wines.

The Ruländer or Pinot Gris of Burgundy, is one of the most widely grown varieties in the Baden-Württemberg wine districts of southwestern Germany. It can and does produce some charming wines of discreet aroma and flavor.

vintage

For the most part the vintage is similar to that of the other white wine regions. When the summer has been sunny and the rain has been considerate enough to fall at the right time, and there is a late fall, the grapes are allowed to remain on the vine until *pourriture noble*, here called *edelfaule*, accomplishes its work.

The date on which the harvest starts is set by each communal council. No one is permitted to start harvesting before that date. After the general harvest, the *Spätlese* (Spät—late; lese—picking) starts. The grower must register with the communal council his intention to make a Spätlese, designating the vineyard. For this he must gather only fully ripened bunches of grapes. Any which have been sorted to eliminate sick and unripe grapes have the right to be called *Auslese* wines (Aus—selected; lese—picking).

If the grapes are over-ripe or are covered by a mold of edelfaule and individually selected, they are called *Beerenauslese* (selected berry picking).

Typical German aging cellar, hewn from the solid chalk sub-soil. (Courtesy German-American Trade Promotion Office, New York)

If the individual grapes are dried out, shrunken to raisin-like consistency, and attacked by the edelfaule mold, they are called *Trockenbeerenauslese* (dry berries, selective picking). Each berry is individually selected, either by being placed in a small basket which the pickers carry, or by selection at the press house. Such a wine will be very rich.

All wines claiming the right to Spätlese or better, have to pass an official tasting panel under Government Control as of July 19, 1971. An inspection number is assigned to the cask, which must be carried on the label of every bottle sold.

The principal difference in the vintage process occurs at bottling time. In the first place, the wines are bottled very young—from six to eighteen months. (Even the great wines are now bottled young; they live longer in bottle that way.) Secondly, unlike the French wine regions where the product of a famous vineyard is equalized by blending the wine of many casks before bottling, the wine from each cask is bottled separately and the price is determined by the quality of each cask.

GERMAN WINE LAW

THE German Government published a new Wine Law on July 19, 1969 which became effective as of July 19, 1971. It aligned the old German Law to the laws prevailing or being promulgated in other wine-producing countries of the European Economic Community. It also defines and controls more specifically the different types of wine being made in Germany through the selective picking method. All German wines being sold as of 1971 and later vintages are subject to this law.

Under this new wine law three broad categories of German wines: *Deutscher Tafelwein, Qualitätswein,* and *Qualitätswein mit Prädikat.* Tafelwein is an ordinary wine, which need not attain any particular strength, or come from any particular grape or place. However, it must be produced from approved grape varieties grown in Germany in one of the five major table wine regions, which are: Mosel, Rhein, Main, Neckar, and Oberrhein. The label may carry the name of the region or even a smaller community within the region but it cannot specify the name of a vineyard. The name of the bottler (abfuller) must appear on the label and brand names may appear for further identification. However, since most of the German wines which will reach our shores will be Qualitätswein or Qualitätswein mit Prädikat, let us see how these two categories are defined by Law.

Qualitätswein and Qualitätswein mit Prädikat are wines which are made from permitted grape varieties and fermented in their area of production. They have to contain a minimum must weight and be passed by a tasting panel which will assign a control number, printed on their label. They are

The inspection control number as it appears on the label of a bottle of German wine. (Courtesy German Wine Information Bureau, New York)

to come from one region and their taste has to be according to that region. If they specify a grape variety, that grape variety has to be predominate by 75 per cent and also by taste. They are required to come from one *lage* (vineyard property) or one *bereich* (area of several vineyard properties in which the grapes are similar in taste). If they carry a vintage year, the vintage year specified on the label must constitute 75 per cent of the wines in the blend and be recognized by taste as coming from that vintage year.

If Qualitätswein, the wines under this category can be sugared prior to fermentation to bring up the alcoholic content of the wine (as is customary in Burgundy and Bordeaux), but Qualitätswein mit Prädikat has to be *without* the addition of sugar in the must. The must weight of these wines has to be 75 (the equivalent of 10 per cent alcohol). Qualitätswein mit Prädikat include Kabinett, Spätlese, Auslese, Beerenauslese, Trockenbeerenauslese, and Eiswein wines.

Kabinett wines must be made from fully ripe grapes which can be fermented without the aid of additional sugar; the minimum *must weight* of 75 (or 72 in certain cold areas like the Mosel).

Spätlese wines must be made from fully ripe grapes gathered after the general harvest; the minimum *must weight* 80.

Auslese wines must be made from grapes gathered after the general harvest from over-ripe grapes without any sick or unripe grapes; minimum *must weight* about 90.

Beerenauslese wines must be made from single-selected, over-ripe grapes; minimum *must weight* about 120.

Trockenbeerenauslese wines must be made from over-ripe, shrunken grapes which are attacked by the mold of edelfaule; minimum *must weight* about 150 (weight may vary slightly by area).

114

Eiswein wines must be wines which qualify at least as Spätlese wines but are made from grapes which were frozen during the harvest and pressing.

All these wines, Qualitätswein and Qualitätswein mit Prädikat must be made solely from permitted grape varieties. When sold, they must specify if they are Qualitätswein or Qualitätswein mit Prädikat and carry the control number. As a still further guarantee of quality, the German wine law has special provisions for listing the name of the producer . . . the person responsible for the wine. Every quality wine has to list the bottler (the abfuller) on the label. The producer's name can also be listed. If the wine is bottled by the actual producer, who himself owns the vineyard, then the new label will state "Erzeugerabfullung" (bottled by the producer) and "aus eigenem Lesegut" (from his own grapes)—which is similar to estate bottling in France. Furthermore, it is permissible that a shipper bottle wines under this designation, specifying the property from which the grapes came and the wine was made.

Germany's wine quality control occurs in three stages:

1. During the grape harvest, a wine grower must officially register the quality wines he intends to produce. He does this with the mayor of his town. Thus, the government controls not only the grapes in the vineyard, but the must in the cellar.

2. When bottling begins, the wine has to be analyzed by government officials. Only officially designated wine laboratories can make the chemical analysis.

3. Finally, the wine is tasted by a panel of experts. Clarity, bouquet, color, and flavor are checked along lines of a standard point system. Official certification number is awarded only when the necessary points are recorded. Sealed samples of the wine are retained by the tasting commission, in case of consumer complaints.

All other wines made in Germany which do not come up to the quality of Qualitätswein or Qualitätswein mit Prädikat may only be sold henceforth as Tafelwein through it also might well bear the regional (gebiet) designation. Therefore, there will no longer be German wines that will be labeled Naturrein or Naturwein.

The following designations are to be found on German wine labels: *labeling*

Qualitalswein bestimmter Anbaugebiete—(quality wine of designated regions). A quality wine bears the control number of the tasting panel. It can be labeled by region (bestimmtes Anbaugebiet), sub-region (Bereich), or vineyard (Lage) in connection with the name of village.

Qualitätswein mit Prädikat—(quality wine with distinction)—which is divided into: Kabinett, Spätlese, Auslese, Beerenauslese, Trockenbeerenauslese, and Eiswein, as described previously.

Corks—It is also customary for each fine wine to bear the branded cork of its producer, but not of the vineyard.

The new German Wine Law has decreed an elimination of vineyard names. Germany has had 50,000 individual vineyards in the past, which the government consolidated in the two years before the law went into effect. Today no vineyard has survived that has less than 12½ acres. As in Burgundy, these vineyards have many owners, each tending his own row of vines and making his own wine. The wine-growing regions (now called gebiets) of Germany that produce the finest wines will still be known by their wines.

WINES OF THE RHEINGAU

ON the right bank of the Rhine, from Asmannshausen to Hochheim, is the celebrated Rheingau, one of the most famous viticultural districts in the world. Compared with other wine-growing districts of Germany, this is one of the smallest . . . but its wines are famous—many of them unsurpassed—anywhere. Among the better-known villages in the Rheingau which have become famous over the years on wine labels are:

Eltville	Johannisberg
Erbach	Kiedrich
Geisenheim	Oestrich-Winkel
Hallgarten	Rauenthal
Hattenheim	Rudesheim
Hochheim	

The German Wine tasting panel at "work." (Courtesy German Wine Information Bureau, New York)

Harvesting grapes near the ruins of Castle Ehrenfels at Rudesheim on the Rhine. (Courtesy German Wine Information Bureau, New York)

In this area are the well-known estates of Schloss Johannisberg, Schloss Vollrads, Schloss Eltz, Schloss Schönborn, and Schloss Reinhartshausen of the Prinz zu Preusen. The most famous vineyard properties of this area are likely to survive any new classification. They are: Marcobrunn (Spring of St. Marcus), Steinberger—the largest single vineyard under one ownership in this region, belonging to the Federal Government and bearing a German eagle on its label—and Schloss Johannisberg.

Charlemagne is supposed to have selected the site for Schloss Johannisberg though it is more than likely that wines from the Johannisberg hill vineyards already existed in his time. During the French Revolution the vineyard and castle on the crest of the hill came into possession of William, Prince of Orange, who lost it to Napoleon by the simple process of confiscation after the battle of Jena. The prize was presented by Napoleon to Marshall Kellermann, Duke of Valmy, whose name, appropriately enough, means cellarman.

After the battle of Waterloo the vineyard again changed hands, passing to the Austrian Emperor Francis who, in gratitude for "services rendered," presented the castle and vineyards in perpetuity to his great Chancellor, Prince von Metternich-Winneburg, whose descendants still own it.

The wines of all these vineyards combine every attribute of greatness in a good year. They have bouquet, body, flavor, character, and breed. Generally speaking, the Rheingau wines have an austere fruitiness and a certain hardness, in which lies their character. They are the longest-lived of all German wines.

RHEINHESSE WINES

THE Rheinhessen is Germany's second largest producing district. Wines from here are softer and fuller than those of the Rheingau. The main villages producing fine wines are:

Bingen	Nackenheim
Bodenheim	Nierstein
Deinheim	Oppenheim
Laubenheim	Worms
Mettenheim	

One of the greatest discoveries in German wine, for the majority who have considered this a simple synonym for Rhine and Moselle, is the delicate wines grown along the river Nahe. Just as the stream lies between the Moselle and the Rhine, into which it flows at historic Bingen, so the wines harmoniously blend the hearty masculine quality of good Rhines with the light tingle of Moselles. They are not so sweet and heavy as the one, not so tart as the other. Growing and shipping both center in Bad Kreuznach, where the wizard Professor Dr. Faustus once taught. Even in Germany you find Nahe vintages on the wine list only in establishments that could count connoisseurs among their steady patrons; these restaurateurs know that people who really want Nahes regard anything else as second best.

At the southern border of the Rheinhesse is the rather dull, smoky gray town of Worms. Not dull or gray are the legends about Worms for it is the locale of the ancient Nibelung story of Siegfried's marriage to Brunhilde and his death by treachery.

Within the city limits of Worms stands the *Liebfrauenkirche* (Church of Our Beloved Lady). Immediately behind it and around it lie three vineyards that have produced wines of some renown for many centuries—first under monastic or ecclesiastic control, but since secularization at the beginning of the nineteenth century they have been the property of a number of private people. The vineyards are: Liebfrauenstift, Liebfrauenstift Kirchenstuck, and Liebfrauenstift Klostergarten, owned principally by Langenbach and Valckenberg. (They are the only two who remain as owners.)

The wines from these sites (lage) or vineyards will nearly always be estate bottled and the labels will normally read: *Wormser Liebfrauenstift, Wormser Liebrauenstift Kirchenstuck*, etc. The word or name Liebfraumilch will not appear on the label. They are pleasant, good wines but somewhat lighter in body and character than those from the better Hessian vineyards of Nierstein and Oppenheim.

LIEBFRAUMILCH

LIEBFRAUMILCH is without question the best-known German wine name.

Before describing what it is, perhaps it is better to explain what it is not. Liebfraumilch is not a vineyard nor a district. It is a collective name for Rhine wine just as Moselbluemchen is for Moselle wine.

Tradition has it that the name derives from the Liebfrauenkirche of Worms.

Who invented and first used the name is not clear but it has been in use for over 200 years, or at least since 1744. Originally Liebfraumilch was only Rheinhesse wines, but today, and since a court decision of 1910, "the name of Liebfraumilch applies exclusively to Rhine wines of good quality and delightful character." This is recognized by present-day German wine labeling regulations. It also permits some latitude in determining what is "good quality and delightful character" and results in the labeling of all sorts of wines with the name Liebfraumilch, wines that will be offered to the public at prices that range from a dollar to over $5.00.

In all cases, Liebfraumilch will be a blended wine. The better, more responsible shippers will only employ the finer Hessian wines for their Liebfraumilch blends. To protect themselves against the competition of those who are less concerned with quality, they have identified their Liebfraumilch with an added registered trade-mark name as well, for example: Blue Nun Liebfraumilch, Liebfraumilch "Hanns Christof Wein," Liebfraumilch "Crown of Crowns," Liebfraumilch "Madonna," Liebfraumilch "Sonne des Rheins," etc.

Workers in the vineyards of the Rheinhessen district. (Courtesy German Wine Information Bureau, New York.)

Simply bear in mind that you will get what you pay for, and there are no bargains in fine wines. The better quality Liebfraumilch blends are generally rather soft and full bodied. They are enjoyable with practically all foods.

RHEINPFALZ WINES

THE Palatinate (Rheinpfalz district) is the largest wine-growing area in Germany. The Upper Palatinate (Oberhaardt) produces the largest amount of table wine in Germany, the wine which is the daily diet in the German *weinstube*. In addition to several good white wines, this area produces a good half of all German red wines, most of which are drunk locally and seldom exported. Palatinate wines are known for their attractive balance.

The area best known for wines of great quality is the Mittelhaardt in the Palatinate. Unlike other German wines, those produced here are heavy, earthy, and long-lived. The finest communities producing wine in the Rheinpfalz district are:

Bad Durkheim	Koningbach
Deidesheim	Mussbach
Edenkoben	Neustadt
Forst	Ruppertsberg
Hambach	Wachenheim
Kallstadt	

MOSELLE WINES

MOSELLE wines have a charming lightness, delicacy, fruity bouquet, elegance, and dryness that is most pleasing. But their most appealing quality is their *spritz* or tingling sharpness, as though they were trying to be sparkling wines, and almost succeeding. The quality disappears after a few years as the buoyancy of youth does from man, and for this reason Moselles are best when young because they are livelier and racier.

The soil of the Moselle Valley is, if possible, more forbidding than in any other region, and vintaging is proportionately more difficult. The vineyard owners carry up the steep slopes pieces of slate which have been washed down the hillsides by the spring freshets, and as they go through the vineyards, they laboriously arrange and rearrange the bits of slate so that they will preserve the warmth of the sun during the cool nights in the earth, and help the development of the roots. It is to this backbreaking toil and infinite patience that we owe an exquisite glass of wine!

These are the lightest fine wines made, for only in rare years does the natural wine exceed 10 per cent of alcohol, as a rule having between 8 and 9 per cent.

There are two ways of recognizing the difference between Rhine and

Moselle wines, without opening the tall flute-shaped bottle or tasting the wine. One is the color of the bottle, for Rhine wines always come in brown-colored bottles, and the Moselle bottles are always dark green. The other is by the township names. The towns along the Rhine as a rule end in "heim," while those of the Moselle do not. There are, however, exceptions to this rule.

It is simple to detect the marked differences in character between the wines of the Rheingau, Rheinhesse, and Pfalz, but we have never found anyone who can make a similar claim about the wines of the Moselle, Saar, and Ruwer. They are all equally pleasant and intriguing, so it isn't a matter of great importance.

The most famous vineyard of the Moselle is the Doktor at Bernkastel. In the year 1360, according to the legend, Boemund II, Archbishop of Trier, fell ill with a fever while on a visit to Bernkastel. The doctors of the region were baffled, muttered in their beards, and just did not know what to do for him. But Ritter von Hunolstein, an old veteran of the wars, whom the good Bishop had helped, hearing of his friend's plight, recalled that he had cured himself of a similar ailment. He filled a bottle with his finest Bernkastel wine, went to the house where the Bishop was staying, and ignoring all protests slipped into the sickroom.

"Drink this," he told the Bishop, "and it will cure you."

Boemund regarded the wine dubiously, but in his condition he had nothing to lose, and it was as pleasant a way to die as any. So he obeyed. The old soldier poured him a brimming beaker, and a second, and the Bishop fell into a sound sleep. The next day he awoke to find the fever had gone. "This wine," he cried. "this spendid doctor cured me!"

Since that day, six hundred odd years ago, the vineyard which produced the healing wine has been known as the Doktor vineyard, and not as some mistakenly believe because a part of the vineyard is today the property of the Estate of Dr. H. Thanisch. According to the records the Bernkasteler Doktor *lage* was the property of the Grafs von Hunolstein until the middle of the seventeenth century when it passed to the Grafs von der Leyen who held possession until 1804 when it was acquired by Anton Cetto, Mayor of Bernkastel, from whom it was eventually inherited by his nephew Nikolaus Lauerburg. In 1882 the Lauerbergs sold a part of the vineyard to the Thanisch family and in 1900 they sold another portion to the Deinhards of Coblenz. The portion of the vineyard which Karl and Walter Lauerburg own today is planted with the original ungrafted Riesling vines.

The Bernkasteler Doktor wines are generally full bodied and richer than most Moselles. Because of the fame of the vineyard, the demand always exceeds the supply and, like Château Yquem, fetches considerably higher prices than its neighbors. While it is the outstanding wine, it is not twice as fine as its nearest rival, which is often the difference in price, as people have a tendency to buy name rather than quality.

Other well-known villages which produce excellent, even superb wines are:

The sun dial on the Moselle at Zeltingen. (Courtesy German Wine Information Bureau, New York)

Bernkastel	Piesport
Erden	Traben-Trarbach
Graach	Urzig
Klusserath	Wehlen
Krov	Zell
Oberemmel	Zeltingen

A vineyard equally famous to the Bernkasteler Doktor is the Wehlener Sonnenuhr (the sundial of Wehlen), and demands almost as high a price in the market place.

The outstanding villages on the Saar are Ayl, Ockfen, Saarburg, Serrig, and Wiltingen, whereas the ones of the Ruwer are Eitelsbach, Kasel, and Waldrach.

The wines of the Saar and Ruwer in fine years have a delicacy and raciness all their own. Moselbluemchen (little flower of the Moselle), like Liebfraumilch, is not a vineyard but a wine which is blended from different Moselle wines. It is usually a pleasant Moselle wine with no distinct village character.

BADEN-WÜRTTEMBERG WINES

While the states of Baden and Württemberg have been officially merged, their wine districts remain distinctively separate, each with wines of its own special taste. The Black Forest separates most of Baden and Württemberg but in the northern section there is little difference in wines grown along stretches of the Neckar River.

Along the shores of Lake Constance in southern Baen, the so-called "lake-wine" or seewein is the traditionally pink-tinted Weissherbst, a white wine pressed from red Spatburgunder grapes. Actually, the better quality red wines of the Baden-Württemberg region are made from the Spatburgunder grape. The Gutedel (the Swiss Chasselas) and Rulander (the French Pinot Gris) produce the popular white wines, which are both very rich and fruity, and in the big years quite full bodied.

Württemberg produces more red wine than white, but the latter are better known. The best white wines are Riesling, followed by Sylvaner, and to a lesser extent Rulander and Traminer. The important red-wine grape variety in Württemberg from the view point of quality is the Trollinger, which produces a rather harsh wine. Better red wines are obtained from the Spatburgunder vine, originally the Pinot Noir of Burgundy.

STEINWEIN IN BOCKSBEUTEL

FINALLY we come to Würzburg and its squat flasklike *bocksbeutel*. These robust wines made largely from Sylvaner possess more body, hardness, and keeping qualities than the Rhine and Moselle wines. They also take longer to develop. The outstanding communities are Würzburg, Escherndorf, Iphofen, Randersacker, and Veitshocheim. The outstanding vineyards are the Würzburger Stein and Würzburger Leiste, which are parceled out among a number of proprietors, including two public institutions—the Juliusspital and Burgerspital, and also the Bavarian Staatliche Kellerei (the organization controlling the Bavarian state-owned vineyards).

All Franconian wines are sold in the traditional flat, squat bocksbeutel (see page 8).

notes on German vintages

The wide variation in vintage conditions cause considerable difference in delicate wines, but the practice of bottling the wine from each cask separately sometimes makes the estimates of a given vintage unreliable. Evaluation of recent German vintages is given on page 471.

to sum up

It is not true that a wine must bear a famous name to be good. Much excellent, clean, pleasant wine comes to us simply labeled with the township name, such as Bernkasteler, Piesporter, Brauneberger, Rudesheimer, Hochheimer, Niersteiner, Moselblumchen, or Liebfraumilch. Inevitably, in describing the wines of a region, one talks more about the great names than about the smaller. But what we have said about the fine wines of a locality applies generally, in a lesser degree, to the other wines of the same place.

Most German wines are at their best when the fresh bloom of youth is on them. This is particularly true of the smaller wines. In fact, we recommend that they be drunk under ten years old, except for the very fine Auslese and Trockenbeerenauslese wines. Since the war there have been a series of good to great vintages. Almost any one of them from 1964 through 1972 will be enjoyable. These are not, however, wines to keep for years. We have had several opportunities to verify this on examining old cellars. Old Champagnes were usually in good condition, while the German wines of the same vintages were undrinkable, having been so maderisé (woody in taste) they reminded us of Vermouth.

THE PLACE OF GERMAN WINES ON THE MENU

WHITE wines, light wines, fresh wines, go well with almost all foods, particularly those which, like Aphrodite, come forth from the sea to grace our table. They are dry and sharp, without being acid, and when they are sweet they are not cloying. A well-chilled bottle of Moselle wine is the summer luncheon or dinner wine par excellence. All German white wines, in fact, are meant to be served chilled.

Another pleasant way to drink Rhine wines is with seltzer, mixing them half and half. This is called a *spritzer*. Having a pleasing, flowery perfume, they lend themselves admirably to *bowles,* cups, and punches.

West Germany is the world's largest producer and consumer of sparkling wine. Something over 100,000,000 bottles are consumed annually in Germany. (Worldwide consumption of Champagne from France averages about 50,000,000 bottles yearly.) Most of this wine is marketed in West Germany under the name of *Sekt* or *Schaumwein* (the use of the word "Champagne" is forbidden in Germany by treaty with France for any but true French Champagne) as Sparkling Hock (Rhine wine only), Sparkling Liebfraumilch or Sparkling Moselle when exported, although the term *Sekt* is being used more and more for the export trade. Its enormous sale in Germany can be attributed directly to the Federal Republic's realistic tax policy. Shortly after the war in the early fifties the tax was reduced from DM3 to DM1, making it possible for the public to buy *Sekt* at four or five marks, or little more than a dollar a bottle. The result has been a consumption of over 100,000,000 bottles as compared with some 15,000,000, before the tax cut.

Sekt is made by all the known sparkling wine production methods. The more reputable houses employ the traditional *méthode champenoise. Sekt* is a pleasantly fruity wine, usually fairly sweet in taste. In addition, Cold Duck, which is a blend of red and white sparkling wines is now being exported in good quantities to the United States. It must be remembered that this popular *Sekt* was first produced in Germany in late 1800s.

8. The Wines of Hungary

WHEN the great lovers of wine gather around in that Valhalla where all good men go who appreciate the finer things, the heated arguments will never be concluded as to which is the greatest natural white wine. There will be backers for Yquem, for Montrachet, for Schloss Johannisberg and for Tokay Aszu, the sweetest of all natural wines. When we think of Hungary and wine, we think first of Tokay.

> *"Happy is the country which grows them*
> *Happy is the queen who sends them*
> *And happier still am I who drink them."*

wrote Pope Benedict XIV to the Empress Maria Theresa in grateful acknowledgment of a gift of Tokay wines.

TOKAY

FOR generations only kings and princes could obtain the all too few bottles of Tokay produced each year, and so it came to be known as a Royal wine. The finest vineyards in the heart of the district belonged to the Royal household, and the Emperor Franz Joseph made the princely gesture of sending Queen Victoria a gift of Tokay every year on her birthday, a dozen bottles for each year of her age. Year by year, as the perennial queen grew older, the present augmented in size, until on her 81st birthday, in 1900, the Emperor sent 972 bottles of the rarest of all wines, Tokay Aszu, which Professor Saintsbury called "No more a wine but a prince of liqueurs."

The virtues of Tokay are many, as may be gathered from the statement of one Robert Druitt, as quoted by P. Morton Shand. Delivering "A Treatise on Intemperance" before the Ladies Sanitary Association, he remarked: "Nor need I mince matters and refrain from saying that when childless families despair, when January is wedded to May, and when old men wish to be young, then Tokay is in request."

125

Tokay wine derives its name from the small village of Tokaj in the Hegyalja country (northeastern Hungary) at the foot of the Carpathian Mountains. The area which can produce Tokay was delimited in 1908 by a very stringent law. A closed district was established which prohibited wine made outside the district from being brought in.

Like a cupped hand, the delimited Tokay district is a small plateau, less than half the size of New York City, around which rise the Carpathians. Though this district is 1,500 feet above sea level, the protecting mountains produce a special condition which makes possible extremes of weather highly beneficial to the growing of the grape. These climatic changes vary from cool dry weather in the spring to very hot summer weather. The rains of early fall give way to a fine, dry "Old Wives Summer" or Indian summer, important for the hanging grapes, as it is during this season that they shrivel and become *trockenbeeren*. The bitterly cold winters are accompanied by howling winds. The soil is rich in iron and has some lime. It is of volcanic origin and the dominant rock of the region is the volcanic *trachyte*.

Tokay is the product of one informing vine, *Io Furmint*. The grapes are quite thick-skinned, but as they ripen the skin becomes thinner and more transparent. The sun penetrates it, evaporating most of the water in the juice, with a consequent concentration of the natural sugar. Sometimes the grapes that ripen earliest are so full of juice that the skin bursts and some of the juice runs out; oddly enough, a new skin forms over the crack and the grapes

WINE REGIONS OF HUNGARY

do not rot, as normally happens. The grapes are allowed to hang on the vine until they are in the state of *pourriture noble*. They are called *trockenbeeren*.

The combination of the Furmint, the soil, climatic conditions, and the special manner in which it is treated are unique to the Hungarian Tokaj-Hegyalja. For this reason, no other wine-producing region has been able to imitate in any degree Tokay, although wines made from so-called Tokay grapes° are produced in other countries. These wines do not resemble in taste or characteristics their famed namesake.

The grapes are gathered in wooden vessels known as *puttonyos*, holding about 25 quarts. The universal measure in the Hegyalja is the *gyöncz* or *gönz* cask, which holds 136 liters (about 35 gallons). It is the number of *puttonyos* of over-ripe Furmint grapes per *gyöncz* cask that determines the quality and richness of the Tokay.

At harvest time, from late October through November, the pickers carry two *puttonyos*, one of regular size, the other smaller. In the latter are placed the *trockenbeeren* grapes which are culled from each bunch picked, and in the larger go the ripe but not shriveled berries.

There are three main types of Tokay—Eszencia, Aszu, and Szamorodni. Others, such as Aztali, Máslás, and Forditás, are made from the marc or lees of Aszu pressings, but they are rarely shipped out of the country.

making the wines

SZAMORODNI. This is made much the same as any other white wine, in the lower sections of the plateau where the grapes do not shrivel and in those years when weather conditions have not been favorable for the *trockenbeeren*. Szamorodni is an excellent dry wine, with a "fresh bread-crust" flavor. It is, however, a fiery, full-blown wine, with an alcoholic strength of some 14 per cent. In years when there are not enough *trockenbeeren* to make a commercial quantity of Aszu, they are pressed with the other grapes and a sweet Szamorodni results, like the dry in character. It does not, of course, begin to approach the richness of the Aszu.

ASZU. When one considers that the average yield of all the vines in the Tokaj-Hegyalja is only some 100,000 hectoliters, or about 2,650,000 gallons, of which Aszu wine represents less than one per cent, it is apparent that this wine is extremely rare. Little wonder it is spoken of as a Royal or Princely wine.

In making Aszu or Ausbruch (very rich Tokay) the *trockenbeeren* are first kneaded into a pulp in a trough. Then the proper proportion of must, expressed from ordinarily ripened grapes, is poured over it and stirred up at intervals. It is left to stand from twelve to forty-eight hours, depending on climatic conditions. When fermentation begins, the whole mixture is placed in canvas

° Tokay grapes are not the produce of *Io Furmint* but are really eating grapes said to have originated in Algeria.

Typical Hungarian vintage scene. Gathering grapes to produce the red Egri Bikaver at Eger, Hungary.

bags and thoroughly trodden out, the resulting juice being put into casks. From this point on, the must is handled like any other white wine.

It is the number of *puttonyos* of over-ripe Furmint that determines the quality of the wine. A label reading "1 puttony" contains about 10 per cent; "3 puttonyos" about 30 per cent; and "5 puttonyos" about 50 per cent *trockenbeeren*, the richest and finest quality. Aszu wines are not made every year. They can be made only in years when the vintage is moderately successful.

P. Morton Shand says: "Druitt considered that Tokay has a flavor of green tea, but an amalgam of the scents of meadow-sweet, acacia-blossom, and the lime-tree in flower, rendered perceptible to the palate . . . is possibly somewhere nearer the mark. No wine possesses such a tremendous force and volume of flavor."

It is the natural sweetness and natural alcoholic richness (it is never fortified) that raises Aszu Tokay wine so high in the estimation of wine lovers.

ESSENZ—ESZENCIA—ESSENCE. In exceptionally successful and plentiful years, the *trockenbeeren*, before they are kneaded, are put in a cask which has a bung with a goose-quill in the bottom. The juice which drips out through the quill, without any pressure other than the weight of the *trockenbeeren* is allowed to ferment apart and is called Essence. This is a fabulous wine that takes years to develop and will live for centuries. There were Eszencias, notably in Poland, over 200 years old. A newspaper account of the marriage of the president of Poland in 1933 reported that toasts were made with 250-year old wine: "The wine, if good, could only have been Essence of Tokay, and the centuries old traditional friendship between Poland and Hungary would seem to support his conclusion."

Eszencias are kept in open bottles and never have more than 7 or 8 per cent of alcohol. Very little is ever made. It is rare and almost unprocurable, as what little is produced is used mostly for improving the Aszus of poorer years.

HOW AND WHEN TO SERVE TOKAY

Dry Szamorodni should be served well chilled. With its full-bodied dryness, it makes an excellent apéritif or all-around table wine.

Sweet Szamorodni may be served at room temperature or cooled. It can be used as any sweet white wine, but is more properly a dessert wine.

Aszus have a ripe, luscious quality and should not be chilled. They are dessert wines of the very first order. A small glass is often one of the most tonic and wholesome restoratives one can take.

Tokay wines, as they come to us, are generally blends of various vintages, but the wines are kept in cask some three or four years before bottling. Tokay wines take a long time to ripen and are rarely shipped much under ten years. There are some vintage wines available. They are not cheap. Their prices range from $4.50 on up for a ½ liter (17 oz.) long-necked bottle, the standard size and shape used for generations.

OTHER HUNGARIAN TABLE WINES

Wine-making is an important part of Hungarian agriculture, as wine is produced in fifty of her sixty-three *Megye* (counties). Most of this wine is drunk locally, but Hungary also produces some very fine red and white table wines, whose quality is known and appreciated wherever Magyars have lived. The wine-producing regions are scattered. Aside from the Tokaj-Hegyalja, in the northeastern corner, of which we have already spoken, there is Eger nearby, whence comes the famous Egri Bikaver; in the central western part of the country is Somlyó; below that, on the northern shores of Lake Balaton (the Plattensee), is Badacsony, center of the vineland producing the best quality of white table wines; and finally, on the southwestern border, is Villány-Pécs, where both white and red table wines are produced.

Hungary contains rough hilly and mountainous country as well as plains. The quality wines are not produced in the plains, but in the hilly country where the top soil appears to be, in many cases, of volcanic origin. Perhaps this explains the fiery character most of the white wines display.

grape varieties The Rizling (Riesling) is generally found in the fine vineyards, as well as the Furmint. For white wines, the Szilvany (Sylvaner), Keknyelu, Leanyka, Harslevelu (which means "like the leaves of the ash"), and Muskotaly (Muscatel) are used; while the principal variety employed for red wines is the Kadarka.

labeling The nomenclature employed is generic, both grape and place-names being used separately and in combination. In one particular instance, a fine, medium sweet wine is made, around Badacsony, which is called Szurke-Barat or Auvergnac Gris (the French translation means "Wine of the Gray Friar").

The descriptive terms used on Hungarian labels mean the following:

Edes	(A'-desh)	Sweet
Szaraz	(Shah'-rahsh)	Dry
Zöld	(Zuld)	Green
Szemelt	(Sem'-melt)	Selected like *Auslese*
Bor	(Bore)	Wine (plural—Borok)
Pecsenyebor	(Pake'-shenny-bore)	Dessert wine
Féherbor	(Fay'-ehr-bore)	White wine
Vörösbor	(Vo'-rosh-bore)	Red wine

While the table wines are made in the same manner as in the wine regions of France and Germany, a wide variety is obtained by the use of different grape species and because of the different soil conditions in the several districts. Only one characteristic is common to all Hungarian table wines, and that is a certain heady, fiery quality.

Typical Hungarian wine names, and descriptions of their taste, follow:

RIZLING-SZEMELT (Riesling Sem'-melt). A light dry wine with Riesling character.

CSOPAKI FURMINT (Cho'-pa-key Foor'-mint). A full-bodied dry wine resembling Tokay, as it is produced from the Furmint grape. In Hungarian, the letter "i" affixed to a name denotes "from." In this case it means Furmint wine from the town of Csopak, which is on Lake Balaton.

SOMLOI FURMINT (Shom'-loy-ee Foor'-mint). A fragrant dry wine, resembling the Csopaki Furmint. Somlyó is also on Lake Balaton.

BADACSONYI RIZLING (Bahd'-ah-chony Riesling). Usually a pale dry full-bodied wine.

BADACSONYI SZURKE-BARAT (Bahd'-ah-chony Soor'-key Bah'-raht). From the Badacsony district comes this lovely, medium sweet wine, whose delicate bouquet reminds one of new-mown hay.

BADACSONYI AUVERGNAC GRIS (Bahd'-ah-chony Oh'-ver-niak Gree). This is the French spelling for Szurke-Barat.

DEBROI HARSLEVELU (Deh'-broy Harsh'-level-you). A medium-sweet wine with a pleasing perfume, produced in the Eger district from the Harslevelu grape.

LEANYKA SZARAZ and LEANYKA EDES (Lay'-on-kah Shah'-rahsh and A'-desh). Dry and sweet Leanyka. These are light table wines with a delicate flavor. The dry is quite dry, but the sweet is only moderately sweet. A great deal of Leanyka comes from Eger.

MUSKOTALY (Moosh'-ko-tah-lee). One of the lightest and most highly perfumed wines of Hungary. It has a pronounced Muscat flavor. Made in various districts, it is always a pleasant wine, though not one of the finest.

SZILVANYI ZOLD (Sil'-vahn-ee Zuld). Literally this means "Green Sylvaner" which it derives from the hint of green in its pale color. It is on the sweeter side of dryness, with a delicate bouquet and flavor.

EGRI BIKAVER (Egg'-ree Bee'-kah-verr). Because of its deep, very dark red color, it is called Bikaver (Bull's Blood). It has a splendid bouquet and is a big, full-bodied dry wine with a character all its own.

From Villány-Pécs (Vill'-ah-nyee Peh'-ch) in the Komitat or County of Pécs come some good red and white wines. The white wines are generally shipped in long fluted Rhine wine bottles, while the red travel in the standard Claret bottles of Bordeaux.

The white wines are served like Alsatian or German wines. In fact, many people who find German wines expensive or hard to get have taken up these wines enthusiastically, pleasantly surprised by their fine quality. The red wines, served at room temperature, can be used, like any other red wine, with almost all foods.

SPARKLING WINE

HUNGARY, like all wine-producing countries, has her sparkling wine. Some of it is sold in America and can be found primarily in restaurants or stores catering to a Magyar clientele. It is one of the better sparkling wines, having a pleasant bouquet and a lot of body. Both the very dry and medium dry are shipped. The very dry seems to be the better quality for our taste.

9. *Sherry and the Wines of Spain*

CULTURE and civilization, like the sun, rise in the East. The first records of Iberia tell of intrepid Phoenician sailors and merchants establishing trading posts. Before long the vine was planted, for nothing else would grow on the hard, sandy, clay soil.

During the period of Rome's greatness, the peninsula did a thriving business with the Romans, as is indicated by the wine jars of Spanish make found among the ruins of Pompeii.

Even during the suzerainty of the Moors, the vine flourished and prospered under the patronage of the Alhambra Caliphs.

It is Jerez de la Frontera and its renowned Sherry wine that concerns us most when we think, of Spanish viniculture. Jerez has been a formally constituted trading post, town, and city for at least 3,000 years. First it was a Phoenician outpost and town called Xera. During the Roman era it was called Seritium, while later the Moorish kings and caliphs spelled it Scherris. The addition of de la Frontera to the actual name of Jerez was granted officially by King Juan I, in his royal decree of April 21, 1380.

The first impression one has of Jerez is that of a clean, peaceful city with the endless, high, windowless, white-washed walls of the bodegas, where Sherry is stored and aged. Charming balconied houses, small parks, and even the blocks of houses recently built give the city the feeling of old-world permanence.

history   Throughout the centuries the region has produced wines that have always won high praise. Those who have written praise include, for instance, Chaucer, Shakespeare, and Samuel Pepys. But the history of Sherry wine, as we know it today, began at least four centuries ago, when an enterprising wine merchant decided to take some wine to England.

Arriving on the Thames, he discovered that the English not only could neither read nor speak Spanish but that they refused to try. If they had to

use foreign words, and they did not take kindly to the idea, at least they would see that the words sounded as English as possible. The word Jerez (Heh-rehz) they promptly Anglicized to Sherries, and finally to its present form, Sherry.°
Wine for export had been designated *saca* by the Spanish and this gave rise to another English word—"Sack†." In Elizabethan times it was common to call Sherry wine "Sack."

Jerez de la Frontera is the city around which the Sherry vineyards lie and the Sherry trade revolves. The principal shippers have their *bodegas* (warehouses) there, and the vast reserves of wine which make possible Sherry as we know it, are kept in Jerez, Puerto de Santa Maria, and Sanlucar de Barrameda.

Jerez de la Frontera is in the district of Andalucia, the southernmost part of Spain, and to understand the wine of the region, one must know something about the Spaniard, particularly the Andaluz.

Spain is a confederation of the thirteen ancient petty kingdoms and peoples who have always inhabited the Iberian Peninsula. It has never been and perhaps will never be one people. Even today, the Catalan from Barcelona speaks a different language from the Castilian of Madrid; he has different customs and, though he carries a Spanish passport, he will always, and with pride, call himself a Catalan—not a Spaniard. Most Spaniards, then, are regionally rather than nationally minded.

In Andalucia there is brilliant sunshine and the people are gay; they dress in flaming colors and worship objects of beauty, whether they be women, gardens, Arabian stallions, or the magnificent Sherry wine. The Andaluz is the Spaniard of romantic song and story.

"Para los gustos, Dios hizo los colores (To please our tastes, God created colors),"* say the Andalucians, a proverb which applies most aptly to the wines of Jerez. For in Sherry, as in a rainbow, almost any shade of color and taste may be found.

Pasquil's *Palinodia* (1619) contains one of the countless encomiums to Sherry:

> "Give me Sacke, old Sacke, Boys!
>   To make the muses merry
> The life of mirth and the joy of the earth
>   Is a cup of good old Sherry."

° Manuel Ma. González Gordon in his definitive "Jerez-Xerez-Scherris" attributes the present-day English spelling of *Sherry* as "obviously a corruption of *Scherrisch*, the old Moorish name of the town."

† The word "Sack" as a term meaning Sherry is archaic. Its rightful use today is limited to the registered trade-mark "Dry Sack," property of the Sherry shippers Williams & Humbert.

The greatest and best salesman Sherry ever had was not, strictly speaking, in the "trade," but he liked Sherry so much that he was always writing about it. His name was William Shakespeare.

Sherry and Sack crop up often in his plays, but most of all in *Henry IV*, in the words of Falstaff. "A good Sherris-sack," said the immortal rogue, "hath a two-fold operation in it. It ascends me into the brain; dries me there all the foolish and dull and crudy vapours which environ it; makes it apprehensive, quick, forgetive, full of nimble, fiery, and delectable shapes; which delivered o'er to the voice—the tongue—which is the birth, becomes excellent wit."

And Samuel Pepys, most famous of all diarists, refers often to "Sack," indicating that he must have been very partial to it.

geography   Andalucia, the most southern region of Spain, extends from the Portuguese frontier on the west to the Mediterranean on the east.

The Sherry district lies roughly between the Guadalquivir and the Guadalete Rivers, with the Atlantic seaboard on the west, and a line paralleling the coast a few miles north of Jerez. Nature has endowed this little piece of land with qualities which are unique. The Sherry produced from it cannot be duplicated

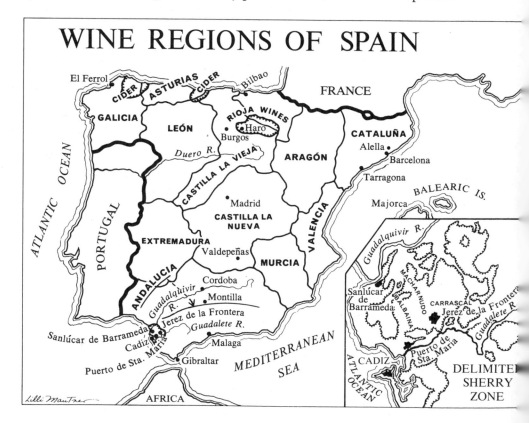

in any part of the world, although Sherry-type wines are made in most wine producing countries of the world.

soil

Three predominating types of soil divide the region into three sections. Around and a little to the north of Jerez itself is found the *albariza*—a soil composed primarily of chalk, magnesium, clay, and lime—where the finest Sherries are produced. South of Jerez is the *barros* (clay). This clay produces Sherry of lesser quality.

The *arenas* (sandy) soil is found toward the seashore and near the river. The arenas nowadays have very little vineyard lands, but nearby all Sherry is produced—at a rate of up to 9 butts° an acre—from albariza soil.

grape varieties

The Palomino is the classic and finest grape variety grown for the making of Sherry wine. Ninety per cent of the vines planted in the Jerez region are Palomino. The albariza vineyards are planted almost exclusively with it. The Mantúo Castellano, Mantúo de Pila, and Cañocazo are of secondary importance; and finally, the Pedro Ximénez, which is used for making very sweet wines and for "blending Sherries," which are important to distillers in making their blended whiskies.

All the Jerez vineyards were destroyed by the phylloxera which invaded the region toward the end of the nineteenth century. Since then the traditional varieties have had to be grafted on to American phylloxera-resistant root stocks.

Jerez is the only place where there has been an increase of about 20 per cent in production since the grafting of the old vines upon American roots, after the phylloxera attacked the vines.

vintage

The actual gathering of the grapes begins when they are fully ripened. This will vary from year to year, from the last week of August to the second week of September, depending on the climatic conditions of the preceding summer months. However, the Feast of the Nativity of the Virgin, which falls on September 8, is the usual "official" commencement of the vintages.

Under the auspices of Saint Ginés de la Jara, patron of vintners, the gay, very colorful Fiesta de la Vendimia (Vintage Festival) is celebrated for four days. There is pageantry, fireworks, a horse show, a solemn Te Deum . . . and much happy singing and dancing of flamencos.

Hundreds of homing pigeons, each bearing an original verse in praise of Sherry, are released into the bright, sunlit sky from the steps of the Real é Insigne Iglesia Colegial, to announce to all Spain the glad tidings of the beginning of the new Sherry vintage.

Following the solemn Te Deum within the church a colorful ceremony takes place upon the steps, before the image of San Ginés de la Jara. Baskets of

° 1 butt = 132 United States gallons

Palomino grapes, borne by the vintage queen and her maids of honor, dressed in traditional local costumes, are blessed by the Monsignor and then emptied into a specially erected lagar. Four treaders, who have won the "honor," tread and press out the "first" butt (cask) of the new vintage.

Meantime, in the vineyards the work of the vintage goes on in all its intensity. The heavily laden rows of Palomino vines growing on the grayish-white albariza soil of the top districts of Macharnudo, Balbaina, and Carrascal are invaded by men with sharp knives. They cut the large bunches of grapes, placing them in baskets. Until the early 1960s, these were then carried by cart or in panniers on mule-back to the white-washed pressing house near the center of each vineyard. Here the baskets were emptied on round woven *esparto*-grass mats in the yard. The grapes were allowed to dry in the sun 12 to 14 hours. If they remained overnight they were covered by similar mats to protect them against the dew.

In the cool of early morning, beginning at three o'clock and continuing until noon, the grapes were brought into the pressing hall. This was a long narrow room, lined along one side with a battery of wooden pressing troughs. The trough was called a *lagar*. It was some eleven to twelve feet square, about two feet deep, tilted forward from the wall to permit the juice to run freely through a doorlike opening. The lagar was raised some three feet above the floor. Sixty baskets or 1,500 pounds of golden Palomino grapes were handled in each lagar to fill one butt.

Four men worked each lagar, wearing special treading shoes, with properly spaced hobnails, (see illustration). The mass was then sprinkled with several handfuls of gypsum (calcium sulphate) to assure an increased tartaric acid content in the wine. Then came the actual pressing. From the center of the lagar a screw post rose about seven feet. Using wooden spades the grape mass was piled evenly and wrapped around it and held in place by an 82-foot-long woven-grass ribbon. A wooden block was fitted and above it a screw with two 3-foot handles, which the men grasped and began to turn. The juice gushed forth, filtered through the grass ribbon, out of the lagar and into the waiting butt.

That, at any rate, was the traditional way of producing Sherry. Today, because of increasing labor costs, the growers have been modernizing the process. Nowadays grapes are carried by truck into modern pressing stations, which are fully automated. That is, most of the grapes of Jerez are now pressed by mechanical means.

The butts of freshly expressed must (juice) are trucked at once to the shippers' bodegas in Jerez, Puerto de Santa Maria, or Sanlucar de Barrameda. They are placed in the fermenting warehouse and allowed to go about the business of becoming wine. For the first week or so, the fermentation process is very violent. The must hisses, bubbles, and boils until most of the grape

LEFT. *Palomino grapes arriving at pressing house yard in panniers, and spread upon esparto grass mats to dry in the sun.*

BELOW. *Typical Jerez vineyard pressing house, showing treaders working ten* lagares *(pressing troughs).*

ABOVE. *Grape mass being built up about the central post in the lagar. Note that the mass is held in place by a ribbon of woven esparto grass wrapped around it.*

RIGHT. *Hob-nail Jerez treading shoes.* (Courtesy Julius Wile, New York)

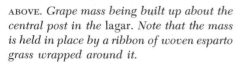

sugar has been converted. Fermentation continues at a quieter, more leisurely pace, through December, when the wine "falls bright." This means that the insolubles have precipitated to form the lees and the wine has clarified itself. It will be racked off into fresh butts which are filled only to seven-eights of their capacity.

In the ordinary sense of wine-making, the grape juice has become wine, however it is still called mosto since it has not yet become sherry. For this to occur, the unique phenomenon of the *flor* (flowering) must take place.

Flowering is peculiar to sherry. We know of no other major wine growing region, except in the Jura Mountains of France, where flowering has occurred naturally.

flowering　Flowering is a term used to describe the yeast film which develops and grows on the surface of the wines, sometimes to a thickness of over a quarter inch. This is a natural yeast associated with that which produced the original fermentation. The flor appears most strongly each spring and autumn. Together with matters of soil and climate, the flor contributes to sherry's distinctive characteristics, especially its delicacy, aroma and nuttiness.

new wines
classified　The new wine is carefully examined and classified. This is important because sherry is ruggedly individualistic. It is the most unpredictable of all wines. When the vintner presses his grapes, he has not the slightest idea of the type of sherry wine which will result. No two butts of must will have fermented into identical wines, even though the must came from grapes of the same vineyard, was pressed at the same time and treated in an identical manner. No man knows what causes this variation. Perhaps some day another Pasteur will come along and give us the answer.

Oloroso group　Some butts will show signs of developing into the pale-colored light, delicate Fino type; others will have a deeper color and fuller body, indicating that they will become the Oloroso type, while other butts will develop coarsely and will be separated for distilling or will become vinegar.

A simple system of chalk marks has been evolved through the centuries to identify these various qualities. The butts of the palest and finest wines will be marked with one stroke ╱ (*raya*) destined for finos, the heavier wines will receive two strokes ╱╱ (*dos rayas*), destined for olorosos, lower quality will be marked with three strokes ╱╱╱ (*tres rayas*), ordinary wines to be used for seasoning and cleaning casks, four strokes ╱╱╱╱ (*cuatro rayas*) or a grid ⧣ (*parilla*) wines to be distilled ⩙ to be hastily removed from the winery and turned into vinegar.

It must be noted that these and the additional marks used in further classification vary somewhat from one sherry shipper to another.

At the time of the first classification, the new wines are lightly fortified with brandy. The rayas will have their alcoholic content raised to 15 or $15\frac{1}{2}$ per cent, and the dos rayas will be fortified more strongly to 17 per cent. Since flor disappears at 16% only the rayas continue to be affected by it during further development.

During the next year or two, the master taster or *capataz* continues the tasting and classification with the eventual purpose of deciding on the final type of wine which will develop and which *solera* it will eventually refresh.

He uses an instrument called the venencia, employed only in Jerez—a tall, narrow, silver cup attached to the end of a long, springy, whalebone handle. It is a tricky gadget, the use of which requires considerable skill. The cup is dipped deep into the butt through the bung, in order to get a sample of clear wine, then it is withdrawn and the wine poured into a glass with one motion. This looks simple until the uninitiated tries it, when he will discover that he is more likely to pour the wine down his sleeve than into the glass.

The original rayas are divided into Palmas, one ⟋ two ⟋⟋ three ⟋⟋⟋ and four ⟋⟋⟋⟋ according to quality and age and these are true finos.

Manzanilla applies to a fino made or matured in Sanlucar de Barrameda, where the sea air imparts an echo of saltiness to the wine.

Amontillado is a raya which has become nuttier, more full-bodied and darker than the finos.

Some original dos rayas are divided into Palo Cortado, one ⟋ two ⟋ three ⟋ and four ⟋ (*cut sticks*) according to quality. These are rather rare, however, and most of the wines will become Olorosos.

An Oloroso in accordance with its name has a characteristic aroma and also possesses more body than the finos. Cream sherry is a full oloroso.

The wines which develop body but not the proper finesse retain the original raya markings and are called either Raya or Raya Oloroso.

The sherries are now ready to enter into the solera system.

The heart of the entire Sherry trade is the *solera* system by which a uniform style, character, and quality will be maintained year in and year out . . . for

the solera system

Deft use of the venencia. *Williams & Humbert's Capataz (bodega master) pouring a sample which he has just drawn from the Dry Sack solera.* (Courtesy Julius Wile, New York)

generations. Every Sherry shipped from the Jerez region has gone through its *solera.*

Solera comes from the word *suelo* (ground) and means the butts nearest the ground. It is created by laying down a number of butts of particularly fine quality of wine of a given style. The next year an equal number of butts of wine of the same style and character are set aside to form a second tier or scale, and the next year another scale is set aside. Depending upon the needs and the desired quality of age, further lots of similar wine will be set aside in succeeding years, which might be described as additional scales to back up the original three.

All the tiers before the first one are called *criaderas* or nursery reserves. The number will vary from one solera to another and one house to another. Each criadera tier is numbered. We have seen soleras which were backed up with six criaderas and others with as many as eight. There is always a year's difference between each criadera number.

It is only when the shipper has established his full line of criadera tiers that he is ready to begin selling wine from the solera. He will then draw wine from the original tier of butts. The wine he withdraws will be replaced from the next youngest criadera tier and so on. When the wine from the youngest criadera is used up, it is replaced with vintage wine of one to two years that has been set aside for the particular solera. Never more than half the wine in the oldest tier is ever withdrawn in one single year. Once a solera is started, it can go on forever. The wine that will be vintaged this year will take from six to eight years or longer to travel through the solera system before it reaches the bottle. In this way, a constant process of blending goes on year after year, and thus a definite standard of quality can be maintained indefinitely.

Consequently, there is no such thing as a Vintage Sherry. *Sherry is always a blended wine.* Occasionally a solera is dated, such as "Solera 1870." This indicates the year when the solera was started, but it does not mean that the wine in the bottle is of the 1870 vintage. When you see a bottle labeled "Vintage of 1900" you are being misled. Vintage Sherry is not sold commercially.

The Sherry shipper, indeed, can supply the finest shades of difference in color and taste by judicious and intelligent blending. Basically, all Sherries are dry. The various degrees of sweetness are the result of the careful use of a special sweetening wine made from raisinized Pedro Ximenez grapes, and the depth of color is obtained by blending in a small amount of color wine (*vino de color*).

Vino de color is made by boiling the must before fermentation begins. The result is a very dark, heavy, syrupy concentration of grape sugar. If, in this process, the must is reduced to one-third of its original content it is called *sancocho;* if down to one-fifth, *arrope.* To this are added some eight or ten parts of regular Sherry wine of the same vintage, and the whole is known as vino de color. The color wines are of great importance to the shipper, who maintains soleras of them, blends them, and ages them for many years. As he uses small amounts in each blend of Sherry, the quality must be on a par with the wine it is to color or sweeten.

The final blending of the wine to be bottled will include the proper proportion of color wine.

It is interesting to note that, due to evaporation, the strength of the wine increases slightly, so that wine which started out with 16 per cent of alcohol, may have 18 per cent or even more after a few years. This varies with the type of wine and with the bodega. Some shippers send their pale dry wines out with an alcoholic content of 17 to 19 per cent, while others fortify all of their wines up to 20½ per cent.

The final step, before bottling or shipping the wine, is to *fine* it, in order

FLOWLINE CHART OF A SOLERA SYSTEM

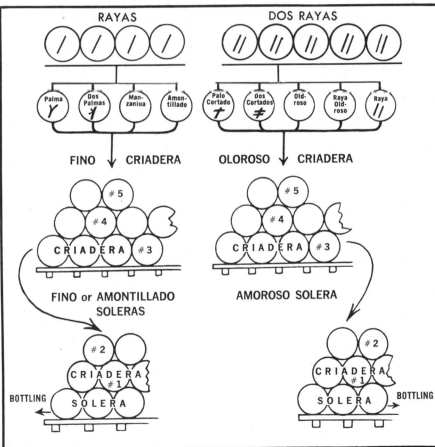

to ensure clarity and brilliance. The best fining material for Sherry is the whites of egg mixed with a small amount of wine.

Spain's best Sherry export customers are England, Holland and other EEC countries as well as the United States. England has always bought most of her Sherry in the cask, while we have bought almost all of our drinking Sherry in bottles. Now, because of the difficulty of shipping, together with higher freight and insurance rates, the practice of bottling in this country has increased greatly. Some importers, indeed, are bottling all their Sherries here.

Bottling a sturdy, fortified wine, such as Sherry, presents few problems, although it is not as simple as merely broaching a butt and running the wine into bottles, Bottling must take place on a bright, clear day, the wines must have rested quietly for at least a month, and occasionally it is necessary to filter them first and then fine them before bottling. Naturally all this requires experience, and when buying an American-bottled Sherry, therefore, our suggestion is that you buy from an importer whom you know to be experienced.

SHERRY TYPES

THE same general types of Sherry are produced by all shippers. Each shipper, however, offers various qualities of each type, and in order to differentiate not only the various qualities but his own brand from that of his competitors, the shipper has developed the custom of giving his solera a trade name.

The Sherry shipper further subdivides the Fino and Oloroso styles as follows:

FINOS

TYPE	DESCRIPTION
Manzanilla	Very dry, very pale, light body
Fino	Very dry, very pale, medium body
Amontillado	Dry, pale to light gold, full body, nutty

OLOROSOS

Oloroso	Usually sweet, deep golden, full body, nutty
Cream	Sweet, deep golden, full body, nutty
Brown	Very sweet, dark brown, full body, nutty

Fino group MANZANILLA. This is a very pale, very dry Fino that has developed in the bodegas located at Sanlucar de Barrameda, where the salt air of the Atlantic ocean has a very definite influence and contributes to the wine's fragrance, lightness, and even slightly bitter tonic undertone. Must from the same vintage and vineyard developed in Jerez will become a Fino, without Manzanilla characteristics. As a matter of fact, if a butt of Manzanilla is moved to Jerez it will lose its Manzanilla character and turn into a typical Jerez Fino.

FINO.   The basic very pale, very dry, elegant wine of Jerez. It is a wine of sturdy body.

AMONTILLADO.   This is deeper-colored Fino, which has developed considerable nuttiness and body. Usually it will be a fairly dry wine. However, some shippers blend their Amontillados less dry.

OLOROSO.   A deeper-golden wine, which can be quite dry, but generally is fairly sweet. It has a full body and is nutty. The term *amoroso* was formerly used for a somewhat sweet and velvety oloroso.

CREAM.   A rich, golden, sweet, soft wine of full body. Cream wines are usually from old, extensive Oloroso and color wine soleras.

BROWN.   This is always a very dark walnut-brown, very sweet wine of full-bodied nuttiness. This type is very popular in England and Scotland, but it has lost much of its appeal in the United States where it has been replaced by the Cream type.

Note: The Sherry styles described are the basic types generally shipped today. Each shipper will vary his final blends according to what he believes will have the widest appeal and will bring in the most money.

Transferring of wines in a solera system. (Courtesy Julius Wile, New York)

PEDRO XIMENEZ

P.X. is made from the Pedro Ximenez grape which, according to legend, was brought to Jerez from Germany by a man named Peter Siemens, whose name was Hispanicized into Pedro Ximenez.

Wine made from this grape is treated differently from regular Sherry. The grapes are lusciously sweet and very low in acid. Before pressing, they are spread on straw mats and left in the sun to dry for ten days to two weeks. After the sunning, the grapes become almost raisin-like. The must that is obtained is not allowed to ferment, because it is so syrupy that fermentation would be slow and arduous. Instead, the must is run into butts containing a small amount of brandy so that all the natural sugar remains in the wine. P.X. wines go through their own soleras.

Obviously, this is an expensive wine to produce. In Spain and in the Latin American countries Pedro Ximenez wine is popular with the ladies, but its main use is to lend richness and softness to the blends of rich Oloroso and brown Sherries. In our own country, this is the blending Sherry used to soften blended whiskies.

SHIPPERS

SHERRY shipping firms do not spring up, like mushrooms, overnight. It takes years to form the soleras and, unless a firm could purchase a complete bodega, as sometimes happens, it would take many years to become established. That is why most of the well-known firms have been in existence for over a hundred years. As a firm does not stay in business for any length of time unless it gives quality and deals fairly with its customers, the people managing these old firms obviously handle fine wines and have solid reputations. In many cases, the directors of these firms are direct descendants of the founders, and well aware of the responsibility with which they are charged in maintaining the reputation of the firm on the same high plane as that of their forebears.

For this reason, and because Sherry is always a blended wine, the shipper's name is of paramount importance in selecting a Sherry. Every bottle bearing his label carries his assurance of honesty, ability, skill, and reputation for shipping wines of consistently high quality.

Every shipper, of course, handles both fine wines and inexpensive wines. Do not compare one shipper's fine wine with another's cheap wine, in trying to establish their merits as shippers.

Each shipper prepares what he thinks is the ideal blend for each quality of wine. You may prefer one and dislike another. This does not mean that the second is a poor wine; it merely means that it does not appeal to your particular taste.

HOW AND WHEN TO SERVE SHERRIES

PALE dry Sherries, such as Manzanilla, Fino, and Amontillado are ideal appetizers. They lose nothing by chilling and we recommend that they be served cold. Serve at any time as an apéritif, before meals, or with hors d'oeuvres or soup.

Although, if you prefer the drier wines, there is no reason why you cannot enjoy equally a Fino, Amontillado, or an Amoroso at any time, afternoon or evening. In fact, Sherry of any type is an ideal wine of hospitality.

The dry and medium Olorosos may be served, like the drier wines, slightly chilled or at room temperature or on the rocks. It is a matter of personal taste preference.

The richer Oloroso or brown wines are too full bodied to be chilled, and should be served at room temperature. They make delightful afternoon drinks to serve at the bridge table or after dinner.

Sherry has many virtues. It can be used in mixed drinks, such as a cooler, cobbler, or flip, and it is indispensable in the kitchen where dishes of character are prepared. Increasingly in the United States, medium Sherry is enjoyed straight from the bottle, and served on the rocks.

Because Sherry is fortified and has a higher percentage of alcohol than table wines, it is a wine whose flavor is in no way impaired by smoking. It is sturdy, does not suffer from travel and therefore is an ideal wine to take traveling or on a picnic. Furthermore, it is an economical wine as a bottle once opened does not deteriorate and will keep almost indefinitely either in the bottle or in a decanter.

Naturally, there always are exceptions to any rule. Manzanillas and Finos deteriorate in the bottle. Their color deepens perceptibly and they lose their freshness. Our advice is always try to buy freshly bottled Manzanilla or Fino Sherry, and do not keep it overlong . . . a year at most.

Note: Sherry occasionally deposits a fairly substantial sediment. This is cream of tartar, which is natural to the wine. Stand the bottle up for an hour and it will fall to the bottom so that clear wine may be poured. This deposit will vary from one shipment to another of the same wine and there is no explaining this variation, except to it being due to fluctuation of temperature.

MONTILLA

BECAUSE the Jerez houses shipped the wines of Montilla for many, many years, they were accepted as Sherry wine. Today the Spanish wine laws delimit the

Jerez and the Montilla regions, and henceforth Montilla can no longer be classified as Sherry.

Montilla is produced near Cordoba, over a hundred miles away from the Sherry region. Named Montilla because it is made from grapes grown on the Montilla Mountains, it is made in the same way as the wine in Jerez except that it is fermented in enormous earthenware jars, called *tinajas,* instead of in oak butts. As a general rule the wine is shipped without additional fortification and average from $15\frac{1}{2}$ to 16 per cent alcohol.

OTHER WINES OF SPAIN

SPAIN'S annual production of wine now exceeds eight hundred million gallons and gives work to about 15 per cent of the population. The bulk of this production is not Sherry, but light, fresh table wine, most of which is consumed locally during the year of the vintage, as in France and Italy. However, certain regions of Spain besides Jerez export quality wines, and the future of Spanish table wine on the world market seems very bright.

The name with the most prestige among natural dry wines of Spain is unquestionably Rioja. In the northern province of Logrono, in Navarre, lies the triangular basin of the Rio Oja, whence rises the Ebro River, and where lie the vineyards which produce the most famous of Spanish table wines, Rioja. The production and exportation of the wines from this strictly defined zone is controlled by an official authority (about twenty-eight producers are entitled to the Rioja certificate of origin), and only those produced in this area may be labeled as Rioja wines.

The grapes of Rioja are native Spanish varieties—for white wines, the Calgrano and Viura; for red wines, the Graciano, the Mazuela, the Tempranillo, and the internationally known Garnacha, or Grenache. Rioja wines are best left to mature in oak casks for not less than two years to allow them to get over their "teething" troubles, and from then onward they will begin to improve out of all recognition, for, like all good wines, they will improve in bottle for many years, attaining a mellowness and character that is a delight to lovers of wine.

From this Rioja zone the best growths are classified as "Reservas," or "Vintages," and are shipped under the bodega's or shipper's brand name. These wines are allowed to mature in cask for some years and then, when bottled, not sold until they have acquired a "bottle age," which gives the wine that velvety flavor and beautiful aroma by which good quality, well-matured wines are recognized. Actually, red Rioja wines continue to improve in the bottle for fully twenty years.

Younger or lesser wines of the Rioja can be somewhat rough, but are still well suited to an outdoor meal or to accompany highly seasoned food. They are also pleasant for wine cups—what the Spanish call *sangria*—whether you make your own or buy the conveniently flavored product from Spain. One brand, Yago Sant'gria, has recently become one of the two or three largest-selling imported wines in America. It is a red wine, flavored with citrus fruit juice and usually sweetened (though also available in a drier version), that goes well with almost any food, or simply by itself as an occasional drink. Rioja Santiago, the firm that makes Yago wines, is a century-old company that exports wine to sixty-seven countries. See page 365 for instructions on how to mix your own sangria.

The favorite table wine of the Madrileños is Valdepeña, produced on the plains of La Mancha around the town of Valdepeña. Both red and white are available everywhere in Madrid. The white Valdepeña is a dry, rather full-bodied, golden wine, with plenty of character and flavor. The red is almost as light in color as a dark rosé, well-balanced, fairly high in alcohol, with a considerably fruity taste. The wines of La Mancha and Valdepeña are drunk when very young, and are exported at about ten to twelve months old, when they are still fresh and vigorous.

Many of Spain's better-known wines of former times have gone out of fashion in a world that, temporarily at least has turned against sweet wine. An important wine region for many centuries has been the Province of Malaga on the Southern Mediterranean coast. Before Prohibition, Malaga wines were extremely popular in the United States, but since Repeal they have not regained their popularity.

Several types of Malaga wine are made, all very sweet. Some come from the Pedro Ximenez, to whose juice has been added not only brandy but also vino de color to make a sweet but full-bodied and dark wine.

Much wine is made from the Muscat grape. This is usually a lighter-colored and lighter-bodied wine, but it too is very sweet, as the grapes are dried in the sun until they are almost raisins before being pressed. This Moscatel de Malaga has the characteristic Muscat flavor. It is served chiefly as a dessert wine in Spain and Latin America.

Along the Levantine coast of Spain, in Valencia, much beverage and fortified wine is produced.

The highly individualistic region of Catalonia, with its beautiful capital, Barcelona, produces interesting fortified wines of Tarragona and Sitges, and beverage wines of Tarragona and Alella. Prior to Prohibition, the United States imported vast quantities of "Tarragona Port." This is a red wine made in a manner similar to that employed in Portugal. The wine, however, is not as fine. In Spain it is called Priorato. According to our present regulations it can no longer be labeled Port, and its sale is not very important.

Tarragona also produces white fortified wines from the Malvasia, Muscat, and Macabeo grapes, for use as altar or sacramental wines. The famous old firm of Augusto de Muller was the accredited purveyor of altar wines to the Vatican and the various cardinals of Spain.

Further north, but still south of Barcelona, around the seaport of Sitges, are produced the most famous Moscatel wines of Spain. These are prepared in the same manner as the Pedro Ximenez wines. They are light golden in color, have a pronounced Muscat flavor, and are very rich and soft. As a rule, they have an alcoholic strength of 16 to 18 per cent. These wines are popular in Spain and in Latin America, though they are unknown to the American market.

The Catalonians also produce several table wines of good quality, particularly dry white and rosé wines suitable to drink with their excellent fish. From the Alella vineyards north of Barcelona comes a pleasant, light, dry beverage wine named Alella, which is shipped in the typical, long, flute-shaped Rhine wine bottle. It does not taste like a Hock or Moselle, but it is, none the less, a clean, good wine.

During the last few years, Spain has come to the fore with her tasty sparkling wines, known in Spain as Espumosos. Most are produced by the *méthode champenoise*. Some are quite good, especially those from Villafranca de Panades, but many are too sweet.

10. The Wines of Portugal

"CLARET is for boys, Port for men," declared Dr. Samuel Johnson, affirming not only his own but England's preference for the wine of Portugal. Indeed, we generally think of it as an English wine, for it was the English who changed it from a natural wine to the rich fortified wine it is today, the English who created the markets for it, and the English who control the trade in Portugal today. The Portuguese themselves, in fact, prefer the light beverage wines of their country, as Port—or Porto, the official name in the United States—is a bit rich for their climate. In fact, we think it would be safe to assume that two-thirds of the citizens of Portugal have never tasted Porto, which the rest of us imagine to be their celebrated, classic, and favorite tipple. Actually, the state of California produces ten times as much "Port" as Portugal.

In Roman times, Portus Cale, the port at the mouth of the Douro River, was the most important center of life and trade of ancient Lusitania. It eventually gave its name to the country (modernized to Portugal) and retained for itself the simple title of O Porto, the Port. In ancient days it was customary to close the Port each night to prevent pirates from coming in. They were able to do this in ports that had a narrow mouth by swinging heavy chains across from one bank to the other, which they called a "bar."

The history of the Port wine trade, like that of Burgundy, is wrapped up in politics and wars. Although Port has been sold in England since the fourteenth century, it was not until the Methuen treaty, signed in 1703, that the wine trade began to develop. English merchants had first settled in Lisbon and Oporto in the sixteenth century, after the discovery of Brazil led to increased trading possibilities; and when the crews of English boats began stopping there, as the years went on, England gradually became acquainted with the Portuguese wines.

history

In 1703 Queen Anne's forces were at war with France; and as a blow to the French wine trade had the English ambassador, John Methuen, draw up a commercial treaty with Don Pedro II whereby, in exchange for free entry of English woolens, Port wine was given an advantageous preferential duty over all other wines coming into England.

149

At first, however, the wine, in spite of its low price, was not popular, being both harsh and sharp. After long experimentation, however, the enterprising English wine merchants in Oporto discovered that by adding brandy to the wine before all the sugar had been fermented out, they had a wine suited to the English taste and climate. It won ready acceptance at home, and the Port trade was established on a firm foundation.

Like so many of our great wines, Port takes its name from the place whence it was first shipped. It is defined by the Anglo-Portuguese Treaty of 1916 as "A fortified wine produced in the delimited Douro region and exported through the Bar of Oporto." Any wine not answering this description cannot be sold in England as Port, even though it should bear a qualifying name, such as "Tarragona Port." Until 1968, the same held true in this country, according to the regulations of the Federal Alcohol Administration, except in the case of a qualifying term such as "California Port." But in 1968, it was established legally, with the concurrence of the United States authorities, that Porto is a geographical product made only from grapes grown in a small demarcated area in the Douro region of Portugal. To protect the genuineness of this unique and esteemed drink, it was to be known in the United States as Porto, or Vinho do Porto. Shippers' labels of wines bottled after 1968 must conform with the ruling. In other English-speaking markets, however, where the origin is legally recognized, it will continue to be known by the traditional name of Port or Port Wine.

The Douro region, one of the most beautiful wine countries in the world, is a rough, mountainous district, with a river winding, twisting, and turning between steep schistous slopes. The vineyards, known as *quintas*, are planted in terraces so that the vines will not be washed down into the river.

grape varieties

There are many varieties of grapes grown in the Douro valley but only two types are essential in the making of Porto. The first, including such *plants nobles* (best vines) as the Turiga, Mourisco, and Bastardo, produces a juice lacking in color, fairly light-bodied, but giving the wine character and finesse; the other, including the Cao, Tinta Francisca, and Souzao, bears grapes that are colored red straight through to the pips and are called *tinturiers*, which contribute the depth of color to the common must.

It is usual for a quinta to be planted with anywhere from ten to fifteen grape varieties, which are all gathered and pressed together, each one contributing its individual characteristic to help produce a balanced wine.

The principal grape varieties employed in the making of white Porto are the Rabigato, Moscatel Branco, Malvasia Fina, and Verdelho.

vintage

The vintage begins at the end of September or the beginning of October, depending on the weather. Men and women gather the grapes, carrying huge baskets on their backs balanced by a crooked stick and supported by a head harness, or piling them in squeaking, two-wheeled oxen-drawn carts, and it is amazing to watch these lumbering beasts cart the grapes down the steep, narrow roads to the pressing house without accident.

As in Spain, vintage time has a festival spirit, and the lively music of the *machete* (guitar) accompanies the work. The grapes, skins, and pips are placed in an oblong stone *lagar* (pressing trough) until it is half full, and men and women tread them until almost all the juice is expressed. In recent years, however, the purple "stockings" of the treaders have begun to disappear. Modern fermenters of the percolation type have entered the scene.

Fermentation begins almost at once and is allowed to continue from two to three days. The difference between Porto and other wines lies in this process, and therefore the fermentation is carefully watched. The sugar content of the must is measured periodically with a mustimeter, and when just the requisite amount of sugar remains unfermented, the must is run off into pipes (casks) which contain sufficient brandy, distilled from wines of the district, to raise the alcoholic content to around 20 per cent. This checks fermentation, and the unfermented grape sugar remains in the wine as sweetening. The amount of sweetness varies with the choice of each vineyard owner; if a lot of sugar is left in, more brandy must be added. Because of this, Porto is invariably a sweet wine.

fermentation

After the must has been run into pipes, there will still be a great deal of juice left in the skins, pips, and stems. Pressure is applied by means of a one thousand pound stone to express the last drop of juice. The wine made from this final pressing sometimes becomes Porto, but usually brandy is distilled from it to be used in fortifying Porto wines.

The new wines are kept at the quintas until the following spring, when they are racked off into fresh pipes and sent down the Douro aboard picturesque sailboats to the shippers' wine lodges in Oporto or Vila Nova de Gaia, twin cities on opposite banks at the mouth of the river. Here the wine is carefully stored until it is decided whether it will be shipped as a Vintage, Crusted, Ruby, or Tawny Porto.

VINTAGE PORTO

BEVERAGE wines such as Bucelas and Colares, made in Portugal in the same manner as those of France, will ripen, mature, and be at their best in eight to ten years, but the richly fortified Vintage Portos require upwards of twenty years before they reach their prime.

Vintage Porto is wine of any exceptional year, bottled two to three years after the vintage. Weather, rain, sun, and soil cooperate to produce a big wine, with character, bouquet, and balanced flavor. On the average, the shippers are able to ship about three vintages in every decade. Bottling rarely takes place in Portugal. The wine is sold to the wine merchants in the cask, and each buyer does his own bottling, although the shipper will do so on request.

Vintage Porto usually bears two dates on the label, the vintage date and the bottling date. The wine must rest for a considerable period of time, varying with different vintages, but at least eight to ten years are required for it to mature, and it will continue developing for many more years.

A generous full wine such as Vintage Porto throws a heavy deposit as it matures, consisting of argol, tartrate of lime, and coloring matter, which settles as a fairly solid crust on the side of the bottle. Once this begins, shipping of the wine becomes difficult, for unless it has the most careful handling the crust may break up, clouding the wine. Once broken, the crust will not re-form. That is why very little Vintage Porto has been shipped to America. What little has come over has been decanted off its crust into new bottles.

The ideal way to bring over Vintage Porto is to ship it as soon as it is bottled and before the crust has a chance to form.

In his *Romance of Wine*, H. Warner Allen tells a story about his great-grandfather's uncle, who was greatly addicted to Porto ". . . and when gout and old age at last drove him to bed, his old servant explained to his nephew how he was nursing his master: 'I keeps a-turning of his Worship,' 'cause you

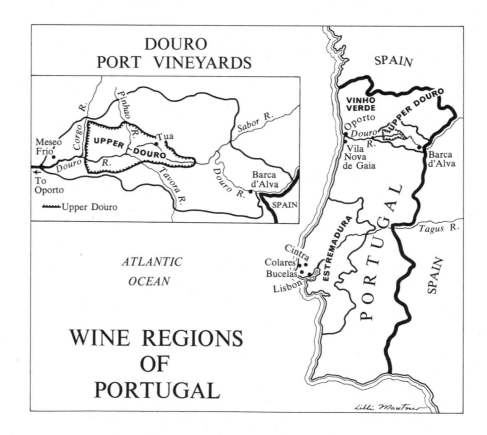

see, Sir, he's got that much Port in his inside, he'd be bound to get crusted, if I let'un stop too long on one side.'"

Vintage Porto has the deepest ruby color, the fruitiest bouquet, and the most body of all styles of Porto. Until fully matured it will be quite rough. Thus is has been customary for the English to lay down a considerable quantity of an approved Vintage Porto, which they buy cheaply, permitting it to mature and treble in value in some twenty odd years. It is no uncommon practice to purchase Vintage Porto at the birth of a son, so that he may enjoy it when they both reach maturity.

CRUSTED PORTO

CRUSTED Porto is a close relative to Vintage Porto in that it is usually wine of a single year. Sometimes, however, it is a blend of vintage wines from several vintages. It may be bottled early or late but, because it does not quite come up to "vintage standard" in quality, it is sold without any date. It is always less expensive, although it resembles Vintage Porto in character, and deposits a crust in the same manner as a vintage wine. It has a deep, dark ruby color and a fine, fruity bouquet.

RUBY AND TAWNY PORTOS

THESE are blended wines which are matured in wood. They are also called "Wooded Portos." The blending, or "vatting," employed in the Porto lodges resembles the Sherry solera system vaguely, in that a definite standard of style and quality is constantly maintained for each brand a shipper offers. The object in blending is to balance the qualities that are lacking in one wine but are present in the other—the wine which has finesse and delicacy but is light bodied will be blended with wine that has a great deal of body but less finesse, and the two will complement each other, giving a more balanced wine. The shipper sometimes uses as many as thirty or more wines in his blend.

While the wine is maturing in the pipe, it throws a deposit (crust) just as it does in the bottle. Some of the deposit is not heavy enough to precipitate and remains in suspension, causing the wine to have a dull or "blind" appearance. This is overcome by fining. Experience has proven that wines will develop best if kept in a good, brilliant condition. They are therefore fined on an average of twice a year. The material used may be a patented fining, but for better wines the shippers generally use white of eggs.

As the film formed by the fining process settles, it carries down with it not only the sediment or fliers which were floating in the wine, but also a certain amount of the coloring matter. As a result, the longer a wine is kept in the wood, the greater will be the number of times it is fined, and the less color it will retain. An old wooded Porto, consequently, is paler in color than a

Gathering the grapes at a typical Upper Douro quinta *during the vintage.* (Courtesy Casa de Portugal, New York)

young wine. This quality of paleness is called "tawniness" because as the wine loses redness, a tawny golden glint appears, which increases with each fining. As it increases in tawniness, a Porto becomes drier, so that an old Tawny will be drier than a young Tawny, though the word dry is used, in this case, in a relative sense.

Ruby Porto is a bright, ruby-colored blend of young wooded Portos. It is generally fruitier and rougher than a Tawny. There are not many true Ruby wines on the market, although there are a number of wines labeled "Ruby" which are, in reality, "Tawny."

A Tawny Porto is a blend of well-matured, wooded Portos; it is softer than Vintage, Crusted, or Ruby wines. It does not possess the fruitiness of the others, but an old Tawny is a soft, delicate, and elegant wine.

There are a few Vintage and Crusted Portos on the market, and the wines generally shipped are the Tawny and Ruby Portos.

WHITE PORTO

THIS is the fifth type of wine produced in the Douro region. Except for the fact that white grapes are used exclusively, it is made in the same manner as the red Porto. It is matured in wood and is generally quite soft and pleasant. It is very popular in France, where it is consumed as an apéritif. Only a small amount is imported into the United States.

PORTO VINTAGES

THOUGH not many Porto vintages are on the market in this country, we are likely to import more of them as time goes on and our wine merchants become more conscious of their function and their duty to their clientele.

Since the turn of the century, the better Porto vintages have been: 1900, 1904, 1908, 1912, 1917, 1920, 1924, 1934, 1935, 1942, 1945, 1947, 1948, 1950, 1955, 1960, and 1966.

USES OF PORTO

PORTO wine is served at the end of the meal with cheese; several cheeses, in fact, are prepared with Porto: such as Stilton, Cheddar, and so forth.

It makes excellent cobblers and flips.

It has many uses in the kitchen: in sauces, in the making of Porto wine jellies, and as an addition to fruit cups.

Colorful Douro rabelo *boat laden with pipes of new wine destined for the Shipper's* *lodges at Oporto or Vila Nova de Gaia.* (Courtesy Casa de Portugal, New York)

OTHER WINES OF PORTUGAL

As previously stated, it is illegal to call a wine Porto unless it has been produced in the delimited Upper Douro region, yet wines of the same type are made in other parts of Portugal, primarily on the Tagus and in the Estremadura region. These wines, shipped from Lisbon, are known as "Lisbon Wine."

The Portuguese themselves prefer wines that are less alcoholic, the best of which are a white and a red beverage wine—Bucelas and Colares respectively.

Bucelas is a town near Lisbon where the wine is made primarily from the Arinto grape. Dry, acidulous, with a recognizable aroma and characteristic straw-white color, this is the wine which according to legend cured King George III when as Prince Regent he suffered from an otherwise incurable ailment. The fine bouquet of this wine increases with age.

Colares is a small town near Cintra in the neighborhood of the cork woods. The vineyards of the region are planted with the Ramisco grape, which produces a clean, full-bodied, ruby-red beverage wine. Incidentally, this grape is immune to the phylloxera which ravaged European vineyards in the last century, making Colares and Periquita possibly the only wines drunk today made from the same grapes as those that gave wine thousands of years ago. Though the very early history of Colares wines is unknown, it is known that in 1385 there was a flourishing trade in Colares.

Carcavelos, located at the mouth of the Tagus of the "sunny coast" of Portugal, produces a wine known and appreciated since the thirteenth century. The climate favors the production of must of the highest quality because the breezes blow away the humidity which otherwise would affect the grapes producing the must. A first-class Carcavelos wine has an average alcoholic content of 19 per cent and is good as apéritif or dessert wine, depending on the sweetness. It has a pleasant bouquet, is smooth to the taste, and ages well.

Setubal Moscatel, a wine with several Royal Charters, is produced in Setubal, a region first acknowledged in 1185, a beautiful area south of Lisbon. It owes its fruity flavor to the distinguishing characteristics of its grapes. It, too, improves with age.

Apart from this Moscatel, the Setubal district is well known for its good quality table wines, the majority being red and made from the Periquita grape. But of Lisbon's (itself) local wines, one of the best is Bucellas—a pleasant, fresh, dry white.

The Dão region, south of the Douro, whose wines were celebrated about 500 years before Christ, has a full-bodied strength and richness. A ruby-red color, delicate bouquet, and smooth taste characterize the red wines; white wines are fresh, light, aromatic, and lemon-colored. The Tourigo grape imparts the principal characteristics to Dão wines. Incidentally, these wines are guaranteed as genuine Dão wines by the Federation of Dão Viniculturists which issues Certificates of Origin to all those wines which are entitled to them.

One of the most pleasant and simple wines of Portugal is the Vinho Verde, produced in the northern province of Entre Douro o Minho. The literal translation of *vinho verde* is "green wine," but the term really means "young wine." It is not green, but either white, red, or rosé. It is always a light, somewhat acid, refreshing, and fragrant wine with an alcoholic content of 8 to 11 per cent. Being light and pleasant and thirst quenching, it is a wine that is generally drunk in large draughts. It is not sipped.

Other districts yielding Portuguese table wines include: Pinhel, which gives a pleasant light wine; Bairrada, producing mostly red table wines which have body with good flavor, and some white wines held in high esteem; Alcobaca, whose fame dates from the twelfth century, whose fine wines are tantalizingly aromatic; Torres Vedras, a large producer of mostly red wines, with body and a high percentage of tannin, as well as some good white wines which are alcoholic, aromatic, and mild in flavor; Ribatejo, a region supplying the most important urban centers of the south of the country, where alcoholic white wines with little acidity are produced, as well as red wines, dark in color and full of body, with a high percentage of alcohol. It should be remembered that Portugal has an unusual number of non-geographical, standard blends, often of good quality, naming the merchant but not the wine's origin.

Most present-day Portugese table wines are fermented in a hermetically sealed cement vat, which enables the vintner to regulate easily. In the past, the must fermented in an open stone lagar where the grapes had been pressed, so that the carbonic acid gas generated by fermentation disappeared and with it many of the subtle and mysterious elements which today give Portuguese wine its appeal. In moderate temperatures this problem does not arise to the same extent, for fermentation is more gradual. With an air-tight vat, the carbon dioxide can be held in the wine as long as desired.

PORTUGUESE ROSÉ WINES

Rosé wines are enjoying a great vogue in the United States and those of Portugal have become very popular here. Both still and crackling rosés are now available. In spite of their higher price, due to higher duties and taxes, the crackling Portuguese rosé wines are widely consumed. They are made crackling (slightly sparkling) by having a small amount of carbonic acid gas added to the wine. These wines are also slightly and pleasantly sweet. Frequently they are shipped in dumpy, glazed earthenware (pottery) bottles.

Of Portugal's sparkling wines, those produced at Bairrada and Lamego, which are prepared by the classic process of fermentation in the bottle, are very good and are available in varying degrees of sweetness.

11. The Wines of Madeira

WHEN Venice dominated the commerce of the Mediterranean, it had a great trade with England in the wines of Candia, which were known as Candy or Malvasia Candiae. The Candia of the thirteenth century is the Crete of today, whose wines have given way to those of Madeira, and, as so often happens, the reasons are political. So long as the wine could be obtained only in Candia, the English submitted to the tyranny of Venice, but as soon as they could obtain similar wines of equal quality from Madeira, no time was lost in giving their trade to the Portuguese island, which is 535 miles south by southwest of Lisbon and some 360 miles off the North African coast in the Atlantic.

history   There is some question as to whether it was Prince Henry or one of his captains, Joao Gonçalves, surnamed Zarco, who discovered the island, in 1418 or 1420. At all events, Zarco was named Captain of Madeira, and founded a settlement there on the Bay of Funchal. The island, which was covered with dense forest from mountain top to seashore, was called Madeira, or "wooded island." When Zarco arrived with his family and a group of colonists he found the island uninhabited and untillable because of the heavy forest. Being a man of action and short of hands, he did not attempt to cut the timber, but fired it instead. It is said to have burned for seven years, but when, at length, the fire went out, there was added to the volcanic quality of the soil, and the accumulation of centuries of leaf mold, the potash ash of the burned forest, which made Madeira one of the most fertile of all islands.

Before long, sugar cane and grape vines were planted, and Portugal had a rich colony. The grape vines were brought primarily from Candia and were of the Malvasia variety which is still grown on the island.

By the end of the fifteenth century, Madeira was exporting wines to Europe where they found favor both in France and England. Shakespeare mentions Madeira in several of his plays, but notably in Henry IV where Poins greets Falstaff:

158

"Jack! how agrees the devil and thee about thy soul, that thou soldest him on Good Friday last for a cup of Madeira and a cold capon's leg?"

And there is the unforgettable story of that early Duke of Clarence who so loved his Madeira that he drowned in a pipe of it.

The sailing vessels of the American colonies, and English ships sailing to America made it a practice to stop at Madeira for water and provisions. Here they invariably loaded a few pipes of Madeira wine, and it became the fashionable wine of the American colonies, a fashion which remained until the turn of the century.

During the early decades of the nineteenth century, Madeira wines were often known by the names of the great shipping families of the Atlantic seaboard whose ship captains brought pipes of wine to their owners. While there were famous Madeiras shipped to Boston, New York, Philadelphia, New Orleans, Charleston, and Savannah, Baltimore was considered the Madeira capital of the United States.

Some of the ship owners gave the wines the name of the ship which brought them to America. Most wine historians credit the name of Rainwater to a Madeira enthusiast, Mr. Habisham of Savannah, who employed a secret fining process which made the wine paler in color without impairing its bouquet or character. Today, "Rainwater" is a trade-marked brand.

Unfortunately Madeira, after being the fashionable wine for many years, receives little attention in the United States today, a condition which can only be explained on the ground that the public is not being informed, by advertising, of the attractiveness of Madeira wines.

grape varieties

The principal grape varieties grown on the island are the Verdelho, which makes up two-thirds of the planted vines; the Sercial (said to be the Riesling of the Rhine transplanted to Madeira); the Boual or Boal; the Malvasia, from which is made the famous Malmsey Madeira. The original Malmsey was produced in Greece in Monemvasia, and in the Middle Ages red and white Malmsey were shipped all over the world. Later this type of wine was produced not only in Madeira, but in Italy, Spain, and the Canary Islands. The name Monemvasia becomes Malvasia in Italy, Malvoisie in France, and Malmsey in England. The Malvasia grape requires a very dry soil and intense heat, and is not gathered until it is shriveled and raisin-like.

Minor grape varieties grown in Madeira are the Tinta or black grape, the Bastardo, the Terentrez, the Listrao, and the Maroto.

Madeira vineyards are generally small, and are planted with several varieties of vines. The cultivator does not bother to separate the different species before pressing them in the lagar. As a result, there is a rich and somewhat deep-colored wine from the admixture of black grapes, some of which are found in every vineyard.

In the larger vineyards, the various kinds of grapes are pressed separately and the must from each kept apart, especially that from the Sercial, Boal, and Malvasia varieties.

The system of viticulture in Madeira differs in some ways from that of other wine regions.

Most of the land is cultivated under the old feudal system of small tenant farmers, known as *caseiros*. The *caseiro* pays half of his grape crop as rent. The cultivation of the small farm is generally managed on holidays and during the evenings, so as not to interfere with the daily work of the tenants, and the business of tending the vineyard is in the nature of an avocation.

Every inch of ground on the island of Madeira is utilized. The hillside is so steep that one can hardly find foothold, and yet it is made up into tiny terraces, each complete with its water channels for irrigation.

Madeira has not sufficient rainfall for its needs, and the land depends on irrigation for its moisture. The water is brought down from the hills in shallow channels which usually run by the roadside. The network of these channels covers the entire island and the water is managed by committees appointed by the caseiros. A farmer may be entitled to so many hours of water every fifteen days and at a given hour—whether it be three o'clock in the morning or three o'clock in the afternoon, he is advised: "It is your turn to get water." The stream will be turned into his farm, and at the end of his time it will be shunted on to the next farm. This organization is extraordinarily efficient.

The Madeira farmer knows little of modern implements or scientific methods and does all his cultivating with the primitive *enchada*, a tool which is a cross between a pick and a hoe. The hillsides are so steep that not even wheel-barrows can be used, and everything is carted in baskets carried on the head or shoulders.

The vines are not carefully pruned as is done on the continent as it has

been found more practical, due to the luxurious growth, to grow them on trellises four or six feet high, with vines fifteen to twenty feet long.

It is the custom on the island for merchants and shippers to buy the produce of the vineyard while the grapes are still on the vine. Their agents watch to see that grape picking is not begun until the proper time, and supervise the work up to the time of the delivery of the must into the shippers' cellars.

As only the ripest grapes are picked, it is often necessary to go over the vineyard four times. The grapes are emptied into a large wooden lagar, where they are trodden out by six men who stand, three on each side of a large central beam, jumping up and down to the tune of a machete.

After the grapes have been thoroughly trodden out, they are piled up in the center and a large stone, weighing well over a ton, is brought to bear on them by means of a wooden screw, until there is practically no juice left in the grapes. This system is ancient, but its results are better than those of the modern press. The contact of the naked feet on the grapes brings out the soft jelly found on the inside of the skin, in which lies the principal flavor.

The must is then placed in goatskins and carried down from the hills by men called *borracheiros*, and is emptied from the goatskins, which hold about 12 gallons and weigh 150 pounds, into casks in the shippers' lodges. Here the must remains until fermentation is completed, usually from two to four weeks, when about 3 per cent of brandy is added. The wine is now known as *Vinho Claro*.

Madeiras are treated in a manner peculiar to the island. They are matured in *estufas* or hot houses. These vary in temperature from 110 to 140 degrees Fahrenheit, according to the length of time the wine is to be baked. If it is to be kept for six months in the estufa, the temperature will be 110°, but if it is going to be kept only three months then a higher temperature will be used. During this treatment, wines which enter a deep purple color undergo a change and emerge amber colored.

This method of maturing the wine is costly as there is quite a loss through evaporation, but a well-matured wine is safe against after-fermentation. All of the work is carried out under government supervision. When the wine comes from the estufa it is known as *Vinho Estufado*. It is then allowed to rest for a period of time and racked into fresh casks, becoming *Vinho Trasfugado*.

The heating process originated many years ago, when it was discovered that Madeira wine was greatly improved by a long voyage in the hold of a ship. At one time, indeed, it was a regular practice to send wines in the hold of sailing vessels bound for India, and thence back to Europe or America, where it was known as East India Madeira. Whether it was the intense heat of the tropical seas through which the wine sailed, or the motion of the ship, which matured the wine, no one knew. In any case, Madeira merchants have learned that the estufas produce the same result.

Model of an old wooden Madeira wine press. (Courtesy Casa de Portugal, New York)

It used to be customary in America for famous shipping families to keep a cask of Madeira slung in a rocking cradle which was placed in the entrance hall of the shipping office. It was the duty of every person who passed through the hall to give the cradle a shove. In this way the wine was kept in motion from morning until night. Of all wines, Madeira is the only one which enjoys motion, and there is none which is a better sailor.

The Vinho Trasfugado is additionally fortified to bring it up to an alcoholic strength of around 20 per cent, and it then becomes known as Vinho Generoso. After this, it is blended with other wines of similar character and matured for a number of years. Wines made from a mixture of grapes are shipped under trade names, while those made entirely from one grape variety are shipped under the grape name. As previously mentioned, there are four, corresponding approximately to degrees of sweetness, though the sweetness is controlled not by the grape but by the amount of brandy and when it is added to the wine.

Malvasia or *Malmsey* is a full-bodied, soft-textured, very fragrant, dark-brown wine. It is the sweetest of all Madeira's wines. In fact, it is of an almost liqueurlike sweetness.

Bual or *Boal* is a golden wine, fragrant and slightly less sweet than the Malmsey. It is distinctly a dessert wine.

Verdelho is a medium rich, golden wine with a dry finish. It is good "all-purpose" wine as it can be taken before or after meals.

Sercial, the driest wine of Madeira, is a pale golden, fruity wine of good body. It is a perfect apéritif, but is suitable for every occasion. There is at least one Sercial that is extraordinarily bone-dry. The one that is most familiar— Gloria Mundi—is produced by Leacock & Company. The late André L. Simon described it as "A Madeira wine so soft and refined that it has no body, no sugar, no color left, and yet it has bouquet and power; the sort of wine that Rabelais, had he known it, would have called 'A Soul with a Nose.'"

Incidentally, the Rainwater Madeira, which we mentioned earlier, is a blend of Sercial, Verdelho, and/or Bual. It is a golden, moderately sweet wine suitable for almost every occasion.

Madeira is one of the most long-lived of all wines, and even 100-year-old wines are magnificent and continue improving as do no other choice wines. In the past it was customary to keep the vintages separate, and the wines were sold as vintage wines.

Since the phylloxera devastated the vineyards, nearly a century ago, the old vintage wines have been used to improve the new. As a result, true vintage Madeiras are very difficult to obtain today.

A few wine merchants have offered such prizes as 1862 and 1898 Verdelho, 1864 and 1898 Sercial, 1869, 1870, 1882 and 1891 Bual, 1880 and 1885 Malmsey, all shipped by the old Funchal house of Blandy.

One basic characteristic which all Madeiras have in common is a subtle acid undertone or tang, which is found in all wines produced from grapes grown in soils of volcanic origin.

USES OF MADEIRA

It may be drunk as an apéritif, served with the soup course in formal dinners, and as a dessert wine. It finds its greatest usefulness, however, as a wine to serve in the afternoon or evening, accompanied by a biscuit, or as a tonic wine. It is rich in phosphates, iron, and minerals.

Madeira is one of the most useful of all wines in the kitchen. It may be used in soups, sauces, or desserts and can be used in place of Sherry in most recipes. Actually the largest export market for Madeira is France where it is used almost exclusively in Sauce Madère and therefore gets eaten and not drunk.

12. Aromatized Wines

"Man first learned to make his wine aromatic," said the late André L. Simon, "when he discovered that by adding honey or sage or some herb to his sour wine, it became more palatable." Since that day, however, great strides have been made in the science of producing aromatized wines.

The ancient Greeks preferred pitched or resinated to natural wine, as do the Greeks of the present day. And the effete Romans liked to flavor their wines with such interesting materials as pepper, spikewood, cypress, wormwood, myrrh, poppy, tar, pitch, bitumen, aloes, chalk, mastic gums, boiled sea water, and asafoetida. Is it strange that one ancient Roman writer said of wine: "It biteth like a serpent?"

Aromatized wine is fourth in the classification of wines, the others, of course, being still, sparkling, and fortified. It is a fortified wine in which herbs, roots, flowers, barks, and other flavoring ingredients have been steeped in order to change the natural flavor of the wine.

Aromatized wines include both dry (French origin) and sweet (Italian origin) Vermouths, and the quinined or other *apéritif* wines of the various countries, such as Dubonnet, Byrrh, Lillet, Punt é Mes, St. Raphaël, Cin, Pikina, Cynar, Positano, Suze, Chambraise, Cherry and Blackberry Julep, and so forth. All, including Vermouths, are *apéritifs*, from the Latin *aperio*, meaning "to open." That is exactly what they are supposed to do. They open . . . whet the appetite pleasantly.

VERMOUTH

The term "vermouth" comes from the German *wermut* but was first used commerically in 1776 by Antonio Benedetto Carpano of Torino, Italy, who may be called the father or founder of the Vermouth industry. He used the white Piedmont wines nearest at hand, especially the fine Canelli muscats, and produced a bitter-sweet Vermouth.

About a generation later, and quite independently, about 1800, Louis Noilly of Lyon, France, developed a somewhat drier Vermouth by employing the thin Herault wines of the French Midi. Thus the sweet type has come to be referred to as Italian and the dry type as French.

Today, however, the Italian producers also make vast quantities of the dry and the French make the sweet type as well. In fact, greater quantities of both types are produced outside of Italy and France since the locally made sweet and dry types are consumed in all wine-producing countries. For example: the United States produces more than 50 per cent of its annual consumption of better than 10,250,000 gallons; and Argentina, whose per capita consumption of Vermouth is probably the highest in the world, does not import any Vermouth from abroad, producing more than fifteen million gallons each year. Much more of the sweet or Italian style Vermouth is drunk throughout the world than of the dry, except in the United States where consumption is about equal of each type. The greater use of the dry variety in the United States is due to the popularity of the Dry Martini cocktail.

The French type is the "dry" Vermouth. According to French law, a Vermouth must consist of at least 80 per cent wine, which must have an alcoholic strength of at least 10 per cent. Later alcohol may be added in order to raise the strength of the wine up to 19 per cent. Sugar, too, may be added in order to get the degree of mildness desired. *dry or French Vermouth*

The wines used for the making of French Vermouth are produced in the Midi in the Department of the Herault, which produces more wine than any other province of France. They are light, thin, and rather characterless, known as Picpouls and Clairettes. In addition, a small proportion of Algerian Grenache wine is used.

The process of maturing the wines plays a very important part in the making of French Vermouth. The dryness of the Vermouth is a perfectly natural development, as the Clairettes and Picpouls become very dry as they mature. In fact, to prevent too much dryness, they are mixed with the less dry Grenache, grown in Algeria, in a proportion of three to one. These wines, which are selected from the finest Herault vineyards, will contain 12 to 14 per cent of alcohol. They are stored from two to three years in thick oak vats called *demi-muids*.

In order to give the Vermouth its mildness the better houses use a *mistelle* or *vin de liqueur* in place of sugar. The mistelles are made by adding to unfermented must the amount of alcohol the must would have produced, had it been allowed to ferment out. In this manner a mistelle contains both natural grape sugar and alcohol (in the form of brandy) at the same time. In making Vermouth, mistelles of Grenache and of Muscat are used. They are aged separately and for the same time as the other wines.

In at least one case, a further aging process is used. When the wines have matured two years, they are placed in casks of 100 gallons, which are stored in the courtyard of the establishment where they can receive the benefits of the sun's rays during the day and the coolness of the night. This daily variation in temperature ages the wines more rapidly. This treatment can be applied only to better quality wines.

After the wines are thus conditioned, they are blended 80 per cent Herault wine and 20 per cent mistelle. This is known as "basic wine." The basic wine is then embodied with the infusion obtained by steeping the special flavoring agents in the wine, according to a duly tested formula. This brings out the characteristic Vermouth bouquet, in which a manifold aroma is blended in the most attractive manner.

Anywhere from 30 to 50 different types of herbs, plants, roots, leaves, peels, seeds, and flowers may go into a single formula for making French Vermouth. Some of these are nutmeg, coriander seeds, cloves, cinnamon, rose leaves from Bengal, Peruvian quinine bark, hyssop, marjoram, angelica root, wormwood, bitter orange peel, camomile, linden tea, centaury, gentian, and flowers of elder.

All the plants are put in a large tank. The basic wine is then poured in and left in contact with the plants for one month; then this wine, which has taken on flavor from the plants, is drawn off and new basic wine is added in its place. This done four times before the flavor of the plants is exhausted, and the basic wine which has acquired the flavoring is now known as the infusion.

The infusion is mixed in a proportion of one to five with other basic wine, and alcohol is added to raise the strength of the wine to 19 per cent.

Casks of maturing wine stored in the open courtyard, exposed to the elements, before being made into dry Vermouth. (Courtesy Noilly Prat & Cie., Marseilles)

This mixture must be allowed to blend thoroughly, and it is put into glass-lined vats where the wines are brought down to a temperature of nearly freezing, constantly stirred by giant paddles to ensure a perfect blending. This refrigeration has a purpose. Vermouth, like all wine, contains some tartaric acid, which is a natural element in the composition of wine. It is invisible, but in time it crystallizes and forms a deposit known as cream of tartar. The formation of this deposit can be forced by abruptly lowering the temperature of the wine.

Vermouth becomes darker in color as it ages, but variations in color have nothing to do with the quality of the Vermouth. The trade, however, insists that it be the same color year in and year out. To ensure this, caramel is added if the color is too light; or, if it is too dark, it is mixed with a lighter Vermouth. But remember that because the formula of each producer is different, no two brands of Vermouth are alike.

It takes three and a half to four years to properly mature, age, and prepare a true French Vermouth. This means that enormous reserve supplies must always be kept on hand and large sums of money are invested in these stocks for a great many years. For this reason, only well-established, financially sound houses can afford to finance the aging process which alone ensures that the wines will acquire the properties of perfect maturity which would not be possible in any other way.

The French Vermouth business must be conducted on a mass-production scale, for otherwise it would not be economical.

sweet or Italian Vermouth

The Italian Vermouth is the "sweet" type, made from white wines. This "sweetness" is due to the fact that the basic wine used for the making of the Vermouth is sweeter and fuller than the thin white Herault wine of the Midi. The law in Italy is specific about Vermouth being made from wines which are at least one year old. Between infusing and final filtering, another year is employed, so that it takes approximately two years to produce an Italian Vermouth.

Most of the wines used for making Italian Vermouth are those from Apulia, although some Moscato di Canelli will always be blended in for flavor and sweetness. These rather bland wines are infused with various herbs, roots, seeds, and a little quinine. They are allowed to mature, and as soon as they have absorbed a sufficient amount of flavor they are drawn off, fortified, filtered, and some sugar and coloring matter are added. The brown color is obtained by the addition of caramel.

There is a reason for the use of quinine. When the European countries started colonizing the Tropics they found that there was a lot of malaria fever, and the best medicine for this was quinine, which has an extremely bitter taste. The soldiers rebelled at the thought of it. Often they preferred the disease to the cure. The solution was found by an ingenious physician who gave his soldiers their quinine in sweetened red wine. Thus was born the taste for *quin-quina*—quinined wine—the apértif wines which the French and Italians have never lost a taste for. Since then, quinined wines have been made with white wine, sherry, and, as a matter of fact, with all types of wines and in all countries.

There are two distinct types of Italian Vermouth: the sweet apéritif type, and the drier cocktail type; the cocktail type is most popular in the United States.

other Vermouths   Vermouths are made in other parts of the world, as well as in France and Italy. There are Spanish, Portuguese, American, Australian, Argentine, and South African Vermouths. In fact, wherever wine is produced, some Vermouth is made. These, however, are for the most part consumed locally.

OTHER AROMATIZED WINES

THE apéritif wines are made in almost all European wine-producing countries in the same manner as French Vermouth, except that the proportion of mistelle is generally greater—the wines being sweeter.

Apéritif wines are basically quinined wines. When the apéritif is white, the basic wine used is white; when red, the basic wine is red. The variation in taste, i.e., sweetness, bitterness, or aromatic flavor, results from the use of different formulae, which are trade secrets of each producing house.

The principal apéritif wines sold in this market are Dubonnet (regular red and white blonde), Raphaël (red and white, but only the red is sold in the United States), Byrrh (red), and Lillet (red and white). Raphaël is slightly sweeter than Dubonnet. Byrrh and Lillet are slightly drier.

Among the more popular recent arrivals on the United States scene are Cynar and Positano. Cynar's name and principal flavor are derived from the artichoke. To the ancient Latins, Cynara (Latin for artichoke) was reputed to help "to keep the liver young," but no one ever bothered to make use of the knowledge until the inquisitive mind of Angelo Dalle Molle recognized its virtues when he was doing research among ancient Latin tomes and manuscripts. As a result, he developed Cynar—a wine apéritif which is now almost as popular as Vermouth in Italy.

Positano is much drier than the average apéritif wine, possessing less than one-third as much sugar. However, it does have the general bitter-sweet character of apéritif wines. All apéritif wines may be served neat, well chilled, or used as cocktail ingredients as you would Vermouth.

Of course, all apéritif wines are not bitter nor do they have a sharp taste. Cherry and Blackberry Julep—both imported from Italy—are in this class. So is Chambraise, a delightfully light drink made from "fraises des bois" (tiny, wild strawberries). By the way, Chambraise can be substituted for the French Vermouth and a strawberry for the olive or lemon peel to make a Strawberry Martini.

USES OF VERMOUTH AND APÉRITIF WINES

IN America we think of Vermouths as wines to be used in the preparation of our favorite cocktails—Martini (French Vermouth) and Manhattan (Italian Vermouth), and that is the principal use made of them and the apéritif wines as well.

In Buenos Aires and the other fashionable centers of South America the invariable gesture of hospitality, no matter what the occasion or the hour, is an invitation to have a *copetin,* which usually means a vermouth. In fact it is a must between 5:00 and 6:00 P.M. This time of day is known as the "Vermouth Hour" and even the movie exhibited at that time is called the "Vermouth" feature.

In other parts of the world, however, Vermouths are widely used as apéritif wines by themselves. The classic ways to drink them are neat, on-the-rocks, or with a splash of soda added. This applies to either Italian or French Vermouths, as well as the apéritif wines.

Another use for these wines is over fruit, or in cooking. By combining wines and savory herbs, Vermouth provides us with a handy, easy-to-use blend of some of the world's most prized seasonings. French Vermouth, for instance, can often be substituted for dry white wine in recipes calling for wines and herbs—and the herbs probably omitted.

The apéritif wines are increasing in popularity in the United States in the past few years as our public is becoming more aware of not spoiling their palates with hard liquor if they are going to drink fine wines with their dinner. Also Americans are traveling more and are drinking more apéritif wines abroad.

13. The Wines of the United States

NEITHER wine grapes nor wine had to be brought to America. They were here long before the Pilgrims came ashore at Plymouth Rock. In fact, about the year 1,000—five hundred years before Columbus "discovered" America —Leif the Lucky and his band of Norse Vikings reached the eastern shores of America—presumably what is today Rhode Island or Massachusetts. He was so impressed by the wild profusion and luxuriance of grape vines he found he called our land Vineland the Good, and so it was known in Icelandic sagas for centuries.

America is one of the richest countries in the world in viticultural natural resources. More than half the known varieties of grape vines (*vitis*) are indigenous to our continent. Logically, it would seem that wine should be a standard daily beverage for Americans.

The Indians used grapes as a staple fruit, and in the narrations of the early voyages, the grape is found in the list of resources and treasures of the new-found continent which indeed proved to be a natural vineyard.

The vintner's life is never an easy one and in the United States it has been more discouraging than in other lands. Our earliest settlers on the eastern seaboard planted the vine and made wine from the grapes it produced. The wines were unlike those of Europe. The consumers, recently arrived, and the folks back in England wanted wines similar to the European types with which they were familiar.

Since the native vines grew so luxuriantly, they reasoned that their problem could be solved easily by planting European (*vitis vinifera*) varieties. However, their efforts were doomed to failure in the east. In California the Missionary Fathers did much the same thing, but there they had greater success.

The reason for the miserable failure of this attempt was due to the fact that the vine growers refused to recognize an important fact; our land, rich though it was in hardy, native grapes, was hostile to the sweet, soft roots of the European varieties. Not only were the soil and climate unsuited for the

170

foreign plants, but the scourge of the grape vine, *phylloxera vastatrix*, attacked the gentle foreigners on American soil, just as it was later to attack them on their own soil, with the same ruinous results.

The *phylloxera vastatrix* is, to the best of our knowledge, a native American. It is a plant pest of the louse family which lives on the roots of the grape vine. Sometime between 1858 and 1863 Europe imported many American vines for experimental purposes. It is practically certain that the deadly phylloxera was brought in on these American root stocks. Within a few years it had become a true scourge and from 1865 to 1890 the phylloxera devastated the vineyards of Europe from France to Greece, from Spain to Germany, even appearing in Russia; the pest then crossed the oceans and appeared in Australia. In our own country it seriously damaged some of the vineyards of California in 1890, where it had been previously unknown.

It is impossible even today to estimate the actual pecuniary loss, but in 1888 M. Lalande, President of the Chamber of Commerce of Bordeaux, calculated that the loss to France alone amounted to two billion dollars, or twice the indemnity paid to Germany in 1871 after the Franco-Prussian War.

The phylloxera has a sharp proboscis with which it pierces the bark of the root. It subsists on the sap of the vine. One solitary louse would do very little damage but each lays many eggs which hatch out in six to ten days. After a few days the young attach themselves to a convenient spot on the root and within three weeks are adults laying more eggs. It has been estimated that a single female which lays a batch of eggs in March and dies, would have 25,000,000 descendants by October.

Every known method of combating diseases of the vine was employed but with little success. It was not until the European viticulturists discovered that the American root stocks were hardier, and immune to the phylloxera, that they found that the solution to their problem was to graft the European vines on American root stocks.

In the meantime, many nurseries and grape scientists have started an intensive program of hybridization between *vitis vinifera* varieties and American varieties to try to produce new selections with the phylloxera resistance of the American parents and the good wine characteristics of the vinifera parents. Although this program never was of great importance in France, it will be noted in Chapter 14 that it now has an impact on Eastern American viticulture.

It is clear that the United States has very radically and vitally influenced European and world viticulture and wine. However, it must be pointed out and borne in mind that even though American root stocks are in fairly general use in Europe, the basic character of the various grape varieties which have been grafted on them, and which form the vine itself, has not changed and the wines made from these grapes are the same as before grafting.

To the best of our knowledge Chile is the only country in the world whose vineyards have never been infested by the *phylloxera*. Every other non-American vineyard region of the world has been invaded and devastated by this louse, and all have had to graft their *vitis vinifera* vines upon American phylloxera-resistant root stocks.

Even in California, where European varieties of grapes are grown almost exclusively, it is necessary to use native American root stocks as a defense against the ever-present, patiently waiting phylloxera, so truly surnamed "vastatrix" (devastating).

Near the end of the nineteenth century the wine industry was producing wines fine enough to win some medals and gain recognition in expositions in France. In fact, there are many strong indications that American wines were well on their way toward becoming firmly established when another and more fatal blight was visited upon the vineyards—National Prohibition.

There was consternation among the vintners in 1919. What were they going to do with the grapes which were good only for the making of wine? Smaller and less sweet than table or raisin grapes, they were poor travelers because of their thin, easily bruised skins. The inevitable happened—many vineyards were uprooted and replanted with more salable types of grapes, and in some cases with other fruits. The thousands of acres of grapes which remained under cultivation during the entire Prohibition period were used in the production of sacramental, medicinal, and cooking wines. Naturally, this business had its limitations and was not large enough to encourage new plantings.

With Repeal, the whole process had to be reversed. While fine wine grapes were growing in the California vineyards, they could not produce enough for the newly established market. There have been quality wines produced in California before, during, and since Prohibition, but it is especially since the 1950s that we are producing quality wines in constantly increasing commerical quantities.

The wines of the United States have fallen into two distinct classes: *California* wines, made from European *vitis vinifera* grape varieties grown only in California and resembling European wines, and *American* wines, made from native American cross-bred grape varieties, grown in the East and elsewhere in the country, which are unlike any other wines in the world. However, in recent years, a new class has emerged in the East: Wines made from French hybrids, newly developed American hybrids, and even vinifera varieties.

14. American Wines

THE wines produced in the United States east of the Rocky Mountains—particularly in the regions of New York, Ohio, New Jersey, Virginia, Missouri and Michigan—are called "American wines" because they are distinctly native to America. When cross-bred with European *vitis viniferas* they dominate and never lose their own definite aroma and flavor characteristics, unless they are cross-bred again and again as French hybridizers have done. It took the early settlers several hundred years to realize this fact, and until they did they could not produce wines with any measure of success.

Today, we do not see the word "American" used to describe native wines as much as it once was. Now, there is a tendency for each state to try to produce their own wines, like "New York State," "Ohio," etc. But to do this in New York State, for instance, 75 per cent of the grapes used in the wine whose label carries an appellation of origin must be grown in the Empire State.

Early settlers left records of the wealth of wild grapes found in many *history* sections along the eastern seaboard. In 1565, Captain John Hawkins spoke of the grapes he found in the Spanish settlements in Florida, and mentioned that the Spaniards had made twenty hogsheads of wine from the wild grapes—probably *vitis rotundifolia*, best represented by the Scuppernong, found along the Atlantic seaboard from Maryland to Florida.

Still later, Thomas Hariot, writing of the advisability of establishing colonies in America, mentioned grapes which were of two kinds, one small and sour, the size of the European grape; while the other was larger, more sweet and luscious.

In 1601, that doughty colonizer Captain John Smith wrote in greater detail. "Of vines," he said, "great abundance in many parts, that climbe the toppes of highest trees in some places, but these beare but few grapes except by the rivers and savage habitations, where they are overshadowed from the sunne; they are covered with fruit though never prunned nor manured. Of 173 these hedge grapes we made neere twentie gallons of wine, which was like our British wine, but certainly they would prove good were they well manured. There is another sort of grape neere as great as cherry, this they [Indians] call messamins; they be fatte and juyce thicks, neither doth the taste so well please when these be made in wine."

It was Lord Delaware, Governor of Virginia, who first suggested that a wine

AMERICAN WINE REGIONS

industry be established in America, when he wrote to the London Company in 1616. The idea was enthusiastically approved, and expert French vine dressers and a wide assortment of the finest European vine cuttings were shipped to this country. There the first mistake was made.

It is understandable that the newly arrived colonists should find the vine made from native grapes with their strange wild taste a shock to their palates. Instead of recognizing the merits of the new wine, they insisted that it be like the old, with which they were familiar. This may seem unreasonable, though it is just what occurs when Americans, traveling abroad, insist that the coffee be like that which they are accustomed to at home.

If these early settlers had attempted to adapt themselves to native wines, it is possible that rising generations would have accepted them and we would have become a wine-drinking nation, instead of having to overcome an inferiority complex about the quality of our native wines.

Numerous attempts were made, vine dressers changed, vines varied, but all to no avail. For two centuries after Lord Delaware's first efforts, wine makers stubbornly continued their efforts to grow the foreign vine, and it was not until the nineteenth century, when they understood the devastation wrought by the phylloxera on foreign vines, that they were able to succeed. Then and only then was a serious effort made to permit our native grape east of the Rockies to stand on its own feet.

The vine can and does prosper in every state in the Union, but not every grape variety makes good wine, and there are certain regions in the United States, as in other countries, where wine grapes grow more successfully than others. In the order of their importance these regions are:

New York. In the Finger Lakes region in the northwestern part of the State; in the Westfield-Fredonia district along Lake Erie and along the Hudson River, around Highland in Sullivan County.

Washington. In the Yakima Valley and in the "bay" area around Puget Sound.

Ohio. From Sandusky to Cleveland along Lake Erie.

Oregon. In the Willamette Valley, south of Portland.

New Jersey. Around Egg Harbor, near Atlantic City.

Southeastern Seaboard. This region includes the coastal plain from Virginia to Florida.

Missouri. Near Harman in the Missouri River valley and in the foothills of the Ozark Mountains in the southern part of the State.

Michigan. Around Benton Harbor.

Pennsylvania. Between the town of North East and the city of Erie along Lake Erie.

Arkansas, Maryland, and other states. Small local districts.

Two types of grapes are grown: native, wild, undomesticated Muscadines (*vitis rotundifolia*), and the hybrids which have been obtained by cross-breeding and careful selection with *vitis labrusca* vines almost exclusively.

There are three principal varieties of Muscadines: the Scuppernong, James, and Misch. The Scuppernong is a white grape and the other two are black. The most famous of these is the Scuppernong, which grows profusely and naturally south of the Mason and Dixon Line, particularly in Virginia, the Carolinas, Tennessee, Georgia, and Florida. It gives a rather sweet, rich white wine with an individual taste all its own. For best results, the vines cannot be pruned, but must grow freely.

The principal cultivated and crossbred varieties—it is impossible to list all *labrusca* varieties within the confines of this book—are:

red grapes   DELAWARE. Originated by A. Thompson, supposedly at Delaware, Ohio, in 1848, these are small, light-red, very sweet grapes and one of the best fine-wine grapes produced in the East. The Delaware is used for white beverage wines and is indispensable for the making of Champagne and sparkling wine.

CATAWBA. Known since 1823 when it was found growing along the banks of the Catawba River in North Carolina and introduced to the wine trade by John Adams. It is a fairly large red grape on a par with the Delaware with which it is often used. From the Catawba, which, when thoroughly ripe has a fairly high sugar content, are produced some of the best sweet white beverage and sparkling wines in America.

DIANA, IONA, AND VERGENNES. These varieties are available now only in small quantities and used in the making of limited amounts of varietal wines.

white grapes   DUCHESS. Originated by A. J. Caywood, according to Valear, "from a white Concord seedling fertilized by Delaware." It is a light green (white), thick-skinned grape, best suited for late picking.

NIAGARA. Originated by Hoagland Clarke of New York in 1872. It is a white grape presumed to have been obtained from a Concord crossed with another *labrusca*.

ELVIRA AND MISSOURI. Seedlings obtained from *Reparia labrusca* crosses. Their use in American wines is decreasing yearly because they are being replaced progressively with newer hybrid varieties.

NOAH, ONTARIO AND PORTLAND. These have ceased to be used in any meaningful quantities.

black grapes   The dark or black grape varieties are not used as widely as the red and white; the only ones of importance are Ives and Isabella. The Fredonia, grown in some parts of the Lake Erie district, is blended with the Concord for juice or wine. The Clinton, Lenoir, and Norton have practically disappeared for use in wine making.

CONCORD. The most important of all American grapes, the Concord, was introduced about 1849 by S. W. Bull. It has since served as a base for cross-

View of a vineyard near the shore of Lake Keuka in the New York Finger Lakes wine region. (Courtesy The Taylor Wine Co., Hammondsport, N.Y.)

breeding, but what is more, it is the most widely used grape we have. From the Concord is produced all the commercial grape juice that is consumed in the United States. Practically all the grape jelly and preserves are made from Concords too, as is most of the kosher wine made both commercially and privately.

NEW VARIETIES

In the years since World War II considerable work has been done to develop new wine grape varieties by cross-breeding viniferas with native American varieties. Curiously enough the outstanding hybrids have been developed in France and introduced to New York State vintners by Philip Wagner who first proved their worth by growing them in his own Boordy Vineyard at Riderwood, Maryland.

The first leading French hybridizer was Louis Seibel. Out of the more than 30,000 hybrids he grew, only a few—less than one in 1,000—have proved satisfactory. Other well-known French hybridizers have been Seyve Villard, Ravat, Landot, Baco, Bertille Seyve, Joannes Seyve, Burdin, Couderc, Galibert, and Kuhlman-Oberlin. A certain number of their hybrids are particularly suited to the Eastern American wine districts. Among them for red and rosé wines, the Seibel 1000, 7053 (Chancellor), 8357 (Colobel), Seibel 5409 (Cascade), and Chelois, Baco Noir, Foch (developed in Alsace), Leon Millot, etc. For white wines, Seibel 5278, 5279 (Aurora), and 9110 (Verdlet), the Seyve Villard 5276, and the Revat 51 (Chardonnay like), etc. Some or all of the foregoing varieties are being grown by the four leading Finger Lakes producers—Gold Seal Vineyards, Pleasant Valley Wine Company, the Taylor Wine Company, and Widmer's Wine Cellars.

For the past few years the New York State Experiment Station in Geneva, New York, is at last very seriously engaged in hybridization and new varieties for testing. The Station is also engaged in a new program of scientific work for the improvement of wine making.

Possibly, one of the most important developments in the New York State wine industry occurred in the early 1950s when Charles Fournier of Gold Seal Vineyards, who always dreamed of growing viniferas in New York State, met Dr. Konstantin Frank at the Geneva Experiment Station. Dr. Frank had great experience in growing vinifera grapes in the Ukraine and persuaded him that it could be done here too. Charles Fournier set aside a piece of land for him to work and the experiments began. Now, the White Riesling, Pinot Chardonnay, and the Aligoté are growing successfully and commercially in the Finger Lakes and the experimental work continues on the Cabernet Sauvignon, Pinot Noir, Pinot Gris, Gewürztraminer, Muscat Ottonel, and some Russian varieties. One outstanding feature of this program has been the discovery that the White Riesling in specific locations of New York State is subject to the *Botrytis Cinerea*. (This is the so-called "noble mold" found on grapes in the German wine regions.) True Spätlese wines are now regularly produced by leaving the grapes on the vine late in the Fall. Dr. Frank at his Vinifera Wine Cellars even made a small quantity of Trockenbeerenauslese wine. Sold at 45 dollars a bottle, this wine made quite a stir.

Mechanical harvester picking grapes in a New York State vineyard. (Courtesy The Taylor Wine Co., Hammondsport, New York)

Vineyards need year'round care. Above workers prune vines in winter. (Courtesy The Taylor Wine Co., Hammondsport, N.Y.)

INDIGENOUS VARIETIES

OF the many grape vines native to our country only a few are of importance to wine production. Besides those referred to as direct producers; i.e., *vitis rotundifolia* and *vitis labrusca*, there are others that are important and which are used throughout the world as root-stocks upon which viniferas are grafted. They are so used because they have been found to be the only successful defense against the ravages of phylloxera and several other diseases of the vine. The principal varieties are: *vitis riparia, vitis rupestris, vitis aestivalis,* and *vitis berlandieri.*

The wines made from our native American grapes have a distinctive flavor unlike those of any other part of the world. As the grapes grew wild, the early settlers attributed the strong, strange taste to the fact that the grapes were not cultivated or domesticated, and called the taste "wild" or "foxy." The term "foxy" has been greatly misunderstood. Its original and only meaning has always been one of strangeness, of wildness, of differing from the familiar (European) wines. It refers to the general character of the wines and has nothing to do with their quality. It derives from the very definite "grapey" aroma and character which all American wines possess.

The native grapes are high in acid and low in sugar, characteristics diametrically unlike those of other countries.

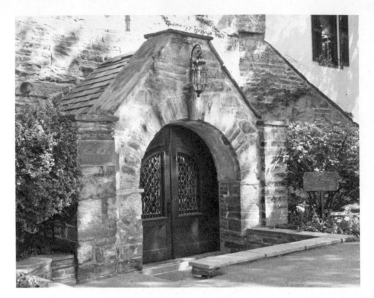

Original entrance to Great Western's Champagne Cellar, which is the oldest continuous one in the United States. (Courtesy of Pleasant Valley Wine Co., New York)

The most important wine-producing section of the East is the Finger Lakes region of upper New York, about 50 miles from Rochester, where the soil, drainage, and climate bear a striking resemblance to that of the French Champagne region. It is a beautiful countryside of rolling hills, dotted with lovely lakes. The region is devoted almost entirely to viticulture. All types of wine are made but sparkling wine predominates as this is the Champagne section of America.

The center of the region is Lake Keuka with Hammondsport at one end, Penn Yan at the other, with Naples and its vineyards nearby, and a section of the west side of Lake Seneca which is becoming quite important.

By 1867, the Pleasant Valley Wine Company at Hammondsport, which made both sparkling and still wine, produced American Champagne of such excellent quality that it won a gold medal at the Paris Exposition. Gold Seal Vineyards was also producing both wine types and received awards in Vienna in 1873 and in Paris in 1878.

The Catawba is one of the mainstays of the blends of grapes used for making Champagne in the East. Because of the color in the skin of this grape it is necessary to remove the juice from the grape pulp as soon as it is pressed in order to produce a white wine.

The Catawba attained its greatest fame prior to Prohibition, due no doubt to the energy of Nicholas Longworth, whose grandson was the late Speaker of the House. As a hobby, Mr. Longworth made a Sparkling Catawba which was so good and so popular that it won gold medals in foreign competitions and made him a fortune. He used to sell upwards of 100,000 bottles a year, produced at his vineyards near Cincinnati, Ohio.

Among his papers is a letter which Mr. Longworth wrote to the Members of the Cincinnati Horticultural Society, dated September 10, 1945, which is particularly interesting because it indicated the progress wines had made and the bright future which lay before them. It read in part:

"The vintage is not only early but the grapes ripen well, and the yield of wine is greater than I have ever known it and of unusual richness. Three of the vine dressers assure me that they have made from 13 to 14 gallons of wine from a flour-barrel of grapes—which I rate at $2\frac{1}{2}$ bushels . . . I have never heard of the grapes of Europe equalling this.

"The day is not distant when the Ohio River will rival the Rhine in the quantity and quality of this wine. I give the Catawba the preference over all other grapes for a general crop for wine. Sugar was formerly added. The Germans have taught us better. Where the fruit is well-ripened, sugar will injure it where intended for long keeping; where the grapes do not ripen well, I should still add from 6 to 10 oz. of sugar to the gallon of must. It rivals the best Hock and makes a superior Champagne.

"The Mission grape makes a fine wine, resembling Madeira, but is less productive than the Catawba. I have heretofore considered this a French Pineau grape, as it is a delicate grower with us; I sent some of the plants to my sister in New Jersey where the soil is bare, stoney and still. It grows perfectly hardy; and I now deem it a native.

"If we intend cultivating the grape for wine, we must rely on our native grapes and new varieties raised from their seed.

"If I could get my lease of life renewed for 20 or 30 years, I would devote my attention to the subject, and I would cross our best native varieties with the best table and wine grapes of Europe. We live in a great age. Discoveries are daily made that confound us, and we know not where we shall stop."

Still widely used in making of both sparkling and still wines, the Catawba is used in conjunction with other varieties, primarily the Delaware, which today has replaced it as the best fine-wine grape. The wine has a pleasant though slightly wild aroma and flavor distinctly different from any European wine.

One of the best sweet white wines we have tasted is a Sweet Catawba produced at Highland on the Hudson. It was bottled as "Sauterne."* A couple of wineries in the Hammondsport area have also developed a semi-sweet Catawba wine which has become extremely popular.

Washington and Oregon

The states of Washington and Oregon are potentially fine wine-producing regions. The great majority of vineyards in Washington are in the Yakima Valley, a famous region of fruit orchards at the Cascade Mountain Range. Such *vitis vinifera* varieties as Pinot Noir, Johannisburg Riesling, Sylvaner,

* The original, produced in the Bordeaux wine region of France, is always spelled Sauternes.

Pinot Blanc, Carignane, Gutedel, and Zinfandel are grown. Along the Puget Sound, Washington's other grape region, the vines popular in New York State—Niagara, Catawba, Delaware, and the hybrids—are planted. The Campbell's Early or Island Belle is also to be found, despite the blatant mediocrity of the wine from its grape.

Oregon has several small vineyards of *vitis vinifera* vines. But wine production in both Washington and Oregon is in its infancy, and their wines have not yet won a great following outside their boundaries. However, the development of good wines from this region of the United States may promise a bright future.

WINE NOMENCLATURE—GENERIC AND VARIETAL

Two basic methods of naming and labeling wines have been adopted by the American wine trade, with the approval of the BATF (Bureau of Alcohol, Tobacco, and Firearms) of the U.S. Treasury Department. The BATF wine labeling regulations refer to them as *generic*° and *varietal* wine labels.

A *generically* labeled wine is one bearing a name which in the judgment of the BATF is in such general use that it has lost its significance of geographical origin. Examples are Burgundy, Champagne, Chianti, Port, Sauterne, Sherry, etc., but to be labeled "New York State" Burgundy, etc., a minimum of 75 per cent of the grapes must be New York State grown.

A *varietally* labeled wine is one bearing the name of the grape variety from which the wine was made. To be so labeled, at least 51 per cent of the grapes employed must be of the variety named on the label. Examples are: Cabernet Sauvignon, Catawba, Chardonnay, Delaware, Johannisberg Riesling, Baco Noir, Aurora, Diamond, Pinot Noir, Traminer, Isabella, Niagara, Dutchess, Chelois, etc. Some wineries are now employing both a varietal and generic name when it is advantageous to best describe its wines to the customer.

On the label of all American wines there must be stated the name of the bottler or packer and the place where bottled or packed. Many purchasers of wine never notice that some labels say the wine was "produced and bottled by" a given company, while other wineries say "made" instead of "produced," and still other wines simply read: "Bottled by . . .". The significance of "produced" is that the vintner named must have crushed, fermented, matured, and bottled at least 75 per cent of the wine in the bottle. Some large wineries, however, often exchange wines with one another to maintain balanced inventories and regularly contract with other cellars to produce wines for them,

---

° "(Regulations under the Federal Alcohol Administration Act). 4.24 (a) (1). A name of geographic significance which is also the designation of a class or type of wine, shall be deemed to have become generic only if so found by the Director. (2) Examples are: Vermouth . . . Burgundy . . . Champagne . . . Sherry, etc."

Four common types of American labels.
TOP LEFT. *Generic label with a state designation.*
TOP RIGHT. *Varietal label.*
BOTTOM LEFT. *Generic varietal label.*
BOTTOM RIGHT. *Varietal label with a region designation.*

and also buy some wines from bulk producers. So, rather than attempt to segregate for separate labeling the lots fermented in their own cellars, they usually compromise with labels saying "made" instead of "produced." However, almost all premium-quality wines are "produced and bottled by so and so at such and such a place." Incidentally, the words "bottled by" simply mean the bottler did not necessarily make a drop of wine that is in that particular bottle.

A few American vintners apply vintage to their wines; other wine makers prefer to blend their wines to the highest possible—and unvarying—standard each year.

AMERICAN WINE TYPES AND THEIR PRODUCTION

ALL classes and types of wines are produced by the Eastern wineries, generally bearing the generic type names. Some are also marketed under varietal labels. William Widmer was a pioneer in vintaging varietal wines and others have followed his leadership.

The Eastern producers have been better known for their white wines. However, due to the planting of black French hybrids, red wines of European type, such as Bully Hill Red, Great Western Chelois, and Boordy Vineyard's Red Wine, are beginning to appear on the American market.

The care exercised in the vineyards while the grapes are maturing and at vintage time is very much the same as in the European wine regions. Winery operations, at least in the New York State Finger Lakes area, include the best of the old-fashioned methods to which the most modern advances have been adapted. Fermentation takes place in large steel tanks and then the wines are racked for aging in oak vats. Pure culture yeast strains are employed to assure continuing uniformity of character to the wines of each succeeding vintage. Some wineries maintain air-conditioning which ensures dry, clean, mold-free cellars, precise and continuous temperature and humidity control. To be perfectly sure of shipping brilliant and stable wines, chilling is practiced.

The table wines are aged at most for at least one year in oak cooperage and up to six months after bottling.

Sherry   The New York State vintners have developed their own unique methods of producing Sherry. They use the Niagara, Concord, and Dutchess grapes which they found suitable to produce a Sherry character.

One method of production is the Tressler process. After fortification, the wines are stored in special vats at a temperature of over 125 degrees for several weeks, during which time oxygen is bubbled throughout the wine. When the Sherry flavor is obtained, they are then aged in other vats for several months or years.

Widmer Wine Cellars store their Sherry in regular, uncharred, fifty-gallon

Special riddling *racks employed to shake down the sediment in New York State Champagne.* (Courtesy The Taylor Wine Co., Hammondsport, N.Y.)

Modern pyrex glass pipes—measuring more than a mile in length—employed to transfer wines from one processing point to another at the Taylor Wine Co. winery, Hammondsport, N.Y.

barrels which are then placed on the roof of the winery establishment and left exposed to the sun and elements for at least three years. After they have developed the desired nuttiness and mellowness, they are returned to the cellars, blended, filtered, and bottled.

The Pleasant Valley Wine Company started a solera system for aging their Sherries and Ports quite a few years ago, which is a series of blending younger wines with older wines periodically, similar to the Spanish method.

It is in the making of sparkling wines that our Eastern vintners excel and have made a name for themselves. The two main grape varieties employed are the Catawba and Delaware. Wines from hybrid grapes are now also used more and more in the blends of Finger Lakes Champagnes and one winery is even using some Pinot Chardonnay in its *cuvée*. The major Champagne

Champagne

districts east of the Rockies are located in the Finger Lakes region of New York and in the small area about Sandusky, Ohio, on Lake Erie.

The American Champagnes which enjoy the greatest repute are all produced in the same manner as the wines of Champagne, France, by means of the secondary fermentation in the bottle. However, the wines reach maturity fairly quickly; after a year of development in the bottle many are ready for marketing but some higher priced brands are aged longer. These wines are clean, have a fine definite flavor, and are most satisfactory examples of quality viniculture.

Sparkling wines are also made by fermenting the wine in large tanks and bottling under pressure. This method is known as the Charmat process or "bulk fermentation" method. Wines made in this manner cannot be labeled "Champagne" but must, under our regulatory laws, be labeled "Champagne style," "Champagne type," or "American Champagne—bulk process." There are more California Champagnes made by this method than in the East.

Bulk-process fermentation has the advantage of saving several years in making the wine available for the market, and consequently is much less costly to produce, but by the same token certain quality factors are sacrificed. The gas does not really become a component part of the wine and tends to escape more rapidly once the bottle is opened. Furthermore, while the basic quality of the Champagne derives from the quality of the still wine employed, its character is influenced and enhanced by the maturation time the Champagne remains aging in contact with the yeast. Obviously, this is minimal in the case of bulk-process production.

There is still another type of sparkling wine made that is artificially carbonated—by adding the carbonic acid gas in much the same way in which soda-pop is made. It cannot be called or labeled "Champagne." It must be labeled "Carbonated Wine."

Cold Duck   The name gives no clue to what it is, yet it has become one of the most popular items all over the country. Cold Duck is a combination of Champagne and Sparkling Burgundy. The story goes that it originated in Bavaria among the hunting set where it was customary to drink Champagne before starting off. Much of it was left in the open bottles, and when the hunters returned, rather than waste it, they mixed it with cold Sparkling Burgundy and called it "Kalte Ende"—Cold End. Before long the "Ende" became "ente," and the Americans translated it literally into Cold Duck.

A couple of wineries in Michigan got the idea to blend the two wines and bottle it. A winery in the East marketed it nationally, and before long everyone got on the band wagon both here and abroad. There is even a Kosher Cold Duck called "Kalta Katchka" which means the same thing. Alcoholic content—12 per cent by volume.

Prices will vary according to the quality of the wine and the method of production. Some are "bottle fermented" while others are made by the Charmat process, which is "bulk fermentation." Read the label.

KOSHER WINES

THE big sale developed in recent years for commercially produced kosher wines is due primarily to the intensive advertising and merchandising effort made by the two or three principal firms specializing in the production of these wines. At the same time it must be recognized that the product must have a wide appeal to the consuming public, or all the advertising and salesmanship in the world would not produce its continuing popularity.

Quality-wise they are quite satisfactory. They are not inexpensive but in our opinion their ready acceptance and wide sale comes from the fact that they are sweet to the taste. The average consumer who has never tasted wine will naturally find their sweetness more appealing to his palate than the very dry red or white table wines of California and Europe. Sampling these wines he finds a beverage with a pleasant, fruity bouquet and flavor and at the same time a rich sweetness in taste. "The proof of the pudding is" that the sale of these wines is reputed to be about four million cases a year.

Although producers of kosher wines offer a wide assortment including Champagne, sparkling wines, table wines, and fruit wines, far and away their largest seller is the wine they make from the Concord grape. While they are made under Rabbinical supervision and meet all Talmudic stipulations for the making of pure, unmixed wine, when the trade speaks of kosher wine it is referring to the sweetened Concord grape wine. It is generally sweetened through the addition of cane sugar.

One thing is certain, the consumption of kosher wines is no longer confined to people of one religious faith. It is also interesting to know that in recent years Israel has had to ship wines labeled "Concord" to satisfy the demand of their American customers, although the wines so labeled do not resemble American Concord wine at all.

Beautiful mountain setting for a Northern California vineyard. (Courtesy Wine Institute, San Francisco, Calif.)

15. California Wines

THE records show that in the year 1518 Cortez, the Spanish conqueror and overlord of Mexico, ordered the establishment of a wine industry in the New World, obliging holders of land grants to plant one thousand vines per year for five years, for every hundred Indians living on the land. This agricultural program proved so successful that the mother country, fearing harm to her own wine industry, ordered wine growing stopped and decreed that wine not imported from Spain should be considered contraband. Like all prohibitions, it failed in its purpose. The vines once planted continued to bear their fruit and wine was made surreptitiously.

Eventually the Spanish colonizers pushed west and then north, into what is today California. This movement was led by the missionaries, whose primary object was the propagation of the Faith.

history

It was only natural that when the Church established its missions with their surrounding settlements, vines should be planted. The Franciscan *padres*, led by Fray Junipero Serra, planted grapes in California as early as 1769 at the San Diego Mission . . . and for the first time found soil in North America where the European vine would prosper and produce good wine. The arid lands of northern Mexico and Lower California did not, and still do not lend themself graciously to viticulture.

The Franciscan missionaries built twenty-one missions, reaching as far north as Sonoma, the northern terminus of the *Camino Real*, i.e., the "King's Highway." Descendants of the vines planted at these missions are still growing. Their largest winery was at the Mission of San Gabriel, near present-day Los Angeles, and the original adobe winery building, where the Indians trod the grapes, still exists with its three wine presses. There too, the famous Trinity vine, planted by the Franciscans, flourished and bore grapes for over 170 years.

Until 1824 the Franciscans were the only wine producers in California. They did not attempt commercial production, confining their efforts to their own sacramental and table needs. At that time one Joseph Chapman, an American,

189

settled near Los Angeles and planted 4,000 vines. He was followed in 1831 by a Bordeaux Frenchman, Jean Louis Vignes, who was shortly producing very excellent wine and brandy. Soon thereafter, a substantial vineyard was established in Sonoma in 1832, by an Indian who grew grapes for sacramental wine for the northernmost of the missions—San Francisco de Solano. Vignes, meantime, was so successful that by 1840 he was chartering vessels to ship his wine and brandy to the ports of Santa Barbara, Monterey, and San Francisco. However, the trade was still small. Then came the Gold Rush of 1849 and with it a boom in all activities. The widening of the market made it financially possible for still another and most important change to be brought about in California wines.

The vines the missionaries planted came from those varieties originally brought to Mexico from Spain during the preceding three centuries. While they were true viniferas, their value for wine making was limited. As a matter of fact, through the years these vines have lost their original European varietal identity, and they are today known and classified as the Mission.

Because the soil and climate of California were so hospitable to the European *vitis vinifera* family of vines, no serious attempt has been made to cultivate the wine growing of our own native American varieties in California, and all grapes grown there, whether for wine, table, or raisin use are from viniferas.

Vignes brought over choice vinifera cuttings from France which prospered in his vineyard, and others then did likewise, but it was not until after the arrival of that amazing gentleman, Count Agoston Haraszthy, in 1849—a sort of "Johnny Appleseed" to the California grape vine—that a real wine industry was developed.

The tireless and far-sighted Haraszthy convinced John G. Downey, the Governor of California, of the important part the wine industry could play in the development of the economy of the new State. As a result, he was sent to Europe in 1861 to select and bring back the widest possible selection of European (vinifera) grape varieties. He returned with over 100,000 cuttings of some 1,400 varieties and in the space of a few short years he had a vineyard in the Sonoma valley with 85,000 vines developed from imported stocks, and a nursery of 460,000 vines. With this effort he set the course for commercial wine growing from which those who have followed him have not deviated.

Haraszthy experimented at his Sonoma valley vineyard and nursery, selecting those vines which showed greatest promise. These were then sold or distributed in all sections of the state. Although at first the wines obtained were rather indifferent, it was not long before the vintners learned to improve their product and were obtaining good, sound, drinkable wine which improved in quality each year. By 1875 California was producing four million gallons of wine a year.

WINE REGIONS
OF
CALIFORNIA

OREGON

NEVADA

NORTH AND CENTRAL COASTAL REGION

Ukiah
Asti
St. Helena
Santa Rosa
Rutherford
Sonoma
Napa
Lodi
San
Francisco
Livermore
Saratoga
San Jose
Los Gatos
Pinnacles
SAN BENITO DISTRICT
MONTEREY DISTRICT

GREAT CENTRAL VALLEY

Fresno
Tulare
Delano

PACIFIC OCEAN

SOUTHERN CALIFORNIA REGION

San Gabriel
ONTARIO
Cucamonga
CUCAMONGA
Los Angeles
ESCONDIDO
Escondido
San Diego

MEXICO

California wine began to acquire a character of its own, and the custom of estate bottling was practiced at some of the best vineyards. In 1895 some 15,000,000 gallons of wine were being made, and most of it was being shipped to other parts of the United States, Mexico, Central America, and Asia.

Gaining confidence in their early success, the vintners began to compete with the European producers and by 1900 they had won gold, silver, and bronze medals, a few blue ribbons, and even grand prizes at the international expositions. Many of the great names associated with the development of California and the Pacific Coast were actively engaged in the wine industry as vineyard owners. They were men like Leland Stanford, George Hearst, James G. Fair, Elias "Lucky" Baldwin, John Sutter, and James Marshall, to mention only a few of the men who made both history and wine in California.

setbacks　　But, as we have pointed out at the beginning of Chapter 4, "Wine in General," the vintner's life is not an easy one. It is a continual struggle against the ravages of the elements, disease, and countless other enemies. The vineyards of California were and are no more immune to these misfortunes than those of other wine regions of the world. So it happened that one day in 1874 a vineyard in Sonoma County was found to be withering from an unknown ailment. Soon other vineyards became similarly affected, and in less than five years the vineyards of Sonoma, Napa, Yolo, El Dorado, and Placer counties were being ravaged by the same blight. The villain turned out to be our own American (phylloxera) grape louse, to which we have referred on page 15. We had quite innocently exported it to Europe on American root stocks and then reimported it into California on the European cuttings.

Still another plague showed up at Anaheim, south of Los Angeles, where a group of vintners of German background had founded a vineyard colony. In 1884 when the mysterious disease struck, the colony had extensive vineyards and eight wineries which were producing over a million gallons of fine-quality wine annually. This ailment which has since become known as the Anaheim disease destroyed every vine in the short space of three years, and the vineyards of Anaheim have never been replanted.

In order to learn the cause and find the remedy for these blights, the California State Board of Viticultural Commissioners was set up in 1880. This agency not only helped to conquer the plant diseases but also did much to improve wine quality and production practices. It also sponsored an experimental station for grape growing and wine production under the auspices of the College of Agriculture of the University of California. This station, located today at Davis, California, has continued its research work and the teaching of viticulture and viniculture. It is considered one of the leading research establishments in its field and is visited by students and scientists from all the wine regions in the world.

One of the University's most important contributions to the wine industry was the development of a disease-resistant root stock called *Rupestris St. George.* Produced in California in collaboration with French scientists, *Rupestris St. George,* with its appropriate variants, is now the basic root stock of all the great vineyards of the world in France, Germany, and California itself.

These were plagues visited upon the vineyards by Mother Nature but they were as nothing compared to the man-made blight which befell the vines as a result of the nineteenth or Prohibition Amendment to the U.S. Constitution which came into force on January 1, 1919.

Thousands upon thousands of acres of vineyards that had been laboriously planted to fine wine-producing varieties, unsuited for any other uses, had to be uprooted and replanted with other crops. This period lasted fifteen years. In 1934, after Repeal, the whole process had to be reversed and the vineyards replanted anew with wine-producing varieties.

Since it takes time for new vines to come into production, and the immediate post-Repeal demand far exceeded supply, many of the wines produced and shipped from California were of necessity of indifferent quality. However, all this has long since changed. In ever-increasing number and quantity fine wines of outstanding quality are being produced, and it is generally accepted that present-day wines are on the whole superior to those California produced prior to 1919 . . . and that some of her premium wines are finer than anything available in the "old days." This is due in great part to the efforts made by the wine producers themselves, to the severe regulations governing standards of quality that have been adopted, and finally to the discriminating taste of the consuming public, which, in the last analysis, is the only effective arbiter in questions of quality.

In California, the climate, soil, and general condition of almost every *geography* viticultural region in the world can be duplicated, for the seven hundred miles of vineyard extend over mountain slopes, irrigated deserts, lush inland valley floors, and the moist plains of the coast. Naturally, the vintner has no difficulty in obtaining a Claret from the Cabernet grape, when he grows it in one of the northern coastal counties.

Every important European grape variety, indeed, can be grown successfully in California by grafting it on the hardy, phylloxera-resisting native root stocks, and every European type has its California prototype.

Viticulturally, California is composed of three great regions: First, the north and central coastal counties grouped around the San Francisco Bay area; secondly, the great central valley; and finally the southern California area.

In the equable climate of the northern and central coastal counties are produced the best table wines. Lying in Sonoma County against the Maya-camas range separating Napa and Sonoma counties is one of the most beautiful valleys in California—the Valley of the Moon. Jack London was a great lover of this locality and many of his stories are centered around it.

The grape and the plum are the two biggest crops, but the valley is rich in everything that California sunshine can grow. It is not artificially irrigated and the best natural wines come from this section.

The Napa valley vineyard district produces wines which are well balanced, not too heavy. The reds resemble Bordeaux rather than Burgundy, the whites are finer than the Sonoma wines. The grapes grow on the valley bottom and on the lower slopes of the hills, averaging a yield of one and one-half to three tons of grapes per acre.

The Sonoma, 40 miles north of San Francisco, produces full-bodied red wines, particularly Cabernet Sauvignon and Pinot Noir, and in recent years, white wines of increasing excellence, particularly Pinot Chardonnay.

The Livermore valley, east of San Francisco, in the arid hills, has a gravelly soil like that of the Graves district in France. Its red wines are soft and mature early, while the white wines are much superior, being full and very fine. Here, the older growers follow French methods of cultivation. Fermentation of the finer growths is carefully watched, separation of the vintages is practiced, and the wine is allowed to develop and mature in accordance with its natural intrinsic worth rather than according to a fixed commercial standard.

In the foothills and on the lower slopes of the Santa Cruz mountains, thirty to seventy miles south of San Francisco, as well as in the hills overlooking Santa Clara valley, grapes are grown from which a fine quality wine is made.

Three new areas have been developed in the north coast counties for production of fine wines in California. This has come about due to two factors. First is the unprecedented prosperity of the California grape growers and the wineries. Second is the fact that intensive industrialization of the counties surrounding southern San Francisco Bay and the equally intensive urbanization of the Livermore, Napa, and Sonoma valleys are steadily making the home vineyard lands of the old established wineries too valuable for further extension into farming purposes.

First of the new districts is the Salinas and adjoining valleys of San Benito and Monterey counties, where thousands of acres of new vineyards are under cultivation. Some of this land had formerly been in lettuce production and some was cattle range. When the viticulturists of the University of California classified this region as suitable from the standpoint of temperature and soil to produce quality grapes, a vast underground sprinkler system was installed to supplement the light rainfall. Here the Paul Masson, Almaden, Mirassou, and Wente Wineries have established extensive plantations of fine varietal grapes.

Similarly, the pressure of urbanization with its tidal wave of new subdivisions, shopping districts, and super highways has caused some of the major wineries of the Napa valley to establish new vineyards in undeveloped lands

ABOVE. *The most modern method known for planting a vineyard. Five rows of new vines are planted simultaneously at Pinnacles vineyard.* (Courtesy Paul Masson Vineyards, San Francisco, Calif.)

BELOW. *A terraced California vineyard nestled high in the foothills. California is blessed with ideal growing conditions for many of the world's finest wine grapes.* (Courtesy Wine Institute, San Francisco, Calif.)

along the northern rim of San Francisco Bay at the Napa-Sonoma County line. This group includes Beaulieu, Beringer Brothers, Louis M. Martini, and Buena Vista Winery, Inc. (the latter owned by Young's Market Company of Los Angeles and not to be confused with Buena Vista Vineyards). This area is just now yielding its initial crops.

The third and newest vineyard area is being established by conversion of the prune orchards of the Alexander valley and of the nearby and misnamed Dry Creek valley in northern Sonoma County. Here, Widmer's Wine Cellars of Naples, New York, has made its debut as a major California grower, in conjunction with the R. T. French Company of Rochester, New York.

The counties of the great central valley—Sacramento, San Joaquin, Merced, Fresno, Madera, Tulare, Kings, and Kern—are hot, must be irrigated, and are more suitable for producing the vast quantities of sweet dessert wines the market requires.

Los Angeles, San Bernardino, and Riverside counties form a region known as the Cucamonga district, which, together with the southern coastal county of San Diego—the Escondido district—make up the third section. The latter two districts, in which the soils, climate, and altitudes at which the vineyards are located differ from those of the central valley, produce some unusual table

A mechanical grape harvester stands in a California vineyard where it is used to pick grapes of perfect ripeness to be made into wine. The grapes, which are crushed on board the harvester, are pumped into a tanker which moves alongside the harvester as it travels down vineyard rows. This immediate crushing assures that the fresh grape juice will arrive at the winery in the best possible condition. (Courtesy Wine Institute, San Francisco, Calif.)

Skilled hands of vineyard worker prepare to gather ripe cluster of Cabernet Sauvignon grapes during harvest season. (Courtesy Wine Institute, San Francisco, Calif.)

wines in addition to the larger quantities of dessert wines for which they are best known. Here they require very little, if any, irrigation.

California may be further subdivided into the following ten districts:

Sonoma—Mendocino. Directly north of San Francisco. It grows all types, but here are obtained primarily red and white table wines and Champagnes.

Napa Valley—Solano County. North of San Francisco. Best known for its fine red and white table wines, although dessert wines are produced.

Livermore—Contra Costa. Just east of San Francisco. Livermore Valley is famous for its white table wines, especially Sauternes, but good red table wines are produced, as well as dessert wines.

Santa Clara—San Benito—Santa Cruz—Monterey. Just south of San Francisco. White and red table wines, sparkling wines, and dessert wines.

Lodi—Sacramento. The northern section of the great central valley. Best known for its dessert wines, but also grows table wines.

Escalon—Modesto. Central portion of the central valley. Primarily a producer of dessert wines, but table wines as well.

Fresno—San Joaquin valley. The southern part of the great valley. Here are produced most of California's dessert wines. Some table wine and Champagne is also produced.

Southern California embraces three distinct districts, namely, Cucamonga, Ontario, east of Los Angeles County, the second district, and the San Diego-Escondido district. All are primarily dessert wine producers, but table wines and Champagne are also made in the region.

California is producing an ever-increasing number of fine premium wines which are bottled and marketed. But, as is to be expected, the quantity is not large in relation to the total amount of wine sold.

Whereas in most other wine-producing countries, discussed in the foregoing chapters, each region or district is devoted to the production of only one wine type, or at most two, in California not only are most wine types produced in each district but often the wines produced in one district are blended with those of one or several other districts. As a result, great continuity and uniformity of quality can be obtained, even though in attaining this objective the individuality of vintage variations is sacrificed. This is the answer to why California wines do not bear vintage dates, as a general rule. A vintage date has no reason to be of interest unless one vintage is very much different from another. Of course, there is also the factor of more uniform weather conditions in all of California than is the case, for example, in any given wine region in Europe.

GRAPE VARIETIES

THE principal grape varieties employed to produce the various types of wine in California are the following:

TO PRODUCE RED WINES

Aleatico	Grenache	Pinot St. George
Alicanté Bouschet	Grignolino	Pinot Noir
Aramon	Gros Manzenc	Raboso Piave
Barbera	Malbec	Refosco
Beclan	Malvoisie	Ruby Cabernet
Cabernet Sauvignon	Marzemino	St. Macaire
Carignane	Mataro	Sangioveto
Charbono	Merlot	Tannat
Duriff	Mondeuse	Valdepeñas
Gamay	Mourestel	Verdot
Gamay Beaujolais	Petite Sirah	Zinfandel

TO PRODUCE WHITE WINES

Aligoté	Malvasia Bianca	Rieslings
Burger	Marsanne	Emerald Riesling
Chasselas Doré	Melon	Franken Riesling
(Golden Chasselas)	Meunier	Grey Riesling
Chenin blanc	Müller-Thurgau	Johannesberg Riesling
(Pineau Blanc de	Muscadelle du	White Riesling
la Loire)	Bordelais	Sauvignon Blanc
Clairette Blanche	Muscat Frontignan	Sauvignon Vert
Flora	Nebbiola	Semillon
Folle Blanche	Negrara Gattinara	Sylvaner
French Colombard	Palomino	Traminer
Gewürztraminer	Pinot Blanc	Ugni Blanc (Trebbiano)
Green Hungarian	Pinot Chardonnay	Veltliner
Gutedel		Vernaccia Sarda
Kleinberger		Pedro Ximenez

Data recorded on each carved cask of wine aging in this California winery cellar is carefully checked by a worker. (Courtesy Wine Institute, San Francisco, Calif.)

TO PRODUCE DESSERT WINES

Aleatico	Grillo	Palomino
Alicante Bouschet	Inzolia Bianca	Petite Bouschet
Alicante Ganzin	Malaga	Petite Sirah
Black Prince	Malmsey	Salvador
Boal di Madeira	Malvasia Bianca	Sauvignon Vert
Burger	Mission	Suzão Teroldico
Carignane	Mourisco Preto	Thompson Seedless
Cinsaut	Muscadelle	Tinta Madeira
Erbalus di Caluso	Muscat of Alexandria	Touriga
Feher Szagos	Muscat of Canelli	Trousseau
Fernaô Pires	Muscat of Frontignan	Valdepeñas
Flame Tokay	Muscat of Hamburg	Verdelho
Grand Noir	Muscat of St. Laurent	Xeres
Green Hungarian	Orange Muscat	Zinfandel
Grenache	Pagadebito	

Among the vast array of European *vitis vinifera* grape varieties grown in *varietal* California, those varieties most likely to be found on varietally labeled wines *wines* will be:

RED TABLE WINES

CABERNET SAUVIGNON: The outstanding claret grape, which produces very fine, big, full-bodied wines in California.

GAMAY: This is the informing grape from the Beaujolais. In California it makes a sprightly wine.

PINOT NOIR: The classic noble grape of Burgundy, which in California produces richly flavored wines.

ZINFANDEL: A California original, grown nowhere else, which produces fruity, spicy, zesty wines.

WHITE TABLE WINES

CHARDONNAY: The white grape of Burgundy and la Champagne, which produces some of the finest crisp, dry, white wines of California.

CHENIN BLANC: A fine variety from the Loire valley which produces a delicate fragrant wine in California.

FOLLE BLANCHE: At one time, the informing grape of the Cognac region. In California it gives a tart, dry, fruity light wine.

PINOT BLANC: Second only to the Chardonnay for good quality, crisp, dry white wines.

EMERALD RIESLING: A unique California hybrid of the white Riesling and Muscadelle. The wine produced from this variety is dry, clean, fresh, fruity, and tart, with a slight prickle on the tongue, suggesting it would like to sparkle.

GREY RIESLING: This is not a true Riesling, but rather the French *chauché gris* variety. In California its wine is soft and mildly spicy.

JOHANNISBERG RIESLING OR WHITE RIESLING: The true Riesling of Germany and one of the finest white wine grapes. It will appear as Johannisberg or Johannisberger Riesling upon wine labels rather than as White Riesling. California wines obtained from this variety will be fairly dry, elegant, with a fine fruity aroma and character.

SAUVIGNON BLANC AND SEMILLON: The classic varieties grown for white wine production in the Bordeaux region of France. These varieties produce in California the medium sweet soft wines with a fruity aroma and flavor and fair richness of body.

SYLVANER OR FRANKEN RIESLING: A variety of German origin, it produces fairly delicate, pleasant wines. It is the most widely used grape in California for the making of all Rhine wines under the general Riesling label.

TRAMINER (GEWÜRZTRAMINER): The wines from this variety possess a fine flowery, fruity aroma, and are usually medium dry. "Gewürz" means spicy, in German. When Traminer wines have it, they will be labeled Gewürztraminer.

ROSÉ WINES

CABERNET ROSÉ: The driest and most tart of all rosé wines, made of the most expensive grapes diverted to this classification, but increasing in popularity and acceptance.

GAMAY ROSÉ: The Beaujolais grape variety, which is used extensively in California to produce pleasant delicate rosés.

GRENACHE ROSÉ: This variety originates from the Rhône valley, France. It makes a fine, sprightly rosé in California.

MAKING OF THE WINE

AT the time of Repeal, American vintners were faced with many problems. During Prohibition nearly all their vineyards had been replanted with other crops or with table and raisin grapes. Repeal came suddenly. *Ipso facto,* overnight, on December 5, 1933, the day of Repeal, the vintner was expected to have wine ready for the thirsty American public, even though until then it was illegal to make wine commercially. Irrespective of what cold storage grapes were used, it still took time to crush the grapes and ferment the must and allow the wine to develop.

The first couple of post-Repeal years were very difficult for American wine producers. However, one problem that did not worry the vintner too much was the question of traditional production methods. With typical American ingenuity they set about resolving their production bottlenecks without fear or inhibition. New methods were tried. Some were discarded, but many were adopted and have become standard practice not only in the United States but in most wine regions of the world today.

Over the years since Repeal the studies and research work of men like Dr. Maynard A. Amerine, Harold H. Berg, Dr. William V. Cruess, Dr. M. A. Joslyn, Dr. Harold P. Olmo, Dr. Albert J. Winkler, and other great oenologists of the University of California at Davis have caused a revolution in viti-viniculture. Today, oenologists and vintners come from all over the world to study at Davis, California, with its experimental vineyards, winery, and distillery.

Uninhibited by grandfatherly tradition, they have made greater contributions to the vintners' science and art in the short period since Repeal than were made in the century since Louis Pasteur explained scientifically the process of vinous fermentation. The effect of their work on commercial wine production has been tremendous, both for the vintner and the consumer. The general quality of wine has been very much improved, within the limitations that soil and climatic conditions permit.

Beginning with wine-producing grape varieties, extensive studies have been made as to the varieties most suited for each wine region of California. In a compact Bulletin 794, titled *California Wine Grapes: Composition and Quality of Their Musts and Wines*, published in March 1963 by the University of California Division of Agricultural Sciences, Drs. M. A. Amerine and A. J. Winkler have analyzed and approved some fifty-one varieties, while rejecting or non-recommending another fifty-nine.

Methods of vinification and treatment for best-quality wine results are given for most of the varieties. Many of these new methods are in use commercially. Among them is stainless steel equipment for grape crushers and fermenting tanks, out in the open, exposed to the elements rather than inside the winery building proper. These out-of-doors fermenters are used only for the first or violent fermentation; the advantage of open-air fermentation is to hold down the natural heat of fermentation so that the open air breezes will blow away any insects which may have come to the crushers with the grapes from the field. Once the wines fall bright (clarify), they are racked into the traditional wood casks.

The method of making wine in California varies, of course, from vineyard to vineyard and region to region. It also depends to some extent upon the size of the vineyard. The smaller vineyards in the northern part of the state in the counties surrounding San Francisco Bay tend to follow the Old World methods, from gathering the grapes to bottling the wine. In the small vineyards of Europe, usually one type of wine is produced, not only in a single vineyard, but in an entire region. Very often the vintner will be a small farmer making, in some instances, only a few hogsheads of wine.

However, in California, where individual vineyards may run to thousands of acres and, in nearly all cases, produce several types and classes of wines, mass production is inevitable. Where the vineyards are extensive and enormous quantities of grapes ripen at the same time, it becomes humanly impossible to follow the rather simple Old World methods. Ergo, new, modern ones must be employed.

The grapes are trucked to the winery as soon as they are picked. After being examined and weighed, they are dumped onto conveyor belts which carry them to a power-driven de-stemmer and crusher. This breaks up the grape skins without breaking the seeds, allows the juice to run freely, and, finally, separates and throws out the stems.

In the making of red wines, the grapes and juice are conveyed directly to the fermenting vats; while in the making of white wine, as in Europe, the juice is separated from the skins before fermentation.

To assure a normal fermentation, as some of the saccharomycetes may have brushed off in transit, the natural yeasts are assisted by the addition of pure culture yeasts—*saccharomycetes ellipsoideus*. Temperature is controlled and the fermenting must is never permitted to go over 85° F., in order to obtain a healthy fermentation. Also, higher temperatures, aside from causing imperfect fermentation, contribute to loss of bouquet and facilitate the action and development of the *mycodermae asceti*, the vinegar-producing bacteria.

The first, or violent, fermentation takes about a week, after which the still fermenting must is run off into closed oak or California redwood vats or stainless steel tanks to complete fermentation. In some California wineries, cement or concrete fermenting tanks are employed. This final fermentation period takes from three to six weeks for both red and white wines.

dessert wines   However, in the production of dessert wines such as Sherry, Port, Muscatel, Angelica, etc., fermentation is arrested before all of the natural sugar of the must has been converted. The alcoholic content is brought up to 19.5 to 20 per cent by the addition of California brandy, that in many cases is distilled by the brandy distillery associated with the winery itself. The wines are aged in large vats or casks and are treated in the same manner as are similar wines all over the world. They are racked periodically so that the wine will not remain on its lees, and then fined and filtered as necessary.

Sherry   California Sherry is obtained by a special treatment or method which was developed in California. When fermentation is arrested in the new wine, it is not cellared in the same manner as other dessert wines. In order to impart the characteristic Sherry flavor it is stored at a high temperature, i.e., it is "baked." This is done by racking the wine into large oak or redwood casks or vats, which sometimes hold 20,000 to 30,000 gallons each, located in cellars where carefully controlled temperatures are maintained. The wine is kept in these baking cellars anywhere from three to six months, at temperatures that will vary from 100° to 140° Fahrenheit, depending upon the length of time the wine is baked. Naturally, wine kept for only three months will be held at a higher temperature and vice versa. Each producer has his own formula for the method that gives the best results. The vats are heated, in some cases by hot water coils in the vat itself, while in other cases the entire cellar room is heated to the desired controlled temperature. In some instances producers obtain like results by the use of smaller cooperage and letting the sun do the baking, through leaving the casks in the open.

The baking process caramelizes the residual sugars, causes the color to deepen somewhat, gives the wine the desired slightly bitter tang, and develops the typical "nutty" flavor of California Sherries.

Upon completion of the baking process the wine is allowed to cool slowly to cellar temperature. It is then stored for aging and treated like other dessert wines to acquire mellowness and to be blended with older wines, and eventually be bottled and marketed.

The essential difference in the method of producing this type of wine between California and the Jerez region of Spain lies in the secondary "flowering" fermentation described on page 138, which occurs in Jerez. It is interesting to note that some California producers have wineries that have had considerable success with "flowering," using film yeast that has given them some unusually fine rancio or nutty flavored Sherries. However, it is apparent that the American public still prefers the traditional "California" type, although with time it could very well be that it will learn to like film yeast Sherries.

Vermouth and the other "aromatized" appetizer wines of California are produced according to the traditional methods described in Chapter 12.

Champagne and the other sparkling wines are produced in California along the lines explained in the previous chapter on American Wines.

Generally speaking, it should be noted that at the large mass production wineries, the most modern and improved methods of treatment of the standard wines are in use, such as refrigeration, to ensure a perfectly bright natural wine . . . a healthy wine, free from heavy sediment.

It must be remembered that wine, table wine in particular, is never standing still. It is constantly developing; minute changes are taking place. This is due to the action of the yeasts that remain in the wine, to the acids, the solids, and the other components of the wine acting and reacting, some with, and others against each other. The result is a state of continual change. One of the natural phenomena of the development of a wine is the crystallization of the bitartrates, which settle in the form of sediment. In the cask, this sediment forms the lees, while in the bottle it forms either a loose sediment or a firm crust. This can be hastened if the wine is held at a low temperature for a short period of time. It is accomplished through refrigeration and ensures a wine that after filtering will be less likely to throw any further sediment or deposit, and therefore less subject to damage from sharp changes of temperature after bottling.

But since the consuming public has become accustomed to seeing so much brilliant, sediment-free wine offered, it has come to believe that a wine that has a very natural sediment or deposit is a wine that is not in good condition for serving, and by the same token, too many retail merchants, rather than explain the facts to their customers, take the easier path and claim against the supplier for refund or replacement of the "unsaleable" wine.

CLASSES AND TYPES OF WINES*

CALIFORNIA is so rich in variety of natural soils and climates that any European wine region finds its counterpart there, and almost every known species of European grape (*vitis vinifera*) may be found; consequently every European wine has its California prototype. The classes and types of California wines have been established by the Wine Institute and the Wine Advisory Board (both of California). Wines are divided into five main classes. Appetizer Wines, Red Table Wines, White Table Wines, Sweet Dessert Wines, and Sparkling Wines.

* Explanatory Note. Lest the reader be confused by what appears to be a direct contradiction to the classification of wines, which appears on page 7 in Chapter 2, "Definitions," we wish to point out that the classifications given above are those adopted and advocated by the Wine Institute. They are included here because they rightfully form part of the California story.

We should also explain at this point that the term "fortified," which has long been and is still used throughout the English-speaking world to describe wines that have brandy added to them for the purpose of arresting fermentation, or simply to increase the alcoholic content above that at which wines will normally ferment out, cannot legally be used in the United States, a rule in effect since 1939, when Regulations No. 4 relating to Labeling and Advertising of Wine (Bureau of Alcohol, Tobacco, and Firearms of U.S. Treasury Department), were adopted, and which include the statement that no advertisement for wine, label, wrapper, container, etc., can contain: "Any statement, design, device, or representation which relates to alcoholic content, or which tends to create the impression that the wine has been 'fortified.'"

The reasons for this were several. It was found, in the first years after Repeal, that a fringe element of the trade, dealers who through ignorance or lack of ethics were promoting or rather exploiting the sale of these wines on the basis of their alcoholic content rather than the basic quality of the wine itself. Also, to Americans during the Prohibition era the word had the connotation of "spiked," and, as a matter of fact, the "spiked beer" of that period was labeled "fortified."

These winery workers "rack" a tank of wine into smaller wooden casks where the wine will continue aging and developing into a delightful smoothness before it is bottled. "Racking" or transferring by pump from a larger to a smaller container, also helps clear the wine of any sediment acquired during fermentation to insure that the wine is brilliantly clear when it reaches the consumer. (Courtesy Wine Institute, San Francisco, Calif.)

California wines fall into two categories: *generics* and *varietals*. Generics are merely generalized wine types, all too often with borrowed names such as Chablis, Claret, and Burgundy from the French, Rhine and Hock from the German, and Chianti from the Italian.

Varietals are the royalty of vintages, each named for the grape variety from which it is made. The premium wineries of the State are successfully diverting California wine tastes into the varietals such as Cabernet Sauvignon, Pinot Noir, or Zinfandel in the reds, and Pinot Chardonnay, Gewürztraminer, and White Riesling in the whites.

Under California regulations a wine bearing a varietal name on the label must be produced from at least 51 per cent of the named variety and in many cases it will be made from 100 per cent of the type of grape used. These wines are under close Federal inspection to guarantee that the wine is exactly as labeled. Here are the various types, of both classes:

GENERICS RED TABLE WINES	VARIETALS RED TABLE WINES
Claret	Barbera
Burgundy	Cabernet Sauvignon
Chianti	Zinfandel
	Charbono
	Gamay
	Gamay Beaujolais
	Pinot Noir
	Petite Sirah
	Grignolino
	Grenache
	Pinot St. George (Red Pinot)
	Merlot
	Aleatico
	Carignane

GENERICS WHITE TABLE WINES	VARIETALS WHITE TABLE WINES
Rhine Wine	Chenin Blanc
Sauterne	° Franken Riesling or Sylvaner
Moselle	Gewürztraminer or Traminer
Hock	Green Hungarian
Chablis	Grey Riesling
White Chianti	Johannisberger Riesling
Muscat	Pinot Blanc
Riesling	Pinot Chardonnay
	Sauvignon Blanc
ROSÉ WINES (are in a class by	Semillon
themselves. In reality, since	Flora
they do not come from a par-	Emerald Riesling
ticular region, they are only	Malvasia Bianca
a varietal when made from a	French Colombard
particular grape variety,	Sauvignon Veit
such as—	Ugni Blanc
Grenache Rosé	Golden Chasselas
Gamay Rosé	Folle Blanche
Cabernet Rosé	
Zinfandel Rosé	
Grignolino Rosé	

° If the wine is labeled "Riesling" it is usually made from the Franken Riesling grape.

In a broad general sense, California produces the following appetizer, dessert, and sparkling wines, which fall between the two categories:

APPETIZER WINES	DESSERT WINES	SPARKLING WINES
Sherry—Pale Dry, Dry Flor	Port—Tawny, Ruby, and White	Champagne
Madeira	Muscatel	Pink Champagne
Marsala	Tokay	Sparkling Burgundy
Vermouth	Malaga	Cold Duck
	Sweet Vermouth	
	Angelica	
	Cream Sherry	
	Medium Flor Sherry	
	Dry Flor Sherry	
	Palomino	

CLASSES OF CALIFORNIA WINES

FORMERLY, California wines were classified as dry, sweet, or sparkling. "Dry" wines were table wines containing less than 14 per cent of alcohol; "sweet" wines were the wines containing up to 20 to 21 per cent of alcohol, irrespective of whether the wine itself had a dry or a sweet taste. Since this led to considerable confusion in the minds of the retail trade and the public, it was found desirable and practical to adopt a uniform classification that would be easily understood by everybody and especially by the consumer of wines.

A committee of the producers under the auspices of Wine Institute proposed the five classes, previously mentioned—Appetizer Wines, White Table Wines, Red Table Wines, Sweet Dessert Wines, and Sparkling Wines.

appetizer wines

Appetizer wines are those which, as the class name implies, are popularly used before meals as appetite sharpeners, such as Sherry (more often the drier types), Vermouth, or apéritif wines.

CALIFORNIA SHERRY is a wine that varies in color from rather pale, in the case of very dry wines produced by the "film-yeast" method, progressing through pale amber, to a very dark amber in the rich sweet wines. It is characterized by its nutty flavor.

CALIFORNIA MADEIRA and MARSALA are wines that resemble the sweeter Sherries. They are produced in a like manner and bear these labels for commercial reasons. California Marsala is generally the sweeter of the two.

CALIFORNIA VERMOUTH is not marketed just as California Vermouth, but rather as the distinctive product of the brand owner who produces it. This is due to the fact that the aromatizing formula used by each producer is his very distinctive secret upon which he capitalizes. Both the dry straw-colored (French type) and sweet dark amber (Italian type) are produced and successfully marketed in ever-increasing volume.

white
table wines

White table wines, as the class name implies, are the light white beverage wines whose alcoholic content can be as low as 10 per cent, does not exceed 14 per cent, but will average about 12½ per cent. It is well to remember that while described as "white," there is no wine that is colorless. White wines vary from a very pale straw to a very dark brown. In taste they vary from the extreme bone dryness of Chablis and Rhine wine types, to the rich lusciousness of the Château-type Sauterne.

CALIFORNIA SAUTERNE (please note spelling without final "s") is usually a light, golden, full-bodied wine with a pleasantly dry taste. It is often labeled "Dry Sauterne."

CALIFORNIA SWEET SAUTERNE, HAUT SAUTERNE, or CHÂTEAU SAUTERNE is a fuller, quite sweet wine. Both the "dry" and "sweet" Sauterne of California are often produced from the traditional Sauvignon Blanc, Semillon, and Muscadelle grape varieties, but at many vineyards a wide assortment of the other white grape varieties listed on page 198 are used as well. Where the foregoing varieties are employed, the resulting wine is rich in fragrant bouquet.

CALIFORNIA SAUVIGNON BLANC and SEMILLON are Sauterne type wines, varietally named because at least 51 per cent of the grapes used in production are of the variety stipulated. Such wines possess the distinctive character which these grape varieties contribute to the perfume and flavor of the wine.

Modern outdoor fermenting tanks at Paul Masson *vineyard, Northern California.* (Courtesy Paul Masson Vineyards, San Francisco, Calif.)

Traditional oak and redwood storage vats, together with modern glass-lined steel tanks in California. (Courtesy Paul Masson Vineyards, San Francisco, Calif.)

CALIFORNIA RIESLING is generally a thoroughly dry, tart wine, with a pale straw color and the delicate fragrance of one of the Riesling grape varieties. There are several varietal California Rieslings available, such as Johannisberg (White Riesling), Traminer, Emerald Riesling, Sylvaner, and Grey Riesling.

CALIFORNIA RHINE WINE, HOCK, or MOSELLE is a light, dry, pale-colored wine resembling the Riesling, but obtained from other varieties whose characteristics are similar.

CALIFORNIA CHABLIS is a delicate straw-colored wine, slightly less tart and with more body than the Rhine wine type. It is generally made from the French grape varieties, principally the Pinot Blanc and the Chardonnay, but Burger, Golden Chasselas, Green Hungarian, and several other varieties are also used to produce Chablis.

CALIFORNIA WHITE CHIANTI is a somewhat dry, medium-bodied, fruity wine usually made from the Trebbiano and one of the muscat-flavored grapes. It is bottled in the traditional straw-covered Chianti bottle.

CALIFORNIA FOLLE BLANCHE, PINOT BLANC, CHARDONNAY, CHENIN BLANC, AND UGNI BLANC are wines of the Chablis type that are varietally named for the grapes from which they are made and possess their distinct characteristics. The Ugni Blanc is also known as the Trebbiano.

CALIFORNIA LIGHT MUSCAT, as the name implies, is a wine made from one of the various muscat varieties. They vary from very dry to very sweet, but all have the pronounced unmistakable muscat aroma. They are sometimes labeled with the exact varietal name of the grape from which they are produced, such as Moscato Canelli, Muscat Frontignan, etc.

red
table wines

Red table wines, like the white, are those whose alcoholic content does not exceed 14 per cent but which generally have about 12 to 12½ per cent. It is well to remember also at this point that any wine which contains any red coloring whatsoever, which is obtained from the grape skins that are allowed to remain in contact with the must during fermentation, is classified as a red wine. There are only two colors in wine—white and red—and red wines vary in color from the very pale pink-hued rosés to the very deep, inky reds of some Barberas.

CALIFORNIA CLARET and CALIFORNIA BURGUNDY are the two best-known red wines and enjoy great popularity in the market. They are bottled in the traditional Bordeaux and Burgundy bottle, illustrated among the bottle sketches on page 7). Claret is a dry, rich red, medium-bodied wine while Burgundy has a deeper, more ruby color, more body and flavor.

CALIFORNIA CHIANTI is a dry medium-bodied deep red and well-flavored wine of Italian character. On the whole we have found these wines to be softer, rounder and less *corsé* than the Italian originals. This wine is usually marketed in the traditional straw-covered Chianti bottle.

CALIFORNIA ZINFANDEL is a distinctly California wine of the Claret type. It is made from and possesses the distinctive fruity flavor, spiciness, and aroma of the Zinfandel grape.

CALIFORNIA BARBERA and BARBERONE are rather full-bodied wines, very deeply colored and having the distinct taste and aroma of the Barbera grape. *Barberone,* meaning literally "small Barbera," is a wine made with a lesser proportion of Barbera grapes.

CALIFORNIA CABERNET SAUVIGNON is the premier claret-type wine of California.

CALIFORNIA CARIGNANE and GRIGNOLINO, are Claret-type wines that have been made from and have the distinct taste and aroma of these grapes.

CALIFORNIA CHARBONO, RED PINOT, PINOT NOIR, and PETITE SIRAH are Burgundy-type wines made from and having the characteristic flavor and bouquet of the grapes named. The Charbono is a very full-bodied wine like a Barbera.

CALIFORNIA ALEATICO is a medium-sweet table wine having the fruity muscat perfume and flavor of the Aleatico grape.

CALIFORNIA GAMAY is a Beaujolais type wine that is lively and fruity with a delicate flavor.

CALIFORNIA ROSÉ is a rather dry, light-bodied wine, lightly colored pink to pale reddish, made pink by removing the skins from the fermenting must before they can impart all their coloring matter to the wine, usually 24 to

48 hours after the first fermentation begins, depending upon the amount of coloring desired in the wine. The Cabernet Gamay, Grenache, and Grignolino are the grape varieties usually preferred for making rosés. These wines have become very popular. They are always served chilled and are delightful, refreshing luncheon and summer wines.

California dessert wines include all the rich, sweet full-bodied wines, which *dessert wines* were formerly known in the trade as "sweet" wines. Their alcoholic content is usually 20 per cent, although for certain markets these wines are sometimes made with a lower alcoholic content. They range in taste from medium to very sweet, and include both white and red wines.

CALIFORNIA SHERRY is rich and sweet in taste, and very properly belongs among the dessert wines.

CALIFORNIA PORT is rightfully one of the more popular dessert wines. Its color will vary from deep red to tawny, and some White Port is also made. The Red Ports are made from a number of grape varieties well known for their high pigmentation, such as the Carignane, Trousseau, Petite Sirah, Zinfandel, to name a few, while the Tawny Ports are produced from grapes that are not so rich in color. White Port is generally obtained from the same grape varieties but the must is fermented without the grape skins. All California Port is very sweet in taste, having anywhere from 10 to 15 per cent of unfermented natural grape sugar in it.

CALIFORNIA MUSCATEL is a rich, sweet white wine possessing the tangy highly perfumed aroma and flavor of any one of the seven or eight muscat varieties cultivated in California. Most Muscatel is a golden color and is obtained primarily from the Muscat of Alexandria variety. Muscat Canelli or Moscato Canelli and Muscat Frontignan are Muscatel obtained from the grape varieties named. Red Muscatel and Black Muscatel are obtained from the Muscat St. Laurent and Muscat Hamburg grapes respectively, and Aleatico is a red Muscatel also.

CALIFORNIA TOKAY is an amber-colored blend of sweet wines, with a slight "nutty" flavor obtained from the Sherry included in the blend. California Tokay should not be confused with the Tokay of Hungary. The only connection is in the name, as it does not resemble it in any way. Nor does the wine get its name from the Flame Tokay grape, which may or may not be used in the production of California Tokay. Insofar as taste is concerned, it is sweeter than most Sherry but never as sweet as Port or Muscatel.

CALIFORNIA ANGELICA is, like the Tokay, a blend of several California dessert wines, but always on the *very* sweet side, having from 10 to 15 per cent unfermented sugar. It is a light-colored wine, ranging from a straw to medium amber. This wine was originated in California.

CALIFORNIA MALAGA is a deep or very dark amber-colored cordial-like wine, obtained in the same manner as Angelica.

sparkling wines   California sparkling wines include Champagne, Pink Champagne, Sparkling Burgundy, Sparkling Moscato, Sparkling Moselle, Sparkling Sonoma, etc. They are produced by the traditional French bottle-fermentation method, exchange method and by the modern Charmat process.

CALIFORNIA CHAMPAGNE is a pale straw to light gold color. In order to satisfy all tastes, the wines are marketed in varying degrees of sweetness, following French Champagne labeling practices, namely—brut, extra dry, dry, and sweet. Often the French equivalents are used on the label. California Champagne is made from a number of grape varieties such as the Pinot Noir, Pinot Blanc, Chardonnay, Folle Blanche, Saint Émilion, Sauvignon Vert, Burger, etc.

CALIFORNIA PINK CHAMPAGNE is a light pink in color. It is produced in the same manner as California Champagne except that it is made with pink or rosé wine.

CALIFORNIA SPARKLING BURGUNDY is a sparkling wine produced in the same way as California Champagne with red wine instead of white wine. It is usually semi-sweet or sweet in taste.

CALIFORNIA COLD DUCK is a combination of California Champagne and Sparkling Burgundy. It is usually semi-sweet or sweet in taste.

CALIFORNIA SPARKLING MOSELLE, SAUTERNE, MUSCAT, MALAVASIA BIANCA, ETC., as the names imply, are sparkling wines made from the white table wines indicated.

CARBONATED WINES are sparkling wines that are made effervescent by artificial carbonation, and are somewhat less expensive than naturally sparkling wines. Both white and red wines are used, and dry and sweet wines are offered.

BRANDY

IN every country of the world where wine is produced, brandy is distilled and California is no exception. Further, as is to be expected, brandies have been distilled from a wide variety of wines and by various methods. In other words, in the few years since Repeal, and they are very few in relation to brandy, no definitive criteria have yet been established as to the grape variety or wines best suited for the production of brandy, nor the ideal distillation method, either. However, progress has been made and it will not be very long before these questions will be answered to the satisfaction of the consumer.

In the meantime, the American public is buying more and more California brandy. In recent years California has provided over 75 per cent of all brandy consumed in the United States. This can only mean that Americans find it appeals to them and satisfies their taste.

California produces three basic types of brandy marketed as such besides the brandies that are distilled for, and are used to produce dessert wines, Vermouths, etc. These are:

CALIFORNIA BRANDY. A brandy produced and treated in somewhat the same manner as is described in Chapter 18, "Brandies," where we speak of the traditional methods followed in France.

The brandies are distilled out as between 140 and 170 proof; reduced to about 100 proof, for barreling; and aged for some years before blending, bottling and being offered for sale. They are matured in oak barrels.

Generally speaking, the beverage brandy of California has a very clean bouquet and taste. It has a character of its own and some unusual brandy of excellent quality is available in limited quantities.

CALIFORNIA MUSCAT BRANDY is brandy distilled from muscat wines, which has the marked bouquet and flavor of the muscat. California is one of the world's largest producers of quality Muscat Brandy.

CALIFORNIA GRAPPA or POMACE BRANDY is brandy distilled from the grape pomace, remaining after the juice is expressed for making wine. Following the Italian custom, Grappa is not aged and normally has very little color, usually being marketed as a white or colorless product.

Modern California outdoor grape crusher. (Courtesy Paul Masson Vineyards)

THE POST REPEAL DEVELOPMENT OF
THE WINE INDUSTRY IN THE UNITED STATES

PRIOR to 1919 the California and American Wine Industry was making slow but steady progress. Whereas in 1900 the record shows 30,100,000 gallons of wine were consumed in the United States, by 1919 consumption reached 55,000,000 gallons (12 per cent of which was imported wine), according to Report No. 134, Second Series, of the United States Tariff Commission. Based on a population of slightly over 100,000,000, this was a per capita consumption of .54 gallons.

Since Repeal in 1933, wine has made steady healthy progress, reaching a per capita consumption of over one and a half gallons. This is not very impressive when compared to per capita consumption figures of fifteen to thirty gallons for wine-consuming countries like Argentina, Chile, France, Germany, Italy, Portugal, etc. However, the most encouraging wine consumption trend which has developed in the United States during the decade of the sixties is the steady, sharp increase in consumption of light table wines containing 14 per cent or less of alcohol. Consumption of these wines is expanding at a rate of between 7 and 8 per cent each year.

All of this is due to several factors. One is that the public is taking a greater interest in wine, possibly in answer to the wealth of advertising which has appeared in the press, radio, and television. Another is the opportunity which so many of our citizens in the armed forces had during their foreign service to sample wine, and, more important perhaps, to observe peoples in other lands who use wine as a regular part of their diet. Following the example of the French, Italian, and other wine-drinking peoples, they too learned to enjoy a glass of wine with their meals, and continued to follow this custom after they returned to their homes.

Still another reason, of a similar nature, is the great increase in travel abroad during the post-war years. The administrator of one of the monopoly state operations told me that he can tell when summer tourists have returned, by the number of "special orders" that flood his office for some particular wine or spirit that the citizens of his state have tasted and liked while on their trip.

The Wine Institute, founded after Repeal, has developed into a very efficient instrument of the industry. Under the able leadership of its management, distribution and merchandising have been organized on an intelligent and effective basis. Practically all California producers are united within Wine Institute as members, and, as a result, subscribe to the self-regulation that has produced such excellent results. Wine Institute has also succeeded in obtaining much of the favorable wine legislation which has been passed in the several States.

Under the Federal Agricultural Adjustment Act of 1933 various states were permitted to pass legislation setting up organizations for the orderly marketing of agricultural products. In 1937 the California legislature enacted the California Marketing Act which permitted the establishment of the Wine Advisory Board, for the purpose of advertising and promoting the marketing of wine. Under this Act the funds for the maintenance of the Wine Advisory Board and its programs are obtained by a special fixed gallonage tax on all wine produced in California. Through this tax substantial sums have been made available to the Wine Advisory Board through the years, with which it conducts an aggressive advertising campaign in favor of California wine, maintains field offices and staffs throughout the country, and conducts an educational program to train all those actively engaged in the marketing of wine to the trade and the public. A free correspondence Wine Study Course was started several years ago in which over a million students have enrolled and more than 200,000 Certificates of Merit have gone out to students who have completed the course satisfactorily. In addition, they have prepared for free distribution to the trade and public a series of handbooks on the uses of wine.

All of this type of work, with time, will produce beneficial results for the entire Wine Trade. There are still many obstacles to overcome, not the least of which is the high taxes levied at almost every step wine makes, from the vineyard to the consumer's table.

We shall not think of light wine as a food until we can buy it in a food store. The only way that naturally fermented wines should be used is with food. It is possible to buy it in food stores in several of the states but not in the most populous—New York and Pennsylvania—to name two. As it is now, wine must either be retailed by specially franchised outlets, which by law cannot engage in any other business, or, as in Pennsylvania, by the state itself. This tends to make wine-drinking a luxury.

Despite the fact that while wine is a food and highly taxed as an alcoholic beverage, the demand for California wines is overwhelming the state's productive capacity. The 1972 annual per capita consumption of 1.61 gallons compares interestingly with the figure of .90 gallons per capita when the preceding edition of this Guide was printed in 1964.

16. Other Wines

WINES OF OTHER LANDS

LUXEMBURG

THE principality of Luxemburg—999 square miles—is surrounded by Belgium on the west and north, Germany on the east, and France on the south, separated from the two last by the bed of the Moselle River. Actually, the Upper Moselle portion of the German Moselle wine regions begins at Wasserbillig, Luxemburg, so wines produced on the opposite bank must be considered Moselle wines just as the German wines are. But, before World War II, Luxemburg wines were, for the most part, consumed within the Duchy while young, and without benefit of bottling. During the last two decades, however, an effort has been made to promote their sales outside the country.

Luxemburg wine bottle labels carry, according to law, name designations of the following three types:

Vin de la Moselle Luxembourgeoise used in combination with the grape variety. This is what appears on most common wines; e.g., *Vin de la Moselle Luxembourgeoise Riesling.*

Locality name, with or without vineyard site, and the grape variety; e.g., *Machtum Sylvaner; Riesling from the Elterberg vineyard near Wormeldange.*

Appellation Complète is the category of fine wines. Labels must indicate grape variety, locality, vineyard site, name grower and his domicile, and the vintage year. (Wines of the first two types may or may not be vintage dated.) There are also strict regulations governing treatment and the type of vine, and wines must pass official tasting tests of the Commission of the Marque Nationale. A small label prominently lettered *Marque Nationale* is affixed to the neck of the certified bottles.

Vinicultural methods are identical with those practiced on the German side of the river. The informing grape is the Riesling, and the wines resemble those of the Upper Moselle in character, with the same light flowery bouquet and prickly tang. The other noble grapes of Luxembourg in addition to the Riesling (or Riesling and Sylvaner) are the Traminer, the Ruländer (Pinot Gris), and the Auxerrois. These are the only grapes which can be used to produce quality Luxembourg wines.

SWITZERLAND

SWITZERLAND is intensely wine conscious; it is both a producer and a major importer of wines. While twenty of its twenty-two cantons produce wine, it is not enough for its own needs, and it is therefore necessary to import large quantities of wine from Hungary, Italy, France, and often all the way from Chile. Notwithstanding, some of its better wines are exported. They are readily available in the United States.

The Rhine and Rhône Rivers, which begin in Switzerland their long journeys to the sea, form a sort of division in Swiss wine regions. While we generally think of Rhine wines as white and Rhône wines as red, the situation is reversed in Switzerland, as though the soil along the rivers changed character beyond the Swiss border. For in Switzerland the wines of the Rhine section are almost all red, while those of the Rhône are predominantly white, with one notable exception—Dôle.

The two major grape-producing regions—Valais and Vaud—are along the Rhône, and about four-fifths of wine made is white. The great grape of both Valais and Vaud is the Chasselas. In the Valais it is called Fendant (Fendant de Sion, Fendant du Valais, Fendant Vert, etc.), and in the Vaud Dorin (Dorin Lutry, Dorin Vaud, Dorin Epesses, etc.). Also in Vaud, the Chasselas makes a wine of lower quality, known as Perlan and a delicious white wine called Dezaley. The Sylvaner (called Johannisberg), the Marsanne of France (called Ermitage), and the local Arvine, Humagne, and Amigne are the other grapes in the two regions that give their names to Swiss white wines.

All the white wines of Valais are heady and powerful (up to 13 per cent alcohol), while those of Vaud are dry, gentle, and fruity. Chablais, the district between Vaud and Valais (though considered part of Vaud region), produces white wines that have characteristics of both regions; that is, they are powerful, but drier and less full than the Valais.

The most popular red wine in the Valais region is called Dôle, which is a blend of Pinot Noir and Gamay. In Vaud, a similar blend is called Salvagnin. Both are very pleasant table wines, deep colored and fairly high in alcohol.

The third major wine-producing region in Switzerland is Neuchâtel, north of Vaud, and is well known for both its red and white wines. Again, the best whites are made from the Chasselas, but here the grape's name is used. These wines of Neuchâtel are generally quite pale in color and have a tendency to be slightly petillant or spritz, showing what the Swiss like to call "the star." This imparts a light and sprightly quality to the wine, prickly to the tongue, which can be seen on the sides of the glass as tiny bubbles that resemble those formed by soda water.

Vines growing on terraced ground above Visperterminen Valais. (Courtesy of Swiss Tourist Bureau, New York)

The best red wine from Neuchâtel is Cortaillod, named after the village which makes a speciality of it. Made of Pinot Noir, it is a pale and light red wine on the order of a Beaujolais.

From the Italian-speaking region of Switzerland, Ticino, come smooth, fruity red wines such as Nostrano, Bondola, Nebbiolo, Merlot. The latter is the one you most likely will find in the United States.

Although several pink Swiss wines are beginning to be known in this country, Oeil de Perdrix, a mellow rosé produced in the Neuchâtel and Vaud, is presently the most popular. A sweet dessert wine known as Malvoisie is produced in the Valais district and is quite good.

Swiss table wines are best when young and fresh. Most of them—even the red Dôle and Cortaillod—are usually served chilled.

AUSTRIA

THERE have always been enough fresh, charming wines produced in Austria to make life enjoyable for the gay Viennese, and to inspire Strauss waltzes. However, the quantities have been limited and lack of knowledge about the wines by those outside of Austria has caused many to overlook some delightful wines. This is a situation which is changing. Austria's wine exports are on the increase and many of them are now available in the United States.

Both red and white table wines are produced, although the whites predominate among the quality wines which are exported. The principal grape varieties grown for white wines are: Riesling, Gewürztraminer, Grüner Veltliner, Furmint, Neuburger, Müller-Thurgau Weissburgunder, Ruländer, and Muskat-Ottonel; while the red wines are obtained principally from the Blaufränkischer, Blauer Portugisser, Sankt Laurent, and Blauburgunder (Pinot Noir) varieties. The predominant characteristic of the white wines is a fragrant freshness, while the red wines are usually quite full in body and flavor.

Of all the wine produced in Austria only the finer qualities are exported. The best-known among the white wines reaching the United States are the Anninger Perle, Gumpoldskirchner, Steiner Hund, Loibner, Kremser, and the famous Klösterneuberger from the old monastery vineyard on the Danube, while three of the most famous, Grinzing, Sievering, and Nussdorf, are grown within the city limits of Vienna itself. From Wachau, Austria's best-known wine area, the principal export is Schluck, a fresh dry wine with a slight sparkle, made from the Sylvaner grape. A Traminer, Trifalter, and the sweet estate-bottled Edelfraulein from the Muscat Oltonel grape, are among other Wachau wines shipped.

The best red wines are those from Vöslau (Vöslauer Rotwein is one of the finest) south of Vienna and Oggan in Burgenland.

Some Austrian wine labels go into full details—village, vintage, grape, and vineyard—while others just give a brand name, such as Edelfraulein. It should be noted, however, that most of Austria's quality wines at least mention the name of the village, followed by the name of vineyard. For example, Steiner Goldberg, designating a wine made from grapes grown in the vineyard of Goldberg in the village of Stein. If the label carried the additional information *Thurgau 1970,* you would know that it was produced from the Müller-Thurgau grape in the year 1970.

CZECHOSLOVAKIA

As its status may be subject to change from time to time, it is simpler to consider the viticulture of Czechoslovakia as it was before 1939.

The most important wine region is around Pressburg, Bratislava. Pressburg, meaning "place or town of the wine press" in German, was known for its wines as early as the thirteenth century. The wines, white for the most part, are light and pleasant. They are obtained from the Dreimanner, or Traminer, Weiss Burgunder, and the Ostreicher or Sylvaner, and are consumed in the country or in Austria.

Very little wine is produced in Bohemia today, though it was, in the past, an important wine region. Both red and white wine is made. The red wine is produced from Blauer Burgunder, Blaufränkischer, St. Laurent, and Portugieser grapes, and the white from the Pinot, Traminer, and Sylvaner. The best Bohemia wines are from Velki Pavlovice, Maltice, and Mikulov—the latter lying due north of Vienna on the frontier between Austria and Czechoslovakia. The white wines have an affinity with German wines, while the red wines are light, not unlike Beaujolais in taste.

At the eastern end of the country around Uzhorod (Ungvar), in what was formerly Hungary and is now in the U.S.S.R., there are two *komitats* or parishes, which border the Tokaj-Hegyalija. A light but spirited white wine, which is delightful, is made in this district, mostly from Riesling grapes. A Czech "Tokay" is made from the Lipovina, Furmint, and Muscatel grapes. This region also produces some good sparkling wines, which are sold under names such as Château Bzenec and Château Melnik.

YUGOSLAVIA

YUGOSLAVIA has recently made remarkable progress as a producer of quality wines. Although an important vineyard area since ancient times, Yugoslavia has, in the last twenty years, undergone a revolutionary modernization of viniculture and wine production. Today, Yugoslavia is among the top ten wine producers of the world, and exports wine to many Western European countries, as well as to the United States.

The forty-fifth parallel which runs through northern Yugoslavia also intersects some of the world's other celebrated wine regions—Bordeaux, the Rhône Valley of France, and Italy's Piedmont District. Consequently, Yugoslav wines share many of the fine qualities recognized in the best bottlings from these great regions. In addition, Yugoslavia's climate and soil varies from Alpine to Continental to Mediterranean, providing a wide selection of fine wines.

Yugoslav wines bear the names of their grape varieties rather than generic labels like "Claret" or "Rhine wine." Some of the grape varieties cultivated are the classic grapes of France and Germany, such as Traminer, Sylvaner Riesling, Cabernet, Gamay, Pinot Noir, and Sauvignon; but many others, including some of the best, are of Yugoslav origin. The Žilavka produces a deep, golden-colored, aromatic white wine of the mountain slopes of Hercegovina. The Šipon, which grows around Maribor harbor in Slovenia, matures into a medium-dry white wine with good fruit and a fresh clean taste. The

Vintage in the vineyards of Smoderovo, near Belgrade. (Courtesy of Yugoslav Information Center, New York)

Plavac, grown in the soil of the Dalmatian Islands, gives a distinctive, full-bodied red wine. It is also from the Plavac grape that the Dalmatians produce the medium-dry, dark-colored rosé wine called Opolo, that is probably the most interesting rosé from Yugoslavia. The most common red variety in Serbia is called the Prokupac, and it is in great demand on the home market as a mellow, fresh, fruity wine to be consumed young, and with typical Yugoslav enthusiasm.

An Association of wine producers was created in Yugoslavia in the late '60's to encourage a serious export effort toward the United States market. This Association markets a complete assortment of quality wines from the leading districts under the Adriatica brand name. These wines are labeled with the name of the grape and with the village or district of origin. Among the names to be seen on the Adriatica label are Rizling from Frŭska Gora, Pinot Blanc from Slavonia, Šipon from Maribor, Prokupac from Yovac, Cabernet from Istria, and Žilavka from Hercegovina. Recently, other wine associations have been marketing wines on our market.

Fruskogorski Biser from Serbia is a typical Yugoslav sparkling wine. It is demi-sec (quite sweet). While the country is not noted for outstanding dessert wines, Prosek Dioklecian from Dalmatia is mildly sweet in taste and has a unique aroma of ripened grapes.

ROMANIA

ROMANIA between World War I and II was the most important wine-producing country in the Balkans. But with the loss of Bessarabia to Russia in 1940, it lost about 40 per cent of its production. Considerable quantities of wine, however, are still made.

The best of Romania's wines today are white and possibly the most popular is the Perla de Tîrnave. This is a well-balanced, light, slightly sweet blend of the main grape varieties grown along the banks of the River Tîrnave. The white blended wines of Tohani and Săhăteni are also well known and well liked. There are other white wines made from a single grape species whose name they carry: Riesling de Dealul-Mare, Fetească de Tirnave, Furmint, Grünsilvaner, Ruländer, Aligoté, Sauvigon de Banat. Most Romanian labels name variety first (and foremost), then may or may not include the region or village.

The Kadarka is the most common red wine in the Balkans and the Romanian Kadarka de Banat is one of the best. The red Băbeasiă of Nicoresti is pleasantly acidic with a clove-like taste. In the south part of the country, on the plain near the Danube, Seyarua Cabernet and Sadova rosés are produced. Both are fairly sweet. The best rosé of Romania is the Menesi Rozsa (Rosé of Menes), a deep-colored wine with a full, fruity bouquet and body.

Speaking of sweetness, Romania has two fine white dessert wines: Cotnari (a strong natural wine based on the Grasă grape, which is subject like the Semillon to the "noble mold" and Murfatlar (a wine with a fine bouquet in which a faint, unique nuance of orange-flower is detectable).

BULGARIA

WINE is produced all over the country, from the Danube valley in the north and the Black Sea coast in the east, to the Maritza valley in the south. As rule, most Bulgarian wines are named after grapes, some of them bearing well-known names, others local ones. Sometimes regional names are also employed. For example, Varna Dimiot is made from the Dimiot grape which flourishes along the coast of the Black Sea and it is produced in the wine center of Varna. The Dimiot produces a dry but fruity wine of a rich golden-green color and will remind one of the German Riesling wines. On the other hand wines from the Misket grapes, in particular the Misket de Karlovo or the Misket Karlova, bring to mind the Sylvaner, as does the Songoularé Misket which is produced on the Black Sea coast.

Other, more common white wines are the Balgarske Slantse (Bulgarian Sun) made from the Furmint grape and the Slantchev Birag (Sunshine Coast) produced from the Rcaizitelli grape. These wines are strong and full bodied. From the Danube basin comes a still fuller white wine, Donau Perla (Pearl of the Danube), made from the Feteasca grape. Of course, one of the most interesting is the Karlovo White Muscatel. It is produced in the same rose valley as the attar of roses, and there is a faint trace of roses in the bouquet of the straw-colored, quite-dry wine—a bouquet which develops with age.

Although there are many more Bulgarian red wines than whites, they are much less varied. The best known, full-flavored but not rich and rather in the style of a Beaujolais, is Gamza, a grape variety. It is produced in various parts of the country. Mavrud is a rather soft red wine from the southern part of the country, sweeter than Gamza and with less acidity. Pamid is sweet and low in acidity, light in color, and suitable for drinking soon after fermentation. For this reason, it is a popular wine for general domestic consumption and none is exported. However, a light, Claret-type wine, Trakia, is made from Mavrud and Pamid grapes in the proportion of about 60 to 40; this blend is exported.

Melnik is a red wine of superior quality, dark and rather heavy. The Melnuk grape variety has been cultivated in Bulgaria since ancient times and is probably a plant of French origin. Another good red wine is made from the Cabernet grape, and is thus labeled as Caberne.

The very popular white Hemus is medium-sweet, while Tamianka and Tirnovo (red) are very sweet. These and numerous other dessert wines are produced in the south.

U.S.S.R.

RUSSIA is the fourth largest wine-producing country in the world, after France, Italy, and Spain. But, until 1972, very little information on Russian wines was obtainable. In that year, a trade agreement with the U.S.S.R. permitted their wines to be exported to the United States.

Although but a few wines are still available for taste, we now know a great deal more about the U.S.S.R.'s wine industry. The viticultural zone sweeps east round the north of the Black Sea from Moldavia to Armenia on the border of Turkey. Two areas, the Crimean peninsula and Georgia on the southern slopes of the Caucasus, have been famous since ancient times for good wine and that remains true today.

Every type of wine is produced in the Crimean region. The most popular dry red wines include Cabernet Levodia, Saperavi Massandra, Alushita, and Bordo Ay-Danil, while dry white wines include Semillon Oreanda, Aligoté Ay-Danil, Riesling Massandra, Silvaner Feodosusky, and Kokur Niznegorsky. The southern Crimea is chiefly noted for dessert wines: white, red, and pink. There are pink (Gourzouf and Alupka) as well as white muscat (Massandra and Livadia) wines. The red muscat wines include Kuchuk-Lambat, Kastel, and Aiou-Dag. Chorny Doktor (red) and Solnechnaya Dolina (white) are sweet dessert wines, while the Pinot Gris Ay-Danil is one of the sweetest in Russia.

Remember the Russian likes sweet wine and the Crimea also produces wines that are made to resemble Tokay, Port, and Madeira. These wines are, of course, named by type, not by origin.

The Crimean vineyard area extends eastward across the straits of Kersch into the Kuban. Anapa is the chief center and Riesling and Cabernet stocks provide good white and red wine. Much brandy and "Soviet Champagne" is also made between Anapa and Gelendshik. Soviet sparkling wine is called "Champagne" in its own country, but bears such names as Krasnodar, Tbilisi, and Tsimlyanskoye when exported.

In Georgia we find some of the oldest vineyard sites in Russia. Some of the best white table wines found here are Ghurdjurni, Myshako Riesling, Napureouli, and Tsinandali. The better reds are Mukuzani, Saperavi, and Mzvane.

Azerbaijan, Armenia, and the region along the Caspian up to Machackalia are the major dessert-wine-producing areas in Russia. About the only table wines made are the Matrasa (red) and Sadilly of Baku (white).

The lower Don River valley, especially near Rostov, produces several good white and red wines, but the region's best-known export is a sparkling wine called Donski.

Moldavia, which was formerly Bessarabia and was part of Rumania until 1940, is primarily known for its table wines. The Negri de Purkar is a dry but fruity red; Fetjaska is a dry white. Romanesti is made with a Bordeaux-type blend of Malbec, Merlot, and Cabernet. And the Cabernet is used in the production of Chumai, a dessert wine. Trifesti (Pinot Gris) and Gratiesti (Rcaizitelli) are popular dessert wines produced in Moldavia region.

HELLENIC WINES

THE vine has been cultivated by the Greeks since time immemorial and their efforts have been praised in prose and poetry by all the ancient poets. "The Greeks had a word for it," and the word was "aromatics." Apparently the natural flavor of the grape itself was too bland for their sophisticated palate, so the wines were stored in *amphorae* (large jars) pitched with tar.

This imparted a resinous flavor to the wine, and, as if this were not enough, bags containing spices, such as peppers, cloves, and aromatic gums, were suspended in the wine to ensure its "preservation" and improved flavor. Present-day Greeks still prefer a resinated to a natural wine, a taste which must be acquired, as the harsh, pungent turpentine bouquet and flavor shocks the unaccustomed palate. These wines are available in the United States. They are labeled Retsina and are a golden or white wine. The resinated red wine is called Kokkinelli and is less resinated than the white variety.

Of course, all Greek wine is not resinated or aromatized. These are several dry white wines such as Hymettus, Mantinia, Santa Helena, Robola, Demestica, Antika, Santa Laoura, Pallini, Lendos, and Marko. The dry red table wines include Castel Danielis, Botrys, Rapsani, Ambelakia, Pendeli, and Nemea. Tegea and Roditys are fairly dry rosés with a highly fragrant bouquet.

The Greek islands of Chios, Crete, Corfu, Cyclades (Santorin), Samos, Thasos, Cos, and Mitylene (Lesbos) all produce wine today, though their product does not enjoy the majestic reputation it had when the Hellenes were masters of the known world.

Everyone in Greece drinks wine, and most of the cultivated area is devoted to vineyards, although the climate is not suitable for the production of the best grapes for table wine making. Most of the Greek islands are volcanic in origin and the wines have a characteristic fiery hotness. The ancient Greeks—as those of today—preferred rich, sweet wines.

The grape varieties cultivated are those which have grown there for ages. The most famous of these is the Malvasia, which originated in the region of Monemvasia, a small town in the Peloponnesian peninsula, and is grown today in almost every wine region of the world, but most notably in Crete and Madeira—where it produces Malmsey.

The muscat is grown generally, and most successfully on the island of Samos. This tiny island, which hugs the Turkish coast, produces another of Greece's venerable dessert wines, Muscat de Samos—a favorite of Lord Byron. It is a pleasant, sweet, fortified white wine. Incidentally, the origin of the muscat is attributed to Samos, but we cannot vouch for this.

The Sultana grape is another native of Greece which produces sweet liqueur wines.

The most popular and widely distributed Greek wine today is the Mavrodaphne, which is obtained from the grape of the same name. This grape was discovered about a century ago by a viticulturist named Gustave Clauss. Because the berry reminded him of the laurel berry, he named it "black laurel"—Mavrodaphne. The wine is sweet, red, and port-like in character. It has an alcoholic content varying from 15½ to 20 per cent, depending on the quality of the must and the amount of brandy used for fortifying.

Cyprus is today an independent nation, and while long held by England she is viticulturally still a Greek island. All types of table, sparkling, and fortified wines are produced and shipped in some volume to the United Kingdom. The most distinguished Cypriot wine is her rich, cream sherry-like Commanderia, which is excellent. Other sherry-type wines are good and a few fine muscat dessert wines (including Muscat de Chypre) are also produced.

Good Cypriot table wines are limited. The best of reds are Othello, Cyprus, and Afames, while Arsinol and Aphrodite top the list of whites. A rosé Kokkinelli is a fresh, semi-sweet wine, although it is slightly darker in color than the majority of rosés.

ISRAEL

THE Bible informs us that the vine was cultivated in Judea in ancient times and that natural, strong, and mixed wines were in use, but it does not tell us either the grape varieties or the names of these wines. With the dispersion of the Jews and the conquest of the country by the Mohammedans, viniculture all but disappeared. Except for a small amount of wine made for religious purposes, none was made commercially in the Holy Land for over 1,500 years.

In the last eighty years, however, and particularly since the war, Palestine has witnessed a viniculture Renaissance. Due chiefly to Baron Edmond de Rothschild, one of the owners of Château Mouton-Rothschild and Mouton d'Armailacq, a beginning was made toward the end of the last century, and today there are many flourishing vineyards in the land which, the Bible tells us, was a land of corn, oil, and wine.

The centers of viticulture are Zichron-Jacob, Nes-Ziona, Gedera, and, most important of all, Rishon-le-Zion (meaning "First in Zion").

For many years the wines were labeled Palestinian Sauterne, Hock, Port, etc. However, Israel recently signed the Madrid International Wine Convention, thus agreeing to rename her wines. In most cases the new names are Hebrew. They clearly identify their Israeli origin. Today some of the popular wines bear names as follows:

Name	Description	Type
Mikve Israel	dry, full-body red	Burgundy
Adom Atic	semi-dry, red	Claret
Avdat White	dry, light-body, white	Rhine wine
Carmel Hock	medium-dry white	Sauterne
Château Richon Vin Blanc d' Israel	medium-dry, golden	Sauterne
Château Richon Vin Rouge d' Israel	moderately sweet, red (Alicanté grape)	
Rosé of Carmel	semi-dry, rosé	Anjou rosé
Binaymina	dry rosé	Rosé
Almog	sweet, red	Malaga
Parton	sweet, full-bodied, red	Port
Sharir	semi-dry, golden	Sherry
Topaz	rich, sweet, golden	Tokay

The courageous pioneers who are rebuilding Israel into a healthy, modern State after its centuries of abandonment deserve all praise for properly giving their wines names that are easily identifiable with their place of origin. The only curious exception we have noted is the Israeli Concord wine, which does not resemble our American Concord wine. In the sparkling wine class, Israel has extra-dry, demi-sec, and pink types available.

Israel exports wine to over twenty-eight countries in Europe, Africa, and North and South America. In the United States, we can choose from a rich selection. All are kosher, involving rabbinical supervision and the ceremonial dumping of a full 10 per cent of the wine. Much of the rest finds its way into the ceremonies of Jewish temples around the world . . . but much more graces the dinner tables of people who simply put their faith in the wines of a land that flowed with wine 4,000 years ago.

NEAR, MIDDLE, AND FAR EAST

ALTHOUGH wine has been produced in Turkey on the Dardanelles and on Mount Lebanon for many centuries, it has always been a minor business. True, there has been some development in the past decade, and some of wines are good enough to get market acceptance in northern Europe.

The best wines of Turkey are produced from native grapes and come from Anatolia and its districts of Ankara, Elazig, and Gaziantep. Still more wine is produced in Thrace, where Turkey joins Europe. The best-known Turkish wines are the Buzbag, a red wine from Anatolia made from the Boguzkere grape, and Trakya, a dry white or red wine from Thrace. Other wines of quality are the red Kalebag and Adabag, as well as the semi-dry white, Beyaz. There are several good dessert wines produced in Turkey, but few are exported.

Iran (modern Persia), fountain of culture and civilization, is, according to the Persians, the place where wine-making really originated. Persia has given us much in philosophy, art, poetry, and one vine which has been planted and has prospered in many wine regions of the world—the Shiraz (Sirrah, Petite Sirah of California). Actually, Shiraz and its wine must have been in the mind of Omar Khayyam, when he wrote:

> "I sometimes wonder what the vintner buys
> One half so precious as the stuff he sells?"

In *A Book of Other Wines*, P. Morton Shand recounts the Persian version of the discovery of wine. The Shah Djemsheed always had a dish of grapes by his bedside, and one day, observing that some of the over-ripe berries were fermented, ordered them to be thrown away, thinking them to be poisonous. A discarded favorite from his harem seized the grapes and drank the juice to put an end to her sorrow. This she did but not in the way she had expected. When the surprised Shah found her, mildly intoxicated but far from melancholy, she revealed the delightful secret of the grapes, thus not only starting the wine industry but restoring the devotion of the Shah.

According to Shand, the principal native Persian vines are the peerless Kishmish white grape of Ispahan, the red Damas, the Kishbaba (seedless), the small and sweet Askeri, the Shahoni (royal grape) of Cashbin, the Imperial of Tauris, and the luscious Samarkand.

The vintage of the Shiraz is in August, when the fresh must is placed in large, glazed earthenware vases of 25 to 40 gallons capacity, which are buried in the ground in cool cellars. When mature, it is filtered and bottled in long-necked flasks, covered with straw, called *Carabas,* holding about 2½ quarts. Both red and white Shiraz are made. It has a pungent, spicy perfumed flavor. Other wine regions of Persia are Ispahan, Tabriz, Yezd, and Teheran.

There is some wine-producing activity in both Syria and Lebanon, but little is exported. Lebanese red wines made from Aramon, Carignan, and Cinsault grapes are very acceptable.

In Egypt, the situation is almost the same. There are, however, three good whites—Crus des Ptolémées, Reine Cléopatre, and Clos Mariout—and two fine reds—Clos Matamir and Omar Khayyam. The latter has an intriguing faint flavor of dates.

In China, wine is supposed to have been "discovered" by I-ty several hundred years before the Christian era, and its use was subsequently prohibited by a Chinese emperor who had the vines uprooted. Even before that, the Chinese made a scented wine from rice, a practice that continues today. The best qualities are called *mandarin,* and are identified by the region from which they come.

Today, in China, white and red wines, dry, sweet, and sparkling, as well as some rosés, are being made from grapes. Some of the wines, especially from Tsingtao (or Shantung) province are very good, but unfortunately little Chinese wine is exported at present. However, this may change shortly, especially because of publicity given Mao Tai—a Chinese rice wine—during President Nixon's trip to China.

Japanese grape table wines range from good to rather poor. However, very few "good" wines ever leave the country; some mediocre wines are exported. Dessert wines and sparkling types are, as rule, of better quality than the table styles. Japanese plum wines are very good and represent some of the best fruit wines of the world.

NORTH AFRICA

THE Koran is specific about its prohibition of alcoholic beverages to the faithful, but the followers of Mohammed have always tended the vine wherever it would grow because they like to eat grapes. Prior to the French, Spanish, and Italian penetrations of North Africa, such wine as was made was produced solely by the Jews for religious purposes. When France controlled North Africa, enormous vineyards in Algeria, Tunisia and Morocco produced vast quantities of wine, most of which was used in the Mother Country to supply the demand for cheap wine for beverage purposes, and for the making of French Vermouth and aperitif wines. But since they won their freedom from France in 1960's, there has been—except in Morocco—a decline in the production of wine from North Africa.

The chief vines cultivated are the varieties of the Midi-Carignane, Clairette, Picpoul, and Mour-vedre; while in the better soils and exposure the best vines of Bordeaux, Burgundy, Jerez, and the Douro are also grown.

The wines of North Africa are generally heady and fiery, with a tendency to heaviness. They are sound, drinkable wines but not great, and when used in France for beverage purposes, are generally blended with the thin light wines of the Midi to which they give body and life.

SOUTH AFRICA

CULTURE of the vine in South Africa began virtually with the founding of the first Dutch settlement by Johan van Riebeeck in 1655 where the city of Cape Town now stands. He brought with him cuttings of European vines

Picking grapes on a farm in Stellenbosch, South Africa. (Courtesy of South African Tourist Corp., New York)

which flourished when planted on the slopes of Table Mountain, and four years later the first Cape wine was made.

In 1688 a large party of French Huguenots arrived and settled in the valleys surrounding the Cape, and later, German immigrants also added their skills to the growing art of South African wine making.

Simon van der Stel, the second governor of the Cape Colony established a vineyard at Groot Constantia and planted over 100,000 new vines. In the eighteenth and nineteenth centuries the wine from this farm—a rich, sweet, liqueur-type—achieved great fame in Europe and was known as Constantia wine.

In 1805 the British occupied the Cape and because of the Napoleonic Wars encouraged wine exports to Great Britain by granting preferential tariffs. This boom period lasted about sixty years and collapsed when the favorable tariffs were removed.

The infamous phylloxera struck the Cape vineyards in 1885 and was only conquered (as it was in Europe) when the vines were grafted onto pest-resistant North American root stocks. By 1918 there was such over-production and low prices that the wine growers, with the backing of the south African Government, formed the Co-operative Winegrowers Association of South Africa, Ltd., better known as the K. W. V., to maintain uniformity of quality, continuity of supply, and to stabilize prices.

Exports to the United Kingdom and the Netherlands resumed again. Initially these were of the dessert-type wines—Ports, sweet Sherries, and Muscatels. When Dr. Charles Niehaus discovered the indigenous *flor* yeast in Cape vineyards in 1935, the production of Sherries of the Fino and Amontillado types became possible. All types of wine are being produced today from the *vitis vinifera* grapes.

The wine-growing region extends in an arc with a radius of approximately one hundred miles with Cape Town as the apex and Vredendal and Oudtshoorn at the northern and eastern points, respectively. There are two main areas: the Coastal Belt, stretching from the sea to the first mountain range where grapes suitable for making fine dry white and red table wines are grown, and the Little Karoon which stretches from the Drakenstein to the Swartberg Mountains and produces mainly sweet Muscatel wines and grapes used for the production of Brandy.

South Africa makes excellent natural table wines. The best white wine comes from the vineyards near Paarl, Stellenbosch, and Tulbagh and is made from the Riesling, Clairvette Blanche, and Steen grapes under controlled pressure and temperature fermentation to maintain their delicacy and fragrance. Alcoholic strengths range from 12 to 12.5 per cent by volume. Sparkling wines ranging from brut to demi-doux are also made, mostly by the Charmat process.

Paarl and Stellenbosch are the centers of the best red wine areas, together with vineyards of Groot Constantia, Drakenstein, and Klapmuts. The finest red wines of the Cape are pressed from Cabernet, Shiraz, Hermitage (Cinsaut) Pinot, Gamay, and Pinotage—the latter a local variety obtained by a cross between the Pinot Noir and the Cinsaut or Hermitage, which creates an exceptional wine. Alcoholic strengths vary from 12 to 14 per cent by volume. Rosés of both the still and petillant types are also produced.

Table wines are sold either under a local geographic name or more often by the varietal name of the principal grape used. European district names are never used as a matter of principal. However, in order to interpret this more clearly for the American market, here are a few of the popular wines and their approximate European type:

Bonne Esperance	Claret
Paarl Roodeberg	Burgundy
Paarl Riesling	Rhine
Steen	Rhine
Late Vintage—"spätlese or auselese"	Rhine

Steen is a varietal wine made from the Steen grape and is now considered a native of South Africa. It is believed to be a "bud mutation" of the famous Sauvignon Blanc.

Production of Sherries and Ports is centered around Paarl and Stellenbosch. The lighter Sherries are fermented under flor yeasts and matured by the traditional solera system from the Palomino and Steen varieties.

Ports are made from grape varieties imported from the Douro region of Portugal. Both Ruby and Tawny styles are popular and are matured in oak "pipes" from five to eight years. Even Vintage Port has been made since 1945 and shipped to London for bottling and maturation.

Sherries and Ports are shipped for export with the phrase "South African" to clearly indicate their country of origin.

Cape Constantia dessert wine is fortified, medium sweet, and has a pronounced Muscat flavor.

AUSTRALIA

GRAPE cultivation in Australia began with Captain Arthur Phillips, who brought vine cuttings with his first fleet when he founded the colony of New South Wales on January 26, 1788. The man primarily responsible for the establishment of the industry on a firm business footing was a Scottish school teacher, James Busby. He selected 20,000 cuttings from 678 varieties from France, Spain, and Portugal, and augmented them with others from Palestine, Syria, Arabia, and Persia.

Australian growing areas are widespread, ranging from the Swan valley, near Perth, to the Hunter River valley, north of Sydney, 2,500 miles across the continent. The stable climatic conditions of Australia's southern half are well suited to the growth and ripening of wine-bearing grapes. Generally, Australia's wine-producing areas are warmer and drier than those of Europe. In the summer, the ripening period, the dry conditions help to ensure clean ripening and disease-free crops. The warmth and dryness also produce more natural sugar in the grapes, with low natural acidity (sugar is not added to Australian wines). There are also many vineyards in the higher and cooler areas where delicate table wines are produced.

In Australia, instead of separate regions being devoted to the making of one type of wine, the principal vignerons make all types—and with no diminution of quality on that account. By judicious buying from independent grape growers and the planting of several grape varieties in their own vineyards, it is common practice for the big wine-making companies to market Sherries, table wines, sparkling wines, dessert wines, and also brandy under their own label. The yield from Australia's wine-grape harvest—the grape-picking season lasting from February until April—averages 250,000 tons, which produces approximately 40 million gallons of wine. (In 1960, the Australians produced only 14 million gallons or wine production increase of almost three times as much.) Of this, half goes to the making of beverage wines of all types, the remainder being used for the distillation of grape spirit and brandy. There are about 200 wineries in Australia, and 60,000 acres are devoted to wine growing. About 60 different grape varieties are found throughout the nation's vineyards, all of them from the *vitis vinifera* stock.

Today most of the wineries in Australia use generic names for their wines—Claret, Burgundy, Chablis, Sherry, Sauternes, Ports, Moselle, and so on. However, many Australian wines are marketed under district names—such as Barossa, Hunter Valley, Coonawarra—and grape varietal names such as Cabernet, Shiraz, Lexia, Pinot Noir, Riesling—and sometimes a combination of both. The latter presents a problem. The exotic Australian place-names are unfamiliar to wine buyers in other countries, which is precisely why wine-makers rely on famous place-names to attract the wine drinker. Unfortunately, the use of famous place-names from France and Germany invariably invites comparisons, which can be unfair to Australian wines. For example, both a Burgundy and a Claret may be made from the same grape, known as the Black Hermitage, and similar to the Syrah or Skiraz used in the Rhône Valley of France. An Australian Moselle—surprisingly dry—may be made from the Riesling, but in Australia this refers to the Semillon of France: the true Riesling of Germany is called the Rhine Riesling in Australia. What all this means to the consumer is simply that he must disregard the generic place-names used on the label, and rely on the skill and reputation of the individual shippers to provide well-made wines under their respective brands.

Of course, all classes and types of wines can be and are produced in

Australia. In addition to a wide array of table wines—many of them vintage wines—dessert wines of various Ports, Sherries, and Muscats types are made. Most of the better sparkling wines and champagnes are made by the authentic French method, although a few are bulk fermented or artificially carbonated. Most producers of Champagne follow the sweetness labeling of *Brut, Extra Sec, Sec, Demi Sec,* and *Doux* (see page 69). Both sweet and dry are also produced in Australia.

Strict government and industry regulations ensure the highest possible quality of exported Australian wines. The provisions of the Pure Food and Drug Regulations are rigidly enforced. Before export is permitted, wines and brandies are inspected by experienced officers of the Federal Government's Department of Customs and Excise, as well as by inspectors appointed by the Australian Wine Board.

CANADA

THE vineyards of Canada are primarily in the Okanagan valley of British Columbia and on the Niagara peninsula of southern Ontario, but the latter, often called "the Garden of Canada," is by far the more important. In fact, about 95 per cent of the wine grapes grown in Canada are from the peninsula.

The grapes employed in Canadian wines are the same as those used in New York State types. That is, while the major portion of the vineyard are still planted with North American varieties (*vitis labrusca*), some viniculturalists are changing over to European hybrids and *vitis vinifera*. From these various grapes, wineries now produce Canadian Sherries, Ports, white and red table wines (both generic and varietal types), sparkling wines, rosés, Tokays, sweet and dry Vermouths, and wine cocktails. With the exception of the table varieties, most Canadian wines are blends of different years and different vineyards. The wines must be marketed by the winery producing them, but in all provinces, they must sell only to the Liquor Control Commissions or Boards, which sell retail through their stores to consumers and to hotel and restaurant establishments. Over the years Canada has only exported a very small quantity of its wine—most of wine produced in the country is consumed there.

LATIN AMERICA

SOUTH of the Rio Grande, wines are produced in a number of the American Republics, but of these only Argentina, Chile, Peru, and Brazil are of interest to us as exporters of wine; and Uruguay and Mexico because of the similarity of their wines to our own American wine types.

The wine regions of Argentina, Chile, and Peru lie almost entirely in the

Andean foothills where the character of the soil, as might be expected, is rough, rocky, and in some cases ferruginous.

Peru   On the Pacific slope and somewhat north of the normal wine belt a fair amount of wine of medium quality is produced in Peru in the regions of Ica, Locumba, Lima, and the Sicamba River valley. The grapes employed are the European varieties, and the wines are all consumed locally. However, the distinguished Pisco muscat brandy, of which we must speak in Chapter 18, "Brandies," is outstanding. It is distilled from wines grown in the Ica region and derives its name from the Port of Pisco, whence it has always been shipped.

Brazil   In Brazil on the Atlantic side of the continent and far from the Andean divide some wine is produced from both *labrusca* and *vinifera* grapes. Most of the wines are consumed locally but small amounts are of exportable quality. Some very satisfactory Champagne has been exported on occasion to the United States. Brazil imports the majority of the wine she consumes.

Uruguay   Lying on the eastern shore of the Rio de la Plata, Uruguay produces small quantities of wines almost entirely from slip-skin varieties, closely resembling our own New York and Ohio wines. Few of these wines are exported, being consumed by the local market.

ARGENTINA

ARGENTINA is the most important wine-producing nation of the Western hemisphere, and ranks fifth among the world's wine producers, being outranked only by France, Italy, Spain and the U.S.S.R.

The three principal wine regions of Argentina are in the provinces of Mendoza and San Juan, and the territory of Rio Negro. Mendoza lies in the west, on the Chilean border, and is the "California" of Argentina. It is only in the last hundred years that the province has been developed. Mendoza was a vast, arid, sandy desert, showing green patches only along the banks of the several rivers that cut through in draining off the melting Andean snows. The Italian immigrants who started coming to the country during the latter part of the nineteenth century pitched in, worked hard, used the waters from the rivers to irrigate the land, and in exactly the same way as their relatives did who went to California they converted the province into a beautiful garden, producing magnificent crops, mostly of all types and classes of fruits. Finding that the grape has been cultivated with success since the establishment of the missions by the Spanish explorers, it was only natural that the first attention was devoted to the expansion of the vineyards and the production of wine. Today Mendoza accounts for 90 per cent of Argentina's annual table-wine production.

The province of San Juan lies immediately north of Mendoza and has similar soil conditions, irrigation being always necessary. Climatic conditions being on the whole somewhat hotter, the San Juan vineyards are the source for dessert wines for Vermouth production and almost all the table or eating grapes, as well as the magnificent raisins that are available in such profusion in Argentina's public markets. San Juan also produces some very pleasant table wines that enjoy wide popularity.

In the territory of Rio Negro and in vineyards along the Rio Negro River, somewhat further south from Mendoza, at a latitude comparable to that at which the Champagne region and the German wine regions lie in Europe, are produced some of Argentina's best white wines and Champagne. By comparison with Mendoza's figures the quantities produced are not large. Very little, if any, irrigation is required and the soil is less sandy, being more argillaceous and containing sections that are quite chalky in character.

While some wine is produced in practically every province of Argentina, all that is obtained outside of Mendoza and San Juan will not amount to more than 2 per cent of the country's total annual production. However, in the mountainous Cordoba province there is a small region around Villa Dolores where the most interesting wine is produced. The quantity is small but both the red and the white are quite uniformly good, bottle after bottle, fruity, full bodied, and well balanced. They are wines of character.

The vinifera varieties are cultivated exclusively for commercial wine production and the leading European varieties are to be found, such as the Cabernet, Malbec, Pinot Noir, Gamay, Barbera, Sangiovese, Sauvignon Vert, Semillon, Muscadelle, Chardonnay, Riesling, all the principal muscats, Palomino. There still remains considerable acreage planted to the criolla (native) grape variety. This variety corresponds roughly to the California Mission, being the descendant of the original varieties brought in and planted by mission padres four hundred odd years ago.

Argentina's vineyards, like those of other wine regions, have suffered and been subjected to attack from various diseases such as mildew, oidium, and the worst of all plagues—the phylloxera, which has caused vast ravages of the vineyards, particularly in Mendoza and San Juan.

On the whole, in Mendoza and San Juan the wines are made on a mass production basis, there being similar conditions to those which occur in California, in addition to which it must be borne in mind that the greater part of the annual production is made by the half dozen "giants" of the Argentine wine industry. Some of the largest wineries and wine cellars in the world are to be found in Mendoza.

The viticultural and vinicultural experiment station, which forms part of the University of Cuyo at Mendoza, has made real contributions to the advances and modernization of wine growing in Argentina. It is an outstanding establishment.

All classes and types of wines are produced in Argentina, almost all of which are absorbed by the local market. Ninety-five per cent or more of the wines produced and consumed are light beverage wines, not containing more than $12\frac{1}{2}$ per cent of alcohol, and those appetizer, dessert wines, and Vermouths as are offered do not reach 16 per cent in alcohol.

Premium wines are often labeled with the brand name Red Wine or White Wine, but labels reading Clarete, Borgona, Barbera, Chianti, Sauternes, Chablis, Rhine, etc. are offered as well as labels reading Viejo and Extra Viejo, meaning "old" and "extra old," respectively.

A number of the leading wine houses also produce sparkling wines by all the methods known in the wine trade. In other words, Argentine Champagne is produced by the traditional bottle-fermented method, the Charmat or bulk-fermentation process, and by the artificial carbonation method. Sparkling Burgundy is also produced, generally by the Charmat method. Champagnes are usually labeled Brut, Extra Sec, Sec, and Dulce to denote the relative dryness or sweetness of the wine.

Sherry and Port wines of very satisfactory quality are offered, but the Muscatels of San Juan are of superior quality, comparable, in fact, to the Muscatel wines of the Mediterranean islands. These wines do not contain more than 16 per cent alcohol.

Argentina is the largest consumer of Vermouth, where one brand alone markets over two million cases a year of the three and a half million sold. Vermouth is consumed almost entirely as an apéritif, served on-the-rocks or with a dash of soda and a dash or two of Italian-style bitters.

Argentine table wines are good, fruity wines. The reds are well balanced, and the whites, especially the Traminer, dry, delicate and as fine as any made. White wines should be drunk young. All are made from vinifera grapes.

One wonders why these wines have not appeared on our market until recently. There were several reasons, some economic and others political. Several attempts were made. Wines shipped for a tasting were not handled properly after the long voyage. The home market was absorbing all that was produced, and then there was a period of paralysis when the Peron government controlled production and prices.

Now at last an energetic importer convinced one of the fine-wine producers in Mendoza to ship four types of wines: two reds and two whites. These are:

	Grape Variety	Bottle
Vina San Felipe Borgono Tinto	Cabernet Sauvignon	Burgundy type
Vasija RFN	Sangiovetto Piccolo and Merlot	Bordeaux type
San Felipe Traminer	Traminer	Alsatian type
San Felipe Blanco	Pinot Blanco and Riesling	Bocksbeutel

There are other wines coming in under two distinct labels: Estanciero for red wine and Pampas for the white, produced by a group of vineyard owners.

In Argentina, wine is part of the people's diet. In every restaurant, whether it be the finest luxury establishment or a simple working-man's eating place, you will see wine on every table, while in the home it will always be found on the host's table as well as the servants'. It is served just as a matter of course, as coffee is served in the United States.

CHILE

By comparison with her sister nation, across the Andes, Chile is a small country both in area and in population, having over 6,000,000 inhabitants. From a wine point of view she is far more important, as she produces the best wines in South America. They are wines of quality and character and have found the greatest acceptance in our market as well as those of Europe.

Chile has been most generously blessed by Mother Nature. She is endowed with a delightfully sunny climate, ideal soil conditions, and, above all, practically disease-free vineyards. No serious plague such as mildew or phylloxera has ever touched the Chilean vines.

The vine has been cultivated in Chile since the beginning of Spanish colonization in the sixteenth century, when the early missionaries, as they did elsewhere, planted the vine for the production of wine for the sacrament. Due to propitious soil, it was not long before these vineyards were producing wines for more mundane purposes. It is presumed that the first vines planted in Chile were cuttings brought down from Cuzco, the ancient capital of the Inca. This must have been before 1551 because in letters of that date Don Pedro de Valdivia, one of Chile's early leaders, mentions eating locally grown grapes; and several years later, he comments upon the wine produced near the city of Santiago.

Chile is a rather long and narrow strip of land which begins at the southern border of Peru and extends 2,800 miles south to icy Tierra del Fuego and the Straits of Magellan. At its back lies the ever-present and imposing massif of the snow-covered Andes range, including the 23,003-foot-high Mount Aconcagua, the tallest peak in the Western Hemisphere; and washing its long shoreline is the equally impressive Pacific Ocean and its cold Humbolt Current. It is this combination of fresh breezes striking against the high wall of the mountain back-drop that produces the ideal climatic conditions that have such a marked effect upon all the fruits of Chile's soil so that whether it be grapes, or peaches, or raspberries, or pears, or melons or lentils, onions or garlic, they are rich in perfume, flavor, and character. Her wines are no exception. They are on the whole better than good, and occasionally capable of greatness.

From Coquimbo, about 30 degrees latitude, south to Temuco, 40 degrees, the vine is generally under cultivation and wine is made. The principal regions are Huasco and Elqui in the north, the central sector which includes the regions of Aconcagua, Maipo, Cachapoal, and Lontué, and to the south are Itata and Cauquenes.

Although in Chile itself the region of the Llano del Maipo, near Santiago, enjoys the reputation for producing the wines of best quality, it is our humble opinion, after continued and repeated tastings, that the wines produced at or near Lontué are equal if not in some cases superior.

The soil of the Chilean wine regions is volcanic in nature, and as we said before, it is one of the most favored wine regions of the world. Such diseases as it suffers are not serious; probably the worst worry the vineyard owner has is that of late spring or early summer hail storms, which are, on occasion, quite devastating.

The principal vinifera varieties are cultivated for wine production, as well as table grapes and raisins. Most of the original cuttings have been brought from the various European wine regions, but in recent years cuttings have also been imported from California. For white wines the varieties most used are the Sauvignon Vert, Semillon, Muscadelle, Pinot Blanc or Chardonnay, Trebbiano, Riesling, Traminer, and the Chilean local variety known as the Loca Blanca, etc., while for red wines, the wine producers use primarily the Cabernet, Malbec, Verdot, Pinot Noir, etc. The table and raisin varieties tend mostly to the various muscats such as the Muscat of Alexandria, Malvasia, Malaga and seedless varieties such as the Corinth and Thompson, of which thousands of boxes are exported annually to the American market.

Cultivation of the vine and production of wine were rather carelessly pursued in Chile for some four centuries. Perhaps haphazardly would be a better term. Then in 1851 Don Silvestre Ochagavia contracted the services of M. Bertrand, a French viticulturer who brought with him the first cuttings of Cabernets, Pinots, etc., and with his arrival began the modernization and vast expansion of wine production, consumption, and appreciation for quality which Chile was capable of producing. During the century that has followed, M. Bertrand has been succeeded by a long series of eminent French viticulturists and oenologists, such as Gaston Canu, Georges Guyot de Granmaison, Leopold Gamerre, O. Brard and Paul Pacottet.

Wine production follows European methods in all respects. Fermentation takes place in vats and the new wine is racked into small or medium-sized cooperage for its development. The wines are generally bottled quite young, one to one and a half years for white wines, and two and a half years for the red wines, i.e., after the vintage.

All classes and types of wines can be and are produced in Chile, but consumption of wines other than red and white table wines is negligible by comparison. Good, but rather sweetish Champagne is produced and some

Sherry and Port type wines, as well as all the Vermouth consumed in Chile.

The largest volume of wine sold in Chile is purchased by the consuming public as simply Tinto or Blanco (red or white), which Mr. Consumer takes home generally from the grocery store, in a typically Chilean type wicker-covered demijohn of 5 to 10 liters, called a *chuico*. He buys his wine, leaving a deposit for the container, which is discounted when he returns it and takes away another filled chuico.

In clubs, restaurants, hotels, and fine groceries, premium wines, of which there is an abundance, are offered in the traditional European bottles. These wines bearing vintage dates sometimes, and resembling quite closely their namesakes, are labeled—Cabernet, Borgoña (Burgundy), Pommard, Pinot, Riesling, Rhine, Chablis, Sauvignon, Semillon, Sauternes, etc. In addition, the labels will bear the name of the vineyard and one of the following phrases, in order of quality (the first being the best): Gran Vino para Banquetes (Great wine for banquets), Gran Vino, or Reservado.

With few exceptions, the Riesling and Rhine are bottled, for sale in Chile, in the boxbeutel of Steinwein fame.

Grape and wine growing in Chile is a very important agricultural endeavor, and one that is of great concern to the people as a whole and to the Government too, particularly the Internal Revenue Department which is charged with controlling every step of the wine's progress from the planting of the grape until its final disposition on the consumer's table. Strict supervision of labeling, quality standards, etc., are maintained.

Chile is the only country we have ever heard of where people actually become completely intoxicated on table wine. As a temperance measure the Chilean legislature passed a law limiting the amount of wine that can be sold within the country to 60 liters (15.85 gallons) per capita. It is interesting to note that there has been a marked decline in absenteeism due to alcoholism. The most recent statistics show that absenteeism due to excessive drinking dropped to only 16 per cent.

In supervising strict compliance of this law, the Internal Revenue Department establishes quotas, governing new plantings, wine production and marketing. This does not mean that production is limited to the 60 liter per capita internal consumption figure. Any wine produced in excess of the statutory limit must be either exported, distilled into brandy or alcohol for fuel purposes, or dumped. Since under the law only some 85/90,000,000 gallons can be marketed internally, and Chile has the potential to produce upwards of 150,000,000 gallons annually, the industry could find a continually expanding export market if it wishes to prosper and progress. Some wine leaders have been able to develop excellent markets for premium wines, exported in bottles to this country and the other American Republics, and for standard quality wines shipped in bulk to a number of European markets, notably Belgium, Holland, the Scandinavian countries, Switzerland, Germany, and France.

Naturally, a much greater volume of exports is made to the European countries than to the American nations.

Chilean wines have justifiably found a very ready acceptance wherever they have been offered. In the United States, where they are very moderately priced, they represent some of the best wine values available to the consuming public.

WINES FROM FRUITS
OTHER THAN THE GRAPE

In a broad sense, the properly fermented, freshly expressed juice of any fruit may be called wine, though we think of wine in its narrower meaning—the product of the juice of the grape.

Commercially, at any rate, wine obtained from other fruits is a minor business. The chief exceptions are cider, obtained from apples; and in a lesser degree, perry, from pears; and blackberry wine.

CIDER AND PERRY

CIDER, or *Sidra*, in Spanish, comes from the Hebrew word *Shekhar*, meaning strong drink. Cider and perry are obtained by the vinous fermentation of the freshly expressed juice of the fruits. Their alcoholic content varies from 2 to 8 per cent and is sometimes slightly higher. This, of course, is the cider which we in America call "hard cider," as opposed to the non-alcoholic sweet cider.

In Spain and England, a secondary fermentation occasionally takes place in the bottle, producing a wine called "Champagne Cider." All Spanish cider, indeed, is treated in this manner.

Just as good eating grapes are poor wine varieties, so apples and pears which are good to eat are poor for making cider or perry.

Both cider and perry are rather sweet beverages which are wholesome and have the pronounced flavor of the fruit. Champagne cider—we are most familiar with the fine Spanish variety—is somewhat sweet and has a pleasant apple flavor. This is made by a secondary fermentation taking place in the bottle, as Champagne is made. The fermentation is produced by adding a small amount of pure cane sugar syrup, the carbon dioxide thus created being retained in the bottle. In Latin America vast quantities of it are sold as the poor man's Champagne, because it is always about half as expensive as Champagne. It is also useful in making punches and cups.

DANISH CHERRY AND BLACK CURRANT WINES

THE most interesting non-grape wine that has found a considerable market in America is the cherry wine of Denmark. Made from the small, black *langeskov* cherries, native to Denmark, the wine possesses not only the lovely cherry flavor but the subtle accent of the cherry stones, which remain present during its production.

Some black currant wine from the same origin has also received acceptance, while the ginger-flavored currant wine from London, England, is also gaining popularity. It is marketed as the "Original Green Ginger Wine."

Both wines are fortified, being shipped with an alcoholic content of approximately $17\frac{1}{2}$ per cent and $19\frac{1}{2}$ per cent, respectively. They are rich in fruitiness and quite sweet—a good reason for their popularity. They are most pleasant if served well chilled, or in mixed drinks, and the cherry wine is finding wide use in the kitchen to give the delightful dash of cherry flavor to fruits and desserts.

Cherry and other fruit wines, such as apple, plum, bilberry, blackberry, black currant, elderberry, gooseberry, honey wine (in reality this is *mead*, i.e., fermented honey, and should not be classified as wine in its true sense), raspberry, red currant, and strawberry, are also imported to the United States from Czechoslovakia, Israel, Holland, Japan, Poland, and Yugoslavia. Each has its own individual flavor appeal. All are very sweet and fruity.

U.S. APPLE, BLACKBERRY, CHERRY, ELDERBERRY, AND LOGANBERRY WINES

MANY fruits besides grapes are used in the United States to make wine but the only ones made commercially today are apple, blackberry, cherry, elderberry, and loganberry. The examples which we have tasted were well-made, clean, fruity wines. They are produced primarily along the eastern seaboard, mostly in New York and Georgia, and in California.

The wines are usually made from fresh frozen fruit or concentrated fruit juice, although some dried fruit may also be added. In all cases it is necessary to add water and pure cane sugar. The fruit musts have to be ameliorated with sugar to balance their high acid content. For example, the acid content of blackberry must is about one per cent, principally isocitric acid, which gives the wine its distinctive character.

Most of the commercial fruit wines are marketed at 12 to $12\frac{1}{2}$ per cent of alcohol, but some are fortified with brandy obtained from the same fruit, to 20 per cent.

In the fabrication of home-made wines, however, the list is quite extensive, including such fruits as gooseberry, elderberry, raspberry, blackberry, strawberry, currant, and cranberry. These ferment and produce good wholesome wine.

Pulpy fruits such as peach, apricot, plum, and cherry are also used occasionally, but they are not, as a rule, as successful in making wine as are berries.

However, all of these fruits require the addition of a substantial proportion of sugar as their acids overbalance their natural sugar content.

A dry or sweet wine of distinctive character is often made from the common dandelion.

"POP" WINES

"POP" or flavored wines are made from a base of natural wine to which herbs, spices, fruit juices and other natural flavorings are added. As a rule they are sweet wines, but brandy is not added as is the case of most sweet dessert wines. In fact, most of today's popular "pop" wines have a relatively low alcohol content—10 to 12 per cent.

Flavored wines have been with us for quite some time. But for years, the low alcohol types were not feasible, in most cases, because of the relatively short shelf life of the product. Therefore, what flavored wines that were produced were in the 20 per cent alcoholic range. Possibly the best known of the group was Gallo's *Thunderbird*. This wine was introduced in 1957 and is still popular today.

In the early sixties thanks to improved filtration methods it became possible to "pasteurize" wine without loosing any of its taste. This made it possible to produce a flavored wine of low alcohol content, but with good shelf life. In 1964, the first of the low alcohol "pop" wines was introduced— Swiss Colony's *Bali Hai*, with its flavorful fruit punch taste. Four years later, Gallo introduced its "pop" fruit flavored—apple, strawberry, cherry, elderberry—wines and a new trend in wine drinking was under way.

The "pop" wines are a very important part of the so-called youth market. While most of the sales of "pop" wines are to people under 30, they are performing a most useful purpose to the entire wine industry. That is, "pop" wines are serving as a means of bridging the gap between the young soft-drink consumer and the neophyte user of light alcoholic beverages. They are starting to educate his taste buds to some small degree to the pleasures of wine drinking.

SACRAMENTAL WINES

FROM the beginning, as we have already pointed out, there has been a close alliance between wine and religion. Even during the era of Prohibition in the United States, wine for religious purposes was permitted. It is, therefore, within the scope of this work to comment on the sacramental use of wine. Almost all of the Western religions use wine in their ritual, the two most important, as regards frequency of use, being the Roman Catholic and Jewish.

USE OF WINE IN THE MASS

THROUGH the kindness of the Dean of Cathedral College, New York, the reference works of the Sacred Congregation of the Holy Office were made available, providing the following information:

To be valid, the wine used in the Eucharistic Sacrifice must be pure grape juice which has passed through the natural period of fermentation. Without the process of fermentation, the juice of the grape does not constitute true wine and consequently cannot be used in the Mass. The Congregation of Sacraments, on July 31, 1890, said: "Provided that the alcohol has been extracted from the fruit of the grape, and the quantity added, together with that which the wine to be treated naturally possesses, does not exceed the proportion of 12 per cent, there is no obstacle in the way of using such wine in the Holy Sacrifice of the Mass." This means that the alcohol contained in the juice from the grape itself, plus that added from an outside source, must not exceed 12 per cent, and the addition must be made soon after the juice is pressed from the grape.

Sour wine is also invalid for use in the Mass, and no chemical process may be resorted to in order to correct the natural tartness of the wine, such as the use of tartrate or potassium. In addition, it was declared by the Sacred Congregation of the Holy Office that sugar should not be added to the wine. To preserve the extra sweet wines, however, the Holy Office, on August 5, 1896, allowed the addition which should not exceed the proportion of 17 or 18 per cent, provided such addition be made when the fermentation had commenced to subside.

As to its color, the wine may be either red or white.°

Wine is also used for the Communion Service by many Protestant denominations.

USE OF WINE IN THE SYNAGOGUE

RABBI A. HYMAN kindly furnished the information as to the use of wine in the Synagogue and in the homes of pious Jews.

° References:
De Sacramentis in Geneve, Tanguerey, page 80.
Matters Liturgical, Wuest Mullaney, page 56.
Catechism of the Council of Trent, McHugh and Collan, pp. 221–223.

In order to be used for ritual purposes, the wine must be made according to the Rabbinical law and must be a pure, natural wine, unmixed, and sound. It may be either red or white. If it becomes sour, or has impurities from the lees, it cannot be used. There is no such thing as a "sanctified wine" in the sense that a special wine is used in the Synagogue. The same wine may be used in the Temple as is used in the home.

Wine is used in the Synagogue in the Friday evening services to announce the incoming of the Sabbath, and also on the eve of the Festivals. It is used at the home service, Friday nights and on Holy Days, its most widespread use being on the two Seder nights of Passover, when it is obligatory for each one to drink four glasses of wine. As a general rule, red wine is used, but white wine is permissible also.

Both at the incoming prayer of the Sabbath, Friday evening, and the outgoing prayer at the end of the Sabbath, Saturday evening, wine is used. In the Synagogue and at home, the amount of wine served at these two services, according to ancient ritual, should equal an egg and a half full—about $2\frac{1}{2}$ ounces—and more than half of it must be drunk.

At wedding ceremonies, a glass of wine must be used by the bride and bridegroom.

PASSOVER WINES

IN America, the home-made Passover wine is being replaced to a large extent by strictly supervised modern wineries, which meet all the requirements of the religious laws.

This wine is made primarily from the Concord grape, grown in the Central and Eastern States, which seems to fit in with the need for a mellow, rich wine.

The Concord wine is rich, sweet, and of a deep purplish color. After the wine has fermented out naturally, pure cane sugar is added as sweetening in order to counteract the natural acidity of the grape, and balance the pronounced flavor.

17. Distilled Spirits in General

THE origin of the art and science of distillation is shrouded in the dim past. It is poetical to call its secret a gift of the gods, but it is more reasonable to suppose that it was discovered by some long-forgotten alchemist.

The essence of the principle of distillation is this: alcohol vaporizes, i.e., becomes a gas, at a lower temperature than water. The boiling point of water is 212° F., when it becomes steam or vapor; while that of alcohol is 176° F. Therefore, if heat is applied to an alcohol-containing liquid, and the temperature is kept below 212° F., all of the alcohol may be separated from the original liquid. If, at the same time, an apparatus is used whereby the alcoholic vapors are gathered and not allowed to escape into the air, it is possible to recondense them into liquid form. The result will be an alcohol of high purity. This sounds simple and so it is, if one wishes to produce alcohol, but if one is trying to produce a potable alcoholic beverage, the problem is more difficult, and, if the product is to be a fine one, more delicate.

Apparently the science of distillation was known to the ancient Egyptians *history* and Chaldeans. Long before the Christian era the Chinese obtained a spirit from rice beer; and Arak has been distilled from sugar cane and rice in the East Indies since 800 B.C. Later we find Aristotle (384–322 B.C.), the great Greek philosopher, stating in his *Meteorology* that "sea water can be made potable by distillation; wine and other liquids can be submitted to the same process." There are many such references to distilled spirits in ancient writings. Even Captain Cook, on his voyage of discovery to the South Pacific, found the natives of the islands familiar with the distillation process.

For our practical purposes, however, the modern history of distillation may be said to date from the Arabs or Saracens. They gave us the words "alcohol" and "alembic"—the word for still, used in all but English-speaking countries. The first mention of distillation is attributed to an Arabian alchemist of the tenth century, one Albukassen; later in the thirteenth century a Majorcan chemist and philosopher, Ramon Lull, described the process. Even before his time, the Celts of Eire and Scotia, unaware of the efforts of the Arabs, were producing a potable spirit which they called *uisgebeatha* or *uisgebaugh*—"water of life."

Curiously enough, every ancient treatise referred to spirits as *acquae vite* or *aqua vitae*—the *eau de vie* of France today. It is strange that the product men have designated from the beginning as the "water of life" should have been regarded by many in this country as dangerous to life.

Although modern science has progressed amazingly, and methods have grown more and more efficient, the apparatus used for distilling most spirits is still much the same, save for a few refinements, as the one used by the original distillers, many centuries ago. Reduced to its two essential parts, it consists of a still and a worm condenser. The still is a copper pot, with a broad, rounded bottom, and a long taper-neck. The worm condenser is a copper spiral tube which is connected to the still by a copper pipe. The worm passes through a jacket containing cold water to assist in a more rapid condensation of the vapors. Such an apparatus is known in the trade as a pot still. Pot stills are used exclusively in the distillation of brandies, Scotch and most Irish whiskies, most liqueurs, Arak, and some rums.

In 1826, Robert Stein, of the famous Scotch whisky distilling family, invented the patent still. This was later perfected by Aeneas Coffey, whose patent replaced Stein's and whose name has come down to us in connection with this type of still, which is known as a Coffey or patent still.

spirits So far in this book we have discussed wines, which are the result of the natural processes of fermentation of the sugar contained in the grape juice. Now we are about to take up those alcoholic beverages which are obtained by distilling out the essence of an alcohol-containing liquid. There are many of these, and while we shall consider each type in separate chapters, it is important to classify and define them now.

BRANDY is a potable spirit, suitably aged in wood, obtained by distilling wine or a fermented mash of fruit. Examples are: Cognac, Armagnac, Spanish brandy, Greek brandy, American brandy, Kirsch or Kirschwasser (cherry brandy), Calvados or Apple Jack (apple brandy), Slivovitz (plum brandy), and other fruit brandies.

WHISKEY is a spirit, suitably aged in wood, usually oak, obtained from the distillation of a fermented mash of grain. Examples are: Scotch whisky, Irish whiskey, Canadian whisky, Rye whiskey, Bourbon whiskey.

RUM is a potable spirit, suitably aged in wood, obtained from the distillation of a fermented mash of sugar-cane juice or molasses. Examples are: Jamaica rum, Demerara rum, Barbadoes rum, Martinique rhum, Cuban ron, Puerto Rican ron, Haitian rhum, Philippine ron, Batavia Arak, and others.

GIN is a flavored beverage, obtained by rectifying a high-proof spirit in the presence of a flavoring agent. Examples are: English London dry and Old Tom gins, Geneva, Schiedam or Hollands gin, American gins similar to these, and fruit-flavored gins.

VODKA is neutral spirits so distilled, or so treated after distillation with charcoal or other material, as to be without distinctive character, aroma, taste, or color. If any flavoring material is added to the distillate, the vodka is usually characterized with the name of the flavoring material used.

CORDIALS or LIQUEURS are flavored beverages, whose flavor is obtained either by infusion or distillation of the flavoring agent, to which is then added simple syrup for sweetening. They may or may not be artificially colored. All liqueurs or cordials are sweet. For tariff and taxation purposes, the regulations specify that a cordial or liqueur must have in excess of $2\frac{1}{2}$ per cent of sugar by volume. Examples are: apricot liqueur, Bénédictine, blackberry liqueur, Cointreau, Crême de Cassis, Crême de Cacao, Crême de Menthe, Chartreuse, Grand Marnier, Prunelle, strawberry liqueur, Triple Sec, and many others.

MISCELLANEOUS SPIRITS are obtained by distilling from various starchy or sugar-containing products. They include: Akvavit, Tequila, Pulque, Okolehao, Bitters.

In other words, we have merely said that a potable spirit, obtained from a given basic material, has an accepted trade name. But it should be explained that the factors which make them differ from one another are the matters, aside from alcohol, which are necessarily distilled out with the alcohol: the flavoring elements, the small amounts of alcohols other than ethyl; the solids and minerals, which differ in fruits, grains, and sugar cane.

While distillation is in progress, it can be carried to the point where all the alcohol is separated. The resultant spirit would be pure, or absolute alcohol of 200 proof. Such a spirit would be the same, whether obtained from fruit, grain, or molasses, and would have no character whatsoever. We are not concerned here with such a pure spirit—in fact, for all practical purposes a spirit of 190 proof is sufficiently neutral for blending, and such spirits are used by the trade daily. The trade term for them is *neutral spirits* or *cologne spirits*.

Newly distilled spirits, whether obtained from fruit, grain, or molasses, are colorless, have little character, and are quite similar. They have a sharp, biting aroma and taste. When they have been matured for a certain length of time in wood, however, the "impurities" or congeners develop, creating products entirely different in aroma, taste, and character.

The various congeners in spirits consist of fusel oils, extracts of mineral salts and solids in minute quantities, acids, esters, aldehydes, and furfural.

Fusel oils are other, or higher alcohols, such as propyl, butyl, amyl, hexyl, heptyl, and the dialcohols and trialcohols.

Acids found in spirits vary with different liquors, but include propionic, butyric, tartaric, lactic, succinic, and so forth.

Esters are produced by the combination of the acids and the alcohols, and form the volatile substance that gives the aroma to the spirit.

Aldehydes are produced by the combination of the alcohols and air, and are a contributing factor in giving a distinctive character to the spirit.

Furfural is an aldehyde. It is mostly obtained during distillation and partly extracted from the oak casks in which spirits are matured.

When the freshly distilled spirit flows from the still it is colorless, has a sharp pungent alcoholic aroma and sharp taste. If distilled out at 180 proof, it would be difficult for any but experienced distillers to differentiate among distillates of grain, fruit (grape), or cane. When the spirit is distilled out at a lower proof, 160 or less, it contains more congeners, and naturally has more character. Such a spirit, upon maturing in wood, undergoes certain changes in its composition, which develop its flavor and character.

Once it is placed in glass, and sealed against air, no further change will take place. But as long as it is in wood, there is constant change, brought about by the oxidizing effect of the air or oxygen on the alcohol. The oxidation, or burning, causes the esters and acids to increase materially, the aldehydes slowly, the fusel oils to remain practically the same, and a certain amount of loss of alcohol to take place in proportion to volume. Furthermore, the spirit will absorb some tannin and other coloring material from the wood container, and become less harsh and, in a sense, sweeter than it was originally.

proof   Before the making of distilled spirits became a science, the primitive distillers had a very simple method for determining the potable strength of the distillate. An equal quantity of spirit and gunpowder were mixed and a flame applied. If the gunpowder failed to burn, the spirit was too weak; if it burned too brightly, it was too strong. But if the mixture burned evenly, with a blue flame, it was said to have been "proved."

Today we know that this potable mean was approximately 50 per cent of alcohol by volume, and we have adopted the term "proof" to describe the strength of alcoholic beverages. In the United States proof spirit is a spirit containing 50 per cent of alcohol by volume at a temperature of 60° F. This is an arbitrary measurement. Each degree of proof is equal to one-half of one per cent of alcohol. Therefore, a spirit of 90 proof contains 45 per cent of alcohol, and a spirit of 150 proof contains 75 per cent of alcohol. The trade term for a spirit of more than 100 proof is "overproof" spirit. See page 492 for Gay Lussac and British Sikes tables.

rectified   What is rectifying? Theoretically, to purify or improve, but practically it
spirits   means anything which changes the character of a spirit, with certain exceptions as provided by law.

Rectified spirits must pay a "rectifying tax" of thirty cents per gallon.

Rectifying must be performed in an establishment which holds a "Rectifier's License."

What constitutes rectifying?

1. Blending two different spirits.

2. Blending two different whiskies, i.e., whiskies distilled in two different distilleries or in two different seasons of the year.

3. Blending whiskey with neutral spirits.

4. Redistillation of a whiskey which has been stored in a barrel.

5. Adding coloring, flavoring, or anything except water.

6. Redistillation of neutral spirits for potable purposes.

7. The distillation of neutral spirits over a flavoring agent.

8. Compounding of spirits, essential oils or other flavors and sugar to make cordials and liqueurs.

The following do NOT constitute rectifying and consequently are not subject to the thirty cents per gallon rectification tax:

1. The blending of whiskies which are four years old or more.

2. The making of gin by original distillation, redistillation, or by mixing spirits with juniper and other flavors.

3. The mere reduction in proof with water only.

Automated barrel-filling at Schenley's Bernheim Distillery in Louisville, Kentucky. (Courtesy of Schenley Industries, Inc.)

THERAPEUTIC VALUE OF SPIRITS

THE whole question of drinking, unhappily, has been invested with so much mumbo-jumbo, loudly proclaimed by badly informed zealots of reform, that the quieter, more restrained voices of the scientific investigators have been drowned out. There is room in all this discussion for a balanced judgment which can recognize the beneficial qualities of alcoholic beverages to man, and at the same time be aware of their faults.

The biggest bugaboo of all is the fact that these beverages contain alcohol. Alcohol is a compound of several elements: carbon, hydrogen, and oxygen, and in itself it not only is not harmful to man but is a necessary constituent of his blood stream. The normal alcoholic content of the average man's blood is .003 per cent, the alcohol being produced by the action of the gastric juices on the sugars and starches consumed.

Alcohol is the only food taken into the system which is unaffected by the digestive system. The stomach and intestines pass it into the blood stream, unchanged, and it is diffused so rapidly, that within a few minutes after swallowing, it has reached every part of the body. It is carried to the liver, then to the right ventricle of the heart, to the lungs, back to the left ventricle of the heart, then through the aorta into the arteries, and throughout the body, finally coming to the brain and the higher nerve centers. Here is where it has its most pronounced effect.

The popular idea is that alcohol is a stimulant. Pathologically, that is not true. There is a false stimulation due to the loss of control of the inhibitory nerve centers which control heart beat, thus increasing the heart beat and causing a sensation of warmth. Actually, the effect is relaxing rather than stimulating.

Again, in regard to this sensation of warmth, there is another general misconception. It is actually only the surface of the body, the skin, which is warmed; and in reality more heat is given off by the body than is supplied by the alcohol. As a matter of fact, alcohol is an excellent way of reducing body heat rapidly. This is why so much rum is drunk in the tropics. It is more cooling than ice water.

All investigations made on the toxic effects of alcohol have been based on doses of pure alcohol. These effects are materially reduced as dilution is increased, and when alcohol is part of other substances, such as the solids of wine or beer, its intoxicating quality is reduced further.

A book which has done much to correct the countless misconceptions about the properties of alcohol is Morris E. Chafetz's *Liquor, the Servant of Man,* which proves conclusively the following points:

"Alcohol is actually manufactured in the human body, but is less toxic than most of the other natural secretions, such as thyroid, pituitary, adrenal, pancreas and bile.

"Alcohol, if taken in anything remotely approaching customary amounts, is harmless to the body and in many cases beneficial.

"Alcohol is one of the most valuable medicines in the world, both as a sedative and as a food, is useful for these and other reasons in many disease conditions, and is almost always indicated in old age.

"Alcohol, to indulge in an understatement, has had a conspicuous position in the history of the race. It fathered religion and science and agriculture, provided more human confidence, and promoted good will toward men. It is the most efficient and practical relaxer of the driving force in the brain; it offers an immediate method of personal enjoyment; it is the greatest medium known for the purpose of permitting man to forget, at least for a little while, the shortness of life and the ludicrously helpless and infinitesimal part he plays in the functions of the universe."

Alcohol is absorbed, in its original state, from the stomach directly into the blood stream.

points to remember about alcohol

Alcohol does not physically damage any of the healthy important organs of the body, such as the heart, liver, kidneys, stomach, brain, or nervous system.

The normal alcoholic strength of human blood (teetotalers included) is .003 per cent. In the average adult, the lethal limit is around .7 per cent.

Alcohol produces energy without making the body work, because it is taken into the blood stream in its original state. Alcohol itself does not produce fat. Other foods, which would normally produce the energy needed by the body, are stored, as an energy reserve, in the form of fat by those who drink regularly in substantial amounts.

The part of the body most quickly and directly affected by alcohol is the brain. Its effect, both on the brain and the nervous system, is relaxing, not stimulating.

Excess of alcohol once absorbed cannot be "worked off" except by oxidation and excretion. The normal rate of elimination is about 10 c.c.° per hour and this remains constant, whether you lie in bed, walk around in the open, or sit in a Turkish bath.

The best insulation against the effects of over-indulgence is food to line the walls of the stomach. The best food is the fat of milk. In the order of their protection value, these are the foods you can take: cream, whole milk, butter, meat fats, olive oil, and meat.

The heart of a hang-over is fatigue poison, lactic acid, physiologically induced by the alcohol. The only cure is rest and time.

There is no evidence that alcohol in itself causes any disease.

° This is one-third of an ounce of absolute alcohol.

The principal danger of too much alcohol is social. One who is drunk—whether from imbibing one or ten drinks—has a narcotized brain—one which is not awake. In a moment of crisis, when a quick decision is necessary, the part of the brain which reasons may be awake, while the part which commands the muscles may be asleep, or vice versa. The result in either case is trouble.

Alcohol is prescribed in many ailments, but is proscribed in some for which the layman believes it most valuable. These are shock, snake bite, fatigue, and colds. In the first two the blood pressure is lowered. That's what alcohol does to you. Fatigue means that you have too much lactic acid in the system and alcohol adds to it.

The conclusion one reaches from the assembled evidence is that alcoholic beverages in themselves, even when consumed in large quantities, are not damaging nor harmful to man, physically. When taken temperately, they are beneficial.

We do not advocate that anyone drink for the "kick." Drinking should be done for pleasure, relaxation, and the release to which the beverage contributes; it should be made a part of the good life.

18. Brandies

BRANDIES OF FRANCE

BRANDY is a potable spirit obtained from the distillation of wine or a fermented mash of fruit, which usually has been suitably aged in wood. An alcoholic beverage answering this description may be produced in any part of the world, except Antartica. However, when we say brandy, we usually mean the delightful "soul" of wine. In this sense, brandy is distilled wherever wine grapes grow and are pressed. There is one brandy which the world has accepted and recognized as superior to all others. This is Cognac brandy.

It is important to understand that *all Cognac is brandy, but all brandies are not Cognac.* Cognac is a brandy distilled from wines made of grapes grown within the legal limits of the Charente and Charente Inférieure Departments of France. Brandies distilled from wines other than these are not legally entitled to the name Cognac, even though they be shipped from the city of Cognac, by a recognized and reputable Cognac shipper.

history The art of distillation, although known to the ancients, was not applied to wine commercially until the sixteenth century, when the brandy trade began. According to legend, a brisk trade in wine existed between the port of La Rochelle, on the Charente River, and Holland. All of this trade was carried on by sea, and the perils of war, which were great then as they are now, placed a premium on shipping.

Casks of wine take up quite a lot of space, particularly if you are using small sailing vessels. So the story is told of one very bright Dutch shipmaster who hit upon the idea of concentrating the wine—eliminating the water—transporting the spirit, or the "soul," of the wine to Holland, where the water could be put back. In his thrifty mind he figured that he could save an enormous amount on the freight charges.

When this enterprising man arrived in Holland, however, with his "concentrated wine," his Dutch friends tasted it and liked it as it was. It would be

253

a waste of water, they decided, to try to make it wine again. And thus the brandy trade had its inception. The Dutch called the new product *brandewijn* (burnt wine), presumably because fire, or heat, is used in the process of distillation. In time this term was Anglicized to the present-day word—brandy.

COGNAC*

THE ancient city of Cognac, on the Charente River, is in the heart of the district which produces the brandies that have carried its fame throughout the world. In fact, they have done the job so well that Cognac is probably the best-known French word in the world. In far-off China, or deep in darkest Africa, the word Cognac will evoke smiles of recognition when any other French word would produce a blank stare.

The story is told of a certain Cardinal who was dining one day in Rome with several other Cardinals, all come to pay their respects to the Holy Father. One of the princes of the Church, turning to the newcomer, asked: "Where is your See?"

"I am Bishop of Angoulême," he replied, and then, amused by their blank expressions, he added, with a twinkle in his eye: "I am also Bishop of Cognac!"

Smiles lit up the faces of his brother Cardinals. "Ah, the magnificent bishopric!" they exclaimed.

The Cognac district, the Charentais, has seven subdivisions, which, in the order of quality, are:

a. Grande Champagne
b. Petite Champagne
c. Borderies
d. Fins Bois
e. Bons Bois
f. Bois Ordinaires
g. Bois communs dits
   à Terroir

The qualities which make Cognac superior to all other brandies are not only the special process of distillation used in this district for centuries, but also the combination of ideal soil, climate, and other conditions. While it might be possible for another section to reproduce one or two of these essentials, the combination of all the factors cannot be achieved elsewhere.

The Cognac region was delimited by law in 1909. The Grande Champagne is a small district which is the kernel of the region. In it lies the town of Cognac about which everything centers, the territory, the commerce, and the fame of the product. Almost completely surrounding it is the Petite Champagne. To the north, and situated about at the point where the encirclement of the Grande Champagne is incomplete, are the Borderies, the smallest district.

* We are indebted to Julius Wile for permission to use his fine report on Cognac for much of the information in this section.

Completely surrounding these first three districts are the Fins Bois. Around all these are the Bons Bois. And advancing from the Bons Bois to the Atlantic Ocean in the west, one passes through the Bois Ordinaires and the Bois à Terroir.

If the Bordeaux system of classifying growths were to be followed, one might say that the two Champagnes plus the Borderies would make up the great *crus;* the Fins Bois, the bourgeois *crus;* and the last three, the ordinary *crus.*

The nature of the soil is limy, and the more lime, the finer the wines produced for distillation.

The grape varieties which produce the wine are predominantly the St. Emilion (elsewhere called the Ugni Blanc) with a small amount of Folle Blanche and Colombar, all white grapes. They produce a white wine which is fruity, thin, and slightly acid, harsh and unpleasant to drink, with an average alcoholic content of 8 to 10 per cent.

In Cognac, the little farmer often has his own still. Big shippers very often own a vineyard or two but they cannot possibly own the amount of vineyard land they need to take care of the demand for wine to produce brandy to supply the world. It is the custom in Cognac, therefore, for all the shippers to buy the brandy from the farmer. Each farmer has his little vineyard, gathers his grapes, makes his wine, and distills it as soon as it falls bright or has it distilled for him by one of the regional distillers. Distillation of brandy in France and in Cognac is supervised by Government inspectors. They have padlocks and seals on every one of these stills. At vintage time the inspectors visit each farm, measure the wine, and tell the farmer how much he can distill from such an amount.

The grapes are picked, pressed, and allowed to ferment, then dumped into stills or alembics—skins, pips, and all. These impurities are necessary to give the full character to the brandy. The stills are the old-fashioned pot stills; there are no modern patent stills in Cognac. Naturally, when you have so many different men carrying out this process of distillation, you will have a variety, so each shipper examines and tastes the young, new brandy. Sometimes the farmers will decide to keep a puncheon or so of brandy, but usually they sell it as soon as it has been distilled. At that time, as with other spirits, it is colorless and has a sharp, but fruity, coppery bouquet and taste. This coppery character, "goût de cuivre," passes after the brandy has been in wood for a year.

At the distillery, the wine is received in large wooden casks, demimuids of about 157 gallons capacity. As the wine producers make wine both for consumption and distillation, there is always the temptation to mix the lees and other deposits from the drinkable wine with the wine to be distilled. The new wine, therefore, passing from the receiving room to the stills, goes through settling basins where gravity draws out the excess impurities. The wine now enters the still.

The distilling apparatus consists of a simple boiler, heated directly by a coal or wood fire. On top of the boiler is a metal hood to collect the vapors before they pass through to the condenser. This condenser is simply a pipe coiled inside of a large container which is continually supplied with cold water to provide the difference in temperature necessary to condense the vapors which then trickle out into a receiving can. All the metal used in a still of this type is pure copper.

The conversion of the wine into *eau-de-vie de Charente* is accomplished in two operations: the *première chauffe* and the *bonne chauffe*. The first gives a distillation of about 30 per cent alcoholic strength, which is then redistilled to give the *eau-de-vie*. The liquid coming from the condenser commences at a very high alcoholic content which eventually goes down to zero when the distillation is finished.

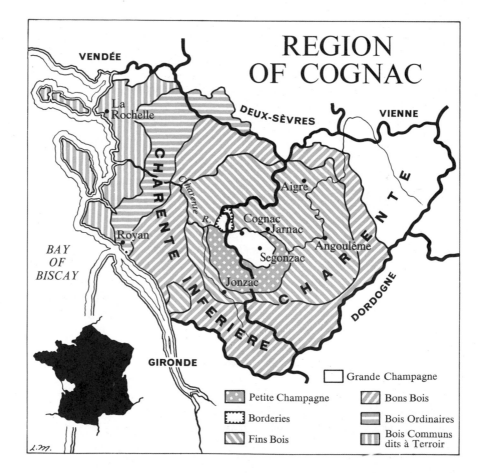

The most important thing in the distillation of Cognac is regularity: regularity of procedure, regularity of heating, and regularity of quantity. The alembics work continuously, twenty-four hours a day, seven days a week, during the distilling season, which lasts from three to eight months, depending on the quantity of the vintage.

As it comes from the alembic, the brandy is colorless, has about 70 per cent of alcohol, and a fruity, coppery taste and smell which come more from the newly formed ethers than from the copper in the still.

Cognac is aged in casks made of "limousin oak," obtained from the forest near Limoges. The cooperage must be very good to stand up for forty to fifty years. The casks are laid away in light-tight cellars or warehouses.

In the cask the Cognac changes by action of the wood and by contact with the oxygen in the air which enters through the pores of the wood, between the staves, and by the bung. In the same way that the air enters, the brandy evaporates, so there is a continual, inevitable loss in volume. As the alcohol evaporates more rapidly than the water and other constituents of the brandy, there is also a diminution of strength, rapid during the first few years, becoming more gradual after that, the average being about 1 per cent per year. During this time the brandy gradually changes from a colorless state, taking on a beautiful amber tone, and the taste and perfume are changed, so that which finally results is a finished Cognac, a delicate mellow liqueur with a natural bouquet of grape blossoms.

Today the demand is for qualities which remain the same, year in and year out, and therefore there are few vintage Cognacs in existence. This requires large stocks being held by the brandy merchant, and judicious and exact blending.

This *coupage*, or blending, is done many months before bottling. The various brandies are put into tremendous oaken vats, brought down to shipping strength—from 40 to 43 per cent alcohol as required—by the addition of distilled water. Coloring matter (caramel) is added to assure uniform color in every bottle. Inside these vats, wooden, propeller-like paddles rotate from time to time, thoroughly mixing the brandies. In several months' time, the blend, thoroughly "married," is put in bottles, cased, and is ready for market.

The French Government has passed laws to protect the public as to what is and is not Cognac. It supplies every purchaser with a certificate, called an *Acquit Régional Jaune d'Or*. This has nothing to do with age; it merely guarantees that the product comes from Cognac.

The various qualities of Cognacs are generally indicated by stars: one, two, or three, in ascending quality. All wine people are superstitious. One of their firmest beliefs is that comet years produce fine wines. The legend goes that in the comet year of 1811, when a superb brandy was produced, one of the shippers decided to designate the brandy of that year with a star. An equally excellent brandy was produced in the following year and this he designated by two stars. By this time he had acquired the habit, but fortunately he stopped when he reached five stars. The firm of Hennessy claims to have originated the system. *The stars on the label have no age significance.* Each house blends its brandies for uniformity of quality, which is maintained year in and year out. The standards represented by the stars vary with the different houses. For instance, all "3 star" brands will not be alike, for with one house it might be a ten-year brandy, with another a six-year brandy, and with still another a twenty-year brandy.

Aside from the matter of stars on the label, all brandy houses handling better quality brandies use letters to indicate quality. And the letters, oddly enough, represent not French words—but English. They represent the following:

E means Especial	S means Superior
F means Fine	P means Pale
V means Very	X means Extra
O means Old	C means Cognac

For instance, when you see on the neck label of a bottle of cognac the letters V.S., they mean Very Superior; S.F.C. means Superior Fine Cognac, and so forth.

There is a good deal of misunderstanding about the question of age in Cognac. It improves in the wood for roughly fifty to fifty-five years. The cost of aging the brandy for this length of time is very high, as the losses through evaporation and the risk of aging too long are considerable, and make the ultimate selling prices so excessive that even millionaires would refuse to pay them. Once the Cognac is bottled, it neither varies nor improves. A Cognac bottled in 1900 will taste exactly the same today as it did the day it was placed in the glass.

The romantic nonsense about the one-hundred-and-more-year-old so-called Napoleon Brandies is nothing but a come-on for the gullible amateur.

The question naturally arises: "What is the best age for Cognac?" To quote the late M. Georges Soullet of Cognac, France: "Cognac is like a woman. She is at her best between the ages of twenty-five and forty." He obviously knew Cognac as well as he knew the ladies.

From the consumer's point of view, there are several questions which are frequently asked.

"What is 'Fine Champagne?'" This means that the brandies have been made from grapes grown either in the Grande or Petite Champagne; consequently a Fine Champagne Cognac should be very good.

"What is *Fine de la Maison?*" In France every restaurant includes among its list of brandies a Fine de la Maison. This is its "bar" brandy, and can be anything the worthy boniface wishes to buy. More than likely it will be "everything but" Cognac, and will usually be a sound enough French brandy.

Cognac still room showing the traditional alembics—*copper pot stills—used for generations.* (Courtesy Cognac Producers of France)

It does not mean that it is "Fine Champagne Cognac." When you order a "Fine" (pronounced feen) all you can expect is brandy of some sort.

As for the "snifters," they are not best for the appreciation of Cognac. The large body and relatively small opening are good, but the size requires too much to be put into each glass. The glass should never be larger than one capable of being held and warmed in one hand. By the same token avoid the tiny, thimble-size, one-ounce pony or cordial glass.

The question of bottles is also important. An old bottle means nothing. Distilled spirits do not change in corked bottles. Much better is an old brandy from the wood in a gleaming, newly labeled container. Large magnum bottles are bad. It is true that a bottle of Cognac need not be consumed at one sitting like a bottle of wine. However, it stands to reason that the larger the bottle, the longer it remains partly full, and the combination of evaporation and oxidation in contact with air in time results in a flat and lifeless drink.

A good test of a fine Cognac is to empty a glass after it has been thoroughly wetted on the inside by the brandy. The glass will retain its delicious aroma for hours, and even days.

ARMAGNAC

SECOND only to Cognac is the Armagnac brandy produced in the Department of Gers, southeast of Bordeaux. The center of the trade is Condom. The principal vine, as in Cognac, is the St. Emilion, plus the Folle Blanche, here called the Piquepoul, plus the Colombard, and others.

The only essential difference in the system of distilling Armagnac and Cognac is that in the former the original and redistillation operations are continuous whereas in the latter they comprise two separate operations. Another difference lies in the fact that the Armagnac aging casks are made of black oak of Gascony instead of the limousin oak of Cognac.

There are some who prefer Armagnac to Cognac, because it is often shipped as vintage brandy, and has a drier, harder taste than the carefully vatted Cognacs. This is a matter of taste.

MARC

BRANDIES distilled from the grape pomace of the wine press are called *Eau de Vie de Marc* (pronounced mar), and are obtained in various parts of France, but notably in Burgundy. They have a straw, woody taste and character much appreciated by some connoisseurs.

Grappa brandy, produced in Italy and California, is also obtained from the grape pomace. In California, Grappa is generally stored in paraffined barrels, which prevents its taking color from the wood. Grappa is usually unaged. It is quite colorless, and sharp in taste.

Substantial quantities of good brandy are distilled in various parts of France, outside of the delimited Cognac and Armagnac regions. These are what you get in France if you order a "Fine" in a Paris or Marseilles bistro. They are, generally speaking, good clean and pleasant brandies, that do not pretend to have the character of quality of Cognac. Logically, they are less costly.

BRANDIES OF OTHER LANDS

SPANISH BRANDY

SOME of the Spanish brandy is distilled from Sherry wine, but today a good part of the blend is made up of brandies distilled from wines of other wine regions of Spain. Spanish brandies are developed and aged by the same solera system used for Sherry wine. Spanish brandy has a distinctive aroma and flavor and is quite different from Cognac or Armagnac. It is a sweeter brandy and can be described as earthier.

The various qualities are distinguished by brand names. The outstanding houses (all Sherry shippers) that produce brandy are: Pedro Domecq, Gonzalez Byass, Terry, and Osborne.

Spanish brandy is one of the best produced outside of France. It has become quite popular in the United States in the years since Repeal.

PORTUGUESE BRANDY

BRANDY has been distilled in Portugal in commercial quantities ever since Porto wine, as we know it today, was developed. Therefore brandy distilling know-how was always there, but very little effort was ever made to develop an export market. It was only when World War II shut off the source of supply for Cognac and French brandies that American importers turned to Portugal. During the war years, vast quantities were imported into the United States, and today, although the quantities brought in are more modest, it is interesting to note that many consumers found the taste of Portuguese brandy to their liking. As a result a steady satisfactory volume is imported annually, which has exceeded the quantity of Spanish brandy imports practically every year since the trade was started in the early 1940s.

Similar to Spanish brandy, with its distinctive flavor from the Sherry wines, Portuguese brandy, being distilled from the same wines of the Douro (Porto) region, has its own bouquet and flavor strongly reminiscent of Porto wine.

AMERICAN BRANDY

ALMOST all of the beverage brandy distilled in the United States is obtained in California from wines of that State, where, since Repeal, production has reached some ten million gallons annually. In addition to this, there is now an average annual production of approximately thirty-three million gallons of "high proof" brandy which is used in the processing of fortified wines and as a base for cordials.

Beverage brandy is produced from selected lots of wine which possess characteristics especially suitable for brandy. The pot still, such as predominates in Cognac, is to be found in some brandy distilleries, but the "patent" or continuous still is preferred in California because it yields an extremely clean distillate and at the same time retains the highly desired congeners of the wine when distillation is performed at appropriate proof strength. It is also more efficient and produces a more uniform product.

White oak barrels of fifty gallons' capacity are used for the storage and aging, during which time the wood imparts the characteristic oak flavor and a light golden color to the brandy.

Ample stocks of sound, mature American brandy, some forty million tax gallons, have now been accumulated, despite the fact that the industry was compelled to start from scratch in 1933. However, official government records show that consumption of California beverage brandy has multiplied more than ten times between 1934 and 1972.

California brandy, like Armagnac or Spanish brandy, is different from Cognac brandy and must stand on its own merits. Time is the only maturer of spirits and each year there will be larger stocks of older and older brandies available for the market.

Some muscat brandy, distilled from muscat wines, is produced in California. It is quite similar in aroma and flavor to the Pisco described below.

PERU

As we have said before, wherever wine is made, brandy is distilled, but outside of South Africa, where a good quality brandy is produced, and the Pisco of Peru, the other wine regions' distillates are not sold with much success outside of their home markets.

Pisco takes its name from the port in southern Peru, whence it is shipped. This brandy is distilled from muscat wines produced in the Ica valley, near Pisco. Pisco is matured in porous clay jars. It is consumed in Peru quite young.

Pisco Punch, which is really a "sour," is the most popular cocktail in Peru, and Chile also. It is a delightfully pleasant drink, but we assure you—most insidious.

Muscat brandies produced both in Chile and Argentina, labeled Pisco, are sold locally, but not exported as such.

GERMANY

FROM Germany comes a soft, mellow grape brandy with characteristic mellow taste and fine aroma and bouquet. It is blended from especially selected distillates of wines from Germany, as well as from France, and matured in oak wood. The most famous German brandy is Asbach Uralt.

SOUTH AFRICA

SOUTH African brandies are made from young white wines, all of which must receive prior approval from Government supervisors before being distilled into brandy. Several grape types are used including Palomino, St. Emilion and Colombard, the most renown varieties of the Cognac region. Distillation and maturation procedures follow closely those of the Charente, the better brandies being matured in limousin oak casks. They must be matured for at least three years before bottling and a five-year-old Cape brandy can rank with many of its cousins from more famous brandy-producing areas. Ten years in cask results in a soft, smooth "liqueur" brandy much sought after in the home market and, therefore, seldom exported.

AUSTRALIA

In the early days of Australia's brandy industry, Lexia-Gordo Blanco (Muscat of Alexandria) grapes were employed. Today, however, the Doradillo—which is almost identical with the Spanish Jaen grape—is almost exclusively used in the making of drinking brandy. The result of switch in grape variety has meant an increase in popularity both at home and in export markets. All good Australian brandy is naturally matured in wood for at least three years.

GREEK BRANDY

A GREAT deal of brandy is distilled in Greece and much of it is exported. Greek brandy is becoming more popular. It usually has a clean flavor, with a touch of sweetness from the caramel used to give it color.

However, the most popular Greek brandy in the United States is Metaxa. In typical Greek fashion this brandy has been "improved." It is a distinctive, pleasant, sweet, flavored brandy, with a deep color.

Another brandy, flavored with anise and licorice, is Ouzo, the national apéritif of Greece. It is always white—colorless—and usually drunk as a long drink, mixed with cold water—four or five parts of water to one of Ouzo. When the water and ice are added, the concoction takes on a milky, opalescent hue. It makes a pleasant, fragrant beverage.

Cyprus is an independent sovereign country today but politics or not, she cannot separate herself from her Greek heritage. Cypriot brandies and Ouzo are good and very similar to those of Greece in all respects.

ISRAEL AND ITALY

GOOD, sound, clean grape brandy has been distilled in the Holy Land for a number of years, but it is only since the State of Israel came into being that any serious efforts have been made to export it. Israeli brandy is always kosher, therefore appropriate for religious use.

Italy produces an excellent, clean grape brandy whose foreign market popularity increases every year.

FRUIT BRANDIES

The fermented mash of fruits, other than grapes, is the source of a wide variety of very pleasant, fine, and enjoyable brandies.

FRUIT	*BRANDY*
Apple	Apple brandy
	Applejack
	Calvados
Plum	Slivovitz
	Mirabelle
	Quetsch
Cherry	Kirschwasser-Kirsch
Strawberry	Fraise
Raspberry	Framboise
Pear	Pear brandy
Blackberry	Blackberry brandy

APPLE BRANDY

THE two principal sources of apple brandy are the United States and France. Here it is commonly called Apple Jack, while in France it is called Calvados, from the town of Calvados in Normandy, center of apple and cider production in France. The chief difference between Calvados and Apple Jack is in the aging. Calvados is generally sold after it has aged in wood for ten years, whereas ours is sold after it is two to five years in wood. Our brandies, too, are often bottled at 100 proof, while theirs are under 90 proof.

The method of production is simple. The cider is made only from perfect, sound, ripe cider apples. After fermentation is complete, and no sugar remains unfermented, it is distilled. In France pot stills are used, and the first, or low, wines must be redistilled to obtain the high wines or brandy. They are distilled out at around 140 proof. Here we use patent stills and distill out at between 140 and 160 proof. Apple brandy is aged in oak barrels and acquires its color from the wood. It has a pleasant, but very definite apple flavor. Incidentally. Apple Jack and Apple brandy are synonymous terms.

OTHER FRUIT BRANDIES

THE most widely used, after the apple, are the plum and the small black wild cherry of the Rhine Valley. All are produced in a similar fashion, except that some are aged, while others are not.

Those which are aged in wood and have a golden brown color are the plum brandies of Central Europe (Hungary, Romania, Yugoslavia) known as Slivovitz, the apricot brandy of Hungary called Barack Palinka, see below.

The group of brandies which are unaged are always colorless, that is, water-white, and are generally referred to as the white alcohols. They include those distilled from a fermented mash of cherries, Kirschwasser; from the mirabelle and quetsch varieties of plums and labeled Mirabelle and Quetsch; from raspberries, known as Framboise; from strawberries, called Fraise; and from the Williams pear, called simply pear brandy.

All of these white brandies are distilled off at a fairly low proof, usually around 100 proof or slightly less. In this way the maximum of fruit aroma and flavor are retained. Since this is their most attractive and desired characteristic, they are bottled promptly so that they will not lose any of their fragrance.

These brandies are made in the following manner. The fully ripened fruit is gathered and thoroughly mixed or mashed with wooden paddles in a wooden tub, where it is allowed to ferment—stones and all. When fermentation is complete, the entire contents of the tub is placed in a pot still. It is distilled twice. In the mixing or mashing some of the stones will have been broken or crushed, and from the stones a small amount of oil will be distilled over with the spirit. This oil imparts the characteristic bitter almond flavor usually found in good Kirschwasser or Slivovitz.

After distillation is complete, Kirschwasser may be stored either in paraffin-lined casks or earthenware containers. If aged in plain oak, it would take on color, which is not desirable. Slivovitz, on the other hand, is preferred with color, so it is matured in wood.

Geographically the source of the finest Kirschwasser is the valley of the Rhine. However, due to geo-politics, the three best sources find themselves in three different countries. They are: Switzerland where the Rhine starts on its way to the sea, Alsace on the French side of the Rhine, and the Black Forest on the opposite side of the Rhine in Germany. One can always find those who will claim that the Kirschwasser of one of these three sources is the superior of the others, but we find them all equal and excellent.

The pear brandies we have tasted, whether from Switzerland or France, have the pronounced fragrance of the Williams pear and are very fine.

A little true blackberry and apricot brandy is distilled in Hungary. The former is shipped under the simple appellation of blackberry brandy, and it is a truly magnificent product. It has the flavor of the blackberry, and the dark color which is imparted by adding some of the darkly colored natural juice to the matured spirit.

Apricot brandy, labeled Barack Palinka, is shipped in a typically Hungarian odd-shaped bottle. It has a short squat body and a long, fairly wide neck.

The brandy is excellent, has the apricot flavor and color, with an undertone of stone (almond), and is rather fiery, but not unpleasantly so.

USES OF BRANDY

ASIDE from their medicinal uses, which are well-established, all brandies, and, of course, those obtained from wine in particular, find their primary use as after-dinner drinks, when they are most attractive neat, although brandy and soda is a pleasant drink, after dinner or at any time when a long, refreshing and relaxing drink is desired. Brandies are also excellent in coffee.

There are many uses in the kitchen, particularly in the case of Kirsch, which is a delightful addition to any fresh fruit cup, and as one of the flavorings in those delicious French pancakes, called *Crêpes au Kirsch*.

The intense fragrance, which all the white fruit brandies possess, makes it possible to impart their flavor by using very small quantities. They are especially good in flavoring desserts, puddings, cakes, and ice creams.

All brandies may be used in making mixed drinks of all kinds.

19. Whiskies

AFTER the process of distillation was discovered, it was inevitable that man should use the product closest at hand, easiest to obtain, and least expensive. As a result, where the grape grows abundantly, brandy is produced; where sugar cane is grown, rum is made; and where there is an abundance of grain, whiskey is distilled.

The word "whiskey" comes from the Celtic *uisgebaugh* or *uisgebeatha,* the Caledonian and Hibernian spellings, respectively. However spelled it is Celtic for "water of life." Whether it was the Scots or the Irish who first used the word or first distilled whiskey is a source of never-ending argument between them.

the word "whiskey"— its origin

> Uisgebaugh is pronounced—whis-geh-BAW
>
> | uis | = whis | as in whisk |
> | ge | = geh | as in get |
> | baugh | = baw | as in ball |

The English found the Celtic word too difficult and too long so they shortened and anglicized it to "whisky." The Canadians use the Scotch spelling and we in America use the Irish spelling.

SCOTCH WHISKY

IN the beginning, every Highland laird had his own still, and the spirits obtained were rough, harsh, with a smoky pungency appreciated only by the Caledonians. The whiskies were distilled freely and paid no taxes. In 1814, distillation from all stills of less than 500 gallons capacity was prohibited in Scotland, and the law almost caused a revolution. However, the Government finally convinced the irate Highlanders that they would be wiser to sell their whisky legally, and within a few years illicit distilling became a rare thing in Scotland. A similar situation prevailed in Ireland at the same time.

Four regions of Scotland produce whisky: the Highlands, the Lowlands, Campbeltown, and Islay (pronounced I-lay). Each produces a whisky with an individual character.

the making of Scotch whisky

Scotch whisky is obtained primarily from barley, which is grown in Scotland preferably, but of late years barley from California, Canada, India, Africa, and other countries has been imported for distilling purposes.

There are five main processes in the making of Scotch: first, malting; second, mashing; third, fermenting; fourth, distilling; and fifth, maturing and blending.

On arrival at the distillery, the barley goes into the barley-receiving room where it is dressed, that is, sieved, or passed over screens so that small and inferior grain will be eliminated, after which the best grain is stored. When required for use, it is placed in tanks, called "steeps," where it is soaked in water until thoroughly softened. It is then spread out on the floor of the malting house, and sprinkled with warm water for about three weeks, during which time the grain begins to germinate, that is, to sprout.

When the sprouts are about three-quarters of an inch long, the water is turned off and the grain is known as "green malt." Please note that it is already malt, for malt is germinated grain. During this germination process, a chemical change has occurred in the grain which is important in its future function of producing whisky. Some of the starches have been changed into diastase, which has the property of converting the balance of the starch into sugars— maltose and dextrin—which are fermentable, whereas the starch in its original state is not.

The green malt is transferred to a kiln, where it rests on a screen directly above a peat° fire. Like green wood, peat gives off a much more acrid and oily smoke than soft coal. This swirls around the grain, which becomes so impregnated with the aroma of the smoke that it is carried over into the spirit later distilled from it.

The kilning, or drying, process is very important, as it is here that the malt acquires a good part of its character, and a variation occurs here in the various regions; that is, the malt in the Lowlands is kilned less than in the Highlands; whereas the Campbeltown and Islay grains are more heavily roasted.

The kilned malt is now screened to remove the culm or dried sprouts, after which it goes to the mill room where it is ground into meal or "grist."

The next step is mashing. The ground malt is thoroughly mixed with warm water in a mash-tub where it soaks until the water has liquefied all of the starches, and the diastase has converted them into sugars. When the water has absorbed all of the goodness from the grain, it is drawn off, cooled, and is known as wort.

° Peat is coal in its primary stage, and consists of partially carbonized vegetable material, usually found in bogs. Pressed and dried peat is generally used for fuel in both Scotland and Ireland.

269

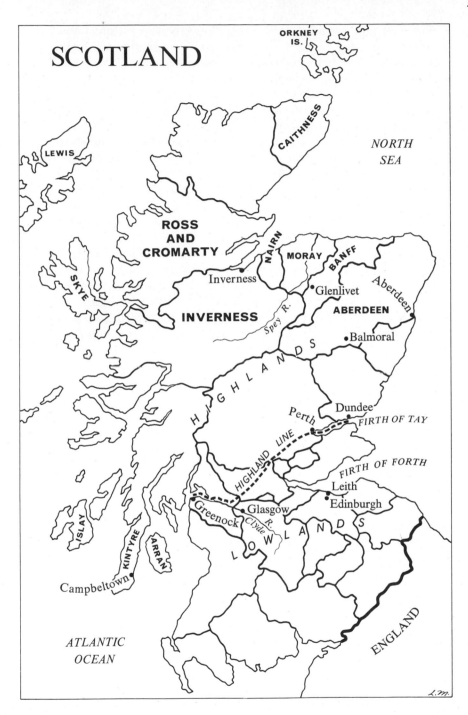

SCOTLAND

The wort now passes into the fermenting vats where a small quantity of carefully cultivated pure yeast is added and fermentation takes place. The yeast acts upon the sugars in the wort in the same manner as the natural yeasts act upon the sugars in grape juice, producing alcohol and carbonic acid gas. When fermentation is completed, the liquid is known as beer, or wash. Up to this point the process is identical with that of the brewing of ales and beers, except for the omission of hops.

The beer now goes into a pot still which is known as the wash still. The result of the first distillation is a distillate of low alcoholic strength, which is known as *low wines*. The low wines pass into the spirit still where they are redistilled. The first and last part of the distillation (the heads and tails—called the *feints*) are gathered separately from the middle portion, which is the useful part of the distillation. At the beginning and at the end of the distillation operation, too high a percentage of impurities is carried over with the spirit, which, if used, would impair the flavor of the spirit when matured. The feints, however, contain a substantial quantity of useful alcohol and are returned to the spirit still with the next charge of low wines, and the alcohol is distilled out. The impurities are disposed of with the residual slop from the spirit still operation, that is, the waste material which is thrown out.

The useful spirit, distilled off at between 140 and 142 proof, is now known as whisky, and flows into a spirit vat from where it is put in casks. These casks, generally made of American white oak, vary in size from 33 to 144 American gallons in capacity. The different sizes are used for convenience. They may be new or old, and very often are casks in which Sherry has been shipped. More often than not, the casks have been previously used for maturing whisky.

At the time of barreling the whisky is reduced in proof to 124 to 126.8 by the addition of water. According to Dr. P. Schidrowitz, whose notes are quoted by Peter Valaer in his excellent paper on Scotch whisky, "it is held that the best water is that which has its origin as a spring served with water which has passed through a red granite formation, and which, after rising from its source, passes through peaty country. Such waters are generally very soft, and possess certain qualities which are apparently due to the peaty soil or heather-clad moor through or over which the water passes on its way to the distillery." The waters of Loch Katrine are reputed to be of the finest for Scotch whisky.

The whisky remains in cask, under government supervision, from the time it is distilled until it is sold for export or home consumption.

Until 1853, Scotch whiskies were always "straight" whiskies, but about that time a few distillers began the practice of blending whiskies from various sources and widely separated distilleries, all in Scotland, of course. The firm of Andrew Usher & Company is credited with beginning this practice. Before this time, the taste for Scotch was confined to Scotland, but after blending

Battery of modern wash and spirit copper pot stills, Tormore Distillery at Advie, Grantown-on-Spey, Morayshire, Scottish Highlands. (Courtesy Long John Distilleries, Ltd., Glasgow)

became a general practice, Scotch whisky became popular in England and throughout the world, as the blend of unmalted grain whisky with malts produced a drink generally liked.

As already pointed out, the four geographical divisions from which whiskies made entirely from malted barley are obtained are the Highlands, Lowlands, Campbeltown, and Islay. To these malted whiskies, we must now add unmalted whisky, known to the trade as grain whisky. Grain whisky in Scotland *is whisky* and not neutral spirits, as some people believe. The Scotch grain whiskies are distilled out at slightly over 180 proof. They are reduced to 124 proof when barreled in Sherry casks for aging.

The blending is done when the whiskies are from three to four years old. A master blender examines them and indicates the exact proportion of Highland, Lowland, Campbeltown, and Islay malts and of grain whisky which are to be married. This is accomplished by placing the whiskies in a large vat where they are thoroughly mixed both by rotating paddles and by compressed air blown up from the bottom. The whisky is then returned to Sherry casks for a further period of maturing.

The Immature Spirits Act of Great Britain specifically states that no whisky may be sold for consumption in the British Isles under three years old. By the reciprocal trade agreement between Great Britain and the United States, Scotch and Irish whiskies imported into this country must be at least four years old to be imported without an age statement on the label.

The usual Scotch blend is composed of from 30 to 50 per cent of malt whisky, the balance being grain whisky. The original object of using grain whiskies, which are always distilled in patent stills, was to reduce the cost, but in doing so a lighter whisky was produced, which appealed much more to the other peoples of the world than had the fuller, smokier Scotch whiskies previously made.

The essential difference between blends consists in the proportions used of the four types of malts. Of these, of course, the Highland malts are considered the finest, and are always the most costly. They are fairly light in body and flavor, and do not have too much smoke. The finest Highland section is Banffshire, and within it the Glenlivet and Speyside regions are considered the best. Next in importance is Moray. Lowland malts are also light in body, but not as smoky in flavor. Incidentally, almost all of the grain whisky distilleries are in the Lowlands. Campbeltown malts are very full in body and quite smoky. The Islay malts are also very full, smoky, and pungent.

In the last analysis, the reasons for blending are to obtain a smoother, more balanced product than any of its single component parts, and to assure uniform continuity of a given brand. In this way the consumer can look for the same character, flavor, taste, and quality year in and year out. A Scotch whisky blend can very easily be the result of a marriage of as many as thirty or forty malt whiskies, together with five or more grain whiskies.

The age of the individual whiskies at the time of blending may vary widely since no single whisky will be employed before it has reached its proper maturity. The time (years) required for this is governed by the character of the whisky itself and the climatic conditions under which it is matured. The fuller-bodied malts of Islay and Campbeltown take much longer, sometimes ten to twelve years, while the Highland and Lowland malts may be ready in six to eight years, and the grain whiskies may only require four years. The greater the climatic dampness, the slower the aging process.

Therefore, the secret of fine Scotch whisky lies in the art of the blender. On his unique ability depends the polish, smoothness, and uniformity of the whisky. There are some 129 distilleries in Scotland (94 Highland Malt, 11 Lowland Malt, 8 Islay Malt, 2 Campbeltown Malt, and 14 Grain Whisky distilleries) producing over 4,000 brands or blends. As we have already indicated, there are many reasons why Scotch whisky from one area differs from Scotches of other areas. Local conditions such as water, peat, and climate and traditional distilling practices of individual distilleries are all contributing factors. But to fully understand the Scotch picture, it is important to remember that there are many distilleries, each one turning out a whisky that has its own individual characteristics. By combining the loud malt whiskies with grain whiskies, the blenders obtain the individuality of a character and quality that distinguishes their brands.

Whereas better than 99 per cent of the Scotch whisky consumed by effete *Sassenach* outside of Scotland is blended whisky as described above, there are also marketed in small quantities straight, unblended Highland Malt whiskies, as well as blends of all malt whiskies, in which no grain whisky has been employed. Such whiskies are much fuller bodied and usually are very fine quality. *all malt whisky*

A Liqueur Scotch Whisky is one which, through proper aging and blending, has acquired a mellow softness. Unfortunately the term is rather loosely employed and amounts to little more than a phrase on the label. It does apply, however, in the case of the finer, older whiskies, particularly the twelve year olds. *liqueur Scotch*

We seem to have a national "age-phobia" which frequently leads us astray. A Scotch whisky with a ten-year-old age statement on the label is not necessarily a better whisky than one with no age statement at all. Naturally, it is during the "aging years" that Scotch or any whisky extracts color from oak casks, plus the smoothness and mellowness characteristic of the product. Fully blended Scotch is laid away in casks for marrying for periods of five to twelve or even twenty years. Although the law stipulates an aging period of at least three years for Scotch whiskies—and none can enter the United States under four years of age unless so labeled—practically all Scotch malts remain in their casks for a minimum of five years. However, it is important to keep in mind that the quality of the whisky and the skill of the blender's hand must be there first. A poor whisky, or one that has been poorly blended, will continue to be a poor whisky, regardless of its age. *age in whisky*

Since World War II there has been an unquestioned trend in the United States towards lightness of flavor and body in most of the beverages Americans consume. Good examples of this are the fashion for vodka drinks and the "very dry" Martini cocktail. *"light" Scotch whisky*

The United States is Scotland's best customer, consuming nearly half of all the Scotch whisky sold each year. Consequently the Scotch whisky blender tries to supply what appeals most to his very important American customer.

Those brands that have been blended for lightness by judicious selection of light-bodied, lighter-flavored malts have not only found a ready acceptance but have succeeded in becoming the largest-selling brands in the United States.

Curiously, the American public has come to associate paleness or lack of color with lightness and dryness. This is, of course, nonsense, since the depth of color or lack of it in a Scotch whisky is governed entirely by the amount of caramel (burnt sugar) which is used in all blends to assure color conformity.

Scotland versus U.S. bottled

The duty and Internal Revenue Tax on imported distilled spirits is levied upon a wine or tax-gallon basis instead of on a proof gallon basis as is the case for domestically produced spirits. This means that a case of imported 86 proof Scotch whisky containing 2.4 liquid gallons pays the same duty and tax as it would if imported at 100 proof. If this same whisky is imported in bulk at 100 proof or higher, the duty and tax are calculated on the proof gallons; i.e., the equivalent wine gallons at 100 proof. When it is reduced to 86 proof, this represents a 14 per cent duty and tax saving. If this lower tax cost is passed along to the consumer it represents a substantial price advantage over the Bottled in Scotland whisky.

Competition for the market being what it is, and as long as the excise tax remains at the excessively high rate of $10.50 per proof gallon, more and more Scotch whisky and other spirits will be imported in bulk for bottling in the United States. In 1973 bulk was 32% of Scotch imports.

IRISH WHISKEY

THERE is a common belief that Irish whiskey is a potato whiskey. This is not true at all. No doubt the misconception stems from the fact that the Irish refer to illicitly distilled whiskey as *poteen*, a term derived from the pot still in which it has traditionally been distilled. Yes, in Ireland they eat potatoes but do not use them for distilling purposes.

Whiskey in Ireland is distilled from a fermented mash of the same grains as are used in Scotland, namely, malted barley, unmalted barley, corn, rye, and other small grains.

The barley malt used is dried in a kiln which has a solid floor, so that the smoke from the fuel—very often peat—has no opportunity to come in contact with the grain. Thus the malt is not "smoke-cured," as is the case in Scotland. All Irish whiskey is triple-distilled.

Irish whiskies are often all pot still distillations, and while often shipped as a blend of whiskies of the same distillery, they are also shipped as unblended straight whiskies, on occasion.

Grain whiskies are also distilled in column or patent stills. Some houses blend their malt whiskies with grain whiskies to produce a lighter-bodied and flavored whiskey.

Most Irish whiskies are seven years old or more before they are shipped.

Irish is a particularly smooth whiskey, but with a great deal of body and a clean, malty flavor.

It is used in the same manner as Scotch whisky.

THE DISTILLING OF WHISKEY IN AMERICA

EARLY American settlers brought spirituous liquors with them, as they were considered essential in withstanding the hardships of an ocean voyage, and a medicine in cases of illness in the new, savage land. For a long time, spirits had to be imported from Europe. *history*

The first commercially distilled spirits in what is the present day United States was New England rum. Distilling of whiskey on a commercial scale began over a century later.

There is a record of experimental distilling in 1660, but it was not until the early eighteenth century that the distilling of whiskey began to develop. The grains used along the Eastern seaboard were rye and barley. As the settlements began extending westward, however, it became apparent that the transportation of newly grown grain back to the populous seaboard cities was difficult for the settlers, particularly those in western Pennsylvania. They found it was simpler to distill their grain, both rye and corn, into whiskey. It not only kept longer, but was easier to transport to the cities. Whiskey and furs, indeed, became the best means of exchange, particularly during the Revolutionary War period when Continental currency was worth less than five cents on the dollar.

Whiskey played a prominent part in our early history, in determining our right and ability to be a self-governed nation. It happened in this way. Whiskey had always been distilled in small, family-owned distilleries, without legal interference from any government. In 1791, not long after George Washington became President, money being a crying need for the new nation, an excise tax was levied on whiskey.

The independent Pennsylvania distillers resented the taxing of their product and said so in no uncertain terms. The tax collectors in some cases were even tarred and feathered. There were rioting and stormy scenes in these "western" communities, and President Washington, in great haste, sent a force of militia to quell the "insurrection." It was done without bloodshed and accomplished its object. While in itself the "insurrection" was of minor importance, it was of tremendous significance to the future of the Federal Government, and is still known as the "Whiskey Rebellion."

Many of the disgruntled Dutch, Scotch, and Irish farmer-distillers decided to move out of reach of the tax collector, which meant going farther west into Indian territory. They found the proper water for distilling in Southern Indiana and Kentucky.

Proportions of grain used in production of Bourbon. LEFT TO RIGHT. *Corn, Rye, Barley Malt. The tanks in rear contain what is shown in glass.* (Courtesy Bourbon Institute, New York)

The first whiskey distilled in Kentucky is generally attributed to the Reverend Elijah Craig at Georgetown, which was in Bourbon County. The grain he employed was corn (maize) as it was more plentiful than rye. It became known as Bourbon County whiskey, and the name Bourbon has remained as the designation of whiskies distilled from a corn mash.

The three important whiskey-distilling areas in the United States are not located where they are from pure chance but because of the most important factor in the making of whiskey—the quality of the water. It comes from springs that pass up through layer on layer of limestone rock. The limestone mantel runs along western Pennsylvania, cuts across southern Indiana and over into Kentucky. There is another isolated limestone region in Maryland around Baltimore.

However, with the advancement of science and the development of inexpensive water technology the distiller has been freed from the necessity of locating his production at or near these limestone mantel outcroppings. Today he can and does distill whiskey in many other parts of the United States.

making of American whiskies

The early distillers used very crude and primitive equipment. Fermentation was carried on in open mash tubs, the yeast being the wild varieties which the air afforded. Since that day tremendous changes have taken place.

The making of American whiskies is basically the same as the making of grain whiskies in Scotland. The grains, of course, are different, and the whiskey is distilled out at a lower proof.

Briefly the steps are as follows:

1. The grain upon arrival at the distillery is carefully inspected and cleaned of all dust.

2. It is ground in the grist mill to a meal.

3. The meal, together with a small amount of malt, is cooked to convert the starches.

4. The cooled "wort" is yeasted with pure culture yeast, and goes to the fermenting vats to become "beer."

5. The beer goes into a patent or double column still. The result is whiskey, which is distilled out as below 160 proof. It is now reduced in proof to 100 to 103 by the addition of pure well water.

The new whiskey is placed in a *new* charred white oak barrel (except for light whiskey—see page 286) to mature in a bonded warehouse, where it must remain under Treasury Department control until the Internal Revenue tax has been paid. The time limit was eight years until recently when it was extended to twenty years. This means that a whiskey or any other distilled spirit still in bond after twenty years is then subject to payment of the Internal Revenue tax, whether it can be sold or not.

origin of charring barrels

No one knows exactly how the advantage of charring barrels was learned. One legend is that as a result of a fire in a warehouse in Jamaica some barrels of rum were heavily charred. After some time, it was learned that the rum in the charred barrels had acquired both color and quality which it had lacked before.

Another explanation is that in order to bend the barrel staves into the proper shape for the barrel, the early Kentuckians heated them before an open fire, and often they became charred. Discovering that the more charred the staves the more palatable the whiskey, charring became an accepted practice. It is unlikely that both of these stories are true, it is possible that neither of them is true. But it is probable that the virtues of charring the barrels in which whiskey was to be stored were stumbled upon quite by accident, as have been many valuable discoveries.

sweet and sour mash

There are two yeasting processes used in America—the "sweet-mash" or yeast-mash process, and the "sour-mash" or yeasting-back process. The sour-mash process is used primarily in making Bourbon whiskey.

A sweet-mash is produced by adding all or almost all freshly developed yeast to the mash, i.e., little or no spent beer from a previous fermentation is mixed with the fresh mash. It is allowed to ferment from thirty-six to fifty hours and the fermenter can be, and usually is, refilled almost immediately upon being emptied.

A sour-mash is produced by adding at least one-third the volume of the fermenter of spent beer (working yeast), from a previous fermentation, to the fresh mash and fresh yeast. The mash is allowed to ferment from seventy-two to ninety-six hours. Fermentation generally takes place in open fermenting vats at low temperatures. Upon being emptied the fermenters are sterilized, aereated and allowed to "sweeten" for twenty-four hours before being used again.

On the contrary, we find "sour-mash" whiskies to be sweet in taste and to be not too different from "sweet-mash" whiskies. Both mashing methods are used widely in the distilling industry, and often in the same distillery.

*proof changes
through aging*

A spirit is made up of alcohol, water, and minute quantities of other substances, the bulk of the liquid being water and alcohol.

Spirits are generally matured in porous containers so that the air can seep in to oxidize and mellow the alcohol. The most common container is made of wood (generally oak). Although it cannot be seen with the naked eye, wood is a porous substance and when liquid is stored in a wooden barrel, even though it be tightly closed, some of it will seep through, that is, evaporate or escape through the pores of the wood.

To the best of our knowledge, all aged spirits such as brandy, rum, Scotch whisky, and so forth, are barreled for aging at proofs varying from 124 up to 150 proof and more. These spirits lose somewhat in alcoholic strength as they mature.

Flow diagram showing entire modern grain distillery operation from the arrival of the grain through to the barrelling of whiskey and grain neutral spirits, and the processing of the spent grain into various types of fodder. (Courtesy Jos. E. Seagram & Sons, Inc.)

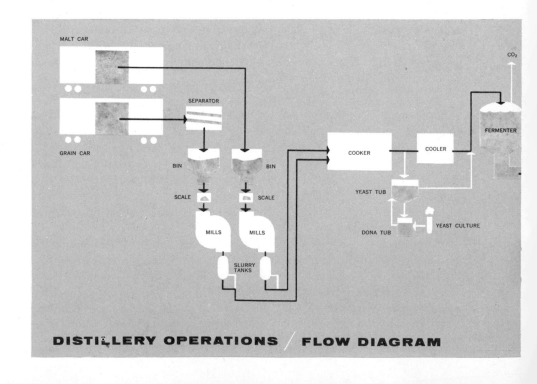

DISTILLERY OPERATIONS / FLOW DIAGRAM

American whiskies, on the other hand, are barreled at 100 to 103 proof (50 to 51 per cent of alcohol) and as they mature their alcoholic strength increases.

To illustrate this point, let us take a fifty-gallon barrel of new whiskey at 100 proof, i.e., twenty-five gallons of alcohol and twenty-five gallons of water. After four years of aging, it is found to have lost ten gallons of liquid, but on measuring the alcoholic strength, it is found to be 110 proof. This means that 55 per cent of the forty gallons remaining in alcohol (twenty-two gallons), and the remaining eighteen gallons is water.

STANDARDS OF IDENTITY FOR DISTILLED SPIRITS*

THE standards of identity for the several classes and types of distilled spirits set forth in this part shall be applicable only to distilled spirits for beverage or other non-industrial purposes. Nothing contained in these standards of identity shall be construed as authorizing the non-industrial use of any distilled spirits produced in an industrial alcohol plant, except that "alcohol" or "neutral spirits," as defined in this part, may be so used if produced pursuant to the basic permit requirements of the Federal Alcohol Administration Act.

the standards of identity

*The standards of identity given here have been taken from United States Revenue Service Regulations under the Federal Alcohol Administration Act.

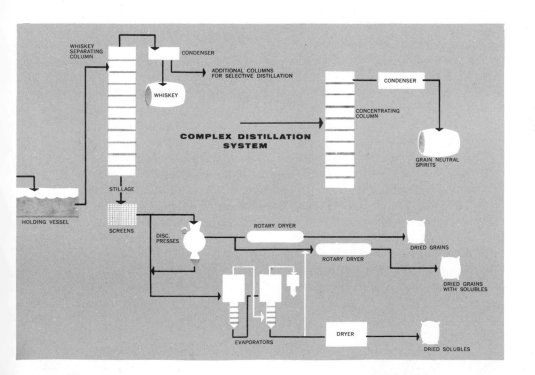

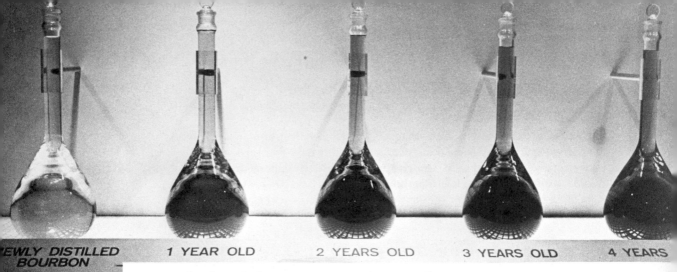

NEWLY DISTILLED BOURBON   1 YEAR OLD   2 YEARS OLD   3 YEARS OLD   4 YEARS

As bourbon whiskey matures in new, charred oak barrels, it picks up color and flavor year by year. Vaporization also takes place, reducing the amount of whiskey in a 50-gallon barrel by as much as 11 gallons in a 4-year period.

application of standards

Standards of identity for the several classes and types of distilled spirits set forth in this part shall be as follows:

(a) *Class 1; Neutral spirits* or *alcohol.* "Neutral spirits" or "alcohol" are distilled spirits produced from any material at or above 190 proof, and if bottled, bottled at not less than 80 proof.

(1) "Vodka" is neutral spirits so distilled, or so treated after distillation with charcoal or other materials, as to be without distinctive character, aroma, taste, or color.

(2) "Grain spirits" are neutral spirits distilled from a fermented mash of grain and stored in oak containers.

(b) *Class 2; Whiskey.* "Whiskey" is an alcoholic distillate from a fermented mash of grain produced at less than 190 proof in such a manner that the distillate possesses the taste, aroma, and characteristics generally attributed to whiskey, stored in oak containers (except that corn whiskey need not be so stored), and bottled at not less than 80 proof, and also includes mixtures of such distillates for which no specific standards of identity are prescribed.

(1) (i) "Bourbon whiskey," "rye whiskey," "wheat whiskey," "malt whiskey," or "rye malt whiskey" is whiskey produced at not exceeding 160 proof from a fermented mash of not less than 51 per cent corn, rye, wheat, malted barley, or malted rye grain, respectively, and stored at not more than 125 proof in charred new oak containers; and also includes mixtures of such whiskies of the same type.

(ii) "Corn whiskey" is whiskey produced at not exceeding 160 proof from a fermented mash of not less than 80 per cent corn grain, and if stored in oak containers stored at not more than 125 proof in used or uncharred new oak containers and not subjected in any manner to treatment with charred wood; and also includes mixtures of such whiskey.

(iii) Whiskies conforming to the standards prescribed in subdivisions (i) and (ii) of this subparagraph, which have been stored in the type of oak containers prescribed, for a period of two years or more shall be further designated as "straight"; for example, "straight bourbon whiskey," "straight corn whiskey," and whiskey conforming to the standards prescribed in subdivision (i) of this subparagraph, except that it was produced from a fermented mash of less than 51 per cent of any one type of grain, and stored for a period of two years or more in charred new oak containers shall be designated "straight." "Straight whiskey" includes mixtures of straight whiskies which are homogeneous and also mixtures of straight whiskies of the same type produced by the same proprietor at the same distillery all of which are not less than four years old.

(2) "Whiskey distilled from bourbon (rye, wheat, malt, or rye malt) mash" is whiskey produced in the United States at not exceeding 160 proof from a fermented mash of not less than 51 per cent corn, rye, wheat, malted barley, or malted rye grain, respectively, and stored in used oak containers; and also includes mixtures of such whiskies of the same type. Whiskey conforming to the standard of identity for corn whiskey must be designated corn whiskey.

(3) "Light whiskey" is whiskey produced in the United States at more than 160 proof, on or after January 26, 1968, and stored in used or uncharred new oak containers; and also includes mixtures of such whiskies. If "light whiskey" is mixed with less than 20 per cent of straight whiskey on a proof gallon basis, the mixture shall be designated "blended light whiskey" (light whiskey—a blend).

(4) "Blended whiskey" (whiskey—a blend) is a mixture which contains at least 20 per cent of straight whiskey on a proof gallon basis and, separately or in combination, whiskey or neutral spirits. A blended whiskey containing not less than 51 per cent on a proof gallon basis of one of the types of straight whiskey shall be further designated by that specific type of straight whiskey; for example, "blended rye whiskey" (rye whiskey—a blend).

(5) "A blend of straight whiskies" (blended straight whiskies) is a mixture of straight whiskies. A blend of straight whiskies consisting entirely of one of the types of straight whiskey, and not conforming to the standard for "straight whiskey," shall be further designated by that specific type of straight whiskey; for example, "a blend of straight rye whiskies" (blended straight rye whiskies).

(6) "Spirit whiskey" is a mixture of neutral spirits and not less than 5 per cent on a proof gallon basis of whiskey, or straight whiskey, or straight whiskey and whiskey, if the straight whiskey component is less than 20 per cent on a proof gallon basis.

(7) "Scotch whisky" is whiskey which is a distinctive product of Scotland, manufactured in Scotland in compliance with the laws of the United Kingdom regulating the manufacture of Scotch whisky for consumption in the United Kingdom: *Provided*, that if such product is a mixture of whiskies, such mixture is "blended Scotch Whisky" (Scotch whisky—a blend).

(8) "Irish whiskey" is a whiskey which is a distinctive product of Ireland, manufactured either in the Republic of Ireland or in Northern Ireland, in compliance with their laws regulating the manufacture of Irish whiskey for home consumption: *Provided,* that if such product is a mixture of whiskies, such mixture is "blended Irish whiskey" (Irish whiskey—a blend).

(9) "Canadian whisky" is whiskey which is a distinctive product of Canada, manufactured in Canada in compliance with the laws of Canada regulating the manufacture of Canadian whisky for consumption in Canada: *Provided,* that if such product is a mixture of whiskies, such mixture is "blended Canadian whisky" (Canadian whisky—a blend).

The balance of the Standards of Identity covering other spirits are discussed in later chapters.

STRAIGHT WHISKEY— BOURBON, RYE, CORN, WHEAT, TENNESSEE, ETC.

A straight whiskey, under Federal Regulations, in one that has been distilled off at a proof not exceeding 160, aged in a new charred white oak barrel for at least two years, and reduced by the addition of water at the time of bottling to no lower than 80 proof. Nothing may be added other than the water.

The higher the proof at which a spirit is distilled out, the lighter it will be in character, flavor, and body. This is due to the fact that more and more of the congeners (flavor and body components) are lost (eliminated) as the purity of the spirit is increased.

Under United States regulations, the theoretical "critical point" is reached at 190 proof (95 per cent alcohol). Any spirit distilled out at 190 proof or higher is called "neutral spirit" and should not possess any noticeable aroma, flavor, or character. Another section of the same regulations requires "the name of the commodity from which such neutral spirits have been distilled." Thus, grain neutral spirits is an alcoholic distillate from a fermented mash of grain distilled at or above 190 degrees proof.

Conversely, the lower the proof of distillation the greater the amount of congeners that will be distilled over and be a part of the distillate to give character, aroma, flavor, and body.

According to United States regulations, a straight whiskey is an alcoholic distillate from a fermented mash of cereal grain (rye, corn, wheat, etc.) and distilled at not exceeding 160 degrees proof, withdrawn from the distillery for maturation purposes at not more than 125 degrees proof and not less than 80 degrees proof, and aged for not less than twenty-four calendar months in new charred oak barrels. Consequently, straight whiskies possess very definite aroma, flavor, and body characteristics, when suitably aged in wood.

The predominant grain used in the mash formula determines the final designation under which the whiskey will be labeled and marketed. If 51 per cent or more of the grain is corn, it will be straight bourbon; 51 per cent or more rye grain makes it a straight rye; 51 per cent wheat, straight wheat whiskey; 51 per cent barley malt or rye malt, straight malt whiskey or straight rye malt whiskey; 80 per cent or more corn, aged in uncharred oak barrels or reused charred oak barrels will be designated as a straight corn whiskey.

Tennessee whiskey is a straight whiskey distilled in Tennessee from a fermented mash containing 51 per cent or more of corn.

Straight whiskies may be mixed, provided the mixture is made up of whiskies of the same distilling period and of the same distillery. Such whiskies do not lose their straight whiskey designation.

Straight whiskies of different distilling periods and from different distilleries may also be mixed or blended, but they must be labeled "blended bourbon whiskey," "blended rye whiskey," etc. When mixing straight whiskies that are homogeneous, the age of this mixture must be identified with the age of the youngest whiskey in the mixture. Most straight whiskies on the market greatly exceed the minimum age requirement because each distiller attempts to age his product until he feels his whiskey has reached the ripeness or maturity which is ideal for that particular whiskey. Most authorities agree that the average bourbon attains this stage in about six years.

Barrels of Ancient Age Bourbon whiskey aging in a modern temperature and humidity-controlled warehouse at Frankfort, Ky. In the background, note the operator and machine "ricking" a barrel. (Courtesy Schenley Industries, Inc.)

A little more than half of the American distilled whiskey consumed in the United States is straight whiskey, bottled in bond and blended straight whiskey. Of these over 97 per cent will be bourbon.

bottled in bond

The term "Bottled in Bond" is generally misunderstood, not only by the layman but too often by people in the retail liquor trade itself. The term is not a guarantee of quality; it has reference only to the Internal Revenue Tax. Only straight whiskies are bottled in bond.

The Bottled in Bond Act of 1894 permitted the distiller to bottle his whiskey (or other distilled spirits) without paying the excise taxes, provided the whiskey was at least four years old, distilled at one plant by the same proprietor, and was bottled at 100 proof and under the supervision of the United States Government Bureau of Alcohol, Tobacco, and Firearm Tax of the Treasury Department. A bottled-in-bond whiskey may contain homogeneous mixtures of whiskies, provided they represent one season, or if consolidated with other seasons, the mixture "shall be the distilling season of the youngest spirits contained therein, and shall consist of not less than 10 per cent of spirits of each such season." After being bottled, however, the whiskey was to remain in the bonded warehouse until the distiller was ready to sell it, at which time the tax had to be paid, before withdrawing the whiskey from bond.

Other distilled spirits may also be bottled in bond provided they meet the specifications of the Bottled in Bond Act of 1894, namely, that they have been distilled out below 160 proof, are straight, four years old or more, and are bottled at 100 proof. Examples are: rum, grape brandy, apple brandy, gin, etc.

If the distiller wishes to bottle his whiskey before it is four years old, he must pay or determine the taxes and withdraw the whiskey to his free warehouse.

"The Bottled-in-Bond stamp," reads the Treasury Department's Decision No. 1299, "is no guarantee as to purity or quality of the spirits, and the government assumes no responsibility with respect to claims by dealers in this connection in advertising Bottled-in-Bond spirits."

BLENDED WHISKEY

NEARLY half of the American-produced whiskey consumed in the United States is blended whiskey. (This includes a small amount of "spirit whiskey." See page 281.)

The blender devotes his art to mixing carefully selected, full-bodied straight whiskies with grain neutral spirits so as to produce a lighter, more harmoniously balanced whole, and to duplicate, day in and day out, an identically uniform product. The straight whiskies contribute aroma, flavor, and body, while the unaged grain spirits give the marriage lightness and smoothness without sacrificing character.

One of the newest and most modern distilleries in the nation, at Lawrenceburg, Ind., showing the towering distilling columns and the complex control panel, whereby precise temperatures and distilling proofs can be maintained scientifically. (Courtesy Schenley Industries, Inc.)

While grain neutral spirits have been and continue to be stored in oak containers by some distillers, no acknowledgment of this practice was permitted by regulations. Grain neutral spirits when stored in reused cooperage possess a distinctive character developed during storage, analogous to that which occurs when whisky is stored in reused cooperage. In order to let the consuming public know about this quality improvement, a new standard "grain spirits" was adopted on June 26, 1968 and became effective on July 1, 1972. Thus, "grain spirits" are neutral spirits distilled from a fermented mash of grain stored in oak containers and bottled at not less than 80 degrees proof. The period of aging in oak barrels may be stated as "stored ————(years and/or months) in oak containers."

Since grain spirits have flavors that are very delicate in nature, they must be stored in oak barrels which have been previously seasoned through the storage of whiskey or grain neutral spirits. It is important that the barrel is compatible with the flavor intensity of the grain neutral spirits, otherwise the woody character of the barrel would overwhelm the light flavor of the grain neutral spirits and thus prevent their proper development during aging.

The regulations also permit the use of certain "blending materials" in blended whiskies, up to $2\frac{1}{2}$ per cent by volume. Those most often employed are Sherry wine (a special heavy blending Sherry made from the Pedro Ximenez grape), prune or peach juice, etc.

Since Repeal there has been an unending discussion as to the merits and demerits of blended whiskey in comparison to straight whiskey. Both usually are fine, very drinkable products. The one you enjoy most—the one that pleases your palate—is the one you should choose. It is absurd to consider one inferior to the other. They are simply different. The straight whiskey is full bodied and full flavored, while the blended whiskey is comparatively light bodied and light in flavor.

Curiously, many people refer to blended whiskey as "rye." It is not. True rye whiskey is described on page 280. As a matter of fact, if by chance they get a true rye whiskey, the pronounced rye flavor and full body may shock their palate.

LIGHT WHISKEY

LIGHT whiskey is whiskey which has been distilled in the United States at more than 160 degrees proof (and less than 190 degrees proof) and stored in used or uncharred new oak containers. This whiskey is permitted to be entered for storage at proofs higher than 125 degrees. If "light whiskey" is mixed with less than 20 per cent by volume of 100 degrees proof straight whiskey, the mixture shall be designated "blended light whiskey." This standard of identity was adopted on January 26, 1968, and became effective July 1, 1972.

The primary purpose for this category was to permit the production of light distillates that could be aged in seasoned oak casks—that is, reused cooperage—which are more compatible in developing the lower flavor intensities found in this type of whiskey.

In general, the production techniques used in the production of straight whiskey and grain neutral spirits are followed in making light whiskey. The proportions and types of cereal grains used in the formula are left entirely to the discretion of the distiller. However, most distillers will use corn (up to 90 per cent) as the major portion of their formula. The main emphasis in this process will be on distillation techniques. The higher proof requirements will permit the use of more sophisticated distillation systems—such as those used in distilling grain spirits. The distiller will also have all of these proofs in which to work. At 161 proof, the whiskey is still flavorful; at 189 proof, it is extremely light in flavor and character. Almost at every level of proof in between, a changing relative amount of flavor components will be left in the distillate to affect the body, flavor, and character of the whiskey. The

Typical distillery tasting room. Note large receptacle where tasters eject samples.

distiller can distill his light whiskey out at any of these proofs and achieve different weights of flavor. He can mix different batches of different proofs of his final brand product.

The age of the light whiskey as it is withdrawn for bottling will affect its final character. As with America's straight whiskeys and the imported whiskeys, a major factor in the character of the light whiskey brands will be their maturity or approach to perfection when bottled. The first light whiskeys were distilled and laid away to age beginning with the formal authorization of this new whiskey on January 26, 1968. Thus, at the entry of light whiskeys into the marketplace, no brand can be more than four years old. As stocks continue to mature, age labels may play an increasingly important role in the market. Federal regulations to that exception provide that where the whiskeys are less than four years old, a back label must identify the whiskeys by volume and age; otherwise the back label is optional.

Light whiskey is available in these three ways:

1. As *light whiskey,* in the bottle as distilled, and including mixtures of these distillates.

2. As *blended light whiskey,* a mixture of less than 20 per cent straight whiskey at 100 proof with light whiskey.

3. In the traditional *blended whiskey,* with its light whiskey *unidentified* in a mixture with 20 per cent or more straight whiskey at 100 proof.

CANADIAN WHISKY

ACCORDING to the U.S. Federal Regulations: *"Canadian whisky* is a distinctive product of Canada, manufactured in Canada in compliance with laws of the Dominion of Canada . . . containing no distilled spirits less than two years old . . . and such whisky is blended *Canadian Whisky*. Canadian whisky shall not be designated as *straight*."

Canadian whisky according to Canadian law must be produced from cereal grain only. While the Canadian Excise Tax Bureau exercises the customary controls to assure proper collection of the tax, the government sets no other limitation as to grain formulas, distilling proofs, or special type of aging cooperage. It believes the distillers are better judges than the government of what the public, both at home and abroad, wants in a Canadian whisky.

Many people believe Canadian whisky is a rye whiskey. Corn, rye, wheat, and barley malt are the grains generally used. The proportions of each in the grain formulas are the trade secret of each individual distiller.

The methods of production are similar but the procedures of maturing differ somewhat from United States standards and practices. For example, any loss from evaporation may be made up by adding new whiskey to replace the amount lost.

Canadian whisky may be bottled in bond when it is two years old, and it can be bottled at 90 proof. However, practically all Canadian whisky is six years old or older when it is marketed. If it is less than four years old, its age must be listed on the label.

The distillers have developed a whisky with a delicate flavor and light body. They obtain these characteristics with mash formulas designed to produce lightness and delicacy and by distilling out at varying strengths, ranging from 140 to 180 proof.

JAPANESE WHISKEY

THE Japanese liquor industry is an old one, going back into their antiquity. However, until relatively recent times (about 1870) it was in large part devoted to such traditional beverages as Sake, Umeshu (a Japanese plum wine made by infusion), and Umechu (a Japanese medicinal wine). But with the advent of the entry of westernizing influences into Japan, distillation was also introduced. Since then products such as Japanese whiskey, liqueurs, brandies, Sochu (a neutral spirit made from grain or sweet potatoes) have become part of their culture.

Although historically much of the technique of distillation was learned from the West, especially Scotland and France, the Japanese adapted the methods to their own economy. For example, their whiskey is primarily a blended whiskey made up of varying percentages of heavier-bodied whiskies produced in pot stills and lighter-bodied whiskies produced by continuous distillation using column stills, many of the column stills adapted from French designs. While the original Japanese whiskies were an attempt to copy the Scotch-type whiskey, due to the Japanese economy the grains employed in these whiskies were of necessity different than those used in Scotland. Japan now produces a whiskey different than any being currently made in the United States or any of the imported whiskies entering the United States.

Much of the heavier-bodied whiskies are made from malted barley, some small portion of which is cured over peat. Most of the whiskey used in the blended Japanese whiskey uses millet, corn, Indian corn, some small quantities of rice, and other grains in varying proportions in their mash bill. Wheat and rye are seldom used. The milling and fermentation procedure is similar to that of the Western methods. The saccharine method differs however in that most of their whiskey uses Japanese Koji Mold, a mold similar to that used in the making of saké (see page 345) to convert the starch to sugar.

The proofs of the whiskies when removed from the stills vary from about 130 proof for the heavier-bodied whiskies to about 180 proof for the lighter-bodied whiskies. The whiskies are aged separately in used charred oak barrels before blending. Blending, the subsequent marrying period, and further aging last from months to years depending on the quality of the whiskey. The laws of Japan define various classes of whiskey primarily for Japanese tax purposes and regulate the aging and handling of whiskey.

Whiskey types are also produced in Holland, Germany, Denmark, and Australia. In the latter country the Scotch method—first producing malt whiskey and then a blend of malts and grains—is followed. Although made on the Scotch pattern, Australian whiskey has a character of its own.

TASTE OF WHISKIES

THE principal taste distinction of Scotch whisky is its smoky peat flavor, whereas Irish whiskey has a similar barley-malt whiskey character without the smoky flavor. Both are somewhat lighter in body than American straight whiskies because high proof, very light-bodied grain whiskies are used for blending. Also, because these whiskies are matured in old, previously used cooperage they require a longer aging period. This is usually seven to eight years, and up to twelve for the finer qualities.

Rye and bourbon whiskies have the distinctive taste and character of the rye and corn grains used. Because of the different methods of mashing and the lower proofs at which they are distilled out, which give them a higher congeneric content, they are both sweeter and fuller bodied than Scotch or Irish. Furthermore, aging in new charred oak cooperage makes it possible for the American whiskies to reach maturity at from three to four years.

USE OF WHISKIES

ASIDE from their most common use as a straight drink or on the rocks, whiskies may be used in numberless cocktails, punches, and other mixed drinks. They are also very popular in long drinks, such as highballs.

20. Gins

GIN is the first liquor in whose production man plays a more important part than nature. In the wines and spirits studied up to now, we have seen that natural forces aged and developed the liquor. But here man has manufactured the whole article. Gin did not happen just by chance. It was created quite intentionally to fulfill a specific purpose. Credit for this belongs to Franciscus de la Boe (1614–1672), also known as Doctor Sylvius, seventeenth-century physician and professor of medicine at Holland's famed University of Leyden.

Doctor Sylvius was not thinking of a beverage spirit, and much less a Dry Martini. His objective was medicinal in the purest sense. Knowing the diuretic properties of the oil of the juniper berry (*juniperus communis*) he felt that by redistilling a pure alcohol with the juniper berry he could obtain its therapeutic oil in a form that would provide an inexpensive medicine. And he succeeded. Within a few years all Holland found itself suffering from ills that could only be cured by Dr. Sylvius' medicine. He named it *Genièvre*, the French name for the juniper berry. The Dutch called it *genever*, which they still do, and today it is also known in the Netherlands as "Hollands" and "Schiedam" (a gin distilling center near Rotterdam). The English shortened and Anglicized it into "gin."

Necessity is said to be the mother of invention, and the popularity of gin in England came about as the result of a demand for distilled spirits which were palatable and also inexpensive. In the reign of Queen Anne (1702–1714) the only way the distillers knew how to satisfy this demand was to take the lees of wine or beer and distill out the alcohol. Such seventeenth-century spirits did not possess a very pleasant flavor and something had to be done about it. The solution was found in gin.

English soldiers returning from the seventeenth-century wars on the Continent brought back a taste for "Dutch Courage," as they dubbed the beverage. In no time at all, gin became the national drink of England, as it has remained ever since. (Contrary to the general belief, popularity of Scotch whisky among the English is quite recent . . . only a little more than a century.)

Queen Anne helped matters along by raising the duties and taxes on French wines and brandies and at the same time lowering the excise tax on English distilled spirits. Naturally the production of this new, inexpensive beverage flourished. In fact, gin was so cheap for a time in England that one innkeeper put up a sign which read:

> "Drunk for a penny,
> Dead drunk for twopence,
> Clean straw for nothing!"

This will give you a mild idea of the kind of gin they made, although it is unlikely it was much worse than the kind many people drank in America during the bathtub gin era of the twenties.

During the course of the years, tremendous improvements have been made in production methods. Today, the making of gin is a highly refined science, with very precise quality controls to ensure continuous uniformity. This does not mean that all gins are identical. Each distiller has his own closely guarded secret formula and method of making his gin.

There are only two basic styles or types of gin:

> DUTCH: Hollands, Genever, or Schiedam gin
> DRY GIN: English or American gin

Dutch gins are very full flavored, full bodied, and possess a clean malty aroma and taste.

English and American gins are quite light in flavor and body by comparison. They have a much more aromatic aroma and taste.

HOLLANDS GIN

IN the Netherlands, gin is generally made in the following manner:

1. A grain formula of approximately equal parts of barley malt, corn, and rye is mashed, cooked, and fermented into a beer.

2. The resulting beer is distilled in a pot still and the distillate may be redistilled once or twice. The final spirits, known as "malt wine," are distilled off at a very low proof, between 100 and 110 proof.

3. The "malt wine" is then redistilled, together with juniper berries, in another pot still. The gin is distilled off at between 94 and 98 proof. (Other "botanicals" are included with the juniper berries, but not in the quantity or variety employed in England and the United States.)

Because of the low proof at which it is distilled *Hollands, Genever,* or *Schiedam* is a very full-bodied gin with a very clean but pronounced malty aroma and flavor. Dutch gin cannot be mixed with other ingredients to make cocktails because its own very definite taste will predominate and overshadow whatever other wine or spirit it is mixed with.

DRY GIN—ENGLISH

ORIGINALLY the term "London Dry Gin" signified gin produced in or near London, where most English gin has always been distilled, but today the use of the term has been adopted by American gin distillers as well as gin producers in other countries. Therefore it has lost its geographical significance. The term "dry" does not have much meaning either, since all English, American, and Dutch gins are equally dry.

English and American gins are very different in character from Dutch gins. This is due to the different production methods used.

In England the making of gin begins with a grain formula made up of 75 per cent corn, 15 per cent barley malt, and 10 per cent of other grains. This is mashed, cooked, and fermented, much the same as the mash is handled for the production of whisky. After fermentation is completed, the *wort* or *beer* is distilled and rectified in a column still to obtain a rather pure spirit of from 180 to 188 proof. This is reduced to 120 proof by the addition of distilled water. The reduced spirit is placed in a gin still, which is a pot still, and redistilled in the presence of the flavoring agents, primarily juniper berries.

Some of the botanicals used to impart distinctive flavor to gin. (Courtesy Calvert Distilling Co.)

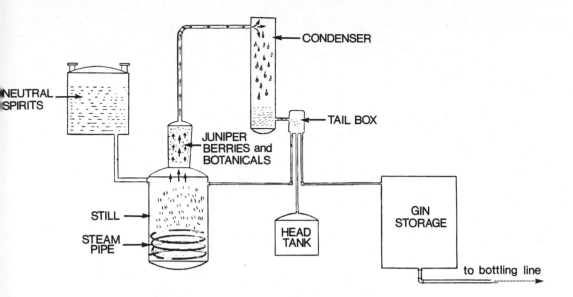

Here is the making of gin reduced to its essential stages. Grain alcohol passes into the still to be evaporated by the heat from a steam coil. The alcohol vapor passes through a still head containing berries and herbs, or in some instances berries are mixed right in with the alcohol in the still. In any event the vapor, rich with the essence of the herbs, passes to a condenser, through a tail box for control, and into the storage tank.

However, other flavoring materials, known as "botanicals," are used in rather small quantities to add flavor nuances to the gin. Among those generally used are dried lemon and orange peel, cardamom and coriander seeds, bitter almonds, angelica and orris root as well as anise, caraway, calamus, fennel, licorice, etc. The precise formula is always a secret. There is also a variation in the method of distilling. Some producers mix the botanicals in with the spirit and distill the entire mash, while others place the botanicals on wire mesh traps which are suspended above the spirit in the still, so that the alcoholic vapors, upon rising, will pass through and around the botanicals, thus becoming impregnated with the aromatic flavoring oils they contain.

The resulting spirit comes off the gin still at 170 to 180 proof and is recovered as gin. It is reduced in proof to bottling strength—80 to 94 proof—and is ready to be marketed. If it is not to be bottled at once, it is stored in glass-lined or stainless steel tanks, since gin is generally not aged.

There is a difference in character between English and American gin. It is due to two basic factors. First and most important is the slightly lower proof of the spirits employed by English distillers; these spirits retain some character. Second is the fact that English water is different from American and does influence the character of the fermented mash and the spirits distilled from it.

English gins different

Dry gin is also produced in Germany, Italy, Israel, Norway, the Balkans, and Africa.

Plymouth Gin

While virtually the whole trade in gin in the British Isles is concerned with London Dry, there are some other varieties. The most important of these minority gins is Plymouth Gin. It is a heavier, more strongly flavored gin than the London dry type.

Old Tom Gin

A few English gin distillers still market a sweetened gin which is labeled "Old Tom Gin." It never proved overly successful in the United States and its availability is rather limited. Old Tom is fine for tall drinks, such as a Tom Collins. Incidentally, there are several stories of its origin. One is that it was named for a man who lived in Plymouth, while Lord Kinross gives a more logical version in his book, *The Kindred Spirit*. He credits the origin of Old Tom to a former government spy, Captain Dudley Bradstreet. It seems "he rented a house in London, nailed the sign of a cat to his ground floor window and put a leaden pipe under its paw, with a funnel inside, at the end of it. Passers-by were invited to put their money in the cat's mouth and to murmur 'Puss! give me 2d. worth of gin.' Then the liquor would come pouring through the tube." This was probably the first coin-in-the-slot vending machine.

DRY GIN—AMERICAN

FEDERAL definition acknowledges the existence of a number of gins, but define only two: distilled gin and compound gin. Practically all gins made in the United States are distilled gins. Compound gin is a simple process that mixes neutral spirits with extract or oil of juniper and other botanicals. There are two methods for producing distilled gin: direct distillation and redistillation.

In direct distillation a fermented mash is pumped into a still. Heat is applied and the spirit vapors rise through the still and through a "gin head" at the top of the still. Prior to the start of the distilling process, this gin head is first packed with juniper berries and other botanicals and as the spirit vapors pass through these flavoring materials, it extracts the flavoring from them. This delicately flavored vapor is then condensed and the resulting liquid is finished gin. The above covers what the government calls "original distillation." In redistillation, neutral spirits are placed in a batch still, reduced in proof, and then a similar procedure to one of those used in England is followed.

A great deal of gin is made by each method—direct distillation and redistillation—although the latter is the more common. The choice between either method has no bearing on the quality of the finished product. But obviously there is a quality difference in gins as everyone knows. To make a quality gin, the producer must start with a high-quality neutral spirit that is clean and free from any foreign flavor. His juniper and other botanicals must also be of the best grades, but once given all of these materials in the highest quality, the producer is still no better off than a housewife who has surrounded herself with a lot of choice groceries and now has to prepare a cake or a sauce. Whereas our regulations do not specify the material from which the neutral spirits should be distilled, most of the United States gins are made with grain neutral spirits.

As was stated earlier, virtually all gins on the market use the word "dry" as descriptive of the brand. The phrase may read "Dry Gin," "Extra Dry Gin," "Very Dry Gin," "London Dry Gin," "English Dry Gin," but they all express the same meaning—lacking in sweetness and lacking in any pronounced aromatic flavor or bouquet. Although the term "London Dry Gin" originally was applied to gin produced in or near London, the name "London" is considered to have become generic, and therefore usable by American-made gins.

FRUIT-FLAVORED AND OTHER GINS

IN all gin-producing countries . . . and which is not? . . . there are people who demand a gin with a special flavor: orange, lemon, pineapple, black-currant, and so forth. These are gins to which the specific flavoring has been added. In the United States these are considered the product of rectification and pay the thirty cents per gallon rectification tax.

"Liqueur" gins are also made in the United States by adding $2\frac{1}{2}$ per cent or more by volume of simple syrup. This is also a rectified product.

For a product to be a "gin" the one requirement *sine qua non* is that its principal flavoring agent be juniper berries. However, there is one exception: sloe gin. Sloe gin is a gin in the name only, since it is a cordial, and it will be discussed in Chapter 23.

ON AGING GIN

UNITED STATES regulations do not permit any age claims to be made for gin. In fact, gin does not require aging to be smooth, palatable, and drinkable. It is ready for consumption when it comes off the gin still and has been reduced to potable strength. However, some producers in the United States do age their gin in wood for short periods of time, which gives the gin a light golden color—often called "golden gin"—even though they cannot advertise or make any age claims upon the label.

There is a general misconception about Dutch gins being aged. In the Netherlands, aging is not recognized by law, although it would still not be illegal to do so. The fact is that whether labeled Hollands, Genever, or Schiedam it is not aged. As they come from the still they are stored for bottling, either in large glazed earthenware vats or more often in glass-lined tanks.

Any slight yellowish or golden color to be found in Dutch gin is the product of a slight amount of caramel coloring that has been added.

USES OF GIN

HOLLANDS gin should be drunk straight; in the East Indies, however, they drink it with bitters: Take a regular whiskey glass, 2 dashes of bitters—roll the glass around until the inside of the glass is covered with the bitters, then throw out the rest; fill with Hollands gin. It is a quick drink and a good appetizer.

The most popular dry gin cocktail, by far, is the Dry Martini, but it is only one of the hundreds of gin cocktail formulas, such as the Alexander, Bronx, Gimlet, etc., etc. Dry gin is also widely used in long drinks, such as the Tom Collins, Rickey, Gin and Ginger Ale, Gin and Tonic, and so forth.

21. *Vodka*

WHEN this book first appeared, in 1940, it was unthinkable that a separate chapter should be required on Vodka. In the short space of three decades, the most neutral of spirits has risen from its "also ran" listing among the "other spirits" to a degree of popularity in America that ranks it second only to Bourbon and Blended Whiskey and Scotch.

The word Vodka is a diminutive of the Russian for water, *voda*, and it is the Russians who originated this particular water of life or *eau-de-vie*. In Russia, Finland, Czechoslovakia, Poland, and elsewhere in northern and eastern Europe, spirits have long been distilled to a very high proof, resulting in a minimum of flavor. They have generally been distilled from the most plentiful and least expensive materials available to the distiller, wherever he might be. It has been popularly and erroneously believed that Vodka was made principally from potato starch. While Vodka *can* be made from potatoes or from any starchy substance susceptible of conversion into sugar and subsequent fermentation and distillation, in practice Vodka has been made from grain in Russia and elsewhere.

According to Mr. R. P. Kunett of Ste. Pierre Smirnoff Fils, Inc., the finest Vodka in Imperial Russia was distilled from various grains, principally corn, with some wheat added. The vast Smirnoff distilleries in Moscow, dating from 1818, passed out of the family's control with the 1917 Revolution. The formula was brought to America in the 1930s via Paris and Smirnoff was the first and only American-made Vodka for many years.

how Vodka is made

The U.S. Treasury Department under Federal Control Regulations No. 5, amended in 1964, has established the definition and the method for producing Vodka in this country as follows: "'Vodka' is neutral spirits distilled from any material at or above 190 proof, and, if bottled, bottled at not less than 80 proof . . . as to be without distinctive character, aroma or taste."

Thus, Vodka, like Whiskey, is an alcoholic distillate from a fermented mash of grain. Whiskey, however, is distilled at low proof to retain flavor

Inspecting activated charcoal used for filtering vodka. (Courtesy Ste Pierre Smirnoff Fls, Hartford, Conn.)

congeners. Vodka, as has been stated, is distilled at high proof, and then processed still further to extract all congeners. In a sense, Vodka is like Gin, yet they have one big difference. Both are made from neutral spirits. Neither has to be aged. But in the making of American Gin, as described in Chapter 20, the neutral spirits are delicately flavored with the addition of juniper and aromatics. In the making of Vodka, nothing is added to the neutral spirits, but instead, all character is subtracted from the spirits leaving it odorless, tasteless, and colorless.

Essentially, two Vodka-making processes are specifically recognized. In the first, neutral spirits flow continuously through tanks containing at least a pound and a half of vegetable charcoal for each gallon of spirits, so that the spirits are in intimate contact with the charcoal for a period of not less than eight hours. It is also required that at least 10 per cent of the charcoal be replaced after each forty hours of operation. In the second, spirits are maintained in constant movement by mechanical means in contact for not less than eight hours with at least six pounds of new vegetable charcoal for every hundred gallons of spirits. Actually, Vodka can be made by purifying or refining the spirits by any other method which the government finds will result in a product equally without distinctive character, aroma, or taste. American Vodka is made at both 80 and 100 proof, the greater majority of sales being at the lower figure, which is milder than all other spirits except Rum.

According to many historians, Vodka was first produced in Russia in the fourteenth century. But, up to the middle of the twentieth century, general consumption was confined almost entirely to Russia, Poland, and the Baltic States. True, Vodka has been produced in the United States since Repeal of Prohibition in 1933, but until 1948 it was just one of those exotic specialties consumed by a few people of eastern European origin who wanted to evoke nostalgic memories. It was drunk straight, ice cold, in a small one-ounce glass, and at one gulp . . . and almost always with a sharp-tasting appetizer. However, drinking Vodka in this way did not have any appeal for Americans, and it would have remained an enigma except for an accident of chance—an accident that had nothing to do with Vodka to begin with. *use of Vodka*

After the end of World War II a Hollywood restaurant man found himself with a large and unsaleable stock of ginger beer. He realized he had to find a new use for it or take a heavy loss. He tried mixing it with any number of products without success, until he used Vodka. He added half a lime, served it in a copper mug and named it "Moscow Mule." The "mule" caught on, and then everybody got in the act creating new drinks. From Hollywood the Vodka fashion swept across the country.

Because it is odorless as well as tasteless, Vodka gained a reputation for leaving the imbiber breathless, in the best sense of the word. Because it had no flavor of its own, it was quickly recognized as the most versatile of all mixers. This fact, perhaps more than any other, accounts for the remarkable growth of Vodka's popularity.

It is a most admirable cocktail ingredient and can be blended with any beverage. One of the most popular cocktails using Vodka is the "Vodka Martini" where Vodka replaces Gin. Others are the "Bloody Mary" with tomato juice, the "Screwdriver" with orange juice, and "Vodka and Tonic" (see recipes p. 356–66). It is often served "On-the-Rocks." In fact, Americans have also begun to enjoy it straight, particularly with caviar, smoked salmon, and spicy appetizers.

Vodka's success has brought an increasing flow of Vodka from abroad, including brands from England, France, Holland, and Israel (kosher Vodka is available) as well as from the traditional Vodka producing and consuming countries of northern and eastern Europe. The most significant and prestigious are those from the original Russian and Polish sources. The Vodkas produced in the United States and Great Britain are, as we previously stated, tasteless, neutral, highly rectified grain spirit whose main virtue is that in mixed drinks *Russian Vodka* the spirit can be "felt but not smelt." This is a far cry from the original eastern European vodkas with characteristic flavor, which are enjoyable on their own. In fact, Russian Vodka is usually drunk neat and served chilled, with caviar or other similar delicacies.

There are several quality Russian and Polish Vodkas on our market today. Some are bottled in these countries, while others are imported in casks and bottled in the United States. In either case, they are distilled from grain, treated with activated birch charcoal, and filtered through quartz sand. They are generally bottled at 80 and 100 proof.

flavored Vodkas

Flavored varieties of Vodka are fairly popular in Poland and Russia, particularly where infusions and mixture with herbs, grasses, leaves, spices, and seeds are involved. Some of these Vodkas are colored and, as Vodka-based liqueurs, sweetened and fruit-flavored. The most common of the flavored Vodkas in the Western world are:

Zubrowka is flavored with a type of grass found only in the forests of eastern Poland. These grasslands are the breeding grounds for a particular species of bison indigenous to Poland and the use of the zubrowka grass gives the Vodka a slightly yellowish tinge and an aromatic bouquet. Exceptionally soft and smooth, it is normally served ice cold and drunk straight. Zubrowka is from 70 to 80 proof.

Starka (starka means old) is an 86 proof Vodka aged for about ten years in special oak casks, previously used for fine-quality wines. This maturing imparts an amber color and flavor to it. Starka is a Vodka for brandy lovers.

Yubileyneya Osobaya, called jubilee Vodka, contains brandy, honey, and other ingredients. It is about 90 proof.

Pertsovka is a dark brown Russian pepper Vodka with a pleasant aroma and burning taste. It is prepared from an infusion of capsicum, cayenne, and cubeb. History records that Czar Peter the Great seasoned his Vodka with pepper, and there are apparently numerous Russians who continue to enjoy the sharp bite of this 70 proof drink.

Okhotnichya, or hunter's Vodka, is a 90 proof spirit flavored with many herbs and has a scent that suggests heather honey.

Russian Vodka makers produce about an additional thirty other Vodkas with a wide range of flavors, some of which are available in the U.S.

22. *Rums*

RUM,* the name of that most versatile of all alcoholic beverages, conjures up pictures of Sir Henry Morgan, the Spanish explorers in the New World, and the smugglers or "rum-runners" of our recent Prohibition era. Its career has been romantic and colorful, and replete with legends, some of which are doubtless apocryphal.

Rum comes from grass—a grass that has given man more genuine enjoyment than any other. Its botanical name is *saccharum officinarum,* more commonly known as sugar cane. The earliest mention we have of sugar cane dates back to 327 B.C. when Alexander the Great returned from his expedition to India. Whether sugar cane originated in the northeastern valleys of India or the islands of the South Pacific we may never know, but it was finally brought to Europe by the Arabs after 636 A.D. Still, crystallized sugar was a costly rarity until Columbus took cane cuttings from the Canary Islands to the West Indies. It prospered so well there that sugar made from cane became inexpensive and could be enjoyed by everyone.

history

Almost at once, distillation of rum sprang up as a by-product of the sugar factory. Today it is made in all parts of the world, wherever sugar cane grows.

Rum is any alcoholic distillate from the fermented juice of sugar cane, sugar cane syrup, sugar cane molasses, or other sugar cane byproducts distilled at less than 190 proof (whether or not such proof is further reduced prior to bottling to not less than 80 proof), in such manner that the distillate possesses the taste, aroma, and characteristics generally attributed to rum; and includes mixtures solely of such distillates.

The early Spanish settlers of the West Indies noted that the residual molasses of their primitive sugar factories fermented easily, so it was natural that they experimented with distilling. The result was a pleasant-tasting alcoholic beverage. The freebooters of the period took the product back to Europe, where it found ready acceptance.

How it got its name—rum—is a matter of conjecture. We do not actually

---

* Ron (Spanish); rhum (French).

301

know. Its origin is lost among the legends of the sixteenth-century swashbuck-ling pirates. The purists—aren't we all—believe it is a contraction of the Latin *saccharum*, which means sugar. Another idea is that the wild lads of the Spanish Main first called the product *rumbullion* or *rumbustion*.

Still others credit the name to the English Navy. In 1745 Admiral Vernon discovered that his men were suffering from scurvy. Not knowing what to do about it, he cut the daily ration of small beer from their diet and replaced it with the strange new West Indian beverage which conquered the scurvy problem and won him the lasting regard of his men, who referred to him affectionately as "Old Rummy" and in his honor called the new drink *rum*. (In eighteenth-century England the term "rum" was a slang expression used to describe people, things, or events that were very good, the very best. Thus, when the British Navy men named the beverage "rum" it was the highest accolade they could bestow upon it.)

For over 300 years rum has been made in the West Indies. While rum is closely associated with the West Indies, it is also produced in other sugar-cane-growing sections of the world and was made in New England, importing molasses from the West Indies for this purpose. Many New England shipping families engaged in an infamous cycle of trade, due to the production of New England rum.

Rum, distilled in New England, was carried to Africa, perhaps with stops at Madeira, the Azores, or the Canaries where some of it was sold. The remainder was exchanged for African blacks who were brought back to the West Indies to become slaves, in exchange for molasses which was brought back to New England to be distilled into rum so that the cycle could be made all over again.

classifications   There are three main classifications of rum: the very dry, light-bodied, brandy-like rums, generally produced in the Spanish-speaking countries, of which Puerto Rican rums are today's outstanding example; the rich, full-bodied, pungent rums usually produced in the English-speaking islands and countries, the best example of which is Jamaica rum; and the light-bodied but pungently aromatic East Indian Batavia Arak rum from Java.

The rums of the various islands of the West Indies as well as those elsewhere all have their own individual character. So we have Cuban rum, Jamacia rum, Puerto Rican rum, and so forth. The Federal Alcohol Administration declares that the word "type" cannot be used in identifying a rum, as is done in the case of many wines, but that it must carry the name of the locality from which it comes. So we cannot have a "Jamaica type" rum made in some other place.

"Light-bodied" rums generally found in international trade today are those of Puerto Rico, Virgin Islands, Haiti, Santo Domingo, Mexico, South Africa, Venezuela, etc. The "full-bodied" pungent rums come from Jamaica, Trinidad, Barbados, Demerara (Guyana), Martinique, Cuba, etc. This does not mean that Puerto Rico produces only "light-bodied" and that Jamaica only "full-bodied" rums. They all can produce both types, but they are better known for their own traditional type.

HOW RUM IS MADE

THE production of rum begins with the harvesting of the cane. The freshly cut cane is brought to the sugar mills, where it is passed through enormous, very heavy crushing rollers that express the juice. The juice is boiled to concentrate the sugar and evaporate the water. Then it is clarified. The result is a heavy thick syrup.

This is pumped into high-speed centrifugal machines, whirling at over 2,200 revolutions per minute, where the sugar in the syrup is crystallized and separated from the other solids. After the sugar is removed what remains is molasses. Sometimes this will still retain up to as much as 5 per cent sugar. The only economical way to recover or shall we say not to lose the residue of sugar is to ferment this molasses and distill it into rum.

PUERTO RICO

THE molasses is placed in large vats holding thousands of gallons. Water is added, together with a substantial proportion of slop from a previous distillation. Cultured yeast is added and fermentation takes place, lasting from two to four days.

After fermentation is completed, the fermented mash, containing about 7 per cent of alcohol, is pumped into a column still, where the spirit is distilled off at 160 proof or higher. Distilling at a high proof produces a spirit low in congeners, light in body, and fairly neutral in flavor.

Only the middle rum (middle part of the distillation), the *madilla,* also called *aguardiente* by the trade, is used for rum. It is aged in uncharred oak barrels, which are used repeatedly.

When the rum has matured—this will vary from one to four years—to the satisfaction of the master distiller, it is passed through a filtering and leaching vat, containing alternate layers of sand and vegetable charcoal. At this point, the rum has very little color, a very light taste, and lightness of body.

A small amount of caramel is added to ensure uniform color and it is placed in large oaken vats to age for a further period. Puerto Rican and Cuban rums are usually blended rums.

"White" or "Silver" are terms used to designate the lighter-colored, more neutral rums, while "Gold" or "Amber" are used to describe the deeper-colored and more flavored rums, which are often older rums and have more caramel to give a uniform deeper color. Today, most of these rums are marketed at 80 proof.

Cutting sugar cane in Puerto Rico, the first step of many towards the eventual distillation of rum. (Courtesy Bar Management, New York)

TASTE OF LIGHT-BODIED RUMS

THE characteristic taste of the White and Gold Label rums is dry, with a very slight molasses flavor, the Gold Label being a bit sweeter and having a more pronounced taste.

The older liqueur rums are usually shipped under brand names. While these rums are generally quite dry, they have a very fine mellow rummy bouquet and flavor, and because of their dryness can be likened to a fine old brandy. Puerto Rico producers now offer full-bodied rums in addition to the light. These may be labeled either Red Label or Heavy Dark, for Planter's Punch.

OTHER LIGHT-BODIED RUMS

WHILE Puerto Rico and the Virgin Islands, and Cuba are the principal areas producing light-bodied rums, this type is also distilled in Santo Domingo, Haiti, Venezuela, Mexico, Brazil, Argentina, Peru, Paraguay, and more recently in Jamaica and Guyana (Demerara). This style of rum is also made in the Philippines, South Africa, and Hawaii.

Some rum is made in Mexico from sugar cane-juice. The product is very light bodied, and as no flavoring ingredients are added, but there is little character in the drink. Also, other parts of Central and South America produce rum in small quantities. It is mostly consumed locally, or exported to nearby markets within the country. Actually, rum is made in limited quantities in most of the sugar-cane districts of the South American mainland. The Bolivian product, made in the rainy forest-slopes just east of La Paz known as the Yungas, has a high local reputation and is shipped out of the country in small quantity. Peruvian rum is made in the valley of the river Maranon, on the border country with Ecuador. Facilities for transport are rather poor in this area and most of the cane grown there is made into rum, which is more economically transported than molasses.

JAMAICA RUM

THE typical Jamaica rum is a full-bodied rum. Its manufacture differs considerably from that of the light-bodied rums.

To the molasses in the fermentation vats, there is added the skimmings from the sugar boilers—the *dunder,* known also as "burnt ale," and water. The natural yeast spores in the air promptly settle on the surface of the liquid mass, multiply rapidly, and cause fermentation to go on apace.

Some call this "wild," and others "spontaneous" fermentation. The correct term is *natural* fermentation. Usually a certain amount of the residue from a previous fermentation is also added. This natural free method of fermentation is slower, taking anywhere from five to twenty days, depending on the abundance of free yeasts spores and climatic or temperature conditions at the time.

This also permits a larger amount of congeners to develop which are carried over in the distillation.

The fermented liquor is pumped into a pot still, where it is distilled, producing a "low wine." This is then redistilled in another pot still. Only the middle rum, taken off after the "heads" and before the "tails" begin to come over, are used.

The new rum is taken off between 140 and 160 proof, and sometimes lower. The result is a very full-bodied, very pungent rummy spirit.

The new rum, like all distillates, is colorless, but with time in oak-puncheon casks it will take on a golden hue. However, the depth of color of Jamaica rum is governed by the amount of caramel added. Jamaica rums are always blended, and being full bodied and rich in congeners they require a longer aging than lighter-bodied rums, anywhere from five to seven years and more.

JAMAICA RUM TYPES

THEIR natural color has always been a rich golden hue, but during the last generation very dark mahogany-colored rums have become very popular. This is due to the fact that they give greater color to the drinks made with them. These darker rums are generally labeled "For Planter's Punch," as this is the drink in which they are used most.

Jamaica's best market is England where much of the rum is shipped for aging and blending. England's damp climate is excellent for maturing rum. (Jamaica rums are usually shipped to Britain at their original high proof. They are reduced to potable strength at the time of bottling, by the addition of water only.) Such rums are known in the trade as London Dock rums, when they are stored and blended in bonded warehouses at the London docks.

Jamaica rums are usually marketed at 86 to 97 proof and occasionally at 151 proof. Most Jamaica rum has a full molasses bouquet and flavor, although some light-bodied, light-flavored types are also made. In all cases, the amount of caramel used determines their color.

HAITI

HAITIAN rums are not so full as those from Jamaica. A major difference is that the rums of Haiti are not made from molasses but from the sap of the sugar cane, fermented and then distilled in old-fashioned pot stills by the same method used in the Cognac country. Because of this, the slightly lighter, slightly less pungent Haitian rums are sometimes called *brandy rums,* as are those of Barbados. The most famous rum of Haiti is Barbancourt, which is made by an old family on the island, and the Five Star Rhum, a straight unblended seven-year-old vintage spirit, is a fine sipping rum that needs no mixer.

Aging is an interesting subject when it comes to rum. No one can really say which is the best age for a fine rum. The light blends of Puerto Rico do not always carry an age label, but by law the youngest spirit in the blend must be at least four years old. Several of the liqueur rums of Jamaica are considerably older, aged in the tropics or in England for twelve, thirteen, or even fifteen years before they are bottled. Age before bottling is all that counts, for like all other distilled spirits and unlike wines, rum does not alter in the bottle. To make matters still more confusing, heat hastens the process and a single year of aging in the tropics may equal two years in England, Scotland, and Kentucky.

DEMERARA RUMS

DEMERARA rums are distilled from sugar cane molasses grown along the Demerara River in Guyana (formerly British Guiana), South America. The chief difference between Jamaica and Demerara rums is due to the variations in character of the sugar cane, the soil, and the climate in the two countries, and the fact that Demerara rums are distilled from column stills. Demerara rums are much darker, not quite as pungent as Jamaica rums, and do not possess the finesse or flavor of the latter.

Demerara rums are obtainable on this market at various proofs. We know of one firm that offers 86, 96, 114, and 151 proofs. The overproof rums are used in Northern lumber camps, by the Grand Banks fishermen, and in Alaska. After exposure to intense cold, they need a very strong bracer to thaw them out. It is generally consumed in the form of grog, that is, mixed half and half with very hot water, as well as in many fancy rum drinks.

When the Zombie became a popular drink, the 151 proof Demerara rum found a new outlet.

VIRGIN ISLANDS RUM

THE Virgin Islands have always been known for three things: rum (the kind you drink), bay rum (the kind you put on your hair), and as pirate hangouts during the days of the Spanish Main.

Purchased by the United States in 1917, they came under our Prohibition laws, and had to confine their efforts to bay rum until Repeal in 1933. The islands were in bad financial circumstances, and our Department of Insular Affairs decided to assist the islands by re-establishing the Virgin Islands rum industry. Eventually the first shipments of the new rum arrived amid the greatest fanfare of free publicity any liquor ever had. The business in rum has not quite solved the islanders' woes, but it has helped them. Virgin Islands rum is today of the light-bodied type. It is generally not aged very long and lacks the finesse of the Puerto Rican rums.

MARTINIQUE AND GUADELOUPE RUMS

MARTINIQUE and Guadeloupe (the French West Indies) rums are the most popular in Paris but not too often encountered in the United States. As a general rule they are full-bodied rums, the color of strong coffee. Sometimes they have the dry, burned flavor of the Demeraras and are used in much the same way, though they are rarely bottled at such high proof. At least one of the Martinique rums, St. James, is made by methods similar to those used in France to make brandy. As in Haiti, the sap of the sugar cane rather than molasses is the base of St. James.

BARBADOS AND TRINIDAD RUMS

SLIGHTLY heavier in flavor than Cuban or Puerto Rican Rum—yet lighter than Jamaica or Martinique—Barbados rums are semi-light in body and color, well

Barcardi distillery at Palo Seco, San Juan—world's largest rum plant.

suited to light punches and cocktails. The distillation of the fermented molasses is carried out with high rectification to over 180 proof, then brought back to 90 proof for bottling. A surprising mixture is placed in the still with the fermented liquid: vegetable-roots, coconut shells, soda, lime, and so on. An equally interesting mixture of flavoring materials is used after fermentation to bring the neutral spirits to the producer's required taste: Sherry, Madeira, bitter almonds, raisins, and spirits of niter. Some of these flavored rums of Barbados are excellent.

Not a great deal of Trinidad's rum is imported into the United States. Quite similar to the rums of Barbados, these rums are considered essential for a proper rum swizzle. When they are used in punches, the drinks are generally enhanced with a dash or "float" of Angostura bitters which are made on the same island.

Trinidad, Barbados, Jamaica, and Guyana form a group whose rums are referred to as the West Indies class.

BATAVIA ARAK

ARAK is a rum produced from molasses that comes from the sugar factories near Batavia, in the Island of Java, Indonesia. Because of the special treatment given the molasses, and the special quality of the river water used in fermentation, a dry, highly aromatic rum results. The quality of Arak owes much, too, to the wild, uncultured yeast, known as the *Saccharomycetes Vordermanni* and the *Monilio Javanica,* and finally to the little cakes of specially cooked and dried red Javanese rice which are placed in the fermenting tubs of molasses.

The Arak is aged for three or four years in Java, after which it is shipped to Holland where it is aged for another four to six years, blended, and then bottled.

Arak is a brandy-like rum of great pungency and rumminess, and is used as any other rum. In Sweden, however, its greatest use is for the making of Swedish Punsch.

USES OF RUM

IN the rum-producing countries, it is drunk straight, rather than in mixtures, and this is the best way to appreciate the qualities of a fine rum. In the United States, however, it is used chiefly in cocktails, such as the Daiquiri, Planter's Punch, rum swizzle, and so forth.

Rums are used extensively in the kitchen for making sauces for desserts and in ice creams and candies. Rums are used also in flavoring tobacco.

23. *Liqueurs or Cordials*

A CLOSELY sheltered room, a thin, ascetic individual wearing a black robe with flowing sleeves bending over strange vessels and retorts, stirring up a fire in search of gold and the everlasting life! This is a picture of the early distiller, the alchemist who was thought to be in communion with the devil. The medieval distiller was the magician of his day, and he was trying to find the chemical secret of obtaining gold from baser metals—in which he failed—and an elixir which would prolong life beyond the normal span. If this medieval magician did not learn how to prolong life at least he learned the secret of making it more interesting, for it was his experiments which produced the first cordials.

Originally cordials were used as medicinal remedies, as love potions, aphrodisiacs, and general cure-alls. It is unnecessary to explain the medicinal and therapeutic value of certain seeds, herbs, and roots which were used at that time, as most of them are to be found in our own pharmacopoeia. To mention just a few: caraway seed, coriander, angelica root, oil of orange, oil of lemon, and various herbs rich in iodine.

In his *Wines and Spirits*, the late André L. Simon says: "In the making of wine . . . the art of man intervenes only to make the best use possible of Nature's own gift . . . but in the making of liqueurs, man has a much wider field wherein to exercise his ingenuity; he is at liberty to give to his liqueurs practically any shade or color he thinks best to attract the attention, raise the curiosity, and charm the eye; he also has at his command all the fruits of the earth from which to extract an almost unlimited variety of aromas and flavors, wherewith to please the most fastidious taste and flatter the most jaded palate."

By the same token, it is theoretically possible to make any liqueur with equal success in any part of the world, but the theory works only up to a certain point. Certain countries have produced such excellent liqueurs that their products are recognized throughout the world as standards of quality. Foremost in this respect are France and Holland, although certain specialties of great repute are produced in other countries, such as Italy's Strega, Flora di Alpi, and Dalmatian Maraschino; Germany's Gilka Kümmel; Sweden's Swedish Punsch; Denmark's Peter Heering; Danzig's Goldwasser; Greece's Ouzo; and here in our own country, Crème Yvette and Forbidden Fruit, two liqueurs which are better known abroad than they are at home.

A liqueur or cordial—the terms are synonymous—is an alcoholic beverage prepared by combining various neutral spirits—brandy, gin, rum, whiskey, or other distilled spirits—with certain flavoring materials, and containing more than $2\frac{1}{2}$ per cent by weight of sugar syrup. Two and a half per cent by weight is a mild form of sweetening material. Most cordials or liqueurs are heavier in sugar content.

The liqueur family is divided into two main branches. These are the natural-colored or "fruit" liqueurs and the "plant" liqueurs, which are colorless. If they have color, it has been added.

The three basic methods used to produce or obtain the flavor for liqueurs are: 1. *infusion;* 2. *percolation;* 3. *distillation.*

FRUIT LIQUEURS

THE infusion or maceration method, very much like making tea, is used primarily for producing fruit liqueurs. As an example, fresh apricots, and perhaps some dried apricots, are placed in a vat or tank containing brandy, as a rule of 120 to 130 proof. The fruit is left to steep in the brandy until it has absorbed almost all the aroma, flavor, and color from the fruit. This will take some six to eight months. The brandy is then drawn off and filtered.

The mass of fruit remaining still contains both useful brandy and some essential flavoring oils. In order to recover them totally, the mass is placed in a still and the last drop of flavor is extracted by distillation. The resultant distillate is then added to the original infused brandy in order to give it more character.

In some cases, where the stones (seeds) of the fruit are present, some of the oil from the fruit stones is also extracted, which accounts for the slight bitter almond undertone sometimes found in such liqueurs as apricot, peach, cherry, etc.

The flavored and naturally colored brandy is then sweetened to the desired richness by the addition of pure sugar syrup, after which it will be stored in a vat for upwards of a year. The principal fruit liqueurs marketed are: apricot, blackberry, cherry, crême de cassis, maraschino, peach, prunelle (plum), and sloe gin.

At this point, the misuse of the word "brandy," as applied to liqueurs, should be explained. In Europe, the word "brandy" is used very loosely in connection with liqueurs, and it is quite common to find these products labeled: "apricot brandy," "cherry brandy," "peach brandy," etc., when they are not brandies

fruit-flavored brandies

as we define brandy. Therefore, in Europe, "apricot brandy" and "apricot liqueur" are the same thing.

The Federal Alcohol Administration defines "brandy" as a distillate obtained solely from the fermented juice, mash, or wine of fruit. Therefore, a liqueur made from fruit by the infusion method cannot be labeled or marketed as a brandy. True fruit brandies are marketed under specific designations such as Kirschwasser, slivovitz, etc. See Chapter 18, page 264.

This regulation caused some confusion for the public who believed "apricot brandy" and "apricot liqueur" were different products. For this reason the Federal Alcohol Administration has, for many years, approved labels for "fruit-flavored brandies" provided the product: 1. is made solely on a brandy base; 2. is 70 proof (minimum); and 3. contains more than $2\frac{1}{2}$ per cent sugar by weight. To the best of our knowledge all "fruit-flavored brandies" marketed in the United States are produced in this country and none are imported.

Most producers make some or all of the following: apricot-flavored brandy; blackberry-flavored brandy; cherry-flavored brandy; coffee-flavored brandy; ginger-flavored brandy, and peach-flavored brandy.

PLANT LIQUEURS

PLANT liqueurs are produced by the percolation and distillation methods.

The percolation or brewing method is somewhat like making coffee. The flavoring agent, in the form of leaves or herbs, is placed in the upper part of an apparatus whose principle is the same as that of a coffee percolator, together with brandy or other spirit, which is in the lower part. The spirit is then pumped up over the flavoring and allowed to "percolate" through it, carrying down, i.e., extracting, the aroma and flavor. The pumping and percolation is repeated continuously for weeks or months until most of the flavor constituents have been obtained. The spirit-soaked flavoring agent is then distilled to obtain whatever flavor remains. This distillate is mixed with the percolate and the whole is sweetened with sugar syrup, filtered and often bottled at once, although some plant liqueurs of this group are aged for a time.

The distillation method is normally carried out in medium-sized copper pot stills, in many cases similar to a gin still, i.e., with a tray upon which the flavoring agent is placed.

The normal procedure is to macerate (soften by soaking) the flavoring agent—plant, seed, root, or herb—in brandy for twenty-four to forty-eight hours, after which it is placed in the still with additional brandy and distilled.

The resultant distillate, always colorless, is sweetened with simple syrup and colored with natural vegetable coloring matter. Thus, it is possible for the producer to give his curaçao or crème de menthe whatever color hue he wishes. We have seen crème de menthe colorless, various shades of green, pink, red, violet, and blue.

Many plant liqueurs are aged in vats for varying periods. In all cases, it is customary to use an aging vat or cask for only one type of liqueur. In other words a liqueur producer will never store his apricot liqueur in a vat that has been used to store or age his curaçao.

Whereas fruit liqueurs derive their color and flavor naturally from one informing fruit, plant liqueurs very often require more than one flavoring agent to balance or bring out the desired flavor. For example, vanilla is always part of the formula in crème de cacao, and plant liqueurs, such as Bénédictine, Chartreuse, Drambuie, etc., result from the blending of flavors obtained from many plants, seeds, roots, and herbs, as many as fifty different ones in some cases. Incidentally, because these herb and spicy liqueurs were originally made by monks, they are sometimes known as "monastery types."

Leading examples of plant liqueurs are: anisette, crème de cacao, crème de menthe, curaçao, kümmel, triple sec, etc.

GENERIC LIQUEURS SHIPPED BY VARIOUS HOUSES

LIQUEURS or cordials have been known by many names and described at one time or another as balms, crèmes, elixirs, oils, and so on. Every producer believes the formula he uses is unique and is his secret, which he goes to great lengths to guard. In the case of many of the famous proprietary brands discussed on the following pages, this is the case.

However, most producers make and market a wide variety of liqueurs under generic or universally used names. In the following list we give you those which are shipped by most general liqueur distillers, together with a description of their principal flavor and usual proof. Since other flavorings will be used by many producers, this will cause variations in the same type of liqueur from one brand to another.

ADVOCAAT. A 40 proof liqueur, sometimes called Egg Brandy, made from egg, sugar, and brandy. It is creamy and thick with an egg nog flavor.

ANESONE. Anis-licorice flavored liqueur made in Italy and the United States. 90 proof.

ANIS. Spanish spelling of anisette, when made in Spain and Latin America. 78 to 96 proof.

ANISETTE. Flavor obtained principally from aniseed. 50 to 60 proof.

APRICOT LIQUEUR. Principal flavor from apricots. Often shipped under a trade name such as Abricotine or Apry. 60 to 70 proof.

BLACKBERRY LIQUEUR. Obtained generally from blackberries, but occasionally has a small amount of red wine added to it. 60 to 70 proof.

CASCARILLA. A popular South American liqueur flavored with spices and various barks. 60 proof.

CHERRY LIQUEUR. Obtained generally from small wild black cherries. 49 to 60 proof.

COFFEE AND BRANDY. A liquid made from Colombian coffee and brandy. 70 proof.

COFFEE LIQUEUR. Based on coffee beans, strictly coffee in taste, and sold all the way from 53 to 60 proof. Many sold under proprietary names.

CRÈME D' ANANAS. Flavor obtained from pineapple. 60 proof.

CRÈME DE BANANES. Flavor obtained from bananas. 60 proof.

CRÈME DE CACAO. Flavor obtained from cacao and vanilla beans. The word "Chouao" often found on Crème de Cacao labels indicates that the beans come from the Chouao region of Venezuela—considered to produce the finest cacao beans in the world. 50 to 60 proof.

CRÈME DE CASSIS. Flavor obtained primarily from black currants. 36 to 50 proof.

CRÈME DE FRAISES. Flavor obtained primarily from strawberries. 40 to 70 proof.

CRÈME DE FRAMBOISES. Flavor obtained primarily from raspberries. 60 proof.

CRÈME DE MANDARINE. Flavor obtained primarily from tangerine peels. 60 proof.

CRÈME DE MENTHE. Flavor obtained from several varieties of mint but principally peppermint. Both white and green are usually shipped. The only difference is that the green has harmless certified coloring added. 54 to 60 proof.

CRÈME DE NOISETTE. Flavor obtained primarily from hazel nuts. 60 proof.

CRÈME DE NOIX. Flavor obtained primarily from walnuts. 60 proof.

CRÈME DE NOYAUX. Flavor obtained primarily from fruit stones, resulting in a bitter almond flavor. Also labeled Crème de Almond. 60 proof.

CRÈME DE PRUNELLE. Flavor obtained primarily from plums. 80 proof.

CRÈME DE ROSE. Flavor obtained primarily from the essential oil of rose petals and vanilla. 60 proof.

CRÈME DE VANILLE. Flavor obtained primarily from the finest Mexican vanilla beans. 60 proof.

CRÈME DE VIOLETTE. Flavor obtained from essential oil of violets and vanilla. 60 proof.

CURAÇAO. Flavor obtained primarily from the dried peel of the famous green oranges from the island of Curaçao. 54 to 60 proof.

DANZIGER GOLDWASSER. Flavor obtained primarily from orange peel and various other spicy herbs and plants. It contains tiny flecks of genuine gold leaf which are harmless if consumed. 80 proof. Also called Gold Liqueur or just Goldwasser.

FRUIT-FLAVORED BRANDY. Apricot, blackberry, cherry, coffee, peach, and ginger are flavors that are employed to produce the several fruit-flavored brandies in the United States. They are all 70 proof.

GOMME. This is a prepared simple syrup. It is non-alcoholic.

GRENADINE. A non-alcoholic flavoring syrup. Flavor obtained from pomegranate.

HIMBEER. Has a delightful raspberry flavor. 60 proof.

KÜMMEL. Flavor obtained principally from caraway seed. Occasionally it has crystallized sugar in it, in which case it will be sold as Kümmel Crystallizé. There is also Allasch Kümmel, Doeppel Kümmel, and Berliner Kümmel. The latter is the dryest of the Kümmel family. 80 to 86 proof.

MANDARINE. Flavor obtained primarily from dried peel of mandarines (tangerines). 60 proof.

MARASCHINO. Flavor obtained from the special Dalmatian Marasca cherry. 60 proof.

MARNIQUE. An Australian liqueur which is based on Australian brandy and tangerines.

MASTIKHA. A Greek liqueur whose flavor is derived primarily from the gum of the mastikha plant and the aniseed. Also known as Mastic. 90 to 92 proof.

OJEN. A dry, high-proof Anis, made from the star aniseed, in the town of Ojen, in southern Spain. 84 to 100 proof.

OUZO. An anis-flavored liqueur made in Greece and Cyprus. 92 proof.

PARFAIT AMOUR. A liqueur of purple shade derived from lemon, citron, coriander, sugar, and alcohol. 60 proof.

PEACH LIQUEUR. Flavor obtained from fresh and dried peaches. 60 proof.

PEPPERMINT SCHNAPPS. A mint liqueur, but lighter bodied than Crème de Menthe. About 60 proof.

PRUNELLE. Flavor obtained from plums. 80 proof.

RAKI. An anis-licorice flavored liqueur from Greece, Turkey, and Cyprus. 92 proof.

ROCK AND RYE. A liqueur with a rye whiskey base, but including grain neutral spirits, rock candy syrup, and fruits—lemons, oranges, and cherries. Another similar product is Rock and Rum, which uses rum as its liquor base.

ROSOLIO. A liqueur, also called Rossolis and Rosoglio, made from petals of red roses, orange blossom water, cinnamon, clove, jasmine, alcohol, and varying amounts of sugar.

SLOE GIN. Flavor obtained from the sloe berry (blackthorn bush). 60 proof.

TIDDY. A liqueur with a Canadian whisky base.

TRIPLE SEC. A white Curaçao, usually 80 proof as against the average orange Curaçao's 60 proof.

WISHNIAK. A Polish liquor made from cherries and spices.

WISNIOWKA. A wild cherry liqueur from Russia and Czechoslovakia. 50 to 70 proof.

FAMOUS PROPRIETARY BRANDS

THESE are, in most cases, world-famous specialty liqueurs, which are produced under closely guarded secret formulas and marketed under registered trademark brands. They are liqueurs made in each case by only one house. Most of them have centuries of tradition behind them and have become household names.

BÉNÉDICTINE.   To the best of our knowledge, the oldest liqueur to survive the test of time is the world-famous D.O.M. Bénédictine, which is still produced on the identical spot where its secret formula was discovered in the year 1510.

If you should visit this corner of France, you could see the duplicate of the original Bénédictine Abbey of Fécamp where Dom Bernardo Vincelli first gave his brother monks his new elixir to comfort them when they were fatigued or ill. D.O.M., which appears on every label, stands for the Latin words Deo Optimo Maximo, "To God, most Good, most Great."

Today, it has no connection with any religious order but is a family-owned corporation, founded by M. Alexandre Le Grand in 1863.

The formula for Bénédictine is one of the most closely guarded secrets in the world. Only three people ever know the complete details. It is a tribute to their ability to keep the secret inviolate that every attempt to imitate this liqueur—and attempts have been made in every part of the world—has failed. At the distillery at Fécamp they point to their Salon de Contrefaçons (Hall of Counterfeits) where the walls are lined with cabinets filled with examples of hundreds of attempted imitations. This is one liqueur of which can be said: "There is only one."

Bénédictine is a plant liqueur made from a number of different herbs, plants, peels, and so forth, on a fine Cognac brandy base. It is made in a number of operations: not all of the flavors are distilled out at the same time. They are obtained separately and then skillfully blended together. Bénédictine is aged for four years before being bottled.

Some years ago the heads of the firm were convinced that a substantial amount of Bénédictine was drunk in the form of B and B (Bénédictine and Brandy) by people who preferred a drier liqueur. They therefore decided to prepare their own B & B liqueur, D.O.M., which makes for a drier or less sweet Bénédictine. 86 proof.

BOLSBERRY.   This is a pleasant drink that derives its mild flavor from a blend of black currants (cassis) and other fruits. Bolsberry is classified by Federal regulations as a liqueur although in Holland where it is most popular, it is looked upon as an apértif. It is not too sweet, nor too dry.

CAFÉ BRIZARD.   This is one of the better-known proprietary brand coffee-type liqueurs. 50 proof.

Battery of copper pot stills employed to distil the various herbs, flowers and plants used to flavor Bénédictine liqueurs at Fécamp, France.

CARLSBAD BECHER is named for the world-famous watering spa, Carlsbad (Czechoslovakia), where it was first created and is still produced today. The thermal waters of the Spa and selected medicinal herbs combine to give this liqueur its special aroma and taste. 76 proof.

CHARTREUSE. The most famous liqueur still made by a religious order is Chartreuse. It is made from a secret formula given to the Carthusian Fathers of the convent of the Grande Chartreuse at Grenoble, France, in 1607 by the Maréchal d' Estrées. The original formula was slightly modified and perfected in 1757 by one of the monks, Brother Gérome Manbec, who was described as a "very clever apothecary" by writers of the period. Two types of Chartreuse—yellow, 86 proof, and green, 110 proof—have been faithfully made according to these formulas.

In 1901, because of a law against religious orders passed in France, the Carthusian Fathers were expelled from their monastery of the Grande Chartreuse, where they had had their headquarters since the founding of the order in 1084 by Saint Bruno of Cologne. Their property, which included their trade marks for Chartreuse liqueurs, were sold at auction, but the secret formula was not available. The clever fathers repaired to another monastery of their order in Tarragona, Spain, where they continued to produce their famous

Stained glass window at Bénédictine Distillerie, Fécamp, France, showing Dom Bernardo Vincelli directing his brother Bénédictines in his medieval laboratory.

liqueurs, according to their ancient secret formulas. The bottles today bear two labels: The original label used before the expulsion from France, and a second which carries the legend, "Liqueur Fabriquée à Tarragona par les Pères Chartreux." After a quarter century of litigation the French Government was obliged by the French Courts to restore to the Carthusian Fathers all their properties and rights. Since 1940 Chartreuse liqueurs have been made again, as of old, at their Charterhouse and distillery at Voiron, near Grenoble, as well.

Both yellow and green Chartreuse are plant liqueurs with a spicy, aromatic flavor, made on a brandy base, the green being much drier and somewhat more aromatic than the yellow. They are also reminiscent of the Green Muse—Artemisia.

CHÉRI-SUISSE is a chocolate-cherry liqueur from Switzerland. 60 proof.

CHERRY HEERING, renamed PETER HEERING, made by him in Copenhagen, Denmark, is recognized as one of the finest cherry liqueurs in the world. Other fine proprietary brands of cherry liqueurs are: Cherristock (Italy), Cherry Bestle (Denmark), Cherry Karise (Denmark), and Cherry Marnier (France). Most of cherry liqueurs are from 48 to 50 proof.

CHOKALU is a Mexican liqueur with a chocolate taste that is moderately sweet. 52 proof.

CHOCOLAT SUISSE is a chocolate-flavored Swiss liqueur, produced with miniature squares of chocolate floating in the bottle. 60 proof.

CORDIAL MÉDOC is a cocktail of liqueurs; a blend of fine brandy, orange Curaçao, and Crème de Cacao, produced in Bordeaux, France. 88 proof.

COINTREAU is a brand name for one of the finest Triple Secs. 80 proof.

DRAMBUIE is a liqueur made by an ancient secret formula brought to Scotland by a French attendant on Prince Charles Edward in 1745, hence its claim to "Prince Charles Edward's Liqueur." It is made with the finest old Highland Malt Scotch whiskey and heather honey. 80 proof.

EXPRESSO is made in Ancona, Italy, on the shores of the sunny Adriatic. The famous and respected firm of A.D.A.L. is the producer. In Italy, Expresso is known as Illy Coffee Liqueur, taking its name from Illy Coffee, from which it is made. This is one of Europe's largest-selling premium coffees. Because "Expresso" is synonymous in the minds of American consumers with coffee, this name was selected as being more meaningful than its Italian designation. The name Illy has been retained in a minor position on the label, for the benefit of Italians now living here and for returned tourists from Italy. 60 proof.

FALERNUM. This is a pleasant flavoring syrup with a small amount of alcohol (6 per cent), made up of simple syrup, lime, almond, ginger, and other spices. It is white in color.

Falernum was invented over 200 years ago in Barbados, B.W.I. Apparently the sugar cane planter who named it was quite erudite for it was named after the ancient and storied Falernian wine of Roman times. Aside from this, Falernum has no connection with wine or Italy for it is made in the West Indies and United States. Its principal use is as a flavoring and sweetening ingredient in rum drinks, a function it performs admirably.

FIOR D' ALPE is an Italian liqueur of the spicy type, bottled with a herb sprig inside of the bottle and made with an excess of sugar which crystallizes on the sprig. The recipe for this cordial is probably centuries old and involves the numerous herbs found in the Alps, such as juniper, mint, thyme, arnica, wild marjoram, hyssop, etc. 92 proof.

FORBIDDEN FRUIT is one of the two liqueurs made in America and exported to Europe. It was made by the famous Bustanoby from a type of grapefruit, called the shaddock, infused in fine brandy. 64 proof.

CRÈME YVETTE is the other American liqueur which is popular in Europe. It is a liqueur colored and flavored violet. 65.5 proof. Both Crème Yvette and Forbidden Fruit are made in Pennsylvania, by Charles Jacquin, Inc.

GILKA KÜMMEL, made in Berlin, Germany, has for almost a century been accepted as the standard of quality, although the old firm of Bols in Holland claims that their Bolskummel was the original Kümmel, distilled by Erven Lucas Bols in 1575. This is said to have so impressed a Russian Czar that he took the recipe back to Russia and eventually made Russia the principal producer and consumer of Kümmel. Kümmel, as previously mentioned, is flavored principally with caraway seed, and cumin seed from which is obtained the highly therapeutic cumin oil. 86 proof.

GLEN MIST, GLAYVA, and LOCHAN ORA are popular liqueurs based on Scotch Whisky.

GRAND MARNIER is a fine liqueur produced in Cognac, France. It is in reality one of the finest orange Curaçao liqueurs. 80 proof.

HALB AND HALB SCHIMMEGESPANN.   A German liqueur drawing its name from a half bitter and half sweet taste. Orange base blended with variety of herb flavors. Halb and Halb Extra Liqueur has less bitter character.

IRISH MIST.   A fine, spicy Irish whiskey and heather honey liqueur whose secret formula was lost for over two centuries. 80 proof.

IZARRA is produced in two forms—green (85 proof) and yellow (64 proof). Production is on a brandy base with flavoring drawn from plants grown in the French Pyrenees.

KAHLÚA is a coffee-flavored liqueur from Mexico. 53 proof.

LIQUEUR D' OR.   Flavor obtained primarily from lemon peel, herbs, and plants. Similar to Danziger Goldwasser, it also has gold-leaf flecks in it. 86 proof.

LIQUORE GALLIANO is a fine, pleasant, spicy, aromatic liqueur from Livorno, Italy, named after Major Guiseppe Galliano, the hero of the defense of Fort Enda Jesus, near Makale. 80 proof.

O-CHA is a green-colored Japanese liqueur with the aroma and taste of fresh green tea. 50 proof.

PASHA is a coffee liqueur from Turkey. 53 proof.

PICON is a popular French bitter cordial which is rarely consumed neat. In France it is drunk as an apéritif by mixing two ounces of Amer Picon with about four ounces of sparkling water. To sweeten the drink, grenadine is sometimes used. In the United States its most popular use is in the pleasantly refreshing Picon Punch, whose recipe is to be found on page 362 of Chapter 26 on cocktails. 78 proof.

PIMM'S CUPS is a drink that dates back more than a century. The story goes that a bartender in a Pimm's restaurant in the London financial district invented the original gin sling many years ago and the patrons liked it so well they used to ask that it be prepared for them in quantity so that they could take it up to the country when they went on holiday. From the numerous requests of this nature, it was natural that the drink be prepared commercially. As it is bottled, Pimm's is a rather heavy cordial, but when mixed with cold lemon soda and garnished with a slice of lemon and a piece of cucumber rind, it makes a very satisfying, cooling, thirst quencher.

SABRA is the popular liqueur of Israel and is made from a blend of Jaffa oranges with an overtone of chocolate. 60 proof.

SAMBUCA ROMANA combines the tang of licorice with the freshness of wild elderbush. The elderbush, whose Latin name is *sambucus*, is a shrub with leaves like honeysuckle and white scented flowers in umbrella-shaped clusters; the berries are violet-black in color. In fact, there are several proprietary brands that carry the sambucus name, including Sambuca di Trevi and Sambuca Molinari Extra. All these liqueur has essentially the same taste and are about 84 proof.

SOUTHERN COMFORT is an American specialty. It was known, originally, as "Cuff and Buttons" around 1875, when this phrase meant "white tie and tails." According to the legend, it was a bartender in St. Louis, Missouri, by the name of Louis Herron, who gave it the very apt name of Southern Comfort.

The Southern Comfort Corporation states that today the drink is prepared in the same manner as Louis Herron made it. To a fine old Bourbon whiskey are added a moderate quantity of peach liqueur and freshly pitted and peeled peaches. This is allowed to age—to blend—from six to eight months in the barrel, after which it is ready to bottle. The fruit and the liqueur help mellow the robust body of the whiskey, and even though it is bottled at 100 proof, Southern Comfort is a velvety drink—albeit with the kick of a mule. It is difficult to know just how to classify this preparation. Its producers call it a cocktail, but in character it seems to be more of a very fine liqueur.

STREGA is a famous spicy plant liqueur which comes from Italy. 80 proof.

SU-MI-RE is a lavender-hued, Japanese cordial about the color of violets. It is a 60-proof liqueur produced by a rather intricate distilling process that begins with a citron base, draws on native fruit, spice, and herb sources, and adds the combined flavors of almonds, oranges, and vanilla beans. Whatever its ingredients, it is full bodied but superbly smooth, distinctly scented but light in bouquet.

TEA BREEZE is a French liqueur that tastes like tea. 50 proof.

TIA MARIA from Jamaica claims to be the original coffee-flavored liqueur. It is made on a rum base and is distinctive. 63 proof.

TUACA is of Italian origin with a sweet, citrus flavor. 82 proof.

VAN DER HUM is a spicy, aromatic liqueur from South Africa, made with fruits, plants, seeds, and barks. Its principal flavor is that of mandarine. 60 proof.

VANDERMINT is a delicious minted, chocolate liqueur from Holland. 60 proof.

USES OF LIQUEURS

LIQUEURS, being sweet and potent and containing certain beneficial essential oils, are natural digestives and for this reason they are most popular as after-dinner drinks. That is their primary use today. During the Prohibition era, however, liqueurs came into wide use as cocktail ingredients because their rich sweetness was helpful in covering up the harsh bite of the spirits the bootlegger supplied. Many cocktails invented during that period call for liqueurs as an important ingredient. In fact, many people have found that a dash of a liqueur in a cocktail gives it added smoothness, texture, and palatability.

In France certain liqueurs are used in various ways aside from their customary use as after-dinner liqueurs. Most of the Crème de Menthe used in France, for instance, is drunk in the form of highballs. Crème de Cassis, made

Bottling and labeling operations in the Benedictine Castle in France. (Courtesy Julius Wile, New York)

from black currants, is drunk mixed with French Vermouth and mineral water, or merely mixed with mineral water. A popular way of serving liqueurs is as frappés, which are made by filling a small glass with finely cracked ice and then pouring the liqueur into it.

liqueurs in the kitchen   In addition to all these uses, liqueurs and syrups are used in cooking, baking, flavoring ices and ice creams, in making sauces for puddings, fruit dishes, and in desserts in general.

SPECIFIC GRAVITY OF CORDIALS

FOR those who are called upon to prepare Pousse-Café or combinations of "floated" liqueurs, we offer this table of proofs and densities of some of the more popular cordials and liqueurs. Of course, not all liqueur manufacturers use the identical formulas and consequently they will vary slightly for various shippers, but this should serve as a fairly good guide. To pour each layer of the Pousse-Café so that the color will settle on color without disturbing the earlier ones in the glass, pour each liqueur over the back of a spoon. The heaviest liqueur goes on the bottom; that is, the lighter product *floats* upon the denser. The result can be a drink as colorful as the rainbow. By the way,

Pousse-Café can be prepared ahead of time and will keep for about an hour in the refrigerator before the layers start to blend together.

CORDIAL OR LIQUEUR	PROOF	DENSITY	CORDIAL OR LIQUEUR	PROOF	DENSITY
Kirschwasser	96	0.938	Peach	60	1.085
Cognac Brandy	84	0.948	Apricot	60	1.085
Green Chartreuse	110	1.015	Anisette	54	1.100
B and B Liqueur			Crème de Menthe	60	1.105
DOM	86	1.045	Mandarine	70	1.110
Prunelle	80	1.045	Crème d'Ananas	60	1.115
Cherry Liqueur	60	1.045	Curaçao	60	1.115
Kümmel	86	1.055	Maraschino	60	1.115
Triple Sec	80	1.055	Parfait Amour	60	1.115
Liqueur d'Or	86	1.065	Vanille	60	1.115
Yellow Chartreuse	86	1.065	Crème de Cacao	60	1.115
Blackberry	60	1.080	Crème de Rose	60	1.130
Strawberry or Crème			Crème de Violette	60	1.130
de Fraises	60	1.080	Crème de Cassis	36	1.170

24. Other Spirits

THE ardent spirit in each country is obtained, as we have already pointed out, from the basic fruit or grain native to the country, and consequently the least costly product obtainable. So we find brandy in France, Spain, and Italy; whiskey and gin in England, Holland, and the United States; and rum wherever the sugar cane grows.

AKVAVIT (AQUAVIT)

THE national beverage of the Scandinavian countries may be made either from grain or from potatoes, and then flavored with caraway seeds. The method of producing Akvavit in Denmark is to obtain from potatoes a highly rectified neutral spirit which is reduced and redistilled in the presence of the flavoring agent. It is distilled at 190 proof, reduced with water back to 120 proof, and redistilled in a still similar to a gin still. The principal flavoring agent is the caraway seed. Other flavorings—orange and lemon peel, cardamom, and so forth—are used, much the same as in preparing a gin, except that in this case they are used in smaller proportion.

Akvavit is not aged. It is filtered as it comes from the still, reduced in proof, and put into a glass-lined vat until it is ready for bottling. Or it may be bottled immediately. There is a general misconception that Akvavit is strictly an unsweetened spirit. In fact, the term Akvavit has been adopted as a general term both for the sweetened and spiced liquor—specifically known in Sweden as Akvavit—and for Brannvin, which is usually (but not always) unsweetened and unspiced. Actually, many people describe it by saying that it is Kümmel before the sweetening syrup is added; it tastes like Kümmel, except that it is much drier. Its alcoholic strength is 90 proof, whereas Kümmel is 60 to 80 proof.

In Norway, Sweden, and Iceland similar methods are used for making Aquavit, but it is recognized by the Scandinavians that the Danish Akvavit is the best product. All Scandinavian spirits are produced under the strictest governmental control.

324

Akvavit is always served ice cold. It is usually taken with food—appetizers, canapes, or sandwiches—and usually with a beer chaser. The usual drink of Akvavit is one ounce, and it is not sipped but is taken at one swallow. It is customarily drunk to the Scandinavian toast:

"Skaal! Min skaal—din skaal,
Alla vackra flickornas skaal!"

"Health! My health—your health,
All the pretty girls' health!"

It is an old Scandinavian custom at formal gatherings to drink as many toasts as there are buttons on the men's dress vests. Our Norse Vikings are sturdy fellows. We do not recommend this method of drinking Akvavit or any other spirit.

A glass or two of Akvavit is an excellent beginning for a party. It makes one relax and is a splendid drink to serve to a group of people for a quick get-together.

OKOLEHAO

ROMANTIC Hawaii has made several exotic contributions to our way of life. In dancing it is the hula, in dress it is the lei, in sport it is the surfboard, while in music it has given us the languorous steel guitar and ukulele. But the most exotic offering is Okolehao or "Oke" as it is known on the island.

According to Ti Root Okolehao Hawaii, Inc., who claim to be the only producers of Okolehao, it is distilled solely from fermented mash of the roots of the sacred Ti plant of Hawaii (*cordyline australis*).

It was first made by an Australian, William Stevenson, about 1790. He cooked the Ti roots, which are rich in levulose (*fructose*), and allowed the mash to ferment in the bottom of a canoe. He then distilled the fermented mash in a still constructed from a ship's cooking pot, with an inverted calabash for a lid and a water-cooled gun barrel for a coil.

Today, of course, it is distilled in a modern distillery employing column stills and all the most advanced scientific mashing and distilling control techniques.

Okolehao is not aged. After distillation it is filtered through charcoal. Both a Crystal Clear and a Golden Oke are produced. Its virtue is an unusual and subtle flavor. Okolehao is marketed at 80 proof.

It is drunk straight, on the rocks, in tall drinks and highballs, and it is employed in the preparation of a number of intriguingly named cocktails such as: Mahalo, which means "thank you" in Hawaiian, Ti A'A Sour, Scratch Me Lani, Okole-Wow, No-Mo-Pain, Aloha, and Coke and Oke, to list only a few.

BITTERS

BITTERS are divided into two classes—medicinal and non-medicinal. Bitters which are medicinal must pass a severe test to satisfy the Federal Alcohol Tax Unit of the Internal Revenue Bureau that they should not be subject to the regular alcohol Internal Revenue Tax. If imported, the regular duty of $2.50 per gallon still applies.

If the bitters are classified as non-medicinal, such as Orange Bitters, the Internal Revenue Tax and the State Tax applies, just as on any other alcoholic beverage.

Medicinal bitters are not considered to be within the province of our alcoholic beverage regulations. They come under the Pure Food Act and may be sold by grocery stores or drug or department stores, and in many states their sale is specifically prohibited in a liquor store. Yet bitters often contain over 40 per cent of alcohol and they are generally consumed either alone or in combination with other liquors (in cocktails). This seems somewhat illogical, but bitters must be considered in a work of this nature because of their many uses in connection with various cocktails.

Most bitters of repute are made from formulas which are closely guarded proprietary secrets. They are the result both of infusion and distillation processes applied to aromatic plants, seeds, herbs, barks, roots, and fruits, all carefully blended on a spirit base. The one common characteristic is their bitterness. They all claim to have stomachic qualities. The best-known of all bitters is Angostura, which is made from a basic formula prepared in Trinidad by the descendants of the creator of the recipe, a German, Dr. Siegert. This basic formula is then amplified by the addition of the spirit.

Abbott's Aged Bitters is the other principal aromatic bitters. It has been prepared in Baltimore since 1865 by the Abbott family.

Other famous bitters are Peychaud's, prepared in New Orleans; Boonekamp (Dutch); Fernet Branca (Italian), also prepared here in America by a branch of the original firm, Fratelli Branca; the German Underberg bitters; and Unicum, made by the Hungarian liqueur firm of Zwack in Italy.

There is little doubt that the most devoted consumers of bitters are the Italians. Today, Campari is the most popular brand in Italy. It is consumed everywhere at all times of the day, particularly in the form of the rose-colored Campari Soda. This is made by fizzing some 3 ounces of club soda onto 1½ ounces of Campari in a small highball glass or a goblet. The Italians drink this the way Americans consume cola drinks.

Campari is gaining favor in the United States, where tourists returning from Italy are beginning to order Campari Soda and the Negroni Cocktail (see page 358). Campari by itself is also a popular apéritif.

The one well-known bitters which is prepared and sold by a number of English firms, primarily, is Orange Bitters. This is obtained from the dried peel of a bitter Seville orange—the same orange which is so popular in England for making orange marmalade.

TEQUILA AND PULQUE

TEQUILA is thought to be the first spirit distilled in the Americas. The Aztecs were distilling it when the Spaniards conquered Mexico, and it is made today as it was then from the fermented juice of a desert cactus plant.

In Mexico, of course, cacti grow plentifully in a thousand varieties. The one used in making Tequila is *agave tequilana weber* of the Amarillyclaceae family, better known as the century plant, or American aloe, and in Mexico as *mezcal*. The plant takes twelve years to reach proper maturity, at which time there is a rush of sap to the base. When the exact moment of maturity is attained, the outer leaves are removed and the base, resembling a pineapple but somewhat larger and heavier, is cut from the plant, leaving only a stump.

These "pineapples" or hearts of the plant are heavy with sweet sap called *aguamiel* (honey water). Upon arrival at the distillery they are split open and placed in an oven where they are steamed for about eight hours. This causes a considerable amount of the aguamiel to run off freely. The "pineapples" are then shredded and the remaining juice is expressed by mechanical means. The juices are placed in large vats to ferment.

To start fermentation and to ensure continuing similarity of character, a small amount of must from a previous fermentation is added to each new batch. Fermentation takes about two and a half days. The fermented product is distilled in pot stills. The finished Tequila, upon distillation, is drawn off at about 106 proof. That which is shipped to this country as white is unaged and bottled at once at 80 to 86 proof, while that shipped as gold is aged in oak vats for from two to over four years. In aging, Tequila becomes golden in color and acquires a pleasant mellowness without altering its inherent taste characteristic.

Tequila has an odd, almost ineffable, taste. It is vaguely sweet, a trifle musty, and whatever else may be said of its flavor, it is certainly pronounced. Tequila has a natural affinity to lime and salt. Actually, the traditional method of drinking Tequila in Mexico, where it is the national drink, is a gracious ceremony in itself. The imbiber takes half a lime or lemon, tilts back his head and squeezes some of the juice on his tongue. Next he puts enough salt on his thumbnail to cover it. This joins the lime juice on his tongue. Then and only then is he prepared to meet his Tequila, which joins the previous preparation in his mouth and is gulped down fast. Not even a Mexican inured to the hottest chile can drink Tequila in any other fashion. Once the draught is down the reaction is pleasant enough. A warm glow suffuses the hero of this episode.

While Mexicans like their Tequila straight in the traditional fashion, we

328

Guillermo Freytag holds the 100,000,000th agave "pineapple" to be harvested at the Cuervo plantation, near Tequila, State of Jalisco, Mexico. (Courtesy Liquor Publications, Inc.)

effete North American Tequila aficionados prefer it in cocktails and mixed drinks. The most likable of these is a cocktail called Margarita, a blend of Tequila, lime or lemon juice, and an orange liqueur such as Cointreau or Triple Sec, shaken and served in a salt-rimmed glass.

Almost equal in popularity with the Margarita in Mexico City is something called a Sangrita, a drink vaguely related to the Bloody Mary with its tomato juices and spices, but different. The Sangrita is taken two ways: with the tequila and the juice mixture served separately, or as a cocktail with the tequila and the tomato juice shaken together and strained. Most Americans seem to prefer the mixed drink.

Pulque is also obtained from mezcal. As a general rule it is not produced in the professional manner as previously described, for the aguamiel obtained is allowed to ferment slowly for about ten days to form *madre pulque* (mother pulque). A small amount is added to fresh aguamiel which ferments rapidly, being ready for consumption in a day or two. Pulque is not readily available very far from its source of origin because it is always consumed freshly made.

Pulque has a rather heavy flavor resembling sour milk, but it is much appreciated by the Mexicans because of its cooling, wholesome, and nutritional properties.

Mescal (mezcal) is made much the same way as Pulque, but a different variety of cactus (*Lathophora williamsi*) is employed. This agave grows particularly in the states to the southwest of Mexico City—Jalisco, Sinaloa, Michoacan—and just to the north of the capital in Hidalgo. Like Tequila, not only the juice but also some cactus pulp is included in the fermentation. Only a single distillation is made and the product is usually colorless and, rather surprisingly, clear. Mescal commonly runs about 90 proof. It is not aged and has a unique "herbaceous, weedy" taste.

THE GREEN MUSE—ABSINTHE

MAN is a perverse creature. Deny him what he considers his inalienable right and by hook or by crook he will get it anyway. Adam and Eve are the classical Biblical examples, and a lot of us who experienced our own dry era are modern examples. But the interesting psychology of prohibition is the aura of mystery with which the prohibited action or thing becomes cloaked.

Of all alcoholic beverages discovered or created by man, none is less understood than Absinthe, poetically described as "the water of the Star Wormwood—the Green Muse." It is supposed to be wicked, to drive the drinker insane, and to have killed many. In France its sale was prohibited before the First World War because of the belief that it would cause a decrease in the birthrate. Possibly it can do all these terrible things, as it is one of the most potent of all alcoholic beverages. It is not because of the wormwood that it is so dangerous but rather because of its alcoholic strength. Absinthe was generally shipped at a proof of 136 or 68 per cent alcohol. In fact the sale of Absinthe is prohibited in Switzerland, where it was invented, in France, the United States, and most other countries.

Just what is this Absinthe of which we hear so much and about which we know so little? The elixir Absinthe is composed of aromatic plants, Artemisia mayoris and vulgaris, balm-mint, hyssop, fennel, star-anis, and high proof spirit, usually brandy. It was invented towards the end of the eighteenth century by a physician and pharmacist, Dr. Ordinaire, a French exile, living in Couvet, Switzerland. In 1797 the recipe was acquired by Henri-Louis Pernod and since that time the Pernod name has been so closely allied with Absinthe as to make it synonymous with it. For the countries to which the importation of Absinthe is prohibited, a similar elixir is prepared which contains everything that Absinthe does except the wormwood.

Absinthe is a light yellow green in color. It has a sharp pronounced aromatic aroma, in which the dominant note is licorice. When it is mixed with water (as it always should be), it changes color, first becoming emerald, then pink, milky, and finally a cloudy opalescent color shot through with glints of green, pink and gold. It is intriguing to look at and to drink.

Only a lunatic, such as it is supposed to produce, would drink Absinthe neat. The proper way to use it is to dilute it with a great deal of water and ice, or use it as an added flavor in a cocktail—a dash is all that is required.

The classic Absinthe drink is the Absinthe Drip, which requires a special drip glass, although a perforated silver "tea-strainer" may be substituted for the "drip" part of the glass. Pour a jigger of Absinthe into the glass, then place a cube of sugar over the drip hole of the upper section, pack with cracked ice and pour cold water to fill the dripper. When all of the water has dripped through, the drink is ready. Some people prefer a slightly sweeter drink, which may be procured by using one ounce of Absinthe and one ounce of Anisette. This drink is an excellent restorative in cases of sea-sickness, air-sickness, and nausea. One is enough.

We should like to point out that the Pernod anis made by Pernod Fils in France and the United States is not Absinthe, but rather a specialty type of anis, reminiscent in flavor and character of Absinthe. There are other similar type products produced throughout the world. They will vary one from another, but none is absinthe, since the formulae do not contain any wormwood (*artemisia vulgaris*). They are usually marketed under trade names.

Anis-licorice flavored liqueurs as described in Chapter 23 are the most popular drinks of the countries bordering the Mediterranean. The product is known in each country by its local name; thus in Spain it is Ojen, in France it is Pastis de Marseilles, the best-known of which is Ricard, in Italy it is Anesone, in Greece it is Ouzo and Mastikha and in Turkey it is often Raki. They are rarely ever drunk neat, but usually mixed with water in a proportion of five parts of water to one of the liqueur, producing a long opalescent cooler. It is served both as an apéritif or as a refresher.

MISCELLANEOUS SPIRITS

OTHER or miscellaneous spirits, like the less eminent members of hagiologies, are innumerable and obscure. Few are now available on the world import market. But with the spirit picture constantly changing it is possible some of them will be obtainable in our liquor stores. If this never comes to pass, it is interesting to learn the more popular spirits the people of the world drink.

As previously stated, any vegetable product which contains sufficient starch or sugar can be employed as a raw material for making spirits; a great many have been. For instance, Kornbranntwein (which in German means "corn-brandy") is in fact a light variant of patent-still whiskey made from fermented cereal grains. As rye is the usual ingredient, it is almost a European equivalent of rye whiskey. In Holland and Germany where it is most popular, this spirit may be flavored, e.g., Wachholderkornbrannt—juniper flavored.

Another German spirit—Kornschnapps—is made of fermented corn. In Germany and Holland, the word *schnapps* is used for any strong, dry spirit, while in Scandinavian countries, the term is synonymous with Akvavit. An aromatic schnapps is produced in Holland from a base of Dutch-type gin flavored with aromatic herbs.

While aguardiente is the name for spirits in Spanish-speaking countries, it refers to an unmatured and very powerful root spirit produced in Spain for medicinal purposes, but sold elsewhere as a spirit. It is especially popular in South America. South America, of course, has its own root spirit. That is, *tiquira,* the Brazilian spirit which is made from tapioca roots, which contain much starch. This is malted and fermented, distilled with unusually high rectification for tropical spirits (it is almost a neutral spirit), and then watered down to 90 proof for drinking.

There are a great number of Eastern spirits, but they are not at all easy to distinguish from one another. Most of them tend to be about the same, and while the basic ingredients vary greatly, the name is always about the same—arak, arack, arrack, or arraki. The original Arabic name of arak means "juice" or "sweet," and today this word, or variations upon it, is used as a general term to describe a multitude of spirits.

Arak was originally, as far as we know, a distillation of toddy, which is the fermented sap from palm trees, produced in the former Dutch and British Far East colonies. Of course, a similar word "aroka" was used to describe a potent spirit made by the Tartar tribesmen centuries ago from mare's milk with added grape juice or sugar. But the modern Oriental spirits known as arak are based on a great variety of materials. That is, they are distilled from dates in the Middle East and Egypt; from fermented palmyra and palm-sap in Ceylon and India; and from fermentation and distillation of Indian mohua flowers. In other countries of the East, arack is made of coconut juice with malted rice; rice and toddy (palm juice); and molasses and malted rice.

The most famous of all arak, of course, is the previously mentioned (see page 309) Batavia arak, the brandy-like rum of Indonesia. This spirit is produced as a rum from molasses fermented with natural yeasts, including specially cooked rice in the mixture. Some Eastern producers include a little coconut juice, or the juice of palm trees is used, in which case the distilled product is called toddy.

In China and Taiwan, Kaoliang Wine, Mui Kive Lu, and Mow Toy Wine are most popular and some is even shipped from Hong Kong. They are crystal-clear liquors with an alcoholic content of 70 to 90 proof. They are distilled from "Kaoliang," a sorghum-like grain, and go down the throat like a gush of liquid-fire.

In India, cereal grains are used for making spirits and Sanskrit words have been current for many centuries for rice-spirit (sura), wheat-spirit (madhulika), and barley-spirit (kohola). The latter, which may or may not resemble whiskey in flavor and aroma, has the distinction of passing into Arabic (al kohl) and hence into every other language (alcohol). It was originally derived from kru (earth) and hala (poison).

25. Beers and Ales

IN Germany in the early part of the present century, excavators discovered a jug whose contents proved to be beer mash, which had been made some sixteen centuries ago—probably the oldest bottle of beer in existence. And yet that mash had been made when the beer industry was thousands of years old, for the history of brewing is as old as recorded history—some seven thousand years.

Archaeologists have found hieroglyphics which mean "brewing." They have found jugs which were used for beer, and chemical analysis has proved that barley was used. They have even found some of the yeast cells by which beer was fermented. In ancient days the brew-master and baker were the same man. Nobility and priesthood were interested in brewing, and there was a close association between religious ceremonies and beer.

According to Pliny, the Egyptians made wine from corn. The Greeks learned the art of preparing beer from the Egyptians.

Through the ages, in every country from Egypt to the New World, evidence of beer has been recorded in all languages. Medieval history is replete with references to brewing and its importance in the development of civilization. Even the Kaffir races of darkest Africa made, and still make, a kind of beer from millet, while the natives of Nubia, Abyssinia, and other parts of Africa prepared a fermented beverage which they called *bousa*.

The Russian *quass* or kvass from black bread (rye), the Chinese *samshu*, the Japanese *saké* from rice, are all beers of ancient origin.

Contrary to popular opinion, the "mead" which Friar Tuck and Little John quaffed in such great quantities in Sherwood Forest with Robin Hood was not a beer. Mead, in reality, was the name for a drink made from fermented honey and water, flavored with herbs.

Had it not been for the lack of beer and food, the Pilgrim Fathers in the *Mayflower* would have continued their journey to Virginia, where they had intended to make their home. Instead, they landed at Plymouth rock, because, as recorded in their Journal: "We could not now take time for further search or considerations, our victuals being spent, especially our beer."

333

Although the Pilgrims called their brew beer, it was really ale that they used, as lager beer was first introduced into America by the Germans in 1840. Although most of the households brewed their own beer, the records show that a brewery was in operation by 1637. Probably William Penn, founder of Pennsylvania, was the first to operate a brewery on a large commercial scale, at Pennsbury in Bucks County. Another early brewery was that of the Dutch brewer Jacobus who had his first brewery and beer garden at what is now the corner of Pearl Street and Old Slip in New York City.

Among early Americans who were brewers or had financial interests in breweries were George Washington, James Oglethorpe, Israel Putnam, Samuel Adams, and Thomas Chittenden, the first Governor of Vermont. They were all men of integrity and standing, so the industry started in America under excellent auspices.

definitions   BEER is a brewed and fermented beverage made from malted barley and other starchy cereals, flavored with hops. Beer is a generic term embracing all malt beverages.

ALE is an aromatic malt or malt and cereal brew, usually fuller bodied and more bitter than beer. Ale is fermented at a higher temperature than beer and the yeast remains at the top of the brew, hence it is a *top-fermentation* brew.

STOUT is a very dark ale with a strong malt flavor, a sweet taste, and a strong hop character.

PORTER is a type of ale having a rich and very heavy foam. Very dark malt is used to give a high extract. It is sweeter and less "hoppy" than regular ale. It is brewed like stout but is not quite as strong.

LAGER is a bright, clear light-bodied beer, which is sparkling and effervescent, brewed from malt—and in some cases prepared cereals such as corn grits or cracked rice—hops and water. The resultant "wort" is fermented and "lagered" (stored) for aging and sedimentation. After this period it is "krausened" or carbonated. All American beers are the lager type.

PILSNER is a term employed universally upon labels of light beers around the world. The original and most famous is the Pilsner Urquell from Pilsen, Bohemia. The intent of the brewer labeling his beer Pilsner is to convey the impression that his beer is similar to that of Pilsen. All are bright, light, lagered beers, but we have yet to taste the first one that comes close to duplicating the original. Pilsner is not a separate type of beer, as Bock Beer is.

BOCK BEER is a special brew of heavy beer, usually somewhat darker and sweeter than regular beer, which is prepared in the winter for use in the spring. Bock Beer Day is supposed to herald the arrival of spring. The bock beer season usually lasts some six weeks.

MALT LIQUOR is a beer that varies considerably among brands. Some are a light pale champagne color, others rather dark; some are quite hoppy, others only mildly so. Their essential characteristic, however, is a higher alcoholic content than most other beers.

SWEET BEER is a combination of beer with a fruit juice—lemon, lime, grape—to give a sweeter drink. In some cases these beverages have a higher alcoholic content than that of lager beers.

SAKÉ is a refermented brew of high alcoholic content produced in Japan, from rice.

Practically all types of beers and ales (except saké) are brewed in the United States, but the bulk of consumption is and no doubt will continue to be the light-colored, light-bodied style. The outstanding characteristic of American beer is its very lightness of character which is what the American public demands. United States beers will vary in alcoholic content from 3.2 per cent to 4.9 per cent by weight, while the specialized beer marketed as *malt liquor* will vary from 4.08 to 6.3 per cent by weight. Ales will average about 4.5 per cent by weight.

The difference between light- and dark-colored beers stems from the amount of kilning or roasting of the barley malt. The more it is roasted the darker it will be and the greater the caramelization of its sugars. Of course, the calorie values of beers and ales vary in accordance with the alcoholic, and carbohydrate content of the individual brand, but the average United States beer will have some $12\frac{1}{2}$ to $13\frac{1}{3}$ calories per ounce. Bock beer, malt liquor, ale, stout, and porter will have a higher caloric value. There are available imported low-carbohydrate beers which have $\frac{1}{3}$ to $\frac{1}{2}$ fewer calories than regular beer.

There are many famous beers and ales produced in the world. Each has its own individual character. Some will appeal to you and perhaps others will not. A partial list of imported beer we have enjoyed can include: Argentina—Schneider and Rio Segundo; Austria—Puntigan; Brazil—Brahma; Canada—Dow's Ale and Labatt's Ale; Czechoslovakia—Pilsner Urquell; Denmark—Carlsberg and Tuborg; France—Kronenbourg; Germany—Dortmunder Union, Beck, Löwenbräu light and dark, and Würzburger Hofbräu; Holland—Amstel and Heineken's; Ireland—Harp Lager Beer and Guinness Stout; Israel—Abir; Italy—Peroni; Japan—Asaki and Kirin; Mexico—Carta Blanca; Norway—Frydenlunds; Sweden—Pripps; United Kingdom—Bass' Ale, Whitbread Ale and Mackeson's Stout; Uruguay—Salus. The United States is the world's largest producer of malt beverages and, of course, there are many fine beers made here—many of them distributed in only "local" areas. Since every beer drinker has his own favorite, we have made no listing of American beers.

The beers of Europe that are most popular in America are the light brews, best exemplified by the magnificent Bohemian Pilsner Urquell of Pilsen, Czechoslovakia. Most of the German, Danish, and Holland beers are similar to the Pilsner. They are very pale-colored, light, fresh-tasting beers. From Munich, Germany, also come some much-flavored, darker-colored, richer, and slightly hoppier-tasting beers. England and Ireland have long supplied the

American market with their famous ales and stout, often shipped in their classical pottery or so-called stone bottles. These brews are of course much darker, richer, and more bitter than those of the Continent.

In the Americas, Canada and Mexico, because of their proximity to the United States, have been the principal suppliers. Canada's very fine ales, in particular, enjoy an appreciative public, as do the very light, delicate Mexican beers that are exported to the United States. Incidentally, some "foreign" beers have a higher alcohol content than those produced in the United States, while others do not. In Sweden you can buy a so-called "motorist beer" which contains only 2.8 per cent alcohol by weight or a beer containing almost 8 per cent alcohol by weight. Some imported beers are full bodied. Many are aged a great deal longer than the average American beer. Most imports, however, are brewed like United States beers.

BREWING PROCESS

IN the brewing of beer, as in the preparation of a fine dish in the kitchen, the resultant product is as good as its ingredients. These will be much the same, whether you wish to produce a light lager beer or a full-bodied creamy ale, the only difference being in the way the ingredients are treated; that is, how long the malt is dried and roasted, quantities used, and the temperature at which fermentation takes place.

ingredients   WATER: Although the quality of each ingredient used is important, none is more so than the quality of the water, not only because it forms from 85 to 89 per cent of the finished beer, but because it is used in every step of the brewing operation and it has a great deal to do with the character of the beer. The first consideration, therefore, is the quality and type of water. It must be biologically pure and its mineral content must be known. If the water contains certain mineral salts that are liable to cause trouble, these salts must be eliminated. Most waters used for brewing are treated to render them suitable.

A water that is well suited for the making of beer will not make a good ale, and vice versa. That is why certain regions are noted for their light beers and others for their ales.

MALT: The second ingredient to consider is the malt. In America only the finest barley malt is used. As a general rule, the breweries do not do their own malting, but buy it from specialists, although the manner in which the malt is to be treated is specified by the brew-master in ordering. But, in general, the malting procedure is as follows: The barley is received, screened, and cleaned. Small grains and foreign matter are eliminated. The barley is then steeped (soaked) for several hours so that it will soften and swell. In some countries, it is then spread out on the malting floor to a depth of four to six

A universal six-roller malt mill, which grinds the barley malt in the brew house. (Courtesy of the F. M. Schaefer Brewing Company)

inches and constantly sprinkled with warm water. This causes the grain to sprout or germinate. The sprinkling will be carried on for several days, until the sprouts are about three quarters of an inch long. The life cycle thus started produces a chemical change in the starch of the grain. The starch is converted into maltose, dextrin, and other fermentable sugars. At the same time, many enzymes, including diastase and amylase are created. By this miracle, the barley is changed entirely and is now malt.

The new or "green malt" must then be dried. This is done by placing it in a kiln. The temperature and the length of time the malt is heated or roasted determine the color and sweetness of the final product. To a great extent the harder the roasting the darker and sweeter the resulting malt. In other words, the exact amount of kilning and the degree of roasting determine to a large degree the dryness or sweetness of the final product: the beer or ale. The dried shoots or culm are removed by screening and the malt is ground to the brew-master's requirements.

OTHER CEREALS: These will either be raw, such as corn and rice, or in varying stages of preparation such as corn grits (cracked corn) and hominy, or may even be like our breakfast cereal, corn flakes. In the making of ales, certain types of sugars or syrups may be used. These are called malt adjuncts.

HOPS: Hops did not come into general use until the fourteenth century and for a while there were laws in Europe forbidding their use in brewing. Up to that time, other substances had been used to give the brews bitterness and character, but it did not take long for the people to realize that hops were the best. The finest hops come from Czechoslovakia, although today fine hops are grown in America, in the States of California, Oregon, Washington, and Idaho. The flower or cone from the female hop vine is most widely used in brewing. The flower is like a small pine cone and has very soft leaves. It must be picked at just the right time, as under- or over-ripeness is detrimental to the brew. It is picked free from leaves and stems, dried carefully to conserve the delicate, fine aroma essential in a choice brewing hop. At the breweries the hops are stored in clean, air-conditioned cold-storage chambers at a temperature of about 35° to 38° F.

It used to be that the brewing value of the hops was judged solely by appearance or physical examination. Today, however, the hops are subjected to careful chemical analysis to determine the exact amount of alpha and beta acids, oils and other minor constituents which they contain. This determines the flavor they impart and bittering value of the hop to the final beer.

YEAST: Finally comes the fermenting agent, the pedigreed brewer's yeast, which converts the wort into beer. This unicellular, microscopic plant is cared for more carefully in a brewery than any other ingredient, because, once the particular strain has been selected, it must not be changed or the character of the beer will be changed. That is why we have used the word "pedigreed." It is just that. It is not merely the fact that the yeast causes the sugars to become alcohol. Another yeast would do that, but it performs other functions as well. These other things are in very small proportion, but they probably influence the character of the beer more than the alcohol does, and it is these secondary products of fermentation which vary according to the types of yeast. Therefore, once a quality or type of beer has given satisfaction to a brewery's customers, you may be sure the brew-master will guard the purity of his yeast more closely than the Treasury guards its gold hoard in Kentucky.

steps in making beer

With the ingredients and the proper plant equipment, the brewer is ready to make the beer. The first step is "mashing."

Mashing: The ground malt first goes through a hopper into a mash tub. This is a horizontal or vertical cylindrical copper or stainless steel vessel with a turbine or ribbon mixer unit. It contains a heating device and a set of temperature controls.

When a raw cereal is used, it is cooked in a cooker, a vessel similar to a mash tub, to gelatinize or liquefy the starch. Prepared or pre-cooked cereals do not require heating. The malt, cereals, and the proper amount of water are thoroughly mixed and stand or are cooked as long as is necessary to obtain the maximum extraction of soluble materials. It is during this mashing operation that the brew-master can determine the composition of the finished beer, for it is the temperature and the length of time at which the mash is maintained at a given temperature that determine the amount of fermentable and non-fermentable substances the wort will contain. It is the non-fermentable substances that give the body to the brew. With modern equipment, all of these operations are scientifically controlled, and the beer from a given brewery will be uniform. The object of malting, as explained in chapter 19, is to create diastase, which has the property of converting the starches in the grain to fermentable sugars. After the cooker mash is added to the main mash in the mash tub the starch is converted into fermentable sugars. Then the total mash is pumped into a lauter tub. This is a circular copper or stainless steel vessel containing a false slotted bottom and a series of movable rakes.

When the stirring is stopped, the solids are allowed to settle. What has been going on is predigestion. Compound things have been made digestible, insoluble substances have been made soluble. The solids, which settle on the bottom, form the filter bed. The liquid, which is now wort, flows through this natural filter and it passes into the brewing kettle. In order to ensure every bit of goodness being obtained from the grain, the solids are sparged (rinsed) with water. This rinse from the sparging is added to the wort. In the kettle, hops are added to the wort, which is then boiled from two to two and a half hours. This accomplishes the following objects:

1. The wort is sterilized.

2. Some excess water is evaporated.

3. Certain volatile materials from the hops and malt which are not needed are lost through evaporation.

4. Some of the soluble substances in the wort are made insoluble by the high heat and coagulate. The brewer calls this the "hot break."

5. A certain amount of darkening of the color, due to a small amount of caramelization, is obtained.

After the hops have done their work, the wort runs from the kettle through a hop-strainer or "hop-jack." There the hops are passed over a screen and the wort, which is now called "hopped-wort," runs through, leaving the spent hops behind. The wort is next cooled down and goes into the fermenting vat.

The temperature to which the wort will be cooled depends on whether the brewer is making beer or ale. In the case of beer, fermentation will take place at a very low temperature—between 37° and 49° F. Ale, on the other hand, is fermented at a temperature of between 50° and 70° F. This is one difference. Another is that the yeast used in fermenting ale is different from that used for beer.

At this point, the yeast is added. There is as much difference between brewer's yeast and ordinary yeast as there is between a Derby winner and a truck horse. The secret of the flavor in many world-famous beers is due, unquestionably, to the strain of yeast used. The difference between lager beer yeast and ale yeast is that lager beer yeast settles to the bottom and does its work there during fermentation and after. Beer is the result of "bottom fermentation."

In the case of ale, the yeast, in multiplying, has a tendency to stick together, creating more of a surface, and does its work from the top of the liquid. Ale is the result of "top fermentation." This is due partly to the higher temperature at which ale is fermented, and partly to the different type of yeast which is used. Beer fermentation takes longer than ale—8 to 11 days being the fermenting time for beer, while 5 to 6 days are usually sufficient for ale.

Beers usually have a lower alcoholic content, while ales have a stronger hop flavor.

During fermentation, the carbonic acid gas which is given off is gathered and stored, to be added, in part, back to the beer later on. After fermentation is over and most of the yeast has settled down, the young beer is run off into glass-lined or otherwise protected storage vats, where it is kept at a very low temperature, close to the freezing point, so that the yeast and other solids which would give it a cloudy appearance may be precipitated by the natural process of sedimentation. During this resting or lagering period certain chemical changes take place which develop the immature beer. During this period, the beer throws off its roughness and, as it matures, it becomes more mellow and pleasing. This is the "lagering," which will take from one to three months.

Finally the beer is carbonated by adding the carbonic acid gas which was released by the wort during fermentation. Another popular method used for the carbonization of beer, known as krausening, is accomplished by adding about 15 per cent of the fermenting wort, or krausen, to the beer in storage and this secondary fermentation carbonates the total product. (It is a sort of

Beer in fermentation in open fermenting vats. Note the foaming, boiling action as the CO_2 gas bubbles and escapes into the air. (Courtesy United States Brewers Association)

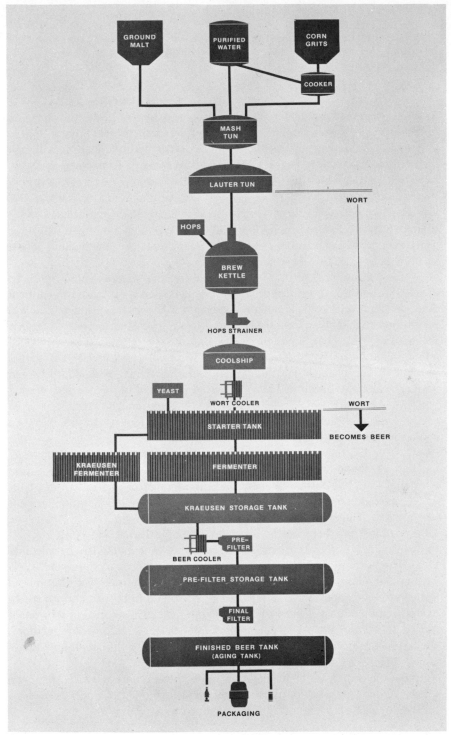

A typical beer flow chart. (Courtesy of the F. M. Schaefer Brewing Company)

bulk Champagne process). But regardless of the method used, once the beer is carbonated, it is passed through a pressure filter and is packaged.

PACKAGING

THE three forms of packaging are: kegs or barrels, bottles, and cans. The beer, under pressure, passes through closed pipe lines into the containers.

Beer cannot be kept or stored in direct contact with wood, as it will take on an unpleasant woody flavor. Once barrels were made from wood and were lined with pitch which was tasteless, did not dissolve in the beer, and kept it from touching the wood. Modern metal kegs of aluminum or stainless steel are used today almost exclusively. These kegs are built to withstand a much greater pressure than is usually found in beer. Wooden cooperage will stand a pressure of 45 pounds per square inch, while metal kegs will stand 300 or so pounds.

As these containers are safe against additional pressure which might be created by additional fermentation, beer so packaged is not pasteurized. Beer packaged in bottles or cans is likely to remain in the package longer and will be shipped farther away from the brewery than the kegs, so, in order to protect the package, this beer is pasteurized, making it sterile and killing any yeast which might be ready to go to work. If this were not done, viable yeast would produce flavor changes and additional carbonic acid gas could form and perhaps burst the bottle or can. This is the principal object in pasteurizing bottled or canned beer. Pasteurization takes place at 140° to 145° F., the temperature at which the beer is kept for about five to ten minutes. It is then cooled rapidly.

As with milk, the pasteurization of beer in the bottle slows down but does not halt the ravages of time. As with milk, it does in some small measure alter the taste. All bottled beers at one time were pasteurized. Draft beers, which are delivered in kegs and kept constantly under refrigeration, are not pasteurized. This was the principal difference between the two. But the difference grows greater as the beer ages. It might be well to point out that the peak quality of pasteurized packaged beer is not indefinite. In cans it is some two to three months, while that of bottles is three to five months.

In recent years, with the advent of microporous materials that filter out all the yeast cells, unpasteurized beer can be packaged in bottles and cans with assurance of a safe shelf-life for the sterile filtered beer, permitting it to retain its so-called draft taste. According to the United States government regulations, the following specifies the use of words "draft beer" on the labels and advertising of both keg beer and bottled or canned beer:

1. Beer in containers of one gallon or more, the contents of which are drawn off through a top or spigot may be described as "draft beer whether the beer has been pasteurized, sterile filtered, or unpasteurized."

2. Bottled or canned may be described as "draft beer" if unpasteurized or has been sterile filtered.

3. Bottled or canned beer may not be described as "draft beer" if it has been pasteurized, but the use of such terms as "draft brewed," "draft beer flavor," and "old-time on-tap taste" is permitted so long as the label or advertisement conspicuously states that the beer has been pasteurized.

DISPENSING TAP BEER

THE three cardinal points of beer service are: 1. Cleanliness 2. Temperature 3. Pressure.

cleanliness

Beer is the most delicate and perishable food product a restaurant handles. It is highly susceptible to extraneous odors, to wild bacteria ever present in the air, and to strong light. It should be stored in a spotless room, which is well-ventilated, in which no other products are stored, and where a constant temperature of 40° F. may be maintained.

The dispensing equipment should be checked and thoroughly cleaned as often as possible, at least once a week. If an establishment wishes to serve perfect beer, no details are too small to be overlooked, no precautions too great in maintaining and ensuring cleanliness of beer service.

temperature

One of the main causes for flat beer is the American tendency to serve it too cold. The ideal temperature is 45° F. for beer and 50° F. for ale, although it is customary to chill as low as 40° for lager and 45° for ale. Do not chill below 40°; and the nearer the beer is to 45°, the better it will taste.

Imported beers should be served at 48° to 50° F., and English ale or Irish stout should be served at 55° F.

Too cold a beer will be flat and cloudy. If it is too warm, the gas will break away from the liquid and you will get too much gas. This condition is called "wild beer." Do not take any chances. Maintain a constant and uniform temperature. Use a thermometer, and store the barrels as close to the dispensing unit or units as possible.

pressure

If an even flow of beer is desired from the tap, the pressure must be carefully watched and controlled. As some of the natural pressure of the carbonic acid gas is bound to be lost between the time the barrel is opened and the last glass of beer is drawn, additional pressure must be supplied. Some people prefer air and others carbon dioxide. Logic points to carbon dioxide, though at first glance it may appear to be more expensive. It ensures a more even supply of gas from the first to the last glass and eliminates the possibility of foul air being drawn into the system, as may happen when air pressure is used. Just as the gasoline gauge on the dashboard of an automobile permits

Final operation in a brewery—the filling of the aluminum kegs. (Courtesy of the F. M. Schaefer Brewing Company)

the driver to check his supply at a glance, so the gas pressure gauge should be at the bar where the operator may check and control the pressure.

HANDLING PACKAGED BEER

BOTTLED beer should be stored in a dark cool place. Beer exposed to the direct rays of the sun in a show window for display cannot be used. It is extremely sensitive to light and will, after a few moments, take on a strange odor and flavor commonly called "skunky."

Beer in cans is not affected by light, but it should be kept in a cool place. In the home, beer should be stored in the lowest, coolest part of the refrigerator. Never store bottled or canned beer in the door shelf of a refrigerator because the constant jostling and drafts of warm air from the kitchen will hasten the beer's deterioration.

opening   Most cans today have the convenient aluminum snap-top openings. But when you must open a flat-topped can, make a small puncture and allow the pressure to equalize, then push opener down as far as it will go.

When serving bottled or canned beer, allow the glass to remain on the table in an upright position. Pour the beer so that the stream flows straight to the center of the glass. Do not tilt and pour down the side, unless you wish very little foam. Pour the beer in a natural manner, neither too fast, which may cause over-foaming, nor too slow.

IMPORTANT SERVING NOTE: Glasses or containers to be used for the service of beer or ale must never be washed with soap or soapy water. The soap leaves a fatty film on the inner surface of the glass which will break down the bubbles of CO_2 destroying the desired collar of foam. Non-soapy detergents may be employed, but always rinse the glass well with plain cold water before filling with beer.

COMPOSITION OF BEER

BEER is one of the most complex of food products. It contains:

Water	89 to 91 per cent by weight
Alcohol	3.5 to 4 per cent by weight
Carbohydrates	
(Sugars and dextrin)	4 to 5 per cent by weight
Protein	0.2 to 0.4 per cent by weight
Carbon Dioxide	0.4 to 0.45 per cent by weight
Mineral Salts	0.02 per cent by weight

As can be seen, the largest part of beer is water. From the point of view of health, beer is one of the finest beverages one can consume. The alcohol with its food value furnishes energy. The carbohydrates give strength. The proteins help us to assimilate food. The carbon dioxide (gas), which gives the beer its "head" or "collar," helps create the cooling or refreshing effect which makes beer so popular in the summertime. The hop bitters help stimulate the appetite.

WHEN TO SERVE BEER

BEER may be served at almost any hour and is equally appropriate at any season of the year. It blends with almost all foods, except heavy cream-sauce dishes and whipped-cream desserts. The characteristic sharp tang of beer adapts it to highly flavored or spicy dishes, and to such foods as hamburger, steak, corned beef and cabbage, Irish stew, sausage, cold cuts, all pork dishes, fried dishes, and particularly broiled lobster, to mention only a few. All the sharper cheeses find themselves at home with either beer or ale.

The use of beer in cooking are legion and many of the old Colonial recipes call for beer as an ingredient, showing that the early American housewives often depended on beer to give their dishes tang and character.

SAKÉ

THE name saké is supposed to derive from the town of Osaka in Japan, which has long been famous for the saké brewed there.

The preparation of saké is interesting. First, steamed rice, called "Koji," is treated with a culture of a special yeast, *Aspergillus oryzae*, which converts the starch into sugar. The koji becomes moto when it is added to a thin paste of fresh-boiled starch in a vat. Fermentation begins and continues slowly for four or five weeks. Next, fresh rice and koji and water are added to the moto. A secondary fermentation, lasting from eight to ten days, takes place. When it is completed, the liquor, now saké, is drawn off, filtered, heated, and run into casks for maturing for a short period. The action of the yeast in this case should be noted. It performs the combined functions of saccharification and fermentation, doing the work of the diastase of malt and the yeast in an American brewery.

Saké is quite strong for a beer, usually having from 14 to 16 per cent of alcohol by volume. It has a sweet first taste and a somewhat bitter aftertaste. Unlike beer, as we know it, it is almost colorless and quite still. It has none of the carbon dioxide in solution that we find in our creamy beers. Because of these facts—its high alcoholic content and its wine appearance—many people call saké Japanese rice wine.

The drinking of saké, like everything Japanese, is accompanied by poetic ceremony. An old Japanese saying states: "Saké should be served warm . . . and by a warm-hearted woman." Traditionally, saké is served warm because heating releases its heady bouquet and allows it to be savored more fully.

To warm saké, place the bottle in a pot of boiling water. Remove when the saké is slightly warmer than skin temperature, about 100° to 105° F. On cold winter nights, or after a day of skiing, some people like it slightly warmer. Saké may be poured directly from the bottle into wine glasses, but many hostesses like the charming ceremony of serving it Japanese style. To serve saké in the Japanese manner, decant the warm saké into small ceramic bottles, called *tokkuri*. The saké is brought to the table in the tokkuri and then poured into tiny porcelain bowls, called *sakazuki*, which hold a little more than an ounce. The saké is sipped. Often these sakazuki have a little tube on the outside, so arranged that as you sip you draw in air and produce a whistling sound. These are called "singing" saké cups. Incidentally, tokkuri and sakazuki may be obtained at any oriental goods store, and some saké producers enclose them with bottles of saké in attractive gift packages.

Many connoisseurs claim that it is not necessary to warm saké before drinking to enjoy its full flavor and bouquet. They prefer to drink it at room temperature, as with any other wine. Others enjoy saké with bitter lemon, Tom Collins mix, or in place of Vermouth in Martinis, or simply chilled or on-the-rocks.

26. Cocktails and Other Mixed Drinks

THE cocktail is a purely American institution, and there are almost as many versions of the origin of its name as there are legends about the beds George Washington is said to have slept in. Actually, of course, the first cocktail was made by that anonymous fellow who first mixed his wine with a bit of honey or an herb or two to give it zest.

history

According to James Fenimore Cooper, of *Leatherstocking* story fame, it was Betsy Flanagan, a spirited Irish lass, who had a tavern near Yorktown, who was responsible for the naming of the cocktail.

In 1779 Betsy's Tavern was a meeting place for the American and French officers of Washington's Army. Here they came to relax, and to fortify themselves for the rigors of the campaign with a concoction called a bracer. The officers used to twit Betsy about the fine chickens owned by a Tory neighbor until one day she threatened to make them eat their words.

Now no true patriot would buy anything from a Tory, but Betsy maneuvered so that the patrons of her tavern had a Tory chicken feast, and when it was over they repaired to the bar to continue the celebration with bracers. To their amusement, they found each bottle of bracer decorated with a cock's tail from the Tory farmer's roost. A toast was called for and one of the Frenchmen exclaimed: "Vive le cocktail," and thenceforth Betsy's concoctions were known as "cocktails," a name which has prevailed to our own day.

The word "cocktail" has been applied to concoctions it was never meant to describe. So we have cocktails of fruit, of oysters, *ad infinitum,* and even a Molotov cocktail that really will blow your head off.

description

The most popular cocktails have always been the Martini and the Manhattan, according to surveys made by the Ahrens Publishing Company. There seem to be several reasons for this:

(1) They are dry, sharp, appetite-whetting drinks.
(2) They are traditional cocktail names which are easy to remember.

347

(3) They are simple to make, requiring less fuss and bother than many other mixtures and consequently are made more often in the home.

(4) Those who make these cocktails at home develop a taste for them and naturally order them when they go to a bar.

These surveys, made over a number of years, have brought out several interesting points in regard to the trend of drinking habits.

The first is that Scotch and soda is the most popular drink in the more important hotels across the country; second, that long gin drinks, considered the summer standby of thirsty America, are on the road to being displaced by rum drinks such as the Daiquiri, Planter's Punch, Rum Collins, and Cuba Libre, although before the Dry era some of these drinks were practically unknown in the United States. The third trend is shown in the increasing popularity of apéritif wines such as Sherry.

A cocktail is a fairly short drink made by mixing liquor and/or wine with fruit juices, eggs, or bitters, either by stirring or shaking in a glass. Because cocktails always contain ice, their strength varies with the length of time they remain in contact with the ice, which dilutes the liquor as it melts.

Cocktails made from liquor and wine are always stirred, except in a few private clubs where the membership insists that they be shaken, such as the Merion Cricket Club of Haverford, Pennsylvania, and the Piping Rock Club of Locust Valley, Long Island.

Cocktails which include fruit juices, cordials, or eggs are always shaken. To the best of our knowledge, there are no exceptions. Mixing in an electric blender gives the same effect as shaking.

A cocktail is as good as its ingredients.

The object of a cocktail is to mix two or more ingredients so that the resulting blend will be a pleasant, palatable drink. No single ingredient should overshadow the rest. It should be a symphony with each ingredient playing its part, contributing its overtones and undertones, but above all, harmonizing with its companions. Lack of such balance produces an unpleasant discord.

If you want to be sure that your Martinis are always the same, use a measure for the ingredients and then always use exactly the same quantities. While experienced bartenders usually measure by "eye," their drinks do vary. This does not necessarily mean that they produce a good cocktail and then a bad one, but simply that at a large bar, where there are several bartenders, no two of them will make identical cocktails unless a measuring jigger is used by all of them.

A jigger is $1\frac{1}{2}$ liquid ounces.

A pony is 1 liquid ounce.

A dash is $\frac{1}{6}$ teaspoon or about four drops.

A teaspoon is $\frac{1}{6}$ ounce.

A wineglass is 4 ounces.

Sometimes recipes are given in parts, because cocktail glasses vary greatly in size. However, exact measurements are given wherever possible. Remember, when you make a cocktail, that melting ice will add from $\frac{1}{2}$ to $\frac{3}{4}$ of an ounce of liquid if it is shaken for ten seconds, and proportionately more if shaken longer. You must use your judgment according to the drink being mixed. For instance, an egg has from $1\frac{1}{2}$ to $2\frac{1}{2}$ ounces of expansion, if properly shaken.

For cocktails that are to be stirred, use cubes of ice. For cocktails that are to be shaken, use small cracked ice.

There is no definite standard recipe on which all "shaker" professionals agree. Tastes change with time. The best example of this is the manner in which the fashion has changed for the *Martini*.

Martini

Today, it is the most popular and most widely consumed cocktail of all. There is some question as to its origin and how it got its name. The earliest recipe we have been able to find is for the *Martinez Cocktail*, which appeared in Professor Jerry Thomas's "The Bon Vivant's Companion or How to Mix Drinks," originally published in 1862. His recipe is a far cry from today's.

Through the years the cocktail became progressively drier. By the time it was referred to as a *Martini*, it had become a mixture of equal parts of dry gin and dry Vermouth. Prior to World War I the accepted standard was two parts of dry gin to one part of dry Vermouth, stirred briskly with large pieces of ice and strained into a cocktail glass. What happened during our Prohibition era of terrible nonsense, with its bathtub gins, was really horrible, but between Repeal in 1933 and World War II the standard recipe became four parts of dry gin to one part dry Vermouth. Then the "tomorrow we die" war psychology led many people to the 15 to 1 Martini, and eventually to the final foolishness of "chilled gin" called a Martini because it was served in a cocktail glass.

Whereas we believe each of us is privileged to drink whatever pleases us and in whatever form we enjoy it most, we also believe firmly that when one of the basic ingredients of a recipe is totally eliminated, it is time to give the recipe a new name.

To give you a clearer picture of the development of the Dry Martini recipe, please note the changes that have taken place over the past century.

MARTINEZ COCKTAIL
(Professor Jerry Thomas' original recipe)

"One dash of bitters
Two dashes maraschino liqueur
One pony Old Tom gin
One wineglass Vermouth
Two small lumps of ice
Shake up thoroughly, and strain into a large cocktail

glass. Put a quarter of a slice of lemon in the glass and serve. If the guest prefers it very sweet, add two dashes of gum syrup."

DRY MARTINI COCKTAIL
(Pre-Prohibition)
2/3 dry gin
1/3 dry Vermouth
Dash orange bitters

MARTINI
(Post-World War II)
15 parts dry gin
1 part dry Vermouth

MARTINI COCKTAIL
(Mauve Decade Recipe)
1/2 dry gin
1/2 dry Vermouth

VERY DRY MARTINI COCKTAIL
(Pre-World War II)
4/5 dry gin
1/5 dry Vermouth
Dash orange bitters or twist lemon peel

Something new has captured popular fancy. It is the:

VODKA MARTINI
7/8 vodka
1/8 dry Vermouth

However, there appears to be a reversal taking place in Martini fashion. Some oldsters who do enjoy a not so "dry" Martini have reverted to the Pre-World War II recipe of a 4 to 1 Martini.

These ingredients are stirred in a mixing glass with ice and in most bars a piece of lemon peel will be twisted over the cocktail, after it is strained into the glass, to give the added "zip" of the oil from the peel. A Martini cocktail can also be served on-the-rocks. It should be garnished with a small olive or pearl onion, which makes it a Gibson.

types of mixed drinks Mixed drinks have a very special nomenclature. Some of these names are: bracers, cobblers, collins, coolers, crustas, cups, daisies, egg nogs, fixes, fizzes, flips, frappés, hot drinks, juleps, pick-me-ups, punches, rickeys, sangarees, slings, smashes, sours, swizzles, toddies.

The following list should be helpful in identifying the types, the glass in which they are currently served, and the ingredients of which they are made.

TYPES OF MIXED DRINKS

DRINK	GLASS	INGREDIENTS	ICE
Apéritifs	Wine or cocktail	Straight and mixed	Chill

DRINK	GLASS	INGREDIENTS	ICE
Cobblers	Water goblet	Liquor, curaçao or sugar, brandy, fruit	Small or shaved
Cocktails	Cocktail (stem glass)	According to cocktail desired	In shaker only
Collins	Collins	Liquor, lemon juice, sugar, seltzer, fruit	Cracked
Coolers	Collins	Liquor, ginger ale or seltzer, syrup or grenadine, fruit if desired	Cracked
Cordials	Cordial, liqueur, Pousse Café, or wine (if frappéed)	By name	Shaved or frappéed
Crustas	Wine	Half orange peeled (sugar rim of glass), lemon juice, Maraschino, Angostura	In shaker only
Cups	Stem (glass pitcher)	Liquor, curaçao, cucumber rind, brandy, fruit, mint	Large ice
Daisies	Highball (special stein)	Liquor, raspberry syrup, lemon juice, seltzer, fruit	Cracked
Egg Nogs	Collins	Liquor, egg, milk, sugar, nutmeg	In shaker only
Fixes	Highball	Liquor, lemon, sugar, water, fruit	Shaved
Fizzes	Highball	Liquor, lemon, sugar, seltzer	One cube
Flips	Delmonico or small 5th Ave.	Liquor, sugar, egg, nutmeg	In shaker only
Highballs	Highball	Liquor, ginger ale or seltzer	One cube
Hot Buttered Rum	Mug	Hard butter, not much sugar, rum	Boiling hot water
Juleps	Tankards or collins	Liquor, sugar, mint (frost glass)	Shaved
Lemonades	Collins	Lemon, sugar, water or seltzer, fruit	Cracked
Orangeade	Collins	Orange juice, water or seltzer, sugar, fruit	Cracked
Punches	Bowls, cups, collins, or tankards	Wine—red or white—rum, brandy, milk, etc. Made according to the recipe	One lump or cracked

DRINK	GLASS	INGREDIENTS	ICE
Puff	Collins	Brandy, fresh milk, Schweppes tonic	One cube
Rickeys	Highball	Liquor, lime, seltzer	One cube
Sangarees	Collins	Liquor, slice lemon, sugar, fruit, nutmeg	Cracked
Shrubs	Tumblers (made in pitcher and bottled)	Special recipes and seltzer	One cube
Slings	Collins	Liquor, fruit juice, cordials	Two cubes
Smashes	Old fashioned	Liquor, lump-sugar, mint, fruit	One cube
Sours	Sour, 5th Ave. or Delmonico	Liquor, lemon juice, sugar, seltzer, fruit	In shaker only
Swizzles	(Pitcher) highball or large 5th Ave.	Liquor, sweetening, seltzer	In pitcher
Toddies	Toddy (hot); old fashioned (cold)	Liquor, slice lemon, sugar, cloves, hot water	—
Tom & Jerry	Coffee cup or special Tom & Jerry sets	Liquor (Jamaica rum) egg beaten, hot water or milk, sugar	—
Twists	Collins	Same as collins	Cracked
Zoom	Wine	Liquor, honey dissolved in boiling water, fresh cream	In shaker only

BASIC MIXING RULES

THERE are a few basic fundamentals, which if followed with care will contribute much to making pleasant, palatable mixed drinks.

1. Mixed drinks are only as good as the ingredients used. They should always be the best whether it be liquor, fruit juices, or mixer.
2. Glassware should sparkle. Use one towel for wiping and another for polishing.
3. Accuracy in the formula assures uniformity. Follow recipes carefully.
4. Measure ingredients. Use a measuring jigger.
5. Stir briskly cocktails that should be stirred. These are generally mixtures of liquor and wine. Stir long enough to mix—approximately seven stirs.

Over-stirring will dilute the drink. A melted ice cube produces about two ounces of water.

6. Shake firmly (do not rock) cocktails that are shaken. These are usually the cocktails whose recipes include sugar, fruit juices, cordials, cream, etc.

7. Always use fresh, clean ice. Never rinse or re-use ice even for making a new batch of the same cocktail. Use cube or cracked ice. Shaved ice is too fine in a hand-shaken cocktail. It will melt and dilute before chilling the drink properly. However, when making drinks in a blender, shaved ice is the most practical to use.

8. Use only perfect fresh fruit. Do not slice oranges or lemons too thinly. They will curl and appear to droop. Cover the sliced fruit with a damp napkin. This will keep it fresh and prevents its drying out. When preparing orange or lemon peel for garnish, remove the white pithy underlining. It is bitter.

9. Use only the best mixer, be it club soda, tonic water, ginger ale, etc. An indifferent or poor mixer will spoil the finest liquor in the world.

10. For bitters or other ingredients where the recipe usually specifies only a dash, use a special "dasher" stopper. This will assure the proper dash, which is $\frac{1}{6}$ of a teaspoon.

11. Lemons and oranges will give more juice if you first soak them in warm water.

12. Serving a cocktail in a pre-chilled glass will keep it cold longer than serving it in a warm glass. If you wish to frost the rim of the cocktail glass, moisten the rim lightly and dip it in powdered sugar spread upon wax paper.

13. To remove the "snowy" look on ice cubes, sprinkle with lukewarm water. Colored ice cubes will make long drinks "colorfully" attractive.

14. Use white of egg only for foaming cocktails.

15. Do not leave ice in the "dividend" remaining in the cocktail shaker. It will dilute the remains and produce a watery second round.

16. Cocktails should always be strained upon serving.

COCKTAILS AND LONG DRINKS

THE following are standard recipes for the most popular cocktails and long drinks. (Wherever aromatic bitters are mentioned, use Angostura or Abbott's)

COCKTAILS

ALEXANDER

½ oz. Crème de Cacao
½ oz. dry gin
½ oz. heavy cream

Shake thoroughly with cracked ice and strain.
Some people prefer brandy to gin.

BACARDI

½ teaspoon granulated sugar
½ large or 1 small green lime (juice)
1½ oz. Bacardi Silver Label rum
1 dash grenadine

First shake up lime juice, sugar, and grenadine with cracked ice until cold.
Then put in the rum and shake until shaker frosts. Strain and serve.

BETWEEN THE SHEETS

½ oz. brandy
½ oz. Triple Sec
½ oz. White Label rum
juice of ¼ lemon

Shake well with cracked ice and strain into cocktail glass.

BLACK RUSSIAN

1 oz. vodka
½ oz. Kahlúa

Pour over ice cubes in 6 oz. glass, on-the-rocks, stir.

BLOODY MARY

1½ oz. vodka
3 oz. tomato juice
juice of ½ lemon
2 dashes Worcestershire sauce
dash of salt and pepper

Shake well with ice; strain and serve.

BRAVE BULL

1 jigger Tequila
1 oz. coffee liqueur

Pour over ice and add twist of lemon.

BRONX

In a mixing glass muddle several pieces of sliced orange that have a bit of the rind on them to give flavor. Into this add:

$\frac{1}{4}$ jigger sweet Vermouth
$\frac{1}{4}$ jigger dry Vermouth
$\frac{1}{2}$ jigger dry gin

Shake thoroughly with cracked ice and strain.

BULL SHOT

1 jigger Vodka
4 oz. clear beef bouillon soup

Pour on-the-rocks in old fashioned glass.

CHAMPAGNE

Place 1 cube of sugar saturated with dash of aromatic bitters in glass. Add cube of ice. Fill glass with chilled Champagne. Twist small piece of lemon rind over glass and insert.

CHERRY WINE COCKTAIL

$\frac{3}{4}$ oz. Danish cherry wine
$\frac{3}{4}$ oz. dry gin
juice of $\frac{1}{2}$ lime

Add ice and shake well. Strain and serve in stem cocktail glass. Note, the gin may be replaced by rum or brandy to suit individual tastes. Also, this may be converted into a Collins by serving in a Collins glass and filling with sparkling water.

CLOVER CLUB

$\frac{3}{4}$ oz. lemon juice
white of 1 egg
$1\frac{1}{2}$ oz. dry gin
1 teaspoon grenadine

Shake thoroughly with cracked ice and strain.

DAIQUIRI

juice of $\frac{1}{2}$ green lime, freshly expressed
1 barspoon granulated sugar

Put some cracked ice in the shaker with lime juice and sugar, and shake it until it gets cold. Add $1\frac{1}{2}$ oz. White Label Puerto Rico rum. Shake until the shaker frosts. Strain and serve.

IMPORTANT! This cocktail should be drunk immediately, because the rum, lime, and sugar tend to separate if the drink is allowed to stand.

Daiquiri　This is the most popular cocktail made with White Label Puerto Rican rum. The origin of the recipe is unknown, but the manner of its naming is another matter.

Shortly after the Spanish-American War of 1898 a group of American engineers were invited to Santiago, Cuba, to help develop the Daiquiri iron mines. The job was hard, the climate was hot, and at the end of the long day's work they needed a refreshing relaxer. It was made from the ingredients most readily available—ice, rum, limes, and sugar to balance the acidity of the lime juice. On week-ends their headquarters in Santiago was the bar of the Venus Hotel where the bartender would make this cocktail for them. On one such occasion, early in 1900, Jennings S. Cox, the chief engineer, suggested that it was a crying shame such a fine cocktail was nameless. After several more rounds of samples, he proposed that it be named the "Daiquiri" after the mines and so it has remained ever since.

Perhaps the biggest Daiquiri made in Cuba at that time was mixed right at the mines in honor of Charles M. Schwab, president of Bethlehem Steel Company, on one of his inspection trips. According to the accounts, the hosts used half an oak barrel into which they emptied two big pails of ice, the juice of 100 limes, a pound of sugar and ten bottles of Bacardi Carta Blanca rum. This was stirred briskly and long with a wooden paddle and ladled out to Schwab and his entourage when they emerged from the mine pits.

If it is properly made, a Daiquiri is truly a most delightful and refreshing cocktail. It must never be made with lemon juice. Only freshly expressed lime juice will make a proper Daiquiri, or you can use the Fresh Frozen Daiquiri Mix which is most satisfactory.

DUBONNET

½ oz. dry gin
1 oz. Dubonnet

Stir thoroughly with cracked ice and strain.

GIMLET

½ oz. Rose's Lime Juice (unsweetened)
1½ oz. dry gin

Stir slightly. Serve in cocktail glass or on-the-rocks in an old fashioned glass. Garnish with a slice of lime.

For a Vodka Gimlet, use Vodka in place of gin.

GOLD CADILLAC

¾ oz. Galliano Liqueur

$\frac{3}{4}$ oz. Crème de Cacao (white)

2 oz. light cream

Shake well with cracked ice and strain into glass.

GRASSHOPPER

$\frac{3}{4}$ oz. green Crème de Menthe

$\frac{3}{4}$ oz. white Crème de Cacao

$\frac{3}{4}$ oz. light cream

Shake hard with cracked ice till very cold. Strain into cocktail glass.

HALF & HALF

2 oz. sweet Vermouth

2 oz. dry Vermouth

Pour in old fashioned glass with ice cubes and twist lemon peel.

HARVEY WALLBANGER

orange juice

1 oz. Vodka

$\frac{1}{2}$ oz. Galliano Liqueur

Fill tall glass with ice cubes. Fill $\frac{3}{4}$ full with orange juice and vodka. Stir and then float the liqueur on top.

JACK ROSE

$\frac{1}{2}$ large green lime (juice)

1 teaspoon grenadine

$1\frac{1}{2}$ oz. Apple Jack

Shake thoroughly with cracked ice and strain.

KIR

4 oz. chilled dry white Burgundy wine

$\frac{1}{4}$ oz. Crème de Cassis (or to taste)

Serve in wine glass or in tumbler with ice cubes.

MAI TAI

$\frac{1}{2}$ teaspoon sugar

1 oz. white rum

$\frac{1}{2}$ oz. orange Curaçao

$\frac{1}{2}$ oz. Orgeat

1 oz. Grenadine

$\frac{1}{2}$ oz. lime juice

Shake with cracked ice; strain into cocktail glass or on-the-rocks. Decorate with fresh pineapple and maraschino cherry.

MANHATTAN

1½ oz. Rye whiskey
¾ oz. sweet Vermouth
1 dash aromatic bitters

Stir well with cracked ice and strain into cocktail glass. Decorate with maraschino cherry.

MARGARITA

1 oz. Tequila
1 dash Triple Sec
juice of ½ lime or lemon with ice

Shake well in with ice, strain and serve in a cocktail glass rimmed with salt.

NEGRONI

1 oz. Campari
1 oz. dry gin
1 oz. sweet Vermouth

Shake with ice and strain into cocktail glass. Serve also as tall drink with soda.

OLD FASHIONED

Place in an old fashioned glass:

1 cube sugar muddled with ½ jigger water
3 dashes aromatic bitters
1 jigger Rye whiskey

Add cube of ice. Stir a little. Garnish with slice of orange and a maraschino cherry. Twist thin piece of lemon rind over glass and insert. Serve with stirrer.

ORANGE BLOSSOM

1 oz. orange juice
1 tsp. sugar
1 jigger dry gin

Shake well with cracked ice and strain into cocktail glass.

PERFECT COCKTAIL

¼ oz. dry Vermouth
¼ oz. sweet Vermouth
1 jigger dry gin
1 dash bitters

Stir well with cracked ice and strain into cocktail glass.

PINK LADY

¾ oz. dry gin

1½ oz. light cream
½ oz. grenadine

Shake well with cracked ice and strain into cocktail glass.

PINK SQUIRREL

1 oz. Crème de Almond
½ oz. Crème de Cacao (white)
1 oz. light cream

Shake well with cracked ice and strain into cocktail glass.

PRESIDENTE

1½ oz. White Label rum
¾ oz. dry Vermouth
2 dashes orange Curaçao
1 dash grenadine

Add ice, stir well, and strain.

RUSTY NAIL

½ oz. Drambuie
1 jigger Scotch whisky

Serve in old fashioned cocktail glass with ice cubes.

ROB ROY

¾ oz. Scotch whisky
¾ oz. sweet Vermouth
2 dashes aromatic bitters

Stir well with cracked ice and strain.

SAZERAC

Muddle in an old fashioned glass:

1 cube sugar with 1 teaspoonful of water
2 dashes bitters
3 dashes Absinthe or a substitute

Add 1½ oz. of Bourbon whiskey, 1 cube of ice. Twist a thin piece of lemon rind over glass and insert. Stir a little, strain and serve.

SCOTCH MIST

Fill old fashioned glass with shaved ice. Pour one jigger of Scotch whisky, twist of lemon peel, and drop peel into glass. Whiskey Mist is prepared as above, except substitute Rye or Bourbon whiskey in place of Scotch whisky.

SIDE CAR

½ oz. lemon juice
½ oz. Triple Sec
½ oz. brandy

Add shaved ice and shake. Strain and serve.

STINGER

¾ oz. brandy
¾ oz. Crème de Menthe (white)

Twist a thin piece of lemon rind over mixing glass and insert. Shake thoroughly with cracked ice and strain.

WHISKEY SOUR

¾ oz. lemon and lime juice
1½ oz. Bourbon or Rye whiskey
1 teaspoon powdered sugar

Shake thoroughly with cracked ice. Put in serving glass a cherry and a slice of orange. Strain mixture and pour into glass. Scotch Sour, Gin Sour, Brandy Sour, Rum Sour, Tequila Sour, or Vodka Sour: Prepare as above, but use Scotch whisky, dry gin, fruit brandy. White Label rum, Tequila, or vodka in place of Bourbon or Rye whiskey. For Tall Sour, pour over ice cubes in highball glass, fill with charged water, stir.

LONG DRINKS

AMERICANO

1 jigger Campari
1 jigger sweet Vermouth

Pour over ice in highball glass. Fill with charged water. Add twist of lemon.

CUBA LIBRE

1½ oz. White Label rum
1 bottle Coca-Cola

Use small highball glass, cube of ice, pour in rum and fill with Coca-Cola. Optional: squeeze and insert quarter of fresh lime.

GIN FIZZ

juice ½ lemon
1 jigger dry gin
1 tsp. sugar

Shake with ice, strain in highball glass, fill with charged water. Add lemon twist. Silver Fizz is made as above but add 1 egg white.

GIN RICKEY

2 oz. dry gin
juice and rind of half a green lime

Insert in glass two cubes of ice. Then the lime juice and rind, the gin, and fill the glass with charged water. Stir and serve.

FRENCH 75

1 jigger brandy
juice of 1 lemon
1 tsp. sugar

Shake with ice, strain into highball glass, fill with chilled Champagne.

HOT BUTTERED RUM

This is the classic warmer-upper of Colonial days, which is still popular today. It is guaranteed to take all the cold stiffness right out of you, if you have been skating, skiing, or out in the cold too long. We do not recommend it if you are going back out into freezing cold weather.

$1\frac{1}{2}$ oz. Jamaica or Demerara rum
5 oz. piping hot water
1 pat cold butter
1 cinnamon stick
ground nutmeg

Rinse an 8-ounce mug or cup with boiling water. Pour in the rum and hot water. Float the pat of butter on the surface and sprinkle with nutmeg. Use the cinnamon stick as a stirrer. Inhale the wonderful aroma and drink it while it is good and hot.

IRISH COFFEE

This drink was made famous by the Buena Vista Café at San Francisco's Fisherman's Wharf shortly after World War II. It has since become popular all around the world.

$1\frac{1}{2}$ oz. Irish whiskey
5 oz. very hot strong black coffee
1 teaspoon sugar
1 spoonful whipped cream

Rinse an 8-ounce stemmed goblet with very hot water. Place the sugar in the glass, pour in the Irish whiskey and coffee; stir to dissolve sugar and top with whipped cream.

COFFEE ROYALE

5 oz. very hot black coffee

$1\frac{1}{2}$ oz. brandy

1 sugar cube

Rinse an 8-ounce stemmed goblet with very hot water. Pour coffee into cup. Place spoon across cup and pour part of brandy into spoon with sugar cube. Place before guest and ignite brandy in spoon.

MINT JULEP

Use 12-ounce glass or pewter cup. Dissolve 1 teaspoonful of granulated sugar in just enough water to cover it. Fill with finely cracked ice. Pour in Bourbon whiskey to within half inch of the top. Stir until glass is thoroughly frosted. Decorate generously with fresh mint.

NOTE: There are two schools of julep makers: the mint-crushers and the non-crushers. If you belong to the second school, follow the recipe above. If you want a more pronounced mint flavor, crush a sprig of mint together with the sugar and water and leave it in the glass. Then pack with ice, add the Bourbon, stir and decorate.

MOSCOW MULE

1 jigger vodka

juice of $\frac{1}{2}$ lime

Pour in 8 oz. copper mug with ice cubes, fill with ginger beer. Garnish with lime.

PICON PUNCH

In a 4-ounce whiskey sour stem glass place two ice cubes; and $1\frac{1}{2}$ ounces Amer Picon. Fill glass with sparkling water, add a twist of lemon peel, stir and serve.

NOTE: A Picon Punch can also be served with a float of Cognac.

PLANTER'S PUNCH

1 oz. lime juice

1 teaspoon granulated sugar

2 oz. Jamaica rum

Dissolve the sugar in the juice of the lime. Next put in the rum and the cracked ice and shake well. Strain into a 10 ounce glass that is half filled with finely cracked ice. Decorate with maraschino cherry, sliver of fresh pineapple, half a slice of orange and sprig of mint. Serve with a straw.

PORT WINE SANGAREE

$2\frac{1}{4}$ oz. Port wine

$\frac{1}{2}$ oz. simple syrup

Stir well with cracked ice and strain into highball glass with two cubes of ice. Grate nutmeg on top.

RUM TODDY

1 cube sugar
1½ oz. Jamaica rum

Fill glass with boiling water. Insert one small piece of cinnamon, one slice of lemon garnished with four cloves and a thin slice of lemon rind twisted over glass and inserted. Stir mixture a little and serve with a spoon. Also serve a small pitcher of hot water on the side.

SCREWDRIVER

1½ oz. Vodka
4 oz. fresh orange juice

Pour the Vodka and orange juice into a highball glass containing several cubes of ice. Stir well to mix thoroughly. It may be served in a cocktail glass if desired. The above recipe would then serve two cocktail portions.

SHERRY COBBLER

¾ oz. simple syrup
2 oz. full-bodied Sherry

Fill glass nearly full with finely cracked ice. Pour in the syrup and Sherry. Stir with a spoon. Decorate with fresh fruits in season, cubed or sliced, a maraschino cherry and a sprig of mint. Serve with straws.

SHERRY FLIP

1 egg
1 teaspoon powdered sugar
1½ oz. Sherry

Shake thoroughly with cracked ice and strain into glass. Sprinkle a little nutmeg on top.

SINGAPORE SLING

1 oz. lime juice
1 oz. cherry liqueur
2 oz. dry gin

Shake well and ice. Top with seltzer and decorate with slice of orange and fresh mint. Then add through middle with a medicine dropper:

4 drops Bénédictine
4 drops brandy

This recipe is the original as used in the Raffles Hotel in Singapore.

SLOE GIN FIZZ

¾ oz. lemon juice

1 teaspoon powdered sugar

$1\frac{1}{2}$ oz. sloe gin

Shake thoroughly with cracked ice, strain, and fill with charged water.

SLOE GIN RICKEY

Made in the same fashion as gin rickey by substituting sloe gin for the dry gin.

TOM AND JERRY

Recipe for one cup (8 ounces). Mix well the yolk of one egg with 1 teaspoonful of powdered sugar. Pour in half a jigger of brandy and half a jigger of Jamaica rum. Stir mixture thoroughly. Put in the white of egg, beaten, and while stirring, pour in hot milk or boiling water, to fill the cup. Nutmeg is sprinkled on top.

TOM COLLINS

$\frac{3}{4}$ oz. lime and lemon juice

1 teaspoon powdered sugar

$1\frac{1}{2}$ oz. dry gin

Shake thoroughly with cracked ice and strain. Add two cubes of ice, fill glass with mineral water and stir a little.

VERMOUTH CASSIS

$1\frac{1}{2}$ oz. dry Vermouth

$\frac{1}{4}$ oz. Crème de Cassis

Place in 5-ounce Delmonico glass, add cube of ice, fill with mineral water, and stir.

WARD EIGHT

1 jigger whiskey

1 oz. lemon juice

1 tsp. grenadine

Shake with crushed ice. Strain into glass with ice cubes and fill with soda or mineral water.

WHISKEY SMASH

Muddle one cube of sugar with a half jigger of water and a few sprigs of mint in glass. Add two cubes of ice. Pour in one jigger of whiskey. Decorate with four or five sprigs of mint. Serve with small barspoon, and club soda on the side.

ZOMBIE°

$\frac{3}{4}$ oz. lime juice

° The original recipe is still supposedly a closely guarded secret of Don the Beachcomber.

¾ oz. pineapple juice

1 teaspoon Falernum or simple syrup

1 oz. White Label rum

2 oz. Gold Label rum

1 oz. Jamaica rum

½ oz. 151 proof Demerara rum

½ oz. apricot liqueur

Shake well and strain into 14-oz. Zombie glass, quarter-filled with ice. Garnish with slice of orange and several sprigs of mint. Serve with straws.

PUNCHES AND WINE CUPS

FISH HOUSE PUNCH

2 quarts Jamaica rum	2 quarts water
1 quart Cognac brandy	¾ pound loaf sugar
1 wine glass peach liqueur	1 quart lemon juice

Slack loaf sugar in punch bowl. When entirely dissolved, add lemon juice. Then all the other ingredients. Put a large piece of solid ice in the punch bowl and allow the mixture to brew for about 2 hours, stirring occasionally. In winter, when ice melts slowly, more water may be used; in summer less; the melting ice dilutes the mixture sufficiently. This will make 1½ gallons, depending on dilution.

This is the original Fish House Punch, made by the Fish House Club, now called the State in Schuylkill, founded in 1732. We are indebted to Anna Wetherill Reed in whose *Philadelphia Cook Book of Town and Country* this recipe appears.

MAYWINE

Soak ½ package Waldmeister° six hours in one bottle of Alsatian wine. Strain and mix with 12 bottles of Alsatian wine. Add 1 bottle Champagne, 2 ounces of Bénédictine, 2 ounces of Cognac. Add ¼ pound cube sugar, dissolved in 1 quart sparkling water. Decorate with strawberries and fresh Waldmeister. When sufficiently cold serve in wine glasses from a punch bowl. To keep it cold, place a pitcher full of shaved ice in the center of the punch bowl.

This will serve approximately 100 cups of 3½ ounces each.

NOTE: Since World War II some German wine shippers have marketed a bottled Maywine. It is usually a pleasant, sweetened, inexpensive wine.

MULLED RED WINE

6 glasses Claret or Burgundy	2 cups of water
2 lemons	4 sticks cinnamon
1 cup granulated sugar	4 cloves

° Waldmeister is the sweet-scented woodruff, a European woodland herb.

Boil the water with the sugar, cinnamon, and cloves for five minutes. Then add the lemons sliced very thin, cover and let stand for ten minutes. Add the wine and heat gradually, but do not allow to boil. Put it in a pitcher or brown jug, and serve it very hot. A silver spoon placed in each glass will prevent it from cracking.

SANGRIA

Throughout the Spanish-speaking world one of the traditional ways of enjoying wine is in the form of a wine cup, the Sangria. The recipe given below is one of the more popular ones.

> ½ cup sugar
> 1 cup water
> 1 orange, thinly sliced
> 1 lime, thinly sliced
> 1 bottle red or white wine

Make simple syrup by adding sugar to the water. Heat, stirring until sugar is dissolved; bring to boiling point. Then remove from heat.

While still hot, add the thin slices of orange and lime. Allow to marinate at least four hours before using.

In a glass pitcher place about 12 ice cubes, six marinated slices of the fruit, and one half cup of syrup. Then add one bottle of red or white wine. This will serve 8 four-ounce portions. Place a slice of orange and a slice of lime in each glass and fill glasses from the pitcher.

For the most dramatic effect, add the wine to the fruit, syrup, and ice at the table and stir with large flat wooden stirrer.

MIXERS

ONE last word about mixed drinks. Since one-half to three-quarters of a highball is made up by the mixer—that is, the water—we cannot stress too strongly the importance of using a quality mineral water. A flat or metallic tasting club soda has ruined more drinks and cost bars more customers than any other cause. It is good business to serve a good water.

PREPARED COCKTAILS

CERTAIN mixed drinks, particularly those whose ingredients include wine and spirits, can be very easily prepared in large quantities, stored and distributed in bottles. These prepared cocktails are practical for those who do not have facilities in the home for mixing them fresh. They have the advantage of being uniform and requiring no fuss to prepare. They can be put in the refrigerator until needed. In other words, with these ready-for-instant-use cocktails, all you have to do is either pre-chill and pour, or simply pour over the rocks.

The most popular varieties are Martinis, Manhattans, Sours, and Daiquiris. But the prepared cocktails run the whole gamut. For instance, they include Tequila Sours, Margaritas, Vodka Martinis, Scotch Mists, high-proof Martinis, Black Russians, Gin Collins and Sours, Gimlets, Screwdrivers, Side Cars, Stingers . . . and many, many others.

The liquor industry has overcome many obstacles in making prepared cocktail mixes that would stand up over a long period of time. The aim was to make drinks that were uniform in quality, that would taste the same a week after the bottle was opened, in which the sugar would not change flavor or crystallize. After extensive research, various companies have developed cocktails which fill the void for people anxious to serve professional cocktails at home.

COCKTAIL MIXES

WITH cocktail mixes you just add the liquor. That just about describes the appeal and convenience of cocktail mixes. Actually they are expertly prepared cocktails with all the necessary ingredients for the finished cocktail except the liquor. To make a Martini, for example, add gin to the appropriate cocktail mix. Add whiskey to create a Manhattan, rum for a Daiquiri.

There are two types of cocktail mixes now on the market. The dry mix type is a comparatively recent development. The other, a liquid mix, has been with us practically since Repeal, although today the range of cocktails has been increased tremendously.

The principle of the liquid mix is simple. Just pour in liquor to make the appropriate cocktail. The dry mix is a powder and water is added in addition to the liquor to dissolve the powder and create the cocktail. Liquid mixes are poured from the bottle. Dry types come in envelopes, each envelope making one cocktail serving.

In addition to convenience, there are other advantages claimed for cocktail mixes. One of these is that it gives the home bartender an opportunity to at least engage in some of the ritual of mixology. Another is that the home bartender can be creative. He can add Scotch to the Manhattan mix and get a Rob Roy. The Martini mix also can produce a Gibson, or Vodka can be used to make a Vodka Martini. The Daiquiri mix is a starting point for a Planter's Punch, Pink Lady, Clover Club, Ward Eight, and Gin Fizz. In addition, of course, the party host can use the liquor brands of his choice.

27. Menu and Wine List Making

THE mauve decade and the years before the First World War were those in which the art of wining and dining reached its height in this country, epitomized, perhaps, in the Waldorf-Astoria with its great Oscar as host to fashionable America.

During the early days of pioneer and frontier America, difficulty in obtaining condiments, in transporting wines, and even in acquiring the necessities let alone the niceties of dining, led to meals of a simple order. The era of Prohibition brought back a period of gastronomical and vinicultural depression. But since Repeal, the country has begun again to cultivate the fine arts of good living, dining, wining, and stimulating conversation.

One evidence of this was the formation, in several metropolitan centers, of branches of the Wine and Food Society, an organization originally founded in London by the late André L. Simon, who so loved his fellow men that he devoted himself to increasing their enjoyment of the better things of life.

The Wine and Food Society functions as a nonprofit organization, holding periodic tastings of wines, spirits, and foods, and occasional dinners. The object of the society is to make available for its members a gathering place where they can become acquainted with the most interesting wines or foods that the community affords, in a manner which would be impossible for a single individual. Its accomplishment is educational in the truest sense, and the society has done much to foster a greater interest in the art of wining and dining since Repeal.

Several other groups have been formed, and each in its own way is contributing to the general interest in better eating and drinking.

The most important of these are the *Confrérie des Chevaliers du Tastevin*, namely, the Brotherhood of Gentlemen of the Tasting Cup, devoted to the greater appreciation of the wines and food of Burgundy; *Commanderie de Bordeaux* whose main interest is the wines and food of Bordeaux, and *Chaîne des Rôtisseurs,* the fraternity of the Turners of the Roasting Spit, who give their allegiance to good food, especially roasts and to the wines that will complement them best.

Whatever the changes in the country's dining habits, and though a new Waldorf-Astoria has arisen to replace the old, the late Oscar Tschirky was the banquet manager par excellence.

The banquet manager serves an important function not only in a hotel but in a community. It is his job to know his menus and to know which dishes the chef prepares best for a small party and which for a large party. He must know his wines and how to sell them. He must be the epitome of tact, for it is his job to advise the host or hostess who consults him, suggest the wine or food they should order, supervise the details of the gathering, and have a shrewd insight into the tastes of the person he is advising. All in all, it is an important position requiring tact, intelligence, and ability.

The following menu is an example of an informal dinner. One wine can be served through the meal and this can be a dry white wine—a Burgundy such as Meursault, a Graves, or an Alsatian Riesling.

Crabmeat Cocktail
Essence of Okra aux quenelles
Celery   Olives   Salted Nuts
Filet of Sea Bass, Bonne Femme
Roast Philadelphia Capon
New Peas and young Carrots au beurre
Pommes Anna
Asparagus, Sauce Vinaigrette
Fresh Strawberries Melba
Parfait glacé à la vanille
Petits Fours
Mocha

For the more formal banquet the following menu with its full complement of wines, was served by the Waldorf-Astoria:

Apértif	Les Canapés Russe
	Amuse-Bouche Gabriel
Sherry	Le Fumet de Gombo
	Paillettes Dorées
	Céleri Amandes Salées Olives
Pouilly Fumé 1970	Les Crabs de Californie
	en Turban
Château Léoville	L'Entrecôte Grillée Vendôme

Poyferré 1961	Bouquetière de Légumes
	Pommes Colorette
	Salade de Floride
Ernest Irroy	Feuillantine Nesselrode
1964	Son Sabayon
Cognac	Moka
Liqueurs	

THE WINE LIST

WE WOULD venture to say that since 1933 well over a million dollars a year has been spent in printing wine lists which are rarely prepared or used as they should be. Many times we have been forced to beg a waiter to bring us the wine list. Why managers invest money in printing these lists without instructing their waiters to use them is an unsolved puzzle to us.

The wine list is as important a silent salesman for wine as the menu is for food, and it should always be presented to a guest along with the menu.

It is not possible to prepare a wine list which would be equally useful in every establishment, as the wine list, like the menu, must reflect the character of one particular restaurant and therefore is prepared with a view to the taste of its patrons. While there is a similarity in certain price groups, each hotel or restaurant has to bear in mind its own clientele in preparing its own wine list. A great hotel or fashionable restaurant will have an elaborate wine list, while a smaller establishment, whose atmosphere is one of simplicity, will plan its list accordingly.

For instance it is not profitable to list a great number and variety of wines when experience shows that there is no demand for them.

The wine list should be simple, and should list wines, spirits, beers, and mineral waters. It is no longer necessary to include a chart, indicating the wine which should be served with a specific dish.

If there is enough space, it will add interest and cause a guest to peruse the entire wine list if short paragraphs describing each type of wine are included, such as a short account of Champagne, Bordeaux wines, and so forth.

Short descriptions of each wine, if there is room for them, will assist a guest in selecting his wine. In this regard, however, avoid use of the word "sour," in describing a wine. "Dry" is the better word.

In making up a wine list, check all spellings carefully, copying them from the labels on the bottles. Correct vintages should also be listed. Avoid repetition of classes of wine. For instance, one regional Sauternes is enough. There is no point in listing three.

One of the best and most balanced wine lists in the United States is that of the New York Hilton at Rockefeller Center. It is very extensive, listing some four hundred wines, but it is practical for the New York Hilton. It embodies all of the points recommended above . . . and we are informed that the hotel's guests have ordered all of the wines listed at one time or another.

There are no arbitrary rules for the order in which wines should appear on a wine list, nor as to whether cocktails and mixed drinks should appear on a left-hand or right-hand page when a large single-fold card is used.

Our preference is for the following order:

Champagne	Sherry
U.S. champagne	Port
Sparkling wines (Burgundy, Italian, etc.)	Madeira
	Cognacs and brandies
Apéritif wines	Whiskies (Rye, Bourbon, and Canadian)
White Bordeaux	
Red Bordeaux (Clarets)	Whiskies (Scotch and Irish)
White Burgundy	Gins
Red Burgundy	Rums
Rhône wines	Miscellaneous spirits
Alsatian French Rhine wines	Liqueurs
Rhine and Moselle wines	Beers
Italian wines	
Wines from other countries	
U.S. wines (all except sparkling)	

We list Champagne first as it is generally the most costly and it is good psychology for the guest to come upon the most glamorous wine when he first opens the list. The balance of the listings seem to us to be in logical order.

Obviously these do not include all the possibilities; on the other hand, not every establishment need have all of them. Where only one or two wines of a given class are stocked, several may be listed under one heading.

Wine lists need not be complicated nor need they be very long. The list should be in line, however, with the type of restaurant in which it is being used. A good selection of five or ten wines is better than a poor selection of fifty. Wine lists should be simple. They should be up to date. And above all, they should be available and used. A menu which has changes and deletions is not acceptable in a good restaurant. Therefore it also follows that a wine list is not acceptable if it has changes or if items are out of stock.

The wine list should be as clear and clean and presentable as the menu from which the diner selects his food. Enough information should be given on the list so that the customer knows what he is ordering without having to ask questions. The type of wine, the size of the bottle, the name of the wine, its vintage if there is any, and the name of the shipper are all important information. Identifying each wine by a number is helpful as this practice eliminates embarrassment in pronunciation.

If the entire list is printed on a large card folded in the center, allowing

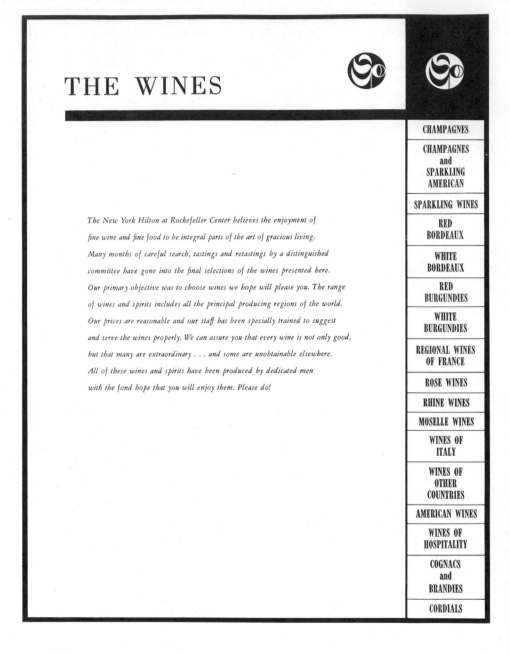

The wine list of The New York Hilton at Rockefeller Center, one of the most complete and well-balanced wine lists in the United States. (Courtesy The New York Hilton)

space for four columns, wines may be listed in the first column, mixed drinks in the two middle columns, and spirits in the fourth column. The two outside columns could be reversed if desired, putting spirits on the left and wines on the right. Listing mixed drinks in the center makes for an orderly and neat arrangement.

In addition to the wine list, many establishments having cocktail rooms find it profitable to print a small secondary list including the most popular bar drinks such as cocktails, mixed drinks, and spirits. This is generally called the Drink List. It should be printed on a card, which may be folded, and it may include a small selection of wines, particularly Champagnes.

Establishments doing a large banquet and function business often have a third list, called the Banquet Wine List, which includes a selection of the more popular mixed drinks, Champagnes, table wines, apéritif wines, spirits and beers; whatever, in short, experience shows to be most frequently ordered at large functions.

It is important for this list to contain a notation in regard to corkage, which it is customary to charge when guests bring their own beverages. In most metropolitan centers, this is $5 to $8 a bottle for Champagne and spirits, and $2.50 to $5 for table wines.

HOTEL ST. REGIS WINE POLICY

ONE of the outstanding wine lists in the country is that of the Hotel St. Regis, New York. This list has been used most profitably because the management believes that its wine list has a selling job to do and has produced one that does it. An interesting feature at this hotel is its announced pricing policy, published in a leaflet entitled "Hotel St. Regis Wine Policy," from which we quote:

"Convinced that poor wine lists and high prices were seriously retarding the use of wine and thus impeding the progress of gracious and temperate living, the Management of the Hotel St. Regis published in the late thirties an extensive and carefully selected list of wines at prices which were recognized as phenomenally low.

"This list attracted wide attention and was generally proclaimed the finest in the country—as it was designed to be.

"In offering well-chosen wines at moderate cost we believed we were performing a public service and at the same time exhibiting intelligent self-interest. We expected, in short, to make up the difference between a small profit per bottle and a large profit per bottle by greatly increasing the volume of our sales."

374

American Champagne

No.		Vintage	Half Bottle	Bottle
93	Waldorf-Astoria, Brut		6.00	11.00
90	Taylor's N. Y., Brut			14.00
*75	Paul Masson, California, Brut			14.00
94	Great Western, N. Y., Extra Dry		7.50	14.00

PINK

80	Paul Masson, California			14.00

American Sparkling Wines

137	Great Western, New York State Sparkling Burgundy			14.00
105	Paul Masson, Very Cold Duck			12.00

American White Wines

828	Chenin Blanc, Clement Colombet, Cal.			5.00
816	Chablis, Clement Colombet, Cal.			5.50
825	Emerald Dry, Paul Masson, Cal.			6.00
781	Pinot Chardonnay, Paul Masson, Cal.		4.75	8.25
798	Pinot Chardonnay, Dr. Konstantin Frank			12.00

American Red Wines

799	Burgundy, Clement Colombet, Cal.			5.00
797	Pinot Noir, Clement Colombet, Cal.			5.00
787	Cabernet Sauvignon, Clement Colombet, Cal.			5.50
778	Pinot Noir, Paul Masson, Cal.		4.00	7.00
786	Cabernet Sauvignon, Paul Masson, Cal.		4.00	7.00

American Rose Wines

840	Vin Rosé, Clement Colombet, California			4.50
841	Vin Rosé Sec, Paul Masson, Cal.			5.00

French Champagne

No.		Vintage	Half Bottle	Bottle
3	Bollinger, Brut	N.V.		24.00
17	Moet & Chandon — White Seal N.V.			21.00
10	Laurent Perrier, Extra Dry	N.V.		20.00
*4	G. H. Mumm, Extra Dry	N.V.	12.00	23.00
32	Piper Heidsieck, Extra Dry	N.V.	14.00	26.00
39	Réserve Baron Philippe de Rothschild	1964/66		24.00
33	G. H. Mumm, Cordon Rouge	1966	15.00	28.00
*9	Piper Heidsieck, Brut	1966	17.00	32.00
61	Laurent Perrier — Grand Siècle	1961/64		36.00

PINK

*26	Moet & Chandon Lovee, Don Pérignon	1962/64		44.00
*44	Taittinger, Blanc de Blancs	1964		40.00

French Pink Champagne

68	Piper Heidsieck, Pink	1966		29.00

French Sparkling Burgundy

122	Chauvenet Red Cap		9.75	18.75

White Burgundy Wines

450	Beaujolais Blanc, *Produced by Maison Louis Jadot*	1971	6.75	12.00
426	Pouilly-Fuissé, *Produced by Sichel Fils Frères*	1970		17.50
457	Meursault, *Produced by Bouchard Père & Fils*	1970		15.00
466	Chablis, *Produced by Barton and Guestier*	1970		12.50
452	Puligny Montrachet, *Produced by Domaine Le Flaive*	1970	8.25	15.50
467	Chablis, Grand Cru, *Estate Bottled by A. Pic & Fils*	1965/68		14.50

Red Burgundy Wines

371	Beaujolais St. Louis, *Produced by Barton and Guestier*	1970		9.25
330	Marquisat Beaujolais Villages 1970/71, *Paquier-Desrognes, St. Léger*		5.00	9.00
413	Côte de Beaune Villages, *Produced by Maison Louis Jadot*	1970		12.50
327	Moulin-à-Vent, *Produced by Maison Louis Jadot*	1970/71		14.00
347	Nuits St. Georges, *Produced by Louis Latour*	1970		22.00
361	Pommard "Clos de la Commaraine", *Estate Bottled by Domaine Jaboulet-Vercherre*	1970	12.50	22.50
412	Chambolle Musigny, *Produced by Louis Latour*	1970		25.50
372	La Tache, *Estate Bottled by Domaine de la Romanèe Conti*	1969		67.50

White Bordeaux Wines

No.		Vintage	Half Bottle	Bottle
285	Graves Extra, *Produced by F. Ginestet*	1969	4.00	7.00
299	Sauternes, *Produced by Barton and Guestier*	1976	3.75	10.50
291	Château d'Yquem, *Appellation Sauternes Controlée*	1967		45.00

Red Bordeaux Wines

284	Château Malbec, *Prats Frères*	1970		9.50
216	Mouton Cadet, *Baron Philippe de Rothschild*	1967/69		10.50
334	St. Emilion, *Produced by Barton and Guestier*	1967		8.50
340	St. Julien, *Produced by F. Ginestet*	1969	8.00	14.50
256	Château Léoville-Barton, *Produced by Barton and Guestier*	1967/69		16.00
138	Château Boucaut, *Appellation Graves Controlée*	1967/69		12.50
260	Château Talbot, *Appellation St. Julien Controlée*	1966		24.00
155	Château Pontet Canet, Cruse, *Appellation Pauillac Controlée*	1967		22.00
255	Château Margaux, Ginestet, *Appellation Margaux Controlée*	1967		45.00

Red Country Wine of France

329	Côte du Languedoc Jules Alby Red			7.50

Rhone Wine

481	Châteauneuf-du-Pape, *Shipped by Barton and Guestier*	1970/71	6.00	10.50

Rose Wines of France

477	Tavel Rosé Château d'Aquéria, *Estate Bottled by J. Olivier*	1970/71		10.50
487	Château de Selle	1970	6.00	11.00

Rose Wines of Portugal

No.		Vintage	Half Bottle	Bottle
483	Mateus Still			8.00
578	Lancers		5.25	10.00

Sparkling Wines of Italy

57	Asti Spumante, Martini & Rossi			16.00

White Wines of Italy

541	Orvieto Secco & Abboccato, *Produced by I. L. Ruffino*		4.25	7.50
544	Soave Ricasoli			6.00

Red Wines of Italy

551	Bardolino, *Riserva Speciale by Ricasoli*	1968/70		6.50
557	Nozzole Chianti Classico Riserva 1967, *Estate Bottled by L. Rincadonini Martini*			9.75

Rhine Wines

606	Kircher Sandgrube, *Original Abfüllung Graf Eltz*	1969/70		10.00
631	Blue Nun Liebfraumilch Superior 1970, *Produced by H. Sichel Soehne*		6.50	11.50
641	Hattenheimer Wisselbrunn Auslese, *Original Abfüllung Schloss Reinhartshausen*	1966/69		24.00

Moselle Wines

670	Bernkasteler Riesling, *Produced by Sonnenhof*	1969/70		8.00
658	Blue Nun Bernkasteler, *Produced by H. Sichel Soehne*	1970/71		9.50
653	Wehlener Sonnenuhr Spatlese 1969/70, *Original Abfüllung Bergweiler-Prum Erben*			15.50
657	Graacher Himmelreich Auslese, *Original Abfüllung Bergweiler-Prum Erben*	1969/70		16.00
652	Piesporter Goldtropfchen, Spatlese	1970	7.00	13.00
665	Bernkasteler Doktor und Beatenbfolchen Spatlese 1970/71, *Original Abfüllung Lauerburg*			30.00

Kosher Wines of Israel

WHITE

65	The President's Sparkling Wine, Extra Dry, *Produced by Carmel*	1970/71		15.00
805	Sauvignon Blanc, *Produced by Carmel*			6.00

ROSE

844	Grenache Rosé, *Produced by Carmel*			6.00

RED

789	Cabernet Sauvignon, *Produced by Carmel*			6.00

3-28-73-100

A partial listing of the wine list offered at the Waldorf Astoria.

"Experience has justified this expectation. The public has cordially supported our wine policy, and now, in our new wine list, we are endeavoring to show our appreciation of that support.

"The new wine list has been months in the making. The wines have been chosen by means of an exhaustive series of 'blind' tastings by experts. Approximately one hundred wines have been added, not a few of them great rarities. And because of our large sale of wines we have been able to scale prices down still further.

"We believe that it is impossible to find upon the St. Regis list a wine which is not a well-selected example of its kind or that is not conspicuously low in price.

"It is our pleasure to show the cellars of which we are so proud."

HOW TO USE THE WINE LIST

ALTHOUGH the wine list is a silent salesman, it cannot perform its selling job unless it receives some assistance from the restaurant's selling staff.

First, the head waiter, waiter, or waitress (whoever takes the order for food) should present the wine list together with the menu. At banquets, two or three banquet wine lists should be on every table.

Second, if the guest or host of a party fails to order a beverage when ordering his meal, he should be asked: "Do you care to order cocktails or wine now?"

Third, to sell you must tell; to tell you must know. It is the duty of the management to have and to impart to the service staff complete information about the wines stocked. This can be done at the regular meetings which all well-organized restaurants hold periodically to instruct the staff on house policies and service, deportment, and so forth. This is important, as we have never yet known anyone who could sell any product successfully if he knew nothing about it.

As most waiters depend on tips for a considerable portion of their income, it should not be difficult to point out to them that they will make more money (through larger tips) when they sell a bottle of wine or some other alcoholic beverage to a guest.

The restaurant has everything to gain and nothing to lose by its wine sales. Wine sales are plus sales because they are made at a time when the guest would normally not drink any other alcoholic beverage, and they are sold at no additional overhead to the restaurant.

It is not our province here to discuss food except as it relates to the wines or other beverages accompanying it. Simplicity is the rule today, even in formal entertaining, and the fourteen-course dinner is practically a thing of the past.

CHAMPAGNE and SPARKLING WINE

Bin		Bottle	½ Bot.
102	BOLLINGER BRUT SPECIAL CUVÉE	13.75	
103	BOLLINGER EXTRA DRY	11.75	
104	LICHTENTHAL KRONE SEKT	6.50	
105	TAYLOR'S COLD DUCK, N. Y. State Split 2.00	6.75	3.50
106	TAYLOR'S EXTRA DRY, N. Y. State Split 2.00	6.75	3.50
107	GREAT WESTERN N. Y. STATE, Dry Champagne	7.50	4.00
111	CHANSON SPARKLING BURGUNDY	9.25	
114	TAYLOR'S SPARKLING BURGUNDY, N. Y. State	6.75	3.50

RED BORDEAUX

Bin		Bottle	½ Bot.
121	CHATEAU LA GARDE, Chanson	6.00	3.50

A fine dry Claret from the world famous Graves District . . . light, yet filled with flavor.

| 123 | CHATEAU MALBEC, Chanson | 4.00 |

A "Bordeaux Rouge Superieur" medium-dry with a gentle bouquet.

| 124 | CABERNET SAUVIGNON, Chanson | 4.50 |

Made 100% from this noble grape — with a remarkable finesse and depth of flavor.

| 125 | MEDOC, Marson & Natier | 3.50 |

Rich, smooth Claret from the best known Bordeaux district.

| 126 | ST. EMILION, Marson & Natier | 4.00 |

Full bodied, red Bordeaux with a delicate bouquet.

RED BURGUNDY

| 131 | BEAUJOLAIS VILLAGES ST. VINCENT, Chanson | 5.25 | 3.00 |

Light, fruity and well-rounded with a pleasant bouquet.

| 132 | CHATEAUNEUF-DU-PAPE, Chanson | 6.50 | 3.75 |

A round, robust, wine from the Rhone Valley.

| 139 | BEAUJOLAIS, Marson & Natier | 4.25 |

Fresh, light Burgundy with a fruity flavor.

| 139A | COTES DU RHONE, Marson & Natier | 3.50 |

Full bodied red wine from the Rhone River region of France.

AMERICAN RED WINE

221	TAYLOR'S LAKE COUNTRY RED	3.00	1.50
222	TAYLOR'S BURGUNDY	3.00	1.50
223	TAYLOR'S ROSÉ	3.00	1.50

AMERICAN WHITE WINE

230	TAYLOR'S LAKE COUNTRY WHITE	3.00	1.50
231	TAYLOR'S SAUTERNE	3.00	1.50
232	TAYLOR'S RHINE	3.00	

after dinner, we recommend the newest thing in coffee, Coffee D.O.M.

after coffee, enjoy

Bénédictine or B and B

have you tried a B and B Stinger?

WHITE BORDEAUX

Bin		Bottle	½ Bot.
161	CHATEAU OLIVIER, Graves, Chanson	4.00	

Dry, soft and elegant. Classified as one of the superior white Graves.

| 163 | SAUVIGNON BLANC, Chanson | 4.00 |

Made 100% from this noble grape— medium dry with a fresh bouquet.

| 164 | GRAVES SEC, Marson & Natier | 3.50 |

Fresh white wine, with a pleasant fruity bouquet.

| 165 | SAUTERNES, Marson & Natier | 4.00 |

Soft, sweet, golden hued Bordeaux from the Sauternes district.

WHITE BURGUNDY

| 172 | CHABLIS ST. VINCENT, Chanson | 7.50 | 4.25 |

The driest and palest of all wines — crisp and delicate with a flinty taste.

| 173 | POUILLY FUISSÉ ST. VINCENT, Chanson | 8.25 | 4.50 |

Dry, crisp and elegant with a delicate bouquet and freshness.

| 177 | PINOT CHARDONNAY ST. VINCENT, Chanson | 7.00 |

Made 100% from this noble grape . . . light and fresh with a full bouquet.

| 178 | CHABLIS, Jouvet | 3.75 |

The driest and palest of all wines — crisp and delicate with a flinty taste.

| 179 | BOURGOGNE ALIGOTÉ, Marson & Natier | 4.00 |

Refreshing white burgundy. With a pleasant bouquet.

RHINE And MOSELLE

| 192 | LICHTENTHAL LIEBFRAUMILCH | 3.50 |

A superior grade of the popular Liebfraumilch — soft, round and well-balanced with a pleasant bouquet.

| 193 | LIEBFRAUMILCH BLUE NUN | 4.75 |

A superior grade of the popular Liebfraumilch — soft, round and well-balanced with a pleasant bouquet.

| 194 | JOHANNISBERGER RIESLING, Deinhard | 6.25 |

Estate bottled by Deinhard . . . an outstanding wine of grace, breed and bouquet.

| 195 | MOSELMAID, Lichtenthal | 3.25 |

Fragrant and light with a fine, fruity flavor.

| 196 | LICHTENTHAL ZELLER SCHWARZE KATZ | 3.25 |

Fresh and light Moselle wine.

| 197 | LICHTENTHAL NIERSTEINER | 3.25 |

Clean, pleasant Rhine wine from the Rheinhessen district.

ALSATIAN WINE

| 201 | RIESLING, Willm | 4.00 |

Beautifully light and dry with a flowery bouquet and a tangy freshness.

ITALIAN WINE — WHITE

| 212 | SOAVE ANTINORI | 4.50 | 2.75 |

A suave Veronese wine . . . light and fairly dry with a pleasant bouquet and a slightly bitter undertone.

| 214 | BIANCO ANTINORI (Fish Bottle) | 5.00 | 3.00 |

A light and fruity, medium dry wine from Tuscany in the unique fish-shaped bottle.

A typical wine list that you may find in your local restaurant.

While there are no set rules about what drinks should be served with specific dishes, there are some traditional customs which are observed because they are practical.

We do not agree with the theory that cocktails should not be served before a dinner at which wine is to be served. If a cocktail whets the appetite, then one should drink it. However, too many drinks on an empty stomach take away the desire for food instead of stimulating it, because the alcohol supplies food value and the system may be satisfied before the meal is begun.

The usual home dinner today consists of an appetizer, a main dish with its accompanying vegetables, a salad, dessert, and coffee. With such a dinner one wine is sufficient. This may be either white or red, depending on the main course and on one's personal preference. When entertaining informally this menu may be expanded to include a soup, but the one wine is still quite correct.

For more formal entertaining, where several wines are in order, the long-accepted order of service should be followed.

(a) Light dry wines
     Full-bodied wines
     Sparkling wines
     Rich, sweet wines

(b) Do not serve a dry Claret or Burgundy after a rich Sauternes (the red wines being dry would taste harsh on the sweetened palate).

(c) When two vintages of the same type of wine are being served, the younger should precede the softer, mellower, older wine. The only exception is Champagne. In this case, the older comes first, because it will seem to lack life and vigor if it follows a fresh young wine.

(d) When serving fine wines, it is advisable to avoid vinegar sauces.

(e) When serving dry red or white wine, avoid dishes with sweet sauces. They will make the wine taste harsh.

(f) Rich, well-seasoned food needs a full-bodied wine. Such food will interfere with the full enjoyment of a delicate wine, while a powerful big wine will completely dominate any delicate, light dish. There should be harmony between them.

In printing menus for formal dinners or banquets, two forms are commonly used for listing the wines. One is to print the wines and spirits on the left side of the menu, listing each opposite the course with which it is to be served. The other is to list the wine or spirit (brandy or liqueurs) as part of the menu, putting each wine immediately below the course with which it is served. In listing wines on a formal dinner menu, full information as to name and vintage should be given. For example, "1959 Château Mouton-Rothschild" or "1969 Gewürztraminer Domaine Willm" would be proper listings.

28. Bar Operation

Bar profits depend on the economical and practical operation of the bar, for if they are not carefully harbored they can easily slip away down the drain pipe.

In most instances, a bar represents a substantial investment in plant, furniture, and decoration. It is imperative to protect this investment by maintaining a standard of service and quality of beverages on a par with the décor and the investment.

The success or failure of the beverage business is squarely in the hands of those who do the dispensing.

THE BARMAN'S JOB

the barman Beverage dispensing should be done quietly and with dignity, creating an atmosphere of refinement and good taste. The job of barman is no different from that of any other retail salesman except that, because of the character of the goods he is selling, he should take extra care to please his customers and look after their welfare.

The barman's day really starts the night before, for without sufficient rest he cannot do his best work on the job.

The barman's smile is one of his best sales arguments and therefore care of the teeth is as important as the most scrupulous cleanliness of the body. Hair should be well brushed and clean, and cut every two weeks. Perfumed hair oils or lotions or medicines with any odor should never be in evidence at the bar. Of course, a clean shave every day is essential. Hands should be washed frequently, nails clipped and cleaned. When a barman finds the necessity of going to the washroom he should take extra pains in seeing that customers observe him cleaning his hands and drying them.

Clothes should be clean and free from perspiration, stains, or spots. Underclothing should be changed frequently and a clean shirt should be worn every day. Colored shirts should never be worn unless they are part of a uniform. Jewelry of any kind should never be worn while on duty. In other words,

378

no person behind the bar should ever make an attempt to "outdress" his customers.

Care of the feet is important for the barman. He cannot show the customer a happy face if his feet are tired and aching. Clean socks help to prevent this. It is a good idea, also, to have two pairs of shoes and change once or twice during the day. Shoes with built-in arches are available in many makes and help to prevent that tired feeling. Rubber heels also relieve the strain.

There is some difference of opinion among barmen as to whether a white vest, vest coat, or white military coat is best for wear while on duty. The vest is admittedly easier to work in, but the coat is more dressy and now, with women to please, the coat is considered better form. If the hotel, club, or restaurant considers a fancy uniform necessary, colors should be confined to the trimming.

The uniform should be kept clean, pressed, and brushed. Standards usually call for white shirt, white collar, and black bow tie. Frayed cuffs may be prevented by having the sleeve length just long enough to allow the cuff to show, but not long enough for it to get in the way or to be soiled. In most places dark trousers are worn with white coats. Aprons are not considered good form today.

While waiting on the trade, the barman should refrain from smoking. Nothing to stop him from taking a little walk and enjoying a moment or two of relaxation with his smoke, but customers as a rule do not like smoking behind the bar. The same is true of drinking—do *not* drink while on duty. Many times the barman is asked to take a drink with the customer, but just pass it up. In the long run it is a profitable gesture.

The first duty of the day, of course, is to report for work on time, whether *the bar* the bartender is to open the bar or to relieve someone else. The bar should be inspected to see that it is spotlessly clean, that the floor, walls, windows, and furniture for table service are in perfect condition, and that the room temperature is right.

At the bar, the woodwork should be polished, back bar dusted, and bottles and glasses neatly arranged. The mirrors should be clean and shining. Liquor bottles should be wiped off with a damp cloth each morning. The work board, drain board, and storage cabinets under the bar should be clean and ready for use.

Supplies of wines and liquors should be carefully checked so that the barman's stock is up to par for the day. His order should be sent to the storeroom and followed up to make sure all supplies are on hand before the first customer arrives. Ice boxes should be filled with ice. Partly used bottles of liquor for mixing purposes should be in the liquor box or in their proper place on the shelves. Then the working equipment should be checked, as well as the draft beer system.

Towels have their proper place behind the bar and not stuck into the belt or over the shoulder of the barman. This careless habit can lose customers.

the fruit   Next the fruits should be prepared. This should be done just before time for opening the bar so that they will be as fresh as possible. If the bar opens an hour or two before luncheon, it is well to prepare only the fruits for which there will be a call during the luncheon hour. Then during the afternoon lull there is time to prepare such additional fruits as might be called for in Champagne cups and other more elaborate drinks most often asked for at the cocktail hour, at dinner, and during the evening.

These fruits will include oranges, lemons, pineapples, olives, cherries; fruit syrups, such as raspberry; and fresh mint. Only a small amount of orange and lemon juice, depending on the ordinary demands, should be prepared in advance, using the less perfect fruit for squeezing, and keeping the finest for slicing and peeling.

Oranges should be of uniform size—about 216 to the crate is a good size—and either California or Florida fruit may be used. Floridas have more juice but Californias have a better color. Oranges are cut in half from top to bottom (use Californias for slicing). Cut slices about a fourth inch thick, discarding the end pieces. Slices should be kept together as much as possible until used, to preserve their freshness. The main supply should be kept, if possible, in a refrigerator, covered with a moist napkin.

Lemon slices should be about one-quarter of an inch thick. Begin by cutting the lemon in half in the middle as for juicing. Then cut back each half, throwing the ends away.

Where pieces of twisted lemon or orange peel are called for, start at one end of the whole fruit and cut a strip about three-quarters of an inch wide, skin deep, the length of the fruit to the other end. If a special piece of lemon or orange peel is called for, start at one end and cut a strip about three-quarters of an inch wide spirally, as when peeling an apple, until the other end is reached.

Fresh pineapple should be used when obtainable, although canned pineapple juice is standard. The best method of preparing this fruit is to cut it into half-inch cubes, with some strips about three inches long. Pineapple should be used only in punches, long drinks, sours, and lemonades.

Olives and cherries should be placed in handy containers so that they may be reached easily. Only pitted green olives, especially prepared for cocktails should be used and the best size is 120s to 130s. Stuffed olives should never be used. Maraschino cherries especially prepared for cocktail use, pitted but with the stems left on, are the best. No broken fruit should be used.

Never use anything but the proper prescribed tongs when serving fruit or ice. It looks smeary to use the fingers and lacks dignity.

The appearance of a drink has great eye-appeal. The professional touch *the drink* is given when it is well-garnished with fruit.

However, appearance implies a clean, neat presentation of the drink. Fill the glass to within $\frac{1}{8}''$ to $\frac{1}{4}''$ from the brim. Never fill the glass to the brim or allow it to overflow. Such service is sloppy. The only exception permissible to this rigid rule of neat service is in the case of draught beer, where it is correct to allow a small amount of foam to overflow.

Finally, the dishes on the bar should be filled with whatever appetizers the rules of the house call for, such as pretzels, cheese crackers, cheese, peanuts, and so forth.

SOME RULES FOR THE BARMAN

1. Your manners will be reflected in your sales. After you have served a drink step back from your customer or move away. Never appear to listen to the conversation and never take part in it unless directly addressed.

2. Cultivate a good memory for the faces and tastes of your regular customers and greet them pleasantly when they come in.

Elegant, intimate small bar at the Regency Hotel, New York. (Courtesy Bar Management)

3. Handle complaints courteously. At the bar the customer is always right unless he is intoxicated. If he complains about his drink, fix it up or mix another. A bar quickly gets a reputation for fine drinks and courteous service— and it can lose it just as quickly.

4. Never hurry a customer or show that you are impatient. Don't show by your manner that you think a customer is drinking too much—or too little.

5. If you must answer a telephone at the bar, do so quietly. If the call is for a patron, never say that he is there. Instead, say that you will inquire, and leave it up to the patron to decide whether or not he wishes to answer the telephone.

6. Be co-operative and friendly with the other employees.

7. You are not a barman until you can fill four glasses to just the right height (about a quarter inch from the top) and not have a drop left over in your bar glass. If you cannot do that, practice until you can. Be sure you know how to mix standard cocktails without referring to a book. A helpful trick in starting is to take a glass cutter and make a few tiny marks on the outside of the bar glass, showing where the main ingredients for Martinis and Manhattans come to for one, two, three, and four drinks. These marks should be invisible to the customer. It is simpler to gauge the ingredients if you put them in before putting in the ice.

8. When a drink is ordered, first place the required glass on top of the bar. If more than one drink is ordered, place the glasses is a straight row with the rims touching. Then place your mixing glass on the bar and pour the ingredients into it where the customer can see it. Allow for the ice melting during the shaking process.

9. In pouring more than one drink, run your mixing glass back and forth over the row of glasses, filling them all first quarter full, then half full, then full. Never fill one glass first and then another.

10. As soon as you have mixed a drink, put the bottles back in their proper places, no matter how rushed you are. This saves time. Rinse your bar glass, shaker, and strainer, and you are ready for the next one.

11. As a rule, standard recipes should be followed. If the barman has regular patrons he should study their likes and dislikes and make their drinks the way they prefer. Adhering too closely to formula for patrons of individual tastes will drive business away.

12. Many houses now require the use of the jigger. Modern types of bar control make it necessary to account for every drink. An inexperienced barman often has a little left over in the shaker, which goes down the sink. This waste is trifling on one drink, but if it is repeated often during a day, the loss is substantial.

13. When properly priced, cocktails, especially those made with gin, Vermouth, wine, or fruit juices, are most profitable, as a higher price is charged

than for straight drinks and a smaller quantity of liquor is required. Drinks of this type should be suggested.

14. When preparing standard cocktails like the Martini and Manhattan, use cubes or large pieces of ice. Finely chopped ice melts too rapidly and dilutes the cocktail too much.

15. Cocktails that are shaken should be shaken briskly and not too long, as the ice will melt and weaken the drink.

16. When serving straight drinks or highballs and the customer has the bottle in front of him, it is a good idea to put the cork back in the bottle each time a drink is served. This will help you keep check on the number of drinks poured.

17. Do not serve a drink from a bottle that is nearly empty, when it can be avoided. Keep this for mixing cocktails.

18. All glasses should be wiped twice. First to dry and second to give a polish.

IMPLEMENTS FOR THE BAR

ASIDE from the necessary glassware, which is discussed in Chapter 29, the man behind the bar needs a number of tools of his trade, some of which are stationary, some movable. The stationary equipment is the province of the architects who design the physical construction of the bar. We might point out that it would be a just punishment for some of these architects to have to work behind the bars they have constructed. They would discover what it is like to mix drinks in a space scarcely big enough for a mole, let alone two men trying to serve a number of people. The space between the front and the back of the bar should be wide enough so that two men can pass each other without jostling. The front section should not be too low, but so arranged that the barman can reach ice, mixing glass, and bottles with ease.

The principal implements needed in a bar are:

Silver cocktail shakers	Ice pick
Mixing glasses (small and large)	Ice tongs
Electric mixing machine (the professional Osterizer is probably the best)	Ice scoop
	Ice shaver
Lime and lemon squeezers	Spoons: long bar; medium bar; mixing;
Electric orange juice extracter	sugar; small old fashioned
Stainless steel fruit knife	Stirrers
A patent cork puller	Muddler (wood)
Corkscrews	Sugar bowls
Bottle opener	Salt shakers; nutmeg shakers
Beer can opener	Beer scraper (bone)

Egg beater

Strainers: silver fruit strainer; wire-
rimmed, handled strainer

Glass pitchers for wine cups

Bitters bottles

Clean towels

SUGGESTIONS TO MANAGERS

1. Keep a barman who *is* a barman.

2. It pays to listen to the barman's suggestions. Napoleon was a very smart man but he had a motto that goes as follows: "There are days when one needs someone smaller than himself."

3. If you have no confidence in your barman, don't keep him.

4. A good barman is worth a good salary in the added business he brings you.

5. Show the barman you are interested in him.

6. Do not set too rigid rules for him, as often he needs to make exception to the rules to please a customer.

7. Many organizations find they do better by training their own barmen. After several weeks of training, the best is picked out as assistant bartender, and gradually given more responsibility in accordance with his abilities.

THE HOME COCKTAIL BAR

IN some homes the closet or pantry where the supply of beverages is stored has to perform the added function of a bar, while in others a corner of the recreation room has an artistically arranged bar with all the necessary ac-coutrements. Whichever one has, these are the implements or gadgets needed to make it a practical working bar and a corner of the house which host and guests will enjoy using.

USEFUL EQUIPMENT FOR A HOME BAR

A generous cocktail shaker

A large heavy mixing glass

A muddler for old fashioned cocktails

A measuring jigger or cup

Long mixing spoons (iced tea spoons will do)

Cocktail, highball, and Sherry glasses (which can be used for other wines, and in a pinch for cordials, too)

A flat bar strainer

Corkscrew, bottle opener, and beer-can opener

Sharp stainless steel knife for cutting fruit

Lemon and lime squeezer

A bucket in which ice may be kept (when cracked ice is needed it should be cracked in the kitchen)

Electric blender

It is difficult to say what supplies are indispensable, as this must be governed by the individual taste and on the assortment of drinks the host wishes to offer his guests. The following list of supplies is consequently offered in the nature of a guide, and no quantities are given, for the same reason. (In Chapter 30, recommendations are made for A Beginner's Cellar, An Amateur's Cellar, An Adventurer's Cellar, and A Gourmet's Cellar.)

USEFUL SUPPLIES FOR A HOME BAR

Lemons	Vodka
Limes	Orange Bitters
Oranges	Aromatic Bitters
Maraschino cherries	Rye whiskey
Small cocktail olives	Bourbon whiskey
Small cocktail onions	Scotch whisky
Fresh mint	Dry gin
Sugar, both granulated and powdered	French Dry Vermouth
Tawny Port	Italian Sweet Vermouth
Cognac brandy	Medium Sherry
Crème de Menthe	Apple Jack
Triple Sec	Bénédictine
Jamaica rum	Crème de Cacao
Grenadine	White Label Puerto Rican rum
Ginger ale	Quality mineral water
Club soda	Coca-Cola or Pepsi Cola

DOS AND DON'TS IN MIXING

Do not make up more cocktails than are needed to fill the exact number of glasses. The custom of "dividends" is one of the horrible inheritances from Prohibition. The remains in the shaker are usually tasteless and watery from melting ice.

Drink a cocktail—do not sip. It tastes better when freshly made. If allowed to stand, some of the ingredients tend to separate. This is particularly the case with mixed drinks that contain fruit juices and sugar.

Cocktails made of liquor and wine may be prepared in quantity in advance of a party, but those which include fruit juices are better if freshly mixed just before drinking.

If the recipe calls for the juice of limes, use fresh green limes for best results. The only exception to this rule is in the use of the Frozen Daiquiri Mix. In many tests we have made we have found it the equal of fresh lime juice. We recommend it highly. This is particularly true with rum drinks, such as the Daiquiri, Planter's Punch, or Swizzle. Lemon juice will not give the sharp acid tang necessary for best results with rum.

29. Beverage Service

GLASSWARE

THE first wine glass is said to have been made from a bubble of seafoam cut in half by Aphrodite as she came forth from the sea—a pretty myth, and one that has a point. The wine glass should be crystal clear.

Undoubtedly, the first cup man used was his hand. As he became more civilized and acquired tools with which to fashion implements, he made himself a drinking vessel. The earliest one was fashioned from a dried gourd. Later on, he experimented with wood, shells, metals, and finally, when he learned how to work with glass, he made the first of our present-day containers. The origin of glass is credited both to the early Assyrians and to the Egyptians. The examples of early glass drinking cups which survive today are misshapen and not very transparent, but even so they were useful and a great improvement on other containers of potables.

As time went on and the art of glass blowing was improved, much beauty and perfection of line were blown into wine bottles and goblets. Later the art of glass cutting further enhanced the elegance and beauty of the container.

The most famous glass-makers were the Venetians and Bohemians. They had a secret for coloring their glass which no one else possessed, and up to the end of the last century colored glasses for wine were still the fashion. There was a definite reason for color in wine glasses. More often than not the wine was not perfectly clear. It had sediment in it and was dull and uninteresting to look at, but since our vintners have learned to "fine" their wines—and wines today should always be perfectly brilliant when shipped—this reason is no longer valid.

The enjoyment of beverages, and wine in particular, calls for the use of three senses: sight, smell, and taste. Before we smell or taste a wine, we see it. There is pleasure in the bright red of a Claret, the deep ruby of a Burgundy, and the limpid, mellow, golden hue of a white wine, to say nothing of the dancing brightness of Champagne as the bubbles rise before your eyes. The very sight of wine shimmering in a clear, transparent, delicately stemmed glass increases the pleasure of anticipation. A colored glass deprives you of this pleasure and we say a plague on it.

386

GLASSWARE FOR THE HOME

THE glassware needed for a well-appointed house and that required for a hotel are two different problems. For the home it is unnecessary to have many different shapes and sizes. Many beverages may be served in the same size glass.

A complete set of glassware to take care of all needs in a home which entertains up to twelve guests at a dinner should include:

> 12 on-the-rocks or old fashioned glasses   8 ounces
> 12 cocktail glasses of a conventional shape to hold 4 or $4\frac{1}{2}$ ounces
> 12 Sherry or dessert wine glasses   4 ounces
> 12 all-purpose wine glasses   8 ounces
> 12 brandy glasses marked with a capacity of 2 ounces
> 12 highball glasses   10 ounces
> 12 champagne goblets   8 ounces

The glassware people in their desire to be of service at the time of Repeal did much to frighten the American public away from wine, by advocating the use of a different glass for every type of wine. The number of types of glass necessary, and some difference of opinion as to what type of glass should be used with certain wines, prevented many people from serving wine at all.

the ideal wine glass

The ideal, all-purpose wine glass (one that is quite proper for red and white table wines and all sparkling wines) should be:

1. Beautiful to look at, with simple, graceful lines.
2. Generous—8 ounces—so that you can pour enough wine (4 ounces) for a satisfying drink and still have room in the glass to swirl the wine around and get the full benefit of its aroma.
3. The mouth should be slightly smaller than the widest part of the bowl so that the bouquet of the wine is gathered to a point for the maximum enjoyment, but the mouth should be wide enough so that the upper edge does not strike the nose when the glass is tilted for drinking.

HOTEL SERVICE

IN a hotel or restaurant, the problem of glass service is entirely different. Tradition and showmanship enter the picture and the requirements are far greater and stricter.

A fine hotel or restaurant must have conventional glassware both for its bar service and its wine service.

The bar must have available the following assortment:

Whiskey $1\frac{1}{2}$ ounces   Sherry   4 ounces

Old fashioned   6 ounces
Delmonico   5 ounces
Small highball   8 ounces
Large highball   10 ounces
Tom Collins or lemonade   12 ounces
Cocktail (various shapes and sizes)
    4 to 4½ ounces
Daiquiri   4½ ounces
Champagne cocktail   5 ounces
Port (Madeira and apéritif wines)   4 ounces

Line brandy (line marks)   1 ounce
Brandy snifter   5 ounces
Punch   5 ounces
Hot Toddy   5 ounces
Tom and Jerry mug   5–6 ounces
Beer shell   8–10 ounces
Beer seidl   16 ounces
Stein   10–12 ounces
Punch bowl, glass or silver
Wine cooler, silver

THE DINING-ROOM WINE SERVICE

Water goblet
Rhine wine, tall, stemmed, squat
    bowled   6 ounces
White wine (Graves, Sauternes,
    white Burgundy)   6 ounces
Champagne goblet   8 ounces

Claret, red Burgundy and red
    Rhône   8 ounces
Sherry   4 ounces
Port   4 ounces
Brandy snifter   5 ounces
Line brandy (line marks)   1 ounce

All of these and such fancy glasses as are the vogue for a short period of time have their place. No hotel or restaurant which lays claim to leadership in a community can hope to get along without them. While in a private home the one all-purpose table wine glass may serve nicely, a hotel or restaurant which serves formal dinners or banquets must serve each wine in its traditional glass. This does not mean that a wine will taste better in it, but, just as dinner clothes invest a formal gathering with a dignity which is lacking when informal dress is the rule, so the proper glassware for each wine lends its dignity and elegance to the affair. In other words, it is good showmanship.

Notwithstanding the foregoing statement, even in large luxury hotels the trend has been to simplify, wherever possible, the service equipment, including glassware. Many new establishments have reduced the glassware for the service of wines to just two sizes of the same shape, namely a six-ounce stemmed glass for the service of rosé and white table wines and a similar style glass but with a capacity of eight ounces for the service of red wines and Champagne or sparkling wine.

placement of glasses   On the table, wine glasses are usually placed at the right of the water glass. If more than one kind of wine is to be served, the glass for the first wine is placed the farthest to the right, so it may be removed first more easily. If, as at elaborate banquets, several wines are to be served, no more than three wine glasses are on the table at any time. The glasses may be arranged in one of two ways. In one, the wine glasses are set to the right of the plate and toward the center of the table—one wine glass in line with knife, one to the right and one below it, forming a triangle. In the other method, the glasses may be set in a straight line in front of and to the right of place—the water goblet and the wine glasses in that order. For additional wines, glasses are exchanged as each course is finished and the next course is served.

HOW TO SERVE WINE

WHAT beverages are served cold? All white wines; all sparkling wines; all pink wines; all beers; all cocktails; most mixed drinks; certain spirits which are consumed as apéritifs such as Vodka and Akvavit; all apéritif wines; very dry Sherry, and very dry Madeira.

temperature

The following generally are served at room temperature: All red wines; medium and rich Sherries, Madeira, Port, Marsala, and all spirits when taken neat, such as whiskey, gin, rum, brandy, and liqueurs. Exceptions are Vodka and Akvavit, mentioned in the preceding paragraph.

Exceptions made the rule, and even a liqueur, with all its sweetness, can be very pleasant in the summer if it is chilled. In fact, many liqueurs are enjoyed on-the-rocks, i.e. served over cracked ice in an old-fashioned glass.

How cold should a wine be when it is served? This is a moot question. It depends, in the last analysis, on the individual taste of the host in each case. The general rule is that the sweeter wines should be served colder than the dry, and that no wine should be chilled below 42° F. (45° is cold enough). This can be accomplished by placing the wine in a refrigerator for two or three hours prior to serving, or by placing it in a wine cooler and packing the bottle with ice for 20 to 30 minutes. Actually, many people store a few bottles and half bottles of white, rosé and sparkling wines in their refrigerators. Contrary to popular belief this will not hurt the wine. However, if possible, these wines should be stored in a horizontal position.

What does room temperature mean? In reality, not quite what it says. The "room temperature" criteria was established in Europe long before central heating was known. Even today rooms are never heated abroad as warmly as is customary in the United States, where 72° to 75° F. is usual. The fact is that "room temperature" for wine is 65° to 68° F., which is ideal, and the temperature at which red wines will be most enjoyable. However, if you enjoy your red table wines either tepid (80°) or very cold (45°), by all means drink them that way since it is your palate which must be pleased.

If the wine has been stored in a cellar where the temperature is lower, it may be brought to room temperature by standing the bottle for a few hours in the room where it is to be served. WARNING! Under no circumstances should the wine be warmed artificially, either by plunging the bottle in hot

FROM LEFT TO RIGHT. *1. Ubiquitous five ounce saucer champagne, which is ideal for the service of ice cream or fruit cups but not for Champagne or sparkling wines. Its flat shallowness exposes too great a surface of wine, allowing the bubbles to escape too rapidly, and not recommended. 2. Nine ounce all-purpose wine goblet employed for red table wines and all sparkling wines by such leading hotels as The Savoy Plaza, The Waldorf-Astoria, The New York Hilton at Rockefeller Center, etc. A good glass. 3. The elegant eight ounce tulip Champagne goblet developed by the Champagne producers of France. Also a good glass for Champagne. 4 & 5. Two Champagne "flute" glasses. The first employed at the Waldorf-Astoria and the second at the Four Seasons Restaurant, New York. 6. The all too well-known two ounce "sherry" which is inadequate. The normal portion of sherry is two ounces, which means this glass must be filled to the brim. Spillage is unavoidable, which is sloppy service. 7. The four and a half ounce sherry, port, madeira, etc., glass is ideal. The two ounce portion can be served cleanly in this glass, which is used at the Plaza Hotel, Savoy Plaza and many other fine hotels and restaurants. 8. Finally, the twenty ounce wine carafe employed by the Brasserie Restaurant, New York.*

FROM LEFT TO RIGHT. *1. Standard "four ounce wine." A bad, inadequate glass should never be used. 2 & 3. Six and a half and eight and a half Libbey "Olympian," which are recommended, as all-purpose wine glasses. 4. Excellent nine ounce glass for red wines and Champagne employed by The New York Hilton at Rockefeller Center, The Waldorf-Astoria, The Plaza, The Savoy Plaza and many other fine hotels and restaurants. 5. The Grossman all-purpose eight ounce lead crystal glass without the four ounce fill line. 6. Exquisite Baccarat ten ounce thin lead crystal wine glass suitable for home use but too fragile for restaurant service. 7. Traditional Roemer for service of German wines, seven ounce capacity. 8 & 9. Dramatic lead crystal glasses, for serving white wine and red wine respectively, used by the fine New York restaurants, Four Seasons and Forum of the Twelve Caesars. (Photo by Al Levine)*

LEFT TO RIGHT. *1. Shot glasses. The etched line on first glass marks the five-eighths of an ounce fill. It is a dishonest glass, properly called a "cheater" in Canada. 2. The second glass is the special shot glass approved by the Liquor License Board of Ontario and which must be used by all Ontario licensees. The etched lines mark the one, one and a quarter, one and a half ounce fill. 3. The one ounce pony brandy or liqueur glass. The normal "pony" portion of one ounce cannot be served in this inadequate glass without spillage. 4 & 5. The two ounce "line brandy" (the etched line marks the one ounce fill) and small three ounce capacity snifter are much more practical for both brandy and liqueurs. 6. The large, dramatic twenty ounce crystal snifter is employed by the Four Seasons, New York, for Cognac and other fine brandies. 7. Traditional ten ounce Pilsner beer. 8. Elegant sixteen ounce footed beer shell used at the Forum of the Twelve Caesars. 9. Absinthe drip glass. 10. Porcelain singing saké bottle and whistling saké cup from Japan.* (Photo by Al Levine)

LEFT TO RIGHT. *1. Inadequate and unrecommended two and a half ounce cocktail still employed by too many restaurants. 2. Ideal four and a half ounce cocktail with an etched line showing the proper three ounce fill used by most good restaurants, hotels and clubs. The example shown is from The Waldorf-Astoria. 3. Six ounce "King's Size" cocktail for dramatic service. Filled to within a quarter inch of the brim permits service of a four and a half ounce cocktail. 4. Waterford Irish crystal glass for service of "Irish Coffee" cocktail. 5. Six ounce "sour" glass from The Waldorf-Astoria, used by nearly all restaurants. 6. Standard eight ounce highball. 7. Standard twelve ounce Collins. 8. Standard five ounce Delmonico, better known today as a "juice" glass. 9. Six ounce "on-the-rocks" or old-fashioned. 10. Seven ounce "footed" on-the-rocks.* (Photo by Al Levine)

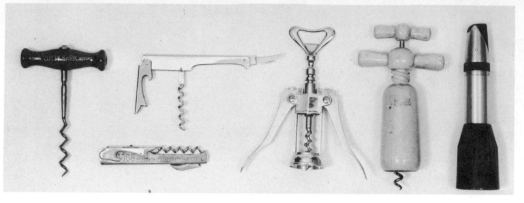

LEFT TO RIGHT. *1. Traditional "T" style. 2. Practical waiter's lever type with knife. 3. Metal "wing" type. 4. Wooden cork-puller with counter-screw. 5. CO_2 cork extractor.* (Photo by Al Levine)

water or by placing it in or near a heater. This will harm the wine. It is better to drink a red wine too cold than to spoil it by heating it.

chilling the wine   There are two ways to chill wine for dining room service. One is to keep pre-chilled in the refrigerator all wines in the main-floor service stock that are to be served cold. In some restaurants, and for luncheon service in almost any restaurant, this is the only kind of chilling needed. The other way is to serve in the conventional wine table-cooler or ice bucket. Since even here some pre-chilling is advisable, the cooler is used mainly for showmanship, to flatter the guest, and is part of the display he is paying for when he orders white dinner wine or sparkling wine with dinner. Serving white wines at luncheon ordinarily does not require the use of the cooler, which takes more time than either the staff or the guests have to spare at midday. Sparkling wines are nearly always served in coolers.

Dining rooms which use coolers usually have them available at the service bar together with stands or trays. A little shaved ice is first placed in the bottom of the cooler, then the bottle is inserted, and finally shaved ice is added to fill the cooler. If ice cubes or cracked ice is used, water must be added so that the bottle can be re-inserted in the cooler between servings. Water and ice chills faster than ice alone.

An important point is to bring the wine to the table immediately after it is ordered. The cooler should be placed on the table if a stand is not available, so that guests at other tables can see it and thereby be influenced to order wine. When the bottle is removed from the cooler it should be wiped dry before the wine is poured. If the wine has not been pre-chilled, it will require about twenty minutes to chill in the cooler. The cooler should be placed conveniently at the host's right so that glasses may be refilled in the waiter's absence. When the bottle is emptied by the waiter, he places it upside down in the cooler, to let the host know it is empty.

OPENING A BOTTLE OF WINE

THERE are three simple steps:

1. Cut and remove the capsule to just below the bulge which is to be found on all wine bottles. With a clean napkin wipe the mold or dirt you will often find between the cork and capsule. The reason for this is that it is impossible to pour wine from a bottle without some of it spilling or slipping over the lip. Since the metal capsule is often corroded or moldy, the wine would taste tainted if it came in contact with the metal.

2. Push down the cork very slightly to loosen the bond between the cork and the glass. Insert the corkscrew (and we recommend the lever type°) in the center of the cork. Drive it in as far as it will go, then lever it out with an even, confident motion. Do not jerk it out nervously, as that will shake up the wine. If you use the T corkscrew, drive it into the cork, then grasp the bottle firmly with the left hand. Hold the bottle so that the shoulder rests in the palm of your hand—grasp the corkscrew with the right hand—hold the bottle between your knees and pull slowly and evenly. Pull straight out. Do not rock or twist the cork in withdrawing it.

3. The cork out, again wipe the mouth of the bottle both inside and out with the napkin. Next smell the cork to see if it is sound. Then you are ready to serve.

Some American and California wines have screw caps or screw-type corks which twist off or open once the capsule has been cut and removed. After the closure has been removed, the mouth of the bottle should be cleaned with the napkin and then the wine can be poured.

° There are many types of corkscrews or cork-pullers available, several of which are illustrated on page 392, but only a few are really practical. The functional objective is to extract the cork from the bottle in one piece and as easily as possible so as to disturb the contents (wine supposedly) as little as possible. Ideally, the screw should be 2 to $2\frac{1}{4}$ inches long. The metal should be rounded, and the point should be a continuation of the spiral. Avoid a corkscrew with a flattened, sharp cutting edge. Avoid any corkscrew that has the appearance of an auger. The lever type referred to is the most practical cork-puller for a waiter to use in a restaurant because it closes into a compact flat instrument easily carried in his pocket. It is also practical for home use.

One of the most practical cork-pullers we have found is the wooden corkscrew with a counter screw. It functions easily and requires a minimum of effort to remove the cork. Steel and brass corkscrews that function on the same principal are also available.

Another addition to cork-extraction is the cork remover that works on the principal of injecting a small amount of harmless carbonic acid gas into the cork by means of a needle. The gas goes through the porous cork back into the bottle. The surface of the wine acts as a platform, stopping the gas which then expands and pushes against the cork until it is ejected or "pops" out. It works satisfactorily. The first question many people ask is—does this gas affect or change the wine in any way? The answer is: *It does not.*

OPENING A BOTTLE OF SPARKLING WINE

Six steps in the business of opening and serving a bottle of Champagne, or any sparkling wine:

1. If the bottle is presented in a Champagne cooler, it should be stood upright in the cooler and fine ice packed tightly well up around the neck.

2. Remove the bottle and wrap a clean napkin around it. The pressure within a bottle of Champagne is around 8 atmospheres, or some 96 pounds to the square inch. The glass of the bottle is quite thick and when the wine has been properly chilled, the glass is cold and contracted. A warm hand against the bottle will cause surface expansion at the point of contact. It is possible, under such conditions, for a bottle to burst. We have seen such an explosion occur, and it is dangerous. True, the chances of it happening are remote, but if the bottle is wrapped in a napkin or cloth, the chances of bursting are greatly reduced, and even if it should happen, no one would be hurt.

3. Remove the foil or metal capsule to a point just below the wire which holds the cork securely. Hold bottle firmly in left hand at an angle of 45°, unwind and remove the wiring. With a clean napkin, wipe neck of bottle and around the cork.

4. Hold the bottle firmly at the same 45° angle. With right hand, grasp the cork so that it will not fly out wildly and strike an innocent bystander. Twist the bottle and ease out the cork. It is quite all right for it to come out with a resounding "pop."

5. After the cork is out, keep the bottle at an angle for about five seconds or until the pressure within has equalized itself with that outside the bottle. If you hold the bottle upright when the cork is released, the gas will rush out and carry a goodly part of the wine with it, to say nothing of giving you a Champagne bath.

6. Once the cork has "popped," remove the napkin as there is no further need of it. Champagne and sparkling wines must be served in two motions. Pour wine until the froth almost reaches the brim of the glass. Stop. Wait a moment until this foaming froth subsides, then continue pouring to fill the glass $\frac{2}{3}$ to $\frac{3}{4}$ full. Be careful not to pour too rapidly or the wine will froth over the lip of the glass. By the way, make sure the Champagne glasses are *dry*, since moisture in a glass kills the bubbles.

It is not necessary to drape either red or white wine in such a manner as to hide the label unless one is ashamed of the wine he is serving. However, a bottle which is in an ice bucket should be carefully wiped dry each time it is withdrawn to insure against drops of ice water trickling down a lady's back.

SERVING WINE

Back in the Middle Ages a popular way of poisoning your enemies was to

1. *Present bottle to guest; then wrap it in napkin.*

2. *Unwind and remove wire basket holding the cork in place.*

3. *Holding bottle firmly in left hand at 45° angle, grasp the cork with the right, then twist the bottle—not the cork—until the cork "pops." Maintain the bottle at 45° angle for a few seconds, until pressure within equalizes with air pressure.*

4. *Remove napkin and serve. Pour in two motions as explained on page 394.*

Serving Champagne at Seven Hills Restaurant, The New York Hilton. (Courtesy Julius Wile Sons & Co., Inc. Photos by Al Levine)

ask them to dine, and sometime during the festivities they would drink a goblet of poisoned wine. A guest had to be wary in those days.

Gradually the custom arose for the host to taste the wine before his guests to allay their fears. Today, too, the host samples the wine before his guests are served, but this practice has a far more reasonable basis. It is the means of assuring the host that his wine is in perfect condition.

When serving at home, when there are no servants, the host should serve himself and then his guests. First he should fill his own glass about $\frac{1}{4}$ full and satisfy himself on the quality of the wine. Then, around the table, clockwise, he should fill the glasses of the ladies first, then those of the gentlemen. Or the glasses may be passed to him and passed back. After all the glasses have been filled, he should fill his own. The wine glass should not be more than $\frac{1}{2}$ to $\frac{2}{3}$ full.

The open wine bottle may be kept at the right of the host. Where there are servants, the bottle is usually placed on the sideboard until it is needed. Wines that are chilled should be kept at the right of the host in a cooler, or, if there are servants, in a cooler on the sideboard.

serving white and rosé wines

As previously stated, white and rosé should be served chilled. Traditionally, they are served with white meats—fowl, fish, and seafood. Turkey may be served with either white or red wine. Tradition does not rule out the possibility that white wine may be drunk with red meat. When a guest orders a particular type and brand of wine, he should be served the wine he orders with no comment by the waiter.

When a guest asks for white wine, the waiter—or *sommelier* (wine steward)—should obtain the bottle from storage, set it into an ice bucket, cover it with a clean, folded napkin, and bring this service into the dining room. The ice bucket, placed on a stand, is set to the right of the person who ordered the wine. The waiter (or *sommelier*) then takes the bottle out of the bucket and presents it to the guest with the label uppermost. The host thus has an opportunity to verify the correctness of his order.

This bottle presentation is an important part of wine service and should not be overlooked. If the waiter misunderstood the guest and brought in the wrong wine—to which the guest will later object—the waiter can now readily exchange this bottle for one the guest prefers. Had the waiter ignored this presentation ritual and opened the bottle without showing it to the guest for his approval, the bottle would have to be returned to storage and may become a loss. Furthermore, this bottle-presentation ceremony shows courtesy to the guest, regardless of his knowledge about wines, and adds to the atmosphere of the dining room.

The glasses in which white wines are to be served are best previously chilled. When chilled glasses are not available, the waiter may chill them in crushed ice. Or the glasses may be filled with crushed ice while the wine is being inspected and opened. The ice should then be dumped into the ice bucket just prior to pouring the wine.

Once the bottle is opened and the mouth cleaned, the waiter should pour one ounce into the glass of the host (or whoever ordered the wine) so that he can approve the wine. Hold a towel in the left hand when serving wine and use it to wipe the bottle, particularly when taking it out of the ice bucket. Do not wrap the bottle in a towel since the guests usually wish to see the label of the wine they are drinking.

When the host has approved the wine, pour wine: (1) *for a couple,* the lady; (2) *for a group,* the person sitting to the host's right. Proceed around the table counterclockwise, filling the host's glass last. White wine glasses should not be filled more than three-fourths full. This gives the guests an opportunity to savor the wine's aroma within the enclosure of the glass before sipping it.

When pouring wine, hold the bottle so that the label is always uppermost and can readily be seen. Bring the bottle to the glass on the table. Do not lift the glass in your hand because the hand warms the glass and spoils the effect of the chilled white wine. When the glass is two-thirds full, twist the bottle to distribute the last drop on the bottle's rim and thus prevent it from dripping. Always pour with the right hand, never with the left. From which side should you serve the wine? Whichever is more convenient. Usually from the right side of the guest as the glass is set at the right of the plate.

When all glasses have been served, place the white wine bottle back into the ice bucket to the host's right. Waiters should always see that every guest's glass is replenished. It often produces the sale of an extra bottle of wine.

Wine should be brought to the table before it is time to serve it. If more than one wine is to be served, all wines should be either on a side table or chilled in coolers where the host and guests can see them.

Red wine is a perfect companion to dark-meated fowl, all kinds of meat however prepared, and is excellent with cheese. As previously noted, it is generally served at room temperature. If brought directly from the wine cellar, it should be served at that temperature—*never warmed.* Some lighter-bodied red wines may be preferred when slightly chilled, particularly in summer.

serving red wines

Red wine often throws a sediment as it grows older. This is a natural occurrence and shows that the wine is maturing in the bottle. For this reason, red wine should be handled carefully and gently. In fact, the Burgundy basket was created in Burgundy for the sole purpose of removing the bottle from the cellar bin in the horizontal position in which it lies, so that the sediment in the bottle is not disturbed. If the bottle in the basket is taken under the arm and stirred up, the object of the basket is wasted. Its sole purpose is to leave the wine undisturbed.

Certain very old red wines should be decanted in the cellar. The object in decanting is to draw off the clear wine and leave any sediment there might be in the bottle. It is not necessary to decant white wines, as they rarely have a heavy deposit. Avoid the use of a filter in decanting wine as it takes out some of the taste. Wine should be decanted a half to three quarters of an hour before serving, to give the wine a chance to breathe, which is the second good reason for decanting. However, if a decanter is not available, we find it a good practice in the home to uncork red table wines (Clarets, Burgundies, and so forth) an hour or two before they are to be served. This is particularly advisable if the wine is young. It will be found that contact with the air expands the bouquet and enhances the enjoyment of the wine.

In decanting, the decanter must be perfectly clean and dry. Remove the capsule completely, then place a candle or a light behind the bottle neck and the moment you see any sediment coming over, stop.

When red wine is presented to a restaurant guest for his approval before opening, care should be taken not to disturb any sediment present. When using a Burgundy basket the bottle should be left in the basket while presenting, opening, and serving the wine.

Red wine glasses are frequently larger than white wine glasses and, therefore, should be filled only one-half to two-thirds full. The serving procedure is the same as for white wine. After filling the glasses return the bottle to its place at the right side of the table's host so that he can pour more wine if he desires to do it himself.

serving appetizer and dessert wines

Appetizer and dessert wines are served in the manner of cocktails and other mixed drinks. These wines are ordered at the bar and brought into the dining room on a small bar tray. Each glass is then set before the guest. But remember that with wines—cocktails and spirits too—no glass should ever be filled to the brim. It is impossible to carry it on a tray without spilling, and the result is sloppy service, and wet glass.

A modern and fast-becoming popular way of serving Sherry and other appetizers is on-the-rocks. Service is over cubed ice in an old-fashioned glass.

In hotel service, when serving Sherry or any product ordered by brand name, it is our opinion that the bottle should be brought to the table. It is not always practical, but wherever it is practical, it makes a better impression on the guest if the waiter does this. Then there is no question that the customer is getting what he ordered.

Burgundy basket.
(Photo by Al Levine)

30. Purchasing

CONFIDENCE is the foundation on which the wine and spirit trade has been built throughout the centuries. The wholesale distributor has confidence in the producer or shipper, the retailer has confidence in the wholesaler, and the consumer has confidence in the retailer.

Just what constitutes the basis for this confidence? It is a combination of factors—quality, price, and service—each in relation to the other.

QUALITY VERSUS PRICE

QUALITY is foremost in importance, for if this is lacking, the other factors do not interest the purchaser. Obviously, a product may be of good, sound quality and yet be inexpensive, while a similar product of better quality will be more costly. In both cases the purchaser gets his money's worth. It is value the purchaser looks for when he buys a product. Value is quality in relation to price.

Naturally the question of determining the quality of a product presents some difficulties unless samples are available. It is important for the buyer to know the product he purchases by actual taste. Comparative qualities can be determined only by comparative tastings. It is important that the salesman, whether wholesale or retail, be sold on a product himself before he can sell it to someone else.

For instance, if two whiskies are under consideration and the price of one is 25 per cent more than the other, the buyer must be satisfied that it is at least 25 per cent better in quality, or the values will not be equal. When quality and price are equal, the intangibles enter the picture. For example, if similar products of similar value at a similar price are offered for sale by different houses, the one which gives the best service will usually get the order.

While the foregoing applies to trade buyers, it is equally important that the consumer or non-licensee purchaser should also sample, in making a quantity purchase of a given type of beverage. In most states, however,

399

sampling in a retail store is not permitted by the regulations. It is wise, in this case, to follow the wine merchant's suggestions on one or two brands and purchase a bottle of each. After tasting them, the purchaser can determine which he prefers in quality, and rate its value in relation to its price.

DISTRIBUTOR'S SALES REPRESENTATIVE

THE sales representative of the distributor or wholesaler is important to the retail trade buyer because he brings information of constant market changes; he can provide merchandising ideas and can render many little services that make the buyer's life an easier one than it might otherwise be.

Of course, the sales representative who approaches his work with an attitude of being eager to render every reasonable service and assistance to his customer will find that the relationship will be a pleasant one of mutual confidence with profit to both. The greatest help a sales representative can give his customer is accurate, honest information about the products he is offering.

The F.A.A. and State A.B.C. Board regulations state very specifically what services a wholesaler is forbidden by law to render to a retail establishment. There are many such prohibitions but they are all designed with one broad principle in mind—to prevent offering inducements to the retailer to use a specific brand to the detriment of competing brands.

The salesman, in offering his brands, should use all the information he has about their quality and usefulness, but he should not disparage his competitor or his brands. This is bad salesmanship. It is always wise to remember that brands which have been selling successfully for generations have stayed on the market because the public has found them satisfactory. The salesman who bases his selling talk on the premise that the public does not know what it is buying is in for a sad awakening.

INVENTORY AND THE ECONOMICS OF TURN-OVER

To operate successfully, a business establishment should have a variety and quantity of stock sufficient to meet all its normal needs. The amounts which must be kept in stock are governed by the nearness of the source of supply. If it is in the same city, and an order can be filled within the day, there is no point in carrying a very large stock. On the other hand, the farther away the source of supply, the greater must be the reserve stock to protect the business from losses due to lack of stock.

During periods when freight, insurance, and costs are likely to rise, it is good business to increase the stock of items affected by conditions substantially beyond normal, as such purchasing and loading of the inventory is not a risky speculation.

A seven to ten time inventory turn-over is considered normal business practice. That is, if the stock required to handle normal business is $20,000, the annual purchases should total $140,000, or a stock turn-over seven times during the year. A slower turn-over means either that the establishment is over-stocked or that something should be done to stimulate more business.

A careful analysis of sales, and perpetual inventory will soon indicate which types and brands of merchandise move most freely and which are dead stock. With the exception of rare, fine-quality, high-priced brands on which a rapid turn-over is not expected (but which may be compensated for by a larger profit), slow-moving brands or items should be culled out of the stock.

A profit is obtained on a given brand of merchandise only when it is sold. Bottles standing on the shelf or lying in a cellar bin cost money. They represent an investment, and unless the merchandise moves, it is costing at least or more than 6 per cent per annum on the purchase price, plus overhead.

Purchasing, therefore, is closely related to merchandising. Buying must always be done in proportion to the establishment's ability to sell. Where savings can be effected by quantity purchases and by cash discounts, it is elementary to avail oneself of the lower price, but if it takes six months to a year to sell a lot so purchased the saving should be greater than the cost of carrying, or there is little advantage in the quantity purchase, and a portion of working capital has been tied up in "dead" stock.

The proper stock for a store, restaurant, or distributor's cellar or warehouse depends entirely on the market that it serves. In the East, for example, the public prefers Blends and Scotch whiskies, while throughout the Middle West, South, and Southwest the public prefers Bourbon.

It is good merchandising to have as complete and varied an assortment on hand as is commensurate with good business practice, as this will make customers feel that they can obtain anything they need. It is impossible, of course, for either a retail or wholesale outlet to carry every brand. A fairly complete assortment of types is possible, however, without too great an investment.

CONSUMER PURCHASING

QUALITY should always be the first consideration—with the consumer as well as with the wholesaler and retailer—although its relation to price and value should not be overlooked.

The most satisfactory system for the consumer who has not had an opportunity to taste many of the products available is to find a supplier in whom he has confidence and ask for his advice. The customer will usually find that it is both sound and helpful. In time each individual discovers, by actual tasting, which products and brands he prefers.

While, in the long run, the contents of a bottle is more important than the label, it must not be forgotten that the brand is important. Any brand which has been marketed successfully for generations—and sometimes for centuries—has maintained its popularity because its quality is satisfactory. People do not continue to accept famous brands because of their reputation and advertising; they continue to buy because of the consistent quality maintained by these brands. The moment quality is lowered, the public turns away.

In purchasing spirits, there is little advantage in stocking more than necessary requirements, as they do not gain in value or in quality after they have been bottled. The only exceptions are very rare old brandies, whiskies, or rums of which only limited supplies are available at any time, and when there is a possibility of a shortage.

There is a different story where wines are concerned. Light beverage wines and Champagnes, being living things, do change, improve, and, in the case of very fine wines, increase in value with time (when properly stored and cared for) and therefore they are worth purchasing with a view to future use.

In general we would recommend allowing light wines several days of rest after receipt before serving. In other words, do not buy a bottle of wine this afternoon to serve for tonight's dinner. If the wine has any deposit, it will be stirred up, giving the wine an unattractive, dull appearance. When possible, do not buy fine wines from hand to mouth. Some of the sturdier wines do not need all this care, but it is safer to err on the side of too much care than to handle wines carelessly.

When preparing to entertain, whether at a cocktail party, reception, or dinner, it is advisable to figure out in advance the quantities of beverages needed. Every host wishes to make sure that his guests have as much as they wish. It is difficult to predict accurately the guests' thirst, but in general it may be said to approximate two drinks per person if the party lasts two hours, and three if it lasts three or four hours. If an allowance of an extra half drink per person is made, there should be no shortage.

The preferences of the guests should govern the class of beverages served. There must be enough mineral water on hand for highballs, lemons and limes for cocktails, and so forth, to take care of the estimated needs. Spirits and fortified wines do not spoil, so a few extra bottles may be purchased as a precaution against a shortage.

To serve as a guide in calculating the number of bottles needed to entertain eight, twenty, or one hundred guests, the following chart has been prepared:

HOW MANY PORTIONS?

PRODUCT	BOTTLE CONTENT	AVERAGE PORTION	NO. OF PORTIONS
Bordeaux wine	24.0 oz.	4 oz.	6
Burgundy wine	24.0 oz.	4 oz.	6
Rhine, Moselle, and Alsatian	23.0 oz.	4 oz.	6
Chianti (flask)	32.0 oz.	4 oz.	8

PRODUCT	BOTTLE CONTENT	AVERAGE PORTION	NO. OF PORTIONS
Champagne	26.0 oz.	4 oz.	6
Sherry, Port, and Madeira	24.0 oz.	2 oz.	12
Vermouth	30.5 oz.	1 oz.	30½
Cognac and brandies	25.6 oz.	1 oz.	25°
Scotch and Irish whiskies	25.6 oz.	1½ oz.	17
Rye‡ and Bourbon whiskies	32.0 oz.	1½ oz.	21
Gins.	32.0 oz.	1½ oz.†	21
Rums	25.6 oz.	2 oz.	12½
Liqueurs	23 to 25.6 oz.	¾ oz.	32
Mixers: water or ginger ale.	32.0 oz.	4 oz.	8
Beer on draft (in kegs)	15.5 gals	8 oz.	250

° Allowance for spillage.

† In a Tom Collins the portion is 2 oz.

‡ The term "Rye" is employed here to describe Canadian Whisky or American Blended Whiskey.

In estimating the wine needed for a dinner party, the following should serve as a guide:

> If one wine is served, 2 glasses (8 oz.) per person
> If two wines are served, 1 glass (4 oz.) of each per person
> If three wines are served, 1 glass (4 oz.) of each per person

Have a reserve of one-half glass per person in case a given wine pleases and the guests wish more.

When Sherry, Madeira, or Champagne is served as an apéritif before the meal, 1½ glasses per person.

WHAT THE CELLAR SHOULD CONTAIN

WHEN one is limited by space or inclination to an inexpensive cellar, it is better to have a small compact assortment of wines and spirits, which provides a sufficient quantity of a given product, rather than a wide assortment of single bottles.

The "cellars" suggested on the following pages can only serve as a guide. Personal taste should govern the selection. However, the only reason for cellaring these products is to have them readily available for serving, both for your own or your guests' enjoyment. Do not buy and store away wines and spirits just to hide them away. Wines will eventually become senile and die and spirits in bottles do not improve. The pleasure in these beverages can only be enjoyed through their consumption.

A BEGINNER'S CELLAR

6 bottles California or American red and white table wine, assorted

6 bottles, French, German, Italian, or Chilean table wine, red and white assorted

2 bottles Champagne

1 bottle Sherry—medium dry

2 bottles whiskey—Rye, Bourbon, or Canadian

2 bottles Scotch whisky

1 bottle Rum—Puerto Rican

2 bottles Gin

2 bottles Vodka

1 bottle dry Vermouth

1 bottle sweet Vermouth

2 half-bottles liqueurs

1 bottle Aromatic Bitters

AN AMATEUR'S CELLAR

If one has twice as much to invest, a wider assortment is possible. Quantities can also be increased. For example, one can include not only California, but American table wines, and several different imported wines of each of the wine regions mentioned above. Additions to the list can include:

Cognac

Jamaica or Demerara rum

Madeira

Port

Sparkling Burgundy

A wider assortment of liqueurs

AN ADVENTURER'S CELLAR

For one who has a real use for the bins and shelves he has put up in the closet, which is the "cellar," and enjoys a variety to please all tastes, this assortment should fill the bill, and, to quote from New York's R. H. Macy & Company's advertisement: "will open a whole new world of taste adventure to you."

6 bottles California red table wine

6 bottles American white table wine

6 bottles Chilean wine—Burgundy and Riesling

12 bottles Bordeaux district Claret

6 bottles of a château-bottled Claret (Latour, Margaux, Mouton, etc.)

3 bottles Canadian whisky

6 bottles Scotch whisky

3 bottles Vodka

4 bottles Gin

3 bottles Cognac

3 bottles dry Rum

6 bottles Italian wine— red and white

3 bottles Rioja wine—red

2 bottles Port

1 bottle Madeira

3 bottles dry Vermouth

3 bottles sweet Vermouth

6 bottles American whiskies

1 bottle Aromatic Bitters

6 bottles Sauternes

6 bottles Pommard or another red Burgundy

6 bottles Chablis

6 bottles Rhine or Moselle wine

6 bottles Vin Rosé

AN ADVENTURER'S CELLAR (cont.)

2 bottles Jamaica rum
1 bottle Apple Jack
1 bottle Bénédictine
1 bottle Cointreau or Triple Sec
1 bottle Tequila

6 bottles Champagne
6 bottles Sherry—dry and medium dry

3 bottles Cherry or other fruit wine

A GOURMET'S CELLAR

The gourmet is desirous not only of enjoying the very finest himself, but of sharing it with his friends. He can stock his "cellar" with the assortment suggested below, or vary it as his "tasting" experience dictates. In either case he and his friends should derive much enjoyment in drinking any of these beverages:

12 bottles California Claret or Zinfandel
12 bottles California Riesling
6 bottles California Sauterne
6 bottles American Sauterne
12 bottles Chilean Burgundy
12 bottles Chilean Riesling
12 bottles St. Julien or Margaux
24 bottles château-bottled Clarets, assorted as to wines and vintages (Châteaux Latour, Lafite, Mouton, Cos d'Estournel, Ausone, Cheval Blanc, etc.)
12 bottles château-bottled white Graves
6 bottles Sauternes (Châteaux Yquem, La Tour Blanche or Coutet)
12 bottles Mâcon or Beaujolais
12 bottles Chambertin or Clos de Vougeot
6 bottles Montrachet or Meursault
6 bottles Cognac—3-star quality
3 bottles Cognac—VSOP quality
6 bottles Puerto Rican rum
3 bottles Jamaica or other full-flavored rum
3 bottles Apple Jack

12 bottles Vin rosé
12 bottles Alsatian wine
12 bottles Chablis or Pouilly Fuissé
12 bottles Moselle wine
12 bottles Rioja
12 bottles Rhine wine
12 bottles Chianti or Valpolicella
12 bottles non-vintage Champagne
12 bottles vintage Champagne
6 bottles Cherry or other fruit wine
6 bottles Sherry—dry and medium dry
6 bottles Tawny Port
2 bottles Boal or Malmsey Madeira
4 bottles Apéritif wine (Dubonnet, Raphaël or Lillet or Byrrh)
4 bottles French Vermouth
4 bottles Italian Vermouth
6 bottles Scotch whisky
8 bottles blended American whiskey (for mixed drinks)
6 bottles Bonded whiskey
6 bottles Canadian whisky
8 bottles Gin
6 bottles Vodka

A GOURMET'S CELLAR (cont.)

6–8 bottles assorted liqueurs, such as Apricot, Bénédictine, Chartreuse, Cointreau or Triple Sec, Crème de Menthe, Kümmel, etc.

1 bottle Aromatic Bitters, Angostura or Abbotts

3 bottles Akvavit

2 bottles Kirsch

3 bottles Tequila

1 bottle Orange Bitters

1 case Beer

1 case Ale

12 bottles Stout

The foregoing are only the suggestions we offer as a beginning, but the Gourmet's Cellar can be varied and expanded as much as the gourmet's taste and pocket book wish to extend it. It can include many of the finer wines, some in Magnums, both table wines and Champagne, and increased quantities of the less costly wines, as well as a supply of older spirits. The selection can be modified considerably, to include the twelve-year-old Scotch whisky quality, Armagnac, etc., some of the rare Rhines and Moselles and some of the other very interesting Italian table wines.

There is one recommendation we wish to make with regard to building up a private cellar. Please do not purchase wines or spirits merely for the sake of collecting and storing them away. Wines, spirits, and beers are produced for only one purpose, and that is to be drunk, thereby giving pleasure, enjoyment and satisfaction to the appreciative consumer of them. Buy them, buy them generously, so that you may enjoy them generously with your guests. We make the admonition because on more than one occasion we have had the sad experience of having to appraise cellars filled with wines that bore magnificent names and vintages, but which had been hidden away and perhaps forgotten until, when we examined them, they were finished and worthless, no longer capable of giving enjoyment and fulfilling their reason for being.

As a final observation, we suggest the purchase of only young vintages of white table wines, rosé wines, and Beaujolais. They are at their best, most attractive, and most enjoyable while they possess the fresh fruity charm of youth. This also means you should drink them young. You may find them disappointing if you keep them four or five years. Of course, there are exceptions.

The sweeter-tasting white table wines such as Sauternes, *spätlese, auslese* and even richer *eiswein* and *trockenbeerenauslese* German wines of the Moselle, Rhine, and Franconia districts can be quite long lived. We have enjoyed and found such wines magnificent after forty years in the bottle. This does not mean that all such rich, white table wines will always last so long. They, like all white wines, tend to maderization with time, but when they are good, they can be extraordinarily good.

31. *Merchandising*

THE principles of successful promotional selling are fundamental. When the public clamors for a particular brand it is usually not only a good product but one that has been intelligently and aggressively merchandised. In our own field the brands most in demand are those that are most widely advertised and intensively merchandised.

The first important consideration is the salesman. Everyone engaged in the wine and spirit trade, whether producer, distributor, retailer, or owner of a restaurant, is necessarily a salesman. The whole object of producing, distributing, or selling these products is to make a profit from them. No one can sell anything about which he knows nothing. The more the salesman knows about the product he is selling, the more successfully he will sell it.

Therefore, it is basic that the members of the sales staff, from the president through the newest salesman down to the telephone operator, who very often takes orders and answers questions, should know as much as possible about the wines, spirits, or beers, their uses and service which they are selling.

RESTAURANT MERCHANDISING

ATMOSPHERE, that intangible, inexplicable something, is the secret of success in some establishments, and its lack is the reason for the failure of others.

We are convinced that if conditions are favorable, if the food is good, the price of the beverages is reasonable, and an effort is made to sell them, the public will buy wine or other beverages when it dines out. It will do this because in the proper atmosphere wine is enjoyed with well-cooked, well-presented meals.

However, after more than a quarter of a century since the Prohibition Amendment to the Constitution was repealed in 1933, the sale of wines (especially), spirits, and beers decreased in public dining places in relation to beverage consumption in the home. Prior to World War II home consumption of alcoholic beverages was some 35 to 40 per cent of total consumption.

407

Today it is exactly the reverse, and in the case of table wines, home consumption is about 90 per cent.

What is the reason for this? The primary reason, in our opinion, is inertia on the part of management . . . a lack of merchandising effort . . . a lazy readiness to accept what the guest orders without even letting him know what is available.

We have never been able to understand why American restaurants work so hard at selling ice water. The moment a guest is seated, a bus boy fills his glass, usually overflowingly, with ice and water . . . and until he leaves, that bus boy sees to it that the glass is never empty. The average cost of this "service" (established by the principal hotel accounting firms of the United States is ten to twelve cents per guest. This is a beverage that produces no revenue or profit. On the other hand, the nearest the restaurant comes to "selling" profitable beverages is "Do you wish a cocktail?"—or "Do you want your coffee now or later?"

Another sales deterrent is over-pricing. That is, in far too many cases wine sales in a restaurant are discouraged by prices which are unrealistic. A study of wine lists and menus from various cities—both large and small—indicates that the ratio of prices of wine vary from the cost of the lowest table d'hôte meal up to 100 or 150 per cent of the highest priced meal. A wine to match the price of the least expensive meal is not a bad starting point. From this point, it is possible to sell up . . . but remember one very important fact; wine is the only item restaurants list that is sold in its original package. It is the item which the patron can most easily relate to a store retail price. While he is willing to pay for service and surroundings, he is not prepared— nor should he be expected—to pay an excessively high premium. Most people resent any pricing that appears to "gouge them." The average patron can be persuaded to enjoy good wines with his dinner if the price is not prohibitive.

Generally, the markup of 100 per cent on a premium quality wine yields the restaurateur a fine profit and is still acceptable to the patron. However, we suggest the "cost plus" system is well worth looking into.

The chart illustrates, for a given cost of a bottle of wine (Column A), the retail store selling price, figuring the usual 50 per cent markup taken by the retail wine merchant (Column B). Columns C and D show the restaurant selling prices based on straight percentage markups of 100 and 150, respectively.

Possibly the best way to price wine is to employ the "cost-plus" system. A restaurant, of course, has certain overhead fixed costs for wine service—use of glassware, depreciation of stock, etc. Let us assume, for example, that these costs are adequately covered by a flat charge of $1.00 per bottle. Now take a look at Columns E and F where $33\frac{1}{3}$ and 50 percent markups are applied, plus a dollar per bottle for fixed expense. By following either of these pricings, higher priced wine such as Champagne can be offered at a more reasonable

Per Bottle Costs and Selling Prices

A	B	C	D	E°	F
	Retail			50%	100%
	Store			+	+
Cost	Price	150%	200%	1.00	1.00
$1.00	$1.50	2.50	3.00	2.50	3.00
1.50	2.25	3.75	4.50	3.25	4.00
2.00	3.00	5.00	6.00	4.00	5.00
2.50	3.75	6.25	7.50	4.75	6.00
3.00	4.50	7.50	9.00	5.50	7.00
3.50	5.25	8.75	10.50	6.25	8.00
4.00	6.00	10.00	12.00	7.00	9.00
4.50	6.75	11.25	13.50	7.75	10.00
5.00	7.50	12.50	15.00	8.50	11.00

° Adjusted to next highest 25 cents.

price and therefore increase sales and increase total profits. If restaurants have wines and are not selling them, the investment in time, space, and money is not paying off. The sale of a bottle of wine with a dinner or a luncheon can yield the restaurateur more solid net profit than the food itself.

How is the restaurant owner going to sell beverages? This is a serious problem, for obviously it is difficult to get the sales staff to learn about something in which they are not interested. How can the interest of the sales staff be aroused so that every member will want to know more about wines and liquors? The answer is—money.

As an object lesson, take two dinner checks as an exhibit. Check A represented a dinner for two people, a man and a girl. The check amounted to $7.50. The tip was $1. Now here is Check B. Another couple. They had cocktails and a half bottle of wine. The check amounted to $13.50. The tip was $2.

Any experienced waiter understands this language, and we recommend to the restaurateurs that this exhibit be duplicated in their own restaurants. It packs a wallop!

The couple that had wine with their dinner enjoyed it, and will remember it as an event to be repeated; the waiter was happier because he made a larger tip; and the restaurant owner made a greater profit through the sale of the beverages.

Of course, before waiters can sell wines, they must be familiar with what they are selling. Here are a few points that they should learn.

1. The first thing to learn is exactly what wines and spirits the restaurant has to offer.

2. They must know which of these are red and which white, and which are dry or sweet.

3. They must know which of the wines are light beverage wines such as Claret, Sauternes, Burgundy, Rhine, and Moselle wines, and so forth; which are sparkling wines such as Champagnes and Sparkling Burgundies, and which are fortified wines such as Sherry, Porto, Madeira.

4. They must know which wines should be chilled and which should be served at room temperature.

5. They should know with what dishes to suggest the various wines they are selling.

6. When they do sell a bottle of wine, they should know the correct manner of presenting, opening, and serving the wine—described in Chapter 29. In this connection, we would like to point out that too frequently wine is casually or sloppily or incorrectly served. While a great deal of absurd ritual has grown up about the serving of wines and spirits, to which we are opposed, it is certainly necessary that a hotel, restaurant, or club know the correct procedure in presenting, opening, and serving wine, simply because it is shrewd sales psychology. There is always a little glamor about ordering wine. Play it up—it flatters the customer.

When the order for wine is taken, the waiter should bring the bottle to the table and present it to the host who has ordered. After the host has said, "Yes, that is the wine I want," it should be opened and served before the food. Then, by all means, leave the bottle on the table where the rest of the diners can see it.

Why? Because people are naturally imitative. Smith and Jones who never bought wine in the restaurant begin to notice first one and then several bottles appearing on the tables of other diners. It will not be long before they too decide that they might as well try it.

These are the bare essentials that a good staff should know in order to sell wines. Any additional information that can be given them will help. No one can expect a staff to learn this overnight. The best way to equip them is to have a weekly class, where these things are explained to them repeatedly until they are thoroughly versed. When waiters are trained, they in turn will be better able to serve guests.

Now for a few practical selling ideas:

1. A good, well-rounded wine list, one that is suited to the needs of the establishment's clientele. Avoid repetition in listings. By this we mean one brand of Sauternes may be quite adequate. Describe each wine as to taste, in two or three words—especially the white wines, which vary greatly between sweet and dry. Often a wine list is placed on every table.

2. Augment the wine list with a listing or mention of wines on the food menu. An appropriate wine suggestion, printed next to the *plat du jour*, will sell lots of wine.

3. Make the wine accessible to serving personnel. Use displays and special bins near the dining area for red wines and a nearby cooler for pink wines, white wines, sparkling wines, and Champagnes.

4. Certain dishes have an affinity for definite beverages. For example, one way to pep up Porto sales is to offer a combination of cheese and Porto for one price. Beer goes well with dishes that have sauerkraut in combination. Offer them together.

5. Arrange a table at the entrance to the dining room with a few wines attractively displayed. This, in itself, suggests gracious dining, and it starts the guest thinking about wine before he is seated.

6. Menu tip-ons, table tents, and menu riders will sell wines, cocktails, cordials, and beer.

7. We are greatly in favor of using measuring cups when making cocktails. Then it makes very little difference which bartender prepares the cocktail. It will always be uniform. Specialize in two or three cocktails made better than others make them.

8. Place wine bottles, half-bottles, or splits (a small 6-ounce bottle which holds enough for two glasses) where customers can see them. It is suggested that actual bottles of wine rather than dummy bottles be placed on each table, for they are more attractive. Use attractive and descriptive price cards.

9. Feature seasonal drinks. Tie up holidays with beverage merchandising.

10. Finally, and most important, while the foregoing nine ideas will help, the actual sale must still be made by the person taking the food order. The wine must be suggested. The wine list or wine card should be presented at the moment the guest finishes ordering the food, and while he is psychologically in the ordering mood. It should be presented naturally, without fanfare, but as a matter of course, with a suggestion such as: "Would you like to *enjoy* a pleasant bottle of Riesling with the fish you have ordered?" In other words SUGGEST wine. You will be surprised by the number of sales.

From experience we know that the best advertisement for wine is the wine itself. We have long maintained that if the wine trade could distribute samples, as the food and cigarette people do, our country would be a wine-drinking nation almost overnight. This is not possible for economic and other reasons.

The closest approach to this is the split. The split can be sold very inexpensively and makes it possible for the person who has never tasted a certain wine to do so without risking too great a sum. It is really a sample size. Actually in tests conducted by leading wine distributors, when splits and half-bottles were featured, the sale of the large bottles of the same wines increased, because the splits perform their "sample" function perfectly.

Another way to promote wine sales, which has been used successfully, is the small 6- to 8-ounce decanters, which perform the same function as the split. In our opinion, the use of the split is better merchandising, because the actual bottle is brought to the customer and he is able to see the label and appearance of the bottle, whereas, with the use of the decanter, he cannot do this.

Splits and half bottles have been merchandised with equal success in retail (off-premise) stores and produced repeat sales of regular size bottles.

Wine sales are best where *all* waiters or waitresses suggest and serve wine to customers. However, for added showmanship, some leading hotels and restaurants like to designate one man to specialize in the sale and service of wine, paying him a commission on the wine he sells. Usually, for practical purposes, this man is simply called "the wine waiter," and his uniform need differ only in color from that of the other waiters. His knowledge of wine types and uses can be acquired by any experienced waiter with a little extra training and inducement from the management. (In turn, he can then aid the

A suitable display for either a liquor store or restaurant. (Courtesy Liquor Store Magazine)

management in training other waiters in wine uses.) Since he is a wine salesman, it is important that the wine waiter have a pleasant personality and the ability to sell without high-pressure tactics.

There is another, more traditional type of wine waiter known as the "sommelier," preferred by a few hotels that want the maximum in wine showmanship. The sommelier is more of a true wine expert, by custom, and he wears a leather cellar apron and a silver chain, with a tasting cup and a medallion or giant key attached. This costume is available from some restaurant supply firms.

It should be emphasized that neither the wine waiter nor the true sommelier is necessary to a profitable wine-selling program, if the regular waiters or waitresses are properly trained. Where a wine specialist is used, however, he can still work hand-in-hand with the regular waiter, and both benefit from the wine sale: one from his wine commission, one from his increased tip. In such an operation, the regular waiter finds out quickly in taking the food order whether the customer likes the idea of wine with dinner. He then summons the wine waiter or sommelier to the table. The latter presents the wine list, suggests a specific type and brand, brings the wine promptly, and serves it. The wine price is added to the regular food check.

An important factor in any merchandising policy is maintenance of a uniform and constant source of supply. The standard quality merchandise should be available to customers at all times. Bargains and close-outs do not build permanent trade. The customer who is pleased by a wine or spirit wants the same quality when he comes back a second time. If he is shifted from one brand or one quality to another, he will lose confidence in the establishment. This is a basic point, applying with equal force to restaurants and to retail establishments, and it should be stressed by the distributor's salesman.

STORE MERCHANDISING AND ADVERTISING

To sell you must tell. This may be accomplished by various methods:
1. In personal conversation with a customer.
2. By display of the merchandise both in the store and in the windows.
3. By the written word in a letter.
4. By the written message in a newspaper or magazine advertisement.
5. By broadcasting the message over the radio.
6. By catalogs and price lists.

The ideal method, of course, is personal discussion with the prospective customer, so that the salesman may use arguments and counter-arguments, answer questions, and render service in the most complete fashion. This method is necessarily limited to the number of people who enter the establishment because of a specific need for merchandise.

However, when a customer does come into an establishment, half of the selling problem has been solved because the customer has come to buy. The other half of the problem is to have the salesman serve his needs if they are specific, or to offer helpful suggestions if he is not certain of what he wishes to purchase. In direct personal selling, even if the customer knows exactly what he wants, the wide-awake merchant can find out by adroit questioning or conversation how the customer plans to use the beverage he contemplates buying and base his selling on this information.

For example, if the merchandise is intended for a party, the merchant can advise the customer as to the quantities he will require for the number of guests he expects to entertain. If it is for daily use, he will be able to tell whether he should buy in half-bottle, bottle, or gallon sizes, depending on the size of the customer's family.

The customer can be told that white wine, after opening, may be kept in the refrigerator, if promptly recorked, and will not spoil for a week or ten days, while red wine, if tightly recorked after opening, will keep almost as long. Champagne and sparkling wines must be consumed when they are opened as they cannot be recorked and will lose their effervescence in a few hours. There are special gadgets which may be purchased whereby the sparkling wine may be drawn off through a miniature spigot without losing all the gas. These are all right in the sick room where small quantities from a bottle are to be used several times a day. However, they are not recommended where the wine is to be kept for several days after drawing the first glass.

Desirable as personal contact with prospective customers is, the scope of such personal contact is limited, and therefore other media are useful and, when properly employed, are profitable. Advertising reaches a far greater audience than anyone could personally, and every advertisement should convey the personality of a store and reflect its character.

What sort of trade does the establishment wish to attract? Are low prices, or special offerings, or a complete range from low priced to the finest quality products to be featured? Even if all three types of merchandise are stocked, start with one and feature it above the others.

Once store policy is decided, select the medium best-suited to reach the widest audience: local magazines, club magazines, fraternal publications, newspapers, local radio stations, or direct mail. First, of course, determine what audience these vehicles reach and which audience contains the largest proportion of potential customers. Check this against the cost of the medium chosen, to determine the most profitable field.

An advertising policy is now established and the medium in which it is to be publicized is decided on. The advertisement must be a projection of the character and personality of the establishment. All advertising has a cumulative effect, and therefore repetition will, in time, produce the wanted sales.

It is advisable to find some merchandising device—a slogan, an illustration, a crest, or the store name—which will always associate the advertisement with the store at first glance.

Feature your merchandise in the advertisement or simply the enjoyment which the purchaser will derive from using it. Perhaps the selling point is a very convenient location, or a fine telephone and delivery service, or perhaps the store has specialized in certain types of beverages or sizes of packages. If so, feature these points.

This is known as "institutional" advertising—that is, selling primarily the store name, its policies, and its services to the public rather than employing the "special offering" form of advertisement, where the primary attraction is price.

direct mail

Direct solicitation by means of a convincingly worded letter has many advantages, although it is one of the more costly methods of advertising. Its principal advantage is that the list of names to which a letter is addressed is made up either of customers who have actually effected purchases in the store, or of those believed to be consumers of alcoholic beverages. The best feature of this audience is its selectivity. Naturally the productiveness of this form of advertising will only be as good as the list itself. In view of this fact, and considering the cost of mailing, it should be immediately apparent that a constant check of the list must be maintained and dead wood culled from it.

Neighborhood stores in residence sections often find that the family butler or chauffeur is charged with the duty of purchasing the alcoholic beverages. As the employees become the actual buyers, it will often be found that by gaining their confidence they will bring business from other families whose purchases are made in the same manner.

newspapers

An important consideration in newspaper advertising is deciding on the right spot for the advertisement. There are society and women's pages, sport pages (read mainly by men), and general news sections. Specify on the order in what part of the paper your ad is to appear. The society page and pages 2, 3, and 4 are generally considered premium spots, and cost more than the general run of the paper. Some dealers prefer to specify these preferred positions, paying the extra rate, as a small advertisement so placed will often be more productive than a larger one in another spot. Try this by test.

The advertisement should be timed in accordance with the buying habits of the public. It is a sound idea to place institutional advertising in the paper on those days when it will have the least competition and therefore greater visibility—generally at the beginning of the week.

catalogs and price lists

The primary object of a catalog or price list is to inform the customer of the products stocked and the price at which they are sold. Price lists fall into two classes—a general catalog listing every item in the inventory, and condensed special offerings of specific products or groups of products.

The general price list or catalog should be designed to have a certain length of life and, in addition to the prices and the list of products, it should contain information that is useful to the customer, such as cocktail recipes, punch recipes, uses of the wines and spirits, and other general information. The more useful this information is to the customer, the longer he will keep the catalog, the more often he will refer to it and be reminded of the name of the store and its products.

special offerings The special offering should state clearly that it is for a limited time only. Its object is to stimulate quick sales. It should therefore be concise, direct, exciting, and dramatic.

These points may be accomplished in several ways. If a lower price than normal is offered, show the regular price and indicate the saving involved.

If it is a new product, describe it briefly.

If it is a seasonal or holiday offering, an illustration or a short paragraph about the seasonal use of the products may be utilized effectively.

The main point to bear in mind is that to be effective, the special offering price list must have a compelling appeal to make people buy at once, to take advantage of a special opportunity.

radio Federal and State regulations cover what can and cannot be said in radio and television advertising. In most states wine and beer may be advertised, while in some states distilled spirits may not be so advertised.

There are a number of different methods of using radio time, such as: one-minute spot announcements; five-minute spots (such as news broadcasts); 10- and 15-minute sustaining spots. Many local radio stations also have what they call "perpetuating" shows, in which the names of different advertisers and their offerings are mentioned from time to time.

importance of window displays Every window display should be designed to be an "interrupting factor" to the eye of the passerby. What will accomplish this? Certainly not a display of standard merchandise with standard prices arranged in rows or even helter skelter. Arrange a window so that attention is focused on *some one thing*. That may be an item of merchandise, or it may be some related subject, a well-set table, for instance, which indicates how a beverage can be used.

ideas 1. A bottle of Rock and Rye, a pair of rubbers, and an umbrella.

2. A brilliant scarlet riding coat, a pair of boots, a riding crop—and a punch bowl and glasses—bottles of Bourbon whiskey and Jamaica rum, and the ingredients for several different punches.

3. A casserole, a chicken (artificial), a bottle of Claret, a chafing dish— pancakes, bottles of brandy and Triple Sec for the sauce.

We feature fine wine.

Lillet Blanc   Mateus Rosé

JUGTOWN MOUNTAIN SMOKEHOUSE

WINE AND FOODS OF ALL NATIONS
FROM THE CORNERS OF THE EARTH

77 Park Ave. Flemington, N.J. • Reply to:
PO Box 366 Flemington, N.J. 08822 • Lord
& Taylor Center Eastchester, N.Y. • The
Fashion Center Paramus, N.J. • The Mall
Short Hills, N.J. • Route 202 Morristown,
N.J. • Route 202 Flemington, N.J.

Our fine wine double feature.

Valckenberg   Krug Reims
Madonna

JUGTOWN MOUNTAIN SMOKEHOUSE

WINE AND FOODS OF ALL NATIONS
FROM THE CORNERS OF THE EARTH

77 Park Ave. Flemington, N.J. • Reply to:
PO Box 366 Flemington, N.J. 08822 • Lord
& Taylor Center Eastchester, N.Y. • The
Fashion Center Paramus, N.J. • The Mall
Short Hills, N.J. • Route 202 Morristown,
N.J. • Route 202 Flemington, N.J.

LEFT. Ads of small wine firm.

WHY NOT A LIBRARY OF WINE FOR CHRISTMAS?

If you have someone on your gift list
who considers a good wine at dinner part
of the good life, why not give them a start
on a library of wine? The expert
in the Wine Cellar is a master librarian.
One he might choose — the host and
hostess choice, for the interested
young moderns, a well-balanced
combination of 12 bottles of fine wines
in a 13" x 17" hardwood and brass
wine rack. 29.95.
Others: the connoisseur's
selection, 49.95; the round-the-world
collection, a superior selection of 48
of the world's most distinguished wines
in a hand-crafted and polished
walnut wine rack, 340.00.

The Wine Cellar
at
NEIMAN-MARCUS

GOOD ADVERTISING

LEFT. *The Wine Cellar at Neiman-Marcus, Dallas, Texas promotes multiple sales with its "wine library" idea.*

BELOW. *This Longchamps ad has attracted more guests . . . and sold additional wine.*

Dinner without _wine_?   Never, says Longchamps.

The wine is free with dinner at Longchamps.

Win a bountiful Christmas basket! Entry blanks at all 9 Longchamps. (Giving a party?
Longchamps has charming banquet rooms and will arrange everything.) PL 9-2600.

ABOVE. *Dramatic mass window display of colorful Chianti flasks and other wine bottles at Berwick's Package Store, Worcester, Mass.* (Courtesy Liquor Store Magazine. Photo by Marvin Richmond)

BELOW. *Educational window display. Note the glasses containing botanicals used to flavor gin and the gin drink-recipe cards resting on the pedestals, at Louis M. Goldberg's store, New York.* (Courtesy Liquor Store Magazine)

4. A top hat, a pair of white gloves, and a cane—a bottle of Champagne and a couple of glasses.

Note: All of the objects used can be obtained from local merchants, who will be glad to lend them for display providing a credit card is placed in the window.

In states where standard merchandise is price-fixed, there is no advantage in a display of bottles with prices affixed, which are identical with competitors'; therefore, it is better merchandising to display fewer bottles, but arrange the display attractively, either with a quantity of a given item, with a picture background, or a seasonal motif with the merchandise of the season featured.

Were a person to be placed in a window under the direct rays of the sun, *warning!* he would get sunburned and possibly sun-struck. Wine, like any other living thing, is also affected by too much light. Wherever possible, use dummy bottles for window displays, and if they are unobtainable, have the awnings down so that the direct rays of the sun do not strike the beverage wines. They become "blind" or dull-looking, and lose their brilliance. The flavor of the wine is affected in the same manner—the wine becomes flattish in taste. Sparkling wine may become overheated and the bottle may burst.

Liqueurs which are artificially colored may change or lose their color if exposed too long to the sun. The afternoon sun is worse than that of the morning, because the actinic rays are stronger after midday.

This is partly the reason for colored glass being used in wine bottles. The dark green, brown, or black glass protects the wine against the light. However, the original reason for dark-colored glass in wine bottles was to hide the cloudy condition of the wines themselves.

Several effective merchandising principles should be considered. One *interior* well-recognized and highly productive principle is the "related sale," that *displays* is, grouping items in relation to each other. For example, cocktail ingredients, the wine for a meal, and the cordial or brandy to finish it, can make an attractive "island display" set in a central spot in the store to attract attention.

The grouping of a dozen half-bottles of wine of different types encourages a customer to buy a few bottles in order to find out which wine he likes best.

The intimate sale display, where merchandise is arranged helter-skelter in a basket so that the customers will not hesitate to pick up and examine a bottle, helps them to overcome the hesitancy they feel about disturbing a neatly arranged stack. It is always good sales psychology to let the customer hold and examine the bottle. Once he has it in his hand, his possessive instinct makes him want it.

Merchandise with which the customer is not familiar and which has a slow *shelf display* sale should be placed in the most prominent part of the store—in the front;

while the standard merchandise could be placed in the center or rear so as to draw the customer back into the store to see the island displays as well as the shelf merchandise.

"Signs," a great merchant once said, "are the tongues that speak best for a store." Put signs on floor stackings; put them on middle-of-the-floor and island displays; put them in the windows (but not directly *on* the windows); and use them as added tongues that tell the sale's story to the customer. They should tell more than just the price and should have a professional look. They can be done by the local sign painter. Keep them clean and neat. Throw away dirty or torn signs.

seasonal promotions   There is a holiday or a seasonal merchandising motif in nearly every month of the year, and these should be tied up with advertising and window displays.

The gift-giving holidays should be featured with the logical type of merchandise for the season or the holiday. Other holidays indicate weekend parties and entertaining. Stress these facts.

In the spring, rums and gins should be featured with the lighter wines.

In the summer, feature all beverages which may be used in preparing cooling drinks; also light white table wines.

In the fall, with approaching cold weather, whiskies, brandies, and fuller bodied wines should be brought forward.

Throughout the winter, the richer products will be more popular.

In May, begin pushing Champagne for the June weddings and the summer garden parties.

For the football season, feature whiskies and brandies.

At Christmas time, the peak selling season in the trade for the entire year, be sure to bring out the finest quality merchandise and the fancy packaged liqueurs. This is the best season for these products, because anyone giving wines and spirits as a gift wants to feel he is making a gift of something that is not only fine, but that will give pleasure and enjoyment to the recipient.

New Year's is the Champagne season for that is the time when everyone wants to celebrate.

sales   Special offerings of slow-moving merchandise help in getting an inventory turn-over.

Keep duplicates of sales slips and, at the end of each month or at the end of six months, find out how many customers bought two bottles of an item, and how many were pint buyers. From these sales slips can be determined the buying habits of customers. If it is found that a goodly portion of them are multiple buyers, try the device which has proven so successful in certain large stores of offering a small discount over the one bottle price in lots of three bottles. Customers who are constant group bottle buyers may be interested in buying a case of the same item if they can save something thereby.

Naturally this cannot apply to price-fixed merchandise, but many shops carry their own brand of merchandise on which they can give a discount for bulk orders.

Study the habits of customers. Feature the items which have seasonal buying appeal.

ABOVE. *Center of store self-service island used to display wine and other beverages in special prices. The motif of this store is of the circa 1901.* (Courtesy Liquor Store Magazine)

BELOW. *Elegant interior decor and layout of Sherry-Lehmann, Inc. in New York, using island wheels to display wines.*

*how to sell
oneself
to one's
customers*

There is only one road to the goal of a flourishing neighborhood business, and that is confidence. The soundest way to establish confidence is by knowledge of the products, courtesy to customers, the quality and value of the merchandise stocked, and the service given. Added to this is personality, a great intangible. Some people have this faculty of approach, the ready smile, the confident air—others do not.

Before customers can be convinced that the merchant's advice is sound, that he is honest in his suggestions, he must know something about the products and how they should be used. Some customers want advice, others feel that they know more about it than the merchant does. Let them have their own way about it or they will go elsewhere.

Watch the daily announcements in the newspapers, and keep alert to the happenings in the lives of your neighborhood—the early bird will catch the worm every time. In the society page announcements there are most valuable leads for bulk sales. Not only large events, such as coming-out parties, engagements, weddings, and births, are cues but organization outings, conventions, and so forth.

All of the foregoing discussion of merchandising is as applicable to the producer's or distributor's salesman as it is to the retail trade.

The service which the salesman, calling on an account, can give to his customer will have a great deal to do with the volume of business the account will produce.

In addition to taking orders, the salesman can render many little services for his customers, such as helping to make up wine and price lists, giving the customer new display or advertising ideas, and new or varied factual information about the products he has sold to the customer. The salesman who brings a customer ideas which he can use profitably is the one who will get the bulk of the business.

WINE TASTINGS

ONE of the best methods of promoting wines for retail dealers, distributors, and producers is through a wine tasting. They are also an easy way to make a home gathering or party a success. Of course, the object of most "commercial" wine tastings is to present a range of wines in the most favorable manner, either to obtain sales or simply to teach more about wine.

According to Gordon Bass, who assisted us in preparing this section, the first point to decide is what type of tasting it is to be, what and how many wines are to be used, and how many people are likely to participate. As a rule, the seriousness and the effectiveness of a tasting are inversely proportionate to the number who attend.

A large, so-called "propaganda" tasting, with over fifty participants, usually requires a big space, a large staff, and very careful organization. Such tastings are usually planned to launch a new branded wine. They are generally confined to salesmen, their customers, and members of the press. At such affairs only a few specific wines are tasted.

The best number of tasters for a wine "lover's" gathering is from twenty to forty. The object here is to learn something about wine—of course, if some wine customers are made, all the better—and it is frequently given in a lecture form. In such cases, a minimum of six and a maximum of twelve carefully selected wines are usually used.

For home wine-tasting parties, five to eight different wines are usually sufficient. Sometimes each couple that attends the affair brings a different bottle of wine or brings a bottle of their favorite wine.

foods, glasses, and other accoutrements

Bland cheese and unsalted crackers are the recommended snacks for use at tastings. A pitcher of water, with tumblers, may be provided for mouth rinsing between tasting.

Buckets should be provided for undesired wines.

Have plenty of glasses on hand. They may be rented very reasonably. Fresh glasses should be freely available, ideally one per person per wine.

Candles add appropriate glamor to the occasion and provide a fine light to check the color of the wine.

Use a white tablecloth or oilcloth. White provides the best background for appreciating the color of the wine. Maps, posters, and literature on the regions of the wines being tasted will stimulate imaginations and conversations.

Have paper available to write notes. It is best to have wine-tasting lists printed (for a small party they may be typed). The list will contain the names of the wines to be tasted, numbered corresponding to the table or bottle numbers. In making such a listing, it is advisable to leave plenty of white space underneath each listing for the guests' written comments, which they should be encouraged to make. When the party is over, it will be interesting to have these comments compared.

Chairs, comfortable though they may be, tend to oppose the vital ingredient of a good tasting party, which is circulation. It is best not to have too many around, unless, of course, some elderly guests would clearly like them.

arrangement of wine tables

In general, the larger the room, the better to allow for free circulation of the guests. At large, professionally-run tastings, every table is numbered (1, 2, 3, etc.), carries its individual wine, and behind each table stands a waiter ready to serve. A wine-tasting folder or sheet, identifying each wine by its table number, is handed to each guest as he enters. He naturally follows the order of tasting, beginning at Table No. 1.

The illustration here shows an arrangement for the tasting of twelve wines with twenty guests around a ping-pong table participating. Ice buckets are

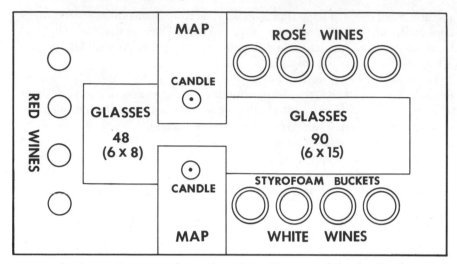

A wine tasting set-up for twelve wines. (Courtesy of Gordon Bass)

used to hold the four white wines and the four rosé wines. The two poster maps shown on the table in the drawing are of the region from which the wines came.

We have found it best to have the snacks—cheese or crackers—on their own table, removed from the wines, making it necessary for the guests to move about, going from the wines to the snacks, and vice versa. If the snacks are placed right next to the wines, little knots of tasters will gather at a particular table, nibbling snacks and tasting, without moving along but with impeding the general flow of traffic.

no smoking   Smoking is a perennial problem. Although smokers will assert they can taste as well while smoking as while not, this is not the case with nonsmokers, many of whom are uncomfortable trying to taste wines in a smoke-filled room. One suggestion would be to have a large ash tray on a table at the entrance to the tasting room, with the request to "drop cigarettes here." Another would be to have all other ash trays out of sight. If it is impossible to control the smokers, see that ventilation keeps the air reasonably free of smoke.

serving the tasters   In small gatherings, it should be made clear that the host, with an aid or two, perhaps some volunteers, does the pouring of the tasting samples, and *not* the guests themselves. There must be some organization in this affair; some control over what is served and how much. Line up the glasses for each wine and pour from 1 to $1\frac{1}{2}$ ounces in each glass for each taster. Later, when the guests have tasted them all, preferably a few times over, and have settled on their favorites, they may request a more generous allotment of the wines they most enjoyed; at this point, the purely educational aspects of the tasting party may be said to have ended and the social side to have begun. (When figuring the amount of wine needed, remember that a bottle holds about 25 ounces.)

The order of serving is as follows: dry before sweet . . . young before old . . . light before full bodied. Not necessarily red before white. A very young, red Beaujolais, for example, should precede a dignified, white Rheingau according to the suggestion "light before full bodied." These sequences should maximize the response to each individual wine.

Suggest to the guests that they should follow these simple steps in making their tasting, using the three senses:

Sight. The professional taster, as previously stated on page 16, judges a wine first by its color. Hold the glass to the light; note color brilliance, clarity. Is it bright and crystal clear? Is the color lively and typical of that particular wine?

Smell. Swirl the wine in the glass; sniff for aroma, bouquet. Is its odor engaging, appealing?

Taste. Sip the wine. Hold in the mouth for a moment, slowly rolling it around with the tongue. Note the pleasant tartness or richness; degree of sweetness, if any; body or consistency; distinctive flavor. Finally, swallow and enjoy the aftertaste. (The professional taster, with perhaps a hundred wines to evaluate in a day, spits out each mouthful, but that is neither necessary nor desirable at most parties.)

Encourage everyone to discuss the wines, compare their reactions to what they see, and smell as well as taste. It will help all to clarify and define responses.

tasting procedure

32. Storage and Cellar Treatment

THE care of wines, spirits, and beers is an important, but a fairly simple problem. In a commercial establishment, these beverages represent an investment on which a profit is expected, and they should be treated both with care and with regard for their perishable qualities. Just as a restaurant operator takes care to store dairy products, meats, and vegetables in a properly refrigerated room, so beverages must be carefully stored. While this applies more to beers and wines than it does to spirits, even the latter need to be safeguarded, preferably under lock and key, for otherwise the profits in them tend to "evaporate" mysteriously.

The main sources of potential harm to a wine are rapid temperature changes, bright light, and constant joggling. Some thought should be given to these factors in choosing a location for wine storage.

TEMPERATURE

THE cardinal requirement of a cellar or storage space where wines are to be kept for some time is an even temperature. The ideal is between 55° and 60° F., but five degrees higher or lower is not important if the temperature is kept constant and violent swings avoided. It is not advisable to store wine in a room where the temperature goes above 70° F.

The cellar should be kept absolutely clean to prevent the formation of mold and to keep it free of odors. Dampness should be guarded against so as to avoid cork mold and label discoloration.

Whether the "cellar" is below ground, or in the closet of an apartment, it should be dry and, if possible, ventilated. A damp cellar is not bad for storing wines, but it is difficult to keep clean. The cellar should be away from a heating plant or a hot-water unit.

426   Modern air-conditioning today makes possible ideal cellar conditions in any

RIGHT. *Ingenious merchandising. Each locked bin contains the private wine stock of a regular guest in the Pipkin at HCA's Royal Orleans Hotel, New Orleans, La.* (Courtesy The Royal Orleans Hotel)

BELOW. *Wine cellar and tasting room of Theodore Hutton's famous La Doña Luz Restaurant at Taos, New Mexico.* (Courtesy La Doña Luz Restaurant)

part of a building. We know of air-conditioned "cellars" five to eight stories above the ground where, by automatic temperature and humidity control, perfect cellar conditions are maintained throughout the year.

Large hotels and restaurants, selling a considerable amount of wine daily, find it economical to have special refrigerators in which the white and sparkling wines for daily use are kept at serving temperature. This ensures giving prompt service to guests. Such refrigerators are also useful for chilling large numbers of bottles for banquet service.

LIGHT

SUNLIGHT is an indispensable friend of the vine, but an implacable enemy of the wine it yields. Susceptibility of some wines to injury by light, as already stated, is the reason many wine bottles are of colored glass. Actually, all bright light is bad, and a wine cellar or storage location should be as dark as possible. No wine, of course, will be damaged by an hour or a day or even a week of any light except bright sunlight.

VIBRATION

CONSTANT vibrations can damage wine. For this reason, do not put wine bottles directly on the floor, but rather keep them on shelves or in racks that are free from vibration. If possible, locate the wine cellar far away from constant jarring machinery or the rumble of traffic.

MANNER OF STORING

LIGHT beverage and sparkling wines should always be stored on their sides in the bins so that the wine is in contact with the inner surface of the cork. This keeps the cork expanded, and prevents it from drying out. If the wine were stored upright and the cork dried out, air could seep through and spoil it. In the case of Champagne and sparkling wines, a dried-out cork permits the gas to escape, resulting in a "flat" wine.

Fortified wines, with the exception of Vintage Porto, are vigorous enough to have no fear of the air, and may be stored in an upright position. Spirits likewise may be stored upright.

White and sparkling wines should be stored in the coolest part of the cellar in the lower bins or shelves, while red wines may be stored in the bins above them, the topmost bins for fortified wines and spirits.

The order of arrangement should be determined by your own practical needs, with items most frequently in demand within easy reach of the cellar-man.

Cased goods should be stored in orderly fashion, stacked off the floor to permit ventilation and to prevent mold from forming. This can be accomplished by laying down two parallel 2 × 4 runners below the stacks.

WINE IN CASK

In states where it is legal to handle cask goods, wine casks should receive careful attention. Upon arrival, they should be examined for damage in transit, and then placed upon scantlings and secured with wood calks so that they will not roll. They should be given at least a month's rest before broaching.

When light beverage wines (14 per cent of alcohol or less) are to be bottled, the bottling must be carried through until all of the useful (bright) wine has been bottled, and then bottles should be corked promptly. This is unnecessary in the case of fortified wines, as the air will not spoil them.

Always bottle on a bright clear day when the barometric pressure is high. Wine bottled on a dull, stormy day will have a dull appearance and will not be as bright as when bottled under proper conditions.

Do not attempt fining and filtering yourself. If, after a month's rest, the wine has not cleared naturally and you believe it needs filtering, have an experienced cellarman from the supplier do it for you. This operation is not as simple as it seems, and it requires costly apparatus. Filtering should be done only in a winery properly equipped for it. Do not attempt it in a retail establishment or in a restaurant cellar.

When the cellar is below the bar and draught beer is stored in it, a separate refrigerated beer room should be maintained for best service.

BOTTLED WATERS

All the adjuncts to beverage service, such as mineral waters, ginger ales, and so forth, may be handled in the wine cellar. Here, too, wine baskets and wine coolers may be stored, but the wine cellar should never become the repository for broken furniture and odds and ends.

The wine cellar should be separated from the rest of the cellar so that it can be locked. In large establishments a time lock should be used or it will be difficult to maintain correct inventory balances.

PACKAGE STORES

Generally speaking, the same principles of cellar storage apply to stores as to hotels and restaurants.

In each case the cellar should be so arranged that the patrons of the establishment may be shown through the cellar. This is good sales promotion as it arouses greater interest in the beverages and the physical view of bottles is far more enticing than a mere printed list.

LEFT. *A closet becomes a wine cellar.* RIGHT. *A wine vault unit which can be installed in a home.*

HOME CELLAR

THE home cellar presents an entirely different problem. But whether it is a cupboard, a closet, or an actual cellar, it can be made efficient and useful.

For an apartment, select a closet which is not near any heating apparatus. Shelves can be built in of strong, inch-thick boards. Leave plenty of space above the top shelves on which to stand the fortified wines and spirits. These bottles average 13 to 14 inches in height when the cork is half out. Then build the other shelves from 12 to 14 inches apart, making them 13 to 14 inches deep, for the wines that are to be stored on their side.

Where a cellar is to be used in a town or country house, a room away from the heating plant or hot water unit should be selected. Bins made of inch planking or of metal should be installed along the walls, 18 inches deep, 3 to 4 feet wide. If the room is large and is to store large quantities of wine, it is advisable to build additional rows of bins in the center of the room. If these are made of wood, we recommend criss-cross bins. If made of metal, the bins should be square. Honeycomb units made of metal, wood or plastic are available in different shapes and capacities and are useful if you have a large number of individual bottles. Oval press-on labels are available at most stationery stores and can be placed on the top of the capsule bearing the bin number or wine name. This eliminates excessive handling.

The cellar should be well-lighted, and contain a table, several chairs, and a cellar book in which a record is kept of all purchases of wines and liquors, together with notes of the menus with which the wines are served, as well as a list of the guests. In time this will become a record of some of your most pleasant memories.

Last but not least, keep a strong lock on the cellar door!

33. *Beverage Control*

1. WINE STEWARDS AND BEVERAGE MANAGERS

THERE is a very apt Spanish proverb: *El ojo del amo engorda el caballo*—"A horse gets fat (and sleek) under the watchful eye of the owner." So it is with your business. A watchful eye will make it prosper.

If you could be present constantly—twenty-four hours a day—buying, receiving, selling, and collecting the cash without depending upon anyone else, you would need few beverage controls. This is never possible. You must have help from others and you can maintain a watchful eye over your "horse" by establishing an orderly control over each phase of your business.

Beverage Control means all the records and checks on the movement of the beverages from their purchase, receipt, storage, through to their use or sale. It is important, since the information obtained will reflect the health, i.e., profit or loss.

We believe strongly in a practical beverage control system. Your accountants will work out the best controls for your specific needs. Our only recommendation is that you employ the necessary inventory and sales records to keep you informed at all times of the state of your business, but avoid excessive, costly control systems that go beyond your needs. We do not believe that the control "tail" should wag the selling part of the "dog."

There is an adage handed down through the ages—"Time changeth many things." That this is true in the likes and dislikes of the public has been proven many times, particularly in their choice of beverages. It is equally true in the business itself. A wine steward need no longer have spent a lifetime in the business, sport a goatee and flowing mustache, or show a portly corporation covered by a leather apron, with a set of symbolic cellar keys hung about his neck. Today the wine steward finds himself emerging as an accredited executive with responsibility for accounting records and statistical information in his department and supervision of the personnel, in addition to being thoroughly experienced in his own specialty.

431

A leading hotel accountant once told us, "The position of wine steward will be one of extreme importance and will rank high among the department heads. He must not only be possessed of technical knowledge, but also should have the requisite executive ability. While the set-up of the organization of the beverage department will vary in different hotels, it is my personal opinion that the responsibility for the administration of this department should rest with the wine steward. This responsibility should extend over the wine cellar, the service bars and public bars, up to the point of service. The wine steward should have charge of the employees in this department, as he will be responsible for their functioning to produce the results and profits expected."

Today even the title itself has been changed and the position is better known as beverage manager, the old name going to the man who actually has charge of the wine cellar. The function of the beverage manager is to maintain constant supervision over all divisions of the department and he usually has an assistant, a wine steward, and a supervisor for the bartenders to help him.

WINE CELLARS

WINE cellars these days need not be cellars at all, but may be located many floors above the street level, as long as they are air-conditioned to maintain the proper temperature for the case storage of wines. The layout of a cellar must, of course, be based on the physical condition of the building, but there are one or two points regarding its construction that can be applied generally. First, the cellar must have only one entrance, and the steward's office should be located at that point. Second, everything pertaining to the cellar or its operation should be confined within the space allotted to it. Third, nothing is to be kept in the cellar that belongs to any other department. In other words, the cellar is to be completely isolated from other departments. Fourth, a generous use of locks within the cellar is advocated and a time lock on the door is usually required.

BEVERAGE DEPARTMENT PROCEDURES

LET us now consider the normal activities of the beverage department of a large hotel and see how the stock is acquired and controlled.

purchasing   When the wine cellar needs an item, whether it be a new one or a repeat, a requisition must be written for it. Any simple form is acceptable, as long as each set of two sheets is numbered in rotation. The requisition is made in duplicate, the original going to the beverage manager's office and the cellar retaining the copy.

On reaching the beverage manager's office, the request is transferred to an order form, which is made out in triplicate. This form should provide plenty of room for writing in the names of the items. Some wines have long names and when the vintage and bottlers' names are added, which should always be done, ample space is needed. The form may also state conditions of the purchase, etc. The original copy of the order is sent to the purveyor; the duplicate, to which is attached the cellar requisition, goes to the beverage auditor; and the triplicate copy is sent back to the cellar as an advice against future delivery.

Upon arrival of the goods, the receiving clerk of the hotel must make out his regular receiving slip in triplicate. The original is sent to the beverage controller; the second copy is kept at the receiving department; and the third copy is delivered to the wine cellar with the merchandise. The receiving slip need not be in detail but should clearly indicate the number of cases received, a type description (such as wine, Scotch, etc.), and the purveyor's name. *receiving*

When the delivery reaches the wine cellar, a detailed delivery slip must be made, listing the items fully and accurately. At this time, the copy of the original order is checked and the number of the wine cellar receipt is written on it. It is then sent to the beverage manager's office, together with the original of the wine cellar receipt and the triplicate copy of the receiving department slip. Some purveyors leave their invoices on delivery of goods and, if this is done, these should also be sent along.

STOCKING THE CELLAR

THE goods for immediate use are now unpacked, inspected, and stamped with the bin numbers. If goods are left in the cases, they must be stored in the proper location for temperature, and it is advisable to stencil the bin number on the case.

If, on unpacking, any of the contents are found broken, leaking, or missing, a form should be made out and included with those sent to the auditor. The same procedure holds true even if the goods are unpacked at a much later date. The necks of all such breakage must be kept to substantiate the claim. If there is a breakage on which no claim can be made, a wholesale cost memo must be written by the cellar and sent to the controller.

When stamping the bottles, care should be taken to get the bin number on a clear portion of the label, either front or back, so that the number is plainly indicated. This is important, particularly for full bottle sales at banquets, since all bottles carrying the stamped bin number are proven property of the house and are identified as such without question. In instances where corkage is charged, this procedure is of the utmost importance, since it will eliminate the possibility of an argument and a disgruntled guest.

Q. P. CO. 10380

NAME _____

MINIMUM REQUIREMENT _____ BIN NO. _____

BOT. $ _____ DRINK ¢ _____ SIZE _____

DATE	No. Bot. Received	NUMBER ISSUED				Balance on Hand
		Front Bar	Rest. Bars	Banq. Bars	Roof Bars	

Bin card.

BIN CARDS

THE use of bin cards (see illustration) is not only desirable but essential in the maintenance of a satisfactory running inventory. A card hangs on the front of each bin in a metal holder and on this card is recorded the movement of the stock as it occurs daily. The card should provide columns for opening inventories, withdrawals for each bar, and closing inventories. If there is more than one bar of the same type, the stock movement can be recorded in different colored pencils. Experience has proven that this detail is not too difficult for the average cellar employee to grasp and that the results obtained are invaluable. A study of the card will show how completely the movement of the beverages is charted. The cards are printed on both sides and can be reversed.

ISSUE OF STOCK

No matter how large or small the place of business or the volume of beverages sold, the bar must give some kind of receipt for goods received from the cellar. An ordinary requisition, similar to one already discussed, is satisfactory. Telautograph machines are sometimes used. In any case, no matter what the system used, a copy of the order must be in the hands of the controller the following day. It is the usual custom for the bar captain of the night shift to make out the replenishing order at the time of closing, so that it will be ready the first thing in the morning for the cellar to work on.

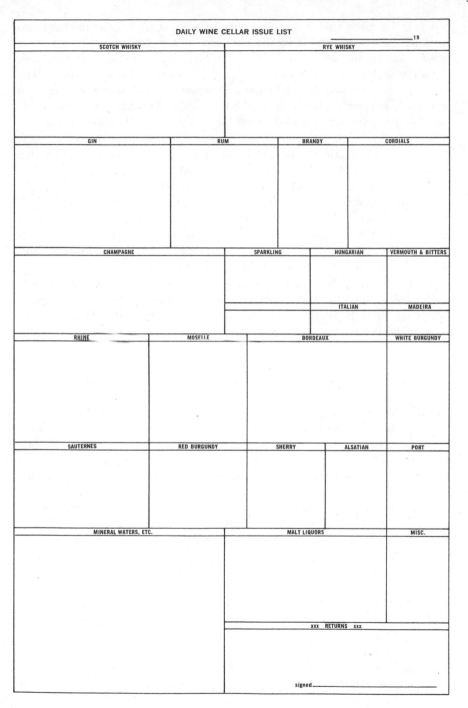

DAILY WINE CELLAR ISSUE LIST

_____ 19

SCOTCH WHISKY	RYE WHISKY

GIN	RUM	BRANDY	CORDIALS

CHAMPAGNE	SPARKLING	HUNGARIAN	VERMOUTH & BITTERS
		ITALIAN	MADEIRA

RHINE	MOSELLE	BORDEAUX	WHITE BURGUNDY

SAUTERNES	RED BURGUNDY	SHERRY	ALSATIAN	PORT

MINERAL WATERS, ETC.	MALT LIQUORS	MISC.

xxx RETURNS xxx

signed _____

The cellar enters each item on a Cellar Issue Sheet after removing the items from the bins and entering on the bin cards, although some hostelries enter prior to filling the order. A Cellar Issue Sheet is used daily for analyzing withdrawals for each type of wine, spirit, or liquor. (See illustration.) The bin number is written in the first space below the type name, and in each space below is written the number of bottles ordered of that particular brand. The following vertical spaces are used for repeat orders. The size of the form should be adjusted to the volume of business and the extent of the cellar stock. Enough horizontal lines should be provided for every item of each type carried in stock, and enough vertical spaces to cover with a safe margin the probable maximum business on the best day of the year. The sheets are dated and should be signed. Attention is directed to the lower-right-hand corner marked "XXX RETURNS XXX," in which are entered items returned to the cellar unused and unopened. For large establishments the use of two wine cellar issue sheets daily is advocated—one for each shift. One man (or one man in each shift) should be assigned exclusively to the task of filling orders.

As in all records, the basic idea is an accurate trace and check on the article itself, with a secondary value as a form of receipt against an order for goods delivered. Since the records already described and particularly the Issue Sheet remain the property of the cellar, it can be checked against the bin cards or order forms at any time and for any given date.

RETURNED GOODS

THE last phase to discuss in the proper operation of cellar detail is the matter of returning goods to a purveyor. A return voucher form is used, in sets of three, numbered consecutively. The cellar makes out the voucher, entering the name of the dealer, the date, and the items being returned. The original is sent to the dealer with the merchandise; the duplicate is signed by the truckman making the delivery and is then forwarded to the beverage controller; and the triplicate is handed to the controller who holds it pending receipt of credit advice (or check) from the dealer. Inventory records are adjusted from entries made from the duplicate copy.

PURCHASE CONTROL

INVOICES for purchases reach the accounting department first and are then sent to the beverage controller where the original cellar requisition, duplicate copy of the purchase order, and receiving slips from the receiving department and the cellar are attached to it. The invoices are now sent to the beverage manager's office and are compared with the original purchase order for price and quantity. After scrutinizing the invoices, the beverage manager should

O.K. each bill, if correct, and return it to the accounting department for payment. However, while the purveyors' bills are in his office, all pertinent details are abstracted from them and entered on a Purchase Control form which is designed to be used in a visible binder. These details include the date, quantity, vendor, price, discount, tax, additional charges, order number, net cost per case and per bottle, and sales price per bottle. This record gives a complete history of purchases by the beverage department and, while a duplication in many aspects of the records maintained by the accounting department and the beverage controller's office, it has the advantage of centering all information on one form. By referring to it, quotations by salesmen can be checked and compared at a moment's notice and data relative to number of cases purchased previously can be found without delay.

CASH REGISTER

THE most practical business control agent ever devised was invented by a tavern owner of Dayton, Ohio, and patented on November 4, 1879. It was called "Ritty's Incorruptible Cashier," later improved and sold as "James Ritty's New Cash Register and Indicator." Today James Ritty's invention, somewhat improved to be sure, is known throughout the world as the National Cash

Typical National Cash Register Inventory Control reports—daily, weekly or monthly. (Photos National Cash Register Co., Dayton, Ohio)

OPTION #1 — HISTORY   INVENTORY CONTROL   6/10/73

STATE CUSTOMER	NUMBER	DESCRIPTION	PER CASE	RETAIL BOTTLE PRICE	RETAIL CASE PRICE	SALES	RECEIPTS	ON HAND	INVENTORY VALUE RETAIL BOTTLE PRICE	ACTUAL $ SALES THIS PERIOD	MONTH TO-DATE	1st MO PREVIOUS	2nd MO PREVIOUS	3rd MO PREVIOUS	YEAR-TO-DATE	REMARKS
1 027:1	0210	10TH CUTTY SARK	24	3.58	81.62	1		44	157.52	3.58	5	24	27	21	77	
1 027:1	0211	5TH CUTTY SARK	12	6.68	76.08	1		26	173.68	6.68	2	9	30	12	53	
1 027:1	0212	QT. CUTTY SARK	12	8.29	94.51			23	190.67		1	4	20	2	27	
1 027:1	0213	10TH DEW WHT LBL	24	3.58	81.62	4	24	28	100.24	14.32	7	20	13	8	48	
1 027:1	0214	5TH DEW WHT LBL	12	6.79	77.21			19	129.01		2	11	17	14	44	
1 027:1	0215	QT. DEW WHT LBL	12	8.39	95.65	1		8	67.12	8.39	1	3	2		6	
1 027:1	0216	10TH GLEN ROSSI	24	2.49	56.77	4		19	47.31	9.96	6	17	15	10	48	
1 027:1	0217	5TH GLEN ROSSI	12	4.99	56.89	2	12	12	59.88	9.98	3	9	10	4	26	
1 027:1	0218	QT. GLEN ROSSI	12	5.99	68.29	2		7	41.93	11.98	4	4	5	2	15	
1 027:1	0219	10TH VL MACNISH	24	3.49	79.57			5	17.45			1	1		2	
1 027:1	0220	5TH VL MACNISH	12	6.66	75.92	1		4	26.64	6.66	1	1	2	1	5	
		GROUP TOTAL				16	36	195	1011.45	71.55	32	103	142	74	351	
1 027:1	0230	10 GRANTS 8 YRS	24	3.65	83.22	1		23	83.95	3.65	1	3		1	5	
1 027:1	0231	5TH GRANTS 8 YRS	12	6.96	79.34	2	6	9	62.64	13.92	3	2	4	1	10	
1 027:1	0232	HAIG & H 5ST	24	3.49	79.57	3		26	87.25	10.47	5	13				

OPTION #2 — COST   INVENTORY CONTROL   7/7/73

STATE CUSTOMER	NUMBER	DESCRIPTION	PER CASE	RETAIL BOTTLE PRICE	BOTTLE COST	SALES	RECEIPTS	ON HAND	INVENTORY VALUE RETAIL BOTTLE PRICE	INVENTORY VALUE @ BOTTLE COST	ACTUAL $ SALES THIS PERIOD	GROSS PROFIT THIS PERIOD	MONTH TO-DATE	1st MO PREVIOUS	2nd MO PREVIOUS	YEAR-TO-DATE	REMARKS
1 027:2	0405	PT. SCHNLY RESRV	24	3.00	2.40	5	24	79	237.00	189.60	15.00	3.00	8	34	95	137	
1 027:2	0406	5TH SCHNLY RESRV	12	4.79	3.83	14		49	234.71	187.67	67.06	13.44	16	25	43	84	
1 027:2	0407	QT. SCHNLY RESRV	12	5.90	4.72	2		28	165.20	132.16	11.80		2	9	20	31	
1 027:2	0408	PT. SEGRM 7 CRWN	24	3.00	2.40	62	48	77	231.00	184.80	186.00	37.20	96	131	212	439	
1 027:2	0409	5TH SEGRM 7 CRWN	12	4.79	3.83	21		15	71.85	57.45	100.59	20.16	38	81	112	231	
		GROUP TOTAL				104	72	248	939.76	751.68	380.45	76.16	160	280	482	922	
1 027:2	0410	PT. SEAGRAM VO	24	3.99	3.19	36		92	367.08	293.48	143.64	28.80	59	84	142	285	
1 027:2	0411	5TH SEAGRAM VO	12	6.40	5.12	15	12	70	448.00	358.40	96.00	19.20	27	46	175	248	
1 027:2	0412	QT. SEAGRAM VO	12	7.95	6.36			52	413.40	330.72					16		

Register. While there are quite a number of cash register manufacturers in the world, National is the leading producer, supplying 80 per cent of all cash registers used anywhere.

Today's registers are mechanical marvels. They will give you practically any information desired for simplified control. In my opinion, no matter how large or small the business operation, the cash register is your most important beverage control tool. It will issue an itemized, mechanically added receipt, print separate and total charges on a waiter's check, and will accumulate and store totals of the several kinds of information you desire for daily verification. It can be equipped with eight or more separate category keys and total separately the transactions of each category. It will even separate the sales made by each cash drawer, when there are several.

Just how you use this most effective beverage control tool is up to you and your individual needs, whether your business is a small tavern, a restaurant, a retail store or a large hotel like the New York Hilton at Rockefeller Center, whose entire data processing system from bar checks, room bills, banquets

RECEIPT				
DATE	NO. PERSONS	AMOUNT OF CHECK		CHECK NO.
				15650
NCR				
1 ¹	MARTINI RKS OLIVE	−1.25 LR		
1 ²	SCOTCH SOUR RKS	−1.50 LR		
1 ³	FILET MIGNON RARE	−7.95 FD		
1 ⁴	LAMB CHOPS	−6.00 FD		
5	TAX	−0.84 TX		
6			17.54 SV	
7				
8				
9				
10				
11				
12				
13				
14				
		TOTAL FROM OTHER SIDE		
		TOTAL AMOUNT OF CHECK		

Tom Collins
Gin & Tonic

−   01.25   LQ
−   01.00   LQ

−   02.25 SV

1327 30 JAN 72

Scotch & Water
Clams Casino
King Crab
Tax

−   01.00   LQ
−   02.25   FD
−   05.25   FD
−   00.45   TX

−   08.95 SV

LEFT & ABOVE. *Typical restaurant guest check and service department requisition or control checks.*

RIGHT. *Standard National Cash Register for restaurant service. Similar registers adapted to retail store are equally practical.*

for 3,000 people, pay rolls, etc., is handled by a whole assortment of National Cash Registers, including a mechanical monster of a computer that collates and analyzes the data from all the small registers.

BARS

WHEN a delivery arrives at the bar, it must be carefully checked in by two barmen by comparing with the bar order. In those instances where the bar orders by telautograph or by telephone, a daily bar order sheet is used by the bar in making up the order for the cellar. Errors or misunderstandings between the bar and the cellar should be cleared up without delay and before the details become vague, in order to place responsibility.

Only one control form is used behind the bar. This is to account for losses through accidents. In the course of each day drinks will be spilled either by employees or customers. When this happens at a standing bar, a regular check must be made for it and the word "Accident" written across its face and signed by the bar captain. If the accident occurs at a table or if for any reason the drink is not acceptable and is returned to the bar, a form is made out by the bar checker and signed by the bar captain. In both instances the cause for the loss or the return of the drink should be stated. Since most of these losses can be prevented, the beverage manager's office scrutinizes such records daily, and may initiate remedial action with the department.

BANQUET BARS

A SEPARATE division of the beverage department is the banquet bar, the importance of which to the hotel is so great that it requires special mention.

Ordering and stocking such bars will follow the procedure previously outlined for bars in general, except that banquet bars require a larger stock both of wine and liquor items because the bulk of the business will be done in full bottle sales. This fact also necessitates keeping a complete record of all bottles of liquor sold so that the proper internal financial adjustment can be made each morning between the beverage controller and the bar. Since the bar has been debited for all beverages at sale prices per drink, the bottle sales will show a decrease from this debit total.

Thus the bar is charged with 16 drinks at $1.20 each, or $19.20
And sells a one-fifth bottle at 15.00
Credit adjustment due to the bar of . . . . $ 4.20

From the record of bottles sold at each party, data are obtained for the beverage manager's future use. Here is a splendid chance to procure a detailed record of these parties and to form a basis of comparison for the following year. A list of wine sold should also be added to the records. One of the most convenient ways to keep such data is on 5 × 8 cards. The name of the person or organization giving the party is essential. The date is very important for future comparison since it sometimes makes a great difference on what day of the week a party is held. The type of function is also important, for if the next party should be a dance instead of a dinner, the beverage results would be entirely different. The number of persons attending and the original number guaranteed are useful too. "Bar Cash" is the à la carte sale of beverages while the "Bar Signed" denotes the inclusive items which may have been ordered in advance by the party. On the face of the card in the left-hand column, the number of bottles sold is entered, followed by the type of beverage, i.e.:

> 54 B Scotch
> 10 B Rye
> 9 B Champagne, etc.

To know the brands used, as reflected in the number of bottles, refer to the bar captain's figures for analysis.

The most common item served at banquets is a cocktail for each guest, either in the reception room or when seated at the tables. A choice of cocktails is invariably offered. In large establishments where there can be anywhere from five to a dozen parties going on at the same time, this basic choice must have attention. If we continue a little further with this idea, and consider the possibility not only of this choice of drinks, but a Sherry with the soup, a dry white wine with the fish, and Champagne with the roast or dessert, then we can understand how complicated the service can become and how necessary it is to give this phase careful advance attention. The detailed information concerning the beverage service of each banquet is, of course, collected at the banquet department where it originates. It is digested and typed on a list six days prior to the date of the function. Enough copies are made so that everyone in the beverage department, and others connected with any of the functions, receives a copy. This includes the wine cellar, each bar, and the beverage manager's office. Every effort is made to eliminate excuses or alibis.

ARRANGEMENT OF THE BAR

THE working arrangement of a bar is of the utmost importance. This matter is too often overlooked when the plans are laid for installations, and nine times out of ten the men who do the work behind the bar are not consulted.

The accompanying sketch shows an ideal layout, insofar as it affects the service for a banquet bar. Note that it follows the same principle as that of food checking: *one* entrance and *one* exit. Some organizations prefer the use of a turnstile at the entrance. If there is none, certainly the rule must be strictly enforced that once a waiter reaches the bar there can be no turning around and going out the way he came in. *The only way out is to pass the checker.*

If the layout in front of the bar is important, certainly also are the working stations behind the bar.

The plan illustrated here is a simple one designed to give some general pointers. Naturally, the more money there is to be expended, the more elaborate the bar fittings and accessories can be.

Special attention is called to the shelf running the length of the bar in back of the working stations. This comes in very handy for additional bottles which cannot be accommodated in the regular stations.

In the center of the stations there are, of course, the ice containers. Make sure these are built oblong, with the longer sides running away from the bartender to facilitate a full scoop of the ice shovel away from the barman.

The height of a bar is more or less a matter of personal preference, but service bars should be built higher than standup bars, particularly when the former are to be in public view. A high bar of, say, forty-seven inches will serve two purposes. First, it will convey the thought automatically to the guest that it is not a standup bar. Second, a bar of this height is convenient for the waiters.

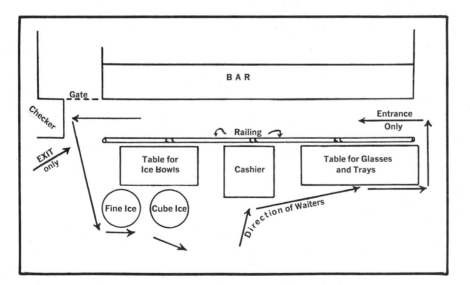

Layout for service bar. (Courtesy Gordon M. VanderBeek)

Back-bars are relatively unimportant except in one respect. Have them built wide and not much higher than the front bar. The width will ensure good cabinet or refrigeration space underneath and enough shelf space on top.

Do not have a lighting system which consists of electric bulbs under glass shelves on which bottles are placed. The heat generated by the lights will

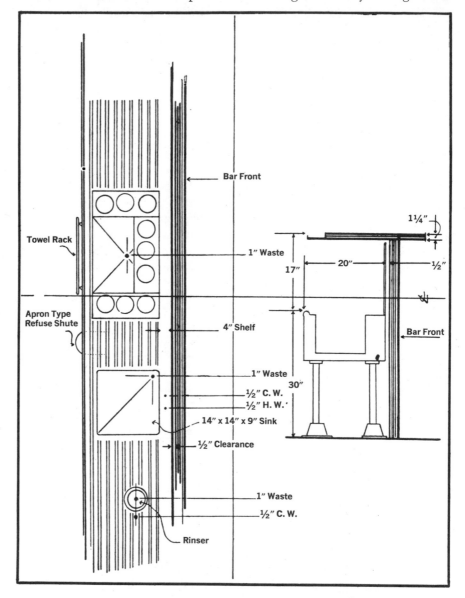

Layout for working stations behind the front bar. (Courtesy Gordon M. VanderBeek)

be detrimental to the liquid contents. Even double shelves with an air space between are not entirely satisfactory.

In laying out the construction of a bar, try to keep the working stations well off the floor. Plumbing repairs will have to be made and if there is plenty of working space the repairs will be completed in less time and at much less expense. But even more important, do not forget that men are going to have to work in the fairly cramped space between the front and back bar. In practically every new large bar layout we have observed over the years the bartender's comfort has been forgotten. The fact that a man must be on his feet for eight hours or longer is not taken into account. The solution is simplicity itself. Wooden racks on the floor make the difference between a smiling, efficient bartender and one that is tired and grouchy after a couple of hours standing on a cold cement floor. These floor racks should be built to the following specifications: Use clear pine laths 3″ wide by 1″ thick by 3′ long; allow 1″ separation between laths and the rack is held together by crosspieces of the same laths. This produces racks with a 2″ clearance off the floor. If the racks are made longer than three feet they become too heavy for easy lifting, to clean the floor daily.

If the bar is oval or some other shape whereby the customers standing on one side can see the working stations on the other, a cover should be hung in front of the stations to conceal the pipes, etc. Under the same circumstances, thought must be given to the floor covering.

For service bars out of the public sight there need be no back bars. This space will be occupied by large refrigerators, while the bottles which ordinarily would be on the back bar are placed on overhead shelves above the counter.

The working space between the service bar and the back wall line must be at least ten feet, particularly if the bar services banquets. This will provide the extra space needed for stacking cases of wines, liquors, and waters when they are to be served in quantities exceeding the capacity of the regular storage space.

The working space between the front and back bars should be at least thirty inches, and thirty-six inches is ideal. Doors of refrigerators set into the back bar should not be so wide that they block traffic when opened.

2. ACCOUNTING FOR RETAIL STORES

ACCOUNTING for stock and sales in a retail liquor store will depend to a great extent on the size of the store and the statutory requirements of the state in which it is located. Prescribed forms will, of course, be in order in state-controlled stores. The forms are too numerous to cite here.

It is our intent to outline roughly the internal control any liquor store needs to assure intelligent operation, without stressing any type of record keeping.

The Requisition Form is used only in stores large enough to have several departments, or where branch stores are operated and centralized control is exercised.

Individual practices may vary, but in general the previously described routine for requisitioning, purchasing, receiving, stocking, and recording of breakage of merchandise, are as applicable to a retail store as to a hotel.

UNIT CONTROL TICKET

In a large number of retail stores it is the general custom to have a Unit Control Ticket which is pasted on the bottle before it is placed in stock. The sale price is entered from the duplicate purchase order and the ticket states the type of merchandise, size of the bottle, the bin, and purchase order number for identification. On sale of the bottle, half the ticket is torn off and either attached to the sales slip or collected for further classification.

PERPETUAL INVENTORY

It is advisable for the retail store to maintain Perpetual Inventory records which provide columns for entering dates, purchase order numbers, and sales ticket numbers; an "In Column" for the units purchased; an "Out Column" for units sold; and a column for units in stock at the close of each day's business. At the bottom of the sheet should be space for the unit (pints, quarts, fifths, etc.) cost price, if the proprietor wishes to enter it; selling price per unit and per case; and the maximum and minimum stock to be carried. This latter, of course, will not be constant but will probably vary according to the time of the year. The name of the item itself is written under "Name or description." An inventory sheet should be made out for each individual brand and size, i.e., if you have quarts, fifths, pints, and half-pints of a Pennsylvania Rye whiskey, have an inventory sheet for each size.

The manner of entering in the Perpetual Inventory record is as follows:

1. Enter in the "In Column" merchandise received as shown by the vendor's invoice and the receiving department ticket. Also enter sales returns from the duplicate tickets.

2. Enter in the "Out Column" total unit daily sales as arrived at by classifying the duplicate sales tickets and/or the Unit Control Tickets; also merchandise returned to vendors as shown on the duplicate return ticket; sales prices should be carefully compared with schedules on inventory sheets, as these provide an opportunity to audit daily sales. Breakages should be entered individually and so labeled.

3. Stock on hand, as reflected in the perpetual inventory at the end of any given day's business, is arrived at by adding to the previous day's inventory the merchandise put into stock and deducting the sales, returns to vendors, and breakages.

Physical Inventory of the merchandise should be taken in sections daily and compared with the perpetual inventory for correctness of quantity.

RETURNED GOODS

MERCHANDISE to be returned to vendors should be taken out of stock, and the unit tickets removed and attached to the returned goods memorandum, which is made out in triplicate. The duplicate copy of the latter is to be sent to the accounting department. The merchandise with the original and triplicate copy of the return ticket should be sent to the shipping department where it is either delivered by the store itself or picked up by the vendor, at which time a receipt is obtained and sent to the accounting department. On the return slip should be indicated the originating department, the date, the vendor, the quantity and description of the merchandise, and the reason for the return. Delays in the actual return of the merchandise should be investigated.

The manager or owner of the store is held responsible for all merchandise returned by customers. The regular "Returned Goods" slip may be used for this purpose and on it should be entered the goods returned, the reason for the return, and the amount of refund involved. The merchandise should then be entered back into stock.

SALES

IN states permitting sales on credit, the same procedure is used for maintaining accounts receivable as is used generally, with a separate ledger account being maintained for each customer.

At the end of each day's business, it is desirable to have an analysis of the sales made, to show the types of merchandise sold. These quantities must agree with the Unit Control Tickets and the Perpetual Inventory posting.

VENDOR'S INVOICES

THESE should be compared with the receiving advices from the receiving department for quantities and condition and then attached to the invoices themselves. After approval by the person making the purchase for price, quantity, discount if any, and type of merchandise, the invoices are approved for payment and entered in the regular purchase register.

LEFT. *Simple blank card which slips over neck of bottle for shipping instructions or other notation.* RIGHT. *Hold card for merchandise to be delivered at a future date.* (Courtesy M. Lehmann, Inc., New York)

MERCHANDISE RECEIVED FOR FUTURE DELIVERY

IT is advisable to use a tag on which the sales ticket number and the name of the customer are entered. At the bottom should be printed "Do not deliver until payment received." In case payment has not been made, the entire tag should be used. If merchandise has been paid for, then the "Do not deliver" half is cut off. At the time the ticket is made out, the date should be stamped on it and a careful check should be made daily to be sure merchandise is not being held too long without reason.

IDENTIFICATION MARK FOR NECK OF BOTTLE

A THREE-by-five-inch card with a one-and-a-half-inch hole near one end is a very handy gadget for identifying a bottle which, because of activity in the store, cannot be handled at the time it is received. These cards are blank so that the necessary information can be written on them, after which they are just slipped over the neck of the bottle to await attention later.

34. Regulatory Bodies and Laws

A GREAT many volumes could be written on the regulation of the alcoholic beverage trade in the United States and all over the world. For the purposes of this work it is essential only to discuss the broader aspects, aims, and purposes of the laws and the regulatory bodies charged with their enforcement—without becoming involved in the many conflicting regulations and systems used.

The first efforts at liquor regulation in this country date from 1791, when the newly formed Federal Government levied a tax on the whiskey distilled in the Thirteen States. As pointed out in chapter 19, this "interference" with the personal liberty of the Pennsylvania distillers was the cause of the "Whiskey Rebellion." From 1791 to the present day, many advances have been made, so that today the industry is more carefully regulated, supervised, and taxed than any other.

There are two broad phases of control: the first protecting the tax revenue which the government, both Federal and State, derives from alcoholic beverages; the second protecting the public from adulterated or misbranded goods. Secondary regulations concern trade practices.

FEDERAL CONTROL

THE liquor trade must comply with all the laws which govern the operations of general business. In addition, there are a great many other special laws which apply only to the alcoholic beverage business. This control is exercised under three broad principles:

1. REVENUE.   All these laws are designed to protect the tax money to which the Federal Government is entitled. This supervision is maintained by the Bureau of Alcohol, Tobacco, and Firearms of the Treasury Department.

2. PUBLIC PROTECTION.   These regulations are to prevent adulteration and

447

misbranding of alcoholic beverages. This is partly the function of the Food and Drug Administration of the United States Department of Agriculture, and partly the function of the Bureau of Alcohol, Tobacco, and Firearms through its control of approved labels which may be used by a member of the industry.

3. TRADE PRACTICES. The control here is exercised by the Bureau of Alcohol, Tobacco, and Firearms and the Federal Trade Commission to ensure fair trade practices in interstate commerce among competitors and among the several branches of the industry.

Through its close cooperation with the customs branch of the Treasury Department, the Bureau of Alcohol, Tobacco, and Firearms, which is also a part of the Treasury Department, exercises a close control over the alcoholic beverages which may be imported into the country.

This control is effected by the Bureau of Alcohol, Tobacco, and Firearms (B.A.T.F.) primarily through the use of its certificate of label approvals. No wine or spirit will be released by the customs unless the importer can furnish an B.A.T.F. certificate of label approval, which must conform, to the last period and comma, with the actual labels on the bottles. The B.A.T.F. will not issue a label approval for a spirit bearing an age statement unless the importer can furnish a certificate of age from the proper authorities in the country of origin which guarantees the stated age of the spirit.

BUREAU OF ALCOHOL, TOBACCO AND FIREARMS OF THE TREASURY DEPARTMENT*

THIS is the most important bureau in regard to Federal control and regulation of the several producing and distributing branches of the industry.

The control takes several forms: licensing, label approvals, approvals of forms of advertising, and supervision of certain trade practices.

The B.A.T.F. issues licenses to producers operating in interstate commerce and to importers. Infringement or nonobservance of its regulations subjects the violator to suspension or loss of license.

All labels used on alcoholic beverages must conform to the B.A.T.F. labeling regulations and must have its approval before they may be used. These regulations are designed primarily to protect the public from misbranded goods. They include certain mandatory information which must appear on the several types of beverages, such as class and type, liquid content, alcoholic content (with certain exceptions such as beer), name and address of the producers or bottlers, and so forth.

Advertisements of any alcoholic beverages must contain the mandatory label

* Prior to July 1, 1940, the functions of the Bureau relating to Alcoholic Beverages were being carried out by the Federal Alcoholic Administration.

information, plus the name of the responsible advertiser, and in addition cannot make any false or exaggerated claim, and cannot claim any medicinal or therapeutic value for the advertised beverage.

The B.A.T.F. further exercises a protective control over the several branches of the industry by stating in its regulations just what services a producer, wholesaler, or importer may or may not render a retailer. The objective of this phase of control is to prevent the use of services or gifts which may serve as an inducement to the retailer to promote the sale of the inducers' brands to the detriment of his competitors.

Distilled spirits in the possession of a retail dealer must be in bottles or similar containers which bear internal revenue tax stamps. This applies to whiskey, gin, rum, brandy, vodka, alcohol, cordials containing distilled spirits, and other similar liquors. A portion of the strip stamp must be kept affixed to each opened bottle. Liquors not stamped in compliance with these requirements are subject to seizure and forfeiture. The penalty for having unstamped liquors is a fine of not more than $10,000 and imprisonment for not more than five years.

New strip stamps are available from the office of the assistant regional commissioner of B.A.T.F. Replacement of the stamp may be necessary when:

1. The strip stamp is missing from an unopened bottle of distilled spirits.

2. The strip stamp is mutilated to the extent that the genuineness of the stamp is in question; or, the contents of the container are available without breaking the stamp.

A retail liquor dealer must for a period of two years keep all records which relate to purchases of, and payment for, distilled spirits, wines, and fermented malt beverages. The invoices and bills covering the period of time must be kept in book form showing the quantity, from whom received, and the date received.

STATE CONTROL

In addition to the Federal Government's control of the industry, the individual states exercise a secondary control. The control of the sale of alcoholic beverages in the states falls into three types:

1. OPEN LICENSE STATES, where private business makes both on-premise and off-premise sales of alcoholic beverages to all types of consumers. (The operations vary in these states because of different taxes imposed on wines, spirits, and beers; and because of different license fees imposed on wholesalers and retailers. Furthermore, each state and, as a rule, each municipality, may have different hours for opening and closing, and different provisions with respect to the number of on-and-off-sale retail premises which will be permitted.)

2. CONTROL OR MONOPOLY STATES, which control the sale of all alcoholic beverages distributed in their territories.

3. CONTROL OR MONOPOLY STATES, which control the sale of distilled spirits and certain kinds of wines. The effect on wines where the state control is based on the percentage of alcohol is rather obvious.

In the Open License States, trade is conducted as in other competitive businesses. In the Control or Monopoly States, however, whether those which control the sale of all alcoholic beverages or those which control only a part of the trade and permit the open sale of other beverages, it must be borne in mind that the states themselves are in the liquor business and their function, public statements to the contrary, is to make as much money as possible. As a result, like any other good businessman, these states stock only those brands which they believe will have the most ready sale.

It might be expected that, due to the regulatory function which the several Federal and State bodies exercise, the trade in general would regard these officers as policemen and live in constant fear of them. As a matter of fact, not only the B.A.T.F. Administrator, but every State Liquor Control Chairman is a public servant, placed in his position to serve the public and the trade, and to assist the trade in performing its services to the public fairly and without favoritism. We can say from personal experience that when one asks any of these functionaries for assistance, he is generally anxious to be of service.

35. Summary

Wʜᴀᴛ has the wine and spirit trade learned in the years since Repeal of Prohibition? It has established the fact that the American public drinks its alcoholic beverages in moderation. Consumption of spirits has remained fairly steady at something less than two gallons per capita, while that of wine and beer has increased progressively to over one and a half gallons and nineteen gallons respectively. This does not mean that individuals are drinking more, but rather that a greater number of people are enjoying the pleasant relaxation that wines, spirits, and beers offer. Also the incidence of alcoholism has decreased, since Repeal, in spite of the stresses and strains and uncertainties of the depression and World War II years.

We are convinced that our consumption of spirits will remain fairly constant, beer will not decrease, and we are ever hopeful that wine consumption will increase steadily until we become one of the wine-drinking countries of the world.

A natural result of Repeal is an increased interest in the art of good living. A dinner accompanied by ice water is a cold and not too interesting or inviting prospect. But a dinner complemented with wine gives the diner greater enjoyment and a feeling that everything is well with the world. The food is more appetizing. Both the diner and the restaurant (or host if it is a home dinner) will be pleased and everyone benefits.

There is little likelihood of Prohibition returning to the United States in the next generation. Too many people still remember the kind of law observance we had until 1933. On the other hand the trade itself, as a matter of protection, must advocate temperance. Temperance education is becoming a function of our public school systems and it is possible that in the future we may see some form of cooperative action between the beverage trade and the educational boards to teach children the real meaning of moderation, and the value as well as the dangers of alcoholic beverages of all types.

Up to now the trade has not made any attempt to place before the medical trade the value of wines in the treatment of nutritional ailments. We believe that this could be done quite successfully, and we hope that in time many of our doctors will prescribe certain types of wines to be used in such cases.

The more accurate information people have about alcoholic beverages the better off they are. Much educational work has been done but much still remains to be done. The future should usher in an era of freedom, but *not* one of unlimited license and abuse.

Of one thing we are convinced. The American public demands the best! It is the best-informed buying public in the world. The person who attempts to fool the public with poor quality or shoddy imitations is fooling only himself. Any brand can be sold provided it has the quality claimed for it. No company can stay in the wine and spirit trade unless people are convinced that the firm's products are good.

The Federal and State regulations are designed not only to protect the public, but honest producers, dealers and dispensers as well.

The increasing interest of the general public in the subject is evidenced by the space devoted to writings on alcoholic beverages in the leading magazines of the country, and the space—more important still—devoted both to the service and the use of beverages appearing on the woman's page of our important dailies. Newspaper editors have a keen sense of their readers' needs, and feature the subject because of public demand for information.

When one walks into an automobile show room to buy a car, one expects the salesman to be able to answer questions about the car's performance, its gas and oil consumption, and other details. Furthermore, one expects that salesman to know comparative values in other cars. When the tables are reversed, and the automobile salesman wants to order a wine or a spirit, he is not unreasonable in expecting an answer to his questions about taste, class, and use of the product he is buying.

The more the wine and spirit merchant learns about the products he is trading in, the prouder he will be to find himself engaged in a profession whose honorable and ancient traditions have been evolved through the centuries.

Our aim has been to compress into this book all available information on alcoholic beverages for producer, seller, and consumer.

The crowning knowledge about the beverages which we have described can come only at first hand, by actual tasting.

We lift our glass to wish you profit in the reading, pleasure in the tasting—and your very good health!

APPENDIX

QUICK GUIDE TO POPULAR WINES AND SPIRITS

NAME	PHONETIC SPELLING†	SOURCE	TYPE	COLOR	TASTE	SERV. TEMP.	SERVE WITH
Abbott's Aged Bitters		Baltimore, Md.	Aromatic Bitters	Dark	Bitter	°	C., & Pun.
Advocaat	AHD-voh-kaht	Holland	Prepared egg nog	Yellow	Sweet	° or °°°	A.D.
Affenthaler	AH-fenn-thah-lehr	Baden, Ger.	Table Wine	Red	Dry	°	R.M.
Aigle	A-gl	Switzerland	Table Wine	White	Med. dry	°°°	F., P., & L.M.
Akvavit	AHK-vah-veet	Denmark	Spirit	White	Caraway	°°°	B.D.
Ale		Various	Malt Beverage	Pale to dark	Bitter-sweet	°°°	Hosp.
Aleatico	Ah-leh-AH-tee-coe	California, Italy	Dessert Wine	Red	Sweet	°	A.D.
Alella	Ah-LEH-yah	Spain	Table Wine	White, Red	Dry	° & °°°	
Aloxe Corton	Ah-lowx-Core-TOH	Côte de Beaune, Fr.	Table Wine	Red	Dry	°	Ch., G., & R.M.
Amarone della Valpolicella	Ah-mah-roh-nch deh-lah Vahl-poe-lee-CHEHL-ah	Verona, It.	Table Wine	Red	Dry	°	Ch., G., & R.M.
Amer Picon	Ah-mehr PEA-coh	France	Apéritif	Dark	Bitter	°°°	B.D.
Amontillado	Ah-mohn-tee YAH-dough	Jerez, Spain	Sherry	Pale	Dry	°°	Hosp.
Angelica	Ahn-JELLY-kah	California	Fortified Wine	Golden	Sweet	°	Hosp.
Angostura Bitters	Ahn-gus-TOO-rah	Trinidad	Aromatic Bitters	Dark	Bitter	°	C. & Pun.
Anisette	Ah-nee-ZET	Various	Liqueur	White	Aniseed	°	A.D.
Anjou	Ahn-ZHOO	Anjou, Fr.	Table Wine	White, Pink	Med. sweet	°°°	F., P., & L.M.
Anninger Perle	On-ing-ehr PEHR-luh	Austria	Table Wine	White	Dry	°°°	F., P., & L.M.
Apple Jack		U.S.	Apple Brandy	Brown	Dry, fruity	°	A.D.
Apricot Liqueur		Various	Liqueur	Brown	Sweet, fruity	°	A.D.
Armagnac	Are-mah-N YAHK	Gers, Fr.	Brandy	Brown	Dry	°	A.D.
Assmannshausen	AHSS-mahns-house-enn	Rhine, Ger.	Table Wine	Red	Dry	°	R.M.
Asti Spumante	Ahs-tea Spoo-MAHN-teh	Piedmont, It.	Sparkling	White	Sweet	°°°	Desserts
Aurora	Oh-ROAR-uh	New York State	Table Wine	White	Dry	°°°	F., P., & L.M.
Avelsbacher Hammerstein	Ah-vels-bahkh-ehr HAHM-mehr-shtine	Moselle, Ger.	Table Wine	White	Dry to Med.	°°°	F., P., & L.M.
Baco Noir	Bak-o NWAHR	New York State	Table Wine	Red	Dry	°	P., & R.M.
Badacsonyi Rizling	BAHD-ah-chony Reez-ling	Hungary	Table Wine	White	Dry	°°°	F., P., & L.M.
Badacsonyi Szurke-Barat	BAHD-ah-chony Tsoor-keh BAH-raht	Hungary	Table Wine	White	Med. dry	°°°	F., P., & L.M.
Banyuls	Bahn-YULS	Banyuls, Fr.	Fortified Wine	White	Sweet	°	A.D.
Barack Palinka	BAHR-ahks PAH-lean-kah	Hungary	Apricot Brandy	Orange	Dry	°	A.D.
Barbaresco	Bar-bah-REHZ-coe	Piedmont, It.	Table Wine	Red	Dry	°	Ch., G., & R.M.
Barbera	Bar-BEH-rah	Piedmont, It., Calif.	Table Wine	Red	Dry	°	Ch., G., & R.M.

SYMBOLS: *Service Temperature* ° (Room Temperature)—°° (Slightly Chilled)—°°° (Cold.) *Serve With:* A.D. (After Dinner)—All F. (All Food)—B.D. (Before Dinner)—C. (Cocktails)—Ch. (Cheese)—F. (Fish)—Fr. (Fruits)—G. (Game)—H. (Highballs)—Hosp. (Hospitality, any time)—L.M. (Light Meats)—P. (Poultry)—Pun. (Punches)—R.M. (Red Meats)—S. (Straight.) † NOTE: Accented syllable is capitalized.

NAME	PHONETIC SPELLING†	SOURCE	TYPE	COLOR	TASTE	SERV. TEMP.	SERVE WITH
Bardolino	Bar-do-LEEN-oh	Verona, It.	Table Wine	Red	Dry	°°	Ch., G., & R.M.
Barolo	Bah-RO-lo	Piedmont, It.	Table Wine	Red	Dry	°	Ch., G., & R.M.
Barsac	Bar-SAHK	Barsac, Fr.	Table Wine	White	Sweet	°°°	Fr., Desserts
Bâtard-Montrachet, Le	Luh Bah-tar Mohn-rah-SHAY	Côte de Beaune, Fr.	Table Wine	White	Dry	°°°	F., P., & L.M.
Batavia Arak	Bah-tah-vee ah AHR-ahk	Java, Indonesia	Rum	Very Pale	Dry, aromatic	°°°	C., Pun., & H.
Beaujolais	Bo-z joe-LAY	Beaujolais, Fr.	Table Wine	Red	Dry	°	All F.
Beaune	BONE	Côte de Beaune, Fr.	Table Wine	Red	Dry	°	Ch., G., & R.M.
Beaune-Les Fèves	Bone-lay FEHV	Côte de Beaune, Fr.	Table Wine	Red	Dry	°	Ch., G., & R.M.
Beaune-Grèves	Bone-GREHV	Côte de Beaune, Fr.	Table Wine	Red	Dry	°	Ch., G., & R.M.
Beer, Lager	LAH-gurr Beer	Various	Malt Beverage	Pale Golden	Dry	°°°	Hosp.
Bénédictine	Ben eh-dick-TEEN	Fécamp, Fr.	Liqueur	Golden	Spicy, sweet	°	A.D.
Bernkasteler Doktor	Behrn-kahss-tell-ehr DAWCK-tohr	Moselle, Ger.	Table Wine	White	Med dry	°°°	F., P., & L.M.
Binger Scharlachberg	Bing-ehr SHAHR-lahk-behrk	Rhine, Ger.	Table Wine	White	Dry	°°°	F., P., & L.M.
Blackberry Liqueur		Various	Liqueur	Dark Red	Sweet, fruity	°	A.D.
Blanc de Blancs	Blahn(g) day-BLAHN	Champagne, Fr.	Sparkling Wine	White	Dry	°°°	All F., Hosp.
Boal (Bual)	BOO WHAL	Madeira	Fortified Wine	Golden	Sweet	°	Hosp.
Bonnes Mares, Les	Lay-Bun MAHR	Côte de Nuits, Fr.	Table Wine	Red	Dry	°	Ch., G., & R.M.
Bordeaux Blanc	Bor-dough BLAHN	Bordeaux, Fr.	Table Wine	White	Med. sweet	°°°	F., P., & L.M.
Bordeaux Rouge	Bor-dough ROOZSH	Bordeaux, Fr.	Table Wine	Red	Dry	°	Ch., G., & R.M.
Bourbon Whiskey		U.S.	Whiskey	Brown	Dry		S., C., H. & Pun.
Bourgogne Blanc	Boor-goy een BLAHN	Burgundy, Fr.	Table Wine	White	Dry	°°°	F., P., & L.M.
Bourgogne Rouge	Boor-goy een ROOZSH	Burgundy, Fr.	Table Wine	Red	Dry	°	Ch., G., & R.M.
Brachetto	Brah-KETT-oh	Piedmont, It.	Table Wine	Red	Dry	°	Ch., G., & R.M.
Brauneberger Juffer	Brown-uh-behrk-ehr YOU-fehr	Moselle, Ger.	Table Wine	White	Dry	°°°	F., P., & L.M.
Brouilly	Brew-YEE	Beaujolais, Fr.	Table Wine	Red	Dry	°	Ch., G., & R.M.
Bucelas	Boo-SELL-uh sh	Portugal	Table Wine	White	Med. sweet	°°°	L.M., & Fr.
Cabernet Sauvignon	Kah-behr-nay Soh-vee-N YOHNG	Various	Table Wine	Red	Dry	°	Ch., G., & R.M.
Calvados	Kahl-vah-DOUGHS	Normandy, Fr.	Apple Brandy	Brown	Dry, fruity	°	A.D.
Campari	KAM-pari	Italy	Apéritif	Red	Bitter	°°°	B.D.
Capri	Kah-PREE	Capri, It.	Table Wine	White	Dry	°°°	F., P., & L.M.
Carema	Kah-REH-mah	Piedmont, It.	Table Wine	Red	Dry	°	Ch., G. & R.M.
Carruades de Château Lafite-Rothschild	Kah-roo-wahd deh Shot-oh Lah-feet roh-SHIELD	Médoc, Fr.	Table Wine	Red	Dry	°	Ch., G. & R.M.
Catawba	Kuh-TAWH-bah	N.Y. & Ohio	Table & Sparkling	Pale	Sweet	°°°	Fr., & Hosp.
Chablis	shah-BLEE	Chablis, Fr.	Table Wine	White	Dry	°°°	Oysters, P., & L.M.
Chablis Bougros	Shah-blee Boo-GROH	Chablis, Fr.	Table Wine	White	Dry	°°°	Oysters, P., & L.M.
Chablis Les Clos	Shah-blee Lay-KLOH	Chablis, Fr.	Table Wine	White	Dry	°°°	Oysters, P., & L.M.
Chablis Les Preuses	Shah-blee Lay-PRUHS	Chablis, Fr.	Table Wine	White	Dry	°°°	Oysters, P., & L.M.

SYMBOLS: *Service Temperature* ° (Room Temperature)—°° (Slightly Chilled)—°°° (Cold.) *Serve With:* A.D. (After Dinner)—All F. (All Food)—B.D. (Before Dinner)—C. (Cocktails)—Ch. (Cheese)—F. (Fish)—Fr. (Fruits)—G. (Game)—H. (Highballs)—Hosp. (Hospitality, any time)—L.M. (Light Meats)—P. (Poultry)—Pun. (Punches)—R.M. (Red Meats)—S. (Straight.) † NOTE: Accented syllable is capitalized.

NAME	PHONETIC SPELLING†	SOURCE	TYPE	COLOR	TASTE	SERV. TEMP.	SERVE WITH
Chablis Montée de Tonnerre	Shah-blee Mohn-tay deh tuh-NEHR	Chablis, Fr.	Table Wine	White	Dry	° ° °	Oysters, P., & L.M.
Chablis Vaudésir	Shah-blee Voh-day-SEER	Chablis, Fr.	Table Wine	White	Dry	° ° °	Oysters, P., & L.M.
Chambertin, Le	Luh Shahm-behr-TAHN	Côte de Nuits, Fr.	Table Wine	Red	Dry	°	Ch., G., & R.M.
Chambertin-Clos de Bèze	Sham-behr-tah(n) Klohd-BAYZ	Côte de Nuits, Fr.	Table Wine	Red	Dry	°	Ch., G., & R.M.
Chambertin-Clos St. Jacques	Sham-behr-tah(n) Klo-sahn ZHAHK	Côte de Nuits, Fr.	Table Wine	Red	Dry	°	Ch., G., & R.M.
Chambertin-Latriciéres	Sham-behr-tah(n) Lah-tree-S YEHR	Côte de Nuits, Fr.	Table Wine	Red	Dry	°	Ch., G., & R.M.
Chambolle-Musigny	Sham-bohl-Moo-see-N YEE	Côte de Nuits, Fr.	Table Wine	Red	Dry	°	Ch., G., & R.M.
Chambolle-Musigny Les Amoureuses	Shahm-bohl Moo-see-n yee Lays-Ah-muh-RUZ	Côte de Nuits, Fr.	Table Wine	Red	Dry	°	Ch., G., & R.M.
Champagne	Shahm-PAHNYE	Champagne, Fr.	Sparkling Wine	White	Dry to Sweet	° ° °	All F., Hosp.
Charbono	Shar-BO-no	California	Table Wine	Red	Dry	°	Ch., G., & R.M.
Charmes-Chambertin	Shahrm-Shahm-behr-TAHN	Côte de Nuits, Fr.	Table Wine	Red	Dry	°	Ch., G., & R.M.
Chartreuse	Shahr-TREHZ	Voiron, Fr.	Liqueur	Yellow & Green	Spicy, sweet	°	A.D.
Chassagne-Montrachet	Shah-sahn-Mohn-rah-SHAY	Côte de Beaune, Fr.	Table Wine	White	Dry	° ° °	F., P., & L.M.
Château d'Arche	Shot-oh DAHRSH	Sauternes, Fr.	Table Wine	White	Sweet	° ° °	Desserts
Château Ausone	Shot-oh-oh-SOHN	St. Emilion, Fr.	Table Wine	Red	Dry	°	Ch., G., & R.M.
Château Batailley	Shot-oh Bah-tay-YAY	Médoc, Fr.	Table Wine	Red	Dry	°	Ch., G., & R.M.
Château Beaulieu	Shot-oh Bo-l-yeu	Pomerol, Fr.	Table Wine	Red	Dry	°	Ch., G., & R.M.
Château Beauséjour	Shot-oh Beau-say-JEW R	St. Emilion, Fr.	Table Wine	Red	Dry	°	Ch., G., & R.M.
Château Belair	Shot-oh Bell-AIR	St. Emilion, Fr.	Table Wine	Red	Dry	°	Ch., G., & R.M.
Château Belgrave	Shot-oh Bell-GRAHV	Médoc, Fr.	Table Wine	Red	Dry	°	Ch., G., & R.M.
Château Bellevue	Shot-oh Bell-VIEW	St. Emilion, Fr.	Table Wine	Red	Dry	°	Ch., G., & R.M.
Château Beychevelle	Shot-oh Bay-sheh-VEHLL	Médoc, Fr.	Table Wine	Red	Dry	°	Ch., G., & R.M.
Château Bouscaut	Shot-oh Boo-SCOE	Graves, Fr.	Table Wine	Red, White	Dry	°, & ° ° °	All F. or Varies with color
Château Boyd-Cantenac	Shot-oh Bwahd Kahn-teh-NAHK	Médoc, Fr.	Table Wine	Red	Dry	°	Ch., G., & R.M.
Château Branaire-Ducru	Shot-oh Brahn-air-Doo-CREW	Médoc, Fr.	Table Wine	Red	Dry	°	Ch., G., & R.M.
Château Brane-Cantenac	Shot-oh Brahn-Kahn-teh-NAHK	Médoc, Fr.	Table Wine	Red	Dry	°	Ch., G., & R.M.
Château Broustet	Shot-oh Brew-STAY	Barsac, Fr.	Table Wine	White	Sweet	° ° °	Desserts
Château Caillou	Shot-oh Kah-YOU	Barsac, Fr.	Table Wine	White	Sweet	° ° °	Desserts
Château Calon-Ségur	Shot-oh Kah-lohn Say-G YOURE	Médoc, Fr.	Table Wine	Red	Dry	°	Ch., G., & R.M.
Château Camensac	Shot-oh Kah-men-SAHK	Médoc, Fr.	Table Wine	Red	Dry	°	Ch., G., & R.M.
Château Canon	Shot-oh KAH-no	St. Emilion, Fr.	Table Wine	Red	Dry	°	Ch., G., & R.M.
Château Cantemerle	Shot-oh Khan-teh-MEHRL	Médoc, Fr.	Table Wine	Red	Dry	°	Ch., G., & R.M.
Château Cantenac-Brown	Shot-oh Kahn-teh-nahk-BROWN	Médoc, Fr.	Table Wine	Red	Dry	°	Ch., G., & R.M.
Château Carbonnieux	Shot-oh Car-bohn-YOU	Graves, Fr.	Table Wine	White	Dry	° ° °	F., P., & L.M.
Château Certan-Giraud	Shot-oh Sehr-TAHN-Zhee-roh	Pomerol, Fr.	Table Wine	Red	Dry	°	Ch., G., & R.M.
Château Châlon	Shot-oh Shah-LOH	Jura, Fr.	Table Wine	White	Dry	° ° °	B.D.

NAME	PHONETIC SPELLING†	SOURCE	TYPE	COLOR	TASTE	SERV. TEMP.	SERVE WITH
Château Cheval Blanc	Shot-oh Sheh-vahl BLAHN	St. Emilion, Fr.	Table Wine	Red	Dry	°	Ch., G., & R.M.
Château Clerc-Milon-Mondon	Shot-oh Klerr-Mee-lohn-Mohn-DOHN	Médoc, Fr.	Table Wine	Red	Dry	°	Ch., G., & R.M.
Château Climens	Shot-oh Klee-MAHNS	Barsac, Fr.	Table Wine	White	Sweet	°°°	Desserts
Château Clos Fourtet	Shot-oh Kloh Foor-TAY	St. Emilion, Fr.	Table Wine	Red	Dry	°	Ch., G., & R.M.
Château Clos Haut-Peyraguey	Shot-oh Kloh oh-Pay-rah-GAY	Sauternes, Fr.	Table Wine	White	Sweet	°°°	Desserts
Château La Conseillante	Shot-oh Lah Kohn-say-AHNT	Pomerol, Fr.	Table Wine	Red	Dry	°	Ch., G., & R.M.
Château Cos d'Estournel	Shot-oh Koh deh-toor-NELL	Médoc, Fr.	Table Wine	Red	Dry	°	Ch., G., & R.M.
Château Cos-Labory	Shot-oh Koh-Lah-BOREE	Médoc, Fr.	Table Wine	Red	Dry	°	Ch., G., R.M.
Château Couhins	Shot-oh KWAHN	Graves, Fr.	Table Wine	White	Dry	°	F., P., & L.M.
Château Coutet	Shot-oh Koo-TAY	Barsac, Fr.	Table Wine	White	Sweet	°°°	Desserts
Château Croizet-Bages	Shot-oh Kwah-zet BAHJE	Médoc, Fr.	Table Wine	Red	Dry	°	Ch., G., & R.M.
Château Dauzac	Shot-oh Dough-ZAHK	Médoc, Fr.	Table Wine	Red	Dry	°	Ch., G., & R.M.
Château Doisy-Daëne	Shot-oh Dwah zee-Dah-AIN	Barsac, Fr.	Table Wine	White	Sweet	°°°	Desserts
Château Doisy-Védrines	Shot-oh Dwah zee-Veh-DREEN	Barsac, Fr.	Table Wine	White	Sweet	°°°	Desserts
Château Ducru-Beaucaillou	Shot-oh Doo-crew-Bo-kah-YOH	Médoc, Fr.	Table Wine	Red	Dry	°	Ch., G., & R.M.
Château Duhart-Milon	Shot-oh Doo-are-Mee-LOHN	Médoc, Fr.	Table Wine	Red	Dry	°	Ch., G., & R.M.
Château Durfort-Vivens	Shot-oh Duhr-for-Vee-VAHN	Médoc, Fr.	Table Wine	Red	Dry	°	Ch., G., & R.M.
Château L'Evangile	Shot-oh Lev-ahn-G EEL	Pomerol, Fr.	Table Wine	Red	Dry	°	Ch., G., & R.M.
Château Ferrière	Shot-oh Feh-ree-EHR	Médoc, Fr.	Table Wine	Red	Dry	°	Ch., G., & R.M.
Château Figeac	Shot-oh Fee-ZHAHK	St. Emilion, Fr.	Table Wine	Red	Dry	°	Ch., G., & R.M.
Château Filhot	Shot-oh Feel-OH	Sauternes, Fr.	Table Wine	White	Sweet	°°°	Desserts
Château Gazin	Shot-oh Gah-ZEEN	Pomerol, Fr.	Table Wine	Red	Dry	°	Ch., G., & R.M.
Château Giscours	Shot-oh Zhis-KOOR	Médoc, Fr.	Table Wine	Red	Dry	°	Ch., G., & R.M.
Château Grand-Puy-Ducasse	Shot-oh Grahn-Poo ee-Duh-KAHS	Médoc, Fr.	Table Wine	Red	Dry	°	Ch., G., & R.M.
Château Grand-Puy-Lacoste	Shot-oh Grahn-Poo ee-Lah-KOHST	Médoc, Fr.	Table Wine	Red	Dry	°	Ch., G., & R.M.
Château Grillet	Shot-oh Gree-YAY	Côtes du Rhóne, Fr.	Table Wine	White	Dry	°°°	F., P., & L.M.
Château Gruaud-Larose	Shot-oh Grew-wahd-Lah-ROHZ	Médoc, Fr.	Table Wine	Red	Dry	°	Ch., G., & R.M.
Château Guiraud	Shot-oh Guee-ROH	Sauternes, Fr.	Table Wine	White	Sweet	°°°	Desserts
Château Haut-Bages-Libéral	Shot-oh Oh-Bahzh-Lee-beh-RAHL	Médoc, Fr.	Table Wine	Red	Dry	°	Ch., G., & R.M.
Château Haut-Bailly	Shot-oh Oh-Bay-YEE	Graves, Fr.	Table Wine	Red	Dry	°	Ch., G., & R.M.
Château Haut-Batailley	Shot-oh Oh-Boh-tie-YEE	Médoc, Fr.	Table Wine	Red	Dry	°	Ch., G., & R.M.
Château Haut-Brion	Shot-oh Oh-Bre-OHN	Graves, Fr.	Table Wine	Red	Dry	°	Ch., G., & R.M.
Château Haut-Brion-Blanc	Shot-oh Oh-Bre-ohn BLAHN	Graves, Fr.	Table Wine	White	Dry	°°°	F., P., & L.M.
Château d'Issan	Shot-oh Dees-SAHN	Médoc, Fr.	Table Wine	Red	Dry	°	Ch., G., & R.M.
Château Kirwan	Shot-oh Kir-WAHN	Médoc, Fr.	Table Wine	Red	Dry	°	Ch., G., & R.M.
Château Lafaurie-Peyraguey	Shot-oh Lah-foh-ree-Pay-rah-GAY	Sauternes, Fr.	Table Wine	White	Sweet	°°°	Desserts
Château Lafite-Rothschild	Shot-oh Lah-feet-Roh-SHIELD	Mèdoc, Fr.	Table Wine	Red	Dry	°	Ch., G., & R.M.

SYMBOLS: *Service Temperature* ° (Room Temperature)—°° (Slightly Chilled)—°°° (Cold.) *Serve With:* A.D. (After Dinner)—All F. (All Food)—B.D. (Before Dinner)—C. (Cocktails)—Ch. (Cheese)—F. (Fish)—Fr. (Fruits)—G. (Game)—H. (Highballs)—Hosp. (Hospitality, any time)—L.M. (Light Meats)—P. (Poultry)—Pun. (Punches)—R.M. (Red Meats)—S. (Straight.) † NOTE: Accented syllable is capitalized.

NAME	PHONETIC SPELLING†	SOURCE	TYPE	COLOR	TASTE	SERV. TEMP.	SERVE WITH
Château La Fleur Petrus	Shot-oh Lah-fluhr Peh-TRUESS	Pomerol, Fr.	Table Wine	Red	Dry	°	Ch., G., & R.M.
Château Lafon Rochet	Shot-oh Lah-foh Rohw-SHAY	Médoc, Fr.	Table Wine	Red	Dry	°	Ch., G., & R.M.
Château La Gaffelière	Shot-oh Lah-Gah-fell-YEE_R	St. Emilion, Fr.	Table Wine	Red	Dry	°	Ch., G., & R.M.
Château La Garde	Shot-oh Lah-GUARD	Graves, Fr.	Table Wine	Red	Dry	°	Ch., G., & R.M.
Château Lagrange	Shot-oh Lah-GRAHN_SH	Médoc, Fr.	Table Wine	Red	Dry	°	Ch., G., & R.M.
Château La Lagune	Shot-oh Lah-Lah-gee-OON	Médoc, Fr.	Table Wine	Red	Dry	°	Ch., G., & R.M.
Château La Mission-Haut-Brion	Shot-oh Lah-Mee-shoh-Oh-Bree-OHN	Graves, Fr.	Table Wine	Red	Dry	°	Ch., G., & R.M.
Château Lamothe	Shot-oh Lah-MOAT	Sauternes, Fr.	Table Wine	White	Sweet	° ° °	Desserts
Château Langoa-Barton	Shot-oh Lahn-go_ah Bahr-TOH	Médoc, Fr.	Table Wine	Red	Dry	°	Ch., G., & R.M.
Château Laroze	Shot-oh Lah-ROSE	St. Emilion, Fr.	Table Wine	Red	Dry	°	Ch., G., & R.M.
Château Larrivet-Haut-Brion	Shot-oh Lah-ree-vay-Oh-Bree-OHN	Graves, Fr.	Table Wine	White	Dry	° ° °	F., P., & L.M.
Château Lascombes	Shot-oh Lahs-COMB	Médoc, Fr.	Table Wine	Red	Dry	°	Ch., G., & R.M.
Château Latour	Shot-oh Lah-TOOR	Médoc, Fr.	Table Wine	Red	Dry	°	Ch., G., & R.M.
Château La Tour Blanche	Shot-oh Lah-Toor BLAHNSH	Sauternes, Fr.	Table Wine	White	Sweet	° ° °	Desserts
Château La Tour Carnet	Shot-oh Lah-Toor Car-NAY	Médoc, Fr.	Table Wine	Red	Dry	°	Ch., G., & R.M.
Château La Tour Haut Brion	Shot-oh Lah-Toor Oh-bree-OHN	Graves, Fr.	Table Wine	Red	Dry	°	Ch., G., & R.M.
Château La Tour Martillac	Shot-oh Lah-Toor Mahr-tee-YAH_K	Graves, Fr.	Table Wine	Red, White	Dry	° & ° ° °	Varies with color
Château Latour-Pomerol	Shot-oh Lah-toor-Pohm-ROHL	Pomerol, Fr.	Table Wine	Red	Dry	°	Ch., G., & R.M.
Château Laville-Haut-Brion	Shot-oh Lah-vee Oh-bree-OHN	Graves, Fr.	Table Wine	White	Dry	° ° °	F., P., & L.M.
Château Léoville-Barton	Shot-oh Lay-oh-veal-Bar-TOHN	Médoc, Fr.	Table Wine	Red	Dry	°	Ch., G., & R.M.
Château Léoville-Las-Casses	Shot-oh Lay-oh-veal-Lahs-KAIIS	Médoc, Fr.	Table Wine	Red	Dry	°	Ch., G., & R.M.
Château Léoville-Poyferré	Shot-oh Lay-oh-veal Pwah-feh-RAY	Médoc, Fr.	Table Wine	Red	Dry	°	Ch., G., & R.M.
Château Lynch-Bages	Shot-oh Leensh-BAHZSH	Médoc, Fr.	Table Wine	Red	Dry	°	Ch., G., & R.M.
Château Lynch-Moussas	Shot-oh Leensh-Moo-SAH	Médoc, Fr.	Table Wine	Red	Dry	°	Ch., G., & R.M.
Château Magdelaine	Shot-oh Mahg-deh-LEHN	St. Emilion, Fr.	Table Wine	Red	Dry	°	Ch., G., & R.M.
Château Malescot-St. Exupéry	Shot-oh Mahl-ehs-coe-Sahnt Ex-uh-PEHREE	Médoc, Fr.	Table Wine	Red	Dry	°	Ch., G., & R.M.
Château de Malle	Shot-oh deh MAHL	Sauternes, Fr.	Table Wine	White	Sweet	° ° °	Desserts
Château Margaux	Shot-oh Mahr-GO	Médoc, Fr.	Table Wine	Red	Dry	°	Ch., G., & R.M.
Château Marquis d'Alesme-Becker	Shot-oh Mahr-key dah-LEHM-Bek-ker	Médoc, Fr.	Table Wine	Red	Dry	°	Ch., G., & R.M.
Château Marquis de Terme	Shot-oh Mahr-key-deh-TEHRM	Médoc, Fr.	Table Wine	Red	Dry	°	Ch., G., & R.M.
Château Montrose	Shot-oh Mohn-ROSE	Médoc, Fr.	Table Wine	Red	Dry	°	Ch., G., & R.M.
Château Mouton Baron Philippe	Shot-oh Moo-tahw(n) Bah-rohn Feel-EEP	Médoc, Fr.	Table Wine	Red	Dry	°	Ch., G., & R.M.
Château Mouton-Rothschild	Shot-oh Moo-tahw-Roh-SHIELD	Médoc, Fr.	Table Wine	Red	Dry	°	Ch., G., & R.M.
Château Myrat	Shot-oh Mee-RAHT	Barsac, Fr.	Table Wine	White	Sweet	° ° °	Desserts
Château Nairac	Shot-oh Nav-RAHK	Barsac, Fr.	Table Wine	White	Sweet	° ° °	Desserts
Château Nenin	Shot-oh Neh-NEH	Pomerol, Fr.	Table Wine	Red	Dry	°	Ch., G., & R.M.

NAME	PHONETIC SPELLING†	SOURCE	TYPE	COLOR	TASTE	SERV. TEMP.	SERVE WITH
Château Olivier	Shot-oh Oh-lee V_YAY	Graves, Fr.	Table Wine	White, Red	Dry	° & °°°	Varies with color
Château Palmer	Shot-oh Pahl-MEHR	Médoc, Fr.	Table Wine	Red	Dry	°	Ch., G., & R.M.
Château Pape-Clément	Shot-oh Pop-Klay-MAHN	Graves, Fr.	Table Wine	Red	Dry	°	Ch., G., & R.M.
Château Pavie	Shot-oh Pah-VEE	St. Emilion, Fr.	Table Wine	Red	Dry	°	Ch., G., & R.M.
Château Pédesclaux	Shot-oh Pay-dehs-KLOH	Médoc, Fr.	Table Wine	Red	Dry	°	Ch., G., & R.M.
Château Petit Village	Shot-oh Peh-tee Vee-LAHZSH	Pomerol, Fr.	Table Wine	Red	Dry	°	Ch., G., & R.M.
Château Petrus	Shot-oh Peh-TRUESS	Pomerol, Fr.	Table Wine	Red	Dry	°	Ch., G., & R.M.
Château Pichon-Longueville-Baron	Shot-oh Pea-shohn-Lohng-veal-Bah-ROHN	Médoc, Fr.	Table Wine	Red	Dry	°	Ch., G., & R.M.
Château Pichon-Longueville-Lalande	Shot-oh Pea-shohn-Lohng-veal-Lah-LAHND	Médoc, Fr.	Table Wine	Red	Dry	°	Ch., G., & R.M.
Château Pontet-Canet	Shot-oh Pohn-tay Kah-NAY	Médoc, Fr.	Table Wine	Red	Dry	°	Ch., G., & R.M.
Château Pouget	Shot-oh Poo-ZHAY	Médoc, Fr.	Table Wine	Red	Dry	°	Ch., G., & R.M.
Château Prieuré-Lichine	Shot-oh Pre-uh-ray Lee-SHEEN	Médoc, Fr.	Table Wine	Red	Dry	°	Ch., G., & R.M.
Château Rabaud-Promis	Shot-oh Rah-boh-Proh-MEE	Sauternes, Fr.	Table Wine	White	Sweet	°°°	Desserts
Château Rausan-Ségla	Shot-oh Roh-zahn-SAY-glah	Médoc, Fr.	Table Wine	Red	Dry	°	Ch., G., & R.M.
Château Rauzan-Gassies	Shot-oh Roh-zahn-Gah-CEASE	Médoc, Fr.	Table Wine	Red	Dry	°	Ch., G., & R.M.
Château de Rayne-Vigneau	Shot-oh Deh-Reign-Vee-N_YOH	Sauternes, Fr.	Table Wine	White	Sweet	°°°	Desserts
Château Rieussec	Shot-oh Ree-uh-SEHK	Sauternes, Fr.	Table Wine	White	Sweet	°°°	Desserts
Château Ripeau	Shot-oh Ree-POH	St. Emilion, Fr.	Table Wine	Red	Dry	°	Ch., G., & R.M.
Château Romer	Shot-oh Roh-MEHR	Sauternes, Fr.	Table Wine	White	Sweet	°°°	Desserts
Château Saint-Pierre	Shot-oh Sahn-Pea-EHR	Médoc, Fr.	Table Wine	Red	Dry	°	Ch., G., & R.M.
Château Sigalas-Rabaud	Shot-oh Seeg-ah-lah-Rab-B_OH	Sauternes, Fr.	Table Wine	White	Sweet	°°°	Desserts
Château Smith-Haut-Lafitte	Shot-oh Smeet-Oh-Lah-FEET	Graves, Fr.	Table Wine	Red	Dry	°	Ch., G., & R.M.
Château Suduiraut	Shot-oh Sue-dee-R_OH	Sauternes, Fr.	Table Wine	White	Sweet	°°°	Desserts
Château Talbot	Shot-oh Tahl-BOH	Médoc, Fr.	Table Wine	Red	Dry	°	Ch., G., & R.M.
Château Du Tertre	Shot-oh Duh-TEHRTR	Médoc, Fr.	Table Wine	Red	Dry	°	Ch., G., & R.M.
Château Trimoulet	Shot-oh Tree-moo-lay	St. Emilion, Fr.	Table Wine	Red	Dry	°	Ch., G., & R.M.
Château Troplong Mondot	Shot-oh Troh-lohn Mohn-DOUGH	St. Emilion, Fr.	Table Wine	Red	Dry	°	Ch., G., & R.M.
Château Trotanoy	Shot-oh Troht-ah NWAH	Pomerol, Fr.	Table Wine	Red	Dry	°	Ch., G., & R.M.
Château Trottevieille	Shot-oh Troht-VEE_YAY	St. Emilion, Fr.	Table Wine	Red	Dry	°	Ch., G., & R.M.
Château Vieux Château-Certan	Shot-oh View-Shot-oh-Sehr-TAHN	Pomerol, Fr.	Table Wine	Red	Dry	°	Ch., G., & R.M.
Château Yquem	Shot-oh Ee-KEM	Sauternes, Fr.	Table Wine	White	Sweet	°°°	Desserts
Châteauneuf-du-Pape	Shot-oh-nuf-due-POP	Rhône, Fr.	Table Wine	Red	Dry	°	Ch., G., & R.M.
Chelois	Shell-OY	New York State	Table Wine	Red	Med. dry	°°	P., & R.M.
Chenin Blanc	Sheh-neen BLAHN	Calif., France	Table Wine	White	Dry	°°	F., P., & L.M.
Cherry Liqueur	Cherry Leek-EHR	Various	Liqueur	Red	Sweet, cherry	°	A.D.
Chevalier-Montrachet	Shehv-ah-lee-ay-Moan-rah-SHAY	Côte de Beaune, Fr.	Table Wine	White	Dry	°°°	F., P., & L.M.

SYMBOLS: *Service Temperature* ° (Room Temperature)—°° (Slightly Chilled)—°°° (Cold.) *Serve With:* A.D. (After Dinner)—All F. (All Food)—B.D. (Before Dinner)—C. (Cocktails)—Ch. (Cheese)—F. (Fish)—Fr. (Fruits)—G. (Game)—H. (Highballs)—Hosp. (Hospitality, any time)—L.M. (Light Meats)—P. (Poultry)—Pun. (Punches)—R.M. (Red Meats)—S. (Straight.) † NOTE: Accented syllable is capitalized.

NAME	PHONETIC SPELLING†	SOURCE	TYPE	COLOR	TASTE	SERV. TEMP.	SERVE WITH
Chianti	Key-AHN-tea	Tuscany, It.	Table Wine	Red	Dry	°	All F.
Chiaretto del Garda	Kee-ah-RETT-oh del Gar-dah	Verona, It.	Table Wine	Pink	Med. Dry	° ° °	All F.
Cider		Spain & England	Sparkling Wine	Straw	Sweet, fruity	° ° °	Hosp.
Clos des Lambrays	Kloh day Lahm-BRAY	Côte de Nuits, Fr.	Table Wine	Red	Dry	°	Ch., G., & R.M.
Clos des Mouches	Kloh-day-MOOSH	Côte de Beaune, Fr.	Table Wine	Red	Dry	°	Ch., G., & R.M.
Clos de la Perrière	Kloh-deh-lah Peh-ree-EHR	Côte de Beaune, Fr.	Table Wine	Red	Dry	°	Ch., G., & R.M.
Clos de la Roche	Kloh-deh-lah ROHSH	Côte de Nuits, Fr.	Table Wine	Red	Dry	°	Ch., G., & R.M.
Clos du Roi	Kloh-due RWAH	Côte de Beaune, Fr.	Table Wine	Red	Dry	°	Ch., G., & R.M.
Clos St. Denis	Kloh Sahn-Deh-KNEE	Côte de Nuits, Fr.	Table Wine	Red	Dry	°	Ch., G., & R.M.
Clos Sainte-Odile	Kloh Sahnt-Oh-DEAL	Alsace, Fr.	Table Wine	White	Med. dry	° ° °	All F.
Clos de Tart	Kloh deh-TAHR	Côte de Nuits, Fr.	Table Wine	Red	Dry	°	Ch., G., & R.M.
Clos de Vougeot	Kloh deh-Voo-ZHOW	Côte de Nuits, Fr.	Table Wine	Red	Dry	°	Ch., G., & R.M.
Cognac	Kohn-YAHK	Cognac, Fr.	Brandy	Brown	Dry	°	A.D.
Cointreau	Kwahn-TROH	Angers, Fr.	Liqueur	White	Sweet, orange	°	A.D.
Colares	Koh-LAHR-ehsh	Portugal	Table Wine	Red	Dry	°	All F.
Les Combettes	Lay Com-BETT	Côte de Beaune, Fr.	Table Wine	White	Dry	° ° °	F., P., & L.M.
Commanderia	Koh-mahn-deh-REE-ah	Cyprus	Dessert Wine	White	Sweet	°	A.D.
Cortaillod	Kohr-tie-OH	Switzerland	Table Wine	Red	Dry	°	Ch., & R.M.
Cortese	Kohr-TEH-seh	Piedmont, It.	Table Wine	White	Dry	° ° °	F., P., & L.M.
Le Corton	Luh-Kohr-TOHN	Côte de Beaune, Fr.	Table Wine	Red	Dry	°	Ch., G., & R.M.
Corton-Charlemagne	Kor-toh-Shahr-leh MAHN-yeh	Côte de Beaune, Fr.	Table Wine	White	Dry	° ° °	F., P., & L.M.
Corton-Pougets	Kor-toh-Poo-JAY	Côte de Beaune, Fr.	Table Wine	Red	Dry	°	Ch., G., & R.M.
Corvo di Casteldaccia	Kohr-voh dee Kah-stell-DAHCHEE-ah	Sicily, Italy	Table Wine	White & Red	Dry	° & ° ° °	Varies with color
Côte Rôtie	Koht Roh TEA	Rhône, Fr.	Table Wine	Red	Dry	°	Ch., G., & R.M.
Côteaux de la Loire	Koh-toh deh-lal-WAHR	Loire, Fr.	Table Wine	White	Med. sweet	° ° °	All F.
Crème de Bananes	Krehm deh-Bah-NAHN	Various	Liqueur	Golden	Sweet, banana	°	A.D.
Crème de Cacao	Krehm de Kah-KAH OH	Various	Liqueur	Chocolate	Sweet, chocolate	°	A.D.
Crème de Cassis	Krehm deh-Kah-SEES	France	Liqueur	Red	Sweet, currant	° ° °	H. & C., Apéritifs
Crème de Menthe	Krehm deh-MAHNT	Various	Liqueur	White & Green	Sweet, minty	° ° °	A.D.
Crème de Noyau	Krehm deh NOY-oh	France	Liqueur	Cream	Sweet	°	A.D.
Crème de Violettes	Krehm deh-Vee-oh-LET	Various	Liqueur	Violet	Sweet, violet	°	A.D.
Crème Yvette	Krehm Ee-VET	Conn., U.S.	Liqueur	Blue & Violet	Sweet, violet	°	A.D.
Csopaki Furmint	CHO-pah-key Foor-mint	Hungary	Table Wine	White	Dry	° ° °	F., P., & L.M.
Curaçao	Kuh-rah-SEW	Various	Liqueur	Orange	Sweet, orange	°	A.D.
Cynar	CHEE-nar	Italy	Apéritif	Brown	Bitter	° ° °	B.D.

NAME	PHONETIC SPELLING†	SOURCE	TYPE	COLOR	TASTE	SERV. TEMP.	SERVE WITH
Danziger Goldwasser	Dahnt-zeeg-ehr GAWLD-vahss-ehr	Danzig	Liqueur	White	Sweet	°	A.D.
Dão	DOW	Portugal	Table Wine	Red & White	Dry	° & °°°	Varies with color
Debroi Harslevelu	DEH-broy Harsh-leh-vell-you	Hungary	Table Wine	White	Med. sweet	°°°	All F.
Deidesheimer Leinhöhle	Die-dehs-high-mehr LINE-hoil-eh	Rhine, Ger.	Table Wine	White	Dry	°°°	F., P., & L.M.
Demerara Rum	Dem-eh-RAH-rah	British Guiana	Rum	Dark	Med. sweet	°°°	C., H., Pu., & S.
Dézaley	Day-zah-LAY	Switzerland	Table Wine	White	Dry	°°°	F., P., & L.M.
Dhroner Hofberg	Drohn-ehr HOHFF-behrk	Moselle, Ger.	Table Wine	White	Dry	°°°	F., P., & L.M.
Dolcetto	Dohl-CHET-toh	Piedmont, It.	Table & Sparkling	Red	Dry & Sweet	° & °°°	All F.
Dôle de Sion	Dohl-deh-SEE OH	Switzerland	Table Wine	Red	Dry	°	Ch., G., & R.M.
Dom Avelsbacher	Dome AH-vels-bahkh-ehr	Moselle, Ger.	Table Wine	White	Dry	°°°	F., P., & L.M.
Domaine de Chevalier	Duh-menn deh Shehv-ah-LEE AY	Graves, Fr.	Table Wine	Red, White	Dry	° & °°°	Varies with color
Drambuie	Dram-BOO EE	Scotland	Liqueur	Golden	Sweet, spicy	°	A.D.
Dubonnet	Do-boh-NAY	France	Apéritif	Red	Sweet	°°°	B.D.
Dürkheimer Michelsberg	Dirk-high-mehr MEEKELS-behrk	Rheinpfalz, Ger.	Table Wine	White	Med. dry	°°°	F., P., & L.M.
Dürkheimer Spielberg	Dirk-high-mehr-SHPEEL-behrk	Rheinpfalz, Ger.	Table Wine	White	Med. dry	°°°	F., P., & L.M.
Eau de Vie de Marc	Ode-vee deh MAHR	France	Brandy	Brown	Dry	°	A.D.
Eau de Vie de Poire	Ode-vee deh PWAHR	Various	Pear Brandy	White	Dry, pear	°°°	A.D.
Echézeaux, Les	Lays A-sheh-ZOH	Côte de Nuits, Fr.	Table Wine	Red	Dry	°	Ch., G., & R.M.
Egri Bikaver	Egg-ree BEE-kah-vehr	Hungary	Table Wine	Red	Dry	°	Ch., G., & R.M.
Eiswein	ICE-wine	Rhine & Moselle, Ger.	Table Wine	White	Sweet	°°°	Desserts
Enkircher Steffensberg	Eng-keerr kh-ehr SHTEFF-ens-behrk	Moselle, Ger	Table Wine	White	Dry	°°°	F., P., & L.M.
Erdener Treppchen	Ehrd-nehr TREPPF-shen	Moselle, Ger	Table Wine	White	Dry	°°°	F., P., & L.M.
Escherndorfer Lump	Eh-shehrn-dorf-ehr LOOMP	Franconia, Ger.	Table Wine	White	Dry	°°°	F., P., & L.M.
Est! Est!! Est!!!	Ehst—Ehst—EHST	Latium, It.	Table Wine	White	Dry	°°°	F., P., & L.M.
Falerno	Fah-LEHR-no	Campania, It.	Table Wine	Red & White	Dry	° & °°°	Varies with color
Fendent de Sion	Fahn-dah deh SEE OH	Switzerland	Table Wine	White	Dry	°°°	F., P., & L.M.
Fernet Branca	Fehr-nett BRAHN-kah	Italy & U.S.	Bitters	Dark	Bitter	°	C. & H.
Fino	FEE-noh	Jerez, Spain	Sherry	White	Dry	° °	B.D.
Fior d'Alpe	Fee ore DOLL-peh	Italy	Liqueur	Golden	Sweet	°	A.D.
Fleurie	Fluh-REE	Beaujolais, Fr.	Table Wine	Red	Dry	°	All F.
Folle Blanche	Fohl BLONSH	Calif.	Table Wine	White	Dry	° °	F., P., & L.M.
Forbidden Fruit		Pennsylvania, U.S.	Liqueur	Orange	Sweet	°	A.D.
Forster Kirchenstück	Fours-tehr KEERR KH-enn-shtick	Rhine, Ger.	Table Wine	White	Dry	°°°	F., P., & L.M.
Forster Ungeheuer	Four-stir UHNGEH-hoy-ehr	Rheinpfalz, Ger.	Table Wine	White	Dry	°°°	F., P., & L.M.
Fraise	Frehz	Various	Strawberry Brandy	White	Dry, Strawberry	°°°	A.D.
Framboise	Frahm-BWAHZ	Various	Raspberry Brandy	White	Dry, Raspberry	°°°	A.D.

SYMBOLS: *Service Temperature* ° (Room Temperature)—°° (Slightly Chilled)—°°° (Cold.) *Serve With:* A.D. (After Dinner)—All F. (All Food)—B.D. (Before Dinner)—C. (Cocktails)—Ch. (Cheese)—F. (Fish)—Fr. (Fruits)—G. (Game)—H. (Highballs)—Hosp. (Hospitality, any time)—L.M. (Light Meats)—P. (Poultry)—Pun. (Punches)—R.M. (Red Meats)—S. (Straight.) † NOTE: Accented syllable is capitalized.

NAME	PHONETIC SPELLING†	SOURCE	TYPE	COLOR	TASTE	SERV. TEMP.	SERVE WITH
Frascati	Frahs-KAH-tea	Latium, Italy	Table Wine	White	Med. sweet	° ° °	F., P., & L.M.
Frecciarossa	Frett-chah-ROH_SAH	Lombardy, It.	Table Wine	Red & White	Dry	° & ° ° °	Varies with color
Freisa	FREY-sah	Piedmont, It.	Table Wine	Red	Dry	°	Ch., G., & R.M.
French Vermouth		Midi, France	Aromatized Wine	White	Dry	° ° °	B.D. & C.
Galliano	Gah-lee-AH-no	Milan, Italy	Liqueur	Golden	Sweet	°	A.D.
Gamay	Gah-MAY	Calif. France	Table Wine	Red	Dry	° °	Ch., G., & R.M.
Gattinara	Gah-teen-AH-rah	Piedmont, It.	Table Wine	Red	Dry	°	Ch., G., & R.M.
Geisenheimer Mäuerchen	Guy-zen-high-mehr M_OWEHR-shen	Rhinegau, Ger.	Table Wine	White	Dry	° ° °	F., P., & L.M.
Geisenheimer Rothenberg	Guy-zen-high-mehr ROE-ten-behrk	Rhinegau, Ger.	Table Wine	White	Dry	° ° °	F., P., & L.M.
Geneva, Genever		Holland	Gin	White	Dry	°	B.D. & H.
Gentil	Zhahn-TEEL	Alsace, Fr.	Table Wine	White	Med. dry	° ° °	All F.
Gevrey-Chambertin	Zhev-ray Shahm-behr-TAHN	Côte de Nuits, Fr.	Table Wine	Red	Dry	°	Ch., G., & R.M.
Gewurztraminer	Geh-vurz-trah-mean-EHR	Alsace, Fr., California	Table Wine	White	Med. dry	° ° °	All F.
Gin, Dry		Various	Gin	White	Dry	° ° °	C., H., & S.
Gin, Old Tom		Eng. & U.S.	Gin	White	Med. sweet	° ° °	H. & S.
Giro di Sardegna	Gee-roh dee Sahr-deh N_YAH	Sardinia, It.	Dessert Wine	Red	Sweet	°	A.D.
Gomme, Syrop de	Seer_up-deh GAWM	France	Syrup	Grey	Sweet	° ° °	C. & Pu.
Graacher Himmelreich	Grah-her HIMM-ell-rye_kh	Moselle, Ger.	Table Wine	White	Dry	° ° °	F., P., & L.M.
Gragnano	Grah-N_YAII-no	Campania, It.	Table Wine	Red	Dry	°	Ch., G., & R.M.
Grand Marnier	Grahn Mahr-N_YAY	Cognac, Fr.	Liqueur	Orange	Sweet, orange	°	A.D.
Grands Echézeaux, Les	Lay-Grahns-A-sheh-ZOH	Côte de Nuits, Fr.	Table Wine	Red	Dry	°	Ch., G., & R.M.
Grao Vasco	Gray-OH Vas-Ko	Portugal	Table Wine	Red & White	Dry	° or ° ° °	Varies with color
Graves	GRAHV	Bordeaux, Fr.	Table Wine	White	Med. dry	° ° °	F., P., & L.M.
Greco di Gerace	Greh-koh dee Jeh-RAH-cheh	Calabria, It.	Table Wine	White	Med. dry	° ° °	F., P., & L.M.
Grenadine		Various	Syrup	Red	Sweet	° ° °	C. & Pu.
Grignolino	Gree-n_yoh-LEE-no	Piedmont, It.	Table Wine	Red	Dry	°	Ch., G., & R.M.
Grinzinger	GRIN-zing-ehr	Austria	Table Wine	White	Dry	° ° °	F., P., & L.M.
Grumello	Groo-MELL-oh	Lombardy, It.	Table Wine	Red	Dry	°	Ch., G., & R.M.
Gumpoldskirschner	GOOM-polls-keerr_kh-nchr	Austria	Table Wine	White	Dry	° ° °	F., P., & L.M.
Haitian Rum		Haiti	Rum	Straw	Dry	° ° °	C., Pun., H., & S.
Hallgartener Deutelsberg	Hahl-garten-ehr DOY-tells-behrk	Rhinegau, Ger.	Table Wine	White	Dry	° ° °	F., P., & L.M.
Hallgartener Schönhell	Hahl-garten-ehr SHOYN-hell	Rhinegau, Ger.	Table Wine	White	Dry	° ° °	F., P., & L.M.
Hattenheimer Engelmannsberg	Hahtten-high-mehr ENG-el-mahns-behrk	Rhinegau, Ger.	Table Wine	White	Dry	° ° °	F., P., & L.M.
Hattenheimer Nussbrunnen	Hahtten-high-mehr NOOSS-broonn-en	Rhinegau, Ger.	Table Wine	White	Dry	° ° °	F., P., & L.M.
Haut Barsac	Oh-Bar-SAHK	Barsac, Fr.	Table Wine	White	Sweet	° ° °	Desserts
Haut Sauterne	Oh-Soh-TURN	U.S.	Table Wine	White	Sweet	° ° °	Desserts
Haut Sauternes	Oh-Soh-TURN	Sauternes, Fr.	Table Wine	White	Sweet	° ° °	Desserts
Hermitage	Ehr-mee-TAHZH	Rhône, Fr.	Table Wine	Red & White	Dry	° & ° ° °	Varies with color
Hochheimer	HOH_KH-high-mehr	Rhine, Ger.	Table Wine	White	Dry	° ° °	F., P., & L.M.
Hochheimer Domdechaney	Hoh_kh-high-mehr DOME-deh-shah-nay	Rhinegau, Ger.	Table Wine	White	Dry	° ° °	F., P., & L.M.
Hochheimer Kirchenstück	Hoh_kh-high-mehr KEERR_KH en-shtick	Rhine, Ger.	Table Wine	White	Dry	° ° °	F., P., & L.M.

NAME	PHONETIC SPELLING†	SOURCE	TYPE	COLOR	TASTE	SERV. TEMP.	SERVE WITH
Hohenwarther	HOH-hen-Vahr-tehr	Austria	Table Wine	White	Dry	° ° °	F., P., & L.M.
Hollands		Holland	Gin	White	Dry	°	H., & S.
Hospices de Beaune	Uhs-peace-deh-BONE	Côte de Beaune, Fr.	Table Wine	Red & White	Dry	° & ° ° °	Varies with color
Inferno	Een-FEHR-no	Lombardy, It.	Table Wine	Red	Dry	°	Ch., G., & R.M.
Iphöfer Julius- Echter-Berg	Ipp-hoy-fehr YOOL-ee-uhs-Ehkht-ehr Behrk	Franconia, Ger.	Table Wine	White	Dry	° ° °	F., P., & L.M.
Ischia	EES-key-ah	Campania, It.	Table Wine	White	Dry	° ° °	F., P., & L.M.
Italian Vermouth		Italy	Aromatized Wine	Red	Bitter-sweet	° ° °	C., & B.D.
Jamaica Rum		Jamaica, B.W.I.	Rum	Golden & Dark	Med. sweet	° ° °	C., H., Pun., & S.
Johannisberger Erntebringer	Yoh-hahnn-iss-behrk-ehr EHRN-teh-bring-ehr	Rhinegau, Ger.	Table Wine	White	Dry	° ° °	F., P., & L.M.
Johannisberger Hölle	Yoh-hahnn-iss-behrk-ehr HOY_L-eh	Rhine, Ger.	Table Wine	White	Dry	° ° °	F., P., & L.M.
Johannisberger Riesling	Yoh-hahnn-iss-behrk-ehr REES-ling	California, Rhinegau, Ger.	Table Wine	White	Dry	° ° °	F., P., & L.M.
Josephshöfer	YOH-zeffs-hoy-fehr	Moselle, Ger.	Table Wine	White	Dry	° ° °	F., P., & L.M.
Juliénas	You-lee-EHN_AHS	Beaujolais, Fr.	Table Wine	Red	Dry	°	All F.
Kéknyelü	CAKE-kneel-you	Hungary	Table Wine	White	Dry	° ° °	F., P., & L.M.
Kirsch	KEERSH	Various	Cherry Brandy	White	Dry, cherry	° ° °	A.D.
Kirschwasser	KEERSH-vahss-ehr	Various	Cherry Brandy	White	Dry, cherry	° ° °	A.D.
Klösterneuberger	CLOISTER-new-bahrk-ehr	Austria	Table Wine	White	Dry	° ° °	F., P., & L.M.
Knipperlé	K_nipp-ehr-LAY	Alsace, Fr.	Table Wine	White	Dry	° ° °	All F.
Kokinello	Koh-key-NEHL-oh	Greece	Table Wine	Red	Dry, res-inated	° ° °	F., P., & L.M.
Kremser	KREHM-sir	Austria	Table Wine	White	Dry	° ° °	F., P., & L.M.
Kröver Nacktarsch	Kroy-vehr NAH_KH-tarsh	Moselle, Ger.	Table Wine	White	Med. dry	° ° °	F., P., & L.M.
Kümmel	KIM-mell	Various	Liqueur	White	Sweet, caraway	°	A.D.
Lacryma Christi	Lah-cream-ah CHRIS-tea	Campania, It.	Table Wine	White	Med. dry	° ° °	All F.
Lambrusco	Lahm-BROOS-coe	Emilia, It.	Sparkling Wine	Red	Med. sweet	° ° °	All F.
Leanyka Edes	LAY-ah-in-kah-A-dehsh	Hungary	Table Wine	White	Med. sweet	° ° °	F., P., & L.M.
Leanyka Szaras	LAY-ah-in-kah ZHAH-rahzh	Hungary	Table Wine	White	Dry	° ° °	F., P., & L.M.
Liebfraumilch	LEEB-fr_ow-mill_kh	Rhine, Ger.	Table Wine	White	Med. dry	° ° °	F., P., & L.M.
Lillet	Lee-LAY	France	Apéritif	White	Bitter	° ° °	B.D.
Mâcon	MAH-coh(n)	Mâconnais, Fr.	Table Wine	Red	Dry	°	Ch., G., & R.M.
Madeira	May-DAY-rah	Madeira	Fortified Wine	Golden	Dry & Sweet	°	Hosp.
Malaga	MAH-lah-gah	Malaga, Sp.	Fortified Wine	Dark	Sweet	°	Hosp.
Malmsey	MAHM-zee	Madeira	Fortified Wine	Dark	Sweet	°	Hosp.
Malvasia di Lipari	Mahl-vah-see_ah dee-LEE-pah-ree	Sicily, It.	Fortified Wine	Golden	Sweet	°	Hosp.
Manzanilla	Mahn-sah-KNEE-yah	Jerez, Sp.	Sherry	Straw	Dry	° ° °	Hosp.
Maraschino	Mah-rahs-KEY-no	Various	Liqueur	White	Sweet, cherry	°	A.D.
Marco	MAHR-koh	Greece	Table Wine	Red	Dry	°	Ch., G., & R.M.
Markobrunner	MAHR-koh-brew-nehr	Rhine, Ger.	Table Wine	White	Dry	° ° °	F., P., & L.M.
Marsala	Mahr-SAH-lah	Sicily, It.	Dessert Wine	Brown	Sweet	°	Hosp.

SYMBOLS: *Service Temperature* ° (Room Temperature)—°° (Slightly Chilled)—°°° (Cold.) *Serve With:* A.D. (After Dinner)—All F. (All Food)—B.D. (Before Dinner)—C. (Cocktails)—Ch. (Cheese)—F. (Fish)—Fr. (Fruits)—G. (Game)—H. (Highballs)—Hosp. (Hospitality, any time)—L.M. (Light Meats)—P. (Poultry)—Pun. (Punches)—R.M. (Red Meats)—S. (Straight.) † NOTE: Accented syllable is capitalized.

NAME	PHONETIC SPELLING†	SOURCE	TYPE	COLOR	TASTE	SERV. TEMP.	SERVE WITH
Mastikha	MAHS-tea-kah	Greece	Liqueur	Cloudy White	Sweet	° ° °	B.D., & H.
Mavrodaphne	Mahv-roh-DAHF-neh	Greece	Dessert Wine	Red	Sweet	°	A.D.
Maximin Grünhäuser	Mahx-ee-mean GRUEEN-hoyss-ehr	Moselle, Ger.	Table Wine	White	Dry	° ° °	F., P., & L.M.
May Wine		Germany	Table Wine	White	Med. sweet	° ° °	All F.
Médoc	MAY-dohk	Medoc, Fr.	Table Wine	Red	Dry	°	Ch., G., & R.M.
Mercurey	Mehr-cue-RAY	Chalonnais, Fr.	Table Wine	Red	Dry	°	Ch., G., & R.M.
Meursault	Mere-SOH	Côte de Beaune, Fr.	Table Wine	White	Dry	° ° °	F., P., & L.M.
Meursault-Charmes	Mehr-soh-SHAHRM	Côte de Beaune, Fr.	Table Wine	White	Dry	° ° °	F., P., & L.M.
Meursault-Genevrières	Mere-so Zhahn-eh-VREE EHR	Côte de Beaune, Fr.	Table Wine	White	Dry	° ° °	F., P., & L.M.
Meursault-La Goutte d'Or	Mere-so-lah-goot-DOOR	Côte de Beaune, Fr.	Table Wine	White	Dry	° ° °	F., P., & L.M.
Mirabelle	Mee-rah-BELL	Alsace, Fr.	Plum Brandy	White	Dry, plum	° ° °	A.D.
Monastique	Mon-as-teek	France	Liqueur	Brown	Sweet	°	A.D.
Montilla	Mohn-TEA-yah	Cordova, Sp.	Apéritif Wine	Straw	Dry	° ° °	Hosp. & B.D.
Montrachet, Le	Leh-Mohn-rah-SHAY	Côte de Beaune, Fr.	Table Wine	White	Dry	° ° °	F., P., & L.M.
Moore's Diamond		New York State	Table Wine	White	Dry	° ° °	F., P., & L.M.
Moscatel de Malaga	Mohs-kah-tell deh-MAH-lah-gah	Malaga, Sp.	Fortified Wine	Golden	Sweet	°	Hosp.
Moscatel de Sitges	Mohs-kah-tell deh-SEET-yes	Catalonia, Sp.	Fortified Wine	Golden	Sweet	°	Hosp.
Moscato-Fior d'Arancio	Mohs-kah-toh-Fee or dah-RAHN-choh	Sicily, It.	Fortified Wine	Golden	Sweet	°	Hosp.
Moscato di Pantelleria	Mohs-kah-toh dee-Pahn-tell-eh-REE AH	Sicily, It.	Fortified Wine	Golden	Sweet	°	Hosp.
Moscato di Salento	Mohs-kah-toh dee-sah-LEN-toh	Apulia, It.	Fortified Wine	Golden	Sweet	°	Hosp.
Moselblumchen	MOH-zell-bloom-shehn	Moselle, Ger.	Table Wine	White	Dry	° ° °	F., P., & L.M.
Moulin-à-Vent	Moo-lahn-ah-VAHN	Beaujolais, Fr.	Table Wine	Red	Dry	°	Ch., G., & R.M.
Muscadet	Moos-kah-DAY	Loire, Fr.	Table Wine	White	Dry	° ° °	F., P., & L.M.
Muscatel	Muss-kah-tell	California & New York	Fortified Wine	Gold	Sweet	°	A.D.
Les Musigny	Lay Moo-see N YEE	Côte de Nuits, Fr.	Table Wine	Red	Dry	° ° °	Ch., G., & R.M.
Muskotaly	MUSH-koh-tah-lec	Hungary	Table Wine	White	Dry	° ° °	F., P., & L.M.
Nackenheimer Rotenberg	Knock-enn-high-mehr ROH-ten-behrk	Rhinehesse, Ger.	Table Wine	White	Dry	° ° °	F., P., & L.M.
Nebbiolo	Neh-BEE O-loh	Piedmont, It.	Table Wine	Red	Dry	°	Ch., G., & R.M.
Neuchâtel	Nuh-shot-TELL	Switzerland	Table Wine	White	Dry	° ° °	F., P., & L.M.
Niersteiner Auflangen	Near-shtine-ehr OWF-lahnng-enn	Rhinehesse, Ger.	Table Wine	White	Dry	° ° °	F., P., & L.M.
Niersteiner Domthal	Near-shtine-ehr DOME-tahl	Rhinehesse, Ger.	Table Wine	White	Dry	° ° °	F., P., & L.M.
Niersteiner Heiligenbaum	Near-shtine-ehr HIGH-lee-genn-bahuhm	Rhinehesse, Ger.	Table Wine	White	Dry	° ° °	F., P., & L.M.
Niersteiner Hipping	Near-shtine-ehr HIPP-ing	Rhinehesse, Ger.	Table Wine	White	Dry	° ° °	F., P., & L.M.
Niersteiner Oelberg	Near-shtine-ehr OIL-behrk	Rhinehesse, Ger.	Table Wine	White	Dry	° ° °	F., P., & L.M.
Niersteiner Rehbach	Near-shtine-ehr RAY-bahkh	Rhinehesse, Ger.	Table Wine	White	Dry	° ° °	F., P., & L.M.
Nuit-St. Georges	Nwee-Sahn-Zhorzh	Côte de Nuits, Fr.	Table Wine	Red	Dry	°	Ch., G., & R.M.
Nussberger	NOOSS-behrk-ehr	Austria	Table Wine	White	Dry	° ° °	F., P., & L.M.

NAME	PHONETIC SPELLING†	SOURCE	TYPE	COLOR	TASTE	SERV. TEMP.	SERVE WITH
Oeil de Perdrix	Uh‿y deh-Pehr-DREE	Burgundy, Fr. Switzerland	Sparkling and Still Wine	Pink	Med. sweet	° ° °	All F.
Oloroso	Oh-loh-ROH-soh	Jerez, Sp.	Sherry Wine	Golden	Sweet	°	Hosp.
Oppenheimer Daubhaus	Ah-pen-high-mehr DOWB-house	Rhinehesse, Ger.	Table Wine	White	Dry	° ° °	F., P., & L.M.
Oppenheimer Herrenberg	Ah-pen-high-mehr HEHRR-enn-behrk	Rhinehesse, Ger.	Table Wine	White	Dry	° ° °	F., P., & L.M.
Oppenheimer Kreuz	Ah-pen-high-mehr KROYTS	Rhinehesse, Ger.	Table Wine	White	Dry	° ° °	F., P., & L.M.
Oppenheimer Krottenbrunnen	Ah-pen-high-mehr CROW-ten-brew-nenn	Rhinehesse, Ger.	Table Wine	White	Dry	° ° °	F., P., & L.M.
Oppenheimer Sackträger	Ah-pen-high-mehr ZAHCK-tray-gehr	Rhinehesse, Ger.	Table Wine	White	Dry	° ° °	F., P., & L.M.
Orange Bitters		Eng. & U.S.	Bitters	Orange	Bitter		C. & Pun.
Orgeat	Or-ZHAH	France	Syrup	Grey	Sweet, almond		C. & Pun.
Orvieto	Ohr-VEE‿EH-toh	Umbria, It.	Table Wine	White	Dry & Sweet	° ° °	F., P., Fr.
Ouzo	OOH-zo	Greece	Liqueur	Cloudy White	Sweet, licorice	° ° °	H. & C.
Parfait Amour	Pahr-fayt-Ah-MOOR	Various	Liqueur	Violet	Sweet	°	A.D.
Pastis de Marseilles	Pass-teas-duh-Mahr-SAY	Marseille, Fr.	Liqueur	Cloudy White	Sweet, licorice	° ° °	H., & B.D.
Pavillon Blanc du Château Margaux	Pay-vee-yon Blahn due Shot-oh Mahr-GO	Medoc, Fr.	Table Wine	White	Dry	° ° °	F., P., & L.M.
Peach Liqueur		Various	Liqueur	Brown	Sweet, fruity	°	A.D.
Pernand-Vergelesses	Pehr-nahn-Vehrzh-eh-LESS	Côte de Beaune, Fr.	Table Wine	Red	Dry	°	Ch., G., & R.M.
Pernod	Pehr-NOH	U.S. & Fr.	Liqueur	Green Gold	Sweet, licorice	° ° °	B.D., & H.
Perry		England	Sparkling Pear Wine	Straw	Sweet	° ° °	Desserts
Peter Heering		Denmark	Liqueur	Red	Sweet, cherry	°	A.D.
Pfaffstätter	PFAHFF-stay-tehr	Austria	Table Wine	White	Dry	° ° °	F., P., & L.M.
Piesporter Goldtröpfschen	Peas-porter GAWLD-trape‿f-shehn	Moselle, Ger.	Table Wine	White	Dry	° ° °	F., P., & L.M.
Piesporter Lay	Peas-porter-LIE	Moselle, Ger.	Table Wine	White	Dry	° ° °	F., P., & L.M.
Piesporter Taubengarten	Peas-port-ehr TAU-ben-gart-enn	Moselle, Ger.	Table Wine	White	Dry	° ° °	F., P., & L.M.
Pineau des Charentes	Pea-no day Shah-RAHNT	Cognac, Fr.	Fortified Wine	White	Sweet	° ° °	B.D.
Pinot Blanc	Pea-no BLAHN	Calif., France	Table Wine	White	Dry	° ° °	F., P., & L.M.
Pinot Chardonnay	Pea-no Shahr-dough-NAY	California, France	Table Wine	White	Dry	° ° °	F., P., & L.M.
Pinot Noir	Pee-noh NWAHR	Various	Table Wine	Red	Dry	°	Ch., G., & R.M.
Pisco	PEES-co	Pisco, Peru	Brandy	Golden	Dry	°	A.D.
Pommard	Poh-MAHR	Côte de Beaune, Fr.	Table Wine	Red	Dry	°	Ch., G., & R.M.
Pommard-Clos-de-la-Commareine	Poe-mahr-Kloh-duh-lah-Kuhm-ah-RAIN	Côte de Beaune, Fr.	Table Wine	Red	Dry	°	Ch., G., & R.M.
Pommard-Les-Epenots	Poe-mahr-lays Eh-pen-OH	Côte de Beaune, Fr.	Table Wine	Red	Dry	°	Ch., G., & R.M.
Pommard Jarolières	Poe-mahr-Zhahr-oh-LEE‿EHR	Côte de Beaune, Fr.	Table Wine	Red	Dry	°	Ch., G., & R.M.
Pommard-Platière	Poe-mahr-Plah-TEA‿EHR	Côte de Beaune, Fr.	Table Wine	Red	Dry	°	Ch., G., & R.M.
Pommard-Rugiens	Poe-mahr-Roo-ZHIH‿ENNS	Côte de Beaune, Fr.	Table Wine	Red	Dry	°	Ch., G., & R.M.

SYMBOLS: *Service Temperature* ° (Room Temperature)—° ° (Slightly Chilled)—° ° ° (Cold.) *Serve With:* A.D. (After Dinner)—All F. (All Food)—B.D. (Before Dinner)—C. (Cocktails)—Ch. (Cheese)—F. (Fish)—Fr. (Fruits)—G. (Game)—H. (Highballs)—Hosp. (Hospitality, any time)—L.M. (Light Meats)—P. (Poultry)—Pun. (Punches)—R.M. (Red Meats)—S. (Straight.) † NOTE: Accented syllable is capitalized.

NAME	PHONETIC SPELLING†	SOURCE	TYPE	COLOR	TASTE	SERV. TEMP.	SERVE WITH
Port		U.S.	Fortified	Red	Sweet	°	Hosp.
Porto		Portugal	Fortified Wine	Red	Sweet	°	Hosp.
Porter		England & Ireland	Malt Beverage	Dark	Bitter	° °	Hosp.
Pouilly-Fuissé	Poo-yee-Fwee-ZAY	Mâconnais, Fr.	Table Wine	White	Dry	° ° °	F., P., & L.M.
Pouilly Fumé	Poo-yee Foo-MAY	Loire, Fr.	Table Wine	White	Med. sweet	° ° °	F., P., & L.M.
Pousse Café	Poos Cah-FAY	France	Liqueur	Brown	Sweet	°	A.D.
Prunelle	Pruh-NELL	France	Liqueur	Brown	Sweet, plum	°	A.D.
Puligny-Montrachet	Puh-lee-n yee-Mohn-rah-SHAY	Côte de Beaune, Fr.	Table Wine	White	Dry	° ° °	F., P., & L.M.
Quetsch	KWEHTCH	Alsace, Fr.	Plum Brandy	White	Dry	° ° °	A.D.
Quinquina	Can-key-NAH	France	Apéritif	Red & White	Sweet-bitter	° ° °	B.D.
Raki	RAHK-ee	Turkey	Liqueur	White	Sweet	° ° °	A.D.
Randersackerer Pfülben	Rahn-dehr-zahck-ehrehr FOOL-benn	Franconia, Ger.	Table Wine	White	Dry	° ° °	F., P., & L.M.
Randersackerer Spielberg	Rahn-dehr-zahck-ehrehr SHPEEL-behrk	Franconia, Ger.	Table Wine	White	Dry	° ° °	F., P., & L.M.
Randersackerer Teufelskeller	Rahn-dehr-zahck-ehrehr TOY-fells-kell-ehr	Franconia, Ger.	Table Wine	White	Dry	° ° °	F., P., & L.M.
Raphael	Raf-fa-EL	France	Apéritif	Brown	Bitter	° ° °	B.D.
Rauenthaler Baiken	R ow-enn-tahl-ehr BY-kenn	Rhinegau, Ger.	Table Wine	White	Dry	° ° °	F., P., & L.M.
Rauenthaler Gehrn	R ow-enn-tahl-ehr GAYRN	Rhinegau, Ger.	Table Wine	White	Dry	° ° °	F., P., & L.M.
Rauenthaler Längerstuck	R ow-cnn tahl-ehr LAHNNG-enn-shtuck	Rhinegau, Ger.	Table Wine	White	Dry	° ° °	F., P., & L.M.
Rauenthaler Pfaffenberg	R ow-enn-tahl-ehr FAH-fenn-behrk	Rhinegau, Ger.	Table Wine	White	Dry	° ° °	F., P., & L.M.
Rauenthaler Weishell	R ow-enn-tahl-ehr VICE-hell	Rhinegau, Ger.	Table Wine	White	Dry	° ° °	F., P., & L.M.
Rauenthaler Wülfen	R ow-enn-tahl-ehr VILL-fenn	Rhinegau, Ger.	Table Wine	White	Dry	° ° °	F., P., & L.M.
Recioto Nobile	Reh-CHEEOH-toh Noh-BEEL-eh	Verona, It.	Sparkling Wine	Red	Sweet	° ° °	All F.
Retsina	Reet-SEE-nah	Greece	Table Wine	White	Dry, resinated	° ° °	All F.
Rhum	ROHM	France	Rum	Dark	Sweet	° ° °	C., H., Pun., & S.
Ricard	Ree-KAHR	France	Liqueur	Brown	Semi-Sweet	° ° °	B.D.
Richebourg, Les	Lay-Reesh-eh-BOOR	Côte de Nuits, Fr.	Table Wine	Red	Dry	°	Ch., G., & R.M.
Riesling	REES-ling	Various	Table Wine	White	Dry	° ° °	F., P., & L.M.
Rioja	Ree-OH-hah	Spain	Table Wine	Red, White	Dry	° & ° ° °	Varies with color
Rizling Szemelt	REES-ling Tseh-mehlt	Hungary	Table Wine	White	Dry	° ° °	F., P., & L.M.
Romanée, La	Lah-Roh-mah-NAY	Côte de Nuits, Fr.	Table Wine	Red	Dry	°	Ch., G., & R.M.
Romanée-Conti	Roh-mah-nay-KAHWN-tea	Côte de Nuits, Fr.	Table Wine	Red	Dry	°	Ch., G., & R.M.
Romanée-St. Vivant	Roh-may-nay-Sahn-Vee-VAHN	Côte de Nuits, Fr.	Table Wine	Red	Dry	°	Ch., G., & R.M.
Rosé, Vin	Vahn Roh-ZAY	Various	Table Wine	Pink	Dry	° ° °	All F.
Ruby·Porto		Portugal	Fortified Wine	Red	Sweet	°	Hosp.
Rüdesheimer Berg Bronnen	Ruee-des-high-mehr BEHRK Broh-nenn	Rhinegau, Ger.	Table Wine	White	Dry	° ° °	F., P., & L.M.
Rüdesheimer Berg Rottland	Ruee-des-high-mehr Behrk ROHT-lahnd	Rhinegau, Ger.	Table Wine	White	Dry	° ° °	F., P., & L.M.
Rüdesheimer Berg Schlossberg	Ruee-des-high-mehr Behrk SHLAWSS-behrk	Rhinegau, Ger.	Table Wine	White	Dry	° ° °	F., P., & L.M.

NAME	PHONETIC SPELLING†	SOURCE	TYPE	COLOR	TASTE	SERV. TEMP.	SERVE WITH
Rüdesheimer Häuserweg	Ruee-des-high-mehr HOI-sehr-vehg	Rhinegau, Ger.	Table Wine	White	Dry	°°°	F., P., & L.M.
Rüdesheimer Hinterhaus	Ruee-des-high-mehr HIN-ter-house	Rhinegau, Ger.	Table Wine	White	Dry	°°°	F., P., & L.M.
Rüdesheimer Klosterkiesel	Ruee-des-high-mehr KLOHSS-tehr-kee-zell	Rhinegau, Ger.	Table Wine	White	Dry	°°°	F., P., & L.M.
Ruppertsberger Hoheburg	Ruh-pehrts-behrk-ehr HOH-heh-boorg	Rhinepfalz, Ger.	Table Wine	White	Dry	°°°	F., P., & L.M.
Ruppertsberger Linsenbusch	Rupperts-behrk-ehr LEEN-sen-bush	Rhinepfalz, Ger.	Table Wine	White	Dry	°°°	F., P., & L.M.
Ruppertsberger Nussbien	Rupperts-behrk-ehr NOOSS-bean	Rhinepfalz, Ger.	Table Wine	White	Dry	°°°	F., P., & L.M.
Ruppertsberger Spiess	Rupperts-behrk-ehr SHPIES	Rhinepfalz, Ger.	Table Wine	White	Dry	°°°	F., P., & L.M.
Rye Whiskey		U.S.	Whiskey	Brown	Dry		C., H., Pun., & S.
St. Amour	Sahnt Ah-MOOR	Beaujolais, Fr.	Table Wine	Red	Dry	°	Ch., G., & R.M.
St. Emilion	Sahnt-A-mee-LEE_OHN	St. Emilion, Fr.	Table Wine	Red	Dry	°	Ch., G., & R.M.
St. Estèphe	Sahnt Ehs-TEFF	Médoc, Fr.	Table Wine	Red	Dry	°	Ch., G., & R.M.
St. Julien	Sahn Zhu L_YEN	Médoc, Fr.	Table Wine	Red	Dry	°	Ch., G., & R.M.
Saké	SAH-keh	Japan	Rice Beer	White	Dry	98°F.	All F.
Sancerre	Sahn-SEHR	Loire, Fr.	Table Wine	White	Med. dry	°°°	F., P., & L.M.
Santenay	Sahn-ten-AYE	Côte de Beaune, Fr.	Table Wine	Red	Dry	°	Ch., G., & R.M.
Sassella	Sah-SEH-lah	Lombardy, It.	Table Wine	Red	Dry	°	Ch., G., & R.M.
Saumur	SO-muhr	Anjou, Fr.	Table, Sparkling	White	Med. sweet	°°°	F., P., & L.M.
Sauterne	So-TEHRN	U.S.	Table Wine	White	Dry	°°°	All F.
Sauternes	So-TEHRN	Sauternes, Fr.	Table Wine	White	Sweet	°°°	Desserts
Sauvignon Blanc	So-vee-nyon BLAHN	California, France	Table Wine	White	Dry & Sweet	°°°	All F.
Scharzberg	SHAHRZ-behrk	Saar, Ger.	Table Wine	White	Dry	°°°	F., P., & L.M.
Scharzhofberg	SHAHRZ-hohf-behrk	Saar, Ger.	Table Wine	White	Dry	°°°	F., P., & L.M.
Schaumwein	SH_OWM-wine	Germany	Sparkling Wine	White	Med. & Sweet	°°°	All F.
Scheidam	SHE-dahm	Holland	Gin	White	Dry	°°°	S. & H.
Schloss Böckelheimer	Shlawss BOY_K-ell-high-mehr	Nahe, Ger.	Table Wine	White	Dry	°°°	F., P., & L.M.
Schloss Johannisberg	Shlawss Yoh-HAHNN-iss-behrk	Rhine, Ger.	Table Wine	White	Dry	°°°	F., P., & L.M.
Schloss Vollrads	Shlawss FAWLL-rahds	Rhine, Ger.	Table Wine	White	Dry	°°°	F., P., & L.M.
Scuppernong		Southeastern U.S.	Table Wine	White	Sweet	°°°	All F.
Sekt	SECKT	Germany	Sparkling Wine	White	Med. & Sweet	°°°	All F.
Semillion	Seh-mee-YONH	California	Table Wine	White	Dry & Sweet	°°°	All F.
Sercial	SIR-shahl	Madeira	Dessert Wine	Golden	Med. dry	°°	Hosp.
Sidra	SEED-rah	Northern Spain	Sparkling Cider	Gold	Sweet apple	°°°	Hosp.
Slivovitz	SHLIV-oh-wits	Hungary	Plum Brandy	Brown	Dry	°	A.D.
Sloe Gin		England & U.S.	Liqueur	Reddish	Sweet, astringent	°	A.D.
Soave	SUAH-veh	Verona, It.	Table Wine	White	Dry	°°°	F., P., & L.M.
Somlöyi Furmint	SIIOM-loy_ye Foor-mint	Somlöy, Hungary	Table Wine	White	Dry	°°°	F., P., & L.M.
Spanish Brandy		Jerez, Spain	Brandy	Brown	Med. dry	°	A.D.
Sparkling Burgundy		Burgundy, Fr. & U.S.	Sparkling Wine	Red & White	Med. sweet	°°°	All F.
Sparkling Moselle		Moselle, Ger.	Sparkling Wine	White	Sweet	°°°	All F.

SYMBOLS: *Service Temperature* ° (Room Temperature)—°° (Slightly Chilled)—°°° (Cold.) *Serve With:* A.D. (After Dinner)—All F. (All Food)—B.D. (Before Dinner)—C. (Cocktails)—Ch. (Cheese)—F. (Fish)—Fr. (Fruits)—G. (Game)—H. (Highballs)—Hosp. (Hospitality, any time)—L.M. (Light Meats)—P. (Poultry)—Pun. (Punches)—R.M. (Red Meats)—S. (Straight.) † NOTE: Accented syllable is capitalized.

NAME	PHONETIC SPELLING†	SOURCE	TYPE	COLOR	TASTE	SERV. TEMP.	SERVE WITH
Steinberger	SHTINE-behrk-ehr	Rhine, Ger.	Table Wine	White	Dry	° ° °	F., P., & L.M.
Steinwein	SHTINE-wine	Würzburg, Ger.	Table Wine	White	Dry	° ° °	F., P., & L.M.
Stout		England & Ireland	Malt Beverage	Dark	Bitter	° °	Hosp.
Strega	STRAY-gah	Benevento, It.	Liqueur	Golden	Sweet	°	A.D.
Suze	Souze	France	Aperitif	Brown	Bitter-Sweet	° ° °	B.D.
Swedish Punsch		Sweden	Liqueur	Yellow	Sweet, rummy	° ° °	A.D.
Sweet Catawba		Ohio & New York, U.S.	Table Wine	White	Sweet	° ° °	Desserts
Sylvaner	ZILL-vah-nehr	Alsace, Fr.	Table Wine	White	Med. dry	° ° °	All F.
Szilvanyi Zold	ZILL-vahn-ye Zuhld	Hungary	Table Wine	White	Med. sweet	° ° °	F., P., & L.M.
Tâche, La	Lah-TAHSH	Côte de Nuits, Fr.	Table Wine	Red	Dry	°	Ch., G., & R.M.
Tavel	Tah-VELL	Rhône, Fr.	Table Wine	Pink	Dry	° ° °	All F.
Tawny Porto		Portugal	Fortified Wine	Red	Sweet	°	Hosp.
Tegea	Teh-GAY-ah	Greece	Table Wine	Pink	Dry	° ° °	All F.
Tequila	Teh-KEY-lah	Mexico & U.S.	Spirit	Pale	Dry	°	C. & S.
Tokaji Aszu	TOHK-ah̲ye Ah-sue	Hungary	Tokay	White	Sweet	° °	Hosp., A.D.
Tokaji Szamorodni	TOHK-ah̲ye SAH-mah rohd-knee	Hungary	Tokay	White	Med. dry	° ° °	Hosp.
Traminer	Trah-mean-EHR	Alsace, Fr.	Table Wine	White	Med. dry	° ° °	All F.
Triple Sec		Various	Liqueur	White	Sweet, orange	°	A.D.
Trittenheimer Altarchen	Tritt-enn-high-mehr AHLT-ehr-shen	Moselle, Ger.	Table Wine	White	Dry	° ° °	F., P., & L.M.
Trittenheimer Apotheke	Tritt-enn-high-mehr Ah-poh-TAY-kuh	Moselle, Ger.	Table Wine	White	Dry	° ° °	F., P., & L.M.
Trittenheimer Laurenzuisberg	Tritt-enn-high-mehr L̲OW-rehn-see-uhs-behrk	Moselle, Ger.	Table Wine	White	Dry	° ° °	F., P., & L.M.
Ürziger Kranklay	Uehr-tsee-gehr KRAHNNK-lie	Moselle, Ger.	Table Wine	White	Dry	° ° °	F., P., & L.M.
Ürziger Wurzgarten	Uehr-tsee-gehr VUEHRTZ-gahr-ten	Moselle, Ger.	Table Wine	White	Dry	° ° °	F., P., & L.M.
Van Der Hum	VAN-der-huhm	South Africa	Liqueur	Gold	Sweet	°	A.D.
Valdepeñas	Vahl-deh-PEH-n̲yahs	La Mancha, Sp.	Table Wine	Red	Dry	°	Ch., G., & R.M.
Valpolicella	Vahl-poh lee-CHE-lah	Verona, It.	Table Wine	Red	Dry	°	Ch., G., & R.M.
Valtellina	Vahl-tell-LEE-nah	Lombardy, It.	Table Wine	Red	Dry	°	Ch., G., & R.M.
Verdelho	Vehr-DELL-yo	Madeira	Fortified Wine	White	Sweet	°	A.D., Hosp.
Verdicchio di Jesi	Vehr-deek-yoh dee-YAY̲Zee	Marches, It.	Table Wine	White	Dry	° ° °	Shellfish
Vernaccia	Vehr-NAH-chee-ah	Italy	Table Wine	White	Sweet	° ° °	Fr.
Villányi-Pécs	VILL-ahn-ye-Pehch	Pécs, Hungary	Table Wine	Red	Dry	°	G., & R.M.
Vinho Verde	VEEN̲YOH Vehr-deh	Portugal	Table Wine	Red & White	Dry	° & ° ° °	Varies with color
Vin Santo	Veen-SAHN-toh	Tuscany, It.	Table Wine	White	Sweet	° ° °	All F.
Vodka		Various	Spirit	White	Dry	° ° °	C., H., & S.
Volnay	Vuhl-NAY	Côte de Beaune, Fr.	Table Wine	Red	Dry	°	Ch., G., & R.M.
Vöslau	FOICE-l̲ow	Austria	Table Wine	Red	Dry	°	Ch., G., & R.M.
Vosne-Romanée	VUH-ohn-Roh-may-NAY	Côte de Nuits, Fr.	Table Wine	Red	Dry	°	Ch., G., & R.M.
Vouvray	Vouv-RAY	Touraine, Fr.	Table Wine	White	Sweet	° ° °	Fr.
Wackenheimer Böhlig	Vah̲kh-enn-high-mehr BOY-lick	Rhinepfalz, Ger.	Table Wine	White	Dry	° ° °	F., P., & L.M.
Wackenheimer Gerümpel	Vah̲kh-enn-high-mehr Guh-REEMP-ell	Rhinepfalz, Ger.	Table Wine	White	Dry	° ° °	F., P., & L.M.
Waldracher Hubertusberg	Vahlt-rah̲kh-ehr Uh-BEHR-toos-behrk	Ruwer, Ger.	Table Wine	White	Dry	° ° °	F., P., & L.M.

NAME	PHONETIC SPELLING†	SOURCE	TYPE	COLOR	TASTE	SERV. TEMP.	SERVE WITH
Wehlener Lay	Vay-len-ehr LIE	Moselle, Ger.	Table Wine	White	Dry	°°°	F., P., & L.M.
Wehlener Nonnenberg	Vay-len-ehr NAWNN-enn-behrk	Moselle, Ger.	Table Wine	White	Dry	°°°	F., P., & L.M.
Wehlener Sonnenuhr	Vay-len-ehr ZAWNN-enn-ehr	Moselle, Ger.	Table Wine	White	Dry	°°°	F., P., & L.M.
White Porto		Portugal	Apéritif	Golden	Sweet	°	Hosp., B.D.
Wiltinger Schlangengraben	Vill-teen-gehr SHLAHNNG-enn-grah-ben	Moselle, Ger.	Table Wine	White	Dry	°°°	F., P., & L.M.
Wisniowka	Vish-nyoof-ka	Poland	Liqueur	Red	Sweet	°°	A.D.
Würzburger Inner Leiste	Veertz-behrk-ehr INN-ehr Lice-teh	Franconia, Ger.	Table Wine	White	Dry	°°°	F., P., & L.M.
Würzburger Leiste	Veertz-behrk-ehr LICE-teh	Franconia, Ger.	Table Wine	White	Dry	°°°	F., P., & L.M.
Würzburger Neuberg	Veertz-behrk-ehr NOY-behrk	Franconia, Ger.	Table Wine	White	Dry	°°°	F., P., & L.M.
Würzburger Stein	Veertz-behrk-ehr SHTINE	Franconia, Ger.	Table Wine	White	Dry	°°°	F., P., & L.M.
Zeller Schwarze Katze	Tsel-ehr SHVAHRRTS_EH Kaht-suh	Moselle, Ger.	Table Wine	White	Dry	°°°	F., P., & L.M.
Zeltinger Himmelreich	Tselt-ing-ehr HIMM-mel-rye_kh	Moselle, Ger.	Table Wine	White	Dry	°°°	F., P., & L.M.
Zeltinger Schlossberg	Tselt-ing-ehr SHLAWSS-behrk	Moselle, Ger.	Table Wine	White	Dry	°°°	F., P., & L.M.
Zeltinger Sonnenuhr	Tselt-ing-ehr ZAWNN-enn-oor	Moselle, Ger.	Table Wine	White	Dry	°°°	F., P., & L.M.
Zinfandel	TZIN-fan-dell	Calif., U.S.	Table Wine	Red	Dry	°	Ch., G., & R.M.
Zubrovka	Zoo-BROHV-kah	Russia, Poland	Flavored Spirit	Straw	Dry	°°°	C., H., & S.

SYMBOLS: *Service Temperature* ° (Room Temperature)—°° (Slightly Chilled)—°°° (Cold.) *Serve With:* A.D. (After Dinner)—All F. (All Food)—B.D. (Before Dinner)—C. (Cocktails)—Ch. (Cheese)—F. (Fish)—Fr. (Fruits)—G. (Game)—H. (Highballs)—Hosp. (Hospitality, any time)—L.M. (Light Meats)—P. (Poultry)—Pun. (Punches)—R.M. (Red Meats)—S. (Straight.) † NOTE: Accented syllable is capitalized.

Note:
Any wine can be drunk with any food, and one should choose a wine according to his personal preference. Certain combinations of wine and food have developed, however, because they are generally pleasing. These are listed here for general guidance, but should not be taken as hard and fast rules. The best guide is your own experience.

It should be remembered, also, that many chilled white wines, either still or sparkling, may be drunk by themselves, as hospitality wines, or as apéritifs.

—Harriet Lembeck

VINTAGE CHART

"I abhor a slavish devotion to vintage charts. This vintage chart, like all others, expresses the personal opinion of its author or authors at the moment it is prepared. The relative quality of the wines of any vintage is necessarily very general. Some good wines are made in even 'poor' years and not all wines turn out 'great' in the great years."—Harold Grossman.

VINTAGE	52	53	54	55	56	57	58	59	60	61	62	63	64	65	66	67	68	69	70	71	72
Red Bordeaux	9C	9C	3D	9C	X	7C	6C	9C	6D	10C	8C	2C	8C	1C	9B	8B	3C	8B	9A	8A	7A
Dry White Bordeaux	X	X	X	8	X	7	7	8	7	9	8	5	9	6	9	8	6	8	9	8	8
Sweet White Bordeaux	9	10	2	10	1	4	4	9	1	10	8	1	5	1	7	7	1	8	9	8	6
Red Burgundy Côte d'Or	8D	7D	5D	8D	1D	7D	4D	7D	2D	10C	8D	3C	9C	1D	9C	5C	2C	10B	8B	9A	7A
Red Burgundy Beaujolais	X	X	X	X	X	X	X	X	X	X	X	X	8D	3D	9D	7D	7D	9C	9C	9C	7B
White Burgundy	7	6	X	7	X	7	6	7	3	9	9	3	9	4	10	8	6	10	9	9	7
Loire	9	9	3	9	2	6	3	10	4	9	8	1	9	2	9	9	4	10	10	9	7
Rhône	9	9	5	8	4	8	7	8	8	10	8	4	9	6	9	9	3	8	10	8	9
Rhine	X	X	X	X	X	X	X	10	2	8	7	6	9	2	9	7	3	9	9	10	7
Moselle	X	X	X	X	X	X	X	9	2	7	6	5	10	2	9	6	3	9	9	10	7
Champagne	X	X	X	X	X	X	X	X	X	10	9	X	10	X	8	7	X	8	8	8	X

Letter Code for Red Bordeaux and Burgundy
A = Not at present ready for drinking.
B = Can be drunk now but development still to come.
C = Fully ready for drinking.
D = Approach with caution: could be good, but could be past best.
X = Probably past its prime, or not bottled as vintage.

Number Ratings:
1 to 10 relate to potential quality when fully mature. A mature wine of modest rating should be preferred to an immature wine whatever its *potential* quality. (10 is finest grade.)

Vintage charts are limited in what they can tell you. There is more pleasure in a miniature rose bush than in an acorn—even if the acorn will eventually be an oak tree. Drink red wines for what they can offer you *now*.

Prepared by Austin, Nichols & Co. Inc.

CONSUMPTION OF WINE PER CAPITA
IN DIFFERENT COUNTRIES

POSITION	COUNTRY	YEAR	LITERS	U.S. GALLONS
1	Italy	1972	110.9	29.30
2	France	1972	107.4	28.37
3	Portugal	1972	ca. 100	26.42
4	Argentina	1972	79.2	20.92
5	Spain	1972	63.5	16.78
6	Switzerland	1972	44.4	11.73
7	Chile	1971	ca. 44	11.62
8	Luxembourg	1972	41.5	10.96
9	Hungary	1972	40	10.57
10	Greece	1972	ca. 40	10.57
11	Austria	1972	34.0	8.98
12	Yugoslavia	1971	26.9	7.11
13	Uruguay	1971	26	6.87
14	Roumania	1970	23.1	6.10
15	West Germany	1972	22	5.81
16	Bulgaria	1971	19.3	5.10
17	Belgium	1972	15.6	4.12
18	Czechoslovakia	1971	ca. 12.5	3.30
19	U.S.S.R.	1972	12	3.17
20	Republic of South Africa	1972	9.97	2.63
21	Australia	1971/72	9.0	2.37
22	Cyprus	1972	8.2	2.17
23	Sweden	1972	7.9	2.09
24	Netherlands	1972	7.81	2.06
25	Denmark	1972	7.48	1.98
26	New Zealand	1971	7.14	1.89
27	Poland	1972	6.2	1.64
28	United States	1972	6.12	1.61
29	Canada	1971/72	5.46	1.44
30	East Germany	1972	5.3	1.40
31	Finland	1972	4.8	1.27
32	United Kingdom	1972	4.05	1.07
33	Tunisia	1972	3.7	.98
34	Israel	1972	3.67	.97
35	Lebanon	1971	ca. 3	.79
36	Norway	1972	2.74	.72
37	Iceland	1972	2.11	.56
38	Brazil	1971	ca. 2	.52
39	Paraguay	1971	ca. 2	.52
40	Republic of Ireland	1971	ca. 1.6	.42
41	Morocco	1971	ca. 1.3	.34
42	Peru	1971	1.14	.30
43	Turkey	1972	0.84	.22
44	Cuba	1971	0.8	.21
45	Algeria	1971	ca. 0.7	.19
46	Japan	1972	0.36	.10
47	Venezuela	1971	ca. 0.3	.07
48	Mexico	1972	ca. 0.25	.06

WINE PRODUCTION BY 1.000 HECTOLITER
(in order of magnitude)

POSITION	COUNTRY	1970	1971	U.S. GALLONS (in millions)
1	Italy	68,874	64,271	1,698
2	France	74,373	61,331	1,620
3	U.S.S.R.	26,845	28,723	759
4	Spain	31,344	25,073	662
5	Argentina	18,360	21,783	575
6	United States	11,670	16,807	444
7	Portugal	11,328	8,835	233
8	Algeria	8,692	8,250°	218
9	Roumania	5,040	7.700°	203
10	West Germany	9,890	6,027	159
11	Yugoslavia	5,478	5,546	147
12	Republic of South Africa	4,185	5,533	146
13	Chile	4,006	5,251	139
14	Greece	4,830	5,070	134
15	Hungary	4,380	4,459	118
16	Bulgaria	3,750	4,050	107
17	Australia	2,869	2,514	66
18	Brazil	2,300	2,300°	61
19	Austria	3,096	1,813	48
20	Poland	1,400°	1,400°	37
21	Morocco	1,253	1,150°	30
22	Tunisia	600	941	25
23	Uruguay	857	910°	24
24	Czechoslovakia	721	863	23
25	Switzerland	1,179	861	23
26	Canada	440	600	16
27	Turkey	458	520°	14
28	Cyprus	399	495	13
29	Israel	301	330	9
30	Mexico	144	219	6
31	New Zealand	185	205	5
32	East Germany	200°	200°	5
33	Peru	200	200°	5
34	Azores	158	170	4
35	Japan	152	155	4
36	Madeira	133°	130°	3
37	Luxembourg	242	105	2
38	Cuba	100°	100°	2
39	Albania	40°	70°	1.9
40	Egypt	30°	54	1.5
41	Lebanon	42	38°	1.0
42	Libya	30°	30°	.8
43	Venezuela	25°	25°	.67
44	Malta	20°	20°	.54
45	Madagascar	17°	17°	.46
46	Jordan	15°	15°	.40
47	Netherlands	12	12	.32
48	Syria	7°	7°	.18
49	Bolivia	6°	6°	.16
50	Belgium	5	5	.13
51	Iran	4°	4°	.10
52	Colombia	1°	1°	.02
	WORLD PRODUCTION: (about)	310,000	295,000	

° Estimated

BEER CONSUMPTION PER CAPITA
OF POPULATION IN VARIOUS COUNTRIES

POSITION	COUNTRY	YEAR	LITRES	U.S. GALLONS
1	West Germany	1972	145.30	38.39
2	Czechoslovakia	1971	144.7	38.23
3	Belgium	1972	ca. 140	36.99
4	Australia	1971/72	127.2	33.60
5	Luxembourg	1972	124.0	32.76
6	New Zealand	1971	121.4	32.07
7	Denmark	1972	107.79	28.48
8	East Germany	1972	106.5	28.13
9	United Kingdom	1972	106.0	28.00
10	Austria	1972	103.7	27.40
11	Canada	1971/72	83.5	22.06
12	Switzerland	1972	73.6	19.44
13	United States	1972	73.4	19.39
14	Ireland	1971	73.0	19.28
15	Netherlands	1972	65.88	17.40
16	Hungary	1972	59	15.89
17	Sweden	1972	57.4	15.16
18	Finland	1972	53.8	14.21
19	Norway	1972	41.22	10.89
20	France	1972	40.3	10.64
21	Venezuela	1971	ca. 40	10.57
22	Spain	1972	36	9.51
23	Poland	1972	35.3	9.33
24	Bulgaria	1971	ca. 35	9.25
25	Colombia	1971	33.8	8.93
26	Japan	1972	31.9	8.43
27	Yugoslavia	1971	29.7	7.85
28	Mexico	1972	27.7	7.85
29	Uruguay	1971	ca. 23	6.08
30	Chile	1971	22.3	5.91
31	Surinam	1971	22	5.81
32	Roumania	1970	21.9	5.79
33	Cuba	1971	21.4	5.65
34	Peru	1971	21.07	5.57
35	Cyprus	1972	20.1	5.31
36	U.S.S.R.	1972	ca. 18	4.76
37	Argentina	1972	ca. 17	4.49
38	Portugal	1972	16.3	4.31
39	Iceland	1972	ca. 14	3.70
40	Republic of South Africa	1972	13.0	3.43
41	Italy	1972	12.5	3.30
42	Greece	1972	ca. 11	2.91
43	Israel	1972	10.28	2.72
44	Brazil	1971	9.6	2.54
45	Paraguay	1971	7.8	2.06
46	Tunisia	1972	ca. 4	1.07
47	Algeria	1971	3.5	.93
48	Lebanon	1971	ca. 3	.79
49	Morocco	1971	2.1	.56
50	Turkey	1972	1.31	.35

CONSUMPTION OF DISTILLED SPIRITS PER CAPITA OF POPULATION IN VARIOUS COUNTRIES

POSITION	COUNTRY	YEAR	LITRES 100%	U.S. GALLONS AT 80 PROOF
1	Poland	1972	3.8	2.50
2	Hungary	1972	3.0	1.98
3	United States	1972	2.95	1.94
4	West Germany	1972	2.93	1.94
5	Spain	1972	2.9	1.92
6	Canada	1971/72	2.86	1.88
7	Yugoslavia	1971	2.8	1.84
8	Luxembourg	1972	2.8	1.84
9	East Germany	1972	2.7	1.78
10	Sweden	1972	2.65	1.75
11	Surinam	1971	2.5	1.65
12	Iceland	1972	2.49	1.64
13	Roumania	1970	2.4	1.58
14	Austria	1972	2.36	1.56
15	Czechoslovakia	1971	2.34	1.55
16	France	1972	ca. 2.3	1.51
17	Netherlands	1972	2.28	1.50
18	Finland	1972	2.2	1.45
19	Switzerland	1972	2.04	1.38
20	Bulgaria	1971	ca. 2	1.32
21	Italy	1972	1.9	1.25
22	Cyprus	1972	1.8	1.19
23	Norway	1972	1.66	1.10
24	Belgium	1972	1.59	1.05
25	Denmark	1972	1.54	1.01
26	Ireland	1971	1.46	.96
27	Peru	1971	ca. 1.4	.92
28	Mexico	1972	1.15	.76
29	Israel	1972	1.1	.73
30	Australia	1971/72	1.04	.69
31	United Kingdom	1972	1.03	.68
32	Republic of South Africa	1972	1.01	.67
33	Cuba	1971	1.0	.66
34	New Zealand	1971	ca. 1	.66
35	Portugal	1972	ca. 0.9	.59
36	Turkey	1972	0.36	.24

TOTAL ALCOHOLIC CONSUMPTION
(spirits, beers, and wines)
IN VARIOUS COUNTRIES
(in order of per capita consumption)

POSITION	COUNTRY	YEAR	LITRES 100%	U.S. GALLONS AT 80 PROOF
1	France	1972	16.9	11.16
2	Portugal	1972	13.7	9.05
3	Italy	1972	13.6	8.98
4	Spain	1972	12.3	8.12
5	West Germany	1972	12.1	7.99
6	Austria	1972	11.6	7.66
7	Luxembourg	1972	11.5	7.59
8	Switzerland	1972	10.8	7.13
9	Argentina	1972	10.4	6.86
10	Hungary	1972	9.7	6.41
11	Belgium	1972	9.5	6.27
12	Australia	1971/72	8.5	5.61
13	Czechoslovakia	1971	8.3	5.48
14	New Zealand	1971	7.9	5.22
15	Denmark	1972	7.7	5.09
16	Canada	1971/72	7.7	5.09
17	Yugoslavia	1971	7.5	4.95
18	United Kingdom	1972	6.9	4.55
19	Netherlands	1972	6.8	4.49
20	East Germany	1972	6.5	4.29
21	United States	1972	6.4	4.23
22	Chile	1971	6.4	4.23
23	Roumania	1970	6.3	4.16
24	Poland	1972	6.3	4.16
25	Bulgaria	1971	6.1	4.03
26	Sweden	1972	5.9	3.90
27	Japan	1972	5.7	3.76
28	Greece	1972	5.4	3.56
29	Ireland	1971	5.3	3.50
30	Finland	1972	5.2	3.43
31	Uruguay	1971	4.3	2.84
32	Norway	1972	3.9	2.58
33	Cyprus	1972	3.8	2.51
34	Surinam	1971	3.6	2.38
35	Iceland	1972	3.5	2.31
36	Republic of South Africa	1972	2.9	1.91
37	Peru	1971	2.6	1.72
38	Mexico	1972	2.4	1.58
39	U.S.S.R.	1972	2.3	1.52
40	Cuba	1971	2.2	1.45
41	Israel	1972	2.1	1.39
42	Venezuela	1971	2.0	1.32
43	Brazil	1971	0.7	.46
44	Paraguay	1971	0.6	.40
45	Tunisia	1972	0.6	.40
46	Lebanon	1971	0.5	.33
47	Turkey	1972	0.5	.33
48	Morocco	1971	0.3	.20
49	Algeria	1971	0.3	.20

Vins A Appellation D'Origine Contrôlé

Région d'Alsace

	WHITE BLANC	RED ROUGE	ROSÉ
Alsace ou Vin d'Alsace accompagne ou non d'un nom de cru	x	x	x

Région de Champagne

	WHITE BLANC	RED ROUGE	ROSÉ
Champagne (uniquement vin mousseux)	x		x
Rosé des Riceys			x

Région de Bourgogne, Mâconnais, Beaujolais

	WHITE BLANC	RED ROUGE	ROSÉ
Aloxe-Corton	x	x	
Auxey-Duresses	x	x	
Bâtard-Montrachet	x		
Beaujolais	x	x	x
Beaujolais suivi du nom de la commune d'origine	x	x	x
Beaujolais-Villages	x	x	x
Beaujolais Supérieur	x	x	x
Beaune	x	x	
Bienvenues-Bâtard-Montrachet	x		
Blagny		x	
Bonnes Mares		x	
Bourgogne	x	x	x
Bourgogne Aligoté	x		
Bourgogne-Hautes Côtes de Beaune	x	x	x
Bourgogne-Haute Côtes de Nuits	x	x	x
Bourgogne Marsannay-la-Cote	x	x	x
Bourgogne Mousseux	x	x	x
Bourgogne Ordinaire	x	x	x
Bourgogne Grand Ordinaire	x	x	x
Bourgogne-Passe-Tout-Grain		x	
Brouilly		x	
Chablis	x		
Chablis Grand Cru	x		
Chablis Premier Cru	x		
Chambertin		x	
Chambertin-Clos-de-Bèze		x	
Chambolle-Musigny		x	
Chapelle-Chambertin		x	
Charlemagne	x		
Charmes-Chambertin		x	
Chassagne-Montrachet	x	x	
Cheilly-les-Maranges	x	x	
Chenas		x	
Chevalier-Montrachet	x		
Chiroubles		x	
Chorey-les-Beaune	x	x	
Clos de la Roche		x	

477

Région de Bourgogne; Mâconnais; Beaujolais (cont.)

	WHITE BLANC	RED ROUGE	ROSÉ
Clos de Tart		x	
Clos de Vougeot		x	
Clos Saint-Denis		x	
Corton	x	x	
Corton-Charlemagne	x		
Cote de Beaune	x	x	
Cote de Beaune-Villages		x	
Cote de Beaune précédé du nom de la commune d'origine		x	
Cote de Brouilly		x	
Cote de Nuits-Villages	x	x	
Criots-Bâtard-Montrachet	x		
Dezize-les-Maranges	x	x	
Echezeaux		x	
Fixin	x	x	
Fleurie		x	
Gevrey-Chambertin		x	
Givry	x	x	
Grands-Echezeaux		x	
Griotte-Chambertin		x	
Juliènas		x	
Ladoix	x	x	
Latricières-Chambertin		x	
Mâcon	x	x	x
Mâcon suivi du nom de la commune d'origine	x	x	x
Mâcon-Villages	x		
Mazis-Chambertin		x	
Mazoyères-Chambertin		x	
Mercurey	x	x	
Meursault	x	x	
Montagny	x		
Monthelie	x	x	
Montrachet	x		
Morey-Saint-Denis	x	x	
Morgon		x	
Moulin-à-vent		x	
Musigny	x	x	
Nuits	x	x	
Nuits-Saint-Georges	x	x	
Pernand-Vergelesses	x	x	
Petit Chablis	x		
Pinot-Chardonnay-Mâcon	x		
Pommard		x	
Pouilly-Fuissé	x		
Pouilly-Loché	x		
Pouilly-Vinzelles	x		
Puligny-Montrachet	x	x	
Richebourg		x	
Romanée (la)		x	
Romanée-Conti		x	
Romanée-Saint-Vivant		x	
Ruchottes-Chambertin		x	
Rully	x	x	
Saint-Amour		x	

	WHITE BLANC	RED ROUGE	ROSÉ

Région de Bourgogne; Mâconnais; Beaujolais (cont.)

	WHITE BLANC	RED ROUGE	ROSÉ
Saint-Aubin	x	x	
Saint-Romain	x	x	
Saint-Véran	x		
Sampigny-les-Maranges	x	x	
Santenay	x	x	
Savigny	x	x	
Tache (la)		x	
Vins fins de la Côte des Nuits	x	x	
Volnay		x	
Vosne-Romanée		x	
Vougeot	x	x	

Région de Bordeaux

	WHITE BLANC	RED ROUGE	ROSÉ
Barsac	x		
Blaye ou Blayais	x	x	
Bordeaux	x	x	x
Bordeaux-Côtes de Castillon		x	
Bordeaux-Côtes de Francs	x	x	
Bordeaux-Haut Benauge	x		
Bordeaux mousseux	x		x
Bordeaux Supérieur	x	x	x
Bourg ou Bourgeais	x	x	
Cérons	x		
Côtes de Blaye	x		
Côtes de Bordeaux-Saint-Macaire	x		
Côtes de Bourg	x	x	
Canon Fronsac		x	
Côtes de Fronsac		x	
Entre-Deux-Mers	x		
Entre-Deux-Mers-Haut Benauge	x		
Graves	x	x	
Graves Supérieures	x		
Graves de Vayres	x	x	
Haut-Médoc		x	
Lalande de Pomerol		x	
Listrac		x	
Loupiac	x		
Lussac Saint-Emilion		x	
Margaux		x	
Médoc		x	
Montagne-Saint-Emilion		x	
Moulis ou Moulis-en-Médoc		x	
Néac		x	
Pauillac		x	
Parsac-Saint-Emilion		x	
Pomerol		x	
Premières Côtes de Blaye	x	x	
Premières Côtes de Bordeaux	x	x	
Premières Côtes de Bordeaux-Cadillac	x		
Premières Côtes de Bordeaux-Gabarnac	x		
Puisseguin-Saint-Emilion		x	
Sables-Saint-Emilion		x	
Sainte-Croix-du-Mont	x		

	WHITE BLANC	RED ROUGE	ROSÉ

Région de Bordeaux (cont.)

	WHITE BLANC	RED ROUGE	ROSÉ
Saint-Emilion		x	
Saint-Emilion Grand Cru		x	
Saint-Emilion Grand Cru Classé		x	
Saint-Emilion Premier Grand Cru Classé		x	
Saint-Estèphe		x	
Saint-Foy-Bordeaux	x	x	
Saint-Georges-Saint-Emilion		x	
Saint-Julien		x	
Sauternes	x		

Région du Sud-Ouest

	WHITE BLANC	RED ROUGE	ROSÉ
Bergerac	x	x	x
Blanquette de Limoux (unique ent vin mousseux)	x		
Cahors		x	
Côtes de Bergerac	x	x	
Côtes de Bergerac-Côtes de Saussignac	x		
Côtes de Duras	x	x	
Côtes de Montravel	x		
Fitou		x	
Gaillac	x	x	x
Gaillac Mousseux	x		x
Gaillac Premières Côtes	x		
Haut-Montravel	x		
Irouléguy	x	x	x
Jurançon	x		
Limoux Nature	x		
Madiran		x	
Monbazillac	x		
Montravel	x		
Pacherenc du Vic Bilh	x		
Pécharmant		x	
Rosette	x		
Vin de Blanquette	x		

Région des Côteaux et de la Vallée de La Loire

	WHITE BLANC	RED ROUGE	ROSÉ
Anjou	x	x	
Anjou Mousseux ou Pétillant	x		x
Cabernet de Sauaur			x
Anjou-Côteaux de la Loire	x		
Blanc Fumé de Pouilly	x		
Bonnezeaux	x		
Bourguei		x	x
Chinon	x	x	x
Côteaux de l'Aubance	x		
Côteaux du Layon	x		
Côteaux du Layon suivi de la commune d'origine	x		
Côteaux du Loir	x	x	x
Côteaux de Saumur	x		
Jasnières	x		
Menetou-Salon	x	x	x
Montlouis	x		
Montlouis Mousseux ou Pétillant	x		
Muscadet	x		
Muscadet des Côteaux de la Loire	x		

	WHITE BLANC	RED ROUGE	ROSÉ

Région des Côteaux et de la Vallée de La Loire (cont.)

	WHITE BLANC	RED ROUGE	ROSÉ
Muscadet de Sèvre-et-aine	x		
Pouilly-sur-Loire	x		
Pouilly Fumé	x		
Quarts de Chaumes	x		
Quincy	x		
Reuilly	x	x	x
Rosé d'Anjou			x
Sancerre	x	x	x
Saint-Nacolas de Bourgueil		x	x
Savennières	x		
Savennières-Coulée de Serrant	x		
Savennières-Roche aux Moines	x		
Saumur	x	x	
Saumur-Champigny		x	
Saumur Mousseux ou Pétillant	x		
Touraine	x	x	x
Touraine-Amboise	x	x	x
Touraine-Azay-le-Rideau	x		
Touraine-Mesland	x	x	x
Touraine Mousseux ou Pétillant	x	x	x
Vouvray	x		
Vouvray Mousseux ou Pétillant	x		

Région du Jura, des Côtes Du Rhône et du Sud-Est

	WHITE	RED	ROSÉ	STRAW WINE	YELLOW
Arbois	x	x	x	x	x
Arbois Pupillin	x	x	x	x	x
Arbois Mousseux	x	x	x		
Bandol	x	x	x		
Bellet	x	x	x		
Cassis	x	x	x		
Château-Chalon					x
Château-Grillet	x				
Châteauneuf-du-Pape	x	x			
Clairette de Bellegarde	x				
Clairette de Die	x				
Clairette de Die Mousseux	x				
Clairette du Languedoc	x				
Collioure		x			
Condrieu	x				
Cornas		x			
Côtes-du-Jura	x	x	x	x	x
Côtes du Jura Mousseux	x	x	x		
Côtes-du-Rhône	x	x	x		
Côtes-du-Rhône-Villages	x	x	x		
Côtes-du-Rhône suivi du nom de la commune d'origine	x	x	x		
Côte-Rôtie		x			
Crépy	x				
Crozes-Hermitage	x	x			
Gigondas		x	x		
Hermitage	x	x		x	

Région du Jura, des Côtes Du Rhône et du Sud-Est (cont.)

	WHITE	RED	ROSÉ	STRAW WINE	YELLOW
L'Etoile	x			x	x
L'Etoile Mousseux	x				
Lirac	x	x	x		
Palette	x	x	x		
Saint-Joseph	x	x			
Saint-Péray	x				
Saint-Péray Mousseux	x				
Seyssel	x				
Seyssel Mousseux	x				
Tavel			x		
Vin de Bandol	x	x	x		
Vin de Bellet	x	x	x		

Vins Doux Naturels and Vins de Liqueur

	V.D.N.	V.D.L.	RED	ROSÉ	WHITE	(SWEET DESSERT WINE)
Banyuls	x		x	x	x	x
Banyuls Grand Cru	x		x			x
Frontignan	x	x			x	
Grand Roussillon	x		x	x	x	x
Maury	x		x	x	x	x
Muscat de Beaumes de Venise	x				x	
Muscat de Frontignan	x	x			x	
Muscat de Lunel	x				x	
Muscat de Mireval	x				x	
Muscat de Rivesaltes	x				x	
Muscat de St Jean de Miner-vois	x				x	
Pineau des Charentes		x		x	x	
Pineau Charentais		x		x	x	
Rasteau	x		x	x	x	x
Rivesaltes	x		x	x	x	x
Vin de Frontignan	x	x			x	

Vin Doux Naturel = V.D.N. = sweet fortified wine
Vin de Liqueur = V.D.L. = grape juice plus spirits

Vins Delimités de Qualité Supérieure (V.D.Q.S.)

Lorraine

	WHITE	RED	ROSÉ
Côtes de Teul	x	x	x
Vin de Moselle	x	x	x

Bugey—Savoie

	WHITE	RED	ROSÉ
Vin du Bugey	x	x	x
Vin du Bugey Petillant	x		
Roussette du Bugey	x		
Roussette de Savoie	x		
Vin de Savoie	x	x	x
Vin de Savoie mousseux ou pétillant	x		

	WHITE	RED	ROSÉ

Vallée de la Loire et Centre de la France

	WHITE	RED	ROSÉ
Auvergne (Vin d')	x	x	x
Châteaumeillant		x	x
Côteaux d'Ancenis	x	x	x
Côteaux du Giennois (or Côtes de Gien)	x	x	x
Côtes d'Auvergne	x	x	x
Côtes du Forez		x	x
Gros Plant du Pays Nantais	x		
Haut-Poitou (Vins du)	x	x	x
Mont-Près-Chambord-Cour Cheverny	x		
Orléanais (Vin dal')	x	x	x
Renaison-Côte Roannaise		x	x
Saint-Pourçain sur Sioule (Vin de)	x	x	x
Thouarsais (Vin du)	x	x	x
Valençay	x	x	x
Côteaux du Vendômois			x

Région du Sud-Est

	WHITE	RED	ROSÉ
Chatillon-en-Diois	x	x	x
Côteaux d'Aix en Provence suivi ou non de Côteaux des Baux-en-Provence	x	x	x
Côteaux du Lyonnais ou vin du Lyonnais	x	x	x
Côteaux de Pierrevert	x	x	x
Côteaux du Tricastin	x	x	x
Côteaux du Lubéron	x	x	x
Côtes de Provence	x	x	x
Côtes du Ventoux	x	x	x
Côtes du Vivarais	x	x	x
Haut Comtat		x	x

Région du Sud-Ouest

	WHITE	RED	ROSÉ
Béarn (Vin de)	x	x	x
Côtes de Buzet	x	x	x
Côtes du Marmandais	x	x	x
Estaing (Vin d')	x	x	x
Entraygues et du Fel (Vind')	x	x	x
Fronton-Côtes de Fronton	x	x	x
Lavilledieu	x	x	
Marcillac (Vin de)	x	x	x
Tursan	x	x	x
Villaudric	x	x	
Rousselet de Béarn	x		

Languedoc—Roussillon

	WHITE	RED	ROSÉ
Cabrières			x
Corbières	x	x	x
Corbières supérieures	x	x	x
Côtes du Roussillon suivi ou non de Villages	x	x	x
Costières du Gard	x	x	x
Côteaux du Languedoc	x	x	x
Côteaux de la Méjanelle	x	x	
Côteaux de Saint-Christol		x	x
Faugères	x	x	
La Clape	x	x	x
Minervois	x	x	x
Picpoul de Pinet	x		

	WHITE	RED	ROSÉ
Languedoc—Roussillon (cont.)			
Pic Saint-Loup	x	x	x
Quatourze	x	x	x
Saint-Chinian		x	
Saint-Drezery		x	
Saint-Georges d'Orques		x	
Saint-Saturnin		x	x

Eaux de Vie (Brandy or Spirits) à Appellation d'Origine Contrôlée

Armagnac
Bas-Armagnac
Bons-Bois
Borderies
Calvados du Pays d'Auge
Cognac
Eau-de-vie des Charentes
Esprit de Cognac

Fine Champagne
Fins Bois
Grande Champagne
Grande Fine Champagne
Haut-Armagnac
Petite Champagne
Ténarèze

Eaux-de-Vie (Brandy or Spirits) à Appellation d'Origine Reglementée

Apple Brandy

Calvados
Calvados de l'Avranchin
Calvados du Calvados
Calvados du Cotentin
Calvados du Domfrontais
Calvados du Pays de Bray
Calvados du Pays du Merlerault
Calvados du Pays de la Risle
Calvados du Perche
Calvados de la Vallée de l'Orne
Calvados du Mortainais

Pear Brandy

Eaux-de-vie de Cidre ou de poiré de Bretagne
Eaux-de-vie de Cidre ou de poiré de Normandie
Eaux-de-vie de Cidre ou de poiré du Maine

Spirit Distilled from Grape Pomace

Marc d'Alsace Gewurztraminer
Eaux-de-vie de Marc originaires d'Aquitaine
Eaux-de-vie de Marc d'Auvergne
Eaux-de-vie de Marc de Bourgogne ou Marc de Bourgogne
Eaux-de-vie de Marc originaires du Bugey
Eaux-de-vie de Marc originaires du Centre-Est
Eaux-de-vie de Marc de Champagne ou Marc de Champagne
Eaux-de-vie de Marc originaires des Côteaux de la Loire
Eaux-de-vie de Marc des Côtes-du-Rhône
Eaux-de-vie de Marc originaires de la Franche-Comté

Spirit distilled from Wine (Brandy)

Eaux-de-vie de Marc originaires du Languedoc
Eaux-de-vie de Marc originaires de Provence
Eaux-de-vie de Marc originaires de Savoie
Eaux-de-vie de Vin originaires d'Aquitaine
Eaux-de-vie de Vin de Bourgogne
Eaux-de-vie de Vin originaries du Bugey
Eaux-de-vie de Vin originaires du Centre-Est
Eaux-de-vie de Vin originaires des Coteaux de la Loire
Eaux-de-vie de Vin des Côtes-du-Rhône
Eaux-de-vie de Vin de Faugères
Eaux-de-vie de Vin originaires de la Franche-Comté
Eaux-de-vie de Vin originaires du Languedoc
Eaux-de-vie de Vin de la Marne
Eaux-de-vie de Vin originaires de La Provence
Mirabelle de Lorraine

Appendix **E**

CONVERSION TABLE OF
METRIC WEIGHTS AND MEASURES

TO CHANGE	TO	MULTIPLY BY	TO CHANGE	TO	MULTIPLY BY
centimetres	inches	.394	kilogram	pounds	2.205
inches	centimetres	2.54	pounds	kilograms	.454
metres	feet	3.281	metric ton	long ton	.984
feet	metres	.305	long ton	metric ton	1.016
kilometres	miles	.621	centilitres	liquid ounces	.03378
miles	kolometres	1.609	liquid ounces	centilitres	29.57
hectares	acres	2.471	litres	gallons	.2642
acres	hectares	.405	gallons	litres	3.785
grams	ounces	.035	hectolitre	gallons	26.418
ounces	grams	28.35	gallons	hectolitre	.03785

APPROXIMATE EQUIVALENTS

10 cms.—4 inches
11 metres—12 yards
8 kilometres—5 miles
50 kilometres—31 miles
1 hectare—2½ acres

5 kilograms—11 pounds
1 litre—1.056 quarts
1 hectolitre—26.418 gallons
1 metric ton—2204.6 pounds

212° F.—100° C. Water boils
98.6° F.—37° C. Body Temp.
32° F.—0° C. Water freezes

Appendix **F**

THE CLASSIFIED GROWTHS OF BORDEAUX

OFFICIAL CLASSIFICATION OF 1855

MÉDOC WINES

FIRST GROWTHS

Château Lafite-Rothschild
Château Margaux
Château Latour
Château Haut-Brion°
Château Mouton-Rothschild

SECOND GROWTHS

Château Rausan-Ségla
Château Rauzan-Gassies
Château Léoville-Lascases
Château Léoville-Poyferré
Château Léoville-Barton
Château Durfort-Vivens
Château Gruaud-Larose
Château Lascombes
Château Brane-Cantenac
Château Pichon-Longueville,
  Baron de Pichon
Château Pichon-Longueville,
  Ctesse. de Lalande
Château Ducru-Beaucaillou
Château Cos-d'Estournel
Château Montrose

THIRD GROWTHS

Château Kirwan
Château d'Issan
Château Lagrange
Château Langoa-Barton
Château Giscours
Château Malescot-St-Exupéry
Château Boyd-Cantenac
Château Cantenac-Brown

MÉDOC WINES (cont.)

Château Palmer
Château La Lagune
Château Desmirail
Château Calon-Ségur
Château Ferrière
Château Marquis d'Alesme-Becker

FOURTH GROWTHS

Château Saint-Pierre
Château Talbot
Château Branaire-Duluc
Château Duhart-Milon
Château Pouget
Château La Tour-Carnet
Château Rochet
Château Beychevelle
Château Prieuré-Lichine
Château Marquis de Terme

FIFTH GROWTHS

Château Pontet-Canet
Château Batailley
Château Grand-Puy-Lacoste
Château Grand-Puy-Ducasse
Château Lynch-Bages
Château Lynch-Moussas
Château Dauzac
Château Mouton-Baron Philippe
Château Le Tertre
Château Haut-Bages-Libéral
Château Pédesclaux
Château Belgrave
Château Camensac
Château Cos-Labory
Château Clerc-Milon

MÉDOC WINES (cont.)

Château Croizet-Bages
Château Cantemerle

SAUTERNES AND BARSAC

FIRST SUPERIOR GROWTH

Château d'Yquem

FIRST GROWTHS

Château La Tour Blanche
Château Lafaurie-Peyraguey
Clos Haut-Peyraguey
Château de Rayne-Vigneau
Château Suduiraut
Château Coutet
Château Climens
Château Guiraud
Château Rieussec
Château Rabaud-Promis
Château Sigalas-Rabaud

SECOND GROWTHS

Château de Myrat
Château Doisy-Daëne
Château Doisy-Dubroca
Château Doisy-Védrines
Château d'Arche
Château Filhot
Château Broustet
Château Nairac
Château Caillou
Château Suau
Château de Malle
Château Romer
Château Lamothe

486 ° Haut-Brion, in the Parish of Pessac, Graves, the one red wine outside the Médoc, included.

OFFICIAL CLASSIFICATIONS OF OTHER BORDEAUX

GRAVES
1959 Official Classification
CLASSIFIED RED WINES

Château Bouscaut
Château Carbonnieux
Domaine de Chevalier
Château Fieuzal
Château Haut-Bailly
Château Haut-Brion
Château La Mission-Haut-Brion
Château La Tour-Haut-Brion
Château La Tour-Martillac
Château Malartic-Lagravière
Château Olivier
Château Pape Clément
Château Smith-Haut-Lafitte

CLASSIFIED WHITE WINES

Château Bouscaut
Château Carbonnieux
Domaine de Chevalier
Château Couhins
Château La Tour Martilla
Château Laville-Haut-Brion
Château Malartic-Lagravière
Château Olivier

SAINT-EMILION
1969 Official Classification
FIRST CLASSIFIED
GREAT GROWTHS

Château Ausone
Château Cheval Blanc
Château Beauséjour-Lagarosse
Château Beauséjour-Fagouet
Château Belair
Château Canon
Château Clos Fourtet
Château Figeac
Château La Gaffelière Naudes
Château Magdelaine
Château Pavie
Château Trottevieille

GREAT CLASSIFIED GROWTHS

Château L'Angélus
Château L'Arrosée
Château Baleau

SAINT-EMILION (cont.)
Château Balestard la Tonnelle
Château Bellevue
Château Bergat
Château Cadet Bon
Château Cadet Piola
Château Canon la Gaffelière
Château Cap de Mourlin
Château Chapelle Madeleine
Château Chauvin
Château Corbin Giraud
Château Corbin Michotte
Château Coutet
Château Couvent-des-Jacobins
Château Croque Michotte
Château Curé Bon
Château Dassault
Château Faurie-de-Souchard
Château Fonplegade
Château Fonroque
Château Franc Mayne
Château Grand Barrail Lamarzelle Figeac
Château Grand Corbin Despagne
Château Grand Corbin Pécresse
Château Grand Mayne
Château Grand Pontet
Château Grandes Murailles
Château Guadet Saint Julien
Château Haut-Corbin
Château Haut-Sarpe
Château Jean Faure
Château Clos des Jacobins
Château La Carte
Château La Clotte
Château La Chusière
Château La Couspaude
Château La Dominique
Château Clos La Madeleine
Château Larcis Ducasse
Château Lamarzelle
Château Laniote
Château Larmande
Château Laroze
Château Lasserre
Château La Tour du Pin Figeac-Belivier
Château La Tour du Pin Figeac-Moueix

SAINT-EMILION (cont.)
Château La Tour Figeac
Château Le Chatelet
Château Le Couvent
Château Le Prieuré
Château Matras
Château Mauvezin
Château Moulin du Cadet
Château L'Oratoire
Château Pavie Decesse
Château Pavie Macquin
Château Pavillon Cadet
Château Petit Faurie de Souchard
Château Petit Faurie de Soutard
Château Ripeau
Château Sansonnet
Château Saint Georges Côte Pavie
Château Clos Saint Martin
Château Soutard
Château Tertre Daugay
Château Trimoulet
Château Trois Moulins
Château Troplong Mondot
Château Villemaurine
Château Yon Figeac

POMEROL°
GREAT FIRST GROWTH
Château Pètrus

FIRST GROWTHS

Château Beauregard
Château Certan-Giraud
Château Certan-de-May
Château Gazin
Château La Conseillante
Château La Croix
Château Lafleur
Château Lafleur-Pétrus
Château Lagrange
Château La Pointe
Château Latour-Pomerol
Château Clos de l'Église-Clinet
Château l'Évangile
Château Nénin
Château Petit-Village
Château Rouget
Château Trotanoy
Château Vieux-Château-Certan

° The wines of Pomerol have not been classified officially. However, Château Pétrus is universally recognized as an outstanding growth, on a par with the great First Growths of Médoc and St. Emilion. The other wines listed are considered the First Growths of Pomerol.

BURGUNDY

LIST OF THE PRINCIPAL VINEYARDS OF THE CÔTE D'OR
including those growths most likely to be found on our market; under their own name.

CÔTE DE NUITS

PARISH	GROWTH	PARISH	GROWTH
Fixin	Clos de la Perrière	Chambolle-Musigny	Musigny
	Les Arvelets		Bonnes Mares
	Le Clos-du-Chapitre		Les Amoureuses
	Les Hervelets		
		Vougeot	Clos de Vougeot
			Clos Blanc-de-Vougeot
			(White wine)
Gevrey-Chambertin	Chambertin		
	Chambertin-Clos de Bèze	Flagey-Echézeaux	Les Grands-Echézeaux
	Mazoyères ou		Les Echézeaux
	Charmes-Chambertin	Vosne-Romanée	Romanée-Conti
	Latricières-Chambertin		La Romanée
			La Tâche
	Mazis-Chambertin		Les Richebourg
	Ruchottes-Chambertin		La Grande Rue
	Chapelle-Chambertin		Romanée-St. Vivant
	Clos Saint-Jacques		Les Malconsorts
			Les Gaudichots
			Les Suchots
Morey-St. Denis	Clos de la Roche		
	Clos Saint-Denis	Nuits-Saint-Georges	Les Saint-Georges
	Clos de Tart		Les Cailles
	Clos des Lambrays		Clos des Porrets
	Bonnes Mares		Les Boudots

CÔTE DE BEAUNE

PARISH	GROWTH	PARISH	GROWTH
Aloxe-Corton	Le Corton	Pommard	Les Épenots
	Les Bressandes		Les Rugiens
	Clos du Roi		Le Clos Blanc
	Corton-Pougets		La Platière
	Corton-Charlemagne		Clos de la Commaraine
	(White wine only)		Les Jarollières
Savigny-les-Beaune	Les Vergelesses		
	Les Marconnets	Volnay	Les Caillerets
	Les Jarrons		Les Fremiets
			Les Champans
Beaune	Les Fèves		Les Santenots
	Les Grèves		Clos des Ducs
	Le Clos-des-Mouches		
	Beaune-Grèves l'Enfant Jésus	Auxey-Duresses	Les Duresses
	Hospices de Beaune	Meursault	Les Cras
		—Red Wines	Les Pelures

CÔTE DE BEAUNE (cont.)

PARISH	GROWTH	PARISH	GROWTH
—White Wines	Les Perrières		₤
	Les Genevrières	Chassagne-	
	Les Charmes	Montrachet	
	La Goutte d'Or	—Red Wines	La Maltroie
			Le Clos Saint-Jean
Puligny-Montrachet	Le Cailleret		La Boudriotte
—Red Wines	Le Clavaillon		
		—White Wines	Le Montrachet
—White Wines	Le Montrachet		Le Bâtard-Montrachet
	Le Chevalier-Montra-chet		Criots-Bâtard-Montrachet
	Le Bâtard-Montrachet		
	Bienvenue-Bâtard-Montrachet		
	Blagny Blanc	Santenay	
	Les Pucelles	—Red Wine	Les Gravières

HOSPICES DE BEAUNE

Founded in 1443 by Nicolas Rolin and his wife Guigone de Salins, this is a charity hospital whose entire financial support has always come from the sale of the wines produced on the vineyard parcels deeded to it by charitable Burgundian vineyard owners. Originally the sales were private, but since 1858, the wines have been sold at public auction. The auction is held each year on the third Sunday of November in les Halles de Beaune.

Hospices de Beaune wines are auctioned in lots under the name of the donor, i.e., Cuvée Nicolas Rolin, Cuvée Guigone de Salins, Cuvée Docteur Peste, Cuvée Charlotte Dumay, etc. The buyers purchase the wine in cask with the right to label it "Hospices de Beaune Cuvée Docteur Peste" or whatever the Cuvée may be.

The Hospices de Beaune Cuvées are:

RED WINES

BEAUNE Dames Hospitalières
VOLNAY-SANTENOTS Gauvain
PERNAND Rameau-Lamarosse
BEAUNE Nicolas Rolin
SAVIGNY-LES-BEAUNE Forneret
BEAUNE Clos des Avaux
VOLNAY-SANTENOTS Jehan de Massol
CORTON Docteur Peste
MONTHELIE J. Lebelin
BEAUNE Brunet
VOLNAY Général Muteau
BEAUNE Guigone de Salins
SAVIGNY-LES-BEAUNE Fouquerand
AUXEY-DURESSES Boillot
BEAUNE Rousseau-Deslandes
POMMARD Billardet
BEAUNE Hugues et Louis Bétault

RED WINES (cont.)

VOLNAY Blondeau
CORTON Charlotte Dumay
SAVIGNY Arthur Girard
BEAUNE Maurice Drouhin
POMMARD Dames de la Charité

WHITE WINES

MEURSAULT-GENEVRIERE Ph. le Bon
MEURSAULT-GOUREAU
MEURSAULT-CHARMES A. Grivault
CORTON-CHARLEMAGNE
   François de Salins
MEURSAULT-CHARMES
   de Bahèzre de Lanlay
MEURSAULT Loppin
MEURSAULT Humblot
MEURSAULT-GENEVRIERES Baudot

WINE AND SPIRIT CASK STANDARDS, WITH LITRE EQUIVALENTS

	APPROX. GALLONS	APPROX. LITRES
Pipe of Port, Tarragona or Lisbon	138	522.37
Pipe of Madeira	110	416.38
Butt of Sherry	132	500.00
Hogshead of Sherry	66	250.00
Quarter-cask Sherry	33	125.00
Octave Sherry	16.5	62.50
Tonneau-Bordeaux (4 barriques)	238	900.00
Barrique-Bordalais	59	225.00
Pièce-Burgundy	60	228.00
Queue-Burgundy (2 pièces)	120	456.00
Hogshead-Cognac	71.8	272.00
Puncheon-Rum (varies-average)	111.6	422.34

AMERICAN EQUIVALENTS OF FOREIGN STANDARDS

Litre	1.0567 quarts		0.26418 gallons
Quart	0.9463 litres		
Gallon	4	quarts	3.7853 litres
Hectolitre	100	litres	26.4178 gallons
9 Litres (average content case of wine)			2.3776 gallons
Kilogram	2.204 pounds		

BOTTLE SIZES

DISTILLED SPIRITS		WINE (Bottled in U.S.A.)		CHAMPANGE[a] (Traditional)	OZ	BOTTLES
1 Gallon—128	oz	4.9 Gallons	627.2 oz	Nebuchadnezzar[c]	520	(20)
½ Gallon— 64	oz	3 Gallons	384 oz	Balthazar[c]	416	(16)
1 Quart — 32	oz	1 Gallon	128 oz	Salmanazar[c]	312	(12)
4/5 Quart — 25.6 oz		4/5 Gallon	102.4 oz	Methuselah[d]	208	(8)

490

DISTILLED SPIRITS				WINE (Bottled in U.S.A.)			CHAMPANGE[a] (Traditional)	OZ	BOTTLES
1 Pint	—	16	oz	$\frac{1}{2}$ Gallon	64	oz	Rehoboam[d]	156	(6)
$\frac{4}{5}$ Pint	—	12.8	oz	$\frac{2}{5}$ Gallon	51.2	oz	Jeroboam	104	(4)
$\frac{1}{2}$ Pint	—	8	oz	1 Quart	32	oz	Magnum	52	(2)
$\frac{1}{8}$ Pint	—	2	oz	$\frac{4}{5}$ Quart	25.6	oz	Bottle	26	(1)
$\frac{1}{10}$ Pint	—	1.6	oz	1 Pint	16	oz	Imperial	19	($\frac{3}{4}$)
$\frac{1}{16}$ Pint	—	1	oz[b]	$\frac{4}{5}$ Pint	12.8	oz	Half Bottle	13	($\frac{1}{2}$)
				$\frac{1}{2}$ Pint	8	oz	Split	6.5	($\frac{1}{4}$)
				$\frac{2}{5}$ Pint	6.4	oz			
				4 Ounces	4	oz			
				3 Ounces	3	oz			
				2 Ounces	2	oz			

NOTE: Bottle sizes are mandatory except for wines bottled outside the United States, liqueurs, alcoholic drinks, bitters and some specialties as specified.

[a] Champagne is bottled fermented only in half bottles, imperials, bottles, magnum, and infrequently in jeroboams. Other sizes are refills.

[b] Brandy only.

[c] Obsolete

[d] These bottles are handmade and vary considerably in capacity.

The California Wine Institute has proposed standard bottle sizes for wines based on the Metric System, hopefully some version of this plan will be adopted world-wide. Presently a "bottle" ranges from 22 ounces to 33.8 ounces.

COMPARISON OF U.S. PROOF, BRITISH "SIKES" AND METRIC "GAY LUSSAC" TABLES OF ALCOHOLIC STRENGTHS—at 60° F.

U.S. PROOF	BRITISH SIKES U.P.°	GAY LUSSAC Alcohol by volume	U.S. PROOF	BRITISH SIKES U.P.	GAY LUSSAC Alcohol by volume	U.S. PROOF	BRITISH SIKES U.P.	GAY LUSSAC Alcohol by volume	U.S. PROOF	BRITISH SIKES O.P.	GAY LUSSAC Alcohol by volume	U.S. PROOF	BRITISH SIKES O.P.	GAY LUSSAC Alcohol by volume
0	100.	0												
1	99.1	0.5	53	53.6	26.5	105	8.1	52.5				149	30.5	74.5
2	98.2	1.0	54	52.7	27.0	106	7.2	53.0				150	31.3	75.0
3	97.4	1.5	55	51.8	27.5	107	6.3	53.5				151	32.2	75.5
4	96.5	2.0	56	51.0	28.0	108	5.4	54.0				152	33.1	76.0
5	95.6	2.5	57	50.1	28.5	109	4.6	54.5				153	34.0	76.5
6	94.7	3.0	58	49.2	29.0	110	3.7	55.0				154	34.9	77.0
7	93.9	3.5	59	48.3	29.5	111	2.8	55.5				155	35.7	77.5
8	93.0	4.0	60	47.5	30.0	112	1.9	56.0				156	36.6	78.0
9	92.1	4.5	61	46.6	30.5	113	1.1	56.5				157	37.5	78.5
10	91.2	5.0	62	45.7	31.0	114	0.2	· 57.0				158	38.4	79.0
11	90.4	5.5	63	44.8	31.5							159	39.2	79.5
12	89.5	6.0	64	44.0	32.0							160	40.1	80.0
13	88.6	6.5	65	43.1	32.5							161	41.0	80.5
14	87.7	7.0	66	42.2	33.0							162	41.9	81.0
15	86.9	7.5	67	41.3	33.5							163	42.7	81.5
16	86.0	8.0	68	40.5	34.0							164	43.6	82.0
17	85.1	8.5	69	39.6	34.5					O.P.		165	44.5	82.5
18	84.2	9.0	70	38.7	35.0							166	45.4	83.0
19	83.4	9.5	71	37.8	35.5				115	0.7	57.5	167	46.2	83.5
20	82.5	10.0	72	37.0	36.0				116	1.6	58.0	168	47.1	84.0
21	81.6	10.5	73	36.1	36.5				117	2.3	58.5	169	48.0	84.5
22	80.7	11.0	74	35.2	37.0				118	3.3	59.0	170	48.9	85.0
23	79.9	11.5	75	34.3	37.5				119	4.2	59.5	171	49.7	85.5
24	79.0	12.0	76	33.5	38.0				120	5.1	60.0	172	50.6	86.0
25	78.1	12.5	77	32.6	38.5				121	6.0	60.5	173	51.5	86.5
26	77.2	13.0	78	31.7	39.0				122	6.8	61.0	174	52.4	87.0
27	76.4	13.5	79	30.8	39.5				123	7.7	61.5	175	53.2	87.5
28	75.5	14.0	80	29.9	40.0				124	8.6	62.0	176	54.1	88.0
29	74.6	14.5	81	29.1	40.5				125	9.5	62.5	177	55.0	88.5
30	73.7	15.0	82	28.2	41.0				126	10.3	63.0	178	55.9	89.0
31	72.9	15.5	83	27.3	41.5				127	11.2	63.5	179	56.7	89.5
32	72.0	16.0	84	26.4	42.0				128	12.1	64.0	180	57.6	90.0
33	71.1	16.5	85	25.6	42.5				129	13.0	64.5	181	58.5	90.5
34	70.2	17.0	86	24.7	43.0				130	13.8	65.0	182	59.4	91.0
35	69.4	17.5	87	23.8	43.5				131	14.7	65.5	183	60.2	91.5
36	68.5	18.0	88	22.9	44.0				132	15.6	66.0	184	61.1	92.0
37	67.6	18.5	89	22.1	44.5				133	16.5	66.5	185	62.0	92.5
38	66.7	19.0	90	21.2	45.0				134	17.3	67.0	186	62.9	93.0
39	65.8	19.5	91	20.3	45.5				135	18.2	67.5	187	63.7	93.5
40	65.0	20.0	92	19.4	46.0				136	19.1	68.0	188	64.6	94.0
41	64.1	20.5	93	18.6	46.5				137	20.0	68.5	189	65.5	94.5
42	63.2	21.0	94	17.7	47.0				138	20.8	69.0	190	66.4	95.0
43	62.3	21.5	95	16.8	47.5				139	21.7	69.5	191	67.3	95.5
44	61.5	22.0	96	15.9	48.0				140	22.6	70.0	192	68.1	96.0
45	60.6	22.5	97	15.1	48.5				141	23.5	70.5	193	69.0	96.5
46	59.7	23.0	98	14.2	49.0				142	24.3	71.0	194	69.9	97.0
47	58.8	23.5	99	13.3	49.5				143	25.2	71.5	195	70.8	97.5
48	58.0	24.0	100	12.4	50.0				144	26.1	72.0	196	71.6	98.0
49	57.1	24.5	101	11.6	50.5				145	27.0	72.5	197	72.5	98.5
50	56.2	25.0	102	10.7	51.0				146	27.8	73.0	198	73.4	99.0
51	55.3	25.5	103	9.8	51.5				147	28.7	73.5	199	74.3	99.5
52	54.5	26.0	104	8.9	52.0				148	29.6	74.0	200	75.1	100.0

° U.P. = Under proof; O.P. = Over proof.

GLOSSARY OF TERMS

(The abbreviations Aut., Eng., Hun., It., Port., Rom., Sp., Yug., etc. represent the countries of origin Austria, England, Hungery, Italy, Portugal, Romania, Spain, Yugoslavia respectively.)

abboccato—(It.) Medium sweet.

abfüllung—(Ger.) Abbreviation: abf. Bottling.

abstich—(Ger.) Racking.

acerbe—(Fr.) Green, acid wine.

Acquit Régional Jaune d'Or—(Fr.) Gold certificate of French Excise, guarantees authenticity of origin of Cognac.

adegas—(Port.) Portuguese for bodegas—wine warehouses.

agrafes—(Fr.) Metal clips used in Champagne cellars to hold the cellar corks in place.

aguardiente—(Sp.) Spirits.

aigre—(Fr.) Wine with an acid undertone.

albariza—(Sp.) Chalky-white soil of best Jerez-Sherry vineyards.

alcohol—Chemically C_2H_5OH, one of the results of fermented sugar-containing liquids.

aldehydes—By-product of alcoholic liquids resulting from the combination of alcohol, acid, and air.

alembic, alambic, alambique—(Fr. & Sp.) Still.

aligoté—(Fr.) White grape variety of Burgundy.

almijar—(Sp.) The courtyard, outside the pressing house where the grapes are spread on esparto mats to dry in the sun before pressing, in the Sherry region of Spain.

alt—(Ger.) Old.

amabile—(It.) Medium sweet.

amaro—(It.) Bitter or very dry.

amélioré—(Fr.) Improved, usually addition of sugar to *must* before fermentation.

amertume—(Fr.) Bitter.

Amontillado—(Sp.) Dry type of Sherry.

Amoroso—(Sp.) Medium dry type of Sherry.

ampelography—Science of grape vine culture.

añada—(Sp.) Wine of one vintage, i.e., vintage wine.

ansprechend—(Ger.) Attractive, engaging wine.

apéritif—(Fr.) Appetizer.

Appelation d'Origine or Appelation Contrôlé—(Fr.) Term which appears on labels of fine French wines—signifying origin and right to the name it bears are guaranteed by French Law.

apre—(Fr.) Harsh, rough wine.

aqua vita, acqua vitae—(It. & Latin) Water of life—spirits.

arenas—(Sp.) Sandy soils of the Jerez-Sherry vineyard region.

aroma, arome—(Sp. & Fr.) Odor or bouquet of wine or spirit.

arroba—(Sp.) Wine measure holding $16\frac{2}{3}$ litres.

arrope—(Sp.) Concentrated wine used for sweetening and giving color to Sherries.

art—(Ger.) Character.

artig—(Ger.) Smooth, rounded wine.

asciato—(It.) A dry wine.

astringent—(Fr.) A wine which puckers the mouth unpleasantly.

asztali bor—(Hun.) Table wine.

aszu, aszubor—(Hun.) Sweeter type of Tokay wine.

aum or ohm—(Ger.) German wine cask, usually 160 litres.

ausbruch—(Ger.) German term for Aszu Tokays.

aus eigenem Lesegut—(Ger.) From the producer's own estate.

auslese—(Ger.) A wine made from selected grapes.

baby—(Eng.) Split, nip or quarter bottle of Champagne, $6\frac{1}{2}$ ounces.

Banvin, Ban de Vendange—(Fr.) Ancient French custom of fixing the date when the gathering of the grapes might begin.

barriques, barricas—(Fr. & Sp.) Hogsheads, i.e., casks.

barros—(Sp.) Clayish soils of the Jerez-Sherry vineyard region.

basto—(Sp.) Coarse wine.

Baumé—Instrument for measuring degree of sweetness in wines and spirits.

beerenauslese—(Ger.) Wine made from individually selected perfectly ripe berries (grapes).

besitz—(Ger.) Sole owner.

bestes—(Ger.) Best.

bianco—(It.) White.

493

bijelo—(Yug.) White.

binning—(Eng.) Storing wines in bins in cellar for development.

biser—(Yug.) Sparkling.

bitter—(Ger.) Bitter.

blanc de Blancs—(Fr.) Made from the juice of white grapes only.

blanco—(Sp.) White

blending—Marrying two or more similar products to obtain a more perfect and uniform quality.

blume—(Ger.) Bouquet, aroma.

blumig—(Ger.) Good bouquet.

bocksbeutel, boxbeutel—(Ger.) Squat, flask-like bottle used for Steinwein.

bocoy—(Sp.) Large cask used in North of Spain, approx. 162 gals.

bodega—(Sp.) Ground level wine warehouses.

body—The term employed to describe the consistency of beverages, for example: a thin wine has less *body* than a full one.

bois, goût de—(Fr.) Wine or spirit with a woody taste.

bon goût—(Fr.) A wine with a good or pleasant taste.

Bond, In—Wine or spirit on which duty and internal revenue tax has not been paid must remain under government supervision as "bond" that same will be paid.

bonded warehouse—Warehouse under government supervision.

bór—(Hung.) Wine. Fehérbór is white wine; vörösbór is red wine and they are pluralized with the suffix ok as in *borok*.

Borkülönlegessége szölögazdaságának—(Hun.) A speciality from the vineyards of the region named.

bota—(Sp.) Butt, Sherry cask, 132 gals.

bottle, botella, bouteille—(Eng., Sp. & Fr.) A wine bottle containing from 23 to 26 ounces.

Bottled in Bond—U.S.A. A straight whiskey, at least four years old, bottled at 100 proof, under government supervision, before taxes have been paid on same.

bouchonné, goût de bouchon—(Fr.) A corky wine—one that has taken on an unpleasant taste of cork.

bouquet—(Fr.) Aroma or fragrance of a wine or spirit.

bowle—(Ger.) Wine cup prepared with fresh fruit, wine, herbs and liqueurs or brandy.

brandewijn—(Dutch); branntwein—(Ger.) Brandy, literally "burnt wine."

breed—The character or degree of perfection a wine attains.

brut—(Fr.) Driest type of Champagne.

bukettreich—(Ger.) Rich, pronounced bouquet.

butt—Standard shipping cask for Sherry, 132 gals.

butte, buttig—(Ger.) Measure used in Tokaj-Hegyalja, 13.6 litres.

cabinett-wein—(Ger.) The finest quality of certain Rhine wines is specially reserved and so marked. Notably at Schloss Johannisberg.

caña—(Sp.) Tall straight-sided glass, used for drinking Sherry in Jerez. Also name for sugar cane from which molasses and finally rum are obtained. In South America rum is called "caña."

cantina—(It.) Cellar, winery, or bar.

cantina sociale (or cooperative)—(It.) Wine growers co-operative.

capataz—(Sp.) Foreman, usually of the Sherry bodega or of the vintage.

capiteux, Vin—(Fr.) Spirity, heady wine.

capsule—Protectors for wine and spirit bottle corks made of metal, plastic or cellulose.

caque—(Fr.) Basket in which grapes are carried from vineyard to the press.

casco—(Sp.) Cask—large barrel usually made of oak, used for developing (aging) and/or shipping wines and spirits.

cask—Large container for wines or spirits usually made of oak.

casse—(Fr.) Chemical disease of wines resulting from excess iron.

catalyst—Chemical agent which induces chemical changes in other substances by its pressence but itself remains unchanged.

caves, celler; cellier—(Fr.) Underground (usually) warehouse or cellar for storing wines and/or spirits.

cellar—Warehouse for storing wines.

centilitre—(Fr.) 1/100th part of a litre.

cep—(Fr.); cepa—(Sp.) The vine stock.

cépage—(Fr.) The vine stock.

Certificate of Age—Government certificate guaranteeing age of spirits.

chais, chaix—(Fr.) Ground level or above-ground warehouse, usually kept totally dark, for wines and/or spirits.

chambrer—(Fr.) To bring red wine to room temperature (65°–68°F.) gradually.

chaptalization, chaptalizer—(Fr.) The practice of increasing the natural sugar content of the grape juice, before fermentation begins, by the addition of sugar or concentrated grape *must*, when there is such a deficiency, especially in poor vintage years.

charnu—(Fr.) A wine of full body.

château, château-bottled—(Fr.) Applies to Bordeaux wines primarily. Wine bottled at the château, estate or vineyard where grapes from which it was made are grown.

chiaretto—(It.) Very light red.

clarete—(Sp.) Light red or dark rose.

classico—(It.) From the central and best area of its region.

classified growths—Classification of 1855: 61 Clarets and 21 Sauternes, now 25, classed according to merit in 1855.

climat—(Fr.) Vineyard.

cochylis—A disease of the vine.

collage—(Fr.) Fining or clearing a wine.

color—(Sp.); couleur—(Fr.) The color of a wine.

color, vino de—(Sp.) color wine, i.e. concentrated wine used to give color and sweetness to Sherry.

commune or finage—(Fr.) Parish.

Confréries—(Fr.) Wine and gastronomic fraternities, mostly of ancient "guild" origin, such as the *Confrérie des Chevaliers du Tastevin* (Burgundy); *Le Bontemps de Médoc* and *La Jurade de St. Emilion* (Bordeaux); *Confrérie de la Chaîne des Rôtisseurs* (Fraternity of the Roasting Spit); etc.

consejo regulator—(Sp.) Organization for the defense, control and promotion of a denominacion de origen.

conservato—(It.) A wine to which concentrated or boiled wine has been added.

consoczio—(It.) Local growers' association with legal standing.

consumo—(Port. & Sp.) Ordinary wine for local consumption.

corks—Stoppers for bottles made from the spongy bark of the cork-oak. Spanish cork is the world's finest for this purpose.

corky wine—A wine with an unpleasant odor which has been imparted by a diseased cork. This can happen even with the finest wines.

corps—(Fr.) Body, i.e. richness in alcohol and other substances.

corredor—(Sp.); courtier—(Fr.) Wine broker.

corsé—(Fr.) A full bodied wine.

cosecha—(Sp.) Crop, or vintage.

cotto—(It.); cuit—(Fr.) A wine which has been heated or "cooked." In Italy this is done especially in the Marsala region.

coulant—(Fr.) A wine which drinks easily and pleasantly.

coupage—(Fr.) Blending or vatting.

coupé—(Fr.) A blended wine.

crémant—(Fr.) Creaming or slightly sparkling, i.e. crackling.

crezenz—(Ger.) "The growth of."

criadera—(Sp.) Nursery stage in the Sherry maturing system.

criado y embotellado por—(Sp.) Grown and bottled by.

crianza, vino de—(Sp.) A suitable wine destined to become Sherry.

crno—(Yug.) Red.

cru—(Fr.) Vineyard, growth.

cru classé—(Fr.) One of the Bordeaux classified growths of 1855.

crudo, vino—(Sp.) Young or immature wine.

crust—(Eng.) The hardened deposit thrown off by red wines which have been long in bottles; applies principally to Vintage Ports.

cups—Iced wine flavored with fresh fruits, brandy, liqueurs, and/or herbs.

cuvaison—(Fr.) The period of first or violent fermentation during which the *must* remains in contact with the grape skins to obtain its color. Applies only to red wines.

cuvée—(Fr.) The blend.

čuveno vino—(Yug.) Selected wine.

decanter—A glass bottle or container into which wines or spirits are decanted from their original containers, for serving.

decanting—To transfer a wine or spirit from one bottle to another.

dégorgement—(Fr.) Disgorging process used in production of Champagne to remove the sediment.

délicat, délicatesse—(Fr.) Delicate, delicacy; an elegant well balanced wine that is not harsh or coarse.

delimited areas—Certain areas whose regional name is given to the wine or spirit produced within the geographical limits of the region.

demi—(Fr.) Half.

demijohn—A fat-bellied wicker encased bottle holding 4 to 10 gals.

demi-queue—A half queue, a Burgundy cask measuring 228 litres.

demi-sec—(Fr.) Half dry. Term used in describing a fairly sweet type of Champagne.

denominacion de origen—(Sp.) Similar to Appellation Controlee.

density—The specific gravity of a liquid when compared with an equal amount of water.

deposit—Normal sediment precipitated by a wine as it matures in the bottle.

depôt—(Fr.) Natural sediment which all wines will deposit, but more visibly in the case of red wines.

desertno vino—(Yug.) Dessert wine.

Deutscher sekt—(Ger.) Sparkling wine made from at least 60% German wine.

dextrine—One of the sugars resulting from starch exposed to the action of malt.

diastase—The enzyme formed by malting barley, which causes the starch in grains to be converted into sugars.

dolce—(It.) Very sweet.

domaine(s)—(Fr.) Followed by a name denotes ownership, for example: Domaine de la Romanée-Conti.

Domäne—(Ger.) Usually a State-owned and/or State-managed vineyard property.

dosage—(Fr.) The dosage of sugar used in preparing Champagne.

double aum—(Ger.) Wine cask measure of 320 litres used in Germany.

douil—(Fr.) The open casks on carts in which the grapes are carted from the vineyard to the pressing house, in the Bordeaux wine region.

doux—(Fr.) Sweet—the term used to describe the sweetest type of Champagne.

dry—A term used in the wine and spirit trade to denote the opposite of sweet. Literally it means lacking in sugar. In the California Wine Trade the term "dry" is used to describe all beverage wines having 14% of alcohol or less. The term "dry" or "sec" on a Champagne label denotes a medium sweet wine.

duft, duftig—(Ger.) Fragrant, fine bouquet.

dulce—(Sp.) Sweet.

dulce apagado—(Sp.) See mistelle.

dunder—Sugar-cane juice remains, used in making full-bodied rums.

dur—(Fr.) Hard. A term used to describe a harsh too-young wine.

eau de vie—(Fr.) Spirits, generally brandy. Literal translation: water of life.

eau de vie de marc—(Fr.) A brandy distilled from the fermented pomace or husks of grapes after they have been pressed for wine.

echt—(Ger.) Genuine.

edel—(Ger.) Noble, extra fine.

edelbeerenauslese—(Ger.) Wine from extraordinary individual grapes which have not dried out, thus preventing classification as a *trockenbeeren.*

edelfaule or edelreif—(Ger.) Over-ripe grapes as the French *pourriture noble.*

edelgewachs—(Ger.) The finest growths, i.e. only the finest vintages.

edelsuesse—(Ger.) Great natural, noble sweetness.

edes—(Hun.) Sweet

égrappage—(Fr.) Destemming process before grapes are pressed.

égrappoir—(Fr.) Apparatus used to perform the *égrappage.*

ehrwein—(Ger.) Very fine wine.

eigenbaugewächs—(Aut.) From the maker's own vineyard.

eigene abfüllung—(Ger.) Bottled by the producer.

eigengewächs—(Ger.) Own vineyard, i.e. "This is wine from my own vineyard."

eiswein—(Ger.) A wine produced from perfectly ripened grapes that have been partially frozen while still hanging on the vine. It used to be very rare, appearing perhaps once every twenty or twenty-five years. Now, it is made more often but only in very limited quantities. These wines are quite elegant, very rich and may be considered to be someplace between an *auslese* and an *edelbeerenauslese.*

eladorado y añejado por—(Sp.) Made and aged by.

élégance—(Fr.) Wine of a good vintage having delicacy and lightness but does not promise longevity.

elegant—(Ger.) Elegant and fine, a pleasing wine.

élixir—(Fr.) The old term used in France for liqueurs.

embotellado—(Sp.) Bottled.

enzymes—The chemical components of yeast which cause various reactions, among which is alcoholic or vinous fermentation.

erben—(Ger.) Heirs of/or Estate of.

erdig—(Ger.) Earthy.

espumoso—(Sp.) Sparkling

Essenz, Eszencia—(Hun.) Essence. The term applied to the rarest and richest Tokay wine.

estate-bottled—Wine bottled by the vineyard owner-producer.

estates—Term applied to sugar plantations in Jamaica and British West Indies whence basic material for distilling rum is obtained.

esters—The volatile compounds formed by the combination of the acids with the alcohols. The esters give the bouquet of a wine or spirit.

estufa—(Port.) Hot-houses or heated cellars where Madeiras are baked when young.

estufado, estufagem (vinhos)—(Port.) Madeira wines after they have been baked in the *estufa.*

ethers—The minute ethereal qualities which form the bouquet of a wine or spirit together with the esters.

ethyl alcohol—The principal alcohol found in all alcoholic beverages.

évent, goût d'—(Fr.) A flat, lifeless wine that has been in contact with air.

extra sec—extra dry—Term used to denote a type of dry Champagne, sweeter than *brut.*

fad—(Ger.) Insipid.

faible—(Fr.) Thin, weak wine.

fass—(Ger.) Term for a cask of some 490 litres capacity employed in all German wine regions except the Moselle, where the term is *fuder.*

faul—(Ger.) Mouldy, unclean.

fehér—(Hun.) White.

fein, feine, feinste—(Ger.) Fine, very fine, finest.

feints—The heads and tails, i.e. the first and last part of a distillation.

ferme, fermeté (Fr.) A firm, full wine which possesses a hardness when mature that it should have lost.

fermentation—The chemical process whereby sugars are broken down into alcohol, carbonic acid gas, and other by-products.

fett—(Ger.) Literally fat. A full, big wine.

fiasco, fiaschi—(It.) Raffia-wrapped flask(s) employed for bottling Chianti, Orvieto and other Italian wines.

filtering—The processes of clarifying liquids.

fin, finesse—(Fr.) A fine delicate wine of breed and character.

finage—(Fr.) All of the vineyards of a given sub-district.

fine—(Fr.) A term applied to an ordinary brandy served in a café.

fining—Clarifying wines by adding materials which combine with the particles of sediment floating in it and after a short period settle to the bottom, leaving the wine star bright.

Fino—(Sp.) The term applied to the driest type of Sherries.

firn—(Ger.) Tired, woody (maderisé) wine.

flagon—An ancient wine flask.

flask—A flat-sided bottle usually 12½ ozs. but holding anywhere from 8 to 32 ozs.

flor—(Sp.) See flower.

flower—flowering—Unique property of the yeast in the Jerez-Sherry region of Spain. Multiplying profusely, it forms a film on the surface of the wine in the cask, especially in the case of the drier, more delicate *Fino* types. A similar flowering of the yeast also occurs in the casks of the *vin jaune* and *vin de paille* of Château Chalon and Château d'Arlay in the Côtes du Jura region of France.

fluchtig—(Ger.) Light, empty.

foils—The metal or tin foil capsules on Champagne bottles.

fort—(Fr.) Strong—wines of good body.

fortified wines—Wines whose natural alcoholic strength is increased by the addition of brandy.

foudre—(Fr.) Large storage casks for wines.

foxiness—Term used to describe the very pronounced grapey flavor to be found in wines produced from American grapes in the eastern part of the U.S.A.

franc—(Fr.) A natural-tasting, clean wine.

frappé—(Fr.) Iced. Term applied to service of liqueur with finely cracked ice.

Freiherr—(Ger.) Baron.

frisch—(Ger.) Fresh, sprightly.

frizzante—(It.) Half-sparkling.

fruchtig—(Ger.) Fruity.

fructexport—(Rom.) The government exporting agency.

fruité—(Fr.) Fruity.

fruity—A frank taste of the grape found in good wines.

fuder—(Ger.) A Moselle wine cask measure holding 960 litres.

fülle—(Ger.) Richness of great wines.

fumet—(Fr.) A pronounced bouquet.

fumeux—(Fr.) A spirited or heady wine.

fungus—Moulds which appear where wines are kept carelessly and where the most careful hygiene is not observed.

Fürst—(Ger.) Prince.

fusel oil—The higher or other alcohols besides ethyl alcohol found in all spirits.

gallice, spiritus vini de—(Latin) The medical term for Brandy used in England.

gallon—An American and English liquid measure. American gallon, 128 ozs.

GAS (Gaspodanüle Agricole de Stat)—(Rom) State agricultural enterprise.

Gay-Lussac—French inventor of the alcoholometer and the standard metric measures of alcoholic strengths, bearing his name, in use in France today.

gefällig—(Ger.) Pleasing, harmonious wine.

gefullt—(Ger.) Full, rich wine.

gemarkung—(Ger.) The district in which a wine is grown.

généreux—(Fr.) A generous warming wine, rich in alcohol, generally having over 12%.

gering—(Ger.) Rather poor wine.

getaufer—(Ger.) Watered wine.

gewächs—(Ger.) Growth or vineyard of, always followed by the name of the proprietor, to denote ownership.

gezuckert—(Ger.) Sugared, i.e. *verbessert* or improved.

glatt—(Ger.) Smooth.

goldbeerenauslese—(Ger.) Auslese made from fully ripened golden individual grapes.

goût—(Fr.) Taste.

goût Américain—Sweet Champagne to please the taste of South Americans.

goût Anglais—A very dry Champagne for the English taste.

goût de bois—(Fr.) Woody taste.

goût de bouchon—A corky wine.

goût d'évent—A flatish, lifeless taste.

goût de paille—A straw, musty taste.

goût de pierre à fusil—A flinty taste, to be found in Chablis.

goût de pique—(Fr.) Vinegary.

goût de terroir—(Fr.) Earthy taste.

Gradi (or Gradi alcool or Grado alcoolico)—(It.) Followed by a number. Percentage of alcohol by volume.

Graf—(Ger.) Count.

grain spirits—Patent still spirits obtained from malted and unmalted grain.

grand réserve—(Fr.) Wine with over 11% alcohol.

gros producteurs—(Fr.) Vine varieties which produce large quantities but not fine quality wines.

grossier—(Fr.) A big, but hard, coarse wine.

growth—A vineyard (*cru* in French).

grün—(Ger.) Young, green, immature.

gut—(Ger.) Good.

habzó—(Hun.) Sparkling.

halb-fuder—(Ger.) Half-fuder, the standard Moselle wine cask, containing 480 litres.

halb-stück—(Ger.) Half-stück, the standard Rhine and Palatinate wine cask, containing 640 litres.

harmonisch—(Gr.) Harmonious, well balanced wine.

hart—(Ger.) Hard, acid, even vinegary.

heads—The spirits obtained at the beginning of distillation.

hecho—(Sp.) Made. A completed wine ready for bottling and shipping.

hectare—(Fr.) 100 ares equalling 2.47 acres.

hectolitre—(Fr.) 100 litres equalling 26.4178 gals.

hefegeschmack—(Ger.) Yeasty tasting. Not a favorable term.

herb—(Ger.) Bitter.

high wines—The useful spirits obtained in distillation after eliminating heads and tails.

hochgewächs—(Ger.) Superb, superior vine-mentioned in poetry.

Hock—The English abbreviation for Hochheimer which today denotes any Rhine wine but not a Moselle.

Hofkellerei—(Ger.) Wine cellars of a royal court.

hogshead—Cask of varying measure. Hogshead of Sherry contains 66 gals.

holzgeschmack—(Ger.) Woody taste.

honigartig—(Ger.) Honey-like aroma and taste.

hübsch—(Ger.) Nice, delicate wine.

hydrometer—An apparatus used to measure the density of alcoholic beverages.

IAS (Interprinderite Agricole de Stat)—(Rom.) State agricultural enterprise.

imbottigliato—(It.) Estate-bottled.

imbottigliato nello stabilemento della ditta—(It.) Bottled on the premises of the firm.

imbuteliat—(Rom.) Bottled.

imperial, impériale—(Eng. & Fr.) A bottle with a capacity of 8 bottles or 6 litres, also known as a Methuselah.

injerto—(Sp.) Vine graft.

isinglass—Made from fish gelatine; in general use as a fining material.

jarra—(Sp.) Wooden or metal jar holding 11½ to 12½ litres used in all Sherry blending operations (as the basic unit of measure).

Jeroboam or double magnum—Name of an oversize Champagne bottle, holding four regular bottles or 104 ozs.

jigger—the standard 1½ ounce measure used in cocktail and mixed drinks recipes.

jung—(Ger.) Young, immature wine.

kabinett—(Ger.) The basic grade of qualitätswein mit prädikat.

keg—A small stout cask.

keller, kellerei—(Ger.) Cellar.

kellerabfullung, kellerabzug—(Ger.) Bottled at the cellar or estate.

kill-devil—One of the first names applied to Rum in the British West Indies.

kimërt bor—(Hun.) Ordinary wine.

klein—(Ger.) Small.

konsumwein—(Ger.) Vin ordinaire—for home or local consumption.

korkbrand—(Ger.) Branded cork.

körper, koerper—(Ger.) Body.

körperarm—(Ger.) Poor body.

kräftig—(Ger.) Robust, rich in alcohol.

lagar—(Sp. & Port.) The term applied to the pressing trough.

lage—(Ger.) Vineyard site.

lager—(Ger.) To store beer for aging and sedimentation. All American beers today are "lagered."

landing—(applied to Champagne) The length of time that Champagne has been in the country—for instance, Champagne that has been in the country one year is said to have one year's landing.

lebendig—(Ger.) Wine with fresh racy flavor.

leer—(Ger.) Thin, lacking in character.

lees—The sediment which settles on the bottom of a cask of wine.

léger—(Fr.) Light—a wine lacking in body.

LeSigille de la Confrérie St-Etienne—(Fr.) A red seal awarded to particularly good wines by the growers' promotional body in Alsace.

levante—(Sp.) Hot, searing wind that blows over Sherry region, said to originate in the Sahara Desert.

lias—(Sp.) Wine lees.

licoroso—(Sp.) A rich, sweet fortified wine.

lieblich—(Ger.) Pleasant, light wine.

limousin (oak)—(Fr.) The oak used for the casks in which Cognac is aged.

liqueur—(Fr.) Cordial.

liqueur d'expédition—(Fr.) In Champagne—the sugar added to give the varying degrees of sweetness at the time of disgorging.

liqueur de tirage (dosage)—(Fr.) In Champagne—the sugar added at the time of bottling to insure an even secondary fermentation.

liquor—A trade term for the water used to reduce the proof of spirits.

liquoureux—(Fr.) A wine which is rich and sweet.

lodges—(Port.) The warehouses where Port wines are stored in Vila Nova de Gaia, Portugal. The warehouses where Madeira wines are stored in Funchal, Madeira.

low wines—In pot still distillation, the spirits obtained from the first operation.

maderisé—(Fr.) A white wine that has become very dark and taken on a woody character.

maestro, vino—(Sp.) Color wine used in Malaga.

mager—(Ger.) Thin, lacking in body; undistinguished.

magnum—A double-sized bottle, Champagne or Burgundy—52 ozs. Claret, 48 ozs.

magyar allami pincegazdaság—(Hun.) Hungarian state cellars.

malt—Grain, generally barley, which has been allowed to germinate for a short period that the enzyme diastase may be formed.

malts—Scotch whisky made entirely from malted barley.

mandel bitter—(Ger.) Wine having the taste of bitter almonds.

marc—(Fr.) The grapes required to load a Champagne press for a pressing; also the skins, pips, or husks remaining after the grapes have been pressed.

mashing—The operation of mixing ground meal and malt with water to liquefy the starches that they may be converted into sugars by the diastase in the malt.

matt—(Ger.) A flat, insipid wine.

Mickey Finn, Mickey—a drink in which "knockout" drops have been placed.

milde—(Ger.) Pleasantly soft but undistinguished wine.

mildew—A disease which attacks the vines in rainy or damp seasons.

millésime—(Fr.) Vintage date.

minösegi bor—(Hun.) Best quality wine.

mise dans nos caves—(Fr.) Bottled in our cellars (not necessarily those of the grower).

mise du domaine—(Fr.) Bottled at the property where it is made in Bordeaux; bottled by the owner in Burgundy.

mise par le propriétaire—(Fr.) Bottled by the growers.

mistelle—(Fr.) Grape *must* whose fermentation is halted by adding sufficient brandy to give it an alcoholic content of 15 percent. The natural unfermented grape sugar remains as sweetening. Mistelles are used as sweetening wines, particularly in making vermouths and apéritif wines.

moelle, moelleux—(Fr.) Marrow—richness in a wine without it being sweet.

monimpex—(Hun.) The state export monopoly.

monopole—(Fr.) The whole of the vineyard named belongs to the same proprietor.

Montilla-Moriles—(Sp.) Wine district of Spain near Cordoba where the very dry Montilla wines are produced. The Sherries classified as Amontillado are supposed to be in the "Montilla" style.

moot—(Ger.) *Must.* Grape juice before fermentation.

morgen—(Ger.) Land measure. Approximately one acre.

mosto—(Sp.) *Must.*

mou—(Fr.) Flabby. Wine lacking in character.

mouillé—(Fr.) Watered wine.

mountain—Term used in England during the eighteenth century to denote very sweet wines as opposed to sack which was less sweet.

mousseux—(Fr.) Sparkling.

moût—(Fr.) *Must,* i.e. unfermented grape juice.

mûr—(Fr.) Balanced, fruity wine.

must—Grape juice before and while it is fermenting.

mustometer, saccharometer—Apparatus for measuring the sugar content of grapemust.

musty—A wine that has acquired a mouldy unpleasant smell.

muté—(Fr.) Mistelle or a sweet wine whose fermentation has been inhibited by the addition of brandy.

mycoderma aceti—(Latin) The vinegar yeast.

mycoderma vini—(Latin) The yeast responsible for vinous fermentation.

natur, naturrein, naturwein—(Ger.) Perfectly natural wine to which no sugar has been added.

nature—(Fr.) Term used in Champagne labeling interchangeably with *brut.* Also to denote still Champagne.

naturwein—(Aut.) Wine without added sugar.

Nebuchadnezzar—Extraordinary Champagne bottle size holding 20 quarts or 520 ozs.

négociant-éleveur—(Fr.) A merchant who buys wine from the grower in its first year and brings it up in his own cellars.

nel'origine—(It.) Estate-bottled.

nero—(It.) Very dark red.

nerveux—(Fr.) A vigorous wine of long keeping qualities which will travel well.

nervig—(Ger.) Good full-bodied wine.

neutral spirits—Spirits distilled out from any material at a proof of 190 degrees or more, whether or not it is later reduced in proof.

Nicolauswein—(Ger.) Denotes a wine produced from grapes gathered December 6, St. Nicholas day.

nip or nips—Term applied in the trade to miniature bottles of spirits; also applied to a "split" of Champagne.

nose—The bouquet or aroma of a wine or spirit.

nu—(Fr.) Term denoting that the price quoted does not include the cost of cask. In other words, the price is for the "bare" wine.

nube—(Sp.) Cloudiness.

Öchsle—(Ger.) The German scale for measuring the sugar content of the grape *must* (before fermentation). The determination is made by the higher weight in grams of the *must* in relation to an equal volume of water. 25% of this greater weight is known to be sugar. Thus, 100 litres of *must* with a reading of 100° Öchsle will contain 25 kilograms of natural grape sugar.

octavilla, octave—(Sp. & Eng.) An eighth of a cask. In Sherry trade, $16\frac{1}{2}$ gallons.

oeil de perdrix—(Fr.) Partridge eye. Labelling term used to describe pink or rosé sparkling wine, usually from Burgundy or Switzerland.

oelig—(Ger.) A wine of high consistency that gives the impression of being oily as it is poured.

oenology—The science or study of wines.

oidium (oidium tuckeri)—A fungus disease which attacks the vines.

Oloroso—(Sp.) The term applied to the full-bodied, deeper-colored Sherries. Although very dry in their soleras, they are usually shipped as sweet-tasting Sherries by blending sweet wines with them.

ordinaire—(Fr.) The common wine of everyday use in France.

organoleptic examination or judgment—The only known method of judging the quality of wines, spirits and beers is by the human organs of sight, smell and taste, i.e. by organoleptic examination. Mechanical or chemical analysis is never as precise.

originalabfullung, originalabzug—(Ger.) Original bottling. Equivalent to estate bottling.

over proof—Spirits whose alcoholic strength is more than 100 proof.

palackozott—(Hun.) Bottled.

palma—(Sp.) The special chalk marking used to identify a very fine ( ) Fino Sherry.

palo cortado—(Sp.) The special marking used to denote raya( ) Sherries which have developed full and will become Olorosos.

Palomino—(Sp.) The best and most widely

used grape variety in the Sherry-producing region of Spain. It accounts for 90% of the vines planted.

parfum—(Fr.) The fragrance, rather than the bouquet, of a wine.

passe-tous-grains—(Fr.) A Burgundy wine made of a mixture of ⅓ Pinot and ⅔ Gamay grapes.

passito—(It.) Similar.

Pasteur, Louis—Great French scientist whose studies on malt and vinous fermentation gave the first complete explanation of these phenomena.

pasteurization—A process discovered by Pasteur of arresting, making inactive, or killing the ferments in wine, beer, or milk, etc., through heating the liquid and holding it for a brief time at 144° to 149° Fahrenheit.

patent still—The two column or continuous still "Patented" by Aeneas Coffey in 1832.

pauvre—(Fr.) Poor—a wine without charm.

Paxarete—(Sp.) Very rich sweet wine made mostly from the Pedro Ximenez grape and used for sweetening Sherries.

pays, vin du—(Fr.) Wine of the region—to be consumed on the spot.

Pedro Ximenez (P.X.)—(Sp.) Grape variety grown in the Sherry region to produce lusciously sweet wines.

pelure d'oignon—(Fr.) Onion skin. The brown tinge which certain red wines take on when old.

perfume—(Fr.) The fragrance of a wine or spirit.

perlwein—(Ger.) Slightly sparkling wine.

pétillant—(Fr.) A crackling or semi-sparkling wine.

petit—(Fr.) Small. A small poor wine.

Pfarrgut—(Ger.) Vineyard owned by a church whose product is given to the parson or preacher as part of his remuneration.

phylloxera vastatrix—The American grapevine louse which has caused untold damage to the world's vineyards.

pièce—(Fr.) The standard Burgundy cask, measuring 60 gallons.

pikant—(Ger.) Attractive, intriguing wine.

Pinot, Pineau—(Fr.) Grape variety of Burgundy and Champagne.

pint—Liquid measure of 16 ozs. Also a standard of fill for spirits in U.S. bottles of 16 ozs.

pipe—The term applied to the cask used in the Port, Lisbon, and Tarragona wine trades containing 138 gallons and to the Madeira trade where a pipe holds 110 gals.

piquant—(Fr.) A pleasant point of acidity. Generally applied to dry white wines.

piqué—(Fr.) A wine which has begun to turn. Its only use is for vinegar.

piquette—(Fr.) A common ordinary wine used in certain parts of France.

pisador—(Sp.) One who treads the grapes at vintage time in the Sherry region.

plastering—The system of adding *yeso* or gypsum to grapes when they are treaded and pressed in the lagar in Jerez, Spain.

plat—(Fr.) A dull, flat, lifeless sort of wine.

plein—(Fr.) A frank, forward full-bodied wine.

polsuho—(Yug.) Medium dry.

portes-greffes—(Fr.) The hardy phylloxera-resisting American root-stocks on which the fine vines of Europe are grafted.

pot still—The old-fashioned, fat-bellied, tapered neck still which requires two distinct operations to produce its useful spirit.

pourriture noble—(Fr.) "Noble rottenness"— the state of over-ripeness of the grapes of the Sauternes region of Bordeaux. It is in reality a yeast or mold known scientifically as *botrytis cinerea.*

précoce—(Fr.) A precocious wine that develops or matures rapidly.

prensa, pressoir—(Sp., Fr.) Wine press.

pricked wine—Same as piqué.

privnitā—(Rom.) Cellar.

prirodno—(Yug.) Natural.

proizvedeno u vinariji—(Yug.) Produced at.

proizvedeno u viastitoj vinariji poljoprivredne zadruge—(Yug.) Made in the cooperative cellars of the place named.

proof—An arbitrary system of measuring the alcoholic strength of a liquid. A spirit of 100 proof is one which contains exactly 50% of alcohol by volume at 60 degrees Fahrenheit. Each degree of proof represents ½% of alcohol.

punjéno u—(Yug.) Bottled at.

pupitres—(Fr.) The special racks used in the Champagne cellars during the remuage (shaking) operation.

puttony, puttonyos—(Hung.) The measure in which grapes are gathered in the Tokaj-Hegyalja from 13.6 to 25 litres.

qualitätswein—(Ger.) Superior table wine subject to certain controls.

qualitätswein mit prädikat—(Ger.) Strictly controlled top-quality wine.

quart—Liquid measure of 32 ozs. Also a standard of fill for spirits in U.S. bottles of 32 ozs.

quarter bottle—Wine bottle containing 6 to 6½ ozs.—one fourth the size of a regular bottle.

quarter cask—In cases where the standard cask, pipe, or butt is too large for a merchant, casks containing one fourth the original are used. Quarter casks vary in contents, depending on the wine region where they are used.

queue—(Fr.) Burgundy casks holding two *pièces* equal to 120 gallons.

Quinquina—(Fr.) French for quinine. Most of the French apéritif wines use the word as a description because they are quinined wines.

quintal—(Sp.) Spanish for 100-pounds. Also French for 100 kilograms.

quintas—(Port.) Portuguese for the vineyard or estate, much the same as "château" means in the Bordeaux wine region.

race—(Fr.) French for breed.

racking—The drawing of wine off its lees into a fresh clean cask. Also means the transference of any alcoholic beverage from one cask or vat to another.

rancio (Sp.)—Term applied to sweet fortified wines that have lost some color through age in the bottle. Such wines acquire a special aroma.

rassig—(Ger.) Wine of race and breed.

rauh—(Ger.) Raw, harsh.

raya—(Sp.) The chalk mark used in the Sherry region to identify wines that will become Olorosos. (/)

récemment dégorgé—(Fr.) Recently disgorged.

recolta—(Rom.) Vintage.

rectifying—Anything which changes the natural state of a spirit, such as redistilling after it has been barreled, adding coloring matter, sweetening, or any other flavoring material. Adding water to reduce proof does not constitute rectifying.

red wines—Any wine which has the slightest part of red coloring, obtained from the pigment found on the inside of the grape skin.

redondo—(Sp.) Round, well-balanced Sherry wine.

reducing—Term applied to the operation of lowering the alcoholic strength of a spirit by the addition of water.

refreshing—Term applied to the adding of young wine to an older one (in cask) to give the old wine new life. This term is also used in the same manner with respect to spirits, particularly brandies.

reif—(Ger.) Ripe, fine sweet wine.

rein—(Ger.) Pure.

reinsortig—(Aut.) Only this particular type.

reintönig—(Ger.) Well-balanced, very good wine.

remuage—(Fr.) The "shaking-down" operation employed in the preparation of Champagne, whereby the bottles are stood on end and periodically shaken to cause the sediment to settle upon the cork. In the United States the term used is "riddling."

Rentamt—(Ger.) Collection office.

reserva—(Sp.) Mature quality wine.

reserve exceptionnelle—(Fr.) Wine with over 11% alcohol in Alsace.

rich, riche—(Fr.) A wine having a generous bouquet, flavor and fullness of body.

rick—Constructed framework or rack in a warehouse in which barrels of distilled spirits are stored for aging. See illustration page 253.

ricking—Placing or racking barrels of whiskey or other distilled spirits on ricks, for aging.

ried—(Aut.) Vineyard.

riserva—(It.) Better quality wine.

robe—(Fr.) The color of the wine.

rociar—(Sp.) To refresh an old solera with young new wine.

rondeur—(Fr.) Roundness. A wine which drinks easily.

rosado—(Sp.) Rosé.

rosato—(It.) Pink.

rosé—Pink wine. A very pale red wine obtained by removing the grape skins as soon as the required amount of color has been attained by the wine.

rosso—(It.) Red.

rotling—(Ger.) Pink wine made from red and white grapes mixed.

rotwein—(Ger.) Red table wine.

ruby—A Port of a very deep red color, usually quite young, as opposed to one which has been aged for some time in wood and has become "tawny"—that is, pale in color, through repeated finings.

rund—(Ger.) Round, harmonious wine.

ružica—(Yug.) Rosé.

saccharometer—Instrument used to measure the sugar content of *must* or of wines or liquors.

sack, sacke—The old English spelling of the

Spanish *seco*, which became the generic term used to denote the drier fortified wines as opposed to "mountain" which were sweet. The term fell into disuse during the last century. Today it forms part of a trade-marked brand owned by one of the larger Sherry shipping houses.

saftig—(Ger.) Juicy, fine wine of character.

sancocho—(Sp.) Syrup produced by simmering or cooking *must* to one-third its original volume. It is used in the Sherry blend to sweeten and color the wine.

sauber—(Ger.) Clean, pure wine.

scantling—The stout wooden beams or supports on which the casks rest in the cellar.

schal—(Ger.) Musty, tired wine.

schaumwein—(Ger.) Sparkling wine.

schillerwein—(Ger.) Pink wine made from red and white grapes mixed.

schloss—(Ger.) Castle.

schlossabzug—(Ger.) Bottled at the castle's cellars, equivalent to Estate-bottled.

schnapps—Generic Dutch and German term denoting spirituous liquors.

schneewein—(Ger.) Snow wine. A term used with eiswein to describe grapes gathered when the vineyard was snow-covered.

schön—(Ger.) Lovely, charming pleasant wine.

schwefel—(Ger.) Sulphur smell in the bouquet of the wine.

sec—(Fr.) French term for dry. Also term used to denote a medium sweet Champagne.

secco—(It.) Dry.

seco—(Sp.) Dry.

sediment—The natural deposit found in wines as they grow old. It is formed by the crystallization and settling or precipitation of bitartrates, tannins, and pigments.

self whiskies—Term used in the Scotch whisky trade to denote a "straight" or an un-blended Scotch malt whisky.

sekt—(Ger.) Sparkling wine made in Germany.

sève—(Fr.) Literally *spa*. It is the combination of flavor and body which makes wine a pleasant beverage. What bouquet is to the nose, sève is to the palate.

Sikes, Sykes—Inventor of a hydrometer and tables for measuring alcoholic strengths which are in use in England.

slatko—(Yug.) Sweet.

solear—(Sp.) Term meaning "sunning" and describing the exposure of the grapes to the sun (sol) for 24–48 hours in the Sherry region.

solera—(Sp.) The system of blending which is the heart and soul of Sherry. A description of the solera system is to be found in the chapter on Wines of Spain.

sophistiquer—(Fr.) To falsify a wine or to ameliorate a defective wine with anything which will cover up its defects.

souche—(Fr.) Cep or vine root stock.

soutirage—(Fr.) Racking the clear wine from one cask into a fresh one.

soyeux—(Fr.) Silky, smooth, soft roundness. Lacking in roughness.

spätlese—(Ger.) Late gathered. A wine made from late picked grapes. Generally sweeter than wines made from grapes gathered earlier.

spirits—The generic term for distilled liquors. Neutral spirits, cologne spirits—A spirit distilled out at 190° proof or more. Used for blending and the preparation of rectified products.

Spital—(Ger.) Hospital.

spitzengewächs—(Ger.) The very best growth, usually only the beerenauslese and trocken-beerenauslese.

spitzenwein—(Ger.) The very best wine. Similar to spitzengewächs.

split—Same as quarter bottle.

spritzig—(Ger.) Wine which gives the impression of a slight prickling effervescence in the mouth. A much desired quality in fine Moselle wines.

Spumante—(It.) Italian for sparkling wine.

spumos—(Rom.) Sparkling.

Staatsweingut—(Ger.) State (owned) vineyard.

stahlig—(Ger.) Steely, austere.

still—The apparatus in which, by application of heat, the alcohol in a liquid may be separated and recovered.

Pot still—The original form of still or alembic.

Coffey still, patent still, double column still —Three names applied to the more modern continuous operation still.

stirrup-cup—The parting drink. The name comes from the custom in olden days of having a last drink with a guest, either to help him to his saddle or after he had mounted his horse.

stolno vino—(Yug.) Table wine.

stravecchio—(It.) Extra old.

strugure—(Rom.) Grape.

stück, stückfasser—(Ger.) The standard of cask measure, used in the Rhine, containing 1200 litres.

suho—(Yug.) Dry.

süss—(Ger.) Sweet.

szamorodni—(Hun.) Literally 'as it comes.'

száraz—(Hun.) Dry.

tafelwein—(Ger.) Ordinary table wine.

tannin, tannic—An important astringent acid found in all wines, but more so in red wines than in white. The proper amount of tannic acid is necessary to the keeping quality of a fine wine.

tappit-hen—A large Scotch wine bottle holding 3 bottles or more.

tawny—The quality of paleness or golden tinge which Ports acquire when matured in wood. This comes from the loss of red color resulting from repeated finings. Such wines are Tawny Ports.

tendre—(Fr.) A rather light and delicate wine, usually a young wine.

tenementi—(It.) Holding or estate.

tent—The ancient name for sweet Spanish wine.

tête de cuvée—(Fr.) Outstanding growth; term generally used in Burgundy.

tierce, tierçon, tierze—(Eng., Fr., Ger.) Various spellings for a cask holding a third of a butt or pipe.

tilts—Bars used for adjusting casks or scantlings to the desired position.

tinto—(Sp.) Red.

tintourier—(Fr.) French for coloring. The term applied to grapes used primarily for the abundance of color they contribute to the *must*.

tirage—(Fr.) Bottling; also drawing off or filling of wines or spirits into other containers.

tischwein—(Ger.) Common wine for local consumption.

tonelero—(Sp.) Cooper.

tonneau—(Fr.) Tun. Term used in the Bordeaux wine trade representing four barriques of 225 litres or 900 litres. This is the unit of measure in which wines are sold in the bulk trade.

traube—(Ger.) Grape.

traubenkelter—(Ger.) Term for hydraulic grape press in use today.

trocken—(Ger.) Dry.

trockenbeerenauslese—(Ger.) Wine made from selected dry, raisin-like grapes. Weather conditions must be perfect throughout the summer and the late vintage season for trockenbeerenauslese wines to be made. They are very rare and as sweet as the richest Sauternes.

tuica—(Rom.) Plum brandy.

uisgebeatha (Celtic); uisquebaugh (Gaelic)—Meaning "the water of life." It was the first word used to describe whiskey.

ullage—The term used in the trade to describe the loss of wine or spirit from a cask or bottle due to evaporation or leakage.

underproof—A spirit whose alcoholic strength is below proof. In the U.S. this is a spirit of less than 100 proof, as opposed to an overproof spirit having a strength of over 100 proof.

ungezuckert—(Ger.) Unsugared, pure wine.

unharmonisch—(Ger.) Opposite of harmonious. Unbalanced.

usé—(Fr.) A wine that has passed its peak and is on the decline.

uva—(Sp.) Grape.

vatting—Mixing or blending in a vat.

vats—The enormous tubs in which wines ferment, or spirits are blended.

velouté—(Fr.) A wine which has a soft, rich, mellow "velvety" softness. No roughness whatsoever.

velvety—English for velouté.

vendange, vendangeur—(Fr.) Vintage, vintager.

vendange tardive—(Fr.) Late-picked wine, implying more strength and/or sweetness.

vendemmia—(It.) Vintage.

vendimia—(Sp.) Vintage.

venencia—(Sp.) The special cup used for drawing samples from the Sherry butts in the bodega. It is a cylindrical silver cup attached to a long limber strip of whalebone.

Verband Deutscher Naturwein Versteigerer—(Ger.) German Natural Wine Auction-sellers Association.

verbessert—(Ger.) Wine improved by adding sugar to the *must*.

vert—(Fr.) Green—term used to describe a wine that is too young and not ready for drinking.

verwaltung—(Ger.) Administration.

vid—(Sp.) Vine.

vie—(Rom.) Vine.

viejo, viejisimo—(Sp.) Old, very old.

vif—(Fr.) A lively, brisk wine.

vigne—(Fr.) Vine.

vigneron—(Fr.) Vine dresser.

vignoble—(Fr.) Vineyard.

viile—(Rom.) Vineyard.

vin—(Fr.) Wine.

vin alb—(Rom.) White wine.

vin cuit—(Fr.) A concentrated wine used to improve thin wines.

vin de garde—(Fr.) A wine worth keeping, i.e. for laying down.

vin de goutte—(Fr.) Wine made from the last pressing. It is generally of poor quality.

vin de masă—(Rom.) Table wine.

vin de messe—(Fr.) Altar wine.

vin de paille—(Fr.) White wine made from grapes which have been spread on straw (paille) mats to sun, before pressing.

vin de pays—(Fr.) Small wines of each region, consumed locally.

vin doux—(Fr.) A sweet wine.

vin gris—(Fr.) A cheap wine made in the eastern part of France from a mixture of red and white grapes. It is also another name for *vin ordinaire*.

vin mousseux—(Fr.) Sparkling wine.

vin nature—(Fr.) Natural; unsweetened wine.

vin ordinaire—(Fr.) Ordinary cheap wine of general consumption.

vin rosé—(Fr.) A pink wine.

vin rosu—(Rom.) Red wine.

vin sec—(Fr.) A dry wine.

vin superioare—(Rom.) Superior wine.

vin usoare—(Rom.) Light wine.

viña—(Sp.) Vine. Also vineyard in Argentina and Chile.

vine—The plant which produces grapes.

viñedo—(Sp.) Vineyard.

vinello, vinetto, vinettino—(It.) Italian diminutives for wine. Always poor, thin vins ordinaires.

vineux—(Fr.) Vinosity.

vinho—(Port.) Wine.

vinho claro—(Port.) Natural wine.

vinho generoso—(Port.) Fortified wine.

vinho surdo—(Port.) Fortified wine. According to Portuguese law, Port wine must be a "vinho surdo."

vinho verde—(Port.) Light, young white or red wines produced in Northern Portugal.

vini—(It.) Wines.

vini da banco—(It.) Table wine.

vini tipici—(It.) Typical or standard wines.

viniculture—The science of making wine.

vinjak—(Yug.) Brandy.

vino—(It. & Sp.) Wine.

vino corriente—(Sp.) Ordinary wine for local consumption.

vino de añada—(Sp.) Young wine of one vintage, ready for the *criadera* reserves.

vino de color—(Sp.) Color wine used in the Sherry bodega to give color and sweetness to the final blend.

vino de cosecha propria—(Sp.) Wine made by the owner of the vineyard.

vino de mesa—(Sp.) Table wine.

vino frizzante—(It.) A lightly sparkling type of wine consumed locally in Italy.

vino liquoroso—(It.) Very sweet wine.

vino maestro—(Sp.) Master wine. A sweet full wine used to lend character and body to weaker, thinner wine.

vino ordinario—(It.) Ordinary wine, not usually bottled.

vino Santo—(It.) Sweet white wine produced from dried grapes in the Chianti wine region of Tuscany.

vino spumante—(It.) Sparkling wine.

vinosity—The wininess or character of a wine. The balance of bouquet, flavor, and body in a wine.

vinous—Pertaining to wine.

vintage—The gathering of the grape crop and the making of the wine. The date of year when the wine is made, which often appears on wine labels.

vintage wines—In certain wine regions, particularly Champagne and Port, the product of exceptional years only, is dated.

virgin brandy—Term applied to unblended Cognac brandies.

visokokvalitetno—(Yug.) High quality.

viticulture—The science of grape culture.

vitis—(Latin) Vine.

vornehm—(Ger.) Exquisite, delightful wine.

vörös—(Hun.) Red.

wachstum—(Ger.) See gewächs.

wappen—(Ger.) Coat of arms or house crest.

wash—The term applied in a distillery (usually whiskey) to the fermented liquor when it is ready to go to the still. In a Scotch distillery the still which receives the wash is known as the *wash-still*.

wassail—Old English toast derived from the Anglo-Saxon *wes hal* meaning "be of good health."

weepers—Bottles that show leakage through the cork. Applied mostly to Champagne and sparkling wines.

wein—(Ger.) Wine.

weinbau—(Ger.) Viticulture.

weingut—(Ger.) Vineyard or estate.

weinkellerei—(Ger.) Wine cellar.

weissherbst—(Ger.) Pink wine made from red grapes.

weisswein—(Ger.) White wine.

wernig—(Ger.) Vinous, vinosity.

wine—Broadly, the fermented juice of fruit.

In the nice sense, wine is the naturally fermented juice of freshly gathered ripe grapes which have been pressed at or near the place where gathered.

wine-brokers—In many wine regions where there are many small vineyard owners, there would be utter confusion in marketing unless there existed a group of intermediaries—wine-brokers—to act for the buyers from every part of the world and for the vineyard owner. The wine-broker has functioned for many, many generations.

Winzergenossenschaft—(Ger.) Wine growers' cooperative.

Winzerwein—(Ger.) Wine growers' association.

wormwood—A perennial herb, *artemisia absinthium*, aromatic, tonic, and bitter. It is used in the preparation of absinthe, certain liqueurs, and Vermouths.

würzig—(Ger.) Spicy, desirable, pronounced flowery aroma.

Wwe. (Witwe)—(Ger.) Widow.

yayin—A biblical Hebrew term for wine.

yeast—The plant organism whose fermentative qualities cause sugars to break down into alcohol and carbonic acid gas.

yema—(Sp.) The must resulting from the treading before the grapes are subjected to pressure. Yema in Spanish means "yolk of an egg" or the core of any product.

yeso—(Sp.) Powdered gypsum (calcium sulphate) sprinkled on the grapes in the lagar at the time of treading and pressing, to fix the tartaric acid during fermentation of the *must* into Sherry wine.

zapatos de pisar—(Sp.) Special nail-studded shoes worn by the men who tread the grapes in the lagar in the Sherry region of Spain.

zymase—The specific enzyme in yeast-cells which cause vinous fermentation and whose catalytic action converts sugars into alcohol and carbonic acid gas.

TRADE ABBREVIATIONS

Å.—Amontillado
abboc.—abbocato (sweet, Italian)
A.B.C.—Alcoholic Beverage Control (Board)
A.B.C.C.—Alcoholic Beverage Control Commission
abf.—abfüllung (bottled, German)
A.B.I. Permit—Alcoholic Beverage Import Permit
A.C.—Appellation Controlée
Akt. Ges.—Aktiengesellschaft. (German corporation)
alc.—alcohol
a/M.—am Moselle (on the Moselle)
Amer. gal.—American gallon
Amont.—Amontillado
Anon.—Anonyme (Anonymous, French)
A°—anno (year)
a/R—am Rhein (on the Rhine)
Artis—Artisans (Bordeaux classification)
A.S.E.—American Society of Enologists.
Assoc. also Assocn.—association
asst.—assortment
A.T.O.A.—Associated Tavern Owners of America
Aus.—Aussle (German-wine from selected grapes) also Austria

B.A.T.F.—Bureau of Alcohol, Tobacco and Firearms
B & B—Benedictine and brandy
B. & G.—Barton and Guestier (French wine firm)
B/B—bottled in bond
bbl.—barrel
Bbn.—Bourbon
Belg.—Belgium
B^elles—bouteilles (bottles)
bev.—beverage
B.F.W.—Bonded Field Warehouse
B.I.—Bourbon Institute (a trade association)
B.I.B.—bottled in bond
Bl.—blanc (white)
B. of L.—bill of lading (shipping document)
Bord. also Bordx.—Bordeaux
bot. also bott.—bottle, bottled
B.P.S.—British Plain Spirits (unsweetened alcohol-used to describe whisky on shipping papers)
Br.—Brandy

Brit.—British, Britain
brl.—barrel
brwy.—brewery
B.S.—Bonded Storeroom also Bonded shipper
Btle. also Btle.—Bottle
bu.—bushel
Burg.—Burgundy
B.W.—Bonded winery also Bonded warehouse
B.W.I.—British West Indies
Bx.—Bordeaux

C. also Cent.—Centigrade (temperature)
C. & F.—cost and freight
Ca. also C^a.—Compania (Company-Portugal)
Cal. also Calif.—California
Ch. also Chat. also Chau. also Chat^au.—Château
Champ.—Champagne
Chat. Bot.—Château Bottled
Cia.—Compania (Company)
Cie.—Companie (Company)
C.I.F.—Cost. insurance and freight
C.I.F.&E.—Cost, insurance, freight and exchange
C.I.V.B.—Counseil Inter professional du Vin de Bordeaux
C.I.V.C.—Comite interprofessional du Vin de Champagne
cl.—classe (class or classification)
C.L.—club liquor license
cm.—centimeter
C.M.B.W.—Customs Manufacture Bonded Warehouse
Conf. du Chev. du Taste—Confrèriedes chevaliers du Tiste Vin (A Burgundy wine group)
cont.—contents
C.P.—Cape Province (South Africa)
C.P.V.F.—Comite de Propagande des Vins de France
Crezc.—Crezcenz (growth of Germany)
cs. also c/s—case
C.S.B.—Central Spirit Bureau. (Swedish body which issues liquor ration books.)
csk.—cask
C.U.C.S.G.—Central Union of Czecho-Slovakian growers.
cuv.—cuvée.
C.V.F.—Charente Viticulturists Federation.

507

C.W.S.C.—Swedish state controlled company which has the monopoly on alcoholic beverages.
cwt.—hundred weight.

d.—penny (England) pence.
d.b.a.—doing business as.
dbl.—double.
dec.—decanter.
D.E.I.—Dutch East Indies.
Den.—Denmark.
D.I.—Direct importer.
D.I.B.—delivery in bond.
Dist.—distiller also distillery also distilled also district also distributor.
Distrib.—distributor.
D.J.—Demijohn (bottle size).
dl.—decalitre.
D.M.—Dry Monopole (Champagne) also Double Magnum (equal to Jeroboam-bottle size)
dom.—domestic also domaine.
D.O.M.—Deo Optimo Maximo (To God, most good, most great.).
doz.—dozen.
D.P.—duty paid.
D.P.D.—duty paid dock.
D.S.C. (U.S.)—Distilled Spirits Council of the United States (a trade association formed by the merger of Distilled Spirits Institute, Licensed Beverage Industries, and the Bourbon Institute.
D.S.I.—Distilled Spirits Institute (a trade association).

E.B.—Estate Bottling.
E.E.C.—European Economic Community (Common Market).
E.O.M.—end of the month.
Est. Bot.—Estate bottled.
Et. also Etab. also Ets.—Establishments (French).
ex tax—Without tax.
ex tax incl.—excise tax included.
Exp.—exporter.

F.—fifth (bottle size) also Fall (on Bottled in Bond revenue stamps).
F.—Fahrenheit (temperature).
F.A.A.—Federal Alcohol Administration.
F.A.C.A.—Federal Alcohol Control Administration.
Fahr.—Fahrenheit (temperature).
F.A.S.—Free alongoid ship (or streamer).

F.D.—Fruit Distillery.
Fed.—Federal.
fgn—foreign.
filt.—filter also filtered.
fl.—fluid.
flav.—flavor or flavored.
F.O.B.—free on board (shipping term) also Fine Old Blend also Fine Old Bourbon.
F.O.C.—free on canal (shipping term).
F.O.R.—free on rails (shipping term).
F.O.R.M.A.—Fonds d'Orientation et de Regularisation des Marches Agricoles.
fort.—fortified.
Fr.—French also France.
frs. also f^{rcs} also frcs.—francs (currency).
F.T.C.—Federal Trade Commission.
F.W.I.—French West Indies.

gal. also gall.—gallon.
G.B.—Great Britain.
Ger. also Germ.—Germany also German.
G.F.C.—Grande Fine Champagne (Cognac).
G.L.—Gay Lussac (French alcoholic strength) also Gold Label.
GmbH.—Gesellschaft mit beschränkter Haftung. (Joint Stock company under the laws of Germany).
GmbHG.—Gesetz betreffend die Gesellschaft mit beschränkter Haftung (Germany law concerning limited liability companies of April 20, 1892).
g.n.s.—grain neutral spirits (alcohol).
g.p.h.—gallons per hour.
gr.—grain.

h. also H.—Half.
ha.—hectacre.
H.D.W.—Hauptvereinigung der Deutchen Weinbauwirtschaft. (Central Union of the German Wine growing industry).
hecto. also hectol. also hectolit.—hectolitre.
hf.—half.
hf. btls.—half bottles.
hhd. also hghd.—hogshead.
H.I.M.—His (or Her) Imperial Majesty.
hl.—hectolitre.
H.L.—Hotel Liquor License also House of Lords.
H$^{nos.}$—Hermanos (brothers).
H.O.P.—Hotel Off Premise Consumption License.
H.R.H.—His (or Her) Royal Highness.
Hung.—Hungary also Hungarian.
H.W.—Hotel Wine License.

I.B.—in bond.
I.D.V.—International Distillers and Vintners Ltd.
I.F.S.—Irish Free State.
imp.—imported also importer also imperiale (bottle size).
imp. gal.—imperial gallon.
imperial—imperial.
I.N.A.O.—National Institute of Appellations of Origin (Italy).
Inc.—Incorporated.
I.N.E.—Instituto Nazionale per l'Esportazione (Italian export regulating body).
insp.—inspected.
I. Permit No.—import (or importers) permit number.
I.R.—Internal Revenue.
I.R.B.W.—Internal Revenue Bonded Warehouse.
I.R.L.D.P.—Illinois Retail Liquor Dealers Protective Assoc.
I.R.O.—Inland Revenue Office.
I.S.R.L.D.A.—Illinois State Retail Liquor Dealers Assoc.
It.—Italy also Italian.
I.T.C/C.C.C.—Intercontinental Trailsea Corp./Commercial Credit Card Inc. (a commercial credit card for payment of merchandise plus duties and handling services.

Jer.—Jeroboam (bottle size).

K.D.A.—Kentucky Distillers Assoc.
kg.—kilogram.
kilolit. also ko.—kilolitre.
komp.—Company (Poland).
k$^{os.}$—kilograms.
K.W.V.—Ko-operative Winsbouvers vereiniging van Zuid Afrika-Beperkt. (Co-operative Wine Growers Association of South Africa, Ltd.).
Ky.—Kentucky.

L.—Retail Liquor License.
£—Pound sterling (England).
lb.—pound (weight).
L.B.I.—Licensed Beverage Industries (a trade association).
L.C.—letter of credit.
L.C.B.—Liquor Control Board.
Ld.—Limited.
Lda.—Limitada (Spanish or Portuguese).
Lic. No.—license number.
liq.—liquor also liqueur also liquid.

liq. gal.—liquid gallon.
lit.—litre.
L.L.—Wholesale liquor license.
Ltd.—Limited.
Ltda.—Limitada (Spanish or Portuguese).

M.—monsieur (mr.).
Mad.—Madeira.
Mag.—Magnum (bottle size).
Md.—Maryland.
med.—medium.
Meth.—Methuselah (Bottle size).
Mg. also Mgm.—Magnum (bottle size).
mins.—miniatures.
mm.—millimeter.
Mme.—Madame (Mrs.).
Mt.—Mount.
M.W.—Master of Wine.

N.A.A.B.I.—National Association of Alcoholic Beverage Importers.
N.A.B.C.A.—National Alcoholic Beverage Control Assoc.
Nat.—Nature (equal to Brut).
N.B.W.A.—National Beer Wholesalers Assoc. (a trade group).
N.B.W.L.A.—National Beer, Wine, and Liquor Assoc. (a trade group).
N.C.S.L.A.—National Conference of State Liquor Administrators.
N.L.B.A.—National Licensed Beverage Association.
N.L.S.A.—National Liquor Stores Association.
Non Vint also Non Vt.—Non vintage.
N.S.W.—New South Wales (Australia).
N.V.—Non vintage also Naamloze Vennootschaap (similar to incorporated).
N.W.I.— Netherlands West Indies.

O.B.W.—Old Blended Whiskey.
O.B.W.I.—Other British West Indies.
O.F.S.—Orange Free State (South Africa).
O.L.V.—Office International du Vin also known as International Wine Office.
o.p.—over proof.
o/Rhein—On Rhine (river).
ord.—ordinaire (ordinary).
orig.—original.
oz.—ounce.

P.—proof also pint also pale also pipe (cask).
Pa.—Pennsylvania.
pct.—per cent.
Per. Dist.—permissive district.

Per. No.—permit number.
pes.—pesos (Spanish).
pf.—proof also preferential (tariff).
p.g. also pf. gal.—proof gallon.
pH.—symbol for effective acidity.
pkg.—package.
P.L.C.B.—Pennsylvania Liquor Control Board.
ppm.—parts per millions.
P.R.—Puerto Rico.
Prf.—proof.
Prop.—proprietor.
P.S.—proof spirit.
pt.—pint.
Pty.—property also proprietary.
pun.—puncheon (large cask).
putt.—puttonyos (Hungarian hods) about 65 pounds.
pvt.—private.
P.W.T.A.—Port Wine Trade Association.
P.X.—Pedro Ximenez (blending sherry) also name of a grape grown in Spain.
P.X.V.—Pedro Ximenez Viejo (old blending sherry).

qr. also qtr.—quarter also British weight 25 stones.
qt.—quart.
qty. also qy.—quality.
qual. also qy.—quality.

R.—rectifier.
R. & R.—Rock & Rye.
rd.—round (bottle).
Rect.—rectifier.
reg.—regular (usually sweet vermouth) also registered.
regd.—registered.
rep.pt.—reputed pint ($\frac{1}{12}$ imperial gallon) also called a tenth (12.8 oz.).
rep.qt.—reputed quart ($\frac{1}{6}$ imperial gallon) also called a fifth (25.6 oz.).
res.—reserve. also Reserva or Reservado (Spanish).
ret.—retail also retailer.
rH.—symbol for level of oxidation.
R.L.—Restaurant Liquor License.
R.L.D.—Retail Liquor Dealer.
R.L.D.P.A.—Retail Liquor Dealers Protective Assoc.
Rom.—Romania also Romanian.
R.W.—Restaurant Wine License.

S/—Sur (on, French).
S.A.—South Africa also South America.
S.A. also S/A.—Sociedad Anónima (Cuba) also

Societé Anonyme (French) also Società Anonyma (Italy).
S.A.R.L.—Societé Anonyme Responsibilité Limitée (a limited liability company).
Saut.—Sauternes.
Sawfa. also S.A.W.F.A.—South African Wine Farmers Association (subsidiary of K.W.V.g.v.).
S.D.R.L. also S. de R. L.—Sociedad de Responsibilidad Limite.
S. en C.—Sociedad en Comandita (limited partnership company).
S.E.P.C.—Societé pour l'Exportation des Produits des Charentes Ltd.
ser.—serial.
S.F.C.—Superior Fine Cognac also Special Fine Cognac.
S.G.W.—Scotch grain whisky.
S.L.A.—State Liquor Authority
S.M.—Sparkling Moselle also sour mash (Bourbon).
Sp.—Spain also Spanish also sparkling.
spark.—sparkling.
sp. g.—specific gravity.
Spt. Bd.—spirit blend.
Sr. also Sres. (plural)—Señor (Mister, Spain).
S.R.—Societé Responsibilité also straight rye.
S.S.—state stores
St.—Saint.
Sta.—Santa (Spain).
Ste.—Sainte.
Ste. A^{me}—Societé Anonyme (France).
stk.—stock
str.—straight.
sucrs. also succrs.—succesores (successors).
sup. also super.—supérieur also superior.
S.V.C.—Societé Vinicolede Champagne.
S.W.A.—Scotch Whisky Association.
Swed.—Sweden.
Szam.—Szamorodni (natural-used on Tokay label.).

T.—teaspoon also Tawny.
tbsp.—tablespoon.
temp.—temperature.
T-men—Treasury Department Agents. (Alcohol tax unit).
T.M. Reg—Trade Mark Registered.
T.P.B.H.—Tax paid Bottling House.
tsp.—teaspoon.
tx.—tonneaux (unit of measure in French bulk wine sales) also tax.

U.B.I.F.—United Brewers Industrial Foundation.

U.C.V.A.—Union des Cooperatives de l'Armagnac (trade group).
U.K.—United Kingdom.
U.K.B.G.—United Kingdom Bartenders Guild.
u.p.—under proof.
U.S.B.A.—United States Brewers Association also U.S. Brewers Academy.
U.S.D.A.—United States Department of Agriculture.
U.S.P.—United States Pharmacopoeia.
U.S.S.G.—United States Storekeeper Gauger.
U.S.S.R.—Union of Socialist Soviet Republic (Russia).

V. de P. also V.D.P.—Vino de Pasto
V.D.Q.S.—Vins Delimités de Qualité Supérieure (French wine growers syndicate guarantee of quality).
vds.—vineyards.
V.I.—Virgin Islands.
vint.—vintage.
V.N.Gaia also V.N.de G.—Villa Nova de Gaia (Portugal).
V.O.—very old.
vol.—volume.
V.O.X.—Very Old Xerez (Sherry).
V.P.—very pale.
V.S.—very superior also very special.
V.S.E.P.—Very Special Extra Pale also Very Superior Extra Pale.
V.S.O.—Very Superior Old also Very Special Old.
V.S.O.P.—Very Superior Old Pale. Also Very Special Old Pale. Also Very Superior Old Product.
V.S.R.—Very Special Reserve. Also Very Superior Reserve.
vt. also vtg.—vintage.
Vve. also V^e—veuve (window).
V.V.O.—very, very old.

W.—Retail Wine License. Also Winery.
W. & G.—White and Green (Creme de Menthe).
W.A.B.—Wine Advisory Board.
W.C.T.U.—National Women's Christian Temperence Union.
W. & F. Soc.—Wine and Food Society.
W.D.W.—Wholesale Dealer in Wines.
w.g.—wine gallon.
Wh.—white.
whse.—warehouse.
W.I.—Wine Institute. Also West Indies.
W.L.D.—Wholesale Liquor Dealer.
W.R.—Warehouse receipt.
W.S.W.A.—Wine & Spirits Wholesalers of America.
W.W.—Wholesale Wine License.
W^{we}—Witwe (window).

Y.—and (Spanish).
Y.O.—years old.
Yr. also Yrs.—year also years.
Yugo.—Yugoslavia.
Z.A.—Zuid Afrika (South Africa).
Zn.—Zoon (son-Holland).
Z.O.—Zeer Oude (very old-Holland).

Appendix **K**

APPROXIMATE CALORIC VALUES
OF BEVERAGES*

WINES

WINE	MEASURE	CALORIES
Bordeaux Red	4 ounces	67
Bordeaux Graves	4 ounces	80
Bordeaux Sauternes	4 ounces	135
Burgundy Red	4 ounces	70
Burgundy White	4 ounces	70/75
California Red	4 ounces	72
California Riesling or Rhine wine	4 ounces	70/80
California Sauterne	4 ounces	95
Catawba, sweet	4 ounces	121
Chablis	4 ounces	70
Champagne, brut	4 ounces	85
Champagne, extra dry	4 ounces	117
Dubonnet	2 ounces	64
Liebfraumilch	4 ounces	95
Madeira	2 ounces	65
Malaga	2 ounces	87
Moselle	4 ounces	67
Port, Portugal	2 ounces	77.5
Port, U.S.A.	2 ounces	86.5
St. Raphaël	2 ounces	64
Sherry, dry	2 ounces	64
Sherry, sweet	2 ounces	72
Sherry, U.S.A.	2 ounces	72
Vermouth, dry	2 ounces	54.5
Vermouth, sweet	2 ounces	87

* In preparing these tables we have been guided by the "Tables of Food Values—Revised and Enlarged" by Alice V. Bradley, Pub. Chas A. Bennett Co., Inc., Peoria, Ill.

DISTILLED SPIRITS

SPIRIT	CALORIES PER OUNCE
Absinthe substitutes	74
Anisette	77/96
Apple Brandy (Calvados)	74
Apricot Liqueur	84
B and B Liqueur D.O.M.	76
Bénédictine D.O.M.	82
Brandies, Cognac, Armagnac, Marc, Spanish, etc.	70/74
Chartreuse, green	74
Chartreuse, yellow	86
Cherry Liqueur	92
Crème de Cacao	90
Crème de Menthe	88
Curaçao	82
Gin	69
Rum, Jamaica	147
Rum, Puerto Rico	74
Triple Sec (Cointreau, etc.)	80
Vodka, 80 proof	70
Whiskies, Canadian & Scotch	74
Whiskies, Irish and U.S.	84
Ale	15
Beer, Imported	13¼
Beer, U.S.A.	11½

MIXED DRINKS

COCKTAILS	MEASURE	CALORIES
Bacardi	4 ounces	244
Daiquiri	4 ounces	199
Manhattan	4 ounces	236
Martini, dry	4 ounces	102
Old Fashioned	5 ounces	221
Sour—whiskey, rum, etc.	5 ounces	184
LONG DRINKS		
Brandy & Soda	8 ounces	66
Colins—gin or rum	12 ounces	118
Fizzes—gin, brandy, rum	7 ounces	137
Highball—whiskey, gin, rum, etc	8 ounces	111/130
Mint Julep—whiskey or rum	12 ounces	180/260
Rickey—gin or rum	8 ounces	103/112
Tom & Jerry	8 ounces	266

SELECTED BIBLIOGRAPHY

Adams, Leon D., *Commonsense Book of Wine*
Adkins, Jan., *Craft of Winemaking*
Allen, H. Warner., *Romance of Wine*
——*Sherry and Port*
——*White Wines and Cognac*
——*Natural Red Wines*
——*Rum*
——*A Contemplation of Wine*
Allen W. W. *The Romance of Wine*
Amerine, Maynard A. & Berg. H. W. *Technology of Wine Making*
Amerine, Maynard A. & Joslyn, M. A. *Table Wines: The Technology of their Production*
Amerine, Maynard A. & Singleton, V. L. *Wine: An Introduction for Americans*
Amerine, Maynard A. & Wheeler, Louise B. *A Check List of Books & Pamphlets on Grapes & Wine & Related Subjects*
Anderson, Stanley F. & Hull, Raymond. *Art of Making Beer*
——*Art of Making Wine*
Austin, Cedric, *Science of Wine*
Bach, Johann S., *Wine & Taxes*
Balzer, Robert L., *Adventures in Wine: Legends, History, Recipes*
Barnard, Alfred, *Whiskey Distilleries of the United Kingdom*
Beadle, Leigh, *Making Fine Wines & Liqueurs*
Bespaloff, Alexis, *The First Book of Wine*
——*Signet Book of Wine*
Beveridge, N. E. *Cups of Valor*
Birmingham, Frederic. *Complete Beer Book*
Blumberg, Robert S. & Hannum, Hurst. *Fine Wines of California*
Bosdari, C. D. *Wines of the Cape*
Bravery, H. E. *The Science of Wine & Beer Making*
Broadbent, J. M. *Wine Tasting*
Buck, John. *Take a Little Wine*
Carling, T. E. *The Complete Book of Drink*
——*Wine Aristocracy*
Carter, Youngman. *Drinking Burgundy*
Church, Ruth E. *American Guide to Wines*
Churchill, Creighton. *Great Wine Rivers of Europe*
——*A Notebook For The Wines of France*

Cockburn, Ernest. *Port Wine and Oporto*
Conant, James B., ed. *Pasteur's Study of Fermentation*
Croft-Cook, Rupert, *Sherry*
Cruess, W. V. *The Principles and Practice of Wine Making*
DeChambeau, Andre. *Creative Winemaking*
De Klerk, W. A. *White Wines of South Africa*
Dettori, Renato G. *Italian Wines and Liqueurs*
Dingman, Stanley T. *Wine Cellar & Journal Book*
Doxat, John. *Drinks & Drinking: An International Distillation*
Ehle, John. *The Cheeses & Wines of England & France with Notes on Irish Whiskey*
Esquire Magazine Editors. *Esquire Drink Book*
Fisher, M. F. & Yavno. Max. *The Story of Wine in California*
Fisher, M. I. *Liquors, a Dictionary*
Food & Agriculture Organization. *World Wine & Vine Product's Economy*
Forbes, Patrick, *Champagne: The Wine, the Land and the People*
Galasz, Zoltan. *Hungarian Wine Through the Ages*
General Agreement on Tariffs and Trade. *World Trade & Prospects for Ordinary Wine*
Girad, Charles. *The Manufacture of Liquors & Preserves*
Gold, Alec, *Wine and Spirits of the World*
Gordon, Alvin. *Of Vines & Missions*
Grossman, Harold J. *Practical Bar Management*
Gunyon, R. E. *The Wines of Central & South Eastern Europe*
Hallgarten, Peter. *Liqueurs*
Hamio, Oscar. *Cocktail & Wine Digest*
Haszonics, J. J. & Barratt, S. *Wine Merchandising*
James, Margery K. *Studies in the Medieval Wine Trade*
Jeffs, Julian. *Sherry*
——*Wines of Europe*
Johnson, Hugh. *Wine*
——*World Atlas of Wine*
Kressmann, Edouard. *Wonder of Wine*

Lake, Max. *Classic Wines of Australia*
Lausame, Edita. *Great Book of Wine*
Layton, T. A. *Cognac and Other Brandies*
Leedom, William S. *Vintage Wine Book*
Lichine, Alexis. *Alexis Lichine's Encyclopedia of Wines & Spirits*
——*Wines of France*
Lucia, Salvatore P. *A History of Wine as Therapy*
——*Wine & Your Well-Being*
Marrison, L. W. *Wines & Spirits*
——*Wines for Everyone*
Massee, William E. *McCall's Guide to Wines of America*
——*Massee's Wine Handbook*
Massel, A. *Applied Wine Chemistry & Technology*
Melville, John & Morgan, Jefferson. *Guide to California Wines*
Misch, Robert J. *Quick Guide to Wine*
Morgan, Jefferson. *Adventures in the Wine Country*
Murphy, Brian. *Vino*
Murphy, Dan. *Australian Wine—a Complete Guide*
Murray, Samuel W. *Wines of the USA*
Pellegrini, Angelo M. *Wine & the Good Life*
Penning-Rowsell, Edmund. *Wines of Bordeaux*
Pohren, D. E. *Adventures in Taste: The Wines & Folk Food of Spain*
Postgate, Raymond. *Alphabet of Wines*
——*Home Wine Cellar*
——*Plain Man's Guide to Wine*
——*Portuguese Wine*
Poupon, Pierre & Forgeot P. *Book of Burgundy*
Pratt, James N. & De Caso, Jacques. *The Wine Bibber's Bible*
Price, Pamela V. *Wine-Lover's Handbook*
Ray, Cyril. *Wines of Italy*
Rosenbloom, Morris V. & Greenleaf, A. B. *Bottling for Profit: A Treatise on Liquor & Allied Industries*
Rowe, Percy. *The Wines of Canada*
Roy, Mike, ed. *Discovering Italian Wines*
Schoonmaker, Frank. *Encyclopedia of Wine*
Shepherd, C. W. *Wines, Spirits and Liqueurs*

Simmons, Matty, ed. *New Diners Club Drink Book*
Simon, Andre. *Everybody's Guide to Wines & Spirits*
——*History of the Wine Trade in England*
——*Wine Primer*
——*A Dictionary of Wine*
——*A Dictionary of Wines, Spirits and Liqueurs*
——*All About South Africa*
——*All About Wines*
——*The Commonsense of Wine*
——*How to Make Wines & Cordials.*
——*The Supply, the Care and the Sale of Wine*
——*Wines & Spirits: The Connoisseur's Textbook*
——*Wines of the World*
Simon, Andre L. & Hallgarten, S. F. *Great Wines of Germany*
Stanislawski, Dan. *Landscapes of Bacchus: The Vine in Portugal*
Storm, John. *Invitation to Wines*
Street, Julian. *Wines*
Sunset Editors. *California Wine Country*
Taylor, Walter S. & Vine, Richard P. *Home Winemaker's Handbook*
Thorpy, Frank. *Wine in New Zealand*
Torbert, Harold & Torbert, Frances. *Complete Wine Book*
Tritton, S. *Guide to Better Wine & Beer Making for Beginners*
Vizetelly, Henry. *Facts About Champagne.*
Wagner, Philip M. *American Wines and Wine-Making*
Waldo, Myra. *Pleasures of Wine*
Waugh, Alec. *Wines & Spirits*
Waugh, Harry. *Diary of a Winetaster: The New York Times Guide to the Wines of France & California*
Wildman, Frederick S., Jr. *A Wine Tour of France*
Wine & Spirit Trade Directory
Winkler, A. J. *General Viticulture*
Wine Industry Year Book
Younger, William. *Gods, Men & Wine*
Yoxall, H. W. *Wines of Burgundy*

WINE COOKERY BIBLIOGRAPHY

Ald, Roy. *Creative Wine Cookery*

Amunategui, Francis. *Masterpieces of French Cuisine*

Beck, Simone, Bertholle, Louisette, and Julia Child. *Mastering the Art of French Cooking*

Caruba, Rebecca. *Cooking with Wine & High Spirits*

Chamberlain, Samuel. *Bouquet de France*
——*Italian Bouquet*

Chase, Emily, compiled by. *Wine Cookbook of Dinner Menus*
——*Pleasures of Cooking with Wine*

Diat, Louis, *Gourmet's Basic French Cookbook*

Gourmet Editors, ed. *Gourmet Cookbooks I and II*

Hatch, Ted. *American Wine Cook Book*

Heaton, Nell. *Cooking with Wine*

Krieg, Saul. *Spirit of Grand Cuisine*

Lewin, Esther & Lewin, Birdina. *Stewed to the Gills*

Logan, Anne M. *Wine & Wine Cooking: Entertaining & Cooking with American Wines*

McDouall, Robin. *Cooking with Wine*

Price, P. V. *Cooking with Wines etc.*

Reynolds, Mary. *Good Cooking with Wine*

Root, Waverly and de Rochemont, Richard. *Contemporary French Cooking*

Shepard, Jean H. *Cook with Wine!*

Simon, Andre L. and Gaige, Crosby. *Andre Simon's French Cook Book*

Simon, Andre L. and Howe, Robin, *Dictionary of Gastronomy*

Sunset Editors, ed. *Cooking with Wine*

Taylor, Greyton, *Treasury of Wine & Wine Cookery*

Van Zuylen, Guirne. *Eating with Wine*

Wine Advisory Board. *Adventures in Wine Cookery by California Winemakers*
——*Epicurean Recipes of California*
——*Favorite Recipes of California Winemakers*
——*Gourmet Wine Cooking the Easy Way*

Wood, Morrison. *More Recipes with a Jug of Wine*
——*Through Europe with a Jug of Wine*
——*With a Jug of Wine*

Appendix N

TECHNICAL EXPLANATION OF VINOUS FERMENTATION*

I. GRAPE-JUICE

Fermentation consists in a series of complex chemical changes, the most important of which causes the transformation of grape-sugar into ethyl alcohol and carbonic acid gas, a transformation which is rendered possible chiefly by the accelerating or catalyctic action of the fermenting enzyme known as Zymase. But grape-juice is not a mixture of water and grape-sugar with Saccharomycetes in it. It is very complex, and there are in it other enzymes besides Zymase. There are other chemical reactions taking place at the same time as those which are responsible for the presence of ethyl alcohol in wine, and these different reactions depend, in the first place, upon the chemical composition of the must, and the presence of certain enzymes— and, in the second place, upon external conditions existing at the time.

Climatic conditions are beyond the control of man. The soil of the vineyards may be improved to a certain extent by drainage and fertilizers, but its chief characteristics remain unaltered. Species of grapes may be judiciously selected and grafted. Grapes may be carefully picked and they may be pressed by different methods, but the last stage, the fermenting of grape-juice into wine, which is so important, may be controlled by the art of man more than any of the other factors which are responsible for the making of wine.

Different processes of fermentation are suited to the different chemical composition of different "musts," and aim at securing different types of wine.

On the whole, it may be said that the process of fermentation, which is an absolutely natural phenomenon, might be left to transform grape-juice into wine without any interference from man, except in the case of sparkling, fortified, or other such wines. This is true, but like all truths, it is true only up to a point. Grass grows in the fields quite naturally, even in wet fields, but, if no one attends to ditching and hedging, moss may some day grow quite naturally where clover used to grow. Wine left too long to ferment upon its husks will draw colour from the skins if they be those of black grapes, but it will also draw from the pips, stalks or the small peduncles, more acidity and tannin and more of the unsuitable acids which may prove objectionable later.

ALCOHOLIC FERMENTATION

Let us measure a gallon of grape-juice and weigh the quantity of grape-sugar it contains. Say that we find 32 ozs. of grape-sugar present. Then let us look for our 32 ozs. of sugar after the same grape-juice shall have finished fermenting. We shall not find any sugar but, in its place, we shall find about 17 ozs. of ethyl alcohol. What has happened? This. Each molecule of grape-sugar, representing 180 by weight, has been split up by fermentation into two molecules of ethyl alcohol (each 46 by weight) and two molecules of carbon dioxide (each 44 by weight). The carbon dioxide has lost itself in the air and the ethyl alcohol has remained in the wine— hence a gallon of wine will be lighter than a gallon of grape-juice, the difference being that of

*Reprinted from "The Supply, the Care and the Sale of Wine" by permission of the author, André L. Simon.

517

the weight of the escaped carbonic acid gas. At the same time, 17 ozs. of ethyl alcohol take up the same space as 32 ozs. of grape-sugar, so that we shall have a gallon of wine in place of a gallon of grape-juice, the bulk of our wine being practically the same as the bulk of the grape-juice, although its weight will be slightly less.

We could, therefore, describe alcoholic fermentation by means of the following simple formula:—

$$C_6H_{12}O_6 \;=\; 2C_2H_6O \;+\; 2CO_2$$
$$\text{(Grape-sugar)} \;=\; \text{(Alcohol)} \;+\; \text{(Carbon dioxide)}$$

Remembering that the atomic weight of carbon, hydrogen and oxygen are respectively: $C = 12$; $H = 1$; $O = 16$; one molecule of grape-sugar, two of ethyl alcohol and two of carbon dioxide will represent:—

(Grape-sugar).

$C_6 \;=\; 12 \times \;\; 6 = 72$
$H_{12} = \;\; 1 \times 12 = 12$
$O_6 \;=\; 16 \times \;\; 6 = \underline{96}$
180

(Alcohol).

$C_4 \;=\; 12 \times \;\; 4 = 48$
$H_{12} = \;\; 1 \times 12 = 12$
$O_2 \;=\; 16 \times \;\; 2 = \underline{32}$
92

(Carbon dioxide).

$C_2 = 12 \times 2 = 24$
$O_4 = 16 \times 4 = \underline{64}$
88

Alcoholic fermentation is therefore a molecular re-adjustment of the carbon, hydrogen and oxygen of grape-sugar. In theory, it seems quite simple—in practice it is very complicated.

To begin with, grape-sugar is not a compact entity made up of six atoms of carbon, twelve of hydrogen and six of oxygen. On balance, there is that number of atoms to be found in one molecule of grape-sugar, but they are arranged in distinct groups in the following manner:—

Dextrose.

CHO
|
CHOH
|
CHOH
|
CHOH
|
CHOH
|
CH₂OH

+

Fructose.

CH₂OH
|
CO
|
CHOH
|
CHOH
|
CHOH
|
CH₂OH

There are 6 atoms of carbon, 12 of hydrogen, and 6 of oxygen in their grouping; they are knit together in a strictly orderly manner, until the Saccharomycetes give the signal, by a loud rap on the piano, for a wild game of musical chairs. Then all is confusion, order is destroyed, there is a rush, hot pursuit, until, all of a sudden, the music ceases, and order reigns once more. Some have lost their seats, others have changed seats and have new neighbours. Of course, if there is no air in the room there cannot be any game. This is a very rough and unscientific simile, but it may serve to convey to your minds the main idea of alcoholic fermentation; it necessitates someone at the piano, i.e. an enzyme; it begins and ends with order, but the intervening period is very confused, and it is during this confusion that all sorts of things happen. There is a loss incurred in the process, and, above all, oxygen, i.e. fresh air, is wanted all the time.

Although Zymase, the fermenting enzyme, is necessary to the process of alcoholic fermentation, it does not take any active part in the game which it sets going. Its chemical composition is such that it acts as a catalyst, that is to say a remover of hindrance or an accelerator of reactions. It does so without taking anything away or giving up any of its own substance.

TEMPERATURE AND FERMENTATION

A suitable temperature for the immediate growth of the Saccharomycetes is of great importance, since their enzyme "Zymase" is indispensable to alcoholic fermentation. But wine is not merely grape-juice with its grape-sugar changed into alcohol and carbon dioxide: in grape-juice there are many other substances besides grape-sugar, and they cannot be expected to remain unaffected by the internal revolution which destroys the chemical structure of grape-sugar and rebuilds with the same materials, ethyl alcohol and carbon dioxide. This revolution is the work of alcoholic fermentation, but other fermentations take place at the same time, other vegetable substances which were in grape-juice are altered, increased, reduced or may entirely disappear, in ways which differ according to the different enzymes and other catalysts present, as well as according to differences of temperature affecting not only the rate of molecular exchanges, but also the degree of solubility of certain acids.

Temperature is an important factor in fermentation because of the influence it exercises upon the rate of molecular exchanges and upon the solubility of various acids. Grape-juice is so complex, it contains such a large number of various compounds, that any and every variation of temperature is liable to affect some chemical reaction upon which may depend, at a later date, some characteristic of the wine.

To sum up, let it suffice to say that the process known as fermentation is one which consists mainly in the splitting up of each molecule of grape-sugar present in grape-juice into two molecules of carbon dioxide. But let it be remembered (1) that there are other fermentable substances in grape-juice besides grape-sugar; (2) that, besides Zymase, there are other enzymes as well as other catalysts which render possible subsidiary fermentations which take place concurrently or subsequently, and are responsible for the presence, in wine, of compounds which did not exist in grape-juice.

II. WINE

Grape-juice is a very complex aqueous solution. Besides water and grape-sugar, it contains acids and other substances, most of them in very small quantities, either of a vegetable or of a mineral origin.

Wine is a still more complex aqueous solution; besides water and ethyl alcohol, it contains glycerine, acids and many substances in minute quantities, some of which were present in grape-juice in a different form or proportion and others which never were in grape-juice.

Water and ethyl alcohol form generally about 97 per cent of the volume of wine, but the remaining 3 per cent are made up of very small quantities of a large variety of substances which vary and give to different wines the distinctive colour, taste and bouquet which are mainly responsible for the charm or lack of charm of individual specimens of wine.

These substances may be divided into two main groups, one to include all those which were originally present in grape-juice and the other all those which were not.

1.—*Substances, other than water, which are the same in must and wine.*
> Grape-sugar.
> Saccharomycetes.
> Acids.
> Cellulose.
> Essential oils, mucilage, etc.

2.—*Substances other than ethyl alcohol, present in wine, but not in must.*
> Glycerine.
> Various acids.
> Alcohols, other than ethyl alcohol.
> Esters and aldehydes.
> Sundry other substances.

1.—SUBSTANCES, OTHER THAN WATER,
WHICH ARE THE SAME IN MUST AND WINE

grape-sugar

The proportion of grape-sugar which remains in wine after fermentation depends, in the first place, upon the proportion of grape-sugar present in the must and, in the second, upon the process or method of fermentation resorted to.

In the case of "fortified" or "sweet" wines, whether obtained like Port, by the addition of brandy during fermentation, or, like Sauternes, from over-ripe grapes, the sweeter the must, the sweeter the wine. But, in the case of beverage wines, such as Claret, it is often the reverse.

Saccharomycetes

Although Saccharomycetes are microscopic fungi, there are millions of them, and they do not escape in air like carbon dioxide. They remain in suspension in the wine until the end of fermentation or until the proportion of alcohol is such that it arrests their growth. They are so fine and so light that they are neither swept down by finings nor do they fall to the bottom of the cask by their own weight; many are carried down into the lees by the microscopic crystals of cream of tartar to which they adhere, many more lose their identity altogether by reason of the chemical splitting up of their cells, and some remain in the wine for all time.

There are, of course, a very large variety of Saccharomycetes and allied members of the vast tribe of yeasts, bacteria and moulds.

A form of yeast-fungi which is not unusual in wines is the *mycoderma vini*, or "flowers of wine." These micro-organisms multiply very rapidly at the surface of wine and remain on the surface in giant colonies, all holding together, and forming a film which can be so complete as to prevent the outside air having any access to the wine. There are quite a number of different species of film-forming microscopic fungi, all of which require much oxygen to grow and all of which grow with astonishing rapidity.

acids

Generally speaking, the acids which disappear wholly or partly during fermentation are those which are soluble in water and not in alcohol, whilst acids which appear in much larger proportions in wine than in must are those which are formed by the oxidation of ethyl alcohol.

Let us take but one example of each class, i.e. tartaric acid and acetic acid.

Tartaric acid is the principal acid in grape-juice. It forms a white crystalline salt which is potassium hydrogen tartarate, commonly known as cream of tartar. Cream of tartar is soluble in water but not in alcohol, and a good deal of the cream of tartar in solution in grape-juice becomes solidified in the shape of fine crystals in the presence of the alcohol of wine; in that form, it is heavier than wine, settles in the lees and is left behind when the wine is racked. Cream of tartar is also more soluble in a warm than in a cold aqueous solution, so that if the new wine be kept in a cold cellar, the lower temperature together with the alcohol present will help render a greater proportion of cream of tartar insoluble, thus depriving the wine, after racking, of much acidity present in the must.

An acid must does not necessarily ferment into an acid wine. Acidity in must is of great benefit because it assists the normal growth of yeasts and checks the development of bacteria, so that it is favourable to alcoholic fermentation. If as well as acidity there is a fair proportion of grape-sugar in the must, this sugar will ferment and be replaced by a fair proportion of alcohol which, in its turn, will cause the crystallisation of a further proportion of cream of tartar, hitherto in solution. In other words, the more sugar in the must means the more alcohol in the wine and the less cream of tartar. The proof of this is easy to make in Burgundy where Pinot grapes must and Gamay grapes must from the same district may be compared: the first contains more acidity and more sugar than the second, but when both have become wine, the first contains more alcohol and less acidity than the second.

Acetic acid in wine is due to the oxidation of ethyl alcohol, one atom of oxygen replacing two of hydrogen, thus:—

$$\text{Ethyl Alcohol} = CH_2CH_2OH$$
$$\text{Acetic Acid} = CH_2CO\,OH$$

The more alcohol there is in a wine and the less oxygen has access to it the smaller will be the quantity of acetic acid formed. This replacement of two hydrogen atoms by one of oxygen is rendered possible by the presence of an enzyme secreted by the Schitzomycetes, and they cannot grow without a free supply of oxygen from the air. Hence when "flowers of wine" or other film-forming mycoderma cover the surface of wine and prevent all contact with the outside air, no more acetic acid can be formed. On the other hand, wine of a low alcoholic strength kept in a fairly warm place and in contact with the air will soon become vinegar, practically the whole of its ethyl alcohol being changed into acetic acid. Of course, this should be avoided, and it can be avoided with a little care. At the same time, normal and sound wine is seldom free from acetic acid when new and, with time, this acetic acid dissolves certain mineral salts in wine, forming various acetates which are partly responsible for the flavour and bouquet of wine.

Cellulose is a danger in wine because it may fall a prey to certain bacteria which cause its decomposition into fatty acids and carbonic acid gas, the former being particularly objectionable. Decomposed or "fermented" cellulose in red wine is the cause of an extremely light viscous sediment which it is almost impossible to keep out of the decanter and which spoils not only the look but the taste of the wine. *cellulose*

2.—SUBSTANCES, OTHER THAN ETHYL ALCOHOL, PRESENT IN WINE BUT NOT IN MUST

These substances are numerous and they vary according to the chemical composition of the must, the various enzymes or catalysts present, and the rate and mode of fermentation. They consist chiefly of glycerine and other alcohols, various acids, esters and aldehydes.

Most of the sugar in grape-juice is transformed by fermentation into ethyl alcohol and carbon dioxide, but not the whole of it. Pasteur's experiments, which more recent researches have completely confirmed, showed that alcoholic fermentation could not use up more than 95 per cent of the sugar present in grape-juice in the proportion of about 48 per cent ethyl alcohol and 47 carbon dioxide. The remaining 5 per cent of sugar are used up in other ways; a small quantity being used by Saccharomycetes themselves by way of food or means of cellular development; a small percentage being decomposed into minute quantities of various volatile acids, and the greater proportion being used up in the production of glycerine. *glycerine*

Besides glycerine which, after and a long way behind ethyl alcohol, is the most important by-product of vinous fermentation, there are other alcohols in wine. Such are propyl and butyl alcohols, practically in all cases, and amyl alcohol sometimes. Although these and other alcohols are present in normal wines only in minute quantities, they have, like all alcohols, the property of forming esters with acids, and they play quite an important part, compared to their volume, in the formation of the bouquet or aroma of wine. *other alcohols*

Some of the acidity in the must, particularly in the shape of cream of tartar, disappears during fermentation, but on the other hand, there are some acids which were not in the must and which are normally present in the wine as by-products of fermentation. *acids*

First among these is succinic acid, which is the principal cause of the "winy" flavour of wine, its "saveur"; the proportion of succinic acid in a wine, according to Pasteur, is 0.61 per cent of the grape-sugar in the must.

A very small quantity of grape-sugar is also transformed, during fermentation, into acetic acid, propionic acid and traces of valerianic acid. These acids are present in very small quantities and they do not affect the taste of wine, but they are responsible to a certain extent for its bouquet; the esters, which give to a wine its bouquet, being formed by alcohols at the expense of acids. Normal wine, that is wine which is sound and suitably fermented, contains always a little acetic acid, but it is only very little. When acetic acid is present in wine in a noticeable amount, it is not the result of the decomposition of grape-sugar, but the oxidation of ethyl alcohol; it is a sure sign that the wine is not absolutely sound, that it will soon be vinegar, and no longer wine, if the progress of acetification is not promptly checked.

The variety of volatile and non-volatile acids in wine, which differ from those of the must, is very great, and Prior's researches have proved that the differences existing in the acids of different wines were due to the differences existing in the species of Saccharomycetes and other micro-organisms present in the must or introduced in the wine at a later date. In every case those acids are present only in minute quantities, sometimes there are but traces of each, but the importance of the part they play upon the degree of excellence of a wine is out of all proportion to their volume.

aldehydes   Aldehydes are always present in wine. They may be regarded as by-products of alcoholic fermentation and as intermediary organic compound between alcohols and acids. They must eventually become either acids by the action of oxidizing agents, or else alcohols, by the intervention of reducing agents.

esters   The ethyl formates, acetates, propionates, butyrates, lactates and other such esters are due to reactions between alcohols and acetic acid, proprionic acid, butyric acid, lactic acid, etc. They are volatile and give to wines their distinctive aroma.

THE CHEMICAL COMPOSITION OF MUST AND LIGHT BEVERAGE WINE*

I. PRINCIPAL CONSTITUENTS, THEIR ORIGIN AND TRANSFORMATIONS

MATTER	MEASURED IN GRAMMES PER LITRE		NOTES ON TRANSFORMATIONS
	Must	Wine	
Water	700–850	850–950	Increase during fermentation because of disappearance of sugar. Slight loss through evaporation during aging in wood.
Sugars	150–300	1–60	Transformed through fermentation into carbon dioxide and alcohol, a small part into glycerine and other products; some sugar is retained unfermented in certain wines made from very rich over-ripe grapes.
Alcohols: ethyllic	none	7%–15%	Through fermentation of glucose and fructose sugars resulting from the action of the yeast.
Others	none	.4%–.8%	Principally glycerine, products of fermentation.
Organic acids and their salts: *a* tartaric	2–5	1–0	Diminishes as deposit (sediment) of cream of tartar (potassium bitartrate).
b others	+	+	Principally products of the secondary fermentations. A small amount of mallic acid which exists in the must becomes lactic acid in the wine.
Esters or ether-salts	0	+	Formed by the action of the acids on the alcohols in the wine; they are responsible for the wine's bouquet; they increase as the wine becomes older.

Explanation of signs: + means barely present.
0 means total absence.
* From "Le Vin" by Ch. Schmutz. Translated from the French by the author.

MATTER	MEASURED IN GRAMMES PER LITRE		NOTES ON TRANSFORMATIONS
	Must	Wine	
Organic flavoring agents	traces	traces	Formed during fermentation. Besides esters a few less known such as *terpenes, vanilline,* etc.
Other organic substances:			
a aldehydes	0	traces	Formed by the action of the air (oxidation) on the alcohols in the wine.
b essential oils	0	traces	Formed by the action of the yeasts during fermentation.
c coloring matter	+	increase	Obtained from the skins of the grapes.
d albumin	+	+	Coagulates, settles to form part of lees.
e tannin	+	+	Obtained from stems, skins and pips; mostly precipitated by the fining and with the albumin.
Mineral substances:			
a chlorines	<1	<1	
b phosphates			
c silicates			
d sulphates			
e carbonates			
f tartrates			
g sodium	+	+	
h potassium			
i magnesium			
j calcium			
k iron			
l manganese			
Total extracts			Diminish with disappearance of sugar.
Sugar extract deduction			Slight loss through precipitation with the salts and the tartar to the lees.
Foreign substances:			
a sulphurous acid	0 natural	+ up to legal limit	Changes into sulphuric acid.
b calcium			Increased when the must is alkalized with carbonate of chalk.
Gas in solution:			
a carbonic			Results from fermentation. Particularly important in sparkling wines.
b hydrogen sulfide			
c oxygenic			Important for the preservation of the wine, that it may oxidize slowly.

II. VARIETY OF PRODUCTS WHICH MAY BE INVOLVED

MATTER	MEASURED IN GRAMMES PER LITRE		NOTES ON TRANSFORMATIONS
	Must	Wine	
A. SUGARS AND ALCOHOLS			
Sugars:			
a glucose	75–100	<10	Produce ethyl alcohol and other products.
b fructose	75–150	10	Fermentable.

MATTER	MEASURED IN GRAMMES PER LITRE		NOTES ON TRANSFORMATIONS
	Must	Wine	
c saccharose	traces	traces ⎫	Unfermentable sugars formed from the gums and pectines.
d pentoses	traces	traces ⎬	
e inosite	traces	traces ⎭	
Alcohols:			
a monoalcohols:			
methyl	0	traces	Minute quantities formed by fermentation.
ethyl	0	7% to 15% ⎫	
propyl	0	traces ⎪	
butyl	0	traces ⎬ Result from fermentation.	
amyl	0	traces ⎪	
hexyl	0	traces ⎪	
heptyl	0	traces ⎭	
higher alcohols	0	traces	Produced by the empyreumatical oils.
b dialcohols:			
ethyllic glycols	0	traces	Produced by certain yeasts of fermentation.
c trialcohols:			
glycerine	0	traces	Produced during fermentation of a particular alcohol.
d polyalcohol:	0	0 to 3	To be found in certain sick wines said to be *mannités*.

B. ORGANIC ACIDS AND ETHER-SALTS

MATTER	Must	Wine	NOTES ON TRANSFORMATIONS
Acids:			
a acetic	0	traces to 2	To be found in wines which have turned to vinegar due to oxidation and the action of the *mycoderma aceti*.
b proprionic	0 ⎫	traces to 0.5	Fermentation of tartar produces these acids in quantity.
c butyric	0 ⎭		
d tartaric	0.5 to 5	0 to 1	It may be free or it may be present in the form of potassium or calcium salts; it is precipitated to form the lees with the bitartrates.
e malic	0.5 to 1	traces	Transformed into lactic acid by the action of fermentation.
f lactic	0	traces	Results from the malic acid.
g succinic	0	0.5 to 1	To be found in wines made from unripe grapes. In certain sick wines it is present in quantity.
Superior acids:			
h capyroic			
i caprylic			Properties of certain old wines resulting from a special development of the glycerine during fermentation.
j oenanthylic	0	traces	
k lauric			
l salicylic		traces	
Ether-salts			
Ethylic acids:			
a acetic			
b proprionic			
c butyric		. . .	Combine to give the wine its flavor and bouquet.
d caprylic			
e pelargonic			
f lauric			
g oenanthylic			Usually found in the lees.
h etheracetylacetic			Product of certain ferments.

C. OTHER ORGANIC SUBSTANCES

MATTER	Must	Wine	NOTES ON TRANSFORMATIONS
Gums	+	+	Precipitated by the alcohol during fermentation.

MATTER	MEASURED IN GRAMMES PER LITRE		NOTES ON TRANSFORMATIONS
	Must	Wine	
Acetaldehyde	0	+	Product of a poor oxidation of the alcohol.
Coloring matters:			Over-ripe grapes produce it in quantity.
$\quad$ a $\quad$ chlorophyl	+	+	To be found only in red wines.
$\quad$ b $\quad$ oenocyanin	+	+	
Peptones	<	+	
Aurides	+	+	
Combination of mineral acids	+	+	
Organic bases (trimethylamin)	0	+	
Enzymes:			
$\quad$ a $\quad$ invertase	+	+	
$\quad$ b $\quad$ oxydase	+	+	
Fat			Sickness. Wines poor in tannin will become viscous.

D. MINERAL SUBSTANCES

MATTER	Must	Wine	NOTES ON TRANSFORMATIONS
Total ash	3 to 4	2 to 3	About 10% of the total by extracts.
$\quad$ a $\quad$ Basic metallic oxides of:			
$\qquad$ Potassium (K_2O)	+	+	Mostly precipitated in the cream of tartar deposit.
$\qquad$ Sodium (Na_2O)	+	+	Invariable.
$\qquad$ Calcium (CaO)	+	+	Diminishes during fermentation by precipitation. Increases through de-acidification.
$\qquad$ Magnesium (MgO)	+	+	Is precipitated with the coloring matter and with the phosphates in wines that have the *caisse* sickness.
$\qquad$ Iron (FeO and Fe_2O_3)	+	+	Given off by the acids in the must and in wine.
$\qquad$ Aluminum (Al_2O_3)	+	+	
$\qquad$ Manganese (MnO)	+	+	
$\qquad$ Copper (CuO)	traces	traces	Minute amounts find their way into the must and wine as a result of spraying the vines with copper sulphate used to protect them against various diseases, notably the oidium.
$\qquad$ Zinc (ZnO)	traces	traces	
$\qquad$ Lead (PbO)	traces	traces	
$\qquad$ Tin (SnO)	traces	traces	
$\qquad$ Arsenic (As_2O_5)	traces	traces	
$\quad$ b $\quad$ Anhydrids of acids:			
$\qquad$ Carbonic (CO_2)	0	+	
$\qquad$ Phosphoric (P_2O_5)	+	+	
$\qquad$ Chlorin (Cl)	+	+	Invariable.
$\qquad$ Silicic (SiO_2)	+	+	Invariable.
$\qquad$ Boric (B_2O_3)	traces	traces	
$\qquad$ Sulphuric (SO_3)	+	+	Comes from the copper sulphate spraying of the vines and the oxidation of sulphur anhydride during the disinfection of the casks.

INDEX

Wagner, Philip, 176
Waldorf-Astoria Hotel, 368–369
Waldrach, Saar, 122
waldmeister, 365
walnuts, 314
Ward Eight cocktail, 364, 367
warehouse, 32, 133
wash, 270
wash still, 270
Washington State, 175, 181–182, 337
Wasserbillig, Luxemburg, 110
water
  beers, 334, 336
  England, 293
  Java, 309
  Scotland, 270, 272
  U.S., 275
water seal, 33
Wehlen, Moselle, 122
Wehlener Sonnenuhr, 122
weinstube, 120
Weissburgunder grape, 219, 220
Wente Winery, 194
wermut, 164
West Indies
  Falernum, 319
  rum, 301–302, 304–308
wheat, 280–283, 288, 297
wheat spirit, 332
wheat whiskey, 280–282
whiskies, 2, 8, 246, 267–289, 371–373, 385, 404–406
Whiskey Rebellion, 275, 447
Whiskey Smash, 364
Whiskey Sour, 360
White Chianti, 209
white oak, 261, 270, 277
White Pinot grape, 220, 238
White Porto, 154–155
White Riesling grape, 198, 200, 209
White Riesling wine, 200
wholesaler, 400, 449
Widmer's Wine Cellars, 178, 196
wild beer, 343
Wile, Julius, 74, 254
Williams Pear, 265
Williamsburg Art of Cookery, The, 17
Wiltingen, 122
window displays, 416–419
Wine Advisory Board, 204, 215
wine cellars, 403–406, 426–430, 432

Wine, classifications, 7
wine in cooking, 17
wine, definition, 5
Wine and Food Society, 368
Wines, fruit and flower, 5, 241–242
Wines Institute, 204, 214–215
Wine List, 370–377, 410–411, 413
wine merchant, 1, 449
Wines and Spirits, 310
Wine Service, 389–398, 410
wine steward, 431–432, 440
wine tastings, 422–425, 452
wine waiter, 412–413
wineglass, 348
Winkler, Dr. Albert J., 201
Wishniak liqueur, 315
Wisniowka liqueur, 315
Wooded Portos, 153
Worms, Rheinhesse, 118
wormwood, 164, 166, 329–330
wort, 268, 277, 292, 334, 338–340
Würzburg, 110–123
Würzburger Leiste, 123
Würzburger Stein, 123

Xeres grape, 199

Yago Sant'gria, 147
Yakima Valley, 181
Yeast, 10–12, 32–33, 46, 67–68, 184, 186, 202–203, 230–231, 270, 276–277, 303, 305, 309, 331, 333, 338–340, 342
yeasting-back process, 277
Yonne Department, 25, 49, 60
Yovac, Yugoslavia, 221
Yubileyneya Osobaya vodka, 300
Yugoslavia, 220–221, 241, 265
  brandy, 265
  fruit wines, 241
  geography, 220
  grapes, 220–221
  labeling, 220
  soil, 220
Yezd, Persia, 228

Zell, Moselle, 122
Zeltingen, Moselle, 122
Zibibbo Muscat grape, 92–93, 107
Zichron-Jacob, Israel, 226